D0204017

American Literary Scholarship 1988

American Literary Scholarship
An Annual 1988

Edited by J. Albert Robbins

Essays by David M. Robinson, Frederick Newberry, Benjamin Franklin Fisher IV, Brian Higgins, Vivian R. Pollak, Hamlin Hill, Richard A. Hocks, Reed Way Dasenbrock, M. Thomas Inge, Gerry Brenner, William J. Scheick, David J. Nordloh, Stephen L. Tanner, Gary Scharnhorst, Jerome Klinkowitz, Melody M. Zajdel, Richard J. Calhoun, Walter J. Meserve, R. Baxter Miller, Michael J. Hoffman, F. Lyra, Michel Gresset, Rolf Meyn, Massimo Bacigalupo, Hiroko Sato, Jan Nordby Gretlund, Elisabeth Herion-Sarafidis, Hans Skei, José Antonio Gurpegui, and James Woodress

Duke University Press *Durham and London* 1990

© 1990 Duke University Press
LC 65–19450 ISBN 0–8223–1033–3
Printed in the United States of America
by Heritage Printers, Inc.

Foreword

In the foreword to last year's *American Literary Scholarship* James Woodress reminded us that the series had reached the quarter-century mark (*ALS 1987*, p. v)—a remarkable longevity for a scholarly series. In format it has also remained relatively stable. Except for the deletion of one chapter (Folklore), the principal changes over the years have been additions: "Black Literature"; "Themes, Topics, Criticism"; and "Foreign Scholarship." With this volume, coverage of foreign work on American literature, which has gradually been expanding, expands once again with a section on Spanish contributions. We welcome the new contributor, José Antonio Gurpegui, Universidad de Alcala de Henares, Madrid.

ALS 1987 marks the last number edited by James Woodress, and this volume the last edited by J. Albert Robbins. After this, the series will be edited by two new coeditors, who will alternate in supervising preparation of the volumes: Professor David J. Nordloh and Professor Louis Owens, both former editors of or contributors to the series. You may address and send review copies of books and articles to Professor Nordloh at the Department of English, Indiana University, Bloomington, IN 47405. Professor Owens's address is Department of English, University of New Mexico, Albuquerque, NM 87131.

The editor of the next volume (*ALS 1989*), Professor Nordloh, has his roster of contributors virtually complete. Those who are writing chapters again for us are 1. David M. Robinson; 2. Frederick Newberry; 3. Benjamin Franklin Fisher IV; 4. Brian Higgins; 7. Richard A. Hocks; 8. Reed Way Dasenbrock; 11. William J. Scheick; 14. Gary Scharnhorst; 15. Jerome Klinkowitz; 16. Melody Zajdel; 17. Richard J. Calhoun; 19. R. Baxter Miller; 20. Michael J. Hoffman.

Several new contributors have joined the team that will produce *ALS 1989*. For Chapter 5, Whitman and Dickinson, John Carlos Rowe, University of California, Irvine, replaces Vivian Pollak. For Chapter 6, Mark Twain, Robert Sattelmeyer, Georgia State University, substitutes for Hamlin Hill during the latter's visiting professorship in Budapest. For Chapter 9, Faulkner, Ladell Payne, President, Randolph-Macon College, takes over from M. Thomas Inge, who is on leave for the year. Replacing Gerry Brenner for Chapter 10, Fitzgerald and Hemingway, is Susan F. Beegel, University of Massachusetts Field Station, Nantucket. Replacing David Nordloh, Chapter 12, 19th-Century Literature, is Alice Hall Petry, Rhode Island School of Design, Providence. And replacing Walter J. Meserve for Chapter 18, Drama, is Peter Davis, Department of Theater, Tufts University. Chapter 13, Fiction: 1900 to the 1930s, is unfilled as of this writing.

We thank all retiring contributors for their faithful services, with a special mention of Walter J. Meserve for his long tenure in covering drama for us. We thank him for his 18 years of service, which began way back in 1966.

We wish to thank Dean Albert Wertheim, in the office of the College of Arts and Sciences, Indiana University, for support in obtaining a grant for retired faculty to assist in the editing and indexing of this volume. We also would like to thank the editorial staff of Duke University Press for their high standards of editing and production. And thanks to our team of able indexers, John McCammon and Lisa Markgraf.

Virtually every chapter in this year's *ALS* makes reference to a landmark volume in American literary history, the 1,263-page *Columbia Literary History of the United States* (general editor, Emory Elliott). (You can find Michael J. Hoffman's thoughts on the new *CLHUS* in chapter 20 (pp. 431–35).

In the foreword to *ALS 1985* (p. vii) I referred to another new work of literary history in progress—a multivolume study to be called *The Cambridge History of American Literature* (general editor, Sacvan Bercovitch). The publisher hopes soon to have in print the first two chronological volumes.

J. Albert Robbins

Indiana University

Table of Contents

Part I

Part II

Key to Abbreviations

Festschriften, Essay Collections, and Books Discussed in More Than One Chapter

Aesthetic Headaches / Leland S. Person, Jr., *Aesthetic Headaches: Women and a Masculine Poetics in Poe, Melville, and Hawthorne* (Georgia)

Afro-American Poetics / Houston A. Baker, *Afro-American Poetics: Revisions of Harlem and the Black Aesthetic* (Wisconsin)

Alcohol and the Writer / Donald W. Goodwin, *Alcohol and the Writer* (Andrews and McMeel)

Ambiguities in Literature and Film / Hans P. Braendlin, ed., *Ambiguities in Literature and Film: Selected Papers from the Seventh Annual Florida State University Conference on Literature and Film* (Florida State)

The American City / Graham Clarke, ed., *The American City: Literary and Cultural Perspectives* (Vision)

American Crime Fiction / Brian Docherty, ed., *American Crime Fiction: Studies in the Genre* (St. Martin's)

The American Indian / Elizabeth I. Hanson, *The American Indian in American Literature: A Study in Metaphor* (Mellen)

American Literary Landscapes / Ian F. A. Bell and D. K. Adams, eds., *American Literary Landscapes: The Fiction and the Fact* (Vision)

Apocalyptic Visions / JoAnn James and William J. Cloonan, eds., *Apocalyptic Visions Past and Present: Selected Papers from the Eighth and Ninth Annual Florida State University Conferences on Literature and Film* (Florida State)

Audits of Meaning / Louise Z. Smith, ed., *Audits of Meaning: A Festschrift in Honor of Ann E. Berthoff* (Boynton)

Authority, Autonomy, and Representation / Mark R. Patterson, *Authority, Autonomy, and Representation in American Literature, 1776–1865* (Princeton)

Beneath the American Renaissance / David S. Reynolds, *Beneath the American Renaissance: The Subversive Imagination in the Age of Emerson and Melville* (Knopf)

CLHUS / Emory Elliott, gen. ed., *Columbia Literary History of the United States* (Columbia)

Coming to Light / Diane Wood Middlebrook and Marilyn Yalom, eds., *Coming to Light: American Women Poets in the Twentieth Century* (Michigan)

Critical Approaches / John H. Stroupe, ed., *Critical Approaches to O'Neill* (AMS)

Critical Essays on Morrison / Nellie Y. McKay, ed., *Critical Essays on Toni Morrison* (Hall)

E. L. Doctorow / Herwig Friedl and Dieter Schulz, ed., *E. L. Doctorow: A Democracy of Perception—A Symposium with and on E. L. Doctorow* (Blaue Eule)

Equivocal Endings / Joyce A. Rowe, *Equivocal Endings of Classic American Novels: The Scarlet Letter, Adventures of Huckleberry Finn, The Ambassadors, The Great Gatsby* (Cambridge)

European Perspectives on Hispanic Literature of the United States / Geneviève Fabre, ed., *European*

Perspectives on Hispanic Literature of the United States (Arte Publico)

European Revolutions / Larry J. Reynolds, *European Revolutions and the American Literary Renaissance* (Yale)

Faith of a (Woman) Writer / Alice Kessler-Harris and William McBrien, eds., *Faith of a (Woman) Writer* (Greenwood)

Faulkner and Race / Doreen Fowler and Ann J. Abadie, eds., *Faulkner and Race: Faulkner and Yoknapatawpha, 1986—Papers Presented at the 13th Annual Faulkner and Yoknapatawpha Conference at the Oxford Campus of the University of Mississippi, 1986* (Miss., 1987)

Feminist Dialogics / Dale M. Bauer, *Feminist Dialogics: A Theory of Failed Community* (SUNY)

F. O. Matthiessen / William E. Cain, *F. O. Matthiessen and the Politics of Criticism* (Wisconsin)

Form and Society / Thomas C. Foster, *Form and Society in Modern Literature* (No. Ill.)

The Form of American Romance / Edgar A. Dryden, *The Form of American Romance* (Hopkins)

Frammenti di Corpi Immaginiati / Annalisa Goldoni, ed., *Frammenti di Corpi Immaginiati: Un Seminario* (Carucci)

Functions of Style / David Birch and Michael O'Toole, ed., *Functions of Style* (Pinter)

Gertrude Stein and the Making of Literature / Shirley Neuman and Ira B. Nadel, eds., *Gertrude Stein and the Making of Literature* (Northeastern)

Gesta Humanorum / Roy Harvey Pearce, *Gesta Humanorum: Studies in the Historicist Mode* (Columbia)

The Harlem Renaissance Re-Examined / Victor A. Kramer, ed., *The Harlem Renaissance Re-Examined* (AMS)

Heir and Prototype / Dan Ford, ed., *Heir and Prototype: Original and Derived Characterizations in Faulkner* (Central Ark., 1987)

Humor in America / Lawrence E. Mintz, ed., *Humor in America: A Research Guide to Genres and Topics* (Greenwood)

Inventions of Reading / Clayton Koelb, *Inventions of Reading: Rhetoric and the Literary Imagination* (Cornell)

Leon Edel and Literary Art / Lyall H. Powers, ed., *Leon Edel and Literary Art* (UMI Research Press)

Literary History of New England / Perry D. Westbrook, *A Literary History of New England* (Lehigh)

The Literary Mind / Leo Schneiderman, *The Literary Mind: Portraits in Pain and Creativity* (Human Sciences)

Modern American Fiction / Thomas Daniel Young, ed., *Modern American Fiction: Form and Function* (LSU, 1989)

The Modernists / Lawrence B. Gamache and Ian S. MacNiven, eds., *The Modernists: Studies in a Literary Phenomenon—Essays in Honor of Harry T. Moore* (Fairleigh Dickinson, 1987)

Morales et Moralités aux États-Unis / Groupe de Recherche et d'Études Nord-Américaines, *Morales et Moralités aux États-Unis: Actes du Colloque des 4, 5 et 6 Mars 1988* (Provence)

New Views of Mormon History / David Bitton and Maureen Ursenbach Beecher, eds., *New Views of Mormon History: A Collection of Essays in Honor of Leonard J. Arrington* (Utah, 1987)

Patrons and Protégées / Shirley Marchalonis, ed., *Patrons and Protégées: Gender, Friendship, and Writing in Nineteenth-Century America* (Rutgers)

Pelican Guide 9 / Boris Ford, ed., *The New Pelican Guide to English Literature, vol. 9, American Literature* (Penguin)

Perspectives on O'Neill / Shyamal Bagchee, ed., *Perspectives on O'Neill: New Essays* (ELS)

The Pictorial in Modernist Fiction / Deborah Schnitzer, *The Pictorial in Modernist Fiction from Stephen Crane to Ernest Hemingway* (UMI Research Press)
Pisatel' i obshchestvo / V. N. Bogoslovskii, ed., *Pisatel' i obshchestvo: Amerikanskaia i Angliiskaia Literatura XIX–XX vv.: Mezhvuzovskii Sbornik Nauchnykh Trudov* (N. K. Krupskoi, 1987)
Poetry and Epistemology / Roland Hagenbüchle and Laura Skandera, eds., *Poetry and Epistemology: Turning Points in the History of Poetic Knowledge—Papers from the International Poetry Symposium, Eichstatt, 1983* (Pustet, 1986)
The Power of Historical Knowledge / Susan L. Mizruchi, *The Power of Historical Knowledge: Narrating the Past in Hawthorne, James, and Dreiser* (Princeton)
Safe at Last / Margaret Morganroth Gullette, *Safe at Last in the Middle Years: The Invention of the Midlife Progress Novel—Saul Bellow, Margaret Drabble, Anne Tyler, and John Updike* (Calif.)
Sea-Brothers / Bert Bender, *Sea-Brothers: The Tradition of American Sea Fiction from* Moby-Dick *to the Present* (Penn.)
Selected Essays / Dorothy M. Joiner, ed., *Selected Essays: International Conference on Wit and Humor* (West Georgia College)
The Self-Conscious Novel / Brian Stonehill, *The Self-Conscious Novel: Artifice in Fiction from Joyce to Pynchon* (Penn.)
Shifting Gears / Cecelia Tichi, *Shifting Gears: Technology, Literature, Culture in Modernist America* (No. Car., 1987)
The Sleuth and the Scholar / Barbara A. Rader and Howard G. Zettler, eds., *The Sleuth and the Scholar: Origins, Evolution, and Current Trends in Detective Fiction* (Greenwood)
Social Construction / Amy Kaplan, *The Social Construction of American Realism* (Chicago)
Studies in Autobiography / James Olney, ed., *Studies in Autobiography* (Oxford)
Thoreau's Walden / Joel Myerson, ed., *Critical Essays on Henry David Thoreau's* Walden (Hall)
Visionary Compacts / Donald E. Pease, *Visionary Compacts: American Renaissance Writings in Cultural Context* (Wisconsin, 1987)
Women's Studies and Literature / Fritz Fleischmann and Deborah Lucas Schneider, eds., *Women's Studies and Literature: Neun Beitrage aus der Erlanger Amerikanistik* (Palm & Enke, 1987)

Periodicals, Annuals, Series

ABSt / *A/B: Auto/Biography Studies*
AEB / *Analytical and Enumerative Bibliography*
Agenda
AHJ / *Atlanta Historical Journal*
AI / *American Imago*
AL / *American Literature*
ALR / *American Literary Realism, 1870–1910*
AmerFilm / *American Film*
AmerHeritage / *American Heritage*
Americana (Univ. de Paris IV)
AmerP / *American Poetry*
AmerPresbyterians / *American Presbyterians*
AmerR / *American Review*
AmerSS / *American Studies in Scandinavia*
Amst / *Amerikastudien*
Anais
AnHuss / *Analacta Husserliana*
ANQ / *American Notes and Queries*
Anuari d'Anglès (Barcelona)
APR / *American Poetry Review*
AQ / *American Quarterly*
ArAA / *Arbeiten aus Anglistik und Amerikanistik*
Archiv / *Archiv für das Studium der Neueren Sprachen und Literaturen*

Arete / Artest, Tidskrift för litterature, konst och musik (Stockholm)
ArmD / Armchair Detective: A Quarterly Journal Devoted to the Appreciation of Mystery, Detective, and Suspense Fiction
ArQ / Arizona Quarterly
ASch / American Scholar
Atlantis: A Women's Studies Journal / Journal d'Études sur la Femme
ATQ / American Transcendental Quarterly
AUMLA / AUMLA: Journal of the Australasian Universities Language and Literature Association: A Journal of Literary Criticism and Linguistics
BALF / Black American Literature Forum
BB / Bulletin of Bibliography
Biography / Biography: An Interdisciplinary Quarterly
Boundary / Boundary 2
BSUF / Ball State University Forum
BuR / *Bucknell Review: A Scholarly Journal of Letters, Arts and Sciences*
C&L / Christianity and Literature
Caliban (Toulouse)
Callaloo: A Black South Journal of Arts and Letters
Calle Mayor
CCTES / Conference of College Teachers of English Studies
CCV / Cahiers Charles V (Univ. de Paris VII)
CE / College English
CEA / CEA Critic
CentR / Centennial Review
CHA / Cuadernos Hisopanoamericanos
ChiR / Chicago Review
CL / Comparative Literature
CLAJ / College Language Assn. Journal
ClioI / CLIO: A Journal of Literature, History, and the Philosophy of History
CLQ / Colby Library Quarterly
Clues: A Journal of Detection
CML / Classical and Modern Literature
Collections
CollL / College Literature
Colorado Review (Fort Collins)
Columbus
Commentary
Comparatist: A Journal of the Southern Comparative Literature Association
Il Confronto Letterario
ConL / Contemporary Literature
Contesti
Costerus: Essays in English and American Language and Literature
Coup de Théâtre
CP / Concerning Poetry
CQ / Cambridge Quarterly
CRAS / Canadian Review of American Studies
Crit / Critique: Studies in Modern Fiction
CritI / Critical Inquiry
Criticism: A Quarterly for Literature and the Arts
CS / Concord Saunterer
DAI / Dissertation Abstracts International
DeltaES / Delta: Revue du Centre d'Études et de Recherche sur les Écrivains du Sud aux États-Unis (Montpellier)
DGQ / Dramatist Guild Quarterly
Dolphin / The Dolphin: Publications of the English Department, Univ. of Aarhus
DrS / Dreiser Studies
DUJ / Durham University Journal
EA / Études Anglaises
EAL / Early American Literature
EAS / Essays in Arts and Sciences
ECS / Eighteenth-Century Studies
Edda: Nordisk Tidsskrift for Litteraturforskning / Scandinavian Journal of Literary Research
EGN / Ellen Glasgow Newsletter
EigoS / Eigo Seinen (Tokyo)
EIHC / Essex Institute Historical Collections
EiP / Essays in Poetics: The Journal of the British Neo-Formalist School
ELH [formerly *Journal of English Literary History*]
ELN / English Language Notes
ELWIU / Essays in Literature (Western Ill. Univ.)

EON / Eugene O'Neill Newsletter
EQMM / Ellery Queen's Mystery Magazine
ES / English Studies
ESC / English Studies in Canada
ESQ: A Journal of the American Renaissance
EuWN / Eudora Welty Newsletter
EW / East-West Film Journal
EWhN / Edith Wharton Newsletter
Expl / Explicator
Extrapolation: A Journal of Science Fiction and Fantasy
Fabula (Univ. de Lille, France)
Fantasy Macabre
FForum / Folklore Forum
FilmH / Film History
Filologia Moderna
FMLS / Forum for Modern Language Studies (St. Andrews, Scotland)
FNS / Frank Norris Studies
Foundation: The Review of Science Fiction
GaR / Georgia Review
GrandS / Grand Street
Hayden's Ferry Review
HC / Hollins Critic
HDN / H. D. Newsletter
HJR / Henry James Review
HLB / Harvard Library Bulletin
HN / Hemingway Review
Horisont (Malmoe, Sweden)
HTR / Harvard Theological Review
HudR / Hudson Review
IdD / Ilha do Desterro: A Journal of Language and Literature (Florianopolis, Brazil)
IFR / International Fiction Review
L'Indice
Iowa Journal of Literary Studies
IowaR / Iowa Review
JAC / Journal of American Culture (Bowling Green State Univ. Press)
JAmS / Journal of American Studies
JDN / James Dickey Newsletter
JEGP / Journal of English and German Philology
JEP / Journal of Evolutionary Psychology
JISHS / Illinois Historical Journal
JJQ / James Joyce Quarterly
JML / Journal of Modern Literature
JNT / Journal of Narrative Technique
Jour. of the Hist. of Medicine
JPC / Journal of Popular Culture
JSSE / Journal of the Short Story in English [formerly *Cahiers de la Nouvelle*] (Angers, France)
KAL / Kyushu American Literature
KN / Kwartalnik Neofilologiczny (Warsaw)
KPR / Kentucky Philological Review [formerly *Kentucky Philological Assn. Bulletin*]
KR / Kenyon Review
LaLit / Louisiana Literature
LAmer / Letterature d'America: Revista Trimestale
L&B / Literature and Belief
L&H /Literature and History
Lang&S / Language and Style: An International Journal
Leer
Legacy: A Journal of Nineteenth-Century American Women Writers
Letras Femininas
LFQ / Literature/Film Quarterly
LHRev / Langston Hughes Review
Ling&L / Língua e Literatura: Revista dos Departamentos de Letras de Faculdade de Filosofia, Letras e Ciêncas Humanas da Universidade de São Paulo
LitR / Literary Review: An International Journal Devoted to English Studies
Litva Literaturnaya
LJHum / Lamar Journal of the Humanities
MarkhamR / Markham Review
MD / Modern Drama
Menckeniana: A Quarterly Review
MFS / Modern Fiction Studies
MHLS / Mid-Hudson Language Studies
MissFR / Mississippi Folklore Register
MissQ / Mississippi Quarterly
MissR / Missouri Review
MLQ / Modern Language Quarterly
MLR / Modern Language Review
MLS / Modern Language Studies
MMisc / Midwestern Miscellany
Modern Age
Mosaic: A Journal for the Interdisciplinary Study of Literature
MP / Modern Philology

MQ / Midwest Quarterly: A Journal of Contemporary Thought (Pittsburg, Kans.)
MQR / Michigan Quarterly Review
MR / Massachusetts Review
MSE / Massachusetts Studies in English
MSpr / Moderna Språk
MStrR / Mickle Street Review
MTJ / Mark Twain Journal
Nabokovian
N&Q / Notes and Queries
Nauka i zhizn'
NCL / Nineteenth-Century Literature
NConL / Notes on Contemporary Literature
Neohelicon: Acta Comparatonis Litterarum Universarum
Neophil / Neophilologus (Groningen, Netherlands)
NEQ / New England Quarterly
NER / New England Review and Bread Loaf Quarterly
NewC / New Criterion
NewComp / New Comparison: A Journal of Comparative and General Literary Studies
Newsboy
NHR / Nathaniel Hawthorne Review
NLH / New Literary History: A Journal of Theory and Interpretation
NMAL: Notes on Modern American Literature
NMW / Notes on Mississippi Writers
NOR / New Orleans Review
NorthAmerRev / North American Review
Novel: A Forum on Fiction
NWR / Northwest Review
NY / New Yorker
NYQ / New York Quarterly
NYRB / New York Review of Books
NYTBR / New York Times Book Review
Obsidian: Black Literature in Review
OL / Orbis Litterarum: International Review of Literary Studies
OT / Oral Tradition
PAAS / Proceedings of the American Antiquarian Society
Paideuma: A Journal Devoted to Ezra Pound Scholarship
PAPA / Publications of the Arkansas Philological Society
PAR / Performing Arts Resources
PCL / Perspectives on Contemporary Literature
PCP / Pacific Coast Philology
P. D. E., Copenhagen / Publications of the Department of English, Univ. of Copenhagen
Phylon: The Atlanta University Review of Race and Culture
PLL / Papers on Language and Literature
PM / Pembroke Magazine
PMLA: Publications of the Modern Language Assn.
PNotes / Pynchon Notes
PNR / PN Review
PoeS / Poe Studies
PolR / Polish Review
PR / Partisan Review
Problemy Amerikanistiki
PSA Newsletter / Poe Studies Assn. Newsletter
PSt / Prose Studies
PULC / Princeton University Library Chronicle
PUUHS / Proceedings of the Unitarian Universalist Historical Society
QJS / Quarterly Journal of Speech
Quaderni (Bergamo)
Quaderni di Lingue e Letterature (Verona)
RALS / Resources for American Literature
R&L / Religion and Literature
Raritan, A Quarterly Review
RCF / Review of Contemporary Fiction
Reader: Essays in Reader-Oriented Theory, Criticism, and Pedagogy
RECTR / Restoration and 18th Century Theatre Research
Renascence: Essays on Value in Literature
Representations
RFEA / Revue Française d'Études Américaines
RJN / Robinson Jeffers Newsletter
RLT / Russian Literature Triquarterly
RMR / Rocky Mountain Review of Language and Literature

RoR / Romanian Review
RR / Romanic Review
RusR / Russian Review: An American Quarterly Devoted to Russia Past and Present
SAD / Studies in American Drama, 1945–Present
SAF / Studies in American Fiction
Sage: A Scholarly Journal on Black Women (Georgia State Univ.)
Sagetrieb: A Journal Devoted to Poets in the Pound-H.D.-Williams Tradition
SAH / Svenska Akademiens Handlinger
SAJL / Studies in American Jewish Literature
SALit / Chu-Shikoku Studies in American Literature
SAQ / South Atlantic Quarterly
SAR / Studies in the American Renaissance
SB / Studies in Bibliography
Sci&Soc / Science and Society
SCr / Strumenti Critici: Rivista Quadrimestrale di Cultura e Critica Letteraria
SCR / South Carolina Review
Scream
SCRev / South Central Review: The Journal of the South Central Modern Language Association
Scripsi
SDR / South Dakota Review
Seven: An Anglo-American Literary Review
SFS / Science-Fiction Studies
SHR / Southern Humanities Review
Signs: A Journal of Women in Culture and Society
SIR / Studies in Romanticism
SlavR / Slavic Review: American Quarterly of Soviet and East European Studies
SLitI / Studies in the Literary Imagination
SLJ / Southern Literary Journal
SLRev / Stanford Literary Review
SNNTS / Studies in the Novel (North Texas State Univ.)
SoAR / South Atlantic Review
SoQ / Southern Quarterly
SoR / Southern Review
SoSt / Southern Studies
Southerly: A Review of Australian Literature (Sydney, Australia)
SPELL / Swiss Papers in English Language and Literature
SR / Sewanee Review
SSF / Studies in Short Fiction
StAH / Studies in American Humor
La Stampa
StHum / Studies in the Humanities (Indiana, Pa.)
StQ / Steinbeck Quarterly
StTCL / Studies in Twentieth-Century Literature
Style
TCL / Twentieth-Century Literature
TESOLQ / TESOL Quarterly (Teachers of English to Speakers of Other Languages)
Thalia: Studies in Literary Humor
Theater
THStud / Theatre History Studies
Tidskrift för litteraturvetenskap
TLs / Théorie, Littérature, enseignement
Tropismes
TSLL / Texas Studies in Language and Literature
Turia
TWN / Thomas Wolfe Review
Uchenie Zapiski Tartuskogo Universiteta
UDR / University of Dayton Review
UMSE / University of Mississippi Studies in English
Vanity Fair
VC / Virginia Cavalcade
Il Verri: Revista di Letteratura
Vestnik Kievskogo universiteta. Romano-Germanskiya Filologiya
VMHB / Virginia Magazine of History and Biography
VQR / Virginia Quarterly Review
WAL / West American Literature
W&I / Word and Image: A Journal of Verbal/Visual Enquiry
WascanaR / Wascana Review
WCPMN / Willa Cather Pioneer Memorial Newsletter
WCWR / William Carlos Williams Review
WE / Winesburg Eagle: The Official

Publication of the Sherwood Anderson Society
WHR / Western Humanities Review
WLT / World Literature Today
WMQ / William and Mary Quarterly
Woman's Art Journal
WorcesterRev / Worcester Review
The World: Journal of the Unitarian Universalist Association (Boston)
WS / Women's Studies
WSJour / Wallace Stevens Journal
WVUPP / West Virginia University Philological Papers
WWR / Walt Whitman Quarterly Review
XUS / Xavier Review
YER / Yeats Eliot Review
YR / Yale Review
ZAA / Zeitschrift für Anglistik und Americanistik

Publishers

Academic / San Diego, Calif.: Academic Press, Inc. (subs. of Harcourt Brace Jovanovich, Inc.)
ALA / Chicago: American Library Assn.
Alabama / Tuscaloosa: Univ. of Alabama Press
Allen and Unwin / Winchester, Mass.: Unwin Hyman, Inc.
AMS Press / New York: AMS Press, Inc.
Andrews and McMeel (Kansas City, Mo.)
Arkansas / Fayetteville: Univ. of Arkansas Press
Arte Publico / Houston, Tex.: Arte Publico Press (div. of Univ. of Houston)
Aubier / Paris: Editions Aubier-Montaigne
Ballantine / New York: Ballantine Books, Inc. (div. of Random House, Inc.)
Barnes and Noble / New York: Harper & Row Publishers, Inc.
Basilisk / London: Basilisk Press, Ltd.
Beacon / Boston: Beacon Press, Inc.
Belknap / Cambridge, Mass.: Belknap Press of Harvard Univ. Press
Benjamins / Philadelphia: John Benjamins North America, Inc.
Berg / Oxford: Berg Publishers, Ltd.
Black Sparrow / Santa Rosa, Calif.: Black Sparrow Press
Black Swan / Redding Ridge, Conn.: Black Swan Books, Ltd.
Blackwell / Oxford: Basil Blackwell, Ltd.
Blaue Eule / Essen: Die Blaue Eule
Boise State / Boise, Idaho: Boise State Univ.
Bowling Green / Bowling Green, Ohio: Bowling Green State Univ. Popular Press
Boynton / Portsmouth, N.H.: Boynton Cook Publishers, Inc. (subs. of Heinemann Educational Books, Inc.)
Bucknell / Lewisburg, Pa.: Bucknell Univ. Press (dist. by Associated Univ. Presses)
Bulzoni / Rome: Bulzoni Editore
Bunka-shobo Hakubunsha (Tokyo)
Calif. / Berkeley: Univ. of California Press
Cambridge / New York: Cambridge Univ. Press
Carucci (Rome)
Cassell / London: Cassell PLC
Cecil Woolf (London)
Center for Medieval and Early Renaissance Studies / Binghamton: State Univ. of New York at Binghamton
Central Ark. / Conway, Ark.: Univ. of Central Arkansas Press (dist. by Univ. Publishing Associates, Inc.)
Chelsea / New York: Chelsea House Publishers (div. of Main Line Book Co.)
Chicago / Chicago: Univ. of Chicago Press
Columbia / New York: Columbia Univ. Press
Continuum / New York: Continuum Publishing Co. (dist. by Harper & Row Pubs., Inc.)
Cornell / Ithaca, N.Y.: Cornell Univ. Press

Delaware / Newark: Univ. of Delaware Press (dist. by Associated Univ. Presses)
Dell / New York: Dell Publishing Co., Inc. (div. of Bantam Doubleday Dell Publishing Group, Inc.)
Donald I. Fine / New York: Donald I. Fine, Inc.
Doubleday / New York: Doubleday & Co., Inc. (div. of Bantam Doubleday Dell Publishing Group, Inc.)
Duckworth / London: Gerald Duckworth & Co., Ltd.
Duke / Durham, N.C.: Duke Univ. Press
Eakin / Austin, Tex.: Eakin Press
ELS / Victoria, B.C., Can.: English Literary Studies, Univ. of Victoria
Faber / Winchester, Mass.: Faber & Faber, Inc. (affil. of Faber & Faber, Ltd., London; dist. by American International Distribution Corp.)
Fairleigh Dickinson / Teaneck, N.J.: Fairleigh Dickinson Univ. Press (dist. by Associated Univ. Presses)
Farrar / New York: Farrar, Straus & Giroux, Inc.
Florida State / Tallahassee: Florida State Univ. Press
Francke / Tübingen: A. Francke Verlag GmbH
Free University Press / Amsterdam: Vrye Universiteit, Boekhandel
Gale / Detroit: Gale Research, Inc. (subs. of International Thomson Publishing, Inc.)
Garland / New York: Garland Publishing, Inc.
Georgia / Athens: Univ. of Georgia Press
Grasset / Paris: Grasset et Fasquelle
Greenwood / Westport, Conn.: Greenwood Press, Inc.
Grove / New York: Grove Press (dist. by Random House, Inc.)
Gunter Narr / Tübingen: Gunter Narr Verlag
Hall / Boston: G. K. Hall & Co. (div. of Macmillan Publishing Co.)
Harcourt / San Diego, Calif.: Harcourt Brace Jovanovich, Inc.
Harold Shaw / Wheaton, Ill.: Harold Shaw Publishers
Harper / New York: Harper & Row Publishers, Inc.
Harvard / Cambridge: Harvard Univ. Press
Hill & Wang / New York: Hill & Wang, Inc. (div. of Farrar, Straus & Giroux, Inc.)
Holt / New York: Henry Holt & Co. (subs. of Verlagsgruppe Georg von Holtzbrinck)
Hopkins / Baltimore: Johns Hopkins Univ. Press
Human Sciences / New York: Human Sciences Press, Inc.
Idaho / Moscow: Univ. of Idaho Press
Illinois / Champaign: Univ. of Illinois Press
Iowa / Iowa City: Univ. of Iowa Press
Iowa State / Ames: Iowa State Univ. Press
John Donald / Edinburgh: John Donald Publishers
Kaibun-sha / Tokyo: Kaibun-sha Shuppan
Kent State / Kent, Ohio: Kent State Univ. Press
Kentucky / Lexington: Univ. Press of Kentucky
Kluwer / Boston: Kluwer Academic Publishers
Knopf / New York: Alfred A. Knopf, Inc. (subs. of Random House, Inc.)
Kobian-shobo (Tokyo)
Krupskoi / Moscow: N. K. Krupskoi
Kukusho-kankokai (Tokyo)
Lehigh / Bethlehem, Pa.: Lehigh Univ. Press (dist. by Associated Univ. Presses)
Liber / Tokyo: Liber Press
Library of America / New York: Library of America (dist. by Viking Penguin, Inc.)
Little, Brown / Boston: Little, Brown & Co. (div. of Time, Inc.)
Longman / White Plains, N.Y.: Longman, Inc.
Loyola / Chicago: Loyola Univ. Press
LSU / Baton Rouge: Louisiana State Univ. Press
Macmillan / London: Macmillan Publishers, Ltd.
Maisonneuve / Washington, D.C.:

Maisonneuve Press (div. of Institute for Advanced Cultural Studies)
Manchester / Manchester: Manchester Univ. Press (dist. by St. Martin's Press, Inc., subs. of Macmillan Publishing Co.)
Mass. / Amherst: Univ. of Massachusetts Press
Meckler / Westport, Conn.: Meckler Publishing Corp.
Mellen / Lewiston, N.Y.: Edwin Mellen Press
Mentor / New York: Mentor Books (imprint of New American Library, subs. of Pearson, Inc.)
Mercer / Macon, Ga.: Mercer Univ. Press
Methuen / New York: Routledge, Chapman & Hall, Inc.
Michigan / Ann Arbor: Univ. of Michigan Press
Minnesota / Minneapolis: Univ. of Minnesota Press
Miss. / Jackson: Univ. Press of Mississippi
Missouri / Columbia: Univ. of Missouri Press
MIT / Cambridge, Mass.: MIT Press
MLA / New York: Modern Language Assn. of America
Morrow / New York: William Morrow & Co., Inc. (subs. of Hearst Corp.)
NAL / New York: New American Library (subs. of Pearson, Inc.)
Nanundo (Tokyo)
Nebraska / Lincoln: Univ. of Nebraska Press
Newberry / Chicago: Newberry Library
New Directions / New York: New Directions Publishing Corp. (dist. by W. W. Norton & Co., Inc.)
New England / Hanover, N.H.: University Press of New England
New Mexico / Albuquerque: Univ. of New Mexico Press
No. Car. / Chapel Hill: Univ. of North Carolina Press
No. Ill. / DeKalb: Northern Illinois Univ. Press
Norske Samlaget (Oslo)
Northeastern / Boston: Northeastern Univ. Press
Northwestern / Evanston, Ill.: Northwestern Univ. Press
Norton / New York: W. W. Norton & Co., Inc.
Notre Dame / Notre Dame, Ind.: Univ. of Notre Dame Press (dist. by Longwood Publishing Group, Inc.)
Odense / Odense Univ. Press
Ohio / Athens: Ohio Univ. Press
Ohio State / Columbus: Ohio State Univ. Press
Ohshi-sha (Tokyo)
Okla. / Norman: Univ. of Oklahoma Press
Olschki / Florence: Leo S. Olschki
Open / New York: Open Univ. Press (imprint of Taylor & Francis, Inc.)
Overlook / New York: Overlook Press (dist. by Viking Penguin, Inc.)
Oxford / New York: Oxford Univ. Press, Inc.
Palm & Enke (Erlangen)
Pantheon / New York: Pantheon Books (div. of Random House, Inc.)
Paragon / New York: Paragon House Publishers
Penguin / New York: Penguin Books
Penn. State / University Park: Pennsylvania State Univ. Press
Peter Bedrick / New York: Peter Bedrick Books
Peter Lang / New York: Peter Lang Publishing, Inc. (subs. of Verlag Peter Lang AG [Switzerland])
Pinter / Dover, N.H.: Frances Pinter Publishers, Ltd.
Pogo / Saint Paul, Minn.: Pogo Press, Inc.
Princeton / Princeton, N.J.: Princeton Univ. Press
Provence / Aix: Univ. de Provence
Purdue / West Lafayette, Ind.: Purdue Univ. Press
Pustet / Regensburg: Verlag Friedrich Pustet
Random House / New York: Random House, Inc.
Roberts Rinehart / Boulder, Colo.: Roberts Rinehart, Inc., Publishers

Rodopi / Amsterdam: Editions Rodopi BV
Routledge / New York: Routledge, Chapman & Hall, Inc.
Rutgers / New Brunswick, N.J.: Rutgers Univ. Press
St. James / Chicago: St. James Press
St. Martin's / New York: St. Martin's Press, Inc. (subs. of Macmillan Publishing Co.)
Scarecrow / Metuchen, N.J.: Scarecrow Press, Inc. (subs. of Grolier Educational Corp.)
Scribner's / New York: Macmillan Publishing Co., Inc.
Sierra Club / San Francisco: Sierra Club Books (dist. by Random House, Inc.)
Simon & Schuster / New York: Simon & Schuster, Inc. (div. of Paramount Communications, Inc.)
So. Car. / Columbia: Univ. of South Carolina Press
So. Ill. / Carbondale: Southern Illinois Univ. Press
Solum / Lysaker, Norway: Solum Verlag (imprint of Humanities Press International, Inc.)
Stanford / Stanford, Calif.: Stanford Univ. Press
Starmont / Mercer Island, Wash.: Starmont House, Inc.
Steinbeck Society / Muncie, Ind.: Steinbeck Research Institute, Dept. of English, Ball State Univ.
SUNY / Albany: State Univ. of New York Press
Susquehanna / Selinsgrove, Pa.: Susquehanna Univ. Press (dist. by Associated Univ. Presses)
TCG / New York: Theatre Communications Group, Inc.
Tennessee / Knoxville: Univ. of Tennessee Press
Thames / New York: Thames & Hudson (dist. by W. W. Norton & Co., Inc.)
Transcendental / Hartford, Conn.: Transcendental Books
TUSAS / Boston: Twayne Publishers (imprint of G. K. Hall & Co., div. of Macmillan Publishing Co.)
Twayne / Boston: Twayne Publishers (imprint of G. K. Hall & Co., div. of Macmillan Publishing Co.)
UMI / Ann Arbor, Mich.: University Microfilms International (div. of Bell & Howell)
UMI Research Press / Ann Arbor, Mich.: UMI Research Press (affil. of UMI)
Ungar / New York: Ungar Publishing Co.
Univ. Press / Lanham, Md.: University Press of America
Utah / Salt Lake City: Univ. of Utah Press
Vanderbilt / Nashville, Tenn.: Vanderbilt Univ. Press
Vikas / New Delhi: Vikas Publishing House, Pvt. Ltd.
Viking / New York: Viking Penguin, Inc.
Virginia / Charlottesville: Univ. Press of Virginia
Vision / London: Vision Books (dist. by St. Martin's Press, Inc.)
Wayne State / Detroit: Wayne State Univ. Press
Wesleyan / Middletown, Conn.: Wesleyan Univ. Press
West Georgia College (Carrollton)
Williams / Williamstown, Mass.: Williams College
Wisconsin / Madison: Univ. of Wisconsin Press
Wyndham Hall / Bristol, Ind.: Wyndham Hall Press
Yale / New Haven, Conn.: Yale Univ. Press
York / Fredericton, N.B., Can.: York Press

Part I

1. Emerson, Thoreau, and Transcendentalism

David M. Robinson

Our understanding of the Transcendentalists advanced significantly in 1988, marked by rising interest in Margaret Fuller, who seems to be joining Emerson and Thoreau as a third member of a Transcendentalist triumvirate—if, that is, she is judged to be a Transcendentalist at all. Volumes of two major editions reached completion, and the *Columbia Literary History of the United States* (*CLHUS*) provided new overviews of the movement and its major figures.

i. General Studies, Editions, Source Material

Transcendentalism was represented in *CLHUS* by three astute, historically grounded essays. In a discerning explanation of the origins and maturity of Transcendentalism (*CLHUS*, pp. 364–78), Lawrence Buell proposed that it "achieved movement status . . . as a reform impulse within Unitarianism" by extending the central Unitarian premise "that human nature is improvable through nurture and self-culture." But these religious sources proved epistemologically unsatisfying, forcing the movement beyond its theological roots. Cautious not to claim too much for the movement, he says that "literary transcendentalism was more enduringly important for its ideology than for its actual literary achievement." But he conveys the subtlety of Emerson's epistemology and recognizes Fuller's *Woman in the Nineteenth Century* as "America's first landmark feminist treatise." Buell also identifies eight key figures in the movement—Emerson, Thoreau, Alcott, Ripley, Fuller, Hedge, Brownson, and Parker—and two subgroups of lesser figures, articulating the consensus that Transcendentalism drew a range of personalities and intellectual emphases into its orbit. Barbara Packer's finely crafted essay on Emerson (*CLHUS*, pp. 381–98) has an interpretive originality unusual in such a genre of summary, stressing Emerson's concern with the forms of power as a key to his career. Most of his first collection of *Essays* "derive their energy from the conflicts they explore between the arrogant assumption of spiritual power and the clear-sighted listing of all forces ranged in opposition to that power." "Fate" and "Power," key texts in Emerson's later development, "are among Emerson's strongest essays, intellectually uncompromising, rhetorically violent." Packer's essay, which takes a place in the general reassessment of Emerson in terms of Pragmatism, will certainly call deserved attention to his later work. Frederick Garber's discussion of Thoreau's "home-directed thought and stubborn originality" (*CLHUS*, pp. 399–412) is a persuasive rendering of the continuing call of Thoreau on modern readers. He describes Thoreau's intellectual project as the pursuit of "getting the self to be at home in the world," a task he best accomplished in his journal. In his subtle comparison of Emerson and Thoreau, Garber finds Thoreau's sense of the "answering" of things in nature a more complex and sustaining theory of nature's expression than Emersonian typology; but there remained in Thoreau's work a sense of the "bifurcation" between the self and its grounding in nature.

Stanley Cavell's *In Quest of the Ordinary: Lines of Skepticism and Romanticism* (Chicago), a gathering of essays from the 1980s (six of the seven previously published), is devoted to Cavell's unlikely but persuasive philosophical rehabilitation of Emerson and Thoreau through an analysis of the engagement with skepticism that they share with Wittgenstein. Cavell's description of the Transcendentalist philosophical method as "reading" rather than "argumentation" suggests that the whole personality must be engaged in the work of philosophy, an engagement which, more than any doctrine, confirms their philosophical stature. I learned much from Larry J. Reynolds's *European Revolutions and the American Literary Renaissance* (Yale), an account of American reactions to the European revolutions of 1848–49. The contrasting reactions of Emerson and Fuller seem to me a key to Reynolds's book. Emerson responded to the French Revolution coolly as he viewed it from England, but thawed somewhat to the apocalyptic fervor of the situation when he came to France, though he never abandoned his skepticism of mass movements. Fuller's story is different, for she "alone had the opportunity, the inclination, and ultimately the resolve to align herself whole-heartedly with European democratic liberalism." She recorded her engagement with the Italian revolution in her *Tribune* letters, which Reynolds discusses persuasively as one of her most significant achievements. David S. Reynolds's *Beneath the American Renaissance* (Knopf) reinterprets antebellum American culture through the era's popular literature, and every scholar of our period will salute his voluminous reading. The richness of the key texts of the "American Renaissance" was the product "of a sudden fluidity of textual modes" that Reynolds traces to a largely forgotten range of popular works such as "torrid popular evangelical preaching" (Father Taylor's influence on Emerson is his chief example), reform writings, and Southwest humor. There is a good bit of Parrington in Reynolds's location of populist and Western texts as sources of vitality for the culture, and a good bit of Matthiessen in his depiction of the major writers' project of expressing this democratic energy in new forms. Reynolds would encourage a new respect for the vitality of the popular culture, while preserving an aesthetic elevation of the high culture—a position not without its problems. But his book will open your eyes to the literary world in which the major authors functioned.

In "Science, Religion, and the Transcendentalist Response to a Changing America" (*SAR*, pp. 1–25), Frederick C. Dahlstrand describes the collapse of the Transcendentalist synthesis of science and religion in what some Transcendentalists saw as the new materialism of the Free Religious Association. He identifies Samuel Johnson and John Weiss as important transitional figures and brings the generally neglected FRA into its rightful context as an extender and modifier of Transcendentalism. In "Transcendentalism and Autobiography: Emerson, Whitman and Thoreau," pp. 57–71, in A. Robert Lee, ed., *First Person Singular: Studies in American Autobiography* (Vision/St. Martin's), Brian Harding describes the tendency of Transcendentalist texts to dissolve "the solidity (or continuity) of the self," making Emerson's project "the deconstruction of autobiography." There is little new of a factual or interpretive nature in the four chapters on Transcendentalism in Perry D. Westbrook's *A Literary History of New England* (Lehigh), though it is a competent survey of the movement, useful as an introductory overview. That Fuller is accorded a separate chapter is significant, and Westbrook is right in noting the continuing cultural influence of Transcendentalism in the "national attitude toward nature." I wish there were more essays with the scope and discernment of Giles Gunn's "The Kingdoms of Theory and the New Historicism in America" (*YR* 77:207–36), which assesses several recent New Historicist studies bearing on Transcendentalism. Readers of Transcendentalism will also be interested in chapters 5 and 6 of William E. Cain's *F. O. Matthiessen and the Politics of Criticism* (Wisconsin), which deal with Matthiessen's *American Renaissance.*

Joseph J. Moldenhauer's edition of Thoreau's *Cape Cod* (Princeton) provides the definitive edition of one of Thoreau's most interesting books, which depicts his encounter with the unfamiliar territory of the Cape and his eye for the humors of its inhabitants. *Cape Cod* has particular significance because of the abrupt suspension of its original serialization in *Putnam's.* In the absence of Thoreau's manuscript, those early chapters have textual significance. In his authoritative introduction, Moldenhauer adduces convincing evidence that George William Curtis could not brook the publication of "The Wellfleet Oysterman" because of its potential offense to "mid-nineteenth-century American bourgeois taste." The fifth volume of Robert N. Hudspeth's vitally important *Letters of Margaret Fuller* (Cornell) covers the crucial years 1848–49, during which Fuller was preparing to give birth and becoming ever more deeply committed to the cause of Italian liberty. Hudspeth presents this as a time in which her estrangement from New England grew, replaced by a sense of belonging in Rome. When forced to evacuate Rome in 1849, Fuller for the first time "left a city that she felt to be a home." The letters from this period are crucial texts in any assessment of her career, and Hudspeth's introductory essay is cogent, sympathetic, and very well informed. An important addendum to Hudspeth's edition is Francis B. Dedmond's "The Letters of Caroline Sturgis to Margaret Fuller" (*SAR*, pp. 201–51), which contains 18 letters to Fuller from 1841 to 1846, along with Dedmond's fine account of this key friendship. Guy R. Woodall's "The Selected Sermons of Convers Francis (Part Two)" (*SAR*, pp. 55–131) adds 14 sermons on the themes of nature, reform, and youth to Woodall's previous installment (see *ALS 1987*, p. 5). Woodall's work reminds us that the sermonic record is one of the richest untapped sources in Transcendentalist historiography. Philip F. Gura has provided a new edition of one very significant sermon in "Theodore Parker and the South Boston Ordination: The Textual Tangle of *A Discourse on the Transient and Permanent in Christianity*" (*SAR*, pp. 149–78). Gura reports that Parker made "literally *hundreds* of changes" in the manuscript before publishing it, and, using Parker's appendix of changes, he reconstructs the original text. In "Miss Fuller Among the Literary Lions: Two Essays Read at 'The

Coliseum' in 1838" (*SAR*, 37–53), Tess Hoffman reports the discovery of two essays by Fuller for a Providence literary club, one of which shows "the kernel of the argument" that she later used in her key feminist texts. Gary Scharnhorst has identified an unrecorded Thoreau essay of 1846 in "'Conflict of Laws': A Lost Essay by Henry Thoreau" (*NEQ* 61:569–71), part of the background of "Civil Disobedience." Leonard N. Neufeldt's "Neopragmatism and Convention in Textual Editing" (*A&EB* 1[1987]:225–36) uses the editing of Thoreau's journal to address the question of the permanence of any edited text, concluding that "textual editing is a practical activity performed by specific people under the influence of specific assumptions."

Joel Myerson's *American Transcendentalists*, volume 5 of the *Dictionary of Literary Biography Documentary Series* (Gale), reprints a generous selection of key periodical and pamphlet texts, beautifully illustrated with reproductions of documents from the period. It includes particularly notable sections on the Brook Farm and Fruitlands experiments. Catherine Albanese's *The Spirituality of the American Transcendentalists* (Mercer) includes selections of Emerson, Alcott, Parker, and Thoreau arranged to demonstrate their accessibility through the concept of spirituality, preceded by a solid discussion of the relation of spirituality to self-culture.

ii. Emerson

Among several strong contributions to Emerson studies, two stand out. Robert Milder's "Emerson's Two Conversions" (*ESQ* 33[1987]: 20–34) offers a new account of Emerson's early development, and Lawrence Rosenwald's *Emerson and the Art of the Diary* (Oxford) considers the genesis and form of Emerson's journal. Milder's closely textured explanation of Emerson's "conversions" in 1827 and 1830 is deeply informed by the psychological dynamics of Puritan regeneration and revives with greater subtlety Perry Miller's version of Emerson as a once-removed Puritan. I had considered Miller's view superseded in light of recent reinterpretations of Unitarianism, but Milder makes persuasive use of the Edwardsian notion of the religious affections in this new tracing of Emerson's route to maturity through spiritual experience. His essay should be read in the company of Daniel Walker Howe's *The Unitarian Conscience: Harvard Moral Philosophy, 1805–1861*, now in a new edition (Wesleyan). Howe's description of Unitarian pietism remains the most important, and least acknowledged, description of the native roots of Transcendentalism. A study of the achievement of Emerson's journals has been in order for some time, especially after the completion of *Journals and Miscellaneous Notebooks* in 1982. Rosenwald is brilliant in disabusing readers of the three myths that have prevented a clearer understanding of the journal—the beliefs that it is a private or secret text, that as such it has a privileged claim on truth, and that it is spontaneously artless. The removal of these obstructions allows him to discuss the evolution of the journal as a genre, beginning with Emerson's mediation between the Lockean commonplace book and Mary Moody Emerson's Puritan journal of spiritual experience. Rosenwald is at points too methodologically self-conscious, rehearsing his strategy as a form of argumentation, and too ready to elevate the journal at the expense of other of Emerson's forms. But his conclusion is a challenging proposition to Emerson studies: "The journals are no draft; they are a text," and a text which constitutes "Emerson's chief literary performance."

David Marr takes Emersonian "privatism" as the fundamental problem of American culture in *American Worlds Since Emerson* (Massachusetts), arguing that the doctrine of the infinitude of the private man is politically evasive. His book might be read as a rejoinder to Irving Howe's recent defense of Emerson's political availability in *The American Newness* (see *ALS 1986*, p. 8). For Marr, the poetic appropriation of nature portends its real appropriation, pushing the uncritical affirmation of nature into an uncritical acceptance of America. "Idealism without negativity," Marr argues, "is mere interiority." Although Emerson is the source of our political woes, Marr's opening chapters on Emerson and Whitman are the least persuasive of this wide-ranging book. Emerson's idealism was to my mind far from uncritical, and I am not inclined to blame a thinker for the misappropriation of his work. But Marr's argument has a cumulative power as it approaches our contemporary cultural condition and forces a consideration of how the progressive ideology of one period may become regressive in the next. In *Emerson and Skepticism: The Cipher of the World*, John Michael challenges Stephen E. Whicher's portrait of Emerson by stressing his continuing struggle with skepticism and need for external approval. Michael is astute in stressing Hume's influence on Emerson, a fact that "radically alters his image as the untroubled spokesman for American individualism," although he overstates the pervasiveness of that image in current scholarship. The book is burdened by a long and unpersuasive digression on Montaigne but redeemed by a subtle reading of the end of *Nature*, in which Michael shows how Emerson reifies the split between the me and the not-me, the very problem that had motivated the work itself. It is a book of limited scope—the crucial texts for Emerson's battle with skepticism come after *Nature*, and are not discussed—but his reading of *Nature* will have to be considered in continuing work on Emerson's early development. In a persuasive and potentially important correction to previous readings of the "Idealism" chapter of *Nature*, "Emerson's Unenlightened Child: Some Corrective Notes" (*ATQ* n.s. 2:89–96), Morton L. Ross stresses the "organic process of education by which the materialist child is transformed into the mature idealist." Ann Hostetler's "Emerson and the Visual Arts: Private Response and Public Posture" (*ESQ* 33[1987]:121–36) describes Emerson's early aesthetic development through his experience of Italian art, arguing that its vitality eventually led him to call for a restoration of "art to a central position in his culture" through the open, reader-oriented form of the essay. Hostetler reaffirms the importance of Emerson's first European trip, and suggests his surprisingly deep affinity with the visual arts. A quite different consideration of Emerson's view of the role of poetry is Lisa M. Steinman's "The Houses of Fathers: Stevens and Emerson" (*WSJ* 12:162–72), which compares Emerson with Wallace Stevens and perceptively describes Emerson's struggles with the exclusion of poetry from the culturally sanctioned sphere of male influence. Emerson's attempt to redefine the poetic life, like Stevens's, led him to distance poetry not only from "the world of commerce" but also from "the actual domestic world." In *Authority, Autonomy, and Representation in American Literature, 1776–1865* (Princeton), Mark R. Patterson discusses Emerson's transition from "Scholar" to "Poet" to "Representative Man," explaining it as Emerson's struggle to find a representative figure who could successfully mediate between world and spirit (or politics and intellectual culture). Patterson notes the "diminished status" of the hero in *Representative Men*, seeing it as "more a prototype of pragmatism than a form of idealism." The Pragmatist reading of Emerson, which seems to be gaining momentum, is extended in David Jacobson's "'Compensation': Exteriority Beyond the Spirit of Revenge" (*ESQ* 33[1987]:94–109), which reads "Compensation" as an anticipation of the Pragmatist dictum that thought must be valued for its "consequences of action in the world," and effectively describes a configuration of shared concerns in Emerson, Nietzsche, and Heidegger. In "Power, Politics, and a Sense of History," pp. 94–105 in *A Free and Ordered Space* (Norton), the late A. Bartlett Giamatti sees a dark side to Emerson's Pragmatism, finding him the chief culprit in America's tendency to equate "power" with "mere force." Giamatti focuses on Emerson's "Power," but the straw man that he attacks has only a tenuous relation to the author who worried about power as much as he praised it.

There were several intelligent readings of Emerson from a theological perspective. In "Transcendental Sacramentals: 'The Lord's Supper' and Emerson's Doctrine of Form" (*NEQ* 61:398–418), Ivy Schweitzer views Emerson's rejection of the sacramental forms in the context of Puritan antinomianism and describes Emerson's belief that one develops through and beyond forms, their rejection marking progress and growth. James Duban analyzes Emerson's impact on later Unitarian theology in "From Emerson to Edwards: Henry Whitney Bellows and an 'Ideal' Metaphysics of Sovereignty" (*HTR* 81:389–411). Duban's trenchant account of Bellows's struggles with Emersonian individualism traces his eventual reconciliation of Emerson with the legacy of Edwards. Gary Scharnhorst details the quite different case of an Emerson disciple in "William Rounseville Alger and the Legacy of Emerson" (*PUUHS* 21[1987–88]:43–54), using Alger as an excellent gauge of "the rehabilitation of Emerson's reputation" among Unitarians at mid-century. In "Emerson, Rammohan Roy, and the Unitarians" (*SAR*, pp. 133–48), Alan D. Hodder describes the controversy over Roy's anti-Trinitarian *The Precepts of Jesus* (1820), finding that it provoked Emerson's reconsideration of Hindu doctrines in the 1820s and prepared him for the deeper impact of Oriental scripture later.

Two essays explore the connection of Emerson's metaphors to economics and politics. In " 'Put God in Your Debt': Emerson's Economy of Expenditure" (*PMLA* 103:35–44), Richard Grusin reads Emerson's economic metaphors in terms of the theories of gift exchange of Marcel Mauss and others. The dynamic of these exchanges "resembles the sacrificial economy of expenditure that Emerson sets forth throughout his work." In "Emerson as Expansionist," pp. 65–78, in Wolfgang Binder, ed., *Westward Expansion in America (1830–1860)* (Erlangen 1987), Yves Carlet literalizes the imperial self, finding connections between Emerson's metaphors of the expansion of the soul and his view of American geographical expansion. Alfred Kazin marked the 150th anniversary of "The American Scholar" with a lecture that asked, "Where Would Emerson Find His Scholar Now?" (*The World* 2, vi:4–7). Kazin used the occasion to call for a "renewal of literary discontent as Emerson knew it." Joel Porte's "Emerson: Experiments in Creation," pp. 85–96, in Boris Ford, ed., *American Literature*, volume 9 of *The New Pelican Guide to English Literature* (Penguin), surveys Emerson's struggle to maintain his creative life, with a notable description of the "wild play of intellectual energy" in *Essays*. *On Emerson: The Best From* American Literature, Edwin Cady and Louis J. Budd, eds., was added to Duke's ongoing series. Of special note, in light of the interest in Emerson and Pragmatism, are the articles by Frederick I. Carpenter and William T. Stafford. Kenneth Walter Cameron offers supplements to Burkholder and Myerson's *Emerson: An Annotated Secondary Bibliography* (see *ALS 1985*, pp. 3–4) in *The Emerson Tertiary Bibliography*, also contributing *Toward a Thoreau Tertiary Bibliography*. Teachers of Emerson should also be aware of Cameron's *Emerson's Prose Poem: The Structure and Meaning of* Nature *(1836)* (Transcendental), designed to introduce students to *Nature*.

iii. Thoreau

Two studies that propose different models of Thoreau's development led the year's work: Stephen Adams and Donald Ross, Jr.'s *Revising Mythologies: The Composition of Thoreau's Major Works* (Virginia), and Robert Sattelmeyer's *Thoreau's Reading: A Study in Intellectual History, With Bibliographical Catalogue* (Princeton). Adams and Ross provide a close-grained description of the interrelations among Thoreau's works, surely a fruitful resource for future scholars. They argue that Thoreau underwent a "conversion" to romanticism in 1851 which provided the rush of energy to complete *Walden* and made its latter half a creative high-water mark. Not before 1851 had Thoreau unambiguously referred to himself as a Transcendentalist, and his reappropriation of the Coleridgean view of the imagination, and a return to Wordsworth, confirm this conversion. This argument bears comparison with Robert D. Richardson, Jr.'s recent explanation of the periodic ebbing and flowing of Thoreau's creative powers (see *ALS 1986*, pp. 15–16) and his description of the impact of Thoreau's reading in natural history and in Cato's *De Re Rustica* in 1851. While

Richardson is more convincing about Thoreau's development, the "conversion" theory leads Adams and Ross to a superb analysis of *Walden*'s structure as two climactic sequences, culminating in "Higher Laws" and "Spring." One corollary of their model of Thoreau's development is an assessment of Thoreau's later work as a decline. Sattelmeyer, in contrast, sees the later work as an extension of a creative phase which began in 1850, when a greater domestic stability and a closer devotion to his journal allowed Thoreau to begin a more systematic study of three interests: natural history, early American history, and the American Indian. Sattelmeyer explains the transition to his later interests in a way that makes them difficult to dismiss as a faltering of creative energies. His study is divided into an authoritative survey of Thoreau's intellectual development and a "Bibliographical Catalogue" of his reading, entailing some 1,500 items. *Thoreau's Reading* will be an enduring resource.

In the best new textual reading of Thoreau this past year, " 'The Limits of an Afternoon Walk': Coleridgean Polarity in Thoreau's 'Walking' " (*ESQ* 33[1987]:110–19), William Rossi reads "Walking" in terms of Coleridge's ideas of polarity and describes the essay as "Thoreau's alternative version of the Transcendentalist doctrine of self-culture popularized by Emerson." This original essay will augment the already high place of "Walking" in the Thoreauvian canon. *Walden* was accorded much attention in addition to the analysis by Adams and Ross (see above). In "Unreading Thoreau" (*AL* 60:385–401), Henry Golemba describes the rhetoric of *Walden* as a "blending of 'leading ideas' with dream-like dissolves, of assertions with infinite qualifiers, of clear sentences with the perpetual sense of their imminent erasure," a style grounded in Thoreau's fascination with the fluidity of language and meaning. Golemba's portrayal of Thoreau's keen linguistic sensibility will interest scholars concerned with contemporary theories of the indeterminacy of language, even though these may differ from the Transcendentalists' notion of infinite linguistic creativity. Golemba's concluding discussion of "silence" in Thoreau's thought is a provocative coda to this astute essay. I recommend that everyone read George Hochfield's "Anti-Thoreau" (*SR* 96:433–43), though I find its argument doubtful. Hochfield contends that Thoreauvians "surrender all claim to irony" when they read his sacred texts, and he accuses Thoreau himself of "implacable humorlessness." To anyone who has read the opening of *Walden*, such a claim damages Hochfield's credibility to pronounce about irony and humor. He calls Thoreau a "Puritan in decadent form" who substituted a naively literal faith in the observation of nature for physical immersion in life. That Hochfield's key evidence, "Higher Laws," begins with Thoreau's puzzled description of his own animality, and strains to reconcile that discovery with the spiritual, calls his conclusion into doubt. Still, it is a provocative essay, and Hochfield is exactly right about Thoreau's being "an actor in a cultural mythology." The essay articulates the inarticulate skepticism that every teacher of *Walden* has found in a few of his or her students. Perhaps the best response to Hochfield is to read through Joel Myerson's fine compilation of *Critical Essays on Thoreau's* Walden (Hall), which brings together both early reviews and modern scholarly essays. Among those essays is Robert D. Richardson, Jr.'s new "The Social Ethics of Walden" (pp. 235–48), an incisive answer to the long-standing attack on Thoreau's destructive individualism. Richardson delineates five of the areas of Thoreau's social concern, which, taken together, constitute a compelling social ethic. Myerson's collection also includes Linck C. Johnson's new "Revolution and Renewal: The Genres of *Walden*," (pp. 215–35), which surveys "the subtle interplay among the genres" in *Walden* and is particularly astute on its relation to books of domestic economy. In "Thoreau's *Walden*: The Provocation of Fire," pp. 215–35, in Anna-Teresa Tymieniecka, ed., *Poetics of the Elements in the Human Condition: Part 2* [*Analecta Husserliana*, 23] (Kluwer), John Dolis concentrates on Thoreau's images of fire, building, and dwelling, arguing that "House-Warming" is a hinge on which the book makes a significant turn. Richard Dillman summarizes his findings from over 300 student journals on *Walden* in "Reader Response to Thoreau's *Walden*: A Study of Undergraduate Reading Patterns" (*Reader* 19:21–36). Teachers of *Walden* will be nodding in confirmation at Dillman's descriptions of the patterns of response. In three related articles, "Thoreau's Philosophy of Rhetorical Invention," "Thoreau's Philosophy of Audience," and "Thoreau's Philosophy of Style" (*BuR*, 31:60–96), Dillman describes Thoreau's "organic" rhetoric, which is grounded in the capacity of ideas to generate new ideas in the process of composition; this is an analysis that will make Thoreau a precursor to process-oriented composition theory. I am puzzled that these three articles were not molded into a unified essay.

Readings of other of Thoreau's works include "Thoreau and Mother Nature: 'Ktaadn' as an Oedipal Tale" (*ATQ* n.s. 2:301–11), in which Gregory M. Pfitzer argues that in his ascent, Thoreau "figuratively tries to rape the mountain." One need not accept Pfitzer's reading to make use of his more convincing suggestion that a "new respect for the awesome power of Nature" might be connected with the Ktaadn expedition. In "Thoreau's *Dial* Alterations and *A Week*" (*SAR*, pp. 179–200), E. Earle Stibitz analyzes the *Dial* material that Thoreau revised for use in *A Week*. In the second chapter of *The American Indian in American Literature: A Study in Metaphor* (Mellen), Elizabeth I. Hanson surveys Thoreau's attempt "to reinvent the Indian" in his published writings and unpublished Indian notebooks. Gary L. Collison's "Shadrach in Concord" (*CS* 19, ii:1–12) is a fascinating account of Frederick Minkins's escape to freedom through the Concord underground railroad in 1851 and the possible effects of the incident on Thoreau's journal. In "Thoreau: An American Taoist Sage" (*Comparatist* 11[1987]:86–95), Patricia A. Okker notes similarities between Thoreau and Lao Tzu, reading Thoreau's ethic in the light of the Taoist concept of *wu wei*, or acting by not acting.

iv. Fuller and Other Transcendentalists

Two notable reinterpretations of the Emerson-Fuller relationship alter our sense of its dynamics. In " 'Born and Bred in Different Nations': Margaret Fuller and Ralph Waldo Emerson," pp. 3–30 in Shirley Marchalonis, ed., *Patrons and Protégées: Gender, Friendship, and Writing in Nineteenth Century America* (Rutgers), Dorothy Berkson treats the relationship with sympathy and discernment, noting that Fuller objected to Emerson's "narrow and overly exalted definition of friendship" and fashioned from her need for intimate relationships "a strong philosophy of mutuality, compassion, and connection." She finds that Emerson initiated the dialogue on friendship at the crisis point in the relationship, a fact suggesting that despite his difficulties with personal intimacy, he needed Fuller's friendship. Berkson argues that "in spite of her transcendental and romantic grounding," Fuller "was at odds with some fundamental precepts of the transcendental point of view." I would suggest that, like others of the group, her differences with Emerson led her to modify and extend Transcendentalism rather than depart from it. Despite his influence, Emerson cannot be accorded the entire definition of the movement. In " 'The Liberal Air of All the Zones': Another View of the Emerson-Fuller Relationship" (*CCTES* 52[1987]:28–35), Susan B. Smith makes excellent use of the Hudspeth edition of the correspondence to argue that the relationship might best be understood in terms of "the differences between Emerson's and Fuller's concepts of self-culture." Smith is convincing about Fuller's frustration with "Emerson's lack of attention to a specific mechanism of social change," and she sees Fuller as having some of the characteristics of the "materialist" that Emerson described in "The Transcendentalist." In *Margaret Fuller: An American Romantic* (Berg) David Watson reads Fuller's Transcendentalism as an encumbrance to be overcome on her way to socialism. Watson sees a three-stage development in Fuller's political views: an early period "structured around ideals of moral individualism and leadership, and deeply sceptical about political organisation"; a middle period keyed by her move to New York, in which her "hostility to political movements softened considerably"; and a final European phase in which she "reached a mature and positive appreciation of Fourier and the associationists." Watson feels that Fuller never achieved "a final synthesis of her romanticism, her feminism and her socialism," but he still sees her life as a potential "text" for the modern reader. In "Romantic Prose and Feminine Romanticism" (*PSt* 10[1987]:178–95), Susan M. Levin describes "the particular counterforce" exercised by women in the romantic movement and applies her argument to Fuller's appropriation of Transcendental doctrine. Levin notes that in *Woman in the Nineteenth Century* Fuller turned Emerson's doctrine of self-reliance into "a statement about feminine independence." While this is a persuasive argument for Fuller's extension of Transcendentalist discourse, Levin also argues that the book "backs away from the Transcendentalists." The essay typifies the current dilemma over whether Fuller extended or rejected Transcendentalist thinking; this issue is not unrelated to readings of the nature of the Fuller-Emerson friendship. Fuller plays a small role, and Caroline Dall and Lydia Maria Child significant ones, in Karen Sánchez-Eppler's superb essay "Bodily Bonds: The Intersecting Rhetorics of Feminism and Abolitionism" (*Representations* 24:28–59). Sánchez-Eppler argues that "the bodies of women and slaves were read against them" and that this resulted in a necessity for feminists and abolitionists "to invert patriarchal readings and so reclaim the body." Using examples from Child and Dall, she demonstrates that "sentimental fiction constitutes an intensely bodily genre" and "constantly reinscribes the troubling relation between personhood and corporeality that underlies the projects of both abolitionism and feminism." This is one of the most illuminating readings of the texts of sentimental fiction that I have read. Dall is also prominent in Helen R. Deese's "Alcott's Conversations on the Transcendentalists: The Record of Caroline Dall" (*AL* 60:17–25), which reprints Dall's abstracts of Alcott's "Conversations" on Fuller, Emerson, and Thoreau. Deese notes the difficulty of "reconstructing the appeal" of a conversationalist such as Alcott and points out that Dall's lifelong habit of careful reporting of lectures makes her journals an excellent source on the vanished oral record of Transcendentalism. Michael Thurston analyzes "Alcott's Doctrine of Human Culture" (*CS* 19, ii:47–54) as a significant philosophical underpinning for his educational work. Alcott's personal crisis in the aftermath of the hostile reception of his educational work at Temple school is detailed in Larry A. Carlson's " 'Those Pure Pages of Yours': Bronson Alcott's *Conversations with Children on the Gospels*" (*AL* 60:451–60). Carlson focuses on a new letter of W. H. Furness's which offered Alcott consolation and support. Bryan F. Le Beau's "Frederic Henry Hedge, 1835–1890: Toward *Reason in Religion*" (*SAR*, pp. 253–70) argues rightly for the importance of Hedge's *Reason in Religion* (1865), seeing that work as one of several reasons why Hedge's importance extends beyond the 1830s.

I conclude, exhausted but happy, with a final plea to future scholars not only for clarity of argument, but for brevity of title.

Oregon State University

2. Hawthorne

Frederick Newberry

In several respects, 1988 was a memorable year for Hawthorne studies. Most notably, the Centenary Edition of Hawthorne's letters has finally been completed, with the nonsequential volume 17 on the personal correspondence edited by Thomas Woodson and with volumes 19 and 20 on the consular letters edited by Bill Ellis. Preliminary notification of how the six volumes of letters might aid critics appears in an article by Carol Marie Bensick. Also important is Gary Scharnhorst's bibliography of 19th-century criticism on Hawthorne. Scharnhorst, a comparative newcomer to the field, has less comprehensively but more than adequately anticipated the long-awaited multivolume work of Buford Jones. Of the two book-length studies this year, Gordon Hutner's seems particularly notable for its sensitive, unsurpassed probe into the bonds of secrets and sympathy. But the most remarkable critical studies appeared in chapters or journals; of these, the lengthier and better contributions largely address Hawthorne's political, cultural, or moral vision. In a New Historicist (ideological) approach, for example, Sacvan Bercovitch offers two essays on *The Scarlet Letter* in which Hawthorne's somewhat faded liberalism is refurbished and redefined. Similarly, Susan L. Mizruchi implicitly argues against a conservative reading of *The House of the Seven Gables*. And amid a bumper crop of fine pieces on *The Marble Faun*, John Michael presents an exceptionally smart tribute to Hawthorne as moral historian. As for work on the tales, surprisingly little—and even less rewardingly—was done on the usual mainstays. Yet by way of refreshing compensation, Mary M. Van Tassel unveils serious cultural and aesthetic issues at stake in "Little Annie's Ramble," suggesting that it is now time for a major reevaluation of Hawthorne's oft-trivialized sketches.

i. Bibliography and Edited Texts

In *Nathaniel Hawthorne: An Annotated Bibliography of Comment and Criticism Before 1900* (Scarecrow), Gary Scharnhorst compiles

2,586 notices, reviews, and commentaries on the life, works, and studies of Hawthorne between 1828 and 1900. More than two-thirds of the entries have not received published attention—thus we now have better access to the early development of Hawthorne's reputation between the publication of *Fanshawe* and the appearance of his major romances. With half of the entries dated after Hawthorne's death, we can also more easily trace the process of canonization. Restricting his research to three microfilm series, Scharnhorst is to be commended for this useful work, which anticipates Buford Jones's comprehensive bibliography and will necessarily have to be consulted and compared with it.

Edited by Thomas Woodson, James A. Rubino, L. Neal Smith, and Norman Holmes Pearson, volume 17 of the Centenary Edition of *The Letters, 1853–1856* (Ohio State) followed last year's nonsequential issue of volume 18, mistakenly identified in *ALS 1987*. The volume contains personal letters written during all but the last year of Hawthorne's consulship. Woodson's impressive introduction, like the one for volumes 15 and 16, basically eschews analysis of the letters themselves in favor of providing biographical orientations to and Hawthorne's relations with their recipients. A thematic question does emerge, however: Why did Hawthorne delay for more than two years a visit to London, where he would have been introduced to literary society? Woodson suggests—not fully to his satisfaction, I take it—that Hawthorne scrupled to attend diligently to his consular duties, partly in an effort to help forestall congressional disaffection over extra-official behavior of foreign officers generally and partly in conscientious response to the alleged political foibles behind his dismissal from the Salem Custom House. Still, Woodson suggests that Hawthorne may have feared the London scene in the absence of James T. Fields, upon whose gregarious presence he counted as a social conduit. Exceedingly helpful annotations, an index, a list of repositories for specific letters, and a chronology of Hawthorne's movements and chief events relating to him are included in the volume. Initial efforts to collect Hawthorne's personal correspondence began more than half a century ago, and over the decades the project became increasingly ensnarled with logistics, permission rights, competing egos and conceptions, deaths, and a host of other complications. Not to be niggardly, I believe that Woodson especially deserves commendation for bringing the project to laudable fruition at last.

Volumes 19 and 20 of the Centenary Edition's *The Consular Let-*

ter, admirably edited by Bill Ellis, bring the full project of Hawthorne's correspondence to completion. The acknowledgments, introduction, and annotations establish indispensable contexts within which to comprehend Hawthorne's official missives. They all draw on the astonishingly complete survival of the Liverpool Consulate archives, transmitted to the U.S. National Archives in 1948, and they reveal, as Ellis notes, the meticulous and legible record-keeping of Hawthorne's English secretary, Henry J. Wilding. Thus, together with Hawthorne's letters, the Centenary Edition includes "supporting documents" that clarify official issues with which Hawthorne contended. While Hawthorne certainly exploited his office for minor advantages, Ellis effectively debunks the ill-founded legend of Hawthorne's being a lazy or incompetent consul. Instead, Hawthorne carried out his duties in exemplary fashion, even exceeding his authority when confronting the horrendous inhumanity characteristic of the maritime service. Volume 20, it should be noted, includes an updated comprehensive index to all six volumes.

Thomas Woodson, James A. Rubino, and Jamie Barlowe Kayes, in "With Hawthorne in Wartime Concord: Sophia Hawthorne's 1862 Diary" (*SAR*, pp. 281–359), provide the first edition of this wartime diary, appending helpful notes that identify persons and obscure references, an index of persons, and a bibliography of Sophia's reading. Although Hawthorne appears infrequently, this daily record of domestic occupations, socializing, reading, and matters connected with the war offers valuable information on what, beyond his literary interests, obviously absorbed his attention. Hugh J. Dawson, in "Discovered in Paris: An Earlier First Illustrated Edition of *The Scarlet Letter*" (*SAR*, pp. 271–80), discovers evidence for an imprint of an earlier version of Paul Émile Daurand Forgues's abridged and corrupted translation, *La Lettre rouge A* (1853), printed in cheap format with the first illustrations of the novel in any language. Dawson includes six of these remarkably wretched illustrations by Jules Jacques Veyrassat.

ii. Books

Two of the books this year dwell on familiar issues but often supersede previous studies in their extensive and provocative reconceptions. Gordon Hutner's *Secrets and Sympathy: Forms of Disclosure in Hawthorne's Novels* (Georgia) ambitiously argues that "secrets in

Hawthorne's major narratives serve not only biographical and psychoanalytic themes or stylistic values, but they also function to clarify issues of genre, of history and culture, along with conditions of reception." Yet Hawthorne's rhetoric of secrecy reflects far less a love for secrecy than it does a generative "manner of communication that stipulates how others must come into his sphere, that is, through sympathetic penetration." Hutner astutely explores the "apprehensive" sympathy Hawthorne sought. On the one hand, readers submit to the animating power of secrets in pursuit of resolutions, but on the other, they learn through repeated exposure to such techniques as ambiguity, multiple-choice interpretations, and multivalent symbols to be dissatisfied with ostensible solutions to mysteries. A necessary objective distance develops that affords the "unsaid" to be kept intact, even while the reader participates in mystifying secrets. Thus, paradoxically, sympathy confirms the necessity for keeping secrets by offering a heart-knowledge—based on conjecture—in place of a more radical and thoroughgoing skepticism. The sanctity of the human heart, the "inmost me" behind the veil, is preserved. Perhaps the most valuable reading is of *The Scarlet Letter*, in which Hutner claims that, as the novel develops, "the very notion of the determinate value of a secret—the meaning of the *A* as one that can be ascribed to Hawthorne—really exists to concentrate the psychological, social, and rhetorical range of several secrets."

Kenneth Marc Harris's *Hypocrisy and Self-Deception in Hawthorne's Fiction* (Virginia) runs the risk of redundancy and overstatement, especially in view of its premise that the "overwhelming majority" of Hawthorne's characters are "hypocrites, self-deceivers, or both." And were the unfortunately brief examinations of the tales and sketches a fair representation of the book's quality, one's fears would be justified. But Harris's analyses of three major romances offer necessary refinements in our understanding of Hawthorne's recurring interest in hypocrisy and self-delusion. Drawing from the Puritans John Cotton and Thomas Shepard, Harris creates tentative contexts for Hawthorne's conception of hypocrisy and self-deception, thus laying the moral and ontological foundation upon which characters engage in frustrated searches for authentic selfhood. Vying with prevalent low opinions of Coverdale, Harris is at his controversial best, arguing a rather doubtful though intriguing case for the minor poet's achievement of the only good faith Hawthorne could imagine after years of investigating hypocrisy, an ironic good faith dependent on his accepting the impossibility of good faith, which in turn sanctions his "poetic exploitation of the ultimate impossibility of distinguishing reality from illusion and life from art."

One can only regret that Darrel Abel's *The Moral Picturesque: Studies in Hawthorne's Fiction* (Purdue) did not appear a decade earlier, when its collection of reprinted essays would have been a more timely capstone to Abel's important contributions to Hawthorne studies than they are today. Printed in an extraordinarily handsome format, the 21 essays appear in four sections, chronologically charting Hawthorne's focus on the relation of the "deeper psychology" with the "paradoxes of opposition and affinity" involved in "how the ideal appears in the real world, and the distinction and relation of the sexes." Only two essays have been extensively revised, and only a few gestures in the notes reflect the criticism of the last 15 years. Still, the volume may prove useful to young scholars unacquainted with seminal studies such as those on *The Scarlet Letter*.

Inasmuch as half of *Aesthetic Headaches* by Leland S. Person, Jr., deals directly with Hawthorne, it seems proper to consider it here. Person essays to establish a middle ground between recent gender arguments that Hawthorne's treatment of female characters is essentially phallocentric and those (like Baym's) that it is protofeminist. Through close readings of "Drowne's Wooden Image," "The Birthmark," "Rappaccini's Daughter," *The House of the Seven Gables*, and *The Marble Faun*, Person argues skillfully that Hawthorne "deconstruct[s] conventional masculinity, which manifests itself in objectifying power over women, in order to achieve a 'feminized' creative self, which comes into being through the surrender of power *to* women. . . . Instead of creating Galatea in order to satisfy a need for possessive power, the American Pygmalion wants Galatea to create herself and, in the process, to create him—to create her creator." Hawthorne's central heroines challenge men to become "the one heart and mind of perfect sympathy." The onus of failing to become this ideal reader falls squarely on a figure like Giovanni, who begins as male victimizer but ends as victim. This shift anticipates more subtle gender transformations in the romances: "Dimmesdale's climactic substitution of himself for Hester, Holgrave's complex identification with Phoebe, Coverdale's incorporation of Zenobia's feminist discourse, Kenyon's inspiration by Miriam." Implicitly, the destruction of heroines results less from Hawthorne's assertion of masculine power than from the inability of his weak heroes to respond to women with the very sympathy Hawthorne sought for himself.

The sizable coverage of Hawthorne in David S. Reynolds's *Beneath the American Renaissance* (Knopf) also compels attention in this section. Subtitled *The Subversive Imagination in the Age of Emerson and Melville*, the book seems subversive in its own right, having a dubious methodology and logic, already unmasked by Nina Baym in "Subversion and the American Renaissance" (*ESQ* 33[1987]: 180–87). Demonstrating an impressive familiarity with a host of antebellum works of dark reform, exposé, and sensationalism, Reynolds argues a deterministic case: the subjects, strategies, and style of Hawthorne's works issue from a heightened literary response to these "subliterary" forms. Even Hawthorne's ambiguity originates from the literature of "immoral or dark reformers," whose manipulation of reform rhetoric results in the "transformation of a culture of morality into a culture of ambiguity" or moral relativism. Nowhere, in three sustained treatments, is Hawthorne credited with an original insight into his culture; nor is he afforded any knowledge of historical literature by which to observe that culture. He merely vibrates to contemporaneous strings strummed by less accomplished writers. Add to this reductive, overly determined methodology the facts that Reynolds never demonstrates Hawthorne's knowledge of any of the contemporaneous fiction at issue, fails to cite scholarship to which he is indebted for his readings of Hawthorne's novels and tales, and habitually repeats himself verbatim—add them all up and one feels disappointed with a study that initially captivates and seems so auspicious.

iii. Essays on Novels

a. The Scarlet Letter. Sacvan Bercovitch's "The A-Politics of Ambiguity in *The Scarlet Letter*" (*NLH* 19:629–54) may well rival Charles Feidelson's premier study in *Hawthorne Centenary Essays* (1964). Giving unprecedented attention to Hester's choice to return to America, Bercovitch elaborates the "overarching ideological design" of the scarlet letter's "fourfold office—political, moral, aesthetic, and historical." Instead of confirming Hawthorne's reputed conservatism, Hester's return manifests his liberal telos, the important *process* by which Hester repudiates her radical either/or mode of thought and accepts the moral imperative to compromise, which requires more courage than to rebel. "Hester's return reminds us, first, that the issue is *not* stasis or change (whether transcendentalist or pragmatist), but whether change shall overturn or conserve, whether our heroine of process shall be Hester in the forest or Hester come home. To opt for *both* is to leave the system intact, as Hester does—radically *un*changed, except in rhetoric and vision."

Bercovitch therefore disputes the presence of ambiguity or multiplicity in Hawthorne, proferring instead a pluralism ultimately reconciled or brought under bipolar control by symbol. Thus "anti-authoritarianism is at best a protest for reform through continuity, and pluralism functions in that process as a mystifying *sense* of multiplicity." Hawthorne's "strategy is to convert the threat of diversity into the pleasures of multiple-choice pluralism where the implied answer ('all the above') guarantees consensus." Hawthorne depends on our recognizing the moral and historical "need for Hester's return. In effect, he invites us to participate in a liberal democracy of symbol making." Controversy will be sharp over this ideological argument, including the radical though logically consistent point that "the Puritan community is the novel's interpretive hero."

Controversy will also wage over Bercovitch's "Hawthorne's A-Morality of Compromise" (*Representations* 24:1–27), which focuses less on embedded textual strategies in support of ideology than it does on pressures of ideological contexts on the text. The two essays comprise twin constituents of Bercovitch's thesis on the "grim necessity" of Hester's "compromise," archaically and honorifically understood. Readers are complicit in this process of liberal consensus-making, a process redolent of those in *The American Jeremiad* and *The Puritan Origin of the American Self*. Enlisting Hawthorne's biography of Pierce and "Chiefly About War Matters" might seem to stretch the bounds of the novel's concerns as Bercovitch plots Hawthorne's centrist, gradualist accommodation with progressive ideology. Even more problematic but equally necessary is the view that the American Revolution is the "pivotal link" in the novel's historical symbology (*A* equals American eagle). Perhaps most seriously, if Hester accepts the political compromise of the letter's "office," is Bercovitch's disregarding the uneasy dialectic in the novel's conclusion: however much Hester may conform to public consensus within the second generation of Puritans, her artwork (for Pearl's daughter) continues underground, a telling reminder of her ongoing subversive nature.

Somewhat like Bercovitch, Joyce A. Rowe, "Bleak Dreams: Restriction and Aspiration in *The Scarlet Letter*," in *Equivocal Endings*, pp. 27–45, believes Dimmesdale correctly chooses to remain within the iron framework of Puritanism, thus accommodating the limited self with community and Utopian vision. Pearl's maturity in Europe also advocates "consistency and reciprocity which social structures foster." Contrarily, Hester as Utopian prophetess, in a Puritan commonwealth she repudiates, "is denied" by Hawthorne in the end "any field of action commensurate with even a chastened set of ideals"—a point likely fundamental to a feminist rejoinder to Bercovitch. Beginning as an Emersonian heroine, she concludes as a Hawthornean equivocation between a "gradualist view of redemption" and revolutionary vision.

Overlooked in *ALS 1987*, James M. Cox's "Reflections on Hawthorne's Nature," in *American Letters and the Historical Consciousness: Essays in Honor of Lewis P. Simpson* (LSU), pp. 137–57, synthesizes Hawthorne's mind and art as they generate from the infamous 12 years of solitude. As much a loving evocation as a critical appraisal, the essay results from Cox's long, deep, and humane "reflections" on Hawthorne's embedded concerns with "sin, shame, sympathy, and judgment," which are implicated in the very act of publishing them: "His capacity to feel both the seduction and the sin of art in a single instant is at the heart of his imaginative power." Such a balanced self-consciousness not only applies to Hawthorne's psychology but also extends to his politics, as in *The Scarlet Letter*, wherein "Hawthorne again distributes the motives of the artist and democratizes the guilt among the characters." Integral to his extraordinary humility is Cox's meditation on what he avows as the necessary shame involved in publication, a shame felt by Hawthorne but apparently rarely felt by scholars.

More thoroughly and significantly than anyone heretofore, Mark M. Hennely, Jr.'s "*The Scarlet Letter*: 'A Play-Day for the Whole World?'" (*NEQ* 61:530–54) evaluates all the central characters, including the communities of Salem and Boston, in their readiness to engage in forms of mirth. In his *Notebooks* and in this novel, Hawthorne reveals divided attitudes toward play (puritanic restraint versus gleeful release), which extend to Dimmesdale and Hester. Although Hennely probably errs in castigating Pearl for attacking the diabolic play of Puritan children, he reasonably sees the child as "the spirit of re-creation," a spirit essential to Hester's joyful apocalyptic vision of the future and coherent with the "sweet moral blossom" promised in the opening chapter.

T. Walter Herbert, Jr., in "Nathaniel Hawthorne, Una Hawthorne, and *The Scarlet Letter*" (*PMLA* 103:285–97), "investigate[s] the contests of gender signification that take place" in the subjects of his title, proposing the method by which their "interlinked differences . . . give us access to their joint engagement in the cultural construction of gender and subvert any effort to view them as autonomous individuals." Reiterating claims that Hawthorne was skittish about his manhood, Herbert sees Hawthorne discovering supposedly masculine traits in his daughter, Una, almost from the moment of her birth. These "monstrous" traits, anathema to her Spenserian name and tragically unresolved in Una's life, are conveniently resolved for Pearl, whose access to a culturally determined femininity in the fairy-tale world of the conclusion evidently constitutes Hawthorne's wish-fulfillment for his daughter. Herbert is careful to caution against the dangers of psycho-social-biographical approaches like his; yet, without persuasive evidence, he seems vulnerable to oversexualizing most all of his and Hawthorne's observations.

In *Critical Essays on Hawthorne's* The Scarlet Letter (Hall), editor David B. Kesterson assembles excerpts from familiar early reviews, five essays written before 1950, seven after 1950, and four new ones covered in the next paragraph. Kesterson's introduction, largely devoted to a fine overview of the novel's early reception, shies away from addressing the host of essays written since 1960. Given 112 notes, a wider range of approaches and issues might have been expected than those represented by the 11 cited critics of the last three decades. The unstated criteria for such selectivity bears on the question of his audience. The reprinted materials seem designed for undergraduates, while three of the original essays will appeal to specialists and the fourth, I fear, scarcely to anyone.

Rita K. Gollin's " 'Again a Literary Man': Vocation and *The Scarlet Letter*," pp. 171–83, finds compelling biographical parallels in Hawthorne's rejection of a professional career as a lawyer (Bellingham), doctor (Chillingworth), and minister (Dimmesdale). That Hawthorne "projected his own internalized conformity" onto Bellingham would seem, however, to overstate an otherwise helpful biographical example of Hawthorne's vacillating struggle with himself as fictionmonger. Also helpful is Thomas Woodson's "Hawthorne, Upham, and *The Scarlet Letter*," pp. 183–93, which offers strong biographical evidence in arguing that Hawthorne employs Chillingworth's diabolic torment of Dimmesdale to wreak vengeance on Charles W. Upham, the chief activist in Hawthorne's dismissal from the Custom House. Less helpful is James M. Mellard's "Pearl and Hester: A Lacanian Reading," pp. 193–211, which presents an unusually clear and, save for a troubling dependence on the Freudian castration complex, an almost persuasive case for the psycholinguistic congruence of Hester and Pearl with a simplified Lacanian psychic schema; still, we probably learn more about Lacan than about the novel. Least helpful is Richard D. Rust's " 'Take Shame' and 'Be True': Hawthorne and His Characters in *The Scarlet Letter*," pp. 211–18, which swiftly and multidigressively relates Hawthorne's shame over ancestral cruelty to the shame of characters in the novel.

More cogently, Joanne Feit Diehl's "Re-Reading *The Letter*: Hawthorne, the Fetish, and the (Family) Romance" (*NLH* 19:655–73) psychoanalyzes the forbidden relation of Dimmesdale and Hester as a substitute for Hawthorne's own incestuous anxieties over his mother, whose death, we are invited to believe, serves as the quintessential context for the novel's inception. Like Mellard, Diehl wearisomely finds the preface and the tale replete with castration symbols; like Philip Young, she re-rereads the letter as a symbol of incest. Andrew J. Scheiber, "Public Force, Private Sentiment: Hawthorne and the Gender of Politics" (*ATQ* 2:285–99), would no doubt argue against Diehl, as he does against feminist readings of Hawthorne's siding against Hester's "masculine" mind. For Scheiber, the novel is "less concerned with the politics of gender than with the gender of politics—with the domination of human institutions by a masculine ethos of intellect and power, to the exclusion of the 'moderating' tendencies" of woman's "tenderness and moral sense." Hawthorne applauds these tendencies because he shares them with Hester in his equivalent male-dominated world, wherein the sentiment of male artists is rendered ineffectually effeminate.

b. The House of the Seven Gables. Through New Historicist critics and rereadings of romantic historiography, Susan L. Mizruchi's "From History to Gingerbread: Manufacturing a Republic in *The House of the Seven Gables*," in *The Power of Historical Knowledge*, pp. 83–134, largely reconceptualizes the political, economic, and social issues of *Gables*, Hawthorne's "most theoretical historical fiction." Agreeing with Michael Colacurcio that Hawthorne is our most serious moral historian and a consummate ironist, Mizruchi uncovers strategic details by which, Bakhtin-like, auctorial consciousness subverts the novel's characters' efforts to repress or defuse history. Yearnings for an edenic or aristocratic past, along with ostensible democratic faith in America's future, are everywhere undermined by class struggle; "the novel's deepest vision of its contemporary society" offers "a series of politicized returns of the repressed [history and hearthside legends] that repeatedly emerge to haunt the illusion of harmony in the official American republic." Rather than criticizing Hawthorne for the conservative idealism suggested in his controversial conclusion, Mizruchi reinterprets it, much as Bercovitch reads Hester's return, as a culmination of the text's ideology *in process*: "a picture of modernity that recognizes that ancestral power is no longer the sole basis for authority in the contemporary world. Inherited power must now be combined with a commitment to movement and action, to the possibilities of social and economic change." Troubling this inflated though persuasive reading is Mizruchi's unwillingness to mention Hawthorne's name, to address specifically the presence of Hawthorne's consciousness and craftsmanship in the shaping of the narrator's vacillating intentions in the narrative. In effect, such elision puts forth *Gables* as an unauthored text.

Roy Harvey Pearce's "A Sense of the Present: Hawthorne and *The House of the Seven Gables*," in *Gesta Humanorum: Studies in the Historicist Mode* (Missouri, pp. 55–74), retaining signs of his original lecture delivered in 1975, attempts yet once more to establish the well-established "sense" of Hawthorne's concern for the past. On this occasion, however, Pearce updates this concern by arguing that *Gables* is a "Romance of the present by virtue of being a Romance of the past and vice versa"; ultimately, "it is of the essence that the past be sealed to the present." But the characters, rather than reverting to the crippling typology of the past, must accept and expiate unavoidable historical sins in order to ameliorate their debilitating effects on the present and thus, finally, prepare for a more sanguine future; this view is compatible with Mizruchi's argument. Readers are dialectically involved in this "effective operation" of *Gables*, which Pearce advocates as reflecting Hawthorne's mature historical vision. Deliberately flying in the face of most recent readings (although no criticism about the novel is provided), he sees the marriage of Holgrave and Phoebe, along with the hopeful vision in the last chapter, altogether proper and convincing. Indeed, Pearce essays to jibe Melville's estimation of Hawthorne's "no! in thunder" with the conclusion: "For a condition of *present* things is that, ineluctably linked as they are with past things, they move into the future. One says NO! in thunder, so to say yes, perhaps only in a whisper, yes to the future." Difficulty resides in such logic, just as in Pearce's effort to present *Gables* as Hawthorne's climactic repudiation of the previous 20 years of saying "NO"—as if *Blithedale* and *Faun*, also set in the present, did not follow. Incidentally, readers will be astonished to learn that "it is in fact [Hawthorne's] ancestors who have bid him write [*The Scarlet Letter*]."

In " 'Who Killed Judge Pyncheon?': The Scene of the Crime Revisited" (*SAF* 16:99–103), Clara B. Cox, with dubious circumstantial evidence, answers the question first raised by Alfred H. Marks by submitting Holgrave, who evidently murders the judge through his inherited skill at Maule-mesmerism.

c. The Blithedale Romance. Dale M. Bauer's, " 'A Counterfeit Arcadia'—*The Blithedale Romance*," in *Feminist Dialogics*, pp. 17–50, grafts gender theory onto Bakhtinian dialogics, observing the novel as a "heteroglossic polylogus of ideologic discourses on social structure and community in the Blithedale 'theatre.' " Coverdale and Hollingsworth are intolerant of the dialogic freedom implicit in communitas, preferring instead, out of their fear of social contradictions and the "muscular feminism" of Zenobia, a monologic masculinity that conventionally supports laissez-faire individualism, which in turn translates into a will to mastery over women. Through Zenobia's suicide (an act of resistance to masculine will), Coverdale is able to unmask but not to comprehend "the powerlessness and voicelessness of women." Thus, while Coverdale nostalgically yearns for a romantic faith in an American Arcadia, Zenobia's starkly real self-violence becomes "a subversive strategy against a culture which has interiorized violence, pretending to a bland humanism and liberal progress." This creditable reading includes a remarkable social analysis of the Blithedale masquerade.

The title of Barton L. St. Armand's "The Song of Miles Coverdale: Intimations of Eliot's 'Prufrock' in Hawthorne's *Blithedale Romance*" (*ATQ* 2:97–109) adequately suggests the methodology by which two weak, egocentric, and self-pitying narrators shed light on one another's romantic cynicism. In "Boswell and Johnson at Blithedale: A Source for Hawthorne's Romance" (*NHR* 14, ii:6–8), Charles Zarobila advances a tenuous connection between Boswell-Johnson and Coverdale-Hollingsworth. Raymond Benoit's "An American Hierophany: The Wood-Pile in Hawthorne and Frost" (*ArQ* 44:22–27) connects the entitled artifacts to the hierophany of Mircea Eliade, "the coexistence of contradictory essences: sacred and profane, spirit and matter, eternal and non-eternal." Coverdale's ontological identification with the woodpile results in the " 'softened outline' of harmonized opposites as the right perspective on man and the convergence of his art." Completing such comparatist approaches, Alison Rieke's "Two Women: The Transformations," in *Faith of a (Woman) Writer*, pp. 71–81, enlists *Blithedale* and *The Bostonians* thinly and predictably to reveal Djuna Barnes's *Nightwood* as no more successful than they in "restructuring the female self."

d. The Marble Faun. One of this decade's better essays on Hawthorne is John Michael's "History and Romance, Sympathy and Uncertainty: The Moral of the Stones in Hawthorne's *Marble Faun*" (*PMLA* 103:150–61). Somewhat like Colacurcio, Michael probes Hawthorne's fundamental concern with moral understanding in relation to moral history, revealing the invariable disruptions in Hawthorne's desire for a sympathetic reader by "estrangements of the human heart." Sympathy and estrangement thereby become epistemological principles that "blur the distinctions between the objective and the subjective, the actual and the imaginary, history and romance." Hawthorne seems "skeptical about the power of sympathy to overcome estrangement and ground [moral] understanding." His ambivalent estrangement from the fragmented stones of Rome, more than matched by Hilda's and Kenyon's, dovetails with the narrator's incapacity to resolve the city's "violent juxtapositions of the sacred and the profane, the sublime and the debased." Bewilderment ensues, as is seen in Miriam and Donatello, who, with Hawthorne's sanction, nevertheless accept their burden as sympathetic though imperfect interpreters; this finally allows them to enter the grotesquery and mirth of the carnival, an historical paradigm in itself.

Along with sacrificing Miriam and Donatello, Hilda and Kenyon refuse to grant sympathy to the Roman stones, refuse to enter the spirit of the carnival, choosing a narrow "moral certainty" in the hope of allaying bewilderment but gaining nothing more than "cold moralizing instead of human knowledge, stiff complacencies instead of moral history." With additional provocative readings of Memnius in the catacombs and Miriam's model, Michael arrives at the moral of the stones—ingeniously derived from the bracelet of gems sent by Miriam to Hilda as a wedding present—which is "the moral of romance and history: each one reads according to his or her own lights, and the knowledge of this is all the wisdom there is. This wisdom is to be found not in the stones themselves but in the connecting string, the ties of sympathy and aversion, the narrative thread that constitutes interpretation."

Another rewarding essay, sensitive and graceful, is Judy Schaaf Anhorn's "Pastoral Exile and *The Marble Faun*" (*NCL* 43:24–41). For Anhorn, the essential tension in *Faun* issues from Hawthorne's feeling himself exiled in Italy as well as from his complex, tragic understanding that a return to edenic New England would not, according to a Christianized pastoral formula, regenerate his person or his art. Donatello and Kenyon, alone and uneasily yoked, represent this tension, while the carnival and Tuscan scenes stand for the literary texts of Hawthorne's memory and ambition. Anhorn astutely notes Kenyon's replication of Hawthorne's verbal imagination, his effort to gain from edenic loss, and his brief acquisition of simplicity and the romance gift of "circumnavigating facts" necessary for his bust of Donatello. Yet Donatello, by indulging rather than sacrificing pastoral longings, seems best to reflect Hawthorne's "yearning against expectation" to return home.

Edgar A. Dryden's "The Limits of Romance," in *The Form of American Romance*, pp. 31–60, is a compelling effort to unravel Hawthorne's longing for a "lost, autonomous form" that once "brought together poetic, metaphysical, and intersubjective realms," thereby harmonizing "fiction and reality, imagination and perception, and writer and reader." Confronted, however, by a "dead world" and the accumulated conventions in texts and works of art having intervened between this world and himself, Hawthorne is dominated by the perplexity of writing and reading. *Faun* begins with the artistic spell cast by Rome, with its "natural magic" that fosters the "illusion of a direct and original relation between the sign and its object." But the ruins of Rome, the very source of enchantment and regrettably unavailable in America, finally produce an overwhelming disenchantment—even a foul contamination. Hawthorne knows that the broken lives of his characters cannot be unified with the world or with art; he also recognizes his own disunity with the "gentle reader" whose death "is the equivalent for the narrator of the loss of sympathy that he recounts in his narrative." Dryden's absorbing analysis should be compared to Michael's and Anhorn's.

Margaret Kissam Morris, in "Rhetoric in a Romance: An Unstable Synthesis in *The Marble Faun*" (*ATQ* 2:207–21), submits nothing fresh in an allegorical and dialectical reading that tries to excuse Hilda's moral rectitude (thesis) as an apt reaction to Miriam's passion and creativity (antithesis), the potential yet unsuccessful synthesis of which resides in her marriage to Kenyon.

e. The Elixir of Life Manuscripts. Charles Swann's "Alchemy and Hawthorne's *Elixir of Life Manuscripts*" (*JAmS* 22:371–87) values these unfinished MSS "with the best of Hawthorne's achievements" for their serious concern with life and death, especially as they reveal "Septimius's neo-alchemical studies as *a* metaphor for his art." Considering the *Septimius Norton* MS, Swann makes a plausible case for Hawthorne's potential knowledge of the English alchemist, Thomas Norton, whether that knowledge came about through Norton's *Ordinall* or through Thomas Fuller's *The Worthies of England*. By interweaving the moral dimension and circle imagery of alchemy with Romanticism, Swann reasonably invites further consideration of how, for Hawthorne, "Revolution" contains both the idea of "the circles of fortune's wheel and the modern idea of the word as suggesting some crucial rupture with the past." One quibble: the connection between Chillingworth's (Indian) herbal lore and alchemy was made previously by Melinda B. Parsons and William M. Ramsey (*ESQ* 29 [1983]:197–207).

iv. Essays on Tales and Sketches

In "'*Decies Repetita Placebit*': The Critical Reception of *Twice-Told Tales*, 1837–1842" (*NHR* 14, i:1–6), Buford Jones submits three previously unnoticed reviews and suggests what lies ahead in his forthcoming bibliography. Compared to Scharnhorst's bibliography (see above), which contains 96 items on Hawthorne from 1837 to 1842 and 118 from 1828 to May 1841, Jones has discovered, respectively, "no fewer than 128" and "more than 150." In a distilled list of reviewers covering this period, Jones mentions 16 not found in Scharnhorst. Along the way, Jones gently scolds critics, beginning with Poe and concluding with J. Donald Crowley, for radically underestimating the critical attention Hawthorne received during the period when he was supposedly the "obscurist man of letters."

Concerned with the first two editions of Hawthorne's tales, Richard Dilworth Rust's "*Twice-Told Tales* at the Threshold" (*JSSE* 11 [Autumn]:27–36) briefly yet richly details the manifold ways in which Hawthorne's tales and sketches anticipated Victor Turner's discussions of liminality. Being on the verge, residing in between, coming in contact with, crossing a boundary, and pausing on or passing through a threshold—all these states or actions recur so frequently that they seem to define more adequately than any previous explanation a thematic principle for the collected tales as a whole. Moreover, "liminal themes, images, and characters" in these early tales reveal Hawthorne's developing "artistic subject and stance," as it later becomes defined in "The Custom-House."

Less sweepingly, David C. Cody, "'Of Oddities and Strangenesses': Hawthorne's Debt to Sir Thomas Browne" (*NHR* 14, ii:10–14), discovers convincing parallels between selections from Browne's works and passages in Hawthorne's notebooks and in such tales as "Rappaccini's Daughter," "The Birthmark," "Lady Eleanore's Mantel," and "The Great Stone Face." Margaret B. Moore's "Hawthorne and 'The Lord's Anointed'" (*SAR*, pp. 27–36) admirably though somewhat problematically traces the influence of George Barrell Cheever—a classmate of Hawthorne's at Bowdoin and at times a fellow Salemite—on three works. The case for the subtle expression of Cheever's temperance antics in "A Rill from the Town Pump" is not persuasive, and its essence was anticipated by Alfred H. Marks (*EIHC* 123[1987]:260–77). But the evidence for Hawthorne's references to Cheever's staunch support of capital punishment in "The Hall of Fantasy" and "Earth's Holocaust" seems conclusive. Sketchy and unrewarding, Susan Manning's "Nathaniel Hawthorne" (*CQ* 17, ii:109–25) surveys a few early tales and *The Scarlet Letter*, avowing that Hawthorne was not as deep as Dante, and concluding that "his prose substitutes for the diversity of actuality a dense verbal structure which re-establishes the imaginative relation of observation to belief, and so sustains the complexity of human possibility against the puritan polarities [symbol and significance] from which it springs."

The perennially analyzed "Young Goodman Brown" and "My Kinsman, Major Molineux" received scant attention this year. Terry Martin, in "Anti-allegory and the Reader in 'Young Goodman Brown'"

(*MHLS* 11:31–40), essays with some success to discover fresh gleanings from a well-harvested field, ultimately arguing, interrogatively, that "if we, along with Goodman Brown, continue to read allegorically in a context which no longer supports it—that is, if we mistake the categories of a kind of convenient literary shorthand [allegory] for the reality itself—is not our judgment in Hawthorne's eyes equally reprehensible [as Brown's]?" Much less successful, because it is inaccurate in some details, impatient with irony, and scantily informed in criticism, is Joyce A. Rowe's " 'My Kinsman, Major Molineux': The Several Voices of Independence" in *Equivocal Endings*, pp. 14–26, which finds Hawthorne irresolute or fuzzy over "anarchic energies released" and the problem of "self-definition without guidance."

Clayton Koelb's "The Name of the Self: Hawthorne's 'Rappaccini's Daughter,' " in *Inventions of Reading*, pp. 96–113, connects the flowers of Rappaccini's garden with the "idle weeds and withered flowers" of "The Old Manse" in their cross-pollinated associations with horticulturist creators Hawthorne / Aubepine / Rappaccini. Defining both the Italian lexeme *rapa* and the English "haw" as things of no value, Koelb suggests that the "oscillating valorization of the hawthorn plant taints everything named 'Hawthorne' and serves as a focus for an ambivalence about self and work evident in the author of *The Old Manse* collection." Discounting Koelb's immunity to irony and unfamiliarity with John C. Willoughby's work on *The Old Manse*, this rhetorical reading is worthwhile.

Less worthwhile is Deborah L. Jones's "Hawthorne's Post-Platonic Paradise: The Inversion of Allegory in 'Rappaccini's Daughter' " (*JNT* 18:153–69), which lacks criticism about the story; instead, it is based on Paul de Man's definition of allegory, "a paradigm of the 'autodeconstructive' narrative" that subverts both the ontological assumptions and the epistemological possibilities found in certain medieval allegories that "elaborate a radical convergence between the postlapsarian human realm of discourse and an inexpressible ideality by demonstrating the inability of a sacramental hermeneutic to provide a transparent referential relationship between discrete ontological categories." From such language as this, Jones comes to the essential and familiar conclusion that Giovanni is a faulty interpreter.

More profitably, Norman German, "The Veil of Words in 'The Minister's Black Veil' " (*SSF* 25:41–47), exposes deliberate patterns of etymological and translingual puns and other wordplay that enrich our pleasure as much as they reinforce the tale's themes. Taking sides with Michael Colacurcio and Richard Slotkin on historicist issues, James McIntosh, "Nature and Frontier in 'Roger Malvin's Burial'" (*AL* 60:188–204), adumbrates the shifting effects of wilderness—Nature—on characters, narrator, and reader: "Nature is by turns a figure for secret natural energies, a figure for maternal sympathy, and a figure for the howling wilderness," the latter two figures reflecting "the cognitive dissonance inherent in the Puritan Errand." We sense that, despite all the partial views and permutations of the landscape, Nature dramatically and mysteriously remains itself, a presence that "mediates . . . between the tale as an historical representation of a culture and the tale as a 'time less' psychological drama." The readings here are clear, astute, and teachable.

Adding to recent studies of Hawthorne's knowledge of Maine history, Hugh J. Dawson's "Père Sébastien Racle in History and Fiction: The Background of Hawthorne's 'Bell' Sketches" (*EIHC* 124: 204–12) very nicely details the borrowings and transformations of information on this French priest's life at Norridgewock in *The American Magazine of Useful and Entertaining Knowledge* and in "A Bell's Biography." With respect to Massachusetts's history, a section in Michael Colacurcio's *The Province of Piety* preeminently anticipates Susan Swartzlander's "'Appealing to the Heart': The Use of History and the Role of Fiction in 'Alice Doane's Appeal'" (*SSF* 25:121–28) in which the author, in puzzling ignorance of Colacurcio, is simply wrong in asserting that "a substantial explication remains to be seen."

Mary M. Van Tassel's "Hawthorne, His Narrator, and His Readers in 'Little Annie's Ramble'" (*ESQ* 33[1987]:168–79) gives provocative, unrivaled attention to Hawthorne's sketches, placing them in context with and in contrast to Irving's. Hawthorne's contemporaneously popular sketches "complement the early dramatic fictions, in that both are part of a spectrum of modes Hawthorne used to explore cultural mentality"; in some of them, "the nexus of social and historical stresses produces a doubled narrator who has been split into seemingly opposed embodiments." Thus, in "Annie's Ramble," the narrator's "multiple voices point to the reading method we must use," which means we must see the narrator, in Bakhtinian terms, as dialogic. Among Van Tassel's exciting insights into the sketch itself is one on the childlike "making" activity of the creative process: "It is the child in the man who enables him to create, but it is also for being 'childish' that the writer and his works are relegated to second rank in this busy republic. The heart of the writer's dilemma is th[u]s embodied in Annie. She is both a vital part of the writer and the writer as seen by his readers. What he produces in all seriousness, they regard as childish. Hence the protest at the end of the sketch: the child in him, the writing that child leads him to, is not, he insists, 'a waste of precious moments, an idle matter, a babble of childish talk, and a reverie of childish imaginations, about topics unworthy of a grown man's notice.' But to the extent that his audience so judges his work, the writer is confined within it. Like the canary's in this sketch, his song is shaped by his cage." With analyses such as this, Van Tassel's projected book-length study of Hawthorne's sketches is surely in good hands.

Beth L. Lueck's " 'Meditating on the Varied Congregation of Human Life': Immigrants in Hawthorne's Travel Sketches" (*NHR* 14, ii:1–7) takes the most extensive look at these works since Alfred Weber, finding to little effect that "immigrants are most often stereotyped as lazy, drinking, licentious foreigners," even though the Irish occasionally "can figure positively . . . offering an example of gay, easy living to contrast with American money-grubbing drudgery."

Carol M. Bensick, in "Shaping Superstitions on a Corn-Stalk Fiddle: Hawthorne's *Letters* and the Hawthorne Interpreter" (*ELWIU* 15:63–76), writes insightfully on selections from volumes 15 and 16 of Hawthorne's correspondence, claiming that "from now on we must grapple with the evidence of a man and writer very largely a stranger to us." The claim may be overstated, but Bensick argues well for Hawthorne's not being the frequently perceived "neurasthenic artist," for his having less sympathy than he sought for his works, for his having "a sturdy confidence in the merit of his work" from an early date, and for his belief that the formal demands of a tale required greater craftsmanship than did the novel. More significantly, Bensick (in clear agreement with Colacurcio) ably reflects on diverse comments that point to "Hawthorne's unequivocal endorsement of three things we cannot claim to have invariably or consistently allowed him: namely, research, study, and deep thought."

Duquesne University

3. Poe

Benjamin Franklin Fisher IV

This year's studies display heterogeneous approaches. Critical-theory interpretations have increased, although scholarship of long-standing types maintains vigorous staying powers. In this latter category we find several source studies which, instead of merely illustrating Poe's origins via the maligned deadly parallel, open windows into his artistic workings. Coupled with these readings, and just as illuminating, are several more works on Poe's influence on later writers and visual artists. Many European bonds are either newly examined or, in the case of long-recognized relationships, expanded. Fewer books appeared during 1988 than we saw last year. The chief center for concentration among this year's scholarship is Poe's short fiction, to which the poems and criticism serve as illustrative adjuncts.

i. Textual, Bibliographic, Attribution Studies

The latest installments of the "International Poe Bibliography," compiled by Richard Kopley and a team of Poe scholars, are thorough, revealing that diversity noted above (*PoeS* 20[1987]:36–45; 21:11–20). In the same journal ([1987]:27–35) Henri Justin's "Recent Poe Criticism in France: 1983–1987" and Roger Forclaz's "Poe in Europe: Recent German Criticism" (21:1–10) provide authoritative overviews of Poe's fortunes abroad, indicating the many-sidedness in foreign approaches. Eric W. Carlson's "Poe: I, New Editions" (*ANQ*, n.s. 1:25–32), more descriptive than evaluative, surveys four editions of Poe's writings and four works containing information about Poe. The Poe section in my *The Gothic's Gothic* (Garland, pp. 153–97; items 918–1200), the longest in the book, includes more annotated entries on Poe's Gothicism than any previous bibliography.

The identification of Outis continues to draw students, as I noted last year in citing Burton R. Pollin's argument for Poe himself as "nobody" (*ALS 1987*, p. 36). By dint of impressive external and internal evidence, Kent Ljungquist and Buford Jones propose Lawrence Labree, editor of the New York *Rover*, as a likely candidate—"The Identity of 'Outis': A Further Chapter in the Poe-Longfellow War" (*AL* 60:402–15). They argue that Labree could have known details of the Poe-Longfellow war and that he knew John Neal's writings, especially those in the *Yankee and Boston Literary Gazette*. They also claim that Poe's acquaintance with the Outis letter was vague. The "Whittier" verse quoted by Outis is in fact part of "The Falls of the Housatonick," an 1829 poem by the Reverend Joseph H. Nichols—a widely reprinted piece during early 19th-century years. In " 'Outis': A Gordian Knot Still Beckons," however, Dwight Thomas observes that, despite the persuasiveness of both the Pollin and Jones-Ljungquist articles, most notably in clarifications of long-standing muddled thought, the "Outis" question still remains open (*PSA Newsletter* 16, ii:3).

ii. General Accounts: Books and Parts of Books

Sybil Wuletich-Brinberg's *Poe: The Rationale of the Uncanny* (Peter Lang), deriving from her 1961 dissertation, treats Poe and his writings from a Freudian angle. Such a survey could be useful, particularly for the unseasoned student. Too intent on seeing Poe in his characters, and too careless about facts, scholarship, and style, however, Wuletich-Brinberg generally does not advance our understanding or appreciation of her subject. The "uncanny," as it is used in this book, is never satisfactorily defined, and most of the secondary sources are now many years old. Were there greater use made of Poe studies from the mid-1960s onward, the book would doubtless stand as far richer criticism. An exception to these strictures is her good reading of "The Purloined Letter" (pp. 158–73), which offers a fresh perspective on the love-hate relationship between Dupin and the Minister D—— and on sexual implications throughout the tale. Ideas of Lacan and his school are drawn in without the jargon or in-group tone that now frequently stand out in critical-theory publications.

Michael J. S. Williams, in a book with poststructuralist foundations, furnishes a much more coherent view of Poe's thoughts on the nature of language. The seven chapters in *A World of Words* (Duke) should make pertinent reading for anyone interested in Poe, regardless of whether Williams's readers find his approach wholly convincing. Poe's skepticism regarding human creative abilities reflects his likewise long view toward arbitrariness in language: no Transcendental Poe here. The essays, tales, *Eureka,* and, to a lesser extent, *Pym* are quarried to support examinations of Poe's poetics. The poetics are in turn exemplified in Williams's readings of the tales. Poe's doubts about readers' trustworthiness in their responses to texts are highlighted, although this point is not new (Richard P. Benton, Michael Allen, James W. Gargano, G. R. Thompson, and others have long since called our attention to this outlook). Williams's citations to "Pinakidia" and "Marginalia" for misgivings expressed there about authors' and readers' authority, however, are original aperçus and among the positive features in his book. Poe's humor is given its deserved importance, and under this rubric a number of tales—"Mystification," "Loss of Breath," and "Some Words with a Mummy" among them—come in for greater, and more acute, attention than is usual, another plus. The Poe who emerges in this book is a healthy skeptic who turned weapons of laughter upon anxieties engendered by the Romantic thought in his times. The texts resistant to easy readings (which is what Poe is about, according to Williams) are sometimes vitalized, sometimes not, in these pages. The section on "William Wilson," for example, seems unoriginal, to me, just as those on "Ligeia" and the ratiocinative tales revitalize them. The book is remarkably free of jargon.

In vol. I of David Morse's *American Romanticism* (Barnes and Noble, pp. 88–118), Poe, in tandem with C. B. Brown, is dubbed an explorer of the human mind. His fiction, characterized by "interiority," is his medium for dramatizing emotions. Poe's characters inhabit worlds so intensely cerebral that externals function as extensions of minds. Madness in Poe's works derives from 18th-century traditions, in which the obsession with a fixed idea entraps the psyche. In this framework, action becomes obsessive in otherwise passive protagonists. No startlingly new view of Poe's fiction appears in Morse's screed, but the presentations of individual tales convey original insights. Farther-reaching in scope, G. R. Thompson's chapter "Edgar Allan Poe and the Writers of the Old South" (*CLHUS*, pp. 262–77) gives a balanced placement of Poe among his contemporaries, rather than portraying him as some weird outcropping on the profile of American literature. Rightly designated as the "major national writer" from the antebellum South, Poe is credited with surpassing simplistic geographical or local-color features. Thompson's concise charting of Poe as poet, fiction-writer, and critic, as well as of his keen awareness about literary ethos and marketplace alike, makes this chapter a must for serious readers. Poe's manipulation of conventions in fiction is succinctly, but well, evaluated.

More expansive critiques of Poe the manipulator of literary conventions come in David S. Reynolds's *Beneath the American Renaissance.* Poe repeatedly figures within contexts of popular culture, especially in its subversive elements. He gets extended attention in three of Reynolds's four large divisions (strangely, he does not appear in the feminist portion). Oriental and visionary features in the verse and tales link Poe with other, much-sought, contemporaneous cultural fare, as did his ventures into temperance fiction. Chapter 8 draws in the tales and *Pym* to exemplify what Reynolds discerns as undercurrents of violence, eroticism, and anarchic and murderous impulses common in popular 19th-century fiction. Unlike many of his contemporaries, Poe held no great esteem for criminal heroes as objects for pity, and he customarily portrayed them unsympathetically (I note here that he resembles Thackeray, who lampooned such creations by Bulwer and Ainsworth, although Thackeray is not mentioned by Reynolds). While many others were giving full rein to unregulated, lurid sensationalism, Poe emphasized an ordered, psychologically plausible variety. Thus he differs from George Lippard and George Thompson, who titillated readers with their gruesome and erotic fiction. "Cask," "Usher," "William Wilson," "Ligeia," "Masque," "How to Write a Blackwood Article," and the Dupin tales are analyzed as prime examples of Poe's methods and outlook. We find his literary mirth contrasted to that of Neal and Irving as well as the Southwest (frontier) and Northeast (urban) humorists in general. Poe disliked the directionless comedy in much of what he read, and his own comic endeavors were attempts to question and warn against such chaos, and so he stands on a plane with Hawthorne and Melville. For interesting comparisons, we may turn to the illuminating remarks about Poe's humor that appear throughout the *Encyclopedia of American Humorists*, Steven H. Gale, ed. (Garland). Reynolds also believes that *Pym* demonstrates Poe's inabilities to sustain creative effort in a long work of fiction. Despite some significant fusions of the scientific with the irrational, the novel but shakily yokes these two features of widespread interest in Poe's time (cf. Herbert F. Smith, below, on *Pym*). Reynolds's comments regarding (1) Poe's fears for the state of fiction as suggested in "Usher" and elsewhere in his humor and "carnivalizing" writings, (2) his temperance works, and (3) his modifications of sensational fiction into what we now know as the detective story might acknowledge Burton R. Pollin's, James W. Gargano's, Donald B. Stauffer's, and my own scholarship about these matters. The Poe commentary in *Beneath the American Renaissance*, nonetheless, will elicit divergent reactions, because the book, like Fiedler's *Love and Death in the American Novel*, "provokes" in all senses.

Equally provocative, but less well prepared, is Donald W. Goodwin's hypothesis, in *Alcohol and the Writer*, that Poe's drinking hallucinogenic absinthe, and not his taking opium, may have inspired remarks about opium use in "Usher" and other tales (pp. 9–35). Goodwin, an M.D., depends too much on the 1978 biographies by Julian Symons and Wolf Mankowitz, as well as on Marie Bonaparte's earlier work, and thus he eschews other writing on intoxicants used either by Poe in person or in his creative writings. His remarks about Poe's supposed homosexuality and necrophilia do more to cast Poe as a character from Gothic novels (more so those of recent date than those of Poe's own day) than as a serious literary artist. Had Goodwin gone to *Poe Studies*, a journal he mentions (but which he apparently did not consult), or to the work of John Ward Ostrom and Randolph Church, he would have found supplemental materials on Poe and alcohol that might substantially modify his own thinking.

The Poe chapter in Donald E. Pease's *Visionary Compacts* (Wisconsin, pp. 158–202) devotes considerable space to *Pym*, "Usher," and "The Philosophy of Composition," with passing comments on several more tales. Along with others, Poe appears in this book as an American writer who, in his "visionary compact," sought community feeling and continuity rather than subscribing to the Revolutionary mythos (that emphasized freedom "from" heritages) important in the work of F. O. Matthiessen and his followers. Their notions about effects of the Revolution call up a world of short-term returns in emotional dividends regarding "family, environment, cultural antecedents, and even their former selves." Such thought, Pease believes, is similar to the tenets of modernism, and it is not positive thinking. Presenting Poe from a new viewpoint—that which casts him as an aristocratic mind, like Tocqueville, who sought a lost cultural lineage—Pease offers new perspectives on *Pym*. For him, the adventurer-narrator does not develop, but the novel showcases the terrors that may arise when one cuts off from a cultural past, as do so many other Poe works. Defying death as the book begins, and as he leaves behind a world of stable, albeit unexciting, culture, Pym in the end yields to it in going on to meet the shrouded white figure. "Usher," too, demonstrates an unfolding of the aristocratic impulse in conflict with a crass world. Pease would have done well, though, to read a solid biography, such as that by A. H. Quinn. There, he would have learned that Poe's birth was not illegitimate, as he himself says (pp. 165, 187–89). Other aspects of "violent displacement" we may find in Poe's life, but this dwelling on supposed illegitimacy does not inspire our unquestioning confidence in Pease's criticism. Nor does his misspelling of "Metzengerstein" as "Metzgenstern." Furthermore, Pease's identifying the speaker in "The Philosophy of Composition" with the raven in the famous poem will not win instant or universal assent, nor will the way in which he emphasizes Poe's speaking to modernism gain easy credence. Whether we agree or not with Pease's interpretations, though, his work should be considered as a foundation for further explorations.

The Poe-woman issue is another that never lacks vitality. Witness the chapter about Poe in *Aesthetic Headaches* (pp. 19–47), by Leland S. Person, Jr., who adopts a feminist critical stance. Person treads thoughtfully between those who think that the strong women characters in Poe, Hawthorne, and Melville represent their creators' misogyny and those who detect condescension by these authors toward the contemporaneous cultural milieu. The desire to escape a physical world and psychological limits coalesces with minimizing of flesh-and-blood womanhood throughout the Poe canon. A fascination-repulsion syndrome is unmistakable in portraiture of characters like Helen (in the 1831 poem), Poe's "prototypical woman," and elsewhere. Person also throws interesting light on the Poe–Helen Whitman relationship, interpreting it as Poe's turning toward feminine inspiration for his own creative powers. Person's reading of Poe's poem, however, does not admit sufficient spirituality in the "statue-like" figure at the closing. Likewise, he does not have the final word on feminine implications in "The Assignation" (which he also does not link closely with "To Helen," although Richard P. Benton and I have suggested this derivation). Moreover, Mentoni is confused with the "hero" in terms of the statue-come-to-life in the opening. Despite the death-of-a-beautiful-woman theme, Poe seemed intrigued by women "who have life, if not lives, of their own," as attested in "Ligeia," "Usher," "The Oval Portrait," and "The Spectacles." Person's hypotheses about the Pygmalion myth are refreshing, although the omission of "How to Write a Blackwood Article" and "Eleonora" from his rostering somewhat blunts the point of his larger outlook.

Finally, a more personal relationship is charted in Mary G. De Jong's "Lines from a Partly Published Drama: The Romance of Frances Sargent Osgood and Edgar Allan Poe," a chapter in *Patrons and Protégées* (pp. 31–58). De Jong's verdict: the Osgood-Poe romance was platonic. If Poe yearned toward Mrs. Whitman for imaginative sustenance, as is suggested by Person above, Mrs. Osgood and other women authors looked to Poe the editor as a literary patron, whatever others believed might be involved in such acquaintanceships. Osgood was not above manipulating Poe to further her own literary ambitions. De Jong's essay takes into account the considerable bibliography on the subject, using previous scholarship—and correcting it where necessary—to create a readable, chronological vignette of biography, useful to Poe and Osgood specialists alike.

iii. Critical Studies

a. **Tales.** David Punter promises more than he delivers in "Edgar Allan Poe: Tales of Dark Heat" (*Nineteenth-Century Suspense*, Clive Bloom, et al., eds., St. Martin's, pp. 1–13). His effort to single out the tales of greatest significance does little more than rehash familiar scholarship (e.g., on puns in "Cask"), and his carelessness to detail undercuts the solidity of his general thesis. For example, is "The Pit and the Pendulum" really "the best-known of Poe's stories" and who is hero, who narrator, in "The Assignation"? Punter's bracketing of Poe's language with that of Bob Dylan in *Desire*, whence comes his own title, does little more than imply an aim toward instant "relevance."

"Usher," as we have seen, commands recurrent attention. John Allison turns once again to the Coleridge-Poe relationship in "Coleridgean Self-Development: Entrapment and Incest in 'The Fall of the House of Usher'" (*SCR*: 8:40–47), a sensible assessment of imbalanced selfhood. In Coleridgean terms (which embody disturbing implications), according to Allison, the Ushers have achieved reconciliation of opposites, but that state brings them nothing more than static self-consciousness. Too much self-development, in other words, can produce negative psychological or physical consequences, which lead to madness and death. As siblings, Roderick and Madeline can reproduce nothing but copies of themselves, and so development or creativity within the family is retarded to the point of destruction. Physical and emotional disintegration thus emerges powerfully, ultimately affecting even the narrator, who has come to help Roderick. All that represents the Usher line—Roderick, Madeline, and their mansion—crumbles. Allison nicely supplements previous work on the Sublime and on incest in "Usher." Kent Ljungquist's "Howitt's 'Byronian Rambles' and the Picturesque Setting of 'The Fall of the House of Usher'" (*ESQ* 33[1987]:224–36) carries on his studies in Poe's use of the picturesque, in this case as it derives from William Howitt's descriptions (in the 1830s) of Byron and Mary Chaworth's country estates. Poe actually advanced the genre of travel literature in "Usher," to which Howitt (and probably others) contributed a share in groundwork for setting and psychology. Like Thompson and Reynolds, Ljungquist sheds clear light on Poe's handling of conventions. Beginning with Stanley Fish's idea, in *Self-Consuming Artifacts* (1972), that effects and content in art are often confused, Ronald Bieganowski pairs two famous tales in "The Self-Consuming Narrator in Poe's 'Ligeia' and 'Usher'" (*AL* 60:175–87), in noting how the narrator-protagonists dramatize failures to capture the ideal in language. What these narrators really respond to is the power of words. For "Ligeia," I think, this idea is especially workable. In more grim contexts, Beverly Voloshin's "Transcendence Downward: An Essay on 'Usher' and 'Ligeia'" (*MLS* 18:18–29) contrasts Poe to Emerson, depicting "outward or downward movement" as motifs for moving past confines of Lockean empiricism. Decay and decomposition are customary pathways to transcendence in Poe's vision.

Using a similar methodology, Patricia Robertson explores possibilities for psychological interpretation offered by the imagery on the Montresor coat of arms, in "Poe's 'The Cask of Amontillado'—Again" (*PAPA* 14:39–46). She supplements previous suggestions as to whether Fortunato or Montresor is best characterized by the colors, the serpent biting the foot, and the motto. Montresor must be intended, according to Robertson, because we behold in the coat of arms a subtle emblem of his pride, self-righteousness, and evil. Furthermore, his psychic suffering will not end with his death. This is a well-thought-out, concise explication, providing appealing insights into a tale that will never be fully analyzed to the satisfaction of all.

More about the visual informs a useful reading with a self-explanatory title, Sarah Webster Goodwin's "Poe's 'Masque of the

Red Death' and the Dance of Death," in *Medievalism in American Culture*, Bernard Rosenthal and Paul E. Szarmach, eds. (Center for Medieval and Early Renaissance Studies [1987]; pp. 17–28). Goodwin amplifies our understanding of Poe's folklore and iconographic backgrounds. "Masque" is also made more accessible in "The Coy Reaper: Unmasque-ing the Red Death" (*SSF* 25:317–20). Here, Leonard Cassuto reasonably demonstrates, Death is the narrator because he is the only presence who could enter Prospero's sealed retreat (and thus relate events that transpired within). Moreover, Death alone could narrate in such a deadpan manner as gives tone to this tale. No great leap need be made to take us to Gita Rajan's "A Feminist Rereading of Poe's 'The Tell-Tale Heart'" (*PLL* 24:283–300). Proposing that the narrator is female, Rajan goes on to observe that she "escapes from one captivity to another, to articulate a female discourse." Therefore, this tale becomes one of "feminist rewriting as well as rereading"; consequently, traditional ideas about Oedipal themes in this tale are sturdily challenged in this novel, but plausible, critique.

Fred Madden contributes another new reading, "A Descent Into the Maelstrom: Suggestions of the Tall Tale" (*StHum* 14[1987]:127–38), which may not vigorously challenge previous interpretations, but which places Poe more clearly within the 19th-century literary scene than many other critiques do. Drawing on previous scholarship on "A Descent" and on theories of Poe as hoaxer, Madden demonstrates how Poe employs to artistic advantage many techniques more commonly recalled as those of Southwest humor (a point that I myself have argued). In sum, Poe "played with the reliability of the framing narrator, the verisimilitude of the 'old-timer's' story, and the reader's willingness to believe" (p. 136). More work like this should be undertaken.

The ratiocinative fiction also elicits perennial readings and rereadings. Clive Bloom's "Capitalising on Poe's Detective: The Dollars and Sense of Nineteenth-Century Detective Fiction" (*Nineteenth-Century Suspense*, pp. 14–25) centers on the Dupin tales as renderings of social-class issues. Dupin the aristocrat represents a new secular priesthood which, because of great intuitive and imaginative endowments, can divine the workings of others' souls. A Dupin who unites speculator with technician and artist may not immediately come to mind for many other readers of Poe, nor will Bloom's imperfect knowledge of American slang strengthen his case. Dupin = *du pain*, or "bread" is ingenious, but "bread" = "money" was not such a colloquialism in Poe's era as it has been in the late 20th century. A related opinion is the mainstay in Christopher Rollason's "The Detective Myth in Edgar Allan Poe's Dupin Trilogy" (*American Crime Fiction*, pp. 4–22). Rollason finds emphatic, if subtle, themes of female sexuality pervading these tales, and he draws on a gamut of critics from Bonaparte to Lacan in supporting his ideas. Dupin thus becomes conspirator as well as hero, and he departs empiric thought for guesswork to fathom the mysteries he confronts. In "The Purloined Letter" he and his double, the Minister D——, are actually feminized by means of the much-sought letter. This circumstance aligns Dupin with oppressed social groups, just as it "devalues" D—— in his relationship with the queen. Poe left off writing detective fiction because in his own creations the form disintegrated. That is, we find implicit in the final Dupin tale an exposé of the limits of the ideology of the detective story. Bordering on the tricksey-cutesy, Rollason's essay is, nevertheless, credible; it directs us to think about Poe's probings of the imagination. A cross-light on this approach appears in Richard Bradbury's "Sexuality, Guilt and Detection: Tension between History and Suspense," another essay in *American Crime Fiction* (pp. 88–99). In the novels of James M. Cain, where "a sudden sexual encounter . . . jams sexuality and violence together," Bradbury finds a nightmare world much like those created by Coleridge and Poe. All three writers comprehend how "guilt can inspire the telling of a tale," and their achievements are masterful. George Grella's thesis, in "Poe's Tangled Web" (*ArmD* 21:268–75), that Dupin himself is criminal, detective, and narrator in "The Murders in the Rue Morgue" and "The Purloined Letter," and that Poe carefully plants clues for us to identify Dupin with himself, also merits attention. One wonders, though, given Grella's reiterated reminders about "fudge" in the Dupin tales, whether he did not keep his tongue in his cheek while setting forth his argument. He might also have consulted Dennis Eddings's and W. T. Bandy's analyses of hoax elements in the ratiocinative tales (*UMSE* n.s. 3[1983]: respectively 81–95; 128–35) and my own 1973 article, "Blackwood Articles à La Poe: How to Make a False Start Pay" (*ALS 1973*, pp. 44–45), in which I demonstrated how, via the hoax, Poe modified Gothic sensationalism into what we now know as the detective story (*RLV* 39: 418–32). Whatever fudge of his own he adds, Grella opens a new route into these tales, making "The Murders in the Rue Morgue" a precursor, as I see it, of the narrative technique in Agatha Christie's *The Murder of Roger Ackroyd*—in which the storyteller proves in the end to be the murderer.

Although most of the material in *The Purloined Poe*, John P. Muller and William J. Richardson, eds. (Johns Hopkins), consists of reprinted critiques of "The Purloined Letter," three new essays may occupy us here. Irene Harvey challenges the concept of "exemplarity," as set forth by Lacan, Derrida, and Barbara Johnson between 1966 and 1980 ("Structures of Exemplarity in Poe, Freud, Lacan, and Derrida," pp. 252–67), concluding that the concept itself may require deconstruction. Harvey finds wanting the handling of signifier and signified in the antecedent studies; Poe, unfortunately, seems to get lost here. François Peraldi's "A Note on Time in 'The Purloined Letter'" (pp. 335–42) sticks closer to Poe's tale as its focus, demonstrating how the time sequences, in Freudian and Lacanian contexts, merge with psychoanalytic functionalism. The last essay in the volume, John Muller's "Negation in 'The Purloined Letter': Hegel, Poe, and Lacan" (pp. 343–68), closes with assurances that additional interpretations of Poe's tale are sure to follow. Meanwhile, Muller's own analysis—based on premises of Hegelian ideas about truth (a community rather than an individual possession, and a tenuous possession at that, wherein negative aspects of the term constitute a large share)—brings to the fore the series of negations that give structure to Poe's tale, wherein the letter itself may have "dynamic character" as the "pure signifier" of negation. The entire volume, in its assembling a great quantity of critical writings, makes a handy reference work. Dennis Porter's essay (*ALS 1980*, p. 947) aims at going beyond Shoshana Felman in *The Literary Freud* (1980), by adding a fourth allegorical status to her three evident in "The Purloined Letter." Power relations, as they are dramatized in the interactions of Poe's characters, occupy Porter, who discovers in them an implication for psychoanalysis before and after Lacan. The poet, as he appears in Poe's tale, is caught up in power plays. Just so, Lacan's writings "reenact scenarios of authority that they simultaneously subvert." A similar view about another crime tale is Thomas Joswick's "Who's Master in the House of Poe? A Reading of 'William Wilson'" (*Criticism* 30: 225–51), an article based on Wittgenstein's theories, along with St. Paul's in his Epistle to the Romans, as regards authority in human relationships. Poe's tale stands as an allegory in mastery and authority, particularly when authority resides in language. Wilson and the reader both sense limits of language, for example, when they come to grips with the concept of sin.

b. Pym. Herbert F. Smith's deconstruction of interpretations of *Pym,* which classifies them generally into readings as hoax and readings from a Freudian base, renders disputes over the novel useless because it stands, finally, as metafiction. The Barthesian tack in "P/P . . . Tekelili: *Pym* Decoded" (*ESC* 14:82–93) is arresting, although it will not please enthusiasts (cf. Reynolds, above). Smith emphasizes that *Pym* is no delightful reading experience for all, although he opts for the "lightness and playfulness of the text" as compared with that in *Eureka,* where the profundity "sinks into the bathos of its own specific gravity." Like Smith's, John T. Irwin's reading, "The Quincuncial Network in Poe's *Pym*" (*ArQ* 44:1–14), will occasion repeated readings and debates. Positing that Poe's use of quincunx motifs derives from Sir Thomas Browne's *The Garden of Cyrus,* Irwin extends ideas he earlier expressed in *American Hieroglyphics* (1980). When man encounters design in nature, as is the case with the explorers in *Pym* upon sighting the penguin and albatross nests, questions of meaning arise over the relationship between humankind and the landscape (cf. Ljungquist, on "Usher," above).

iv. Sources and Influences

Burton R. Pollin's repeated explorations of Poe's origins now bring to light—in "Poe's 'Ulalume': Its Likely Source and Sound" (*ANQ* n.s. 1:18–19)—another *Blackwood's* inspiration, Daniel Donnelly's poem "Ullaloo, Gol, or Lamentation Over the Dead," from the May 1820 issue. The sounds in Donnelly's title and the overall theme of mourning a loved one doubtless appealed to Poe's ear and imagination. Michael Wentworth's "A Matter of Taste: Fitz-James O'Brien's 'The Diamond Lens' and Poe's Aesthetic of Beauty" (*ATQ* n.s. 2:271–84) convincingly links the motifs of failure in man's quest for eternal beauty in a renowned short story to Poe's poetic theory. Pollin's "Poe and Bellow: A Literary Connection" (*SBN* 7:15–26) points principally to resonances of "To Helen" in *More Die of Heartbreak,* with sidelight observations of additional Bellow debts to Poe. Another popular American author's responses to Poe and the Poesque are noted in remarks scattered throughout Joseph Reino's *Stephen King: The First Decade* (Twayne).

An ongoing fascination with *Pym* informs two influence studies. Lynette C. Black's "Pym's Vision Transcribed by 'Le Bateau Ivre,'" a poem by Rimbaud (*MissQ* 41[1987–88]:3–19), shows how, in both works, "visionary drunkenness" assists escape from ordinary states of life; the linking of beauty and horror with destruction of the self is important in both; and both constantly bombard us with conflicts between fixity and movement. Rimbaud's poem also functions as a "prism for the whiteness of *Pym*," which it "transcribes" into a rainbow. The ties of Arno Schmidt's novel, *Zettels Traum* (1970) to Poe's works, but chiefly to *Pym*, are recorded in Thomas S. Hansen's "Arno Schmidt's Reception of Edgar Allan Poe; Or, The Domain of Arn(o)-heim" (*RCF* 8:166–81). Schmidt attempted a psychobiography of Poe by reading the man into his works. Both Schmidt and Poe were obsessed with plagiarism.

Several scholars turn our attention toward broader issues in Poe's impact (generally via Baudelaire's translations) on European writers. Roderick Usher, according to Roger C. Lewis ("The Figure of the Decadent Artist in Poe, Baudelaire, and Swinburne," *The Fantastic in World Literature and the Arts*, Greenwood [1987], pp. 103–14), furnishes prototypes for the decadent artist, one who chooses to live in "intensity and artificiality." These states may stem from Poe's own criteria, expressed best in "The Poetic Principle," that effect, not morality, is the province of poetry. Roderick "revels in all forms of the fantastic." Baudelaire, Wilde, and Swinburne carried on a Poesque breaking down of traditions. Amidst such collapsings, however, the artist may bring about his own downfall. In such terms, for D. H. Lawrence, Poe numbers among the first of the moderns. Roxana Sorescu's "Eminescu and Poe" (*RoR* 41, xi [1987]:62–68) juxtaposes "Usher" with Mihail Eminescu's poem "Melancholy" for purposes of analyzing the theme of melancholy. Eminescu knew Poe through Baudelaire's texts, and he and Veronica Micle translated "Morella." Poe's association of melancholy with the death of a beautiful woman in his tale is cast in a lyrical tone, as is the Romanian's—although the latter planned his poem on a grander scale. Both works move from landscape description into the unfolding of states of mind, thus evincing the writers' shared symbolic values and modes of expression.

Poe channeled through the French alembic into Poland provides interesting subject matter in Frank Kujawinski's "Leśmian and Edgar Allan Poe" (*PolR* 33:55–69). The influence of Poe on the Polish writer Boleslaw Leśmian came first through Baudelaire's translations. Later,

Leśmian translated some of Poe's work into Polish. Poe and he were interested in literature of the nonrational, but Leśmian diverged from Poe in that rhythm for him became a metaphysical instead of prosodic engagement. Many critics see in Poe a need to destroy a universe (cf. Voloshin, above). Poe's endings take us into the void and nothingness, but Leśmian's writings, though similar in their themes, conclude with an entry into "an unknown world of newness and dreams." Thus his vision allows for a hope and promise uncommon in Poe. Based on his own great knowledge of Portuguese writing, George Monteiro surveys Poe's influence on an early 20th-century Portuguese man of letters, Fernando Pessoa. Monteiro's "Poe/Pessoa" (*CL* 40:134–49) is a model of its kind, claiming neither too much nor too little for Poe's inspiration. Pessoa wrote about Poe and prepared translations, not all published. He envisioned a multifaceted Poe, sometimes comparable with Baudelaire, sometimes with Zola. Baudelaire's biographical-critical essay, translated into English in *The Choice Works of Edgar Alan Poe* (1902), first led Pessoa to Poe. Pessoa's uppermost interest was Poe's supposed alcoholism, a condition from which the Portuguese writer himself eventually died.

Another kind of interest is evident in a "Poe Special" of *Fantasy Macabre* (no. 11), Jessica Amanda Salmonson and Richard H. Fawcett, eds. Reprinted and original creative writings that obviously betray ancestry in Poe predominate, with special emphasis going to macabre features, as the magazine title indicates. William Henry Poe's tale, "The Pirate," and his poem, "Despair," are also included. Thus Poe's ties to popular culture give impetus to undiminishing revaluations and reworkings. As a like tribute, marking the anniversary of Poe's death, "The Black Cat" is reprinted in *Ellery Queen's Mystery Magazine* for October, "in honor of the father of the detective story."

Poe's impact upon other media, specifically that of painting, is discussed in Robert J. Belton's "Edgar Allan Poe and the Surrealists' Image of Women" (*Woman's Art Journal* 8[1987]:8–12), a brief, readable account. Poesque inspirations for Max Ernst's paintings, as well as Magritte's, are given thoughtful analyses. The image of woman in a patriarchal society is common subject matter, and a sense of fantasy pervades the works of all. Ernst's Poe is reinterpreted in light of psychological and cultural outlooks of the early 20th century, but Magritte deliberately rejected such an approach to Poe, preferring, as he saw it, to identify directly with Poe's own aesthetic in devising his paintings of latter-day femmes fatales and vampire figures. Belton's study might have gained strength had he drawn on William Goldhurst's 1979 study in *The Comparatist* (pp. 3–14), "Literary Images Adapted by the Artist: The Case of Edgar Allan Poe and René Magritte." Pioneer study though Goldhurst's may be, its greater elaboration of Poe's influence on the Belgian maintains great value. Fred Miller Robinson's "The Wizard Proprieties of Poe and Magritte" (*W&I* 3[1987]:156–61) would have additional strength had he taken a look at Goldhurst's article. Robinson's comments about comic propensities shared by both literary and visual artist—who discerned incongruities between the "familiar and the strange"—should not go unnoticed. The nature of paradox, illustrated principally with allusions to "The Domain of Arnheim," "The Poetic Principle," and *Eureka*, reveal that Magritte's knowledge of Poe's work was not cursory. Poe and another kind of visuality are foremost in Kenneth Von Gunden's "Edgar Allan Poe's 'The Black Cat' on Film" (*UMSE* n.s. 6:106–18). From D. W. Griffith, early in this century, through Corman's work in the 1960s, and on into the eighties, this tale has lured filmmakers. Most filmmakers take great liberties with Poe's texts by bringing sensationalism to the fore, although their filmography is often skillful.

University of Mississippi

4. Melville

Brian Higgins

i. Editions, Checklists

Nineteen eighty-eight finally saw publication of the long-awaited Northwestern-Newberry edition of *Moby-Dick*, edited by Harrison Hayford, Hershel Parker, and G. Thomas Tanselle. As befits the work, it is an extraordinarily rich volume, providing not only a meticulously edited text but in the "Editorial Appendix" a wealth of previously unrecorded biographical and textual information. The sections of the "Historical Note" on the book's composition, the publication arrangements for the English and American editions, and the discovery of *The Whale* (and perhaps occasionally *Moby-Dick*) by British literary people, many of them also admirers of Whitman and Thoreau, during the decades before Melville's death especially add to what Melville scholars have previously known. Other sections of the "Historical Note" on the sources of *Moby-Dick* and theories of its genesis marshal an impressive and useful array of information never previously brought together in one place. In addition to listing the hundreds of substantive differences between the English and American editions and the emendations made by the editors in this edition (the text differs at some 200 points from the Norton Critical Edition edited by Hayford and Parker [1967] and at 27 points from the 1983 Library of America edition), the editorial appendix also documents, in the "Note on the Text" and the "Discussions of Adopted Readings," a plethora of textual problems. Many of these "arose from Melville's shifting, expanding, and not altogether seamlessly blending conceptions of the work during the course of its year-and-a-half composition in varying circumstances at four domiciles in New York City and Pittsfield," from his habits of research and composition, and from "a strong characteristic bent" of his literary imagination, "his greater concern for a scene's dramatic qualities than for its local consistency of realistic detail or its consistency with other parts of the manuscript." (The editors report that in no other work in the 15 volumes of the edition have they encountered so many textual problems.) The editorial appendix also reproduces a number of documents relevant to the composition of *Moby-Dick*, including the notes Melville penciled at the end of his edition of Shakespeare and his memoranda on Owen Chase's *Narrative* of the Essex. The editors express the hope that the presence of so much new information about Melville and *Moby-Dick* will stimulate new research. One might add the hope that future writers about *Moby-Dick* will heed their caveat: "a thorough understanding, by critical readers, of Melville's mind and art and of their modes of manifestation in *Moby-Dick* must be grounded in detailed knowledge of the genesis of its textual characteristics and how those characteristics reached their published state in the English and American editions." The Northwestern-Newberry edition itself makes a major contribution to that understanding.

Cause for further celebration in 1988 was the publication—on the heels of Mary K. Bercaw's *Melville's Sources* (see *ALS 1987*, p. 50)—of a revised and enlarged edition of Merton M. Sealts, Jr.'s *Melville's Reading* (So. Car.), which takes into account volumes belonging to Melville and members of his family—for example, his annotated copies of Milton and Dante—that have emerged since the publication of the first edition in 1966, and makes significant use of new evidence, in the Augusta Melville papers, concerning Melville's reading. Sealts's original introductory essay is expanded into nine chapters, relating Melville's reading more closely to the composition of individual works and drawing on Melville's sources beyond the volumes he and his family are known to have owned or borrowed.

ii. General

Drawing on "the social history of mourning in antebellum America" and on "recent findings in the psychology, sociology, and anthropology of mourning," Neal L. Tolchin's *Mourning, Gender, and Creativity in the Art of Herman Melville* (Yale) argues that "the conflicting images of Allan Melvill in his wife Maria's Calvinist and genteel style of bereavement" crucially influenced Melville's adolescent grief for his father, resulting in his lifelong inability to finish mourning. Consequently, throughout his work Melville struggled "to untangle his own conflicted grief from the irreconcilable images of his father—both as idealized figure and as possibly damned—he had internalized from Maria's bereavement." As this might suggest, though he claims to have been "careful not to reduce the richness" of Melville's art to "grief work," Tolchin analyzes the works as repetitive reactions motivated by an essentially unchanging psychological pattern. Thus *Typee* "centrally concerns the conflicts of Melville's unfinished grief"; in *Mardi* Melville "stages an elaborate attempt to exonerate his father"; *Moby-Dick* is Melville's "attempt to rewrite the memory of his father's deathbed mania"; at stake in *Pierre* "are Melville's own conflicts about his chronic grief for his father"; and so on. Narrative incidents, details of setting and characterization, characters' names and dress, relationships among characters, the "experimental energy" of Melville's writings, their "distorted attitude to women," even Melville's "susceptibility" to "shift artistic intention in midstream of the creative process" are all related to Allan's death or Maria's grief and are manifestations of Melville's own essentially static conflicted grief. (According to Tolchin, Melville achieved nothing more than "momentary resolutions" of this "chronic grief" in his fiction.) In all of this the supporting lines of association Tolchin draws between the works and Melville's parents can kindliest be described as tenuous. Tolchin's versions of unpublished Melville family papers should be regarded with caution; Maria Melville's "sense of *Typee*'s contradictions," for instance, which is presented as important supporting evidence in chapter 2, stems from Tolchin's misreading of her letter of February 7, 1846, to Augusta Melville. The letter shows quite unambiguously that it was in fact a letter from Allan Melville to Herman regarding *Typee* (and a copyright problem) and not *Typee* itself (as Tolchin claims) that was "so contradictory in its information." (Hershel Parker, who is working extensively with Melville family papers for the forthcoming new edition of *The Melville Log*, drew my attention to Tolchin's error. He reports that not all of Tolchin's other transcriptions are accurate.)

David S. Reynolds's *Beneath the American Renaissance* (Knopf) is a major, groundbreaking work, an exploration of the ways in which major American renaissance writers "transformed classic themes and devices into truly American texts by fusing them with native literary materials." More specifically, his sections on Melville bring together a wealth of information from "contemporary cultural backgrounds" to illustrate Melville's indebtedness to the "anecdotal sermon style, the visionary mode, the Oriental dialogue, dark temperance, city-mysteries fiction, sensational yellow novels, grotesque native humor," and other "forgotten popular genres." Reynolds draws on areas of popular culture unexplored in the related work of Constance Rourke and Richard Chase, often yielding surprising new insights. (Witness, for example, his analysis of Melville's combined concern for literary effect and "reform statement" in the "Fast Fish and Loose Fish" chapter in *Moby-Dick*, or his explanation of the increasing complexity of Melville's narrative voice as the result in part of his openness to the humorous idioms of the late 1840s). The sections on Melville are far from flawless. Notably missing is any attempt to show what Melville demonstrably had read or knew about; and at times Reynolds too readily assumes Melville's knowledge of popular authors or contemporary "modes" on the basis of rather general similarities. At times too his eagerness to establish connections between Melville's works and their cultural background leads him to reductive or distorted judgments (Ahab "figuratively enacts the highly charged ironies of antebellum reform culture"; Taji, Jackson, Ahab, Bartleby, Babo, and John Paul Jones are all Melville's versions of a contemporary literary phenomenon, the likable criminal—and both the Confidence-Man and Billy Budd are "the ultimate likable criminal"). Reynolds's treatment of Melville is more than welcome, nonetheless, for the remarkably wide research he has brought to bear on the works and for his sustained attempt to understand them as products of their own unique times.

In his two chapters on Melville in *Aesthetic Headaches* (Georgia), pp. 48–93, Leland S. Person attempts to dispel the widespread view of Melville as "fearful, distrustful, or openly hostile to women," arguing that his novels "evidence increasing complexity in his depiction of women," while *Typee*, *Mardi*, and *Pierre* in particular "evidence his increasing sophistication in exploring male-female relationships, his discovery of a connection between relationships to women and creativity." Women, in Person's view, "are identified with the kind of art that Melville most wanted to create: spontaneous, fluid, self-creative and self-propelling, the product of deep 'diving' and an imaginative openness to experience." The increasing complexity in Melville's depiction of women is easier to demonstrate than their association with the kind of art Melville wanted to create; Person's evidence for it is slender at best.

In *Sea-Brothers* (Pennsylvania), a study of American sea fiction from 1851 to the present, Bert Bender argues that the sea's influence on American literature has been "more profound and continuous" than is generally recognized, exceeding even that of the inland frontier. In its development over the last century, Bender finds, the tradition of fiction by working seamen has been most influenced by the values and vision of Dana, Melville, and Darwin; its emphasis on biology and the sea originated with Melville, though his cetology conforms to the kind of biological thought (natural theology) whose foundations were destroyed by the *Origin of Species*, a dominant influence on subsequent sea fiction. Bender's emphasis on the sea's influence on American literature and on Melville's centrality in the tradition of sea fiction is welcome; he provides scant evidence, however, to support his novel thesis that Melville's attitude toward biology was in accord with natural theology and its adherents, who "accepted the increasingly apparent fierceness of the struggle for existence as essentially benign, a necessary part of the creation's balance and harmony," and he otherwise sheds no new light on Melville's works.

Robert Milder's chapter on Melville (*CLHUS*, pp. 429–47) scarcely provides the factually and methodologically groundbreaking essay one might have been led to expect by Columbia's advertising flyer ("The Story of American Literature is About to Unfold as Never Before . . ."), and one has to go to the Northwestern-Newberry *Moby-Dick* and Sealts's new volume (see section *i.* above) for use of new biographical information in the Augusta Melville papers (see *ALS 1984*, p. 69); still, Milder's survey of Melville's concerns over the course of his career is intelligently alive at its best to the psychological implications and historical significance of the characters and conflicts in his works. Marvin Fisher's pamphlet *Herman Melville: Life, Work, and Criticism* (York) includes a "biography" of Melville (not always accurate in its details), a chronological list of Melville's works (which misleadingly lists the first American editions of five of Melville's first six books as reprints), a critical survey, and a 13-page annotated selective bibliography.

Mark R. Patterson's ponderous analysis of the ways Melville's works "recreate the complex relationships between authority, autonomy, and representation" in *Authority, Autonomy, and Representation in American Literature, 1776–1865* (Princeton), pp. 189–239, extends his previous discussion of *Moby-Dick* (*ALS 1984*, p. 72) and treats earlier and later works, in particular *The Confidence-Man.*

On Melville: The Best from American Literature, Louis J. Budd and Edwin H. Cady, eds. (Duke), reprints articles on Melville published in *American Literature* between 1931 and 1983.

iii. Miscellaneous

Merton M. Sealts, Jr.'s "A Sheaf of Melville-Melvill Letters" (*HLB* 35:280–93) reprints the texts of six letters and two postcards written in 1892 and 1893 by Melville's widow, Elizabeth, to his cousin Helen Jean Melvill of Galena, Illinois, a daughter of Thomas Melvill, Jr. (from family papers recently given to the Houghton Library by descendants of Thomas—see *ALS 1987*, p. 51).

Elizabeth I. Hanson slights an important topic in her essay on "Melville and the Indian" in *The American Indian in American Literature: A Study in Metaphor* (Mellen), devoting more space to Melville's portrayal of Polynesian Indians and Queequeg than to his portrayal of American Indians while discussing what she refers to as his "metaphorical indian"; to her, this metaphorical character "represents all the violent divisions which threaten the life of man with its own destruction, as well as an image of radiant health, of imagination itself, which helps to illuminate the despair of the white man."

Without arguing for Melville's direct influence on Robert Frost, Victor Strandberg in "The Frost-Melville Connection" (*Costerus* n.s. 66:17–25) shows that beneath the surface differences "the two writers' affinities rested upon fundamental parallels in theme and technique."

iv. Typee to *White-Jacket*

The year's offerings on the early works were again meager. William Heath in "Melville and Marquesan Eroticism" (*MR* 29:43–65) seeks "to reconstruct the sexual life of the savages" in the Typee Valley with the aid of 19th- and 20th-century accounts of Polynesian eroticism and to illuminate "crucial questions" about Melville's response to Marquesan sexuality and his relationship to Fayaway. Not surprisingly, he finds that "Polynesian eros aroused in Melville a contradictory tangle of impulses and anxieties"; he also concludes that Fayaway was probably "a tangible, flesh-and-blood woman," though the "emotional importance of the relationship to each" remains problematical, and Fayaway's portrait "may be blurred because she was Melville's model for not one but several lovers." Extending his earlier discussion of *Omoo* (*ALS 1986*, p. 57), Stephen de Paul's "The Poetics and Politics of the 'Unmanageable': Cultural Cross-Currents in Melville's *Mardi*" (*ESC* 14:170–83) examines the disruptive effects of "cultural transvaluation" on Polynesian myth and the allegory of American politics in *Mardi.* De Paul finds that both myth and allegory contribute to what he terms "the unmanageability of Melville's novel"; the "unmanageable" of the title thus refers to the "highly intractable" material of *Mardi* and has little to do with the sense in which Melville used the term in his letter of June 5, 1849, to Richard Bentley ("some of us scribblers . . . always have a certain something unmanageable in us"), though that is not apparent from de Paul's article.

Brian Saunders's at times awkwardly repetitive "Melville's Sea Change: From Irving to Emerson" (*SNNTS* 20:374–87) finds in chapter 22 of *Redburn* ("The Highlander Passes a Wreck") rather oblique evidence that Melville "suggests a curious resemblance between the limitations of Irving's sentimental retrospection and Emerson's transcendental intuition"; both are "provincials and sentimentalists in Truth." Dominique Marçais in "Transmutation of Identity in Melville's *White-Jacket or the World in a Man-of-War*" (*LAmer* 6[1985]:51–65) plays with the meanings and associations of several words in *White-Jacket,* usually with little regard to the context in which they appear; she claims that through its veiled allusions Melville "tries to smuggle a revolutionary spirit" into his "Dionysian" text, which "proposes the creation of a new identity and order of the United States implying the dissolution or the rejection of the identity of the white American." In "'Sailing with Sealed Orders': Herman Melville's *White-Jacket* and B. Traven's *The Death Ship,*" in *B. Traven: Life and Work,* Ernst Schürer and Philip Jenkins, eds. (Penn. State), pp. 316–25, Pattie Cowell points to a number of resemblances between the two works, though none are close enough to prove Melville's influence.

v. Moby-Dick

This year brought forth a remarkably mixed bag of essays on *Moby-Dick,* most of them slight, none of them likely to cause much excitement. Two essays examine Melville's literary debts or affinities. Alexandrino Eusébio Severino's "The Adamastor and the Spirit-Spout: Echoes of Camoëns in Herman Melville's *Moby Dick,*" in *From Dante to García Márquez: Studies in Romance Literatures and Linguistics,* Gene H. Bell-Villada, Antonio Giménez, and George Pistorius, eds. (Williams, 1987), makes exaggerated claims for the influence of *The*

Lusiads on *Moby-Dick* but has some value in its discussion of Camoën's possible influence on "The Spirit-Spout" and the *Pequod's* itinerary. Tony Magistrale's unremarkable " 'More Demon than Man': Melville's Ahab as Gothic Villain" (*Extrapolation* 27[1986]:203–7; revised in *Spectrum of the Fantastic,* Donald Palumbo, ed. [Greenwood], pp. 81–86) notes a number of standard Gothic elements in *Moby-Dick.*

One essay examines the book's structure; time is "*the* structuring element," according to David Ketterer, who finds 23 "time-breaks" which divide the work into 24 "temporal blocks" or "books" that parallel the 24 books of Homeric epic and "reinforce a reader's sense of Melville's epic ambition" ("The Time-Break Structure of *Moby-Dick,*" *CRAS* 19:299–323). According to Ketterer, these divisions constitute not only the most obvious but also the most illuminating structural feature of *Moby-Dick*: the time-break structure underlines the interpretive importance of the chapters preceding and following each time-break, especially those chapters which both follow a time-break and precede another one. That this structure is not so obvious as Ketterer claims is suggested not only by the fact that no one else has ever noticed it—at least not in print—but by the lengths that Ketterer has to go in order to "establish" it: "proceeding chapter by chapter, taking account of all the temporal pointers, both explicit and occasionally implicit." One also wonders why, if Melville were consciously following the Homeric model, the length of "books" varies rather un-Homerically, from one chapter to twenty-one chapters.

Joseph A. Boone's "Male Independence and the American Quest Genre: Hidden Sexual Politics in the All-Male Worlds of Melville, Twain, and London" in *Gender Studies: New Directions in Feminist Criticism,* Judith Spector, ed. (Bowling Green, 1986), pp. 187–217, tries to demonstrate that the experimental form of the American quest romance (characterized by "an open series of often jarring or startling narrative expansions and transformations" and by "abrupt refocusings of perspective") in large part owes its existence to the presence of a hidden sexual politics. In the quest narratives he examines (*Moby-Dick, Huckleberry Finn, Billy Budd* [sic], and *The Sea-Wolf*), Boone finds "visions of individuality and mutual relationship that attempt to break down conventional sexual categorization by breaking through the limiting forms of culture and the conventions of love-literature" and "expansive" characters (like Ishmael) "whose inner equanimity rests upon their unselfconscious acceptance of the love and compassion traditionally associated with the female sphere and the heart." Bryce Conrad is on surer ground than Bert Bender (see section ***ii.*** above) when he remarks in "*Moby-Dick*: The Reader and the Act of Cognition" (*Iowa Journal of Lit. Studies* 4 [1983]:91–105) that *Moby-Dick* has taken the "logical simplicities" of late 18th- and early 19th-century natural theology, "with its teleological arguments for the existence of God, and has turned those simplicities into cognitive and metaphysical complexities." But Conrad breaks no new ground in showing ways in which Ishmael "consistently points out the limits of one's habitual and familiar knowledge as a basis for cognition." Samuel Kimball's "Uncanny Narration in *Moby-Dick*" (*AL* 59:528–47) examines instances of Ishmael's repeated use of the word "strange" and plays elaborately with Freud's concept of the "uncanny" (the "unheimlich"), arguing that throughout the book Ishmael "tries to economize the strange home, that is, to domesticate the strange so as to make a narrative home of homelessness." Janine Dove-Rumé's eccentric "Scatology and Eschatology: Digestive Process and Occult Transmutation in Melville's *Moby-Dick; Or, The Whale*" (*LAmer* 6[1985]:67–86) reads *Moby-Dick* as offering "a kind of homeopathic remedy to and redemption of the curse of having to feed oneself, to which living beings are subjected," a reading depending a good deal on an elaborate interplay of meanings Dove-Rumé finds "occulted" in the etymologies of various words in the text. William E. H. Meyer, Jr., in "Melville and O'Connor: The Hypervisual Crisis" (*SLRev* 4 [1987]:211–29), attempts to "critique" *Moby-Dick* and *Wise Blood* "as documents of our American cultural eye-apotheosis or 'eye-dealism,'" seeing *Moby-Dick* as "ultimately the American epic which strives to grasp the mystery of Vision Itself." Meyer proposes a remarkable exercise: the book "must be re-read, substituting in each and every instance the word 'see' for 'sea.'"

Ishmael's struggle with the problem of how to represent the ineffable in fiction is Robert Bain's concern in "Grasping the Ungraspable: Ishmael on the Art of Fiction" (in *The Cast of Consciousness: Concepts of the Mind in British and American Romanticism*, Beverly Taylor and Robert Bain, eds. [Greenwood], pp. 160–72). Most of the essay is devoted to the sixth paragraph of "Loomings," Ishmael's "first meditation on art," which, according to Bain, suggests that the artist can begin to grasp the ungraspable in his work by "hints, indirections, and suggestions—achieved largely through symbol, myth, and archetype." Reuben J. Ellis's "The Interiority of the Weave: Raising the

Shed in Melville's Incomplete 'Mat-Maker'" (*ATQ* 2:111–24) is informative on the subject of weaving, but less rewarding in its attempt to show "how the information about weaving that Ishmael does not explicitly provide develops meaning in his use of the metaphor" in "The Mat-Maker."

Two essays examine Ishmael and Ahab together. Traci Carroll's "Suicide and the Death-Instinct in *Moby-Dick*" (*JEP* 9:96–99) is not entirely novel in finding "recognizable suicidal urges" in both Ishmael and Ahab. David Oberhelman's "An Encounter at Saïs: The Masks of Nietzsche and Melville" (*LJHum* 13[1987]:17–31) analyzes Ishmael and Ahab in terms of Nietzsche's theory of conscious and unconscious masks; Ishmael adopts the former and Ahab the latter, according to Oberhelman.

James D. Benson and William S. Greaves's linguistic study "A Comparison of Process Types in Poe and Melville," in *Language Topics: Essays in Honour of Michael Halliday*, Ross Steele and Terry Threadgold, eds. (Benjamins, 1987), vol. 2, pp. 131–43, compares *Moby-Dick* and "The Fall of the House of Usher." Another comparative study finds a fundamental similarity between *Moby-Dick* and Ralph Ellison's *Invisible Man* in "their epistemological orientation and their attempt to understand the nature of reality itself"; in *Invisible Man*, according to Elizabeth A. Schultz, Ellison confirms Melville's perception of reality as multiple, mutable, and ambiguous ("The Illumination of Darkness: Affinities between *Moby-Dick* and *Invisible Man*," *CLAJ* 32:170–200). Schultz's "*Moby-Dick*: The Little Lower Layers" (*North Amer. Rev.* 273:52–59) gives a readable account of *Moby-Dick*—and Schultz's teaching of *Moby-Dick*—for a general audience.

Donald E. Pease's attempt, in *Visionary Compacts* (Wisconsin, 1987), pp. 235–75, "to show how *Moby-Dick*, the nineteenth-century social text, resists the procedures involved in forming a modern canon, just as its subject matter resisted or . . . disarticulated the ruling mythos in the nineteenth century" extends his earlier discussion of *Moby-Dick* (see *ALS 1986*, p. 60).

vi. Pierre

Related to David Reynolds's work in its concern with Melville's debts to popular literature (see section *ii.* above), Charlene Avallone's "Calculations for Popularity: Melville's *Pierre* and *Holden's Dollar*

Magazine" (*NCL* 43:82–110) gives grounds for thinking that in writing *Pierre* Melville may have had in mind as models the sensational and sentimental pieces and even parodies published in *Holden's*, where not even "the theme of incest" was taboo. The panegyric on Nature Avallone quotes from *Holden's* is particularly worth noting for its correspondences with the paean to Nature in book II of *Pierre*. Nancy Craig Simmons in "Why an Enthusiast? Melville's *Pierre* and the Problem of the Imagination" (*ESQ* 33:146–67) discusses *Pierre* in relation to the literature of enthusiasm, "which discusses the term's inherent ambiguity, often equates enthusiasm with madness, and focuses on the problem of determining the source of supposed inspiration." Simmons may be exaggerating when she claims that *Pierre* reveals a sound knowledge of the literature of enthusiasm and that Pierre "behaves exactly" as Isaac Taylor's "scientific model" in *Natural History of Enthusiasm* "predicts he will." (Taylor is apparently "the only writer on enthusiasm to explore in any detail the consequences of enthusiasm for the individual.") Much of Taylor's thought and imagery, however, as well as the various quotations from other writers that Simmons provides, are clearly relevant to *Pierre*. Simmons attempts less successfully to demonstrate how the term helps explain Melville's use of his story "to explore the problem of the imagination, especially for the writer of fiction, as a guide to action and a means to truth in a modern, secular world."

According to Michael C. Berthold, *Pierre* and "Bartleby" are the "highmarks" of Melville's study of the prison ("The Prison World of Melville's *Pierre* and 'Bartleby,'" *ESQ* 33[1987]:237–52); what is distinct about them, "as opposed to other literary discussions of the prison, both in Melville and in his contemporaries, is the depth of their engagement in the vigorous cultural debate about reform and prisons in mid-nineteenth-century America." There is little in Berthold's essay, however, to support the idea that these two works are engaging in any such debate.

vii. Stories

Nineteen eighty-eight brought forth the usual crop of new readings of "Bartleby," of which Darryl Hattenhauer's "Bartleby as Horological Chronometer: Yet Another View of Bartleby the Doubloon" (*ATQ* 2:35–40) seems the most misguided. As a "horological chronometer," Bartleby, for Hattenhauer, is "a symbol of the confusion of the sacred and profane," a "monk in the temple of capitalism, worshipping at the walls of his secular cathedral and exploiting workers in his vain attempt at upward mobility." The other essays on the story offer conflicting views of the title character, none particularly illuminating. For Peter A. Smith, Bartleby is "a victim of both physical and informational entropy" who uses his own life and death "as graphic examples of the inevitability of entropy and of the futility of existence" for the benefit of the narrator ("Entropy in Melville's 'Bartleby the Scrivener,'" *CentR* 32:155–62). Bartleby is simply one half of an employer-employee relationship for Irving Adler, who draws on the history of the Court of Chancery to argue that the central theme of the story is "Natural Rights vs. Property Rights sanctified by law" ("Equity, Law and Bartleby," *Science & Soc* 51:468–74). Richard Kopley, in "The Circle and Its Center in 'Bartleby the Scrivener'" (*ATQ* 2:191–206), finds a "striking hidden image of a circle with Bartleby at its center" repeated throughout the story and takes a more exalted view of the scrivener, arguing that "the center/Bartleby is Christ and the circle/lawyer's office/prison yard is the Holy Temple," while the lawyer himself can be identified with the high priest of the temple, all or several of Christ's disciples, and Pontius Pilate. The story of Bartleby is no less than the story of the Second Coming; the tragedy of Bartleby/Christ is that he is not recognized and so must die.

According to the year's most ambitious essay, however—William H. Hildebrand's "'Bartleby' and the Black Conceit" (*SIR* 27:289–313)—the misery of "Bartleby" is rooted in a loss of God and a despair of humanity. For Hildebrand, Bartleby is the "noonday demon"—the demon of *acedia*—and a victim of the malaise he represents. Claiming that the influence of Pascal's *Pensées* on "Bartleby" is "extensive and significant, reaching into its symbolic structure and thought," Hildebrand finds in the story "an intricate network of Biblical pericopes" that "occur in a sequence of decisive scenes dramatizing the evil of an empty room." ("In a very urgent sense," we are told, "the entire story exists for the sake of the naked room, with Bartleby at its forlorn center.") According to Hildebrand, the story also "figurally" relates Bartleby to both Job and Abel and the narrator to Cain.

The only other essays on the stories in 1988 concern "Benito Cereno" and the little-discussed late work "Daniel Orme." In "Aftermath: Captain Delano's Claim against Benito Cereno" (*MP* 85:265–

87), Sterling Stuckey and Joshua Leslie print translations of hitherto unpublished documents from the Archivo Nacionale in Santiago, Chile, concerning Delano's attempt to collect a reward from Benito Cereno after the taking of the *Trial.* The documents shed new light on the dispute and the character of the two men involved but relate only tangentially to "Benito Cereno." Stuckey and Leslie suggest that Melville may have sought out the documents and that, along with parts of Delano's *Voyages* that critics have neglected, they may have influenced the story. The case is not compelling. In "Masquerades of Language in Melville's *Benito Cereno*" (*ArQ* 44:5–21), Jon Hauss attempts to show that "the central form of masquerade examined by, and ultimately dominating, the text is linguistic": according to Hauss, the languages of its principal characters serve as both its "overwhelming substance" and central subject and demonstrate the ways in which linguistic masquerades consolidate political hierarchies.

Philip Young's disjointed "Melville's Good-Bye: 'Daniel Orme'" (*SAF* 16:1–11) argues that the force of the story "rests substantially in the realization that it is Melville's portrait of himself as an old man approaching death willingly." Young links the scar across Orme's tattooed crucifix to Melville's discovery in his late teens that he had an illegimate sister (the discovery is an assumption but, according to Young, this "knowledge was the slash in Melville's spiritual history"). Young also relates the remorse attributed to Orme to Melville's own possible unconfessed guilt over his role as husband and father.

viii. *Israel Potter; The Confidence-Man; Billy Budd, Sailor*

The overall design of *Israel Potter* (with its four brief chapters devoted to Israel's 40 years in London and his return to America, and its comic presentation of Israel) is justified by Melville's central concern with the role of accident and bad luck in Israel's life, according to Peter A. Obuchowski, who finds nonetheless that Potter's life leaves Melville with "too uninteresting a major character to sustain the work" ("Technique and Meaning in Melville's *Israel Potter*," *CLAJ* 31:455–71). Obuchowski sensibly relates the book's concern with bad luck and accident to Melville's pondering of the causes of his own predicament in the mid-1850s. Less persuasively, Judith R. Hiltner, in "'A Parallel and a Prophecy': Arrest, Superimposition and Metamorphosis in Melville's *Israel Potter*" (*ATQ* 2:41–55), analyzes a "pattern of images suggesting the untimely arrest of youthful promise," a pattern emphasizing Melville's "concern with the premature extinction of American ideals."

In the year's single essay on *The Confidence-Man*, "Melville's *Confidence-Man*: An Uncharitable Interpretation" (*AL* 59:548–69), Peter J. Bellis takes issue with the "standard line" of interpretation that finds a central Confidence Man, both supernatural and diabolical in nature, operating aboard the *Fidèle*. Bellis argues that while Melville provides his readers with all the "evidence" needed to identify and characterize a single Confidence Man, "the contexts in which such 'evidence' appears work to undermine rather than sustain interpretive certainty"; Melville's dialogues repeatedly "reveal the unreliability of any possible 'evidence' of identity, whether physical or verbal." Playing on the "critical desire for textual integrity and consistency" manifest in the "standard" reading and in other interpretations, *The Confidence-Man*, Bellis argues (like others before him), "cannot finally be said to provide an authoritative textual center upon which to build a reading." Bellis makes his task easier by considerably oversimplifying the "standard line" he seeks to demolish and the evidence it employs; in his own analyses he displays at times an inattention to the actual words of the text more culpable than the critical "blindness" he attributes to proponents of the "standard" reading.

The year's sole essay on *Billy Budd*, Bernhard Radloff's "The Truth of Indirection and the Possibility of the Holy in *Billy Budd*" (*R&L* 20:49–70), argues that the work's narrative structure "allows the possibility of the holy to emerge by way of a reading of the modes of withdrawal, or concealment, signaled by the narrator's indirections." The holy, Radloff informs us, "emerges by way of indirection out of the myriad forms of concealment which import the withdrawal of presence from the empire of signification."

University of Illinois at Chicago

5. Whitman and Dickinson

Vivian R. Pollak

A good year for Whitman, with two new books and several important essays locating Whitman's response to the urgent political and moral issues of his day. Dickinson studies were equally vigorous but somewhat less centered. Attempts to rehistoricize her work were prominent, whether through biography, popular culture, or religious tradition. To the extent that there was a central theme, it was Dickinson's extraordinary responsiveness to the language of other writers, including her family and friends.

i. Whitman

a. **Bibliography, Editing.** Solid work here, much of it by Ed Folsom who claims, however, to have "given up on trying to make an exhaustive bibliography" of new poems about Whitman, as he did in *Walt Whitman: The Measure of His Song* (*ALS 1981*, 83–84). In "The Poets Continue to Respond: More Citations of Whitman as Poetic Subject" (*WWR* 5:35–40), Folsom lists about 200 additional entries, including several tantalizing titles by Sharon Olds, especially "Nurse Whitman" and "The Language of the Brag," from *Satan Says* (1980). Also concerned with "Whitman as Poetic Subject: Additional Citations" is Edward A. Malone, who provides 17 new entries for Folsom's project (*WWR* 5:34–35). Folsom, meanwhile, provides remarkably thorough coverage with "Whitman: A Current Bibliography" (*WWR* 5:48–50; 6:36–38) and coauthors "Whitman: A Current Bibliography," along with William White (*WWR* 5:43–46).

In "A Recovered Harry Stafford Letter to Walt Whitman" (*WWR* 5:40–42), Arthur Golden supplements Charley Shively's *Calamus Lovers* (*ALS 1986*) with a very brief note written by Stafford, who was looking for Walt and hoping to see him. In the same issue of the

Judith L. Richmond and Madelyn Horton provided valuable research assistance.

WWR, Folsom prints "Another Harry Stafford Letter" also missed by Shively (5:43–44). The letter is signed "From your affectionate son." Neither jotting will alter our view of the hapless Stafford, who was perhaps the most pathetic of Walt's young friends.

A more substantial piece is by Kenneth M. Price, who points out in "Whitman's Solutions to 'The Problem of the Blacks'" (*RALS* 15[1985]:205–8) that "in the late 1860s and early 1870s Whitman had racial issues in mind because of his quarrel with William Douglas O'Connor over the voting rights of blacks and because of his reading of Thomas Carlyle's 'Shooting Niagara,' a work notable for its slurs against blacks." In the Perkins Library at Duke, Price has discovered a very short manuscript note, hitherto unpublished, which "reveals how Walt Whitman, in the post-Civil War period, sought solutions to a problem that threatened his ability to encompass and reconcile." In the manuscript, Whitman anticipates the gradual disappearance of the black race, since the alternative—that blacks should develop all the "mental and moral attributes . . . of a leading and dominant race"—is viewed as unlikely. Yet Whitman also seems to be endorsing intermarriage as a possible solution to America's race problem. Price concludes that "Whitman managed both to give credence to certain racist scientific themes of his day and to write *Leaves of Grass*, a book that generally rises above these themes."

Kenneth M. Price and Robert C. Leitz III have edited "The Uncollected Letters of Hamlin Garland to Walt Whitman" (*WWR* 5:1–13), 12 in number, five previously unpublished. The letters were written from 1886 to 1890 and show Garland assiduously cultivating Whitman's favor. The content usually has to do with Garland's efforts to publicize *Leaves of Grass*, which, as he tells it, was finding a ready audience in the Boston area, especially among women.

***b.* Biography.** In "Subversion versus Celebration: The Aborted Friendship of Fanny Fern and Walt Whitman" (pp. 59–93 in *Patrons and Protégées*), Joyce Warren writes against those Whitman scholars who fail to take Fern seriously "as a critic of literature or as a person." In 1856 Fanny Fern (Sara Willis Parton), who was the first woman to praise *Leaves of Grass* in print, thought that she had found in Whitman the kind of unpretentious honesty that she extolled in her columns. But the friendship ended in mid-1857 when Whitman failed to repay the $200 he had borrowed from her husband, James Parton. Warren, who has edited the Rutgers reissue of Fern's novel *Ruth Hall*, argues cogently that Fern was not in love with Whitman and that she was a highly intelligent woman who was only incidentally "the purveyor of sentimental pap," as Gay Wilson Allen has called her. Before the quarrel, Whitman was a regular visitor at the Partons' on Saturday nights, in company with other literary types, one of whom recorded in his diary, "Walt talks *well*—but occasionally too much, being led by the interest with which his remarks are received into monopolizing the converse. I, as a rule, would prefer to play listener, yet it is a violation of good taste to find yourself constrained to become one. And nobody wishes to become a bucket to be pumped into, let the stream be ever so nutritious." So much for Whitman's statement—or the statement of his Walt persona—that in parlors he was a dumb gawk. Perhaps the last third of the article is devoted to demonstrating that Whitman was an antifeminist, and Warren, whose footnotes are scrupulously detailed, makes some telling and disturbing points, but she goes too far when she concludes that "it was not Walt Whitman who was the rebel against American society; it was Fanny Fern."

c. **Criticism: General.** The slippage between Whitman's egalitarian ideology and his less-than-perfect practice also concerns Betsy Erkkila in her *Whitman the Political Poet* (Oxford). Erkkila, the author of *Walt Whitman among the French* (*ALS 1980*), writes out of a deep sympathy for Whitman's project, including his attitudes toward women. Thus, whereas Warren stresses that, in one of his *Eagle* editorials, Whitman opposed equal pay for equal work in arguing for an across-the-board raise for teachers, Erkkila emphasizes that in one of his *Eagle* editorials "Whitman cited poor wages as the primary cause of female criminality, particularly prostitution," and that he was aware of "women's particular oppression in the new economic order." As for Whitman and Fanny Fern, Erkkila suppresses the somewhat sordid personal subtext and concentrates on Fern's favorable review and its role in "the debate over *Leaves of Grass* [which] developed in its initial stage into a battle over the propriety of naming the female body, particularly in its sexual and reproductive capacities." As a gender theorist, Erkkila is fully cognizant of Whitman's occasional lapses from his egalitarian sexual project. As a practical critic, however, she is significantly more interested in Whitman's successes than in his failures.

Erkkila is at her best in discussing racial issues, which she views as central to Whitman's poetic vocation. Within this frame, the close readings she offers are persuasive and well-balanced. For example, in discussing "A Boston Ballad," which was written in response to the arrest of the fugitive slave Anthony Burns in Boston on May 24, 1854, Erkkila cogently observes: "The poem turns on the irony of Burns's arrest and return in Boston. Inverting both the traditions of the ballad and the heritage of the Revolution, Whitman protests the Fugitive Slave Law and the politics of compromise, as well as the larger betrayal of republican values in an orderly, complacent, but ultimately dead America. . . . Burns himself, however, is absent from the poem. The failure to name him as the subject of the poem adds an unintended dimension of irony, which reveals as it conceals the racial phobia of Whitman and his age." Thus Whitman's sometime racism is viewed as representative of a national dilemma, and the poet is not really expected to transcend the ideology of his era. For its wide-ranging scholarship and critical tact, *Whitman the Political Poet* is one of the most impressive contributions to Whitman studies in recent years.

Equally valuable but somewhat harder on Whitman is Kerry Larson's *Whitman's Drama of Consensus* (Chicago). Larson's approach is eclectic, insightful, and somewhat difficult to classify. His introduction suggests that his project depends on rehistoricizing Whitman along the lines suggested by Donald Pease in *Visionary Compacts* (*ALS 1987*). More particularly, Larson proposes to redeem Whitman's democratic idealism from the charge of naïveté and, in so doing, to heal the split between the "poet of the self" and the "bard of democracy." Larson explains, "Whitman effectively subordinates a mimetic or transcendentalist model of art to a contractual one, the integrity of which is continually affirmed and reaffirmed through the give and take between the self and other that identifies the poem's central reason for being." Whitman's verse thus exemplifies a "transactive process." His poems provide the occasion for social cohesion, and the poet is engaged in "national therapy," a point equally advanced by George B. Hutchinson in *The Ecstatic Whitman: Literary Shamanism and the Crisis of the Union* (*ALS 1986*, p. 72). Like Erkkila, Larson believes that Whitman's "shift in allegiance from political to extrapolitical means of realizing his dream of consensus was instrumental in his discovery of a vocation." Unlike Erkkila, however, Larson is not really concerned with charting the impact of the impending political crisis on Whitman's style. Rather, his primary interest is the relationship between rhetoric and psychology. Though he writes against psychoanalytic critics such as Edwin Miller and Stephen Black, he sometimes employs a psychoanalytic vocabulary, deploys a quasi-psychoanalytic vocabulary of excess and deficiency, and, despite some stylistic obscurities, is consistently attentive to Whitman's inability to achieve his political and psychological goals. The drama of consensus, it turns out, is more nearly a tragedy. "That these two subjects—personal trauma and collective tragedy—are only tentatively brought together in the course of the drama reveals, to my mind, its deepest source of interest," Larson writes of "The Sleepers." The same might be said of his own beautifully quirky book.

In *Beneath the American Renaissance*, David S. Reynolds is also concerned with our national dialogue, though in this case Reynolds examines the origins of *Leaves of Grass* in popular culture (pp. 103–12, 309–33, 507–23). Virtually eschewing the slavery debate that Erkkila and Larson emphasize, Reynolds re-creates the "dark reform" impulse which, in appearing to reject violence, criminality, illicit sexuality, and intemperance, covertly gratified the desire to transgress repressive Victorian social and political norms. Whitman's long foreground is described as a period of immersion in the dark reform milieu, and within this model Reynolds is especially good on Whitman's early fiction. His claim that there is a kind of natural and inevitable development toward *Leaves of Grass*—such that "Song of Myself" becomes the exemplar of a purified dark reform sensibility—is more difficult to justify. If Reynolds's transformation scheme cannot fully account for the originality of Whitman's moral and psychological vision, the command of hitherto unknown or neglected popular texts that these chapters reveal is truly impressive. Because of Reynolds's ability to re-create some of the richly detailed sexual discourse available to Whitman and to his sensation-loving antebellum readers, *Beneath the American Renaissance* is one of the most compelling books of the year.

In these historicizing times Jerome Loving dares to assert that "Whitman remains our most successful apologist for a literature that is universal because it is 'native' " (in "Walt Whitman," *CLHUS*, pp. 448–62). Scooping up Whitman's influence on others and influences—mainly biographical and Emersonian—on Whitman, Loving too glances perceptively at Whitman's early fiction with its "uncaring fathers, persevering mothers, and neglected sons." Observing Whitman's fear of *becoming* the father, Loving tracks Whitman's journalistic career through a series of beginnings that failed to sustain themselves, in order to show (pace Reynolds) how the poet "finally liberated himself from the literary conventions," especially the sexual ones, "that had enslaved the American sense of self." Moving chronologically through Whitman's career, Loving lingers over the "Calamus" poems to suggest that "they may well represent Whitman's last on-the-scene account of his experience with experience." With meticulous attention to historical detail, the essay provides a sensible and stimulating overview of Whitman's career as a whole.

A growing concentration in Whitman studies has to do with Whitman and photography. Philip Fisher, for example, in "Democratic Social Space: Whitman, Melville, and the Promise of American Transparency" (*Representations* 24:60–101), describes photography as *the* American art, as opposed to painting, which is less repeatable and in Fisher's terms, less transparent, or quasi-homogeneous. Even more to the point, for Fisher's pathbreaking article is only peripherally concerned with photography, is Graham Clarke's " 'To emanate a look': Whitman, Photography and the Spectacle of Self," in *American Literary Landscapes: The Fiction and the Fact*, Ian F. A. Bell and D. K. Adams, eds. (Vision), pp. 78–101. As he considers "the daguerreotype, the photograph and aspects of early film technology," Clarke elucidates Whitman's relationship to the new visual technology: "What emerges is a language of desire and of spectacle which, in the widest sense, underpins both Hollywood and Madison Avenue. America and Whitman become, and are projected as, images of *desire*: There but unobtainable." Toward the end of his life, however, Whitman came to view the portrait in oils as the more "realistic" medium.

In "Democratic Social Space" (cited above), Philip Fisher argues that the comparative blandness of the American character, including Whitman's, was a necessary compensation for the threatening heterogeneity of our vast geography and immigrant-derived, pluralistic culture. In "Walt Whitman and the American City" (in *The American City: Literary and Cultural Perspectives*, Graham Clarke, ed. [Vision], pp. 179–97), Malcolm Andrews evokes the old world prejudice against cities ("God made the country, and man made the town") to show that in Whitman's imagination "the city is celebrated as an integral element in the grand pastoral hymn that is America." The point is well taken and the article is well written.

d. **Criticism: Individual Works.** Four articles more or less worthwhile here, all but one on "Song of Myself." Perhaps the least balanced, because of its lack of sympathy for Whitman, is by Robert S. Frederickson, "Public Onanism: Whitman's Song of Himself," in a delayed issue of *MLQ* (46[1985]:143–60). The poem, he believes, "has throughout a salacious undertone." More plausibly, Frederickson argues, as have others, that Whitman's "most sexual moments in 'Song of Myself' . . . take place alone." The notion that the poem "is an autoerotic sexual act performed in front of an audience" leads to the dismal view that the persona's "origin seems to be in solipsistic masturbatory fantasies which cannot be passed on to us." Also in a delayed issue of *MLQ* (48[1987]:145–61), is a carefully reasoned and thoroughly documented essay by Herbert J. Levine on " 'Song of Myself' as Whitman's American Bible." Citing the work of John E. Becker, Levine explains that "the secular literature we value most highly keeps its hold on us precisely because it fulfills the cultural role that the Bible performed for earlier generations." In a time of national crisis, as Levine argued in "Union and Disunion in 'Song of Myself' " (*ALS 1987*, pp. 70–71), "the greatest threat to the union was the failure of democracy on a personal level. . . . Whitman's self-assumed task was to reeducate individuals away from either subservience to others or mastery over them." Christianity, Whitman believed, was too hierarchical and even monarchical to function effectively as the religion of a great republic. Hence the need, as recorded by Whitman in one of his notebook entries, for "*The Great Construction* of the *New Bible.*"

In "Whitman's 'Overstaid Fraction': Section 38 of 'Song of Myself' " (*WWR* 5:17–22), R. W. French glosses the persona's "usual mistake" as a failure of the poetic imagination, which causes him to overidentify with others who suffer. The "overstaid fraction" is something like joy, recovered because of Whitman's recognition that "to see the whole pattern is to find cause for rejoicing." French's exegesis highlights the obscurity of this much-debated crisis passage and provides a useful interpretation that is in keeping with surrounding passages. It would also be good to consider why Whitman resorts to such mystifying language to describe the process of recovery at this point in the poem. In other words, there is a crucial tension between Whitman's manner (separateness) and his message (comprehensiveness), if French's interpretation is true. Perhaps too much comprehensiveness, or linguistic vagueness, leads to too much separateness, or incomprehensibility. Thoroughly comprehensible is " 'Whitman's Election Day, November 1884' " (*WWR* 5:14–17) by Nicholas Natanson, a lucid discussion of Whitman's poem of that title, inspired by the election of Cleveland over Blaine. Disillusioned with party politics, Whitman failed to vote, "but in 1884, in the midst of America's dirtiest campaign, Whitman's rhetoric turned heroic instead of cynical." Natanson closes with the interesting point that, in reaffirming democratic myth, Whitman may have been doing more harm than good. He had lost the ability to discriminate and the enthusiasm that, 20 years before, had enabled him to make those distinctions on which credible political poetry depends.

e. **Affinities and Influences.** There were two pieces on Whitman and architecture this year, expanding the growing literature on this subject. The stronger of the two is "Democratic Space: The Ecstatic Geography of Walt Whitman and Frank Lloyd Wright" (*WWR* 6: 16–32), by John Roche. The wide-ranging argument is somewhat difficult to summarize, but one of Roche's central and most interesting points is that both Whitman and Wright were agoraphiles, "reveling in the experience of inexhaustible space as a renewable source of personal and artistic energy." There is a theoretical background in Gaston Bachelard's *The Poetics of Space* which provides a useful vocabulary of "intimate immensity." "Walt Whitman and Louis Sullivan: The Aesthetics of Egalitarianism" (*WWR* 6:1–15) by Kevin Murphy provides a cogent analysis of Sullivan's belief in "the art of reading buildings" and hence in the reader-viewer's part in a building's function. Ornament functions to stimulate the mind's eye of the interpreter. Sullivan's dictum, "Form ever follows function," does not exclude ornament but rather demands it. The illustrations prove the point, but the Whitman connection, at least as presented here, is banal.

A refreshing article is by John Engell, "Walt and Sir Walter or the Bard and the Bart.: Balladeers" (*WWR* 5:1–14). In this briskly paced discussion of Whitman and Sir Walter Scott, Engell points out that "several examples of Whitman's verse published in the period before *Leaves of Grass* are in the traditional ballad form." Encountering *Border Minstrelsy* early, Whitman subsequently turned away from Scott's "feudalism," only to return to his early admiration for Scott's nationalist, partially democratic, theory and practice later in life. Further, Engell's identification of balladesque qualities in some passages of Whitman's poems such as "Song of Myself" seems right on the mark. " 'Virile emotionalism,' " a quality Whitman admired in Scott and in Irish poetry, contributed to his admiration for Thomas Moore, who figures prominently in "The Text of a Whitman Lincoln Lecture Reading: Anacreon's 'The Midnight Visitor' " (*WWR* 6:91–94), by Arthur Golden. It turns out that "throughout his career Whitman had not only been a compulsive revisor of his own poetry, he regularly revised the poetry of others as well," at least for his public readings. Following his five Lincoln lectures, Whitman usually read from *Leaves of Grass* and from works by several other poets, including Moore's translation of Anacreon's "Ode XXXIII," which Whitman called "The Midnight Visitor." Golden's effective short article presents the comparable texts: Moore's original and Whitman's version.

Arguing that "while Whitman's texts have taken on some divergent meanings in various countries as a result of cultural differences, it is remarkable how many similarities in textual interpretation there are from one culture to the next," Walter Grünzweig attributes this consistency less to Whitman's texts or personality than to the "very effective propagandistic effort stimulated by Whitman's admirers and ultimately initiated by Whitman himself." In " 'Collaborators in the Great Cause of Liberty and Fellowship': Whitmania as an Intercultural Phenomenon" (*WWR* 6:16–26), Grünzweig presents this counterintuitive idea somewhat unpersuasively, though there are some moments of local interest, especially those having to do with the interactions of the Whitman Fellowship and "the well-known German poet and dramatist Johannes Schlaf (1862–1941), one of the founders of the naturalist school of German drama and generally recognized as the leading Whitmanite in Germany." A more straightforward essay of wider appeal, also by Grünzweig, is " 'Inundated by this Mississippi of Poetry': Walt Whitman and German Expressionism" (*MStrR* 9:51–63). Grünzweig offers a helpful definition of German Expressionism as a response to dislocating social forces, suggesting that European artists are more alienated from society than Americans and that they found in Whitman the possibility of a " 'new wholeness.' " The provocative notion that "for the period between 1910 and 1920, the 'wound dresser' becomes, for a variety of reasons, the most widely known image of the American poet" is not really developed, but there is a highly instructive and touching tribute from Kafka to Whitman which Grünzweig has translated to good purpose. The essay's title quotation is from Franz Werfel, who used to read Whitman with his wife Alma, and who knew Whitman's poetry well.

Also in the *Mickle Street Review* (a publication of increasing interest to scholars) is Kenneth M. Price's "Whitman's Influence on Hamlin Garland's *Rose of Dutcher's Coolly*" (*MStrR* 5:19–29). Price aptly suggests that "although much attention has been paid to the Whitman tradition in American poetry, it has been largely overlooked that novelists, rather than poets, were the first to make significant use of *Leaves of Grass*." Garland in particular "illustrated how writers dissatisfied with the prevailing marital ideology could gain inspiration from Whitman's candor, his free love themes, his questioning of gender roles, his democratizing of relationships, and his focus on companionship." The novel, for all its Whitmanian power, Price concludes, "is at odds with itself."

As the "soaked sponge of his air and time" (the quotation is from Henry James), Garland had absorbed the vocabulary of evolution, a language which interests Hertha D. Wong in "'This Old Theory Broach'd Anew': Darwinism and Whitman's Poetic Program" (*WWR* 5:27–39). Wong's assertion that "Whitman consciously applies 'the Evolution theory' throughout his work" is overstated, but Wong makes interesting connections, albeit briefly, between Whitman's racial and sexual attitudes and the Darwinian project. Overall, the article is especially useful in its ability to muster significant quotations that illuminate Whitman's interest in evolution, as in the title quotation from his seldom cited short essay "Darwinism—Then Furthermore."

ii. Dickinson

***a.* Bibliography.** In my zeal to tell all the news and tell it first, I anticipated the publication date of Karen Dandurand's *Dickinson Scholarship: An Annotated Bibliography 1969–1985* (Garland) by a year, reviewing it in last year's *ALS*. The correct publication date is 1988. Otherwise, this was a quiet year bibliographically. *Dickinson Studies* published a 25-item bibliography of Dickinson in Russian, 1946–86, which includes translations of poems and eight articles (*DicS* 65:34–36). For now, the compiler is anonymous.

***b.* Editing, Biography.** The Dickinson family figured prominently this year, with my edition of courtship letters and Barton Levi St. Armand's article on the poet's nephew Ned. In *A Poet's Parents: The Courtship Letters of Emily Norcross and Edward Dickinson* (No. Car.), I bring together the letters exchanged by the poet's parents between February 1826 and May 1828, the date of their marriage. During this interval, the couple were physically separated—Emily Norcross at home in Monson, Edward Dickinson completing his training at the Northampton Law School and then establishing his busy law practice in Amherst. They saw each other only infrequently, so that to a remarkable extent theirs was a literary courtship.

I first encountered this correspondence while completing *Dickinson: The Anxiety of Gender* (*ALS 1984*, p. 96), having been alerted to its existence by some tantalizing excerpts in Richard B. Sewall's *The Life of Emily Dickinson* (*ALS 1974*). Reading these previously unpublished manuscripts at Houghton Library, I was struck by their narrative energy, their puzzling ellipses, and by their probable value for Dickinson studies. Though there is no evidence that Dickinson herself read the letters and though it seems to me unlikely that she would have read them before her mother's death in 1882, these letters reveal the personalities of her parents and the relationship between them more directly and with incomparably greater detail than any other biographical source. I emphasize the word "biographical" because Emily Dickinson's poetry may be said to be our single best source for understanding her parents, their relationship, and her relations with them, at least obliquely. Whatever the covert dynamics of their relationship, overtly Edward Dickinson's was the dominant voice. He wrote 69 of the letters, Emily Norcross wrote 24. The edition, which is fully annotated, is supplemented by three additional letters that illuminate their relationship but are not courtship letters as such. As I suggest in the epilogue, their marriage was apparently more gratifying to Edward than to Emily. But then so too, I conclude, was their courtship.

In "'Your Prodigal': Letters from Ned Dickinson 1879–1885" (*NEQ* 61:358–80), Barton Levi St. Armand notes that "throughout American history certain archetypal families have arisen whose personal histories mirror the nation's political fortunes, intellectual aspirations, social destinies, and aesthetic predilections." The Dickinsons, he believes, are one such family: "Its power to fascinate us comes not simply from [Emily Dickinson] . . . its most famous representative, but from all, including the supporting actor Ned Dickinson." Ned, the poet's nephew, was the elder son of Sue and Austin. A somewhat pathetic being who got caught up in the whirlwind of his parents' marriage, after having attracted the attention of Mabel Loomis Todd before she became his father's lover, Ned died in 1898, shortly before his 37th birthday. St. Armand presents a selection of his letters mainly from the 1880s and concentrates on Ned's religious heterodoxy and on his support of his mother during these years against his father. Ned's relationship with his mother was exceptionally flirtatious, and he sometimes writes her as one woman to another. Confused by his father's sexual experimentation, Ned sought refuge from his family's troubles in a variety of personae, including that of the prodigal son. His misdeeds seem to have been restricted to fantasy, however, unless his intense loyalty to his mother be construed as such. One of Ned's letters, which "were considered community property by the Dickinson family and were read regularly to the 'Aunts,' Emily and Lavinia," provided the immediate occasion for Dickinson's late poem 1545, "The Bible is an antique Volume— /Written by faded Men," in which the poet sides with the younger generation against their elders.

c. **Criticism: General.** An attempt to move Dickinson studies away from biography is Elizabeth Phillips's *Emily Dickinson: Personae and Performance* (Penn State). Arguing against the belief that Dickinson is an autobiographical poet, Phillips stakes out the position that "the poems are self-conscious—but not self-enclosed—literary performances." In her view, the poet is "histrionic but hardly hysterical." Yet Dickinson's biographical experience forms the basis for this book and Phillips is really arguing for an expansion of biographical criticism, so that it may include, and quite properly so, an author's reading. Phillips explains, "Having found the histrionic imagination especially congenial, Dickinson disclaimed that she was always writing *in propria persona.* Like many authors, she assumed many personae; and the experiences in the poems are often transformations of episodes in the lives of personal friends, literary characters, and historical figures for whom a fictive 'I' is only a convenient term." There are some promising leads here, but on the whole the book lacks both theoretical sophistication and solid common sense. Can we really believe that Dickinson's life was a "social comedy," that she was almost always competent and cheerful, busy running her home and "at home" in her world?

In her need to portray Dickinson as a healthy role model, Phillips negates the complexity of Dickinson's inner life and offers some extremely strained, if not incredible, readings of well-known poems. But she is right to insist that Dickinson listened to other voices, and Phillips herself is often an attentive reader of Dickinson's letters, as in her nicely contextualized discussion of Civil War poems in chapter 3 and in her evocation of Dickinson the local colorist, who might have written fiction, and who "remained close to the life about her." The notes are consistently judicious, and there is an excellent index, which includes references to Dickinson and such more or less contemporary women writers as the predictable English foursome—Charlotte and Emily Brontë, Elizabeth Barrett Browning, and George Eliot—along with less expected entries: Louisa May Alcott, Frances Hodgson Burnett, Rebecca Harding (Davis), Helen Hunt Jackson, Alice James, Frances Sargent Osgood, George Sand, and Harriet Prescott Spofford.

A shorter, more elegantly presented piece of work is by Margaret Dickie, "Dickinson's Discontinuous Lyric Self" (*AL* 60:537–53). Dickie suggests that readers of lyric poetry should not look for consistency of representation when it comes to plot and character. Consistency of representation, she believes, is "foreign to the lyric 'I'." Thus, Dickinson's choice of the lyric genre "is a deliberate choice of self-presentation, expressive of a particular sense of the self (of herself or a self) as shifting, changing, reforming." The genre-defining terms Dickie wishes to use seem somewhat arbitrary—she suggests brevity, repetition, figuration—and indeed Dickie acknowledges that her method is tautological. "In concentrating on the brevity, the repetition, and the figuration of the lyric form," she writes, "I have attempted to read Dickinson's poems by the qualities they possess. These terms may only be useful for Dickinson's work; they will not all serve Wordsworth's lyrics or Milton's or Shakespeare's, for example. Thus, they cannot be worked into a model for reading all lyric poetry." But the article is brilliant in its evocation of a Dickinson who cannot be totalized and who, as a consequence, is *more* rather than less self-reliant.

A more general article is by Wendy Martin, "Emily Dickinson," in the *CLHUS*, pp. 609–26, a format that perhaps necessitates some kind of totalizing. Martin's scheme involves four crises, skirmishes in Dickinson's "battle for self-reliance." The first was "with the traditional religious concept of an all-powerful God"; second, "she struggled with her father for intellectual independence"; third, "she reclaimed the energy that she had invested in the ideal of the romantic hero"; finally, she struggled to receive validation as an artist. The Dickinson who emerges from this feminist civil war is a strong woman "whose relative isolation was a self-imposed strategy that gave her time and space in which to write."

There were two articles that highlight oral imagery in Dickinson's poetry. The first, "Emily Dickinson's 'Renunciation' and Anorexia Nervosa," is by Heather Kirk Thomas (*AL* 60:205–25). As Thomas notes, "Several critics have suggested a metaphorical link between Dickinson and anorexia but have always stopped short of tendering a literal diagnosis." Is this lack of imagination on their part? I think not. The biographical evidence, though suggestive, is finally unpersuasive. As a young woman, Dickinson apparently had a tendency toward anorexia, but there is a significant difference between a tendency and a full-blown disease. Thomas believes that Dickinson had the disease, that her "enmeshed" family conspired to hide this weakness, and that subsequent generations of critics have participated in this conspiracy. There is good material here, but there is also too much melodrama. A more restrained (in the good sense of the term) essay is by M. K. Louis, "Emily Dickinson's Sacrament of Starvation" (*NCF* 43:346–60). In this well-written piece, Louis shows that Dickinson viewed the sacrament of communion as an exclusionary "test of personal attachment": "It is as if the sacrament itself represents to her a sense of alienation, of the evasiveness of the sacred."

Correcting misconceptions about Dickinson's sacramental experience, in "Emily Dickinson and the Calvinist Sacramental Tradition" (*ESQ* 33[1987]:67–81), Jane Donahue Eberwein provides a dense historical context for understanding Dickinson's imaginative use of sacramental language. Contrary to popular critical belief, marriage was no sacrament among the Calvinists. And "of the two sacraments [baptism and communion] recognized within her religious culture, Dickinson received only the first."

In "The Development of Dickinson's Style" (*AL* 60:26–43) Timothy Morris analyzes patterns of rhyme and enjambment, to show that "these formal contours of her verse changed over time, especially from 1858 to 1865." Morris charts a pattern of diminishing use of exact rhyme and a significant increase in enjambed quatrains. This latter feature sharply distinguishes Dickinson's prosody from Isaac Watts's. However, Morris treats a stanza that ends in a dash as though it had no punctuation at all; he also exhibits too much confidence in the Johnson-Ward-Franklin chronology. The article nevertheless focuses much-needed attention on the particulars of Dickinson's versification, as it may have evolved over time. Also dealing with a neglected area is Judith Weissman. In " 'Transport's Working Classes': Sanity, Sex, and Solidarity in Dickinson's Late Poetry" (*MQ*

29:407–24), she finds in the late poems not volcanic intensity but "lucidity, sanity, and generosity." By "late," she means poems written after 1864, a date that errs on the side of earliness. A comparatively neglected subject is also tackled by Sharon M. Harris, in "The 'Cloth of Dreams': Dream Imagery in Dickinson's Poetry and Prose" (*DicS* 68:3–16). She writes persuasively that "though dreams allow her to expand the boundaries of her 'Demurer Circuit' and afford a security and freedom seldom found at dawn, the illusions of her dream-world also make confronting daylight realities even more burdensome."

A well-balanced and well-written essay (the title typo notwithstanding) is by Raymond A. Mazurek. In " 'I Have [sic] no Monarch in My Life': Feminism, Poetry, and Politics in Dickinson and Higginson," in *Patrons and Protégées*, he suggests that "Higginson, as first critic, stands in for us . . . embarrassed as we are to acknowledge him." Along the way, there is an excellent discussion of Higginson's career, but Mazurek's larger point is that the modernism of Dickinson's poetry made it difficult for Higginson to appreciate her project.

***d.* Criticism: Individual Works.** In "Emily Dickinson, the Master, and the Loaded Gun: The Violence of Re-figuration" (*ESQ* 33:137–45), Jeanne Holland treats the Master figure as male precursor who is engaged in an exchange relation with the Gun/Speaker. The "power to kill" is the "art of naming and objectification." In "Narrative Technique in Emily Dickinson's 'My life had stood a loaded gun' " (*JNT* 18:258–68), Helmut Bonheim uses a corrupt text, thereby significantly weakening the effectiveness of his close linguistic analysis. Ernest Fontana, in "Dickinson's 'Go not too near a House of Rose' (Poem 1434) and Keats' 'Ode on Melancholy' " (*DicS* 68:26–29), disputes the belief that the poem is based on a passage from Emerson's "Nature." Rather, he contends, "a text that is closer in its speech act, subject matter, and imagery to Dickinson's poem is Keats' 'Ode on Melancholy.' " Writing about a perhaps deservedly neglected poem, Dorothy Huff Oberhaus, in "Dickinson's 'Poem 698' " (*Expl* 46:21–25), attempts to show that "Life—is what we make it—" is "a dense and complex text that is of poetic interest as well as of great importance to understanding her portrait of Jesus Christ in other poems." In "Emily Dickinson's 'My Life Closed Twice': The Archetypal Import of Its Imagistic Number Two" (*AI* 45:225–27), Eli Flatto asks: "Is it possible that our conceptions of heaven and hell . . . stem from our childhood experiences, disguised as memories?" He suggests an oedipal origin for the losses which in his view are best understood as psychologically universal rather than biographically particular. Despite the relevance of this interpretation to Freudian theory, most readers, I suspect, will not agree.

e. **Influences and Affinities.** Linking Dickinson to the popular women writers of her day, David S. Reynolds (*Beneath the American Renaissance*, pp. 412–37) argues that her poetry should be viewed "as the highest product of a rich literary moment, roughly between 1855 and 1865." This "American Women's Renaissance" was composed of "conventional literature, women's rights fiction, and the literature of misery. Conventional literature generally avoided gender-specific issues and invested the redemptive moral exemplar with unprecedented power." Given these choices, Reynolds associates Dickinson with Samuel Bowles's category, "the literature of misery." Potentially, this nomenclature is reductive, and feminist critics would not agree that domestic or sensational fiction avoided gender-specific issues. As deployed by Reynolds, however, who focuses less on Dickinson's alienation from her culture than on her participation in a "rebellious American sisterhood," the literature of misery includes an extraordinary "flexibility of tone." Indeed, Reynolds praises this literature for its "intellectual probing," especially along religious lines. Though there are gaps in his argument—Dickinson's indebtedness to English literature, for example—Reynolds effectively deepens our understanding of Dickinson's contemporary context and of her position within it.

A useful short article is by Michael E. Staub, "White Moth and Ox: The Friendship of ED with H. H. Jackson" (*DicS* 68:17–25). Biographically, there is nothing new here, but Staub examines Jackson's verse from a feminist perspective so as to link the two writers. His comments about Jackson's cult of antidomesticity are shrewder than his observations about Dickinson's style.

Moving across national boundaries and back in time, Shira Wolosky, in "Rhetoric or Not: Hymnal Tropes in Emily Dickinson and Isaac Watts" (*NEQ* 61:214–32), presents a densely reasoned extension of her study of Dickinson's religious themes in *Emily Dickinson: A Voice of War* (*ALS 1984*, pp. 96–97). Initially, Wolosky contends that "a surprising number of Dickinson poems seem written in direct response to particular Watts hymns. Furthermore, Dickinson's relation to Watts is not simply parodic. The hymnal frame of so much

Dickinson verse asserts a genuine and profound effort to accept doctrines that she cannot, however, help but question, leading her in turn to question her own doubts." Ultimately, though, "Dickinson's art fails to close the gap between faith and figure, even when she attempts to turn against her own rhetoricity." Wolosky's larger point is that Dickinson wishes to reclaim "the religious state beyond language and beyond figuration." There are some superb close readings, though some of the juxtaposed passages from Dickinson and Watts (pp. 216–17) are not persuasive, in that they do not demonstrate that Dickinson was responding to Watts as a unique source. Despite a tendency to overstate her case, Wolosky shows Dickinson wrestling with cultural issues of such complexity that they cannot finally be resolved. This sense of dynamic irresolution—whether moral, psychological, or linguistic—informed many of the best works I read this year, and for both poets.

University of Washington

6. Mark Twain

Hamlin Hill

The big news for 1988—maybe for the decade—was the publication of the Iowa/California edition of *Adventures of Huckleberry Finn*. The first volume of the new edition of *Letters* came in a close second; and a number of important books and articles saw the light of day. *South Central Review* devoted most of an issue to Mark Twain, and there is every indication that 1989 will be another banner year.

i. Biography

One of the most useful biographical items of 1988 was Edgar M. Branch's "A Proposed Calendar of Samuel Clemens's Steamboats, 15 April 1857 to 8 May 1861, with Commentary" (*MTJ* 24, ii:2–24). An extremely helpful itinerary of Clemens's service as a cub, pilot, or copilot on 64 assignments, Branch's calendar is enhanced with old photographs of the boats and is supplemented by extensive and authoritative narrative commentary. This is a significant resource for Mark Twain biography. George Moss's equally fascinating "Popular Entertainment in Virginia City, Nevada, 1859–1863" (*JPC* 22:1–31) is a cultural portrait of Sam Clemens's western "home" during his period of residency. Per capita alcoholic consumption was 22 gallons a year; gambling was legal and endemic; boxing matches, horse races, and cockfighting were common sports. No wonder the Langdon family expressed some reluctance at welcoming a stranger from there to their fireside hearth!

Wallace Shugg fleshes out details of the burglary of Stormfield on September 18, 1908, with extensive evidence from Twain, Clara, Isabel Lyon, and one of the two burglars himself, in "The Humorist and the Burglar: The Untold Story of the Mark Twain Burglary" (*MTJ* 25, i:2–11). And Ursula Thomas updates the story of Mark Twain's assault on the German language with *Notebooks & Journals* (volumes 1 and 2) and Alan Gribben's *Mark Twain's Library*, in her

"Mark Twain's German Language Learning Experiences" (in *Teaching German in America* [Wisconsin], pp. 133–43).

More extensive is Miriam Jones Shillingsburg's *At Home Abroad: Mark Twain in Australasia* (Mississippi). This study traces in minute detail Mark Twain's three-and-a-half month lecture tour of New Zealand and Australia. Shillingsburg's research has turned up new interviews of the author, described the social and political background in which the tour took place, retrieved reports of his lecture subjects and manner, and documented the adulation (and occasional hostility) which greeted him. Final chapters record the reception and evaluation of Mark Twain and American humor by Australasian journalists and critics.

Finally, Isabelle Budd's "Clara Samossoud's Will" (*MTJ* 25, i:17–29) is of interest to Twainians because the ultimate beneficiary was the Mark Twain Foundation, because it reveals details of Clara's and Nina's personalities, and because it has all the possibilities and ingredients for a hit soap opera!

ii. Editions

"It is finished," to borrow a phrase: the Iowa/California *Huckleberry Finn* (Calif.), co-edited by Walter Blair and Victor Fischer, is in print! It is a cornucopia—362 pages of text, and 539 pages of apparatus. Almost everything a person could want is here—a detailed introduction by Blair, a meticulous and precise textual introduction by Fischer, the working notes and printed texts revised for lecture readings, Webster & Co.'s advertisements and announcements of the first publication, maps, glossaries, and lists of emendations. The only item missing from the feast is the running heads which were on the tops of the odd-numbered pages of the first edition, with which Mark Twain probably tampered.

To make up for absence, though, the "Raftsmen" passage from *Life on the Mississippi* is restored to its original position in chapter 16. I personally remain unconvinced that its inclusion represented Mark Twain's final intention, and I am bothered by the unfamiliar lowercase *aunt*, *uncle*, and *widow* when Huck is referring to specific characters. But the volume is a monument to scholarship, historical investigation, and precise and painstaking research.

Mark Twain's Letters, I, 1853–1866, Edgar Marquess Branch, Michael B. Frank, and Kenneth M. Sanderson, eds. (Calif.) is the first in a set of complete correspondence which will ultimately run to over 10,000 letters. The first volume covers the apprentice years and, as the editors point out, traces "the transformation of the cocksure but callow printer of 1853 into the worldly journalist and public figure of 1866." Clemens was almost literally incapable of writing a dull letter (excluding the bread-and-butter and RSVP notes gathered by Cyril Clemens in *Mark Twain the Letter Writer* over a half century ago), and these record the most famous rites of passage in American literary history and legend. Since Clemens was a typesetter himself, Robert H. Hirst's "Guide to Editorial Practice" is an especially informative addition to the volume, detailing how the edition handles the problem of Clemens's own printer's marks. Also fascinating is the use of photographic reproduction of holographs in the "Textual Commentaries" section when readings are ambiguous or conjectural.

Two letters saw print in brief journal notes, as well. Howard Kany prints "A Letter from Mark Twain" to his father, Arthur S. Kany, thanking him (probably on August 22, 1902), for sending a high school biography of Clemens (*MTJ* 25, i:31). And John O. Stark publishes a March 15, 1881, letter from Clemens to Ulysses Grant in "Mark Twain and the Chinese" (*MTJ* 24, ii:36). This one thanks Grant for his presumed intervention with the Chinese viceroy on behalf of the Chinese Educational Mission in Hartford and a student named Yung Wing.

iii. General Interpretations

John C. Gerber's *Mark Twain* (Twayne) moves sensitively through the major works from *Innocents* through to selected later writings. Given the austere constraints on space in the TUSAS volumes, Gerber's adroit combination of the major biographical facts and perceptive interpretation of the major (and a few of the minor) works is a tour de force, an ideal distillation of facts and insights. Less satisfactory is Philip Fisher's "Mark Twain" in *CLHUS*. A curiously quirky and disorganized combination of truisms, facts, and original insights—literary commercialism and fraud; the mass media of journalism, lecture platform, and subscription book; multiple narrative voices; picaresque form, ultimately internalized or fantasized; transcendent strangers who bring the apocalypse. They are all here, in roughly that order, but somehow they do not jell as Dixon Wecter's old essay did in the original LHUS. "In Twain's works there are no plots, only local complications," Fisher avers; the same might be said, and more accurately, of this essay.

Equally disappointing is Elizabeth I. Hanson's chapter "Mark Twain and the Indian" (in *The American Indian*, pp. 77–85). She traces, mostly by plot summary, Mark Twain's attitudes toward the Indians in *Roughing It*, *Tom Sawyer*, and (indirectly) "To the Person Sitting in Darkness." But she curiously ignores the work which treats the Native American most extensively—*Huck Finn and Tom Sawyer Among the Indians.*

Edward W. Huffstetler's "Mark Twain's Unique Brand of Cultural Relativism" (*DQR* 18:59–67) probes many titles superficially—*Roughing It*, *Huck*, *Connecticut Yankee*, "To the Person Sitting in Darkness," "In Defense of General Funston," and "The United States of Lyncherdom"—to explain Mark Twain's opposition to the Christian conversion of pagan cultures. According to Huffstetler, Mark Twain believed that "at least uncivilized man is not yet totally contaminated," as civilized man is. In "Twain's Early Writing and Theories of Realism," Walter Shear argues that Realism balances an external objective world with a subjective internal perception of that world (*MQ* 30:93–103). Shear focuses on "Old Times" and *Huck Finn*; the correct balance is achieved by Bixby in the former, and in *Huck* by alternative "communal" and pastoral episodes.

In "Mark Twain's Public Private Correspondence" (*SCR* 5:22–28) I have analyzed the "My Dear Bro" letter of October 19, 1865, to Orion and the 1890 "Belly and Members" letter to Andrew Lang to suggest that they were in fact "public" literary performances rather than private correspondence. In each of them, Mark Twain tried "to justify and define a talent and a profession about which he never achieved a reconciliation." In the same journal, Pascal Covici, Jr., confronts "Mark Twain and the Failure of Humor: The Puritan Legacy" (*SCR* 5:2–14). Playing Mark Twain off against Benjamin Franklin, Hawthorne, and Nathaniel Ward, Covici suggests that the Puritan tradition which contrasts "the materially practical" with the "authoritatively moralistic" permits us to laugh at other "transgressors" but only rarely to proceed to self-indictment. Humor "gives us momentary stays against chaos; it provides flashes of self-understanding that then flicker and vanish," Covici maintains.

Two broadly based book-length studies conclude this General Interpretations section for 1988. Andrew Jay Hoffman's *Twain's*

Heroes, Twain's Worlds (Penn.) is a richly textured analysis of Huck, Hank, and David Wilson as a kind of triad of heroic models who successively try to find "a kind of heroism which could at the very least survive the world as he saw it." But "at the end of their novels, they betray our trust in their heroism and fail to make material the hopes their heroism leads us to invest in them." Moving comfortably among a host of earlier scholarly studies, Hoffman delineates a Huck who is emblematic of the failure of Jacksonian idealism, a Hank who represents the failure of Industrial/Imperial America, and a Pudd'nhead who, "perhaps nothing but a cog in an existential situation," nevertheless "finds that the knowledge of identity brings him an alloyed success far above what his more powerful heroes achieve. In him, we find a hero to believe in."

In *Mark Twain and Science* (LSU) Sherwood Cummings investigates Clemens's grounding in the popular science of the intellectual magazines of the 1870s, a topic inflamed by religious controversy. At first, Mark Twain's own journalistic humor on the topic vacillated; Calvinism, deism, evangelism, and post-Darwinian science all held him captive at various times in his early career. Slowly, as evidenced in Cummings's broad-ranging survey of a multitude of works, Mark Twain became permanently if reluctantly enslaved by his mechanistic determinism, with only rare and sporadic outbursts of his earlier idealism. Penetrating readings of *Huck*, *Connecticut Yankee*, *Pudd'nhead Wilson*, and many lesser works punctuate Cummings's study, which would have been more felicitously described by its subtitle, *Adventures of a Mind.*

iv. Individual Works Through 1885

Brigit Wetzel-Sahm's "Deadpan Emotionalized: American Humor in a German Translation of Mark Twain's 'Journalism in Tennessee'" (*SAH* 5:3–16) is a meticulous analysis of an 1895 German translation of the 1869 tale. This essay shows how the translator, August Schacht, altered the original to make it comprehensible to a German audience: he emphasized with stronger language, removed deadpan sentences, and substituted versions of German local color for American ones. John E. Bassett, "*Roughing It*: Authority through Comic Performance" (*NCL* 43:220–34), argues that *Roughing It*, as the first book Mark Twain wrote as a book, contains a blueprint for "controlling audience and subject matter" to assert his own authority as author.

Throughout the book, "by centering language and communication in many episodes," Mark Twain shares or withholds information to develop "a mode that could thrive on internal contradiction and undermine signification itself." Philip Burns mines the same vein in "Fabrication and Faultline: Language as Experience in *Roughing It*" (*MQ* 29:249–63). The narrator's experience, according to Burns, is basically linguistic, with lies and tall tales, vernacular language and slang, embodied in "legend," "pure fabrication," and "a kind of evasive writing one might call the nonstory"—all producing a gap between reality and language.

Lawrence I. Berkove nominates William Wright's anecdote "Pilot Wylie" (1875) as a source for Mark Twain's reminiscences of Strother Wiley in the sixth *Atlantic* installment of "Old Times on the Mississippi" in "Dan DeQuille and 'Old Times on the Mississippi'" (*MTJ* 24, ii:28–34), but Edgar M. Branch disagrees (pp. 24–27). Elizabeth G. Peck, in "Tom Sawyer: Character in Search of an Audience" (*ATQ* 2:23–36), undertakes to "redefine what normality and maturity mean in St. Petersburg" to gauge Tom's growth. Not surprisingly, the adults approve false theatricality and Tom is gradually "molded into an actor constantly in search of an audience." Trygve Thoreson "liberates" Aunt Polly from her role as chief guardian of St. Petersburg's social values in "Aunt Polly's Predicament" (*StAH* 5:17–26). He argues that Aunt Polly shows her "recognition that spontaneous demonstrations of affection and concern can have more value than perfectly 'proper' behavior."

John Daniel Stahl's "Mark Twain and Female Power" (*SAF* 16: 51–63) explicates "A Memorable Midnight Experience" and *1601* as ambivalent fictions regarding female sexuality, power, and authority as opposed to traditional Victorian stereotyping.

David E. E. Sloane's *Adventures of Huckleberry Finn: American Comic Vision* (Twayne) is a less flamboyant study than Harold Beaver's 1987 book-length analysis of the novel, but it moves authoritatively through the historical contexts and the book's significance and critical reception to a detailed analysis of themes and motifs, chapter by chapter. Along the way, Sloane provides analogues and parallels in the works of Mark Twain's contemporaries—John T. Trowbridge, particularly, in whose novel *Cudjo's Cave* Sloane finds a convincing source for Pap's speech against the "gov'ment."

Alan Gribben suggests, in "Manipulating a Genre: *Huckleberry Finn* as Boy Book" (*SCR* 5:15–21), that *Huck* includes a number of the standard qualities that define the Boy Book genre—an orphan central character, a schoolboy crush, a gang, a test of courage, an almost fatal illness, authoritative adults, and a grown narrator. Twain selected some of these elements for his novel, and "what literary critics nowadays dislike most" about *Huck* "are actually the vestigial parts of the conventions in which it originated." In "*Adventures of Huckleberry Finn, The Bostonians,* and Henry Ward Beecher: Discourse on the Idealization of Suffering" (*SCR* 5:42–52), Janet Gabler-Hover argues that both novels "explore the integral relationship between social reform in America and a contemporary idealization of suffering," a concept popularized in Beecher's preaching. Beecher's argument that suffering produces empathy and compassion functions negatively throughout most of *Huck*, where "suffering is concertedly avoided" in favor of selfishness and self-interest, except of course for Huck himself.

Steven Blakemore, "Huck Finn's Written Word" (*ALR* 20:21–29), confronts the increasingly popular topic of Huck as author of words rather than as a character in his novel and argues that as Huck "refers to learning and books, he locks himself into a language of guilt, a language of bad conscience and civilization." Dennis Patrick Slattery's "The Via Dollarosa: Money Matters in *Huckleberry Finn*" (*SCR* 5:29–41) juggles an enormous number of concepts (perhaps too many, since they tend to blur) regarding the theme of money in the novel: mythic and talismanic backgrounds, symbolic equivalents, the "central icon" (along with Jim) in the novel, the metaphor for culture as opposed to Nature. Money is a goddess who complements "the generous river god of the Mississippi," and ultimately "Huck reconciles money with Providence, death, and justice."

Forrest Robinson's "The Characterization of Jim in *Huckleberry Finn*" (*NCL* 43:361–91) is a sensitive addition to recent revisionist interpretations of Jim. He argues that Jim tries to be " 'visible,' and frank, opinionated, assertive, even argumentative with Huck, and the invariable result has been trouble." As a result, and with special emphasis on the separation in the fog and the incident of the slave traders in chapters 15 and 16, Robinson suggests that Jim must deliberately assume the stereotype mask which Huck expects of him and "turn this stereotype to his own advantage." Joyce A. Rowe's chapter "Mark Twain's Great Evasion: *Adventures of Huckleberry Finn*" (pp. 46–74 in her book *Equivocal Endings*) sees the novel as "centrally concerned with the defeat of a visionary ideal that is at once national and individual." Rowe catalogs Huck's loss of control of the novel action in the "Evasion," suggesting that the entire episode has the sense of "a kind of blasphemy." Events at the Phelps' Farm make "clear the impossibility for Huck of ever achieving a visionary ideal based on those energies nurtured on the raft." That doesn't sound very equivocal to me!

Two pedagogically oriented examinations of *Huck* appeared in 1988. Elaine Cheesman and Earl French edited a *Twain-Stowe Sourcebook* (Mark Twain Memorial and Stowe-Day Foundation), which contains the proceedings of a July 1987 institute for Connecticut schoolteachers. Among the Mark Twain materials are summaries of lectures by Louis Budd, Shelley Fisher Fishkin, Hamlin Hill, Justin Kaplan, and David E. E. Sloane; chronologies and bibliographies; and suggestions for thematic approaches to the novel such as "Feminism," "Humor/Satire/Irony," and "Literature as History." More compact is Randy Mills's "Using Tom and Huck to Develop Moral Reasoning in Adolescents: A Strategy for the Classroom" (*Adolescence* 23:325–31). Mills proposes sets of questions for students that require them to examine closely (1) Tom's actions in the "Evasion," (2) Huck's debate with his conscience in chapter 31, (3) Jim's decision to withhold from Huck his knowledge of Pap's death, and (4) Colonel Sherburn's behavior. This will, Mills asserts, help adolescents "face the difficult task of developing their own value system." The question is, if they come up with the right answers to these events in the novel, how will we be able to tolerate them?

v. Individual Works After 1885

Two articles dealt with *A Connecticut Yankee in King Arthur's Court.* Earl F. Briden's "Chromo-Civilization and Mark Twain's *Connecticut Yankee*" (*ANQ* 1:137–39) links Hank's homesickness for chromos with a handful of articles debating this cultural artifact of popular culture in magazines of the 1870s and 80s. More substantial is Thomas H. Fick's "Mark Twain's Machine Politics: Unmetaphoring *A Connecticut Yankee in King Arthur's Court*" (*ALR* 20:30–42). Fick provides a 19th-century political context for Hank's technological terminology ("boss," "machine," and "practicality"). The Catholic Church—"only a political machine," as Hank calls it—is his adversary in its Tammany Hall, Boss Tweed facet. Hank's reforms are doomed to failure because of his "maintaining a willful ignorance of political engineering."

The two articles on *Pudd'nhead Wilson* for 1988 follow complementary, and often identical, lines of development. Susan Gillman's " 'Sure Identifiers': Race, Science, and the Law in Twain's *Pudd'nhead Wilson*" (*SAQ* 87:195–218) argues that, in order to distinguish slave from free and establish identity, American legal systems in the 19th century and scientific theories aimed to "fix racial identity as an absolute quantity with clear boundaries rather than on a continuum of gradations." In the courtroom climax of *Pudd'nhead*, Mark Twain confronts these two false premises with the science of fingerprinting revealing "identity" and the law intervening to declare Tom "property." Ironically, though, *Pudd'nhead* exposes "the artificial character of essential social measures of identity." Eric J. Sundquist's "Mark Twain and Homer Plessy" (*Representations* 24:102–28) complements Gillman by analyzing *Plessy v. Ferguson*, which, although not decided by the Supreme Court until 1896, was initiated in 1893 and was preceded by a host of earlier court cases which foreshadowed the "separate but equal" doctrine and which Sundquist summarizes helpfully. In addition, he fleshes out extensive historical background about anti-immigration sentiment in the 1890s, which has a bearing on the arrival of the Italian twins in Dawson's Landing.

Susan Gillman confronts the issues of identity, gender, and legality again in " 'Dementia Americana': Mark Twain, 'Wapping Alice,' and the Harry K. Thaw Trial" (*CritI* 14:296–314). She conflates the Thaw murder of Stanford White in 1906 with Mark Twain's renewed interest in his 1898 story of alleged seduction in the Clemens's household staff in 1877. The trial, and the story, raise complex questions about gender, stereotyping, and sexuality. As Alice shifts from pregnant female to unpregnant male transvestite to unpregnant female in Twain's revisions of the story, she embodies, like Evelyn Nesbit Thaw, characteristics of the sexually aggressive New Woman and raises "confusions between factuality and fictionality and between stereotypical male and female roles." In confronting both of their stories, Mark Twain assumed the role of Victorian father, outraged and ambiguous about what those stories meant.

Finally, in "Rude Awakenings and Swift Recoveries: The Problem of Reality in Mark Twain's 'The Great Dark' and 'Three Thousand Years Among the Microbes'" (*ALR* 21:19–28), Kathleen Walsh explicates the two fragments to show that Mark Twain "is experimenting with new outlooks and techniques and not simply railing against new times and his personal difficulties." To reconcile himself to a relativist universe, "he experiments with characters who are aware of and living with competing realities."

It appears, at midyear, that 1989 will have some special delights for Twainians. The *Connecticut Yankee* Conference at Elmira College was a splendid success. Susan Gillman's book *Dark Twins* (containing versions of the two essays published in 1988) has appeared and is enormously thought-provoking. And *Huck Finn and Tom Sawyer Among the Indians*, with the title story, "Tom Sawyer's Conspiracy," "Villagers of 1840–3," and many lesser works, has come out in the Mark Twain Library in paperback for classroom use. Robert Sattelmeyer will have the delight of summarizing them all next year.

Texas A&M University

7. Henry James

Richard A. Hocks

Work on Henry James certainly stays plentiful, with six critical books, an edition of letters, and just over 100 journal essays or chapters from books. The international flavor of James scholarship remains strong, and parallel studies still dominate. *The Bostonians, What Maisie Knew*, and (of course) *The Turn of the Screw* drew the most work; also "Maud-Evelyn" merited several analyses. New, or nearly new, approaches address the short story sequences, the precise "stylistics" of the late prose, and the issue of historicism. Because of a small number of scholars who, for one reason or another, fail to cite previous work on the same topic or else claim new insights already in print, my sense is that perhaps 1988, though high in quantity, shows a slight "dip" in quality from, say, 1983 to 1986. Yet there is excellent work by Paul Armstrong, Susan Mizruchi, and David Smit, as well as strong work by a considerable number of others as noted below. My favorite 1988 quote is Dorothea Krook's, on recent criticism of *The Figure in the Carpet*: "I can always see what Henry James's story is doing for their theories, but I can't always see so clearly what their theories are doing for James's story."

i. Editions, Biographical Studies

Rayburn S. Moore's finely edited *Selected Letters of Henry James to Edmund Gosse, 1882–1915* (LSU) prints 317 letters of over 400 written by James to Gosse, 224 for the first time (Edel prints 41), recording a literary friendship of three decades reminiscent of James's with Stevenson, their mutual friend ("R.L.S."). This edition is a labor of love: the texts are derived from original manuscripts; they retain James's distinctive ampersands and punctuation, and the annotations are so thorough as to be well-nigh obtrusive, yet ideal for a reader who uses the edition as a reference work (though James's French stays untranslated). Reflections on his lack of popularity as a dramatist, his British naturalization process, a recounting of William's death, and the constant flavor of British and American slang are some of the high spots.

I include *Leon Edel and Literary Art*, Lyall H. Powers, ed. (UMI Research Press), within this subheading, although most of its 23 contributions honoring Edel—poems, essays, letters, artwork—are neither biographical studies nor on James. Those that are include Daniel M. Fogel's "Leon Edel's Henry James," pp. 73–82, which updates and revises his solid *HJR* essay (*ALS 1982*, p. 119) and again meticulously compares and prefers the two-volume *Life* over the five-volume *Henry James*; Dennis W. Petrie's "Vision of the Artist: Leon Edel's Henry James," pp. 63–71, a shorter segment from his *Ultimately Fiction* (*ALS 1982*, p. 112); Sergio Perosa's translation of his essay, "Henry James's " 'The Aspern Papers,' " pp. 125–33, which treats the tale's "fusion" of gothic elements, its "exchange value" theme, and the effective use of its Venice setting; Adeline R. Tintner's latest "Source for James's *The Ambassadors* in Holbein's *The Ambassadors* (1533)," pp. 135–50, a plausible claim that James named his book, already under way, after seeing—and perhaps studying the *carpe diem/memento mori* icons of—Holbein's newly named portrait of two French ambassadors to England on view at the National Gallery; Joseph A. Ward's " 'The Amazing Hotel World' of James, Dreiser, and Wharton," pp. 151–60, which explores James's repulsion-attraction to the Waldorf in *American Scene* as a key signature for the luxury hotel as "microcosm" of America itself, its horror as well as its realm of "fantasy" and "escapism"; editor Lyall Powers's "James's 'Maud Evelyn,' " pp. 117–24, which first situates the tale in the context of works of the "compensatory *imagined*" experience (including "Hugh Merrow"), then contends "Maud-Evelyn" takes a different turn—largely through its narrator—in showing the beneficial consequences of Marmaduke's imaginary life with the Dedrick's daughter: practical consequences so as to embody William's pragmatism. Powers's versatile volume also reprints David A. Leeming's moving "Interview with James Baldwin on Henry James," pp. 171–81, whose extensive comments on Strether, Newman, and on James as the "only writer" who understood the failure of Americans to "perceive the reality of others," are important statements. (Leeming also published "A Conversation with Stephen Spender on Henry James" [*HJR* 9:128–35], which contains reflections on *The Ivory Tower* as crucial for Spender's *The Destructive Element*.)

No homage to Edel is Cheryl B. Torsney's "The Traditions of Gender: Constance Fenimore Woolson and Henry James" in *Patrons and Protégées*, pp. 161–83, which seeks to correct Edel's "male fantasy" reading of Woolson's death as a rejected lover of James with a view of them as "compatriots sharing the literary life of the age." She attributes Woolson's suicide to illness and depression, including Seasonal Affective Disorder, and encourages a comparative rereading of *Portrait* and *Anne* as contemporary novels about a "woman's struggle for independence and identity." Citing Henry Adams's well-known remark that James had written "pure autobiography," Marnie Jones in "Telling His Own Story: Henry James's *William Wetmore Story* (*Biography*: 10[1987]:241–56) affirms that James replaces "his own inward history for that of Story," a tendency found earlier in *Hawthorne* and of course prominent in James's own late memoirs, augmented by his belief in the "meagreness of the material." Revealing a "retrospective envy" of Story's expatriate opportunity, James exhibits the "transference" Edel warns of when writing biography of James himself. Timothy Materer in "From Henry James to Ezra Pound: John Quinn and the Art of Patronage" (*Paideuma* 17, 2/3:47–68) argues that knowing Quinn's devotion to James, it is impossible not to see a Jamesian " 'perfectly rounded' vision in Quinn's life," since he was Pound's ideal patron—one of the first to recognize the value of modern art and a staunch supporter of experimenters like James, Joyce, and Pound. Materer links James's themes of art acquisition and money by Verver in *Golden Bowl* to Quinn, who shared certain flaws of the "accumulators." Spouses Henry Janowitz and Adeline Tintner recount in detail James's visits to his doctors between 1909 and 1915 while he was suffering from coronary artery disease in "An Anglo-American Consultation: Sir William Osler Refers Henry James to Sir James Mackenzie" (*Jour. of the Hist. of Medicine* 43, iii:297–308). In different ways each doctor tried to relieve James's anxiety with sound advice in accord with the medical practice of the era as set forth in Mackenzie's notes on Angina Pectoris; these notes even cite James as exemplum. An interesting twist is that Mackenzie drew out James's confirmation that in *Turn of the Screw* "the basis of terror is mystery," so he reversed the psychology with the worried James by reassurances "less than candid." Finally, Robert Gale has updated his valuable DLB entry, "Henry James," in the *Concise Dictionary of Literary Biography: Realism, Naturalism, and Local Color, 1865–1917*, (Gale), pp. 214–43.

ii. Sources, Influences, Parallels

A model source study replete with thoroughness and intelligence is Marijane Roundtree Davis's "'A Fine Bewilderment': The Influence of Henry James's *William Wetmore Story* on *The Golden Bowl* (*HJR* 9:17–34) for the convincing way she clarifies why James undertook the Story biography and then, especially, how both his research and emotional ties to Story's background (both Italian and American) provided important materials—characterization, imagery, even numerous verbal echoes—for *The Golden Bowl.* An added bonus is Davis's broadening while incorporating previous good work by Adeline Tintner and Cheryl Torsney (an example of good "colleagueship") and her further elaboration of James's reworking of Poe and Hawthorne in the novel. Another interesting piece is Celeste Goodridge's "Towards a Poetics of Disclosure: Marianne Moore and Henry James" (*Sagetrieb* 6, 3[1987]:31–43), which charts the influence of James's concept in his memoir of the "orphan self" and his "aesthetic of disclosure and concealment" on the mind and art of Moore, especially her poem "An Octopus." Moore's connection with James's niece at Bryn Mawr, where James lectured on Balzac, is itself interesting. More conventional is Susan Elizabeth Gunter's "The Russian Connection: Sources for Miriam Rooth of James's *The Tragic Muse* (*SoAR* 53, 2:77–91), which finds in Miriam elements of Turgenev's Gemma Roselli of *Spring Freshets* (her acting ability), Marianna of *The Virgin Soil* (her independence), and Clara Milich (her physical appearance) of "Clara Milich." Yet despite the Turgenev "imprint," James transcends the prototypes and creates a figure with "tensile strength," an "architect of her own being."

Using effectively the deconstructive assumptions that texts are as filled with absences as with presences and that history is best interpreted through the traces it leaves in texts, Eileen Sypher in "Anarchism and Gender: James's *The Princess Casamassima* and Conrad's *The Secret Agent*" (*HJR* 9:1–16) asserts that both male authors domesticate political acts in an attempt to deal with the "new women" and gender relations. The plot of *The Princess* insinuates that "women motivate anarachist acts," that "they sow confusion," and that their infidelity prompts self-destruction. Judith Ryan's "Validating the Possible: Thoughts and Things in James, Rilke, and Musil" (*CL* 40:305–17) briefly examines several James characters—Strether, "The Real Thing" narrator, Maggie Verver, the Governess—who have a special kind of vision "that both creates and validates the possible," comparing them to similar characters in Rilke and Musil. Her further claim that in James's art the validation of the possible and the seamless, continuous relation between thoughts and things parallel William James's later empiricism is legitimate—but no longer original. Alison Rieke's "Two Women: The Transformations" in *Faith of a (Woman) Writer*, Alice Kessler-Harris and William McBrien, eds. (Greenwood), pp. 71–81, places Barnes's *Nightwood*, Hawthorne's *Blithedale*, and James's *Bostonians* together to examine the problems between women in situations where a stronger woman tends to dominate a weaker, more passive type. All three writers connect the "passive girls" with "mesmerism, sleepwalking or mediumship," yet James's main focus is on Olive's neurotic need to "own" Verena.

"A Wilde Subtext for *The Awkward Age*" (*HJR* 9:199–208) by Paula V. Smith argues cogently that James's rivalry and ambivalence toward Wilde are preserved in the novel's "oddities of structure" and dramatic resemblance to *The Importance of Being Earnest*—especially the many references to books: the "bookness" of characters (who discuss one another as books), the "corrupting power" of books, and "the implications of reading, interpreting and being shaped by a printed text." James's scenic text suggests *Earnest*, but his subtext hints at *Dorian Gray*. Elizabeth Kaspar Aldrich, in "Musing on the Model, or An American Tradition of Female Life into Art: Henry James in Context" (*SPELL* 4:159–78), draws an arresting analogy between Picasso's "fractured" portrait of Gertrude Stein and James's "translated" portrait of Minny Temple in his autobiography in order to answer Alfred Habegger's accusation of Jamesian distortion of her letters with a counterclaim of artistic representation—a point similar to mine in my review of Habegger (*ALS 1986*: pp. 112–13). However, Elisabeth Bronfen's "Dialogue with the Dead: The Deceased Beloved as Muse" (*NewComp.* 6:101–18) keenly places James's "reanimated" Minny (as well as the characters George Stransom [Mary Antrim] and Marmaduke [Maud-Evelyn]) alongside disturbingly similar "muse-poet relations" in Poe and Novalis. Adeline Tintner's "*The Aspern Papers*: Argento's Opera & James's Tale" (*Dallas Opera Program*, November:21–27) explains that composer Dominick Argento did an "ingenious adaptation" of the tale in his opera by shifting the setting from Venice to Lake Como, changing Aspern from poet to composer, and refocusing the plot on a love affair which James only alludes to in the story. Similarly, Beverly Branch's "François Truffaut and Henry James: The Encounter of Two Master Craftsmen," in *Transformations: From Literature to Film*, Douglas Radcliff-Umstead, ed. (Kent State [1987]), pp. 184–90, shows how *La Chambre verte* artfully weaves together elements from *Beast in the Jungle, Friends of the Friends*, and especially *Altar of the Dead*, while conveying "universal human tragedy" though formal "circularity" as analyzed by Georges Poulet. "Inconscience: Henry James and the Unreliable Speaker of the Dramatic Monolog" by James R. Bennett (*BSUF* 28[1987]:74–84) treats mostly poetic monologues, yet stresses James's "special identification of character and reader produced by the 'inside view' " and his positive "restorative element" by contrast with most dramatic monologists. Given Bennett's emphasis on James and Browning's *Ring and the Book*, William Buckler and Ross Posnock (*ALS 1984*, p. 130; *1985*, pp. 106–07) needed to be cited.

Ira B. Nadel's "Gertrude Stein and Henry James," pp. 81–97 in *Gertrude Stein and the Making of Literature*, Shirley Neuman and Ira B. Nadel, eds. (Northeastern), argues a "theory of *tessera*, the completing link," whereby Stein "extends and expands the work of James" but "denies his influence," although she remains much preoccupied with his artistic medium and "modernizing his pronouncements." According to Toklas, he is "*the precursor*" with "pure Gertrude phrases" in *Wings of the Dove*. Alternatively, Carol M. Dole's "Oppression, Obsession: Virginia Woolf and Henry James" (*SoR* 24: 253–71) examines closely the disparity between Woolf's public praise and private distaste for James and his work, as well as the "undercutting" irritation even in the praise. Dole presents copious evidence that Woolf complains of the very elements in James that others complained of in her own work, then acutely dissects exactly how, for both, "external events of any importance do not occur 'onstage' "—though, unlike Joyce, neither "transcribes" the stream of consciousness they dramatize through metaphor and adapted soliloquy. Dole thinks Woolf's reaction was against the symbolic patriarchal "fellowship" of James, her father and grandfather. This excellent essay lays the groundwork for a major anxiety-of-influence study. Finally, Gordon Hutner's subtle last chapter on Hawthorne and James in *Secrets and Sympathy: Forms of Disclosure in Hawthorne's Novels* (Georgia), pp. 184–220, continues (and acknowledges) last year's fine work by Richard Broadhead (*ALS 1987*, p. 97) in charting the evolution of Hawthorne on James's literary imagination. Ranging from *Hawthorne* to *Wings* to *American Scene* (and elsewhere), Hutner reveals perceptively that Hawthorne's preoccupations with secrecy and sympathy are converted by James to "curiosity," "appropriation," "appreciation"—at once thematic and structural for his art and ideal reader-critic.

iii. Interpretive Books

Perhaps the most interesting 1988 book on James is a tough-minded language study by David W. Smit, *The Language of a Master* (So. Ill.); it is the most extensive examination of James's late style via stylistic theory since the work of Seymour Chatman in the early seventies. Its subtitle should be "the limits of stylistic criticism," for Smit means to demonstrate that all extant critical response to the late style "has been—to put it bluntly—rather glib." What follows is not, however, ponderous scientism designed to persuade (or mystify) through almighty data, but rather a highly reasoned, often whimsical, critique of every major attempt to explain, account for, or interpret the late style. Smit classifies such attempts as follows: Style by Identification (distinctively Jamesian); Style as Expression (of James's aesthetic quality, personality, view of reality); and Style as Imitation (of character's thought processes). Citing innumerable scholars, Smit says precisely where each falls short; and he is far tougher on the hard linguistics approach of someone like Roger Fowler than on, say, Ian Watt's venerable analysis of the first paragraph of *The Ambassadors*. His own solution to the elusive variety of James's late style—fiction, letters, notebooks—lies in the "psychology" of each critic (Smit's adaptation of Ingarden-Iser reader-response) together with James's "patterning imagery," rhetorical periodicity, and an "aesthetic register" intoned during dictation, compensating for his personal shyness and insecurity. Like David Hume, whose thinking he resembles, Smit is more impressive pinpointing the inadequacies of others' views than in his own alternatives; besides, he really resides in his own Category Two. Smit may not change James criticism, but he makes us newly conscious of the imprecision of our claims. (For some additional criticism of this book, see my forthcoming review in *MLR.*)

Equally worthy is *The Power of Historical Knowledge* by Susan L. Mizruchi (Princeton), a fine study which locates James centrally between Hawthorne and Dreiser in a broader context of novels that represent and critique "the very process of historical mystification." Her analysis of *The Bostonians* probes deftly the narrator's ambivalent "politics of temporality" and the opposing historical myths employed by Olive and Basil as part of their sexual politics; most astute is the analysis of Verena's growing capacity for awareness of historical change. Her sophisticated analysis of *Wings of the Dove* reassesses all major characters: Kate rewrites the past, Milly engages in "mutuality of exchange" with her deceivers, Densher's past remains "static" and escapist, whether of Milly's memory or Kate's lovemaking. Even the narrative "plot" does not unfold but "evades and suppresses" like the characters (a structural problem with the novel, James thought, but maybe not).

When the Master Relents: The Neglected Short Fictions of Henry James by George Bishop (UMI Research Press) addresses the Michel Foucault-John Rowe issue of Jamesian "mastery" by exploring six tales which "somehow limit the power of the interpreter" in a way that mitigates James's mastery—thus accounting for their neglect. Bishop's highly visible conceptual stance regarding James's "canonicity" is evenly divided between prolix ingenuity and genuine illumination as he sketches "the outlines of a competing collection, an 'unauthorized edition'" of artist and writers tales. Interestingly, like many postmodernist studies, its strength is not really in its theory but in the freshness of individual readings of "A Bundle of Letters," "Glasses," "The Liar," "The Third Person," "Collaboration," and "Hugh Merrow." Some of this analysis is formalist-like close reading of specific passages, though there are strategic intertextual connections made with the *Notebooks*. Ultimately, it is hard to finish this book without feeling the Master has been reasserted after all, even when he relents. Bishop's brief analysis of "Maud-Evelyn" (in the "Hugh Merrow" section) is stunning, an example of what is best in the study rather than the repeated claims about authorship and criticism being power plays and other deconstructivist soon-to-be clichés. Another study informed by contemporary thought is Lloyd Davis's *Sexuality and Textuality in Henry James* (Peter Lang), a Foucauldian and Lacanian analysis that charts "James's use of the virginal" as the key to the "interdependent and generative relationship between sexuality and textuality in his novels." James's "virgin" (whether male or female, married or single) is always "the product of psychological and sociosymbolic forces of power and knowledge." Davis applies this perspective competently to *Watch and Ward*, *The American*, *The Spoils of Poynton*, and *The Golden Bowl*, highlighting the interplay between "sociosexual" experience and "sociosymbolic" structures with virgin characters Nora Lambert, Christopher Newman, Fleda Vetch, Maggie Verver, and others. One advantage to this kind of criticism is that the thesis is usually de facto "unified," since sexuality, in some form and at some level, hovers always at the core of things, a uniquely human drive, which is then perforce inscribed in texts. One disadvantage to this approach, however, is that a reader must exert an awfully strong "willing suspension of disbelief" at the expense of so many other subjects present in the same novels, even when the same reader is constantly assured that those very subjects are merely the playing out of this one. Finally, veteran James critic Alan Bellringer has penned a fine introductory-overview monograph on James in the Modern Novelists Series (St. Martin's), surveying his life and 15 representative works divided about equally between novels and tales and—like many English critics—just a bit weighted away (so to speak) from the "major phase." Bellringer's very explicit ranking of James in the history of American, English, and (Western?) world literature, both poetry and prose, is surely arresting: James is number 8!

iv. Criticism: General Essays

"History and Epistemology: The Example of *The Turn of the Screw*" by Paul B. Armstrong (*NLH* 19:693–712) is a beautifully lucid and cogent analysis of the interdependence of history and epistemology in the act of interpreting literary texts, and a convincing rebuttal to those who "view history as a way out of the impasses of epistemology." Using the perennial *Turn of the Screw* debate as his locus classicus, Armstrong shows time and again that epistemology is always the condition of interpretive choice and evidence, however "historical"; but he also explains how history, in its very symbiosis with epistemology, is essential to the enterprise. Among the splendid elements in this essay are his phenomenological critique of "object-based" criticism, his whole handling of Edmund Wilson–Robert Heilman and other disputants surrounding James's tale, his helpful concept of a "heteronomous" literary work, and his dissection of the "part-whole relations" that underlie the historian's claim. Since Aristotle we have known that history and philosophy are two sides of one coin with respect to a work of the imagination, but Armstrong's phenomenological essay gives this idea fresh currency and context. In "Text, Author-Function, and Appropriation of Modern Narrative: Toward a Sociology of Representation" (*CritI* 14, iii:431–47), Robert Weimann situates James's fiction historically within the crisis of representation by asserting that later works like *The Tragic Muse* reveal "the precariousness of the links between traditional forms of representation and the eroding relations of representativeness." What his fictional artists lose in representation James himself regains ("fills the gaps") in narrative technique. Peter Collister in "Taking Care of Yourself: Henry James and the Life of George Sand" (*MLR* 83:556–70) presents the familiar view that the "drama of [James's] writing on Sand derives from the confrontation between a [private] sensibility" and the "profligate" detail of an "artist who has the capacity to thrive at the cost of anything else." Addressing Sand's relationship with Alfred de Musset, Collister unsurprisingly notes James's admiration for her "practice of life," while he found her art limited. Eloise Knapp Hay's "Proust, James, Conrad, and Impressionism" (*Style* 22: 368–81) adds to the perennial conundrum of James and the Impressionists the point that he found their "great surface of life" a "simplification" lacking in "brooding reflection." She claims that because the Impressionist movement "was tied to a materialist account of how the mind uses impressions, its theory was persistently eroded and finally dismissed by James." A couple of James scholars not cited would quarrel with or qualify this assertion, yet Hay makes a good case.

Dorothea Krook's lively tour de force " 'As a Man Is, So He Sees': The Reader in Henry James" (*Neophil* 72, 2:300–15) uses *Figure in the Carpet* to showcase her approach to the "all-ambiguous" mature stories. Taking off from James's plea for "appreciation, speculation, imagination," she posits two readers in the tale, the narrator and Corvick, as prototypes of two generic Jamesian analysts, the "Insensitive Critic" (narrator) and the "Sensitive Critic" (Corvick). What is delightful and cogent in her essay are the many permutations or possibilities Krook improvises from this postulate. Kaja Silverman's long, Freudian "Too Early / Too Late: Subjectivity and the Primal Scene in Henry James" (*Novel* 21:147–73) argues that James's primary subjective "authorial phantasmatic" parallels the passive sexual awakening of his major characters; some awaken too late (Strether, Marcher, Isabel), others too early (Miles, Maisie, Nanda). Silverman further claims that just as James's bisexual author "inside" the text is nothing like the Jacobite Master, so his most "scenic" works, like *Awkward Age*, are in fact the most subjective—his literary "going behind" issue full of "pederastic identification." Stuart Hutchinson's "Henry James:

The American City and the Structure of Experience," in *The American City*, pp. 198–216, extrapolates James's views of city and culture from *Washington Square, Bostonians, American Scene,* and several tales set in New York. James defines American experience through a juxtaposition between "attendant forms" (the older English tradition) and the new "dauntless power" of America, which exhibits ugly skyscrapers but also an "expansive power" that "energizes" and "appalls" him. Yet neither structure, old or new, has "moral pre-eminence." In "Henry James in *The Critic*: 1883–1885" (*HJR* 9:136–41), Arthur Sherbo reprints a number of assessments of James from the periodical not found in extant reference guides by Foley, Ricks, or Taylor; he suggests that "some Jamesian should take it upon himself to go through the whole run." Finally, Ruth B. Yeazell's "Henry James" in *CLHUS*, pp. 668–89, is a worthy successor to Blackmur's esteemed *LHUS* chapter; still, it is consciously different, in line with the new editorial policy of "modest postmodern[ism]" and "contradiction." A model of graceful prose and acute biographical-critical discrimination, Yeazell's essay avoids Blackmur's broad cultural crosscurrents and focuses more directly and sequentially on the fiction itself, her beginning and end framed by James's memoirs in line with recent biography-theory like Paul John Eakin's. The result, best with *The Golden Bowl*, is very much the "portal" effect named by the editors, and only inadequate—given her space strictures—by not sufficiently registering James's achievement in short fiction and the ghostly realm.

v. Criticism: Individual Novels

Armand Michaux's "The Innocent and the Puritan: Henry James' *Roderick Hudson*" (*Costerus* n.s. 66:43–54) unoriginally puts the center of the novel in James's "unresolved tension" between Roderick and Rowland, "art and morality"—and accents Rowland's destructiveness. Steven H. Jobe's "The Discrimination of Stoicisms in *The American*" (*SAF* 16:181–93) shows that, in line with James's nondoctrinaire Stoicism, Newman becomes not happier but a "more excellent" man by adopting the stoic principle of "sublime indifference to the unchangeable circumstances of life," particularly in the face of the novel's "murder-suicide pattern."

"Playing the Game of Life: The Dilemma of Christopher Newman and Isabel Archer" by Nancy Morrow (*SAF* 16:65–82) can be classified with either *The American* or *Portrait.* Her formal analysis explores the way the protagonists respond as "players" to "the systems that structure social experience," Newman taking the "open game" of life for granted and Isabel being given the means to play it. Isabel's own "playful" imagination (stressed in James's revisions) is gradually suppressed in accordance with her "loss," but she chooses to live among her adversaries rather than opt for a life like that of Merle or Gemini. Yet Newman's ostensible "winning" by moral rules is qualified by a sense of "diminishing possibilities." So these endings in tandem show James breaking new ground with "a certain ambiguity" surrounding "the issues of victory and defeat." Using several elements of the feminist paradigm, Kumkum Sangari in "Of Ladies, Gentlemen, and 'The Short Cut' " (*NLH* 19:713–37) analyzes numerous aspects of Isabel Archer's femininity—her being a lady, being free, being mannered—in order to demonstrate that through his portrait James creates "a set of values through which an emergent section of the middle class and its women find a voice," thus "activating a real social need, addressing a real social configuration." The author sees a need for more studies that address the interconnections between literary representation, cultural process, and gender difference. In "Parable, Secrecy, and the Form of Fiction: The Example of 'The Figure in the Carpet' and *The Portrait of a Lady*" (*JEGP* 87:230–50), Warren Johnson ably constructs a hermeneutics of secrecy-parable-narrative with "Figure," and especially *Portrait*, by probing parallels between ways of knowing and James's composition and reticence as moral author, a situation evoking Ralph's with Isabel. "The invitation to interpret consists in the announcement of a secret which excludes us, hence the work—and the difficulty of it—of interpretation." This foundation informs "Figure" and turns parable in *Portrait*, which is organized around "acts of exclusion which announce secrets and refuse to name them"—imparting to the novel its "mystery of form." George McFadden's "A Note on 'Goodwood's Lie' in *The Portrait of a Lady* (*HJR* 9:212–14) tries without much success to "contextualize" Gordon Hutner's thesis of last year regarding Caspar's "lie" that Ralph asked him to take care of Isabel. In his *Gothic Manners and the Classic English Novel* (Wisconsin), Joseph Wiesenfarth's chapter on *Portrait*, pp. 120–40, explores James's reformulation of Gothic elements as the "decay of contemporary manners in the cultural centers of Europe," the "horrifying version of a Gothic world with Osmond" where "life turns deadly as manners" (with tomb imagery), and

Ralph's role with Isabel as beloved "affined souls." Wiesenfarth's is also just an excellent overview essay on the novel.

There were many studies of *The Bostonians* this year. In "Elizabeth Peabody Revisited" (*HJR* 9:209–11) Mary Frew Molstad gives circumstantial evidence that William James was right to believe Henry modeled Miss Birdseye on Elizabeth Peabody, and that Henry's attribution of the character to his "moral consciousness" was a defensive evasion. Joan Maxwell's "Delighting in a Bite: James's Seduction of His Readers in *The Bostonians*" (*JNT* 18:18–33) argues adroitly that James delivers a "triple-barrelled" satire in the novel which hits not only Olive's ideological world and Ransom's "chivalric mode of relations between the sexes" but especially his 1886 audience who wanted novels to end in marriage after courtship—which James provided while "undercut[ting]" with "narrative devices." In line with her thesis, Maxwell feels contemporary academic "audiences" still want to simplify this novel with post-Freudian labels and "homosexual-feminist" phobias. A related thesis is Robert K. Martin's "Picturesque Misperception in *The Bostonians*" (*HJR* 9:77–86), which examines James's treatment of a "faulty" romantic vision coinciding with "his own inclinations" in favor of a "chastened realism," and shows that several instances of landscape misperception emblematize this broader thematic pattern. The novel's tone, "precariously balanced between high Romantic indulgence and ironic distance," focuses ultimately on Olive Chancellor's "Romantic folly at its height," someone "who can find meaning only in her own defeat." But against *all* such critical "balancing act[s]" is Alfred Habegger's "*The Bostonians* and Henry James Sr.'s Crusade Against Feminism and Free Love" (*WS* 15:323–42), which argues that James stands right behind Basil Ransom as the result of an "untold story," a son's uneasy loyalty to his recently deceased father's weird, paternalist, often publicly controversial views on marriage and women, views that went through wild sea-changes all chronicled by Habegger with lively iconoclasm. The historical basis for James's hostility toward figures like the journalist Matthias Pardon is most convincing, but Habegger's whole argument is worth hearing: "Our" James of that book has narrative virtuosity, whereas Habegger's has, like the book, "instability." Habegger gives the exact same thesis with a bit more evidence—that is, William's robust support of his father's views—and also better explains Henry's "self-cancelling" narration in "Henry

James's *Bostonians* and the Fiction of Democratic Vulgarity" in *American Literary Landscapes*, Ian F. A. Bell and D. K. Adams, eds. (St. Martin's), pp. 102–21. Somewhere between Habegger and the rest is Ian F. A. Bell's "The Emersonian Irony of James's Basil Ransom" (*N&Q* 35:328–30), which claims that Ransom's surname comes from James's memory of Emerson's abolitionist "Boston Hymn," recited by the poet in Boston Music Hall for Lincoln's proclamation—thus suggesting irony and "equivocation" in James's portrait of the Southerner.

Building on work by John Kimmey (whose work on *Princess* [*ALS 1986*, p. 105] should be cited), Mark Chapman in "Physical Mobility and Social Power in *The Princess Casamassima*" (*HJR* 9:165–75) shows close parallels between Hyacinth's various walks throughout London and the unfolding social and psychological drama of the novel. Chapman stresses two walks along the Thames, one to Millbank Prison and the sight of Hyacinth's mother, the second with Paul past the Traitor's Gate. Hyacinth's last walk before his suicide is aimless, for (unlike James in his Preface) "he has no place left to walk." More conceptual is Mike Fischer's "The Jamesian Revolution in *The Princess Casamassima*: A Lesson in Bookbinding" (*HJR* 9:87–104), a fine Marxist-Althusserian approach which, building on John Rowe, Mark Seltzer, and Taylor Stoehr, dissects the master-slave dynamics and the various networks of power through mystification and secrecy in the novel. Hyacinth's craft, bookbinding, covers or "hides the material conditions and forces of production" that make a book to begin with. As artisans like him co-opt the proletariat, so is he (as on his Continental vacation) "out of it" compared to the real "secret" source of power, Hoffendahl, and, to some extent, James. Peter Faulkner's more conventional reading, "*The Princess Casamassima* and the Politics of Betrayal" (*DUJ* 82:287–93) mostly cites long passages to show that Hyacinth is betrayed by civilization.

Daniel James Sundahl in "The High Altar of Henry James: *The Tragic Muse* and 'The Art of Figuring Synthetically' " (*CLQ* 24:212–24) probes the structural elements of James's long novel. Ironically, James (like Gauguin or Stevenson) sought a "synthetic" principle at odds with "analytic" empiricism by which to organize his book, yet the book "remains in disequilibrium" by never finding its subjective "citidel of interest"—despite James's success with multiplied Tintorettoesque "aspects," cinematic framing, or triangulation of its main characters.

Employing elaborate wordplay on "to square" in order to emphasize the parody and self-parody of the novel, Barbara Eckstein's "Unsquaring the Squared Route of *What Maisie Knew*" (*HJR* 9:177–87) squares the narrator/James with Maisie's "disreputable guardians" who are trying to "square up" their relationship with Maisie by "squaring off" against each other, and with Maisie herself, who practices "the rules of squaring" when she offers to sacrifice Mrs. Wix if Sir Claude will sacrifice Miss Beale. Using Derrida's notion of reading through other writing, Eckstein admits she reads *Maisie* through *Lolita*, so that all the issues of "control, manipulation, attraction" between Maisie and her narrator/author are ones Nabokov addresses between Lolita and "her Humbert/author." Less ingenious but also quite suggestive is Lee E. Heller's "The Paradox of the Individual Triumph: Instrumentality and the Family in *What Maisie Knew*" (*SoAR* 53, 4:77–85), which likens the house of fiction to Maisie's unstable house, for unlike the "traditional nineteenth-century plot about placelessness and the family," which moves "progressively towards the resolution of conflict between the individual and the family world," James's novel "depends on shifts in character roles that do not point to a clear line of reconciliation but multiply impossible possibilities." Despite her mediating role as James's "tennis ball," Maisie simply disappears at the end when she rejects her "instrumentality" in James's subversion of the "family romance." Finally, James Lowe's "Color in *What Maisie Knew*: An Expression of Authorial Presence" (*HJR* 9:188–98) analyzes well James's literal and figurative use of color to show Maisie's development of consciousness through increased "sensory perception," her "moral transcendence" over "corruptive circumstances," and the "ironic difference between her perceptions and those of the reader." By adhering to her "very limited context," James is the "first American writer to use color so extensively and adroitly to render thematic development"—an interesting claim considering Crane's *Red Badge* published two years earlier.

"Iconological Characterization in James's *The Ambassadors*" (*AL* 60:416–32) by Robin P. Hoople challenges Todorov and Derrida by arguing that Chad Newsome (compared to a " 'new edition of an old book' " by Bilham) is the core "iconic character in the text of the novel," whom Strether with New England "typology" ultimately sees "right" as neither absence nor free signifier but "equation between word and thing." Mrs. Newsome and Mme de Vionnet are also iconic characters who do not "change for [Strether], they only signify more fully." Joyce A. Rowe's "Strether Unbound: The Selective Vision of Henry James's Ambassador," in *Equivocal Endings*, pp. 75–99, tests Pater's aesthetic vision of the problematic modern consciousness against James's ending and argues that Strether secures instead Emersonian "self-reliance" with consciousness "its own sanctification," the result of a "costly" moral idealism whose isolation from the real (encountered in Chad, Marie, and Maria) is "absolute." Rowe's Strether takes back no "new recognition of himself and his limitations" but a "more absolute vision of ideal possibility and a deeper disgust with the world as it is." Finally, Bernard Richards's "An Ornithological Mistake in Henry James's *The Ambassadors*" (*N&Q* 35:334–35) shows by deduction that the swallows Strether espies at Chester would not have arrived yet in early March.

In "Henry James's Remorse for *The Wings of the Dove*" (*HJR* 9:114–27) George McFadden reconsiders fully James's lament in the preface for certain failures—"one's plan, alas, is one thing, and one's result another"—to figure out how justified it is. McFadden feels James does not "dodge" in Books Fifth and Sixth, as he thought, yet does succumb to "Millyolatry" and invents the poetic "entrapment" conceit because he inadequately conveyed "Densher's history with Kate Croy—hers with him" (as he wrote Hueffer in 1902). The essay is rather disjointed and at times unconvincing, yet it is also stocked with some good, discrete points. Paul W. Harland's " 'Disconcerting Poetry': James's Use of Romance in *The Wings of the Dove*" (*ESC* 14:310–25) repeats a familiar argument, that James renews and transforms Hawthornean romance in *Wings* by incorporating its "mystery, distancing, . . . psychological depth" and its "heighten[ed] moral value." James's romantic-real distinction in his Preface to *The American* is put by Harland to good use, though his pure pro-Milly/anti-Kate reading is hardly au courant.

Dale M. Bauer's *Feminist Dialogics*, a creative attempt to apply Bakhtin to gender theory, has a fresh substantial chapter on *The Golden Bowl*, pp. 51–88, which explores Amerigo's "double-voicedness" and Maggie's "internal dialogiz[ing]" in Parts One and Two—both against Adam's patriarchal monologic/monolithic "discourse of money" governing the social community. Bauer reads radically the Charlotte-Prince affair as good "dialogic resistance" and part of the "social carnival" in James's "permutations of rivalry," yet feels that despite Maggie's "ritual sacrifice" of her father, her ambiguous union with Amerigo (which many critics praise) does not affirm her own dialogic voice and may only show she masters the "male gaze."

vi. Criticism: Tales

Richard Gage tackles major new ground with *Order and Design: Henry James' Titled Story Sequences* (Peter Lang), an ambitious attempt to show "organic unity," "thematic continuity, and architectural form" in James's six short story volumes with "evocative titles," as well as in Volume 18 in the New York Edition. Gage's true interest is thematic unity, and his analysis works well with the first four collections, *Terminations, Embarrassments, The Two Magics,* and *The Soft Side,* where he explores variations on the ideas of death, misperception, black-white magic, and identity. Then he strains and overclaims with *The Better Sort* and especially with Volume 18, where the unifying theme of society's "infringements" on "private lives" breaks down after the first three tales despite Gage's attempts to invert and vary it; besides, if James is here the "conscious artist arranging and placing each tale with careful attention," then surely "Julia Bride" would be the copestone for this volume (Gage oddly thinks "Julia," which ends Volume 17, is not in the New York Edition). Scholars like Michael Anesko should be kept in mind. Nevertheless, Gage is quite convincing with *The Finer Grain,* where he follows James's publisher's description and develops the "grain"-women leitmotif and necessary "graining" of male protagonists, "tested and proven in the furnace of human experience." His "pointillism" thesis at the end is unfortunate; I feel this book has an excellent topic and would be fine if just the right (wrong?) 25 percent were trimmed away.

W. R. Martin and Warren U. Ober's " '5 M.S. Pages': Henry James's Addition to 'A Day of Days' " (*SSF* 25:153–55) proposes that the 640-word passage beginning with the words, "As the minutes elapsed, Adela found herself drifting . . ." is the one James added for *Galaxy* editors to soften the terms of her "virtual marriage proposal" to Ludlow. In "The Illness of the Passionate Pilgrim" (*ALR* 21:3–18) Gerard M. Sweeney makes the startling hypothesis that Clement Searle's "real and specific" illness is terminal syphilis, suggesting that dissipated Americans carry "to Europe the seeds of their own destruction." In this context, Sweeney perceives the narrator (obviously) as romantic and myopic and Searle's English kinswoman lucky that Searle died before they could marry. I still see "Passionate Pilgrim" wrestling with the "superstitious-valuation-of-Europe" theme of the 1870s, and I only wish Sweeney's thesis were more resonant therewith.

"Unambiguous Ambiguity: The International Theme of *Daisy Miller*" (*SAF* 16:209–16) by Paul Lukacs misclaims that critics fail to see any ambiguity in Daisy or the meaning of her story, and even that they dismiss it as "minor"! This will surprise the umpteen number of us who have tried to interpret the great tale. More enlightening is John Needham's "The Limits of Analysis" (*PNR* 46, 6:35–38), which effectively applies Michael Polanyi's theories of "tacit awareness" and "boundary conditions" to two episodes in "Daisy Miller."

Arnold E. Davidson's "Transformations of Text in Henry James's *The Aspern Papers*" (*ESC* 14:39–48) is a sinuous Lacanian argument that the failed narrator's text "elides" into a multifaceted parody of Aspern's own dubious "seduction" text (the papers), a text "mastered" instead by Tina, who "unwrites" it, foils the narrator, and keeps us guessing who she is. Davidson is also innovative discussing Aspern and his protégé-narrator as parodic/inverted Orpheus figures in a tale which "subvert[s]" any "text of male mastery." Dennis A. Foster's astute reader-response study, *Confession and Complicity in Narrative* (Cambridge [1987]), cites "Figure in the Carpet," pp. 39–51, as an "exemplary" "confessional" form wherein "the critic's failure is the figure's success," since the narrator's "transgression" provides the reader pleasure and "involvement," even as the "image" (figure) itself is propagated "from character to character."

Here we go again, another year (in more or less descending order). Karen Halttunen's "'Through the Cracked and Fragmented Self': William James and *The Turn of the Screw*" (*AQ* 40:472–90) is just the sort of "historicist" explanation Paul Armstrong challenged earlier. Yet Halttunen carefully grounds the tale in the context of 19th-century psychology, specifically William James's lecture notes on "Exceptional Mental States," whereby the governess could be partly hypnagogic, part multiple personality, or a medium. In "A Question of Values: Culture and Cognition in *The Turn of the Screw*" (*L&C* 8:147–54) Joann P. Krieg uses cognition theory to explore the "train of communication" in the tale by which moral values are transmitted and circumscribed by James's "blanks" for the reader to fill in his or hers. "Stylistics and the Ghost Story: Punctuation, Revisions, and

Meaning in *The Turn of the Screw*" by Norman Macleod, pp. 133–55 in *Edinburgh Studies in the English Language*, Macleod and John M. Anderson, eds. (John Donald), claims on linguistic grounds that James's structure, arrangement, and especially revision add (guess what) ambiguity, "making it always more rather than less difficult" to separate the story and its telling. Dennis Chase's "The Ambiguity of Innocence: *The Turn of the Screw*" (*Extrapolation* 27:197–202) strains too hard to support Freudianism in the tale by forever pointing to sexual double entendre (even "get off") between Miles and the governess, though each is too innocent to know quite what they mean. Lastly, Robert Emmet Whelan's "Ordinary Human Virtue: The Key to *The Turn of the Screw*" (*Renascence* 4:247–67) is a tedious blow-by-blow allegory of the governess' "spiritual growth" by resisting her "cowardice," confronting demons Quint and Jessel, and ultimately serving as Miles's "guardian angel" at his death! This reading worries me, and, although much exhausted by *Screw* scholarship, I wish Whelan had included some.

In "Pragmatism and 'The Beast in the Jungle' " (*SSF* 25:275–84) Paul J. Lindholdt states that "The Sick Soul" chapter from *Varieties of Religious Experience* is a "paradigm" for the character of John Marcher. The essay's title is misleading and its main ideas, though suggestive, are too diffuse and finally unconvincing: for example, that William's morbid hallucination is like Marcher's epiphany, or, especially, that May Bartram is a version of Minny Temple. That the Jameses "secularized" Puritan "experience" is not news, but the claim that, "had [Minny] lived," the "tale probably would never have been written" is too much news. The author rightly senses apposite generic themes arising from the family consciousness but tends to look past the distinctive vehicles of each brother. James Phelan's interesting "Character in Fictional Narrative: The Case of John Marcher" (*HJR* 9:105–13) tests a "theory of literary character" by offering a rhetorical analysis of James's "rare fusion" between the "mimetic" and "thematic" functions of his character Marcher with additional emphasis on the drama of "outward and inward instabilities" (the "synthetic" aspect?). Finally, "The Bench in *The Bench of Desolation*" (*KAL* 29:23–30) by Shigemi Satomi makes the altogether pedestrian point that the bench changes in the fourth "chapter" (section?) from a desolate spot to a restorative place in line with the return of Kate Cookham to Herbert Dodd.

vii. Criticism: Nonfictional Works

In "Henry James's *The American Scene: A Vade Mecum* for Writing American Culture" (*ATQ* 2:313–26) Joseph Fargnoli affirms James's volume (often "deconstructed" these days) as a model for observation and written interpretation, a true "semiotics of American culture." The romantic view from the "restless analyst" addresses male-female relations and other critical issues, disclosing a vision of a "potentially great culture flawed by commercialism, wastefulness, social disorganization, and a devaluation of history." Martha Banta's " 'There's Surely a Story in It': James's Notebooks and the Working Artist" (*HJR* 9:153–64) is a readable, incisive analysis of the contrast between Hawthorne's "thought-silence" notebooks "straight from idea to product" and James's "access to the writer's workplace" in his, with recurrent expressions of crisis, goading, marketability, self-flagellation/self-coercion, and communion with his genius ("mon Bon"). To Banta, James's notebooks resemble Thoreau's journal, and a reader's "delight" with them is to see "the frightening principle of rank organicism let loose upon the world." Paul John Eakin's "Henry James's 'Obscure Hurt': Can Autobiography Serve Biography?" (*NLH* 19:675–92) continues his valuable thesis of James's autobiographical exchange of wound for war (*ALS 1984*, pp. 130–31), but this time reveals his theoretical foundations: that autobiography is biographical fact, that memory as "palimpsest" does not undermine Eriksonian "identity," even while (vide Hayden White) it does contextualize the past. Eakin incorporates James Cox (*ALS 1986*, p. 112), Carol Holly (*ALS 1987*, p. 96) and Howard Feinstein into his extremely complex, deceptively simple claim that "autobiography can serve the biographer's quest for referential truth."

University of Missouri

8. Pound and Eliot

Reed Way Dasenbrock

Nineteen eighty-eight was the year of Eliot's centennial, with celebrations on at least three continents and a good deal of important new work published. Pound, however, was not forgotten in the process. Some of the work on Eliot published this year—here I would mention particularly books by Richard Shusterman, Lyndall Gordon, and Christopher Ricks—promises to change our view of Eliot more profoundly than any work done on Pound this year, but taken as a whole Pound criticism remains at a higher level than the flood of new work on Eliot.

i. Pound

***a.* Text, Biography, and Bibliography.** This continues to be an active area of Pound studies, with two new volumes of correspondence and a new biography this year. Omar Pound and Robert Spoo have edited *Ezra Pound and Margaret Cravens: A Tragic Friendship, 1910–1912* (Duke), and this concise, well-edited volume presents Pound's letters to Cravens (the other side has not survived), an American pianist living in Paris who befriended Pound and assisted him financially. These letters clear up certain mysteries in Pound's biography, in particular the source of the income with which he proposed to her father to support Dorothy Shakespear in 1912, but it can't be said that Pound behaved very well toward Cravens, who abruptly committed suicide the same year.

The second volume of Pound's correspondence published this year is *Pound/The Little Review: The Letters of Ezra Pound to Margaret Anderson*, Thomas L. Scott, Melvin J. Friedman, and Jackson R. Bryer, eds. (New Directions). This handsome volume is informative on one of Pound's crucial editorial interventions, his two-year stint as foreign editor of the *Little Review* during which much of *Ulysses*, important work by Yeats, Eliot, and Lewis, and other interesting material was shepherded by Pound into print. I do think, however, that a selection of the correspondence would have made a better book than this complete correspondence: it is interesting to see how closely Pound worked with Margaret Anderson, but surely we don't need every detail of every *Little Review* subscription Pound solicited and garnered. The other textual contribution this year is Ira Nadel's "Ezra Pound: Two Poems" (*JML* 15:141–45), which reprints and introduces two uncollected "Alfred Venison" poems published in the *New England Weekly* in 1935 and 1936.

Humphrey Carpenter has entered the Pound biographical sweepstakes with the biggest biography of Pound yet, one of over 1,000 pages, *A Serious Character: The Life of Ezra Pound* (Faber and Houghton Mifflin). The sheer bulk of the book as well as its coming after a great deal of other work on Pound means that it is more complete than any previous biography and will need to be read by every Pound scholar. But it is a rather disappointing book. Carpenter gets so lost amid his facts and file cards that the narrative line needed for a good biography is missing. He is also absurdly unfair to various people surrounding Pound, particularly in the St. Elizabeths period—to Dorothy Pound, to Pound's lawyer Julian Cornell, and to the director of St. Elizabeths, Winfred Overholser—and he clearly takes sides on issues where a biographer needs to try to be objective. Finally, and most seriously, Carpenter simply has no appreciation for Pound or his poetry. He describes Richard Aldington's relation to Pound as "the cultivated Englishman laughing at the brash American, whom he supposed to be at least partially a mountebank." He could be describing his own attitude here and does so in a way that exposes its limitations, for the English laughter at the "brash American" shows a lack of comprehension (and perhaps cultivation as well). This is not to say that biography must be hagiography, but a biographer must at least manifest some interest in and understanding of his subject.

Carpenter's biography is already not the last word, as the new volumes of correspondence and three biographical essays in *Paideuma* show. Jeffrey Meyers goes over familiar ground in "Ezra Pound and the Russian Avant-Garde" (17, ii–iii:171–76). But James J. Wilhelm usefully supplements his own biographical labors with "Addenda and Corrigenda for *The American Roots of Ezra Pound*" (17, ii–iii:239–44), and Timothy Materer's "From Henry James to Ezra Pound: John Quinn and the Art of Patronage" (17, ii–iii:47–68) adds to our knowledge of Pound's relations with Quinn, arguing that Quinn's patronage of the arts exemplified what Pound admired in Renaissance patronage. Hugh Witemeyer's "The Making of Pound's *Selected Poems* (1949) and Rolfe Humphries' Unpublished Introduction" (*JML* 15:73–91) is a fascinating discussion of the manuevering that surrounded the *Selected Poems* and includes an unpublished introduction to the volume by Rolfe Humphries with an explanation of why it remained unpublished. Tim Redman's "Poking Around Pound's Library" (*Pembroke Magazine* 20:184–87) provides some interesting details on Pound's library that supplement his earlier listing of Pound's books.

***b.* General Studies.** Robert Casillo's *The Genealogy of Demons: Anti-Semitism, Fascism, and the Myths of Ezra Pound* (Northwestern) is the general study of Pound most likely to attract attention this year, if only because of his blanket condemnation of the "Pound industry" for ignoring the centrality of anti-Semitism in Pound's life and work. I have reviewed Casillo's book at length elsewhere (*AmLH* 1:231–39), but briefly it is a treasure trove of research into aspects of Pound's work that few have wanted to investigate, weakened unfortunately by a desire to make its case so strongly that lots of evidence running the other way gets ignored. *The Genealogy of Demons* in fact resembles *The Cantos*: no one will be able to ignore it, but everyone will wish that its author had been less dogmatic in making his case.

If one surveys work on Pound in 1988 against Casillo's blanket condemnation, one has to say that a lot of interesting work is being done. At least three outstanding general essays on Pound were published this year. Hugh Kenner hasn't published a lot on Pound in recent years, and "Self-Similarity, Fractals, Cantos" (ELH 55:721–30) tells us how much we have missed as a result. Vintage Kenner, it takes a principle of mathematics I had never heard of, renders it easily explicable, and then uses it to make some of the most illuminating remarks ever made about the issue of form in Pound's poetry, particularly "Mauberley" and *The Cantos*. Another very good essay is James Longenbach's "Ezra Pound and the Vicissitudes of Post-Romantic Ambition" (*SoR* 24:481–501), which presents Pound as the most romantic poet of his generation, romantic in his conception of the poet's social function. Finally, the best essay on Pound published this year is Michael North's "Where Memory Faileth: Forgetfulness and a Poem Including History" (in *Ezra Pound: The Legacy of Kulchur*, Marcel Smith and William A. Ulmer, eds. [Alabama]: pp. 145–65), which investigates the themes of memory and forgetting in Pound's work in some extremely suggestive ways. The rest of that volume—papers from the Pound Centennial symposium at the University of Alabama—isn't as strong and might be said to support Casillo's critique of Pound criticism, except that its problem is that many of the people invited to speak at the symposium (Leslie Fiedler is the most egregious example) aren't Pound scholars and didn't have much to say about him.

But that isn't the end of good general studies on Pound this year. Steven Helmling's "Unmasking Pound" (*SoR* 24:505–19) goes over familiar ground when it argues that Pound's use of masks is closer to Yeats than to Eliot, but gets into more interesting territory discussing Pound's attempt to get beyond masks in "Propertius" and "Mauberley." Helmling's most interesting contention is that Pound meant to dismiss the early poetry by titling it *Personae* in 1926. Michael Coyle's "'A Profounder Didacticism': Ruskin, Orage and Pound's Reception of Social Credit" (*Paideuma* 17, i:7–28) is an excellent essay relating Pound's initial interest in politics to Orage, Guild Socialism, and a Ruskinian tradition in English culture. Two less successful studies on potentially interesting subjects also in *Paideuma* are Mohammed Shaheen's "Pound's Transmission of *Ittisal* in Canto 76" (17, i:133–45) and Ellen Keck Stauder's "Towards a Grammar of Relationships: The Rhetoric of Music in Pound and Rousseau" (17, i:45–57). Shaheen presents more on the Islamic concept of *ittisal* than Pound could have known, while Stauder lapses into a Yale-formulaic reading in which "Pound's musical rhetoric calls into question the apparently mimetic thrust of his ideas of language and representation." A much more successful study relating Pound and music is Milton A. Cohen's "Subversive Pedagogies: Schoenberg's *Theory of Harmony* and Pound's 'A Few Don't by an Imagiste'" (*Mosaic* 21, i:49–65), which presents both Pound and Schoenberg as utilizing pedagogy to consolidate their modernist innovations. V. G. Paleolog's "Brancusi and Ezra Pound" (*RoR* 42, 8:69–73) is another cross-artistic study, but it doesn't add anything new to our knowledge of the relationship between these two figures.

Three very general studies include chapters on Ezra Pound; the *CLHUS* has a chapter written by A. Walton Litz on "Ezra Pound and T. S. Eliot" (pp. 947–71), while David Perkins's *A History of Mod-*

ern Poetry: Modernism and After (Harvard) and Albert Gelpi's *A Coherent Splendor: The American Poetic Renaissance, 1910–1950* (Cambridge) both give each poet a chapter. The writing of literary history is an increasingly impossible task, I suppose, but though Litz contents himself with a rather neutral survey of his two poets, the *CLHUS* in general and Litz's chapter in particular are more successful than Perkins's *History*. Perkins begins his *History* with Eliot and ends with a full chapter on James Merrill, the only living poet so honored, and there is not a line that makes much sense either of Pound's work or his contribution to contemporary poetry. Perkins's *History* slights the wackier current of American poetry initiated by Pound and, more tellingly, almost all non-Anglo-American poets, in favor of a modern Genteel tradition Perkins feels more comfortable with. Albert Gelpi has many of the gifts a literary historian needs: he is a good reader of poetry and can find virtues in—but not oversell—works by minor poets. But it is in keeping with these gifts that the more interesting parts of *A Coherent Splendor* are the discussions of less widely studied poets such as John Crowe Ransom and Yvor Winters. The long chapters devoted to Eliot and Pound go over familiar ground surely but not with outstanding authority, and I didn't find enough of a thesis or argument to make the familiar journey worth making again.

c. Relation to Other Writers. The four books published this year treating Pound's relation to other writers tend less to open up new ground than to say interestingly new things about familiar ground. The exception is Norwood Andrews's terrible *The Case against Camões: A Seldom Considered Chapter from Ezra Pound's Campaign to Discredit Rhetorical Poetry* (Peter Lang). Camões is an underappreciated poet in the English-language world; according to Andrews, it is all Ezra Pound's fault. Though it is useful for correcting a few errors in Pound's (and Pound criticism's) citation of Camões, the book absurdly overstates Pound's influence and quickly becomes tiresome in its denunciation of Pound for his "lies" and "deceit." A book elucidating Camões would have been more to the point than this diatribe. In contrast, Daniel M. Hooley's *The Classics in Paraphrase: Ezra Pound and Modern Translators of Latin Poetry* (Susquehanna) is a good book that traces the influence of Pound's *Propertius* on a number of subsequent translations. Hooley is very good at the difficult task of comparing originals and translations, and the most interesting part of the book for Pound scholars is likely to be his look at Pound's late translations of Horace. I would have liked this to be a more ambitious book, however, as there are quite a few Pound-influenced translators Hooley could have discussed but didn't. To move closer to the present, George Bornstein's *Poetic Remaking: The Art of Browning, Yeats and Pound* (Penn State) is more on Browning and Yeats than on Pound, but is valuable for its rethinking of the relation between Romanticism and Modernism, arguing that Bloom's monolingual anxiety model doesn't seem to work for the modernists. Finally, the most important book this year on Pound's debt to other writers is James Longenbach's *Stone Cottage: Pound, Yeats and the Secret Society of Modernism* (Oxford). Longenbach has a story to tell about the winters Pound and Yeats spent together at Stone Cottage, and he has a point to make, which is that in a number of respects Pound's modernism is more Yeatsian than we have previously recognized. He is good on the way *The Cantos* is seance-like in its invocation of ghosts, on the links between the Noh and Yeats's occultist interests, and on how Pound was more interested in Yeats's occultism than he usually let on. But the book oversells its revelations and often pushes points farther than they can be made to go: Longenbach has found some pieces of the puzzle, not its secret key.

A number of essays trace more specific and limited debts of Pound to other writers. In "'Akin to Nothing but Language': Pound, Laforgue, and Logopoeia" (*ELH* 55:259–85), Jane Hoogestraat is concerned with distinguishing Pound's concept of logopoeia from his interest in visual impressions and sound. The most valuable part of her essay is that she also distinguishes Pound's theory from contemporary notions of linguistic free play. Bruce Fogelman's "Whitman in Pound's Mirror" (*AL* 59[1987]:639–44) looks at "On His Own Face in a Glass" as a response to Whitman. JoAnn Gardner's "Yeats, Pound and the Inheritance of the Nineties" (*JML* 14:431–43) is a competent survey of Pound's relation to that decade. Paul Skinner's "Of Owls and Waterspouts" (*Paideuma* 17, i:59–68) traces some more debts of Pound to Allan Upward and to the fiction of Ford Madox Ford, and Massimo Bacigalupo gives us an informed if overly dichotomized comparison of Pound's and Joyce's different responses to Italy in "Pound/Joyce: Style, Politics and Language" (in *Joyce Studies in Italy* 2, Carla de Petris, ed. [Bulzoni], pp. 161–70). A. D. Moody contrasts Pound's and H.D.'s differing versions of Imagism in "H.D., 'Imagiste': An Elemental Mind" (*Agenda* 25, iii–iv:77–96). Mohammed Shaheen discusses the relationship between "Pound and T. E. Lawrence: Two Self-Crowned Laureates of the Time" (*Paideuma* 17, ii–iii:223–38); the correspondence he prints shows a rather cross Pound rudely responding to friendly overtures from Lawrence in the 1930s. Lois Bar-Yaacov describes "The Odd Couple: The Correspondence between Marianne Moore and Ezra Pound, 1918–1939" (*TCL* 34:507–27). But probably the most unusual comparison made this year is found in George Nemeth's "Freud and reason or fraud and treason: E. Pound and W. Reich; the trials and tribulations of two famous mavericks in postwar America" (*Discours Social/Social Discourse* 1:229–38); Nemeth finds some striking parallels between Pound and Reich and then asks the provocative question of why Reich was prosecuted with so much more zeal than Pound.

***d.* The Shorter Poems and Translations.** Pound's poems other than *The Cantos* received a good deal more attention than usual this year. The major work here is Bruce Fogelman's *Shapes of Power: The Development of Ezra Pound's Poetic Sequences* (UMI Research Press), which looks at the organization of Pound's early books of poetry and at the sequences they contain more closely than anyone else has before. Much useful information is collected, and Fogelman speculates, generally persuasively, about how the early collections experiment with and develop techniques that later shaped *Propertius*, *Mauberley*, and *The Cantos*. The weakest part of the book is the extension of his argument to *The Cantos*: he argues unpersuasively that "the foundation for all that follows is solidly established in the first three cantos," and this is the more regrettable as his work on lyric structure could be an important help in understanding *The Cantos*. But Fogelman makes the very early poetry more interesting than anyone has since Hugh Witemeyer's 1969 book *Forms and Renewal.*

Fogelman continues his work on neglected early poems of Pound in "The Structure of Pound's 'Und Drang'" (*Paideuma* 17, ii–iii:191–99), a look at the structural devices employed in this early sequence, which Fogelman again finds anticipatory of later work, and in "The Evolution of Ezra Pound's 'Contemporania'" (*JML* 15:93–103), which focuses on Pound's revision of the order of this sequence. The only other piece on the very early poetry this year is David Roessel's "'Near Perigord' and a Mycenaean Trade War" (*Paideuma* 17, i:105–7), which rather too briefly relates "Near Perigord" to Homeric criticism of the time. Steve Ellis usefully traces the changing history of

"The Punctuation of 'In a Station of the Metro,'" (*Paideuma* 17, ii–iii:201–7). And Russell J. Reising's "Condensing the James Novel: *The American* in *Hugh Selwyn Mauberley*" (*JML* 15:17–34) argues that *The American* is the central James novel for *Mauberley*.

But most of the articles on Pound's shorter poems this year are on the translations. Anne S. Chapple, in her long, detailed article "Ezra Pound's *Cathay*: Compilation from the Fenollosa Notebooks" (*Paideuma* 17, ii–iii:9–46) is quite good on the process by which Pound selected poems from the Fenollosa manuscripts to include in *Cathay* and on the links between Imagism and these poems. Her reading of the sequence that emerges, however, is less convincing in arguing that Pound was only interested in these links and not in the subject matter of the poems. In "Pound's 'The Beautiful Toilet'" (*Expl* 47, i:29–31), Yu Zhang examines some of the differences between Pound's poem and the Chinese original. Chang Yao-Xin combines some useful remarks about *The Confucian Odes* with some less useful general remarks in "Pound's Chinese Translations" (*Paideuma* 17, i:113–32). Brian Atkins's "Pound's *Propertius*: What Kind of Homage?" (*Paideuma* 17, i:29–44) is a careful look at Pound's translation that doesn't really add anything that is new. A more interesting study is Alan J. Peacock's "Pound's Propertian Distortions: A Possible Rationale" (*Paideuma* 17, ii–iii:211–19), which coins the term "induced mistranslation" for what Pound is up to in the *Homage*. Thus the questions surrounding Pound's Chinese and Propertius translations are as alive as ever, and Edward H. Baker's good "Historical Mediation in Two Translations of Ezra Pound" (*Paideuma* 17, i:69–86) links the discussion of the two by looking at the form of both *Cathay* and *Propertius*. Baker concludes somewhat contradictorily by criticizing the lack of attention to the content of these poems, a lack exemplified by the essay itself. I basically agree with Baker, however; Pound's translations have been looked at as translations often enough, and the next advance in our understanding of these key poems of Pound will come from reading them more closely as poems by Pound. A good model for this can be found in C. B. Coleman's "Pound's *Elektra* at CSC" (*Theater* 19, iii:83–86). Pound's translation of Sophocles' *Elektra* was produced for the first time just last year, yet Coleman's piece is far more than just a report on the performance; he briefly but perceptively comes to grips with the creative, original aspects of Pound's version.

e. The Cantos. Last year I noted a slowdown in studies of *The Cantos,* a slowdown only partially reversed this year, though work already discussed by Longenbach, Fogelman, Kenner, and others also contain discussions of *The Cantos.* Good recent work on *The Cantos* seems to be sharply but not narrowly focused; less successful work tries to cover too much ground to cover it well. Taking on too much ground is Jerome J. McGann's "The *Cantos* of Ezra Pound, the Truth in Contradiction" (*CritI* 15:1–25), which is in a sense more about McGann's struggle with Pound than with Pound himself, but with an elusive focus on how the quest for a totalitarian form in *The Cantos* self-deconstructs. Also in need of a sharper focus is K. Narayana Chandran's "Making Cosmos: Building/Creation in *The Cantos*" (*Paideuma* 17, ii–iii:177–89), which attempts to talk about every building project in the poem, and Elizabeth Dodd's "Metamorphosis and Vorticism in *The Cantos*: How to Read the Allusive Image" (*MQ* 29:425–37), which says nothing about Vorticism and little about metamorphosis, focusing mostly on an unoriginal discussion of the role of allusions in the work. I was frankly confused by Eli Goldblatt's "Gender Matters in Pound's *Cantos*" (*JML* 15:35–53), which argues for a cult of maleness in the Malatesta Cantos but sees Pound as identifying the poet with the feminine. And Victor Li's "The Rhetoric of Presence: Reading Pound's *Cantos* I to III" (*ESC* 14:296–309) provides an overly predictable account of these three cantos through a perspective provided by Paul de Man and Derrida.

Much more useful and perceptive is Stephen Sicari's excellent "Reading Pound's Politics: Ulysses as Fascist Hero" (*Paideuma* 17, ii–iii:145–68). Sicari has two central points, both of which seem well-founded: first, that the figure of Ulysses in *The Cantos* is more Dante's Ulysses than Homer's; second, that, far from condemning the roving Ulysses as Dante does, Pound finds in him the type of the active Fascist hero he also finds in Mussolini. My own "Jefferson and/or Adams: A Shifting Mirror for Mussolini in the Middle Cantos" (*ELH* 55:505–26) explores Pound's perception of a relation between Jefferson and Adams and Renaissance and contemporary Italy; I argue that Pound's shift in attention from Jefferson to Adams reveals an important shift in his politics and in his conception of Mussolini. Also discussing the Middle Cantos is a very long and detailed essay by Carol H. Cantrell and Ward Swinson, "Cantos LII–LXXI: Pound's Textbook for Princes," the first half of which is published in *Paideuma*

(17, ii–iii:111–44). This installment is a close discussion of the China Cantos, primarily concerned with showing how these cantos violate Pound's own stated aesthetic and historiographic principles. Also detailing Pound's Chinese sources is Elizabeth Bruce's "Yao and Shun in *The Cantos*: Chinese Emperors Placed in the Context of Frazer's *Golden Bough*" (*Paideuma* 17, ii–iii:69–92). Bruce presents Pound's use of these ancient legendary Chinese kings as influenced by Frazer's notion of magician-kings. Finally, Stephen J. Adams describes "The Metrical Contract of *The Cantos*" (*JML* 15:55–72). This interesting and ambitious article on the metrics of Pound's "free verse epic" argues that Pound's rhythm rises "in lyrical passages into syllabic patterns that resemble Greek meters": at key moments, stress gives way to quantity.

These essays show that interpretive criticism of *The Cantos* is flourishing. We are getting a better handle on how the poetry and the politics interrelate and on all the parts of the poem, particularly the middle and late sections that have been previously less studied. What we are getting less of, however, is explications of specific passages. C. J. Ackerley finds an allusion to Shelley's drowning in "Canto 82: Pound, Swinburne (Shelley) Aeschylus, Whitman" (*Paideuma* 17, ii–iii:209–10). Finally, David Roussel's "The 'Repeat in History': Canto XXVI and Greece's Asia Minor Disaster" (*TCL* 34:180–90) provides a model of the kind of local readings of *The Cantos* we need more of, relating Canto 26 to contemporary issues in Asia Minor and to Hemingway.

ii. Eliot

***a.* Text and Biography.** It's pleasant to have something substantial to put in this category for the first time in several years, two things in fact, the long-awaited *The Letters of T.S. Eliot, Volume I 1898–1922*, Valerie Eliot, ed. (Faber & Faber), and Lyndall Gordon's second volume of biography, *Eliot's New Life* (Oxford). *The Letters* represent the major addition to Eliot's texts since the manuscripts of *The Waste Land* were edited almost twenty years ago, and it is something every reader of Eliot will want to have and consult. It must be said, however, that Eliot was not one of the great letter writers of the century. His letters, like Joyce's, are interesting primarily for their content and for what they add to our biographical knowledge; they are mostly business correspondence, revealing less about Eliot himself than about the literary world (or minefield) he entered in literary London after 1915. Here, as elsewhere, he played the Possum. Valerie Eliot has done a generally good editorial job, adding many letters from Vivien or to Eliot that help fill in the picture. The glacial pace of this project and the veto of publication of other manuscript material for the sake of the *Letters* means, however, that our understanding of Eliot is still a good deal more obstructed than aided by the Eliot Estate.

The next volume of letters is either going to have a substantial lacuna or be truly glacial in its pace of arrival, for many of the thousand letters to Emily Hale sealed (at Eliot's desire) until 2019 come from the late 1920s and 1930s. And Gordon's *Eliot's New Life* is in a sense an attempt to imagine what is in (and behind) those letters and what Eliot's tie to Emily Hale meant to the poetry. This means that *Eliot's New Life* is necessarily more provisional, filled with more guesswork, than Gordon's *Eliot's Early Years* (1977), and my major reservation about the new book is that Gordon doesn't keep this as firmly in view as she should. She presents her theories about the relation between the life and the work almost as if they were biographical facts, not interpretive constructs. But what I like about the book is that these theories do help us read the later poetry and plays in interesting and fresh ways. In particular, Gordon does more to open up the plays to reading than anyone has in a long time. Another biographical study is Loretta Johnson's "A Temporary Marriage of Two Minds: T. S. and Vivien Eliot" (*TCL* 34, i:48–61), which continues the rehabilitation of the first Mrs. Eliot through a look at her work published in *The Criterion.*

***b.* General Studies.** The most substantial general study this year is Christopher Ricks's *T. S. Eliot and Prejudice* (Faber & Faber). Almost as hard to paraphrase as Eliot's poetry, Ricks's study moves among and connects the issue of Eliot's own (racial and political) prejudices, some of the ways readers and critics have prejudged Eliot's own poetry, and some larger issues about the connection between prejudging and interpretation. Ricks's study contains many interesting nuggets along the way, a number of new sources or allusions in Eliot, a fascinating explanation of Eliot's way of reading his own poetry, and an excellent account of Eliot's evolution from *The Waste*

Land to *Four Quartets* in terms of the gradual disappearance of names in the poetry. Ricks is a very good (and very Eliotic) reader of Eliot, and everyone will learn something from this book.

Two British general introductions to Eliot were published this year, Martin Scofield's *T. S. Eliot: The Poems* (Cambridge) and Ronald Tamplin's *A Preface to T. S. Eliot* (Longmans). Though both Scofield's and Tamplin's are good books, these are in addition to two similar studies published last year by Angus Calder and F. B. Pinion, and I wonder if we need such a profusion of general introductions to the life and works. Tamplin's is the more introductory study of the two, and he spends a good deal more time sketching a context for Eliot's work than looking at it directly. Scofield's book is clearly the best of all these recent introductions to Eliot. He devotes the majority of the book to a close reading of virtually all of Eliot's poems, and what he says is fresh, makes sense, and would serve well to introduce Eliot to a novice reader. Another English study, Erik Svarny's *"The Men of 1914": T. S. Eliot and early modernism* (Open University Press), is more specialized. Svarny's emphasis on the debt Eliot owes to Pound, Lewis, and the Vorticist milieu is a welcome corrective to much Eliot criticism, but his otherwise intelligent study is seriously flawed by his failure to cite virtually any work done in this area in the last 15 years. This frankly looks like something that sat in a box for a long time and didn't quite get dusted off.

An emphatically American collection in its address to the teacher—not to the common reader—is *Approaches to Teaching Eliot's Poetry and Plays* (MLA), a collection of 27 brief, pedagogically oriented essays and some bibliographical aids ably edited by Jewel Spears Brooker as part of the MLA's Approaches to Teaching World Literature series. Brooker has done a good job in getting her contributors to focus on pedagogical rather than scholarly issues and in gathering together different approaches to Eliot and different contexts in which he can be put, and this is a volume any teacher of Eliot will learn something from. My only reservation is that these teachers report nothing but success, sweetness, and light in teaching Eliot. I personally encounter a good deal of resistance to a number of aspects of Eliot's work (for some of the reasons Ricks treats). And this resistance is not just among students, as we shall see below, for Eliot-bashing remains still very much in vogue, at least along the Raritan River. Brooker's useful collection would have been even more useful if some of her contributors had addressed this important issue. Another pedagogically oriented essay is Mariolina Salvatori's "Toward a Hermeneutics of Difficulty" (in *Audits of Meaning*, pp. 80–95), which by following a student's reaction (and resistance) to *The Waste Land* through a series of papers on the poem provides one of the kinds of studies missing from Brooker's collection.

Other fairly general looks at Eliot's career include a 1985 special issue of *Agenda* devoted to Eliot reprinted in this country by Black Swan, and *T. S. Eliot: Essays from the* Southern Review, James Olney, ed., (Oxford), a similar collection of centennial essays from the *Southern Review* (see *ALS 1985*). Seamus Heaney's "The Government of the Tongue" (*Partisan Review* 55:292–308)—also included in *The Government of the Tongue: Selected Prose, 1978–1987* (Farrar, pp. 91–108)—is a general reflection on the power of poetry that takes off from and returns to Eliot's work. Hugh Kenner's *A Sinking Island: The Modern English Writers*, a general look at writing in England in this century, contains a chapter on *The Waste Land* which usefully places the poem less as an English poem or as an American poem than as one of the central gestures towards an International Modernism that seeks to escape such national categories. A briefer piece by Kenner is "Tradition Revisited" (*Renascence* 40, iii:171–75), which is concerned with establishing the difference between Eliot's attitude toward the past and that prevalent in England before his work. Two Dutch scholars are concerned with defining the relation between Eliot and modernism: L. R. Leavis, in "T. S. Eliot and the Poetry of the Future" (*ES* 69:481–96), argues that Eliot's modernism has not dated and is still in a vital relation to contemporary poetry. Douwe Fokkema's "Modernist Poetry? On the Interference of Genre and Group Code: The Case of T. S. Eliot" (in *Approaches to Discourse, Poetics and Psychiatry*, Iris M. Zavala, Teun A. van Dijk, and Myriam Diaz-Diocaretz, eds., [Benjamins, 1987], pp. 181–86), seems to be working with too restrictive a notion of modernism to get anything of much interest said. He has a most bizarre notion that there isn't much modernist poetry and therefore that modernism is primarily to be found in fiction.

Several studies focus on Eliot's politics. Michael Long's "The Politics of English Modernism: Eliot, Pound and Joyce" (in *Visions and Blueprints: Avant-garde culture and radical politics in early twentieth-century Europe*, Edward Timms and Peter Collier, eds. [Manchester], pp. 98–112) tries to cover too much ground too quickly and is therefore mostly summary. Kenneth Asher's "T. S. Eliot and Ideology" (*ELH* 55:895–915) delineates the "French reactionary matrix of Eliot's thought." In "'Meeting Mr. Eugenides': T. S. Eliot and Eugenic Anxiety" (*YER* 9:169–77), Juan Leon interestingly relates themes in Eliot's work to the Anglo-American eugenics movement. John Carey's "Eliot and the Mass" (*SPELL* 4:49–64) argues that Eliot's impersonalist critique of individuality is connected to his hostility toward the modern masses and mass society. Finally, the best essay on this subject this year is Jeffrey M. Perl's "The Law of the Excluded Middle" (*Renascence* 40, iii:159–70), which relates Eliot's philosophical skepticism to his political detachment and sees in Eliot's politics a consistent and Bradleyan attempt to dissolve either/or dichotomies and choices.

The humor of Eliot's work is often ignored by critics, but several essays this year redress this gap. Russell Kirk's "Cats, Eliot, and the Dance of Life" (*Renascence* 40, iii:197–303) uses the poems on cats as an entry into Eliot's work. More substantively, C. A. Patrides's "T. S. Eliot: Alliances of Levity and Seriousness" (*SR* 96:77–94) uses the poems on cats as an entry into the jostling of the comic and tragic in Eliot's work, and while Elizabeth Kraft's "'A Great Humour which is serious': Caricature and the Development of T. S. Eliot's Poetic Vision" (*ELWIU* 15:221–35) argues that Eliot's use of caricature is not meant to be funny as much as an exposé of our shortcomings. Steven Helmling's "The Humor of Eliot from 'Prufrock' to *The Waste Land*" (*YER* 9:153–56) takes a different and more incisive tack: Helmling argues that Eliot increasingly rejects the humor of "Prufrock" as a response to the problem of self-consciousness. And a related essay by Helmling, "The Success and Failure of T. S. Eliot" (*SR* 96:55–76) perceptively explores Eliot's attachment to the idea of failure.

Other good general studies include Marc Manganaro's "Beating a Drum in a Jungle: T. S. Eliot on the Artist as 'Primitive'" (*MLQ* 47[1986]:393–421), and Michael Beehler's "Metaphysics and Dramatic *Praxis*: Eliot on the Rhetoric of Drama" (*CEA* 51:103–13). Manganaro, extending previous work of his in this area, traces the influence of Lévy-Bruhl on Eliot's concept of the primitive and of literature; Beehler usefully traces Eliot's critique in his essays of the realistic assumptions of the Western dramatic traditions. This was interesting enough that I wanted to hear more, to have the argument applied to Eliot's own subsequent dramatic work. Two other general studies offer little illumination. Dan Pearce's "Repetition Compulsion and 'Undoing': T. S. Eliot's 'Anxiety of Influence'" (*Mosaic* 21, iv: 45–54) is a psychological study of Eliot's "poetic perversity," which the author solemnly assures us is not meant as a derogatory term; T. H. B. M. Harmsen's "T. S. Eliot's Poetic Testament: The Personality of the Impersonality Seeker" (*ES* 69:509–17) offers nothing new on Eliot's quest for impersonal poetry.

c. Relation to Other Writers. Much of the work in this category this year is concerned with placing Eliot more accurately in the context of his British contemporaries. Sonjoy Dutta-Roy assumes a sharp contrast between "The Rooted Bard and the Rootless Satirist: Tradition and Modernity in Yeats and Eliot" (*YER* 9:119–24), but this is correctly challenged by Grover Smith's "Yeats, Eliot, and the Use of Memory" (*YER* 9:131–39) and Max Stewart's "The 'Gout pour la Vie Spirituelle': T. S. Eliot's Anglican Profession and His View of Bishop Lancelot Andrewes" (*YER* 9:54–63). Smith provides an interesting discussion of the "dialogue" between Yeats's and Eliot's works in the 1920s and 1930s, mostly on the question of ghosts, while Stewart tries to save Eliot from Yeats's and Tate's critique of his spirituality as insufficiently emotional and overly ecclesiastical. But the Anglican Eliot is portrayed in all his lack of color in Alzina Stone Dale's hagiographic *T. S. Eliot, the Philosopher Poet* (H. Shaw), an intellectual biography of no great substance that presents Eliot as if he were a composite of C. S. Lewis, Charles Williams, G. K. Chesterton and Dorothy Sayers. John Martin's "Voices of Fire: Eliot, Lewis, Sayers and Chesterton" (in *The Taste of the Pineapple: Essays on C. S. Lewis as Reader, Critic, and Imaginative Writer*, Bruce L. Edwards, ed. [Bowling Green], pp. 219–39) continues in this biographical vein, summarizing the lives and works of his four writers and unintentionally showing how little there really was in common among them. Donald G. Keesee shows Eliot's influence on the other of these writers in "Specters of T. S. Eliot's City in the Novels of Charles Williams" (*Seven* 9:47–55); Williams (or perhaps Keesee) misread Eliot, however, in seeing his vision of the city as entirely negative, entirely infernal. And Charles Doyle studies the troubled relationship between "Richard Aldington and T. S. Eliot" (*Richard Aldington: Papers from the Reading Symposium*, Lionel Kelly, ed. [University of Reading, 1987], pp. 122–36). Tom Gibbons puts Eliot in better and more appropriate company in "Yeats, Joyce, Eliot and the Contemporary Revival of Cyclical Theories of History" (*AUMLA* 69:151–63), a good though overly brief treatment of an important topic.

The studies of Eliot's relation to American writers are generally more interesting. Two studies of the relation of Marianne Moore and Eliot appear in a special issue of *Sagetrieb* (6, iii [1987]) on Moore: in "Consanguinities: T. S. Eliot and Marianne Moore" (pp. 45–56), Cleo McNelly Kearns narrates the two writers' attitudes toward each other and argues unpersuasively for Moore's influence on Eliot; Alan Nadel's "Marianne Moore and the Art of Delineation" (pp. 169–80) makes the more persuasive argument that Moore is an Eliotic modernist and that her work has been misread because this affinity hasn't been seen. Cyrena N. Pondrom argues for a relation between H. D.'s "*Trilogy* and *Four Quartets*: Contrapuntal Visions of Spiritual Quest" (*Agenda* 25, iii–iv:155–65), though, as often in studies of this kind, it is unclear whether she is arguing for influence or a significant parallel. Finally, Kieran Quinlan contrasts the two critics in "Sacred Eliot, Secular Ransom: Dead Opposites" (*KR* 10, iv:1–14).

To move to work on Eliot's relation to the past, it seems as if Eliot's sense of literary history isn't undergoing quite as much of an attack as it was some years ago. For example, Todd H. Sammons's "A Note on the Milton Criticism of Ezra Pound and T. S. Eliot" (*Paideuma* 17, i:87–97), argues that Eliot's "recantation" of his attack on Milton isn't as much of a change as it has been presented as being and, less interestingly, that the initial attack was deeply indebted to Pound. Another of Eliot's quarrels with literary history is presented by Patrick D. Murphy, in "Eliot's Problems with Keats in *The Waste Land*" (*PLL* 24:91–93), who sees *The Waste Land* as an attack on the romantic treatment of the nightingale. Christopher Coates, in "Eliot's Baudelaire: 'Christ the Tiger' in the 'Fourmillante Cite' " (*YER* 9: 149–52), sketches how Eliot could see Baudelaire as a spiritual poet. Leslie Higgins's "T. S. Eliot and the Poetry of Gerard Manley Hopkins" (*SoR* 24:291–302) depicts Eliot's changing and ultimately more positive reaction to Hopkins. But Richard Poirier gives us a bit of old-fashioned (or more precisely, recent-fashion) Eliot-bashing when he argues in "Pater, Joyce, Eliot" (*JJQ* 26:21–35) that Eliot has mislead us into seeing Pater and Joyce as opposites when Pater is really central for Joyce's (and Eliot's) work. And that veteran Eliot-basher, Harold Bloom, goes to bat one more time in "Reflections on T. S. Eliot" (*Raritan* 8, ii:70–87). Though not acknowledged as such, this piece is a reprint of the introduction to Bloom's terrible Chelsea House volume on *The Waste Land* (see *ALS 1987*), and I can't quite see why it deserved reprinting. Sadly, Bloom is still utterly paranoid about Eliot, "the spiritual enemy": he speaks of entering in the 1950s a "discipline virtually enslaved not only by Eliot's insights but by the entire span of his preferences and prejudices."

Precisely how Eliot attained his power to "enslave" us and shape (or cloud) our perceptions of literary history is the subject of a number of studies. Craig S. Abbott tries to argue in "Untermeyer on Eliot" (*JML* 15:105–19) that Untermeyer's long-lived anthology, *Modern American Poetry*, helped canonize Eliot, but the evidence he presents suggests rather that Untermeyer's text simply reflected Eliot's canonization. William E. Cain focuses on one of Eliot's influential early critics in "F. O. Mattheissen's Labor of Translation: From Sarah Orne Jewett to T. S. Eliot" (*SAQ* 87:355–84); his real focus is on Mattheissen, whom Cain sees as a mirror for contemporary criticism in his inability to reconcile his Eliotic formalism with his radical political leanings. Cain assumes an identity between Eliot's poetry and his criticism, an assumption implicitly challenged in James Longenbach's interesting if again a little overly dramatic "Hart Crane and T. S. Eliot: Poets in the Sacred Grove" (*DQ* 23, i:82–103). Longenbach's argument is that Crane was a better reader of Eliot's (and of his own) poetry than his friends Munson and Tate were and that *The Bridge* in particular needs to be judged by criteria other than those of Eliot's criticism, which, from Munson's and Tate's early comments, have shaped the critical tradition on Crane's poem. Louis Menand makes a parallel argument in "T. S. Eliot after His Time" (*Raritan* 8, ii:88–102), in a good article that answers the negative view of Eliot advanced by Poirier and Bloom by distinguishing Eliot's verse from later appropriations of it, including Eliot's own. Finally, James E. Morrison focuses on one of Eliot's explicit acts of canon formation in "The Preface as Criticism: T. S. Eliot on *Nightwood*" (*CentR* 32: 414–27), though his argument is that Eliot was reflecting on his own work and the evolution of his own self-consciousness as much as on Barnes's novel. This renewed attention to the process by which Eliot shaped the literary history of his own time (as well as perceptions of the past) is potentially an extremely valuable one, as long as it is not just an excuse for Poirier- and Bloom-style Eliot-bashing. I think we long ago moved beyond the need to dethrone Eliot, for it is only in Bloom's and Poirier's memories that he is still on a throne.

Three studies trace Eliot's influence on contemporary writers. Guido Kums compares the most famous works of Eliot and Malcolm Lowry in "Dovetailing in Depth: *The Waste Land* and *Under the Volcano*" (*New Comp* 5:150–61), but seems to misread the novel in pursuing its resemblance to the poem. Marsha Peterson White briefly traces the influence of "East Coker" on Galway Kinnell in "Trusting the Hours: On 'Wait' " (in *On the Poetry of Galway Kinnell: The Wages of Dying*, Howard Nelson, ed. [Michigan, 1987], pp. 251–55). More substantive is Patrick Deane's "A Line of Complicity: Baudelaire–T. S. Eliot–Adrienne Rich" (*CRAS* 18[1987]:463–81), which shows Eliot's influence on Rich's particular appropriation of Baudelaire in "Snapshots of a Daughter-in-Law."

Finally, there are two comparisons of Eliot to Eastern European writers, not influence studies as much as explorations of significant parallels. David Ayers compares "Two Bald Men: Eliot and Dostoyevsky" (*FMLS* 24:287–300) in terms of the concept of the double, which he sees as pertinent to the "you and I" of "Prufrock"; Jesse T. Airaudi's "Eliot, Milosz and the Enduring Modernist Protest" (*TCL* 34:453–67) compares the two poets as modernist critics of modernity.

***d.* The Poems and Plays.** "Prufrock" is the only early poem that receives separate attention this year, but it receives a good deal of it, with four essays and one book devoted to the poem. Lloyd F. Dickson's "Prufrock in a Labyrinth: A Text without Exits" (*YER* 9:140–44) doesn't add much to our knowledge of the poem. In a not particularly illuminating comparison, Linda J. Taylor's "Form, Process and the Dialectic of Self-construction: 'After Great Pain' and Three Modern Poems" (*UDR* 19:91–101) compares "Prufrock" to poems by Dickinson, Yeats, and Stevens. Donald J. Childs's "*Knowledge and Experience* in 'The Love Song of J. Alfred Prufrock' " (*ELH* 55:685–99) makes some interesting connections between "Prufrock" and Bradley; however, since the poem was written before Eliot read Bradley, the argument focuses, a little oddly, on how Bradley shaped Eliot's subsequent reading of "Prufrock." Couldn't a poem influence the reading of a philosopher as well as the other way around? The best essay on "Prufrock" this year is Joseph Bentley's "Action and the Absence of Speech in 'The Love Song of J. Alfred Prufrock' " (*YER* 9:145–48), which focuses on the fear of language expressed in the poem and is interesting on the prevalance of questions in the poem. Finally, Robert F. Fleissner's *Ascending the Prufrockian Stair: Studies* *in a Dissociated Sensibility* (Peter Lang) collects the numerous studies he has made of the poem over the past 20 years. He hasn't made a well-structured book out of these separate essays, unfortunately, but in any case most of his studies strike me as over-reading, exercises in eisegesis rather than exegesis. It may be that "Prufrock" doesn't need the honor of having a whole book written about it.

However, the two books about *The Waste Land* this year are considerably worse. Nancy K. Gish's *The Waste Land: A Poem of Memory and Desire* (Twayne) is part of another unnecessary Twayne series devoted to rereadings of major poems. Publishers have a greater appetite for such books than I do; this one adds little to our understanding of *The Waste Land.* And Robert L. Schwarz's *Broken Images: A Study of The Waste Land* (Bucknell) is simply a terrible book, a line-by-line explication of the poem devoted to a number of bizarre and unpersuasive theories. Schwarz's ambition is to do for Eliot what John Livingston Lowes did for Coleridge in *The Road to Xanadu,* but he can't really be said to succeed even in that eccentric ambition. According to him, the poem is largely about Marie Larisch, and his local readings are as unhelpful as his large-scale assumptions.

The 13 essays on *The Waste Land* start at the beginning, with Michael Alexander's "The Dedication to *The Waste Land*" (*Scripsi* 4, i[1986]:7–9), in which Alexander, ignoring Eliot's fairly superficial knowledge of Italian, tries to make too much of Eliot's changing of *miglior fabbro* into the superlative *il miglior fabbro.* Three local explications add to the density of the poem: Raymond J. S. Grant's "On *The Waste Land,* line 8: 'Coming over the Starnbergersee' " (*YER* 9: 93–105) sees this line as a reference to King Ludwig II of Bavaria; P. K. Saha's "Eliot's *The Wasteland*" (*Expl* 46, iii:31–32) relates lines 38–41 to passages in the final cantos of the *Inferno* and *Paradiso*; and Randy Malamud's "Frankenstein's Monster: The Gothic Voice in *The Waste Land*" (*ELN* 26, i:41–45) finds a reference to *Frankenstein* in line 182, "by the waters of Leman." Two essays in the *Yeats Eliot Review* make unpersuasive broader arguments. David Spurr's "*The Waste Land*: Mourning, Writing, Disappearance" (9:161–64) argues in an overly theoretical way that the poem is "mourning for the loss or disappearance of the subject." Purnima Bose's "End-Anxiety in T. S. Eliot's *The Waste Land*: Narrative Closure and the End of Empire" (9:157–60) is utterly unpersuasive in its attempt to read the Indic allusions at the end of the poem as simply a reference to the collapse of the British Empire. No more persuasive is Alison Tate's

"The Master-Narrative of Modernism: Discourses of Gender and Class in *The Waste Land*" (*L&H* 14:160–71), which presents the poem as a replication of the English literary tradition in its hierarchical subordination of women and the working class. Tate's logic is purely circular: her evidence for the subordination of these voices in the poem is simply the fact they always have been subordinated. Thomas C. Foster devotes a chapter of his *Form and Society* to *The Waste Land* (pp. 57–76), but what he offers is a quite traditional reading of the poem as a pessimistic reaction to the War.

Two essays in *Twentieth Century Literature* advance more interesting but not entirely persuasive arguments about the poem that focus on the role of Ezra Pound. Leon Surette's "*The Waste Land* and Jesse Weston: A Reassessment" (34:223–44) relates Weston to occultism and sees Pound as revising out much of the poem's occultism. The source study is valuable, but Pound seems much more interested in occultism than Eliot (as Surette's own work has informed us), so it's not clear why he would want to edit this material out. Wayne Kostenbaum's prizewinning "*The Waste Land*: T. S. Eliot's and Ezra Pound's Collaboration on Hysteria" (34:113–39) presents the manuscript of *The Waste Land* as akin to the hysterical discourse worked on by Pound and Eliot. William Burke's "Reading Through *The Waste Land*" (*YER* 9:75–92) argues that the poem calls for primarily an emotional, not an intellectual, response. Stephen Medcalf continues the rediscovery of the Latin influences on Eliot in a good essay on "Ovid and *The Waste Land*" (in *Ovid Renewed: Ovidian influences on literature and art from the Middle Ages to the twentieth century*, Charles Martindale, ed. [Cambridge], pp. 233–46); Medcalf's central claim is that the poem is Ovidian in its shifting and transformations, though Eliot's Ovid is an Ovid seen through Frazerian anthropology. Finally, the best essay on *The Waste Land* this year is Donald J. Childs's "Stetson in *The Waste Land*" (*EIC* 38:131–48), which argues that the reference to Stetson is metonymically a reference to ANZAC soldiers in the War (who wore Stetson hats). Gallipoli therefore lies behind this reference, as does Jean Verdenal. This is a carefully argued combination of local explication and interpretive criticism—my only reservation, one that extends to much Eliot criticism, is that I wonder if Eliot was (or if any poet could be) this deliberate in his concatenation of references.

There are two good essays on *Ash-Wednesday* in the *Yeats Eliot Review* this year. Marguerite Murphy finds a source for the poem in

"Henri de Régnier's 'L'Escalier': The Hidden Stairway of T. S. Eliot's *Ash-Wednesday*" (9:178–82). Melissa A. Eiles argues, in "The Inform Glory of the Positive Hour: Re-Conversion in *Ash-Wednesday*" (9: 106–18), that the poem is not about conversion but about a reconversion. "Animula" received a close study emphasizing its critique of the contemporary world in Slawomir Wacior's "A Horror Syndrom: A Study of T. S. Eliot's 'Animula' and Louis MacNeice's 'Prayer before Birth'" (*KN* 31[1984]:199–209). Brian M. Barbour's "Poetic Form in 'Journey of the Magi'" (*Renascence* 40, iii:189–96) argues that the poem is the response of one of the magi to St. Matthew asking about the events of long ago.

Criticism of *Four Quartets* remains at a fairly low level of vitality this year. John D. Boyd, S.J., discusses "The Paschal Action in Eliot's *Four Quartets*" (*Renascence* 40, iii:176–88) in a rather opaque piece of theology. John A. Sinclair's "Eliot's Burnt Norton II" (*Expl* 46, iii: 30–31) briefly but persuasively relates the axle tree of "Burnt Norton" to Hindu and Buddhist thought. In "A Condition of Complete Simplicity: Poetic Returns and Frost's 'Directive'" (*Worcester Rev.* 10, i:32–41), E. D. Lloyd-Kimbrel compares "Little Gidding" to Frost's poem in terms of their common theme of return.

There are six essays and parts of two books on the plays this year. David Galef discusses a rarely discussed work in "Fragments of a Journey: The Drama in T. S. Eliot's *Sweeney Agonistes*" (*ES* 69:497–508); Galef argues that the play has a Christian basis, but that Eliot couldn't finish the play because at this stage in his career he wasn't able to view religion comically as his conception of the play demanded. Scott Samuelson's "The Word as Sword: Power and Paradox in *Murder in the Cathedral*" (*L&B* 7[1987]:73–81) superficially modernizes the play by arguing that the struggle in the play is about interpretation. A more useful study is Mohit K. Ray's "Eliot's Use of Eyewitness Accounts in *Murder in the Cathedral*" (in *Modern Studies and Other Essays in Honour of Dr. D. K. Sinha*, R. C. Prasad and A. K. Sharma, eds., [Vikas, 1987], pp. 152–66), which looks at Eliot's use of original sources for the play. There are three essays on *The Cocktail Party*: Virginia Phelan's fine "Eliot *contre* Sartre: Reversing the Proposition" (*YER* 9:183–86) reads *The Cocktail Party* as a critical response to Sartre's assertion in *Huis Clos* that "Hell is other people"; Michael Selmon's "Logician, Heal Thy Self: Poetry and Drama in Eliot's *The Cocktail Party*" (*MD* 31:495–511) sees the play not as achieving Eliot's ideal of blending verse unobtrusively with content as much as dramatizing a struggle with language. Another less interesting essay in the same issue of *Modern Drama* is Lesley Chamberlain's "Through a Cocktail Glass Darkly" (pp. 512–19), which simply sees the play as unstagable. Niloufer Harben's *Twentieth Century English History Plays* (Macmillan) has a chapter on *Murder in the Cathedral*; mostly fairly flat plot summary, it does start by making the interesting suggestion that Brecht may have been an influence on the play. Glenda Leeming has a more inclusive context for Eliot's drama in her study of 20th-century English *Poetic Drama* (St. Martin's), but her discussion of Eliot is also mostly summary. This renewed level of attention to the plays is encouraging, but as I said above, Lyndall Gordon's *Eliot's New Life* is the best work on the plays in some time, much more interesting than these other books.

***e.* The Criticism.** There has been a similar rebirth of interest in Eliot's criticism, but of the three books and five articles on the criticism this year, everything but Richard Shusterman's superb *T. S. Eliot and the Philosophy of Criticism* (Duckworth) illustrates why Eliot's reputation as a critic is in the doldrums. Harold F. Brooks's *T. S. Eliot as Literary Critic* (Cecil Woolf, 1987) is almost entirely occupied with old questions about the accuracy of Eliot's critical judgments, and K. N. Phukan's "T. S. Eliot as a Poet-Critic" (in *Modern Studies and Other Essays in Honour of Dr. D. K. Sinha*, R. C. Prasad and A. K. Sharma, eds. [Vikas, 1987], pp. 182–94), similarly worries about an old category and where Eliot fits into it. With no such doubts on this (or any other) score, Samuel Hazo's "Standpoint Eliot's: Outlook Mine" (*Renascence* 40, iii:204–23) is an appropriation of Eliot's critical terms to praise and criticize a variety of living writers Eliot knew nothing about. Blanche Goren is in Hazo's camp, presenting in "Silence from the Sacred Wood" (*Modern Age* 31, ii [1987]:115–24) an Eliot whose criticism was deeply spiritual from the very beginning and offers an absolute critique of the entire modern world. None of these critics seems aware (or perhaps wants to be aware) that anything has happened in literary criticism since Eliot's work, and their Eliot is therefore without significant relation to our critical situation today. The same is unfortunately true of Lawrence Venuti's "The Ideology of the Individual in Anglo-American Criticism: The Example of Coleridge and Eliot" (*Boundary* 14, i–ii[1986]: 161–93). Venuti presents his study as establishing the superiority of Marxist criticism in terms of its "historical awareness," but he seems lamentably unhistorical in his criticism of Eliot's failure to "move beyond" the bourgeois concept of the individual to a post-structuralist conception of the self not available to Eliot, particularly when Eliot's work in fact played a role in creating that contemporary concept Venuti smugly criticizes Eliot for not accepting. Peter Davidhazi's "The Case of Instrumental vs. 'Autotelic' Criticism: From T. S. Eliot to Deconstruction" (*Neohelicon* 15:237–53) similarly builds a wall between Eliot and contemporary criticism, using the work of Hartman and others to argue against Eliot's view of the instrumental nature of criticism.

These dismal failures to move beyond stereotypical views of Eliot make Shusterman's study, easily the best book on Eliot this year and in my opinion the most important book on him since Ronald Bush's in 1984, all the more valuable. I have reviewed it at length and with enthusiasm elsewhere (*YER* 9:126–29), but briefly Shusterman shows the indebtedness of Eliot's early criticism to the analytic philosophy of Moore and Russell, describes how Eliot himself quickly realized the inadequacies of his early "objectivist" criticism and moved in a more historicist direction, and argues that this anticipates the directions of later critics and philosophers including Gadamer, Wittgenstein, and others. Each of these contributions is extremely valuable in understanding and placing Eliot's criticism; Shusterman doesn't superficially modernize Eliot's criticism, but he shows its relation to and importance for contemporary criticism. In sum, what Shusterman manages to do is to make Eliot's criticism interesting again. Twenty years ago, Eliot's work had been monumentalized to the point that it was almost uninteresting. Since then, the poetry (except perhaps for *Four Quartets*) has been demonumentalized and made interesting again; now Shusterman has reopened the criticism and Gordon has made a start on the plays; and we shall see in the years to come what gets built on these promising foundations.

New Mexico State University

9. Faulkner

M. Thomas Inge

The amount of scholarship on Faulkner declined this year. The usual dozen books are reviewed here, but only a little over 40 articles are considered (the number was 100 in 1986 and 70 in 1987). This may simply be a lull of some kind, since quite a few books announced for publication this year were delayed until 1989, including a weighty fourth biography, and Faulkner continues to be an attractive topic for commercial and university presses. His popularity abroad remains on the increase among readers and scholars. There were no major developments this year, although the subject of Faulkner and race was given a thorough reworking, and some advances were made in bibliography and our understanding of the development of Faulkner's reputation. A good many critical challenges, of course, remain to be addressed satisfactorily by the scholarly community.

i. Bibliography, Editions, and Manuscripts

Between William Boozer's quarterly checklists in *The Faulkner Newsletter*, the annual checklist of scholarship on Southern literature in each Spring issue of *MissQ*, and the annual MLA bibliography, fairly effective control of scholarship on Faulkner is maintained. The first two include helpful annotations and comments, and the *Newsletter* is always a small treasury of new information about Faulkner's life, career, and manuscripts. A William Faulkner Society has been organized by Judith Wittenberg of Simmons College; its *Newsletter*, so far, has been devoted to professional conference activities and news of members.

Thomas E. Connolly's *Faulkner's World: A Directory of His People and Synopses of Actions in His Published Works* (Univ. Press) is another in a series of such guides; but Connolly makes his more thorough by including every major and minor character, named and unnamed, and the works are arranged in chronological order with a comprehensive index to named characters. The guide lends itself to a variety of scholarly uses. An imaginatively structured reference work is *The Yoknapatawpha Chronicle of Gavin Stevens* by John Kenny Crane (Susquehanna), in which the author adopts the persona of Gavin Stevens, one of Faulkner's most dependable narrators, to retell the entire history of Yoknapatawpha County in a chronicle with annually arranged entries from 1540 to 1947 when Isaac McCaslin dies. Crane provides genealogical charts for 28 families and a character index that allows the user to chart the history of a single character chronologically throughout the fiction. Placing characters into historic conjunction with each other provides some interesting insights, but Crane's approach does require some debatable solutions to Faulkner's own internal contradictions in terms of time and place.

The Mansion: *A Concordance to the Novel* (UMI), ed. Noel Polk and John D. Hart, is the tenth in the invaluable series of concordances issued by the Faulkner Concordance Advisory Board. Each set makes research easier in numerous ways. Louis Daniel Brodsky's "William Faulkner's 1962 Gold Medal Speech" (*SB* 41:315–21) provides carefully edited texts of the existing versions of a speech made upon the occasion of an award from the American Academy of Arts and Letters. In "William Faulkner" (*ConL* 29:140–54) Alan Warren Friedman reviews a dozen books about Faulkner of 1983–85 with little enthusiasm, unlike Calvin S. Brown's survey of another seven books of 1985–86 (*SR* 96:271–79), which enthusiastically declares in its title "No Faulkner Moratorium Needed." Clifton Fadiman, who reviewed Faulkner negatively throughout his career, has grudgingly admitted he may be wrong in his entry on Faulkner in *The Lifetime Reading Plan*, third edition (Harper), but he misspells Flem Snopes first name as "Lem."

In addition to her excellent study *The Origins of Faulkner's Art* (1984) and her careful textual work on an edition of Faulkner's poem sequence *Vision in Spring* (1984), Judith L. Sensibar has now published a complete description of all known poetry by Faulkner, published and unpublished, and an annotated checklist of criticism on the poetic efforts, in *Faulkner's Poetry: A Bibliographical Guide to Texts and Criticism* (UMI Research Press). Together, the three volumes make a definitive statement about the power and importance of Faulkner's apprenticeship work as an aspiring poet in the larger context of his literary accomplishment.

ii. Biography

In *Dangerous Dossiers: Exposing the Secret War Against America's Authors* (Donald I. Fine), Herbert Mitgang finds that Faulkner's dossier at the FBI is a light one and mainly expresses concerns over his liberal political and civil rights views. A fellow Mississippian of another generation provides some interesting insights on Faulkner's cultural milieu and his visit in Faulkner's home in *Fabulous Provinces: A Memoir* (Mississippi) by Thomas Daniel Young. Young has the advantage of being a first-rate critic of Faulkner's fiction.

Donald W. Goodwin's chapter on Faulkner in *Alcohol and the Writer* summarizes every second-hand rumor, myth, and piece of gossip about his drinking problem as if it were fact, and except for a suggestion that Faulkner may have suffered from dipsomania, characterized by occasional binges, says little that is new. Without fully documenting his opinion, as a good psychiatric doctor should, Goodwin finds Faulkner the most severe alcoholic among all American writers, and he demonstrates a naive grasp of the fiction (since Faulkner's short stories "really go nowhere and have a thousand loose ends, lacking plot and structure, alcohol may have been the cause"). A better book on the subject by Tom Dardis will appear in 1989. Leo Schneiderman's *The Literary Mind: Portraits in Pain and Creativity* (Insight Books) locates the source of great literature in deep personal suffering and suggests, in the case of Faulkner, that "by reverting to a fantasy world peopled by charismatic ancestors, Faulkner was able to escape the painful reality of parental rejection." Much of what Schneiderman says is sensible, but once again craftsmanship is made out to be a matter of neurotic response: "The lack of coherence that some literary critics have noted in Faulkner's writing, including his major works, was a product of long-standing ego defects." Such reductive statements tax one's patience. Also, Dr. Goodwin needs to talk to Dr. Schneiderman about the nature of alcoholism; the latter views it as simply a "dramatic expression of Faulkner's self-hatred and need to punish himself."

iii. Criticism: General

Creating Faulkner's Reputation: The Politics of Modern Literary Criticism (Tennessee), by Lawrence H. Schwartz, is a carefully researched and impressively argued case study of the ways political trends, social forces, and aesthetic movements can be brought to bear on the creation of a writer's reputation. His analysis of the conjunction of interests between the New Critics, the New York intellectuals, and the Rockefeller Foundation explores new territory and requires some adjustments in previously held perceptions. Some will wish to argue with matters of interpretation, and the whole story is in danger of being read as a conspiracy theory, but Schwartz clearly demonstrates the usefulness of examining literature in its full historical-political-cultural milieu, especially in the case of Faulkner.

Gene D. Phillips's *Fiction, Film, and Faulkner: The Art of Adaptation* (Tennessee) is an engaging overview of the film scripts on which Faulkner worked and the motion pictures based on his fiction, with an emphasis on the latter. Phillips assembles all the facts, reflects on the personalities involved, and summarizes the relevant plots, and he sensibly accepts the principle that fiction and film are very different art forms, and adaptations should be judged primarily on their merits as film. The criteria being used by Phillips are not always clear, however, and more thorough analyses of the films would have been desirable.

Donald M. Kartiganer's chapter on Faulkner (pp. 887–909 in the new *CLHUS*) is as informative and concise a survey of his work and accomplishment as one can expect in 23 pages, with appropriate emphases on his style, his narrative structure, and his use of myth. The major themes and critical cruces are briefly elucidated, and the whole is engagingly written. In his general essay on regionalism for the *History* (pp. 779–81), James M. Cox in only three pages incredibly says a good deal of what is worth saying about Faulkner; in many ways, this one sentence says it all: "To read his work is to enter a wilderness of loss and degeneration replete with ruin, defeat, decay, venality, guilt, and shame, yet imbued with honor, courage, struggle, and endurance as it dies into our possession."

In the only general essay in *Heir and Prototype: Original and Derived Characterizations in Faulkner* (Central Ark.) David L. Vanderwerken's "Faulkner's 'Psychic Maturity'" (pp. 1–7) briefly supports the idea that Faulkner's protagonists confront their destinies rather than try to escape their selves and responsibilities by lighting out for the territories, as in most American fiction. Joseph Blotner's contribution to *The Incarnate Imagination: Essays in Theology, the Arts and Social Sciences* (Bowling Green), ed. Ingrid H. Shafer, is an essay on "Faulkner's Religious Sensibility" (pp. 185–96) which effectively draws together what there is to know about the writer's opinions on religion.

iv. Criticism: Special Studies

a. **Ideas, Influences, Intellectual Background.** A number of influence and parallel studies with other European and American writers appeared this year, three of them in *Heir and Prototype.* Lisa Holiman Crosthwait finds numerous parallels between central characters in *As I Lay Dying* and George Eliot's *Adam Bede* in "Cash Bundren and Adam Bede" (pp. 82–92), although there is no certain evidence Faulkner read it; F. A. Rodewald argues for the influence of *Wuthering Heights* by Emily Brontë on *Absalom, Absalom!* in "William Faulkner and Emily Brontë" (pp. 93–97); and Alan Perlis provides a thorough analysis of the influences of Thomas Mann in "*The Sound and the Fury: Buddenbrooks* Reconsidered" (pp. 98–112). E. P. Edwards finds good evidence in a brief personal poem that "Faulkner Borrows from Joyce and/or Richard Head and/or The Oxford English Dictionary" (*MissQ* 41:459–61).

Diana Orendi Hinze's "William Faulkner and Thomas Wolfe" (*TWN* 12:25–32) is an exhaustive comparison of *As I Lay Dying* and *Look Homeward, Angel* to demonstrate the influence of Wolfe, and Susan Tuck continues a series of comparisons with Eugene O'Neill in "White Dreams, Black Nightmares: *All God's Chillun Got Wings* and *Light in August*" (*EON* 12:48–55), which strongly supports an O'Neill influence. Randall Waldron's "Faulkner's First Fictional Car—Borrowed from Scott Fitzgerald?" (*AL* 60:281–85) locates the source of Faulkner's first automobile, described in a 1925 sketch called "Country Mice," in a similar passage of *The Great Gatsby*; Faulkner also anticipates his treatment of autos in the fiction to come. A very useful overview of the types and varieties of legendry found in the fiction and their origins has been provided by the expert folklorist George W. Boswell in "The Legendary Background in Faulkner's Work" (*MissFR* 21[1987]:29–39).

b. **Race.** The topic of the 1986 Faulkner and Yoknapatawpha conference at the University of Mississippi, and the title of the published proceedings, was *Faulkner and Race* (Mississippi), ed. Doreen Fowler and Ann J. Abadie. The general essays will be discussed here, but those devoted to specific works will be discussed below in the appropriate sections. Eric J. Sundquist's "Faulkner, Race, and the Forms of American Fiction" (pp. 1–34) is a comprehensive and insightful survey of the ways the black experience has been treated in fiction by both blacks and whites and how Faulkner fits into that larger context. The limitations and extent of Faulkner's accomplishment in treating that experience are thereby more fully elucidated. The comparisons with numerous black writers, from Charles W. Chesnutt to Alice Walker, are especially interesting. "Faulkner's Negroes Twain" (pp. 58–69) by Blyden Jackson finds two types of black characters in the early and late fiction; the first are stereotypes, but the latter reflect his sincere convictions about the essential humanity of blacks despite his training in a society that denied it. Thadious M. Davis turns to music as a way of categorizing Faulkner's blacks—those who reflect the qualities of jazz and those who imbue the spirit of the blues—in her eloquent essay "From Jazz Syncopation to Blues Elegy: Faulkner's Development of Black Characterization" (pp. 70–92). Those unhappy with Faulkner's treatment of blacks in the fiction are forcefully addressed by Noel Polk in "Man in the Middle: Faulkner and the Southern White Moderate" (pp. 130–51), where he asserts: "I believe that we have tried too hard to discover the number and kinds of things that Faulkner *did not* or *could not* write about, and not nearly hard enough to find the profound and perplexing human drama that within his lights . . . he did draw so convincingly." Polk's is one of the best essays I have seen on Faulkner's political and racial attitudes.

"Marginalia: Faulkner's Black Lives" (pp. 170–91), by Philip M. Weinstein, carefully explicates "the detached lives of the black characters Faulkner's art records, and also the undetached, fantasized black life Faulkner imaginatively projects from within himself as he creates these figures." Weinstein argues that Faulkner is best when dealing with racism in the white mind rather than the black experience. Lothar Hönnighausen, in "Black as White Metaphor: A European View of Faulkner's Fiction" (pp. 192–208), brings his expert eye to bear on the imagery and finds that in the early work, black is used as a cultural metaphor, while in the later fiction the black image is more clearly political in its content. Hoke Perkins investigates a strain in Faulkner's fiction—the use of black razor murderers and the emphasis on a bond between the murderer and a white character—in "'Ah Just Cant Quit Thinking': Faulkner's Black Razor Murderers," (pp. 222–35) and concludes that we can come to no final conclusions about Faulkner and race because "there is too much history and circumstance in our way." Sergei Chakovsky's enlightened and enlightening essay, "Lucas Beauchamp and Jim: Mark Twain's Influence on William Faulkner" (pp. 236–54), suggests that while Twain admitted defeat and gave up on the race issue after *Pudd'nhead Wilson,* Faulkner refused to "quit" the issue and moved ahead artistically to integrate blacks and whites as universal humanity. Michael Greenwood believes that Faulkner doubted his ability to deal with the reality of black people and that his anxiety caused a crisis of confidence from which he never recovered, a provocative idea explored in "Faulkner and the Vocational Liabilities of Black Characterization" (pp. 255–71).

Louis Daniel Brodsky throws a good deal of new and interesting light on "Faulkner and the Racial Crisis, 1956" (*SoR* 24:791–807) by examining a package of letters addressed to Faulkner about the time of his controversial interview in *The Reporter* and his "Letter to the North" in *Life* magazine. A good deal is revealed about popular sentiment toward racism and Faulkner in America. Mark W. Lencho takes on a very different but related matter in "Dialect Variation in *The Sound and the Fury*: A Study of Faulkner's Use of Black English" (*MissQ* 41:403–19). Although on the surface variable and inconsistent, Lencho documents the theory that Faulkner's use of dialect is "governed by a more telling underlying consistency." He must have paid careful attention then to black behavior and speech patterns. Faulkner's treatment of another racial group is explored in a chapter of Elizabeth I. Hanson's *The American Indian* (pp. 102–12) and is compared with treatments by Hemingway, Melville, Thoreau, and Cooper. Faulkner was fascinated with the wilderness and made effective use of the symbolic potential of the Native American.

v. Individual Works to 1929

"'I Want You to Be Human': The Potential Sexuality of Narcissa Benbow" (*MissQ* 41:447–58), by Ron Buchanan, is a spirited defense of Narcissa Benbow, who is treated harshly for the shrew she becomes in later fiction but who in the first part of *Flags in the Dust* is portrayed as an earth goddess whose sexuality might have proven comparable to that of Lena Grove or Eula Varner. In "Who Killed Simon Strother, and Why?: Race and Counterplot in *Flags in the Dust*" (*Faulkner and Race,* pp. 93–110), Pamela E. Rhodes's concern is to answer the question in her title. The answer is Faulkner, because he was afraid of where this complex, independent black character might lead—an intriguing thesis, and well argued, but not everyone will be convinced.

Leona Toker addresses the "Diffusion of Information in *The Sound and the Fury*" (*CollL* 15:111–35), that is, "the effect of numerous minor informational gaps which delay pattern recognition," and finds this to be a rhetorical device intended to influence our interpretation of the novel. Her argument is indeed persuasive. Another technical matter is considered in a highly technical analysis by Cheryl Lester, "From Place to Place in *The Sound and the Fury*: The Syntax of Interrogation" (*MFS* 34:141–55), which deals with the extent to which the separate parts of the novel necessarily relate to each other in an interpretation of its meaning. The discussion requires careful concentration. Webb Salmon's "Faulkner's *The Sound and the Fury*" (*Expl* 46, ii:27–29) is an unresolved attempt to clarify references to letters written by Quentin in his section of the novel.

vi. Individual Works, 1930–39

In "William Faulkner and the Drama of Meaning: The Discovery of the Figurative in *As I Lay Dying*" (*SoAR* 53:11–23), Joseph R. Urgo finds that it is the drama of meaning—conflicts in epistemology—that make Faulkner's narratives compelling, especially in *As I Lay Dying*, which Urgo brilliantly explicates. Ronald Emrick tries to determine whether or not Darl is actually insane in his essay "Darl Bundren's Insanity: The Collapse of Community in *As I Lay Dying*" (*Heir and Prototype*, pp. 70–81), and concludes that he has a mental disposition for instability but is not shown to be insane in the novel.

"Women at the 'Crossing of the Ways': Faulkner's Portrayal of Temple Drake" (*Heir and Prototype*, pp. 59–69), by Jeffrey J. Folks, is an admiring examination of the heroine of *Sanctuary* from a variety of modernist perspectives. Her uncompromising character requires a transformation in Faulkner's treatment of women. Karen Aubrey Ellstrom outlines the symbolic uses of passages and doors, and the opening and closing of them, and how they are tied to character development, in "Faulkner's Closing of Doors in *Sanctuary*" (*NMW* 20:63–73). In an essay overlooked here earlier, Charles Chappell effectively demonstrates the importance of determining the role played by the Jewish lawyer from Memphis in the novel in "The

Memphis Lawyer and His Spine: Another Piece in the *Sanctuary* Puzzle" (*ELWIU* 20[1986]:331–38). *William Faulkner's* Sanctuary (Chelsea) is a volume in the Harold Bloom factory-produced series "Modern Critical Interpretations." The essays are mostly reprinted chapters from books already available on the library shelf, and the introduction is the same one for each Faulkner volume, except for a section added at the end on *Sanctuary*. The same goes for another in the series, *William Faulkner's* Light in August (Chelsea), which has as a jacket illustration the strangely irrelevant painting *The Last Civil War Veteran* (1961) by Larry Rivers.

Another fine essay by Joseph R. Urgo is "Menstrual Blood and 'Nigger' Blood: Joe Christmas and the Ideology of Race and Sexism" (*MissQ* 41:391–401), which shows how cultural attitudes toward race and sex come together in a nexus that inevitably spells tragedy in *Light in August*. Glenn Meeter focuses on "Male and Female in *Light in August* and *The Hamlet*: Faulkner's 'Mythical Method'" (*SNNTS* 20:404–16) to clarify and understand better how the mythical process works in those two novels, especially in terms of male/female dichotomies, with an assist from Joseph Campbell. Charles Chappell helpfully sorts out fact from speculation in the final chapter of *Light in August* in "The Infatuated Final Narrator of *Light in August*" (*PAPA* 14:1–12). Although the unnamed furniture dealer is engaging and entertaining, he is not to be trusted in his interpretation of what happens between Lena Grove and Byron Bunch. Using theories of C. G. Jung and Rollo May, Robert Gibb outlines the conflicts confronted by Joe Christmas because of his lack of knowledge about himself ("Joe Christmas: Faulkner's Savage Innocent" [*JEP* 9:331–40]). "*Light in August* and the Rhetorics of Racial Division" (*Faulkner and Race*, pp. 152–69) is a version of a chapter from James A. Snead's *Figures of Division: William Faulkner's Major Novels* (see *ALS 1986*, p. 143).

Edgar A. Dryden's intent is to reassert the importance of the romance as a thematic and generic category in his book *The Form of American Romance* (Johns Hopkins), and his chapter on *Absalom, Absalom!* focuses on the acts of reading and writing in that novel and how they cause the author and reader to question the nature of the fictive world (pp. 137–67). This is a perceptive reading of the novel as a self-reflexive piece of fiction. Renard Doneskey, in "'*that pebbles's watery echo*': The Five Narrators of *Absalom, Absalom!*" (*Heir and Prototype*, pp. 113–33), argues that in addition to Quentin,

Mr. Compson, Rosa, and Shreve, there is an additional external or fifth objective narrator who binds them together and that his search for meaning is as important as that of the others. The complexity of narrative strategies in the novel is also clarified by Rosemary Coleman in "Family Ties: Generating Narratives in *Absalom, Absalom!*" (*MissQ* 41:421–32).

Susan V. Donaldson intelligently recognizes the pitfalls in discussing Faulkner's fictional women in her essay "Subverting History: Women, Narrative and Patriarchy in *Absalom, Absalom!*" (*SoQ* 26: 19–32) and brings off a fine feminist reading of that complex work that lends appreciation and understanding. Equally keen and sensitive to the subtle complexities of the novel is Frederick R. Karl's study of "Race, History, and Technique in *Absalom, Absalom!*" (*Faulkner and Race*, pp. 209–21), which finds interesting buried commentaries in the text on matters of race. Margaret D. Bauers's "Hank Morgan Finds the Flaw in Thomas Sutpen's 'Design': Southern—American—Human" (*SCRev* 5:53–59) throws all sorts of interesting new lights on *Absalom, Absalom!* by bringing Twain's pragmatic Connecticut Yankee and builder of his own shattered dream into conjunction with Faulkner's, and the result reflects on the cultural resonances in both works. This is an imaginative idea, well developed.

vii. Individual Works, 1940–49

Barbara Monroe's "Reading Faulknerian Comedy: Humor and Honor in *The Hamlet*" (*SoQ* 26:33–56) is a thoroughgoing analysis of Faulkner's all-pervasive humor that takes several new tacks. In *The Hamlet* the characters use humor as a "rearguard action to contain creeping Snopesism and to maintain their honor. The Snopeses, in turn, parody honorable conduct by emulating their detractors." Also, Monroe finds that "the text is encoded with alternative readings that accommodate both male and female readers." Her discussion is rich and rewarding. "William Faulkner's *The Hamlet*: A Monument to Footprints" (*IFR* 15:58–62) is a reading of the novel in the light of the theories of Edward Said on authorial control of the literary text. It is an exercise in critical theory. Richard Parker speculates on the sexually suggestive origins of the name of one character in *The Hamlet* in "Two-way Texan: The Name, Symbols, and Function of Faulkner's Buck Hipps" (*NConL* 18:11–12), partly with tongue in cheek, I suspect.

Two essays begin with *The Hamlet* but move through the remainder of the Snopes trilogy, *The Town* and *The Mansion.* John E. Bassett provides an intelligent overview of the development and meanings of the Snopes family saga in "Yoknapatawpha Revised: Demystifying the Snopes" (*CollL* 15:136–52), with attention to changes in Faulkner's own attitude toward them. Keith Louise Fulton's main concern is with the daughter of Eula Snopes in "Linda Snopes Kohl: Faulkner's Radical Woman" (*MFS* 34:425–36), but places her in the broader context of Faulkner's attitudes toward women and finds her to be an extraordinarily admirable example of female power and endurance.

Form and Society in Modern Literature (No. Ill.), by Thomas C. Foster, is the result of the author's attempts to find a satisfactory way of dealing with Modernist literature, which he concludes requires coming to terms with history, society, and literary history, and viewing works of literature as "acts of confronting their culture." The chapter on *Go Down, Moses* is a prime exhibit, which demonstrates how deeply embedded that novel is in individual and collective Southern history. Marion Tangum, in "Rhetorical Clues to *Go Down, Moses*: Who Is Talking to Whom?" (*Heir and Prototype*, pp. 8–21), tries to read behind the language of the narration to the rhetorical intent of the speaker, Roth Edmonds, and finds it to be a good example of Bakhtin's "pure" dialogue. Dorys Crow Grover's "Isaac McCaslin and Roth's Mistress" (*Heir and Prototype*, pp. 22–32) considers Faulkner's treatment of Roth's half-caste mistress as a central issue in the novel.

William J. Sowder examines the young Isaac McCaslin as Faulkner's creative embodiment of his belief in man's ability to survive and as an example of Karl Jaspers's "*beau ideal* of the existential hero" in "Young Ike McCaslin: Travels in *Terra Incognita*" (*Heir and Prototype*, pp. 33–47). The Jaspers categories do seem to fit and explain Ike's actions and behavior. Robert Merrill makes one more effort to explain the poker game in "Was," which forms a part of *Go Down, Moses*, in "Faulknerian Sleight of Hand: The Poker Game in 'Was' " (*SSF* 25:31–40), to prove that Faulkner played loose and fast with the rules and probabilities of the game, partly for dramatic necessity but also because he became confused with the game he had set up. The argument is impressive, but you would have to be a poker player to know for sure. A less detailed explication of the situation is found in Webb Salmon's "Faulkner's *Go Down, Moses*" (*Expl* 46, iv:29–32). *Go Down, Moses, Intruder in the Dust*, and *Absalom, Absalom!* are all compared with selected works by black writers on the Afro-American experience by Craig Werner in "Minstrel Nightmares: Black Dreams of Faulkner's Dreams of Blacks" (*Faulkner and Race*, pp. 35–57). Werner believes that while "he rarely distorts observed facts, Faulkner frequently misperceives the underlying dynamic of Afro-American experience." The essay is both informative and provocative.

viii. Individual Works, 1950–62

The odd structure of *Requiem for a Nun* as novel and play, and its final importance in the Faulkner canon, continue to generate discussion. Karl Zender, in "*Requiem for a Nun* and the Uses of the Imagination" (*Faulkner and Race*, pp. 272–96), reads it as an effort on Faulkner's part to work through a time of creative blockage, and the character of Nancy Mannigoe is important in that regard because she "signifies the dream of a life free of the imagination—free, that is, of the need to exist in a mediated relation to either a past or a future condition of pure being." It is a success and enables Faulkner to move on to his later work. The essay is well written and the points well argued. John E. Bassett places Temple Drake in *Requiem* within the contexts of all the other female characters in his fiction, and the women in Faulkner's personal life, in "*Requiem for a Nun*: Revising Temple Drake" (*Heir and Prototype*, pp. 49–58). This throws considerable light on Temple and leads Bassett to agree with Zender that the work served as therapy for Faulkner: "Both its updating of Temple Drake and its historical narratives reveal central concerns for Faulkner at the time of his Nobel Prize, and prepare the ground for completion of the Snopes Trilogy." In "Imagination and the Rending of Time: The Reader and the Recreated Pasts in *Requiem for a Nun*" (*MissQ* 41:433–46), Marnie Parsons discovers an integrating unity in the work by studying the relationships between the past and the present in the narrative. Like the two essays discussed above, Parsons's also is an imaginative reading which should stimulate further discussion of a work whose problems are far from resolved.

In the one essay on *The Reivers*, "Faulkner's *Reivers*: How to Change the Joke without Slipping the Yoke" (*Faulkner and Race*, pp. 111–129), Walter Taylor charges Faulkner in his last novel with having created in Ned McCaslin a character who causes the entire novel to beam "the very loud political message that Jim Crow was not so bad." Like all the other essays on Faulkner and racism discussed here, however, this one is not likely to be the last or concluding thought on that thorny issue.

ix. The Stories

Except for the discussions above of "Was," which forms a part of *Go Down, Moses*, only that favorite story of anthologists and explicators received any attention. "The Chivalric Narrator of 'A Rose for Emily' " (*UMSE* 6:280–84) by Hal Blythe looks once again at the unnamed narrator and contends that he "possesses a dual vision of his subject that produces an ironic portrait of her [Miss Emily] as well as a surprising self-portrait." The narrator, we learn, is a troubadour in love with Emily himself and perhaps one of her scorned suitors. Some will feel that this does push things a tad far, but then everyone is inclined to do that with this fascinating *nouvelle fatale*. The answer to Peter L. Hays's question, "Who Is Faulkner's Emily?" (*SAF* 16:105–10), is Emily Dickinson. The evidence is not bad, so maybe so, but, then again, we can never know for sure. That continues to be the fun of Faulkner, after all.

Randolph-Macon College

10. Fitzgerald and Hemingway

Gerry Brenner

Not an elegant banquet of Fitzgerald-Hemingway scholarship this year. Items for Fitzgerald continue to dwindle, two books and a dozen articles making up this year's short list. The long list (some 80 items) falls to Hemingway's portion, with far more slender notes than substantial essays. And several critics worked up articles that showed little time in library stacks—as if Baker, Young, and Rovit were the only jolly trio who've worked Hemingway's texts. Nevertheless, no single work dominated the year's scholarship, as in previous years.

i. Text, Biography, and Bibliography

A meager two items fill minor gaps on Fitzgerald. In "Fitzgerald Explodes His Heroine" (*PULC* 49:158–72) James L. W. West III writes an informative introductory essay to an aborted short story, here printed for the first time, "A Full Life." West summarizes Fitzgerald's financial distress in early 1937, discusses his inability to continue writing convincing romantic fictions with spritely heroines, chronicles the difficulties he had in making a salable story out of the materials that became "A Full Life," and hypothesizes that the allegorical piece, which ends with the heroine's explosion, was a private gesture of his feelings about the kind of heroine he had drawn on for so much of his magazine fiction. A complementary essay is Matthew J. Bruccoli's "Where They Belong: The Acquisition of the F. Scott Fitzgerald Papers" (*PULC* 50:30–37), a chronicle of the nine-year rivalry between Julian P. Boyd, Princeton University librarian, and David A. Randall, head of Scribners' rare book department, to buy the Fitzgerald papers (manuscripts, typescripts, proofs, correspondence and memorabilia), which Boyd purchased in 1949 for a whopping $2,500.

The major textual event for Hemingway scholars was the publication by William Braasch Watson of "Hemingway's Spanish Civil War Dispatches" (*HN* 7, ii:4–92), a scrupulously edited collection of the 30 extant dispatches Hemingway wrote for the North American Newspaper Alliance (NANA) during his four stints in Spain between March 1937 and June 1938. Watson includes a detailed introduction to the entire set, maps, and editorial notes for each dispatch, acknowledging that most of the dispatches published here are not facsimiles but "diplomatic texts" with minor changes. Only a handful of the dispatches are of literary merit. But the collection as a whole records Hemingway's involvement in and commitment to the Loyalist cause, his keen sense of terrain and military logistics, and his knack of crafting cameos of war-afflicted humanity. To convey the vexations of publishing the dispatches, in "A Variorum Edition of Dispatch 19" (*HN* 7, ii:93–113) Watson assembles and explains the field notes, two drafts, cable, NANA release, *Boston Globe* printed version, and *New Republic* reprint of one of the best of the Spanish Civil War dispatches, the April 3, 1938, "Flight of Refugees." Charles M. Oliver joins Watson in printing with a brief introduction "In Defense of His Reporting from Spain: A Hemingway Letter to NANA" (*HN* 7, ii: 119–21), Hemingway's letter to John Wheeler, general manager of NANA. Claiming $250 still owed him, he itemizes the hazards, time, and money it cost him to cover the stories asked from him during his May 1938 trip into Spain. In " 'Humanity Will Not Survive This!': The *Pravda* Article" (*HN* 7, ii:114–18) Watson prints the text of, and offers several reasons Hemingway would have agreed to write, the brief but eloquent propaganda piece against the Fascists' "murderous"—because indiscriminate—bombing of innocent civilians in cities and towns during the Spanish Civil War.

Three additional items complete the Spanish Civil War materials. Jeffrey Shulman's "Hemingway's Observations on the Spanish Civil War: Unpublished State Department Reports" (*HN* 7, ii:147–51) introduces two summarized conversations American Ambassador to France Claude G. Bowers had with Hemingway. In his report of early April 1938 Bowers tells of Hemingway's recommendations for evacuating American patients, doctors, and nurses in case of a Loyalist collapse; his mid-May report tells of Hemingway's optimism for Loyalist resistance and of various Loyalist commanders. Richard Allan Davison, in "The Publication of Hemingway's *The Spanish Earth*: An Untold Story" (*HN* 7, ii:122–30), comments on and reprints materials relating to the publication of Hemingway's script for the film "documentary" he and Joris Ivens collaborated on. The materials include telegrams, letters, the introduction by the young editor, Jasper Wood, and the 1938 Cleveland newspaper account of the script's publication. A biographical footnote to Hemingway's Spanish Civil War involvement is Townsend Ludington's "Spain and the Hemingway–Dos Passos Relationship" (*AL* 60:270–73). He responds to recent essays by Scott Donaldson and Donald Pizer on the two authors, rejecting their view that the execution of Dos Passos's friend José Robles triggered the Hemingway–Dos Passos split. Ludington insists that the execution merely ignited their long-smoldering rivalry over who better knew Spain and who correctly viewed bullfighting. Ludington emphasizes that Dos Passos knew Spain well—for he lived and traveled there in 1916 and 1917, again in 1919 and 1920—and prints a 1919 Dos Passos letter that sardonically describes bullfighting's stupidity and splendor.

Part of the FBI file on Hemingway is now available, thanks to Russell J. Boone, editor, and Michael S. Reynold's introduction, "Hemingway: The FBI File" (*Scream* [Raleigh, N.C.] [1987]3, ii:2–21). And Richard Allan Davison's "The Cohn/Hemingway Collection" (*Collections,* [Univ. of Del. Lib. Associates] [1987]2:64–82) lists the items in the University of Delaware Library's Lewis Henry Cohn/Hemingway Collection. Davison prints excerpts and discusses a letter from one of Hemingway's fellow *Kansas City Star* reporters, comments on and reproduces a page from "Up in Michigan," and reprints a 1930 letter to Cohn, Hemingway expressing his aesthetic standards and reasons for not writing and signing an introduction to a limited edition of his first bibliographer's bibliography on him.

Four minor biographical items warrant mention. N. Ann Doyle and Neal B. Houston, in "Hemingway: A Final Meeting with Adriana Ivancich at Nervi" (*HN* 8, i:58–61), report that contrary to previous biographical accounts the correspondence between Hemingway and Adriana was not broken off between 1951 and 1952, "no emotional estrangement" existed between them, and their final meeting took place in June 1954 near Genoa, following Ernest and Mary's return from Spain en route to Cuba. In "Comments on James Brasch's 'José Luis Herrera Sotolongo Remembers Ernest Hemingway'" [*JML* (1986) 13:185–210] (*JML* [1987] 14:147–49) Aden Hayes scolds Brasch, not only for a number of misspellings and accent marks, unidiomatic translations, and various biographical and historical facts, but also for claiming that Hemingway supported Castro's Cuban revolution. James D. Brasch responds in "Professor Brasch's Reply" (*JML* [1987] 14:149–50), expressing gratitude for corrections but contesting Hayes's view of Hemingway's relationship to Castro's revolution and the factual background of the 26th of July Movement. Finally, in "The Way It Wasn't: Hemingway and Gellhorn in Burma" (*HN* 8, i:40–41) Robert A. Martin reprints a March 1988 Martha Gellhorn letter that ridicules her alleged disparagement of Hemingway and some "facts" reported in H. L. Woods's memoir, *Wings over Asia.* Now if *her* version of the facts can be verified . . . .

Megan Floyd Desnoyers, curator of the Hemingway Collection at Boston's John F. Kennedy Library, shares "News from the Hemingway Collection" (*HN* 7, ii:166–68), defining photocopying policy, itemizing the 457 pages of Hadley Richardson Hemingway Mowrer correspondence now available to researchers, and noting the cataloging of the 832-page manuscript of *African Journal,* soon available to scholars. And Al DeFazio assembles the "Hemingway Bibliography" (*HN* 8, i:68–77).

ii. Influences, Sources, and Parallels

Three studies probe for sources to Fitzgerald's two best novels, and one study argues Fitzgerald's influence on a contemporary novelist. In "Dick Diver and the Priest of Nemi" (*JML* [1987] 14:65–81) Erwin R. Steinberg establishes the widespread knowledge of Frazer's *Golden Bough* and Weston's *From Ritual to Romance,* then argues the likelihood of Fitzgerald's familiarity with them and with literary works derivative of them. Citing numerous passages from *Tender Is the Night,* Steinberg points out echoes of and parallels to the Grail Legend and the myths of Adonis and Diana: Nicole resembles Diana and Aphrodite, Tommy Barban the Quester of the Grail Legend, and Dick Diver the Fisher King, Adonis, and the Priest of Nemi. Companion to such lucubration is Jerome Mandel's labored "The Grotesque Rose: Medieval Romance and *The Great Gatsby*" (*MFS* 34:541–58). Drawing on a battery of medieval romances, he finds parallels in Fitzgerald's novel: Lord-King Tom Buchanan, Queen Daisy, Merlin Wolfsheim, Knight Nick, Warrior-Lover Gatsby, Gardens, Courts West and East Egg, and Assorted Romance Details. In "*Nostromo* and *The Great Gatsby*" (*EA* 41:405–17) Peter L. Hays and Pamela Demory itemize correspondences to argue the influence of Conrad's novel on Fitzgerald's, both studying the "taint" brought by "a materialism that infects the entire country of each novel." For techniques of naming, use of colors, thematics, and parallel characters Hays and Demory sift the two novels, finding neither Gould nor Carraway aware of his "complicity with the immorality around him." After a long, derivative rehash of Fitzgerald's motif of emotional bankruptcy in essays and fiction, Mary S. Vásquez, in "Tusquets, Fitzgerald and the Redemptive Power of Love" (*Letras Femininas* 14, i–ii:10–21), turns to three novels by Catalan author Esther Tusquets, finding in them a preoccupation with inevitable—but potentially reversible—failed love relationships that have "a fragile hope-within-despair that Fitzgerald's vision did not contain."

An interesting source study is Linda Patterson Miller's "'Nourished at the Same Source': Ernest Hemingway and Gerald Murphy" (*Mosaic* 21, i:79–91). Her third essay on the Hemingway-Murphy relationship, here Miller analyzes Murphy's artistic stages and compares his Precisionist-Cubist painting *Watch* to Hemingway's "Hills Like White Elephants." The two works, she contends, share a sense of "containment and spaciousness, flatness and depth," represent a scene "in miniature detail but in giant scale," and employ negative space. Miller also remarks Hemingway's alliance with the Precisionists "when he shows people trying to respond to life in a machine-like, orderly way." But Miller's essay is overshadowed by Cecelia Tichi's *Shifting Gears: Technology, Literature, Culture in Modernist America* (No. Car., 1987), a study of the machine world of gear-and-girder technology and "how its assumptions affected diverse areas of American culture, from skyscrapers and autos to popular media and the arts of the written word." In a chapter primarily focusing on Hemingway, "Opportunity: Imagination Ex Machina II" (pp. 216–29), Tichi argues that Hemingway "brought engineering values into prose style," its economy exemplifying "the engineer's aesthetic of functionalism and formal efficiency." Comparing him to the American painter Thomas Eakins and to Frank Lloyd Wright, who shared Hemingway's distaste for nonfunctional ornament, Tichi emphasizes Hemingway's technological interest in the mechanics and structural planes of events he describes, be it Marjorie setting fishing lines in "The End of Something," Nick pitching his tent in "Big Two-Hearted River," or Jake packing trout in ferns in *The Sun Also Rises.* Whether writing of hunting, fishing, bullfighting or boxing, Hemingway exhibits "a machine aesthetic, even when machines or structures play no part in the fiction." "He is full of nostalgia for a preindustrial, 'natural' environment, but his sentences are irrevocably of another, a gear-and-girder, world," showing that Hemingway's style formally "marks the achievement of machine values in imaginative literature."

Three unpersuasive source studies link Hemingway to the "ancients." Mary Ann C. Curtis, in "*The Sun Also Rises*: Its Relation to *The Song of Roland*" (*AL* 60:274–80), establishes Hemingway's familiarity with the French epic but makes farfetched comparisons to show that he had *Roland* "in mind in choosing some of his details, and in ordering the sequence of events in his novel." In "Rounds with Mr. Cervantes: *Don Quijote* and *For Whom the Bell Tolls*" (*OL* 43, ii:108–28) Kevin S. Larsen similarly unearths "numerous parallels between themes, motifs, characters, and even incidents in the two books, indicating not only how closely [Hemingway] had read *Don Quijote*, but also his attempt at systematic one-upsmanship, his almost consuming desire in his 'novel of Spain' to out-Cervantes Mr. C." Larsen exhumes similarities between the two novels' casts and digs up echoing conflicts (chivalric ideals versus modern reason), debates (arms versus letters), and archaic language. Larsen acknowledges that *Bell* lacks *Quijote*'s comedic ironies, but he insists upon "a certain craziness about Robert Jordan, whose idealistic monomania parallels that of Don Quijote." Joseph J. Liggera, "Rereading *Across the River and into the Trees*" (*WVUPP* 34:94–101), worries out the allusions to *Othello*, claiming that Hemingway uses Shakespeare "to show us what a real Othello and Desdemona might be like if we dared look beyond idealized dramatic models."

A half-dozen articles link Hemingway to immediately preceding or contemporary artists. In "*Islands in the Stream* as Hemingway's *Laocöon*" (*ConL* 29, i:26–48) Evelyn J. Hinz and John J. Teunissen discuss Lessing's classic *Laocöon* to argue Hemingway's sustained focus on aesthetic issues in *Islands*, a fictional exploration of "the respective boundaries of the narrative and pictorial arts." They find allusion in the text to nude scenes by Pascin and Cézanne as well as to Cassilly Adams's epic-sized, widely distributed 1886 lithograph "Custer's Last Stand." Sniffing for art allusions everywhere, Hinz and Teunissen seize upon references to Bimini's constable to compare John Constable's paintings and ethic to Thomas Hudson's limited ambitions and refusal to paint Mr. Bobby's requested epics. David Kerner, in "The Origins of Hemingway's Anti-Metronomic Dialogue" (*AEB* n.s. 2, i:12–28), scours O. Henry, Jack London, 1917–18 copy from the *Kansas City Star*, and current examples from the *New York Times* to show that Hemingway's occasional use of end-quoted and newly indented dialogue from the same speaker was and is an honored practice long used to imply an inferable omission or a discontinuity in tone, time, rhythm, event, or addressee. This practice shows that the juxtaposed, unattributed, separate speeches of a single character—the old waiter's in "A Clean Well-Lighted Place" or Frazer's in "The Gambler, the Nun, and the Radio"—were conventional and intentional and should not have been, scolds Kerner, corrupted by Scribners' editors' "corrections."

In "Hemingway, Steinbeck, and the Art of the Short Story" (*StQ* 21, iii–iv:73–84) Richard Allan Davison discusses the men's rivalry as fiction writers, then compares Hemingway's "Big Two-Hearted River" with Steinbeck's "Flight," and "Cat in the Rain" with "Chrysanthemums," concluding that "whether they are writing about men seeking ritualistic escape through the complex forces of nature (as with Nick and Pepé) or women trying to cope with a world of sexual ambivalence (as with the American girl/wife and Elisa), both Hemingway and Steinbeck use their rhythms, onomatopoeic sounds, repetition of key words, and sensuous language to forge a prose that will survive." In "Ivan Turgenev, Sherwood Anderson, and Ernest Hemingway: *The Torrents of Spring* All" (*NewComp* 5:136–49) Richard Chapple trots through routine comparisons of Turgenev and Hemingway's novels of the same titles and Anderson's *Dark Laughter*, pointing out parallel styles and character types: weak males, abandoned wives, seductresses, and "natural" foils. To Pascale Bécel, in "Hemingway and Brancusi: A Relationship Between Writer and Sculptor?" (*WVUPP* 34:83–93), both artists attempt to purify and simplify forms, achieve a reduced "vocabulary," reject abstractions, and share "an interest in ever purer, more reduced means of expression to which they nonetheless give distinctive features by attributing to their subject an environment which functions as an understatement." Kenneth G. Johnston writes an encyclopedia entry on Tristran Tzara and Dadaism in "The Silly Wasters: Tzara and the Poet in 'The Snows of Kilimanjaro' " (*HN* 8, i:50–57). But from manuscript he identifies Malcolm Cowley as the American poet with whom Tzara talks in a flashback section of "Snows," and he contrasts Hemingway, the serious young artist, to Tzara, the brash and extravagantly provocative writer of wasted talent.

A minor source duet ends this section. In "The Doctor and the Doctor's Friend: Logan Clendening and Ernest Hemingway" (*HN* 8, i:37–39) Paul Smith notes that in the last paragraph of *The Human Body* (1928) by Clendening—who received and shared with Hemingway the letter that became "One Reader Writes"—are terms and sentiments about death that strongly resemble a variant conclusion to Hemingway's *Farewell to Arms.* And Robert D. Madison, in "Hemingway and Selous: A Source for 'Snows?' " (*HN* 8, i:62–63), suggests that Hemingway may have gotten the plot ingredients of a man with blood poisoning in his leg and prowling hyenas around an African safari camp, as well as the title for his Kilimanjaro story, from J. G. Millais's biography, *Life of Frederick Courtenay Selous*, a well-known African white hunter whose *A Hunter's Wanderings in Africa* Hemingway owned.

iii. Criticism

***a.* Full-Length Studies.** *Fiction, Film, and F. Scott Fitzgerald* (Loyola, 1986) by Gene D. Phillips, S.J., is a companion to his 1980 *Hemingway and Film.* Assembling biography, plot summary, film history, photographs, a filmography, and commentary on Fitzgerald's Hollywood screenwriting experience, Phillips also discusses the films made from Fitzgerald's fiction. Much here is already known—Fitzgerald's failure as a screenwriter, his dislike of collaboration, his fiasco on scripting *Winter Carnival* with Budd Schulberg. And Phillips's commentary is often negligible: reviewers' opinions, quibbles over the merits of various film endings, alterations to the texts, and comments on and by such film figures as Elliott Nugent, David O. Selznick, Henry King, Elia Kazan and Francis Ford Coppola. This makes for some interesting reading, but it lacks the acumen of Wheeler Dixon's critical close-ups of selected Fitzgerald scripts and analysis of Fitzgerald's acquisition of film techniques for *The Last Tycoon* in his *The Cinematic Vision of F. Scott Fitzgerald* (1986).

Sarah Beebe Fryer's *Fitzgerald's New Women: Harbingers of Change* (UMI) is a good study of the women in Fitzgerald's five novels, sympathetically analyzing the recurrent pressure to be both dependent, submissive wives and independent, assertive women. Backgrounding Fitzgerald's male characters, Fryer shows Fitzgerald's alertness to his heroines' ill-sorted blending of confidence and uncertainty, autonomy and vulnerability. She cogently refutes the facile dichotomizing of Fitzgerald's women as frivolous goddesses or impudently insincere bitches and shows their complexity and difficult conflicts, for example, Gloria Patch's recognition in *Beautiful and Damned* of her need to free herself from—and to help—her dissolute husband. Good chapters focus on the "plight" of Daisy Buchanan and compare *Tender* and Zelda's *Save Me the Waltz*. But best is Fryer's chapter on *Tender*. Convincingly she argues Dick Diver's "fundamental unsuitability to be practicing psychiatry," citing casebook studies and psychoanalytic texts to explain both his inept diagnosis of Nicole as a schizophrenic (she's a hysteric) and the symbolic import of Nicole's victimization by a patriarchal world. Oddly, while Fryer credits Fitzgerald with charting the "progression of the social and sexual revolution of the 1920s," she faults him for doing so "inadvertently," as if he were blind to the feminist subtexts in his novels. The book's major defect is the omission of a chapter on heroines from the stories.

Of the three books on Hemingway, Susan F. Beegel's *Hemingway's Craft of Omission: Four Manuscript Samples* (UMI) is the most interesting. She examines deleted manuscript material from "Fifty Grand," the manuscript coda to "A Natural History of the Dead," the deleted introduction to the last chapter of *Death in the Afternoon*, and the changes in successive drafts of "After the Storm." On "Fifty Grand" Beegel comments on the story's first three manuscript pages, which Fitzgerald recommended cutting, and thematically ties in the cut material to the story, "an ironic tale of courage and professional integrity at the service of sordid ends." Along with printing some of the deleted manuscript, Beegel discusses the publication history of the story and Hemingway's feelings that Fitzgerald tried to get him to prostitute his genius for money. On "Natural History" Beegel gives background history and shows that the "rather vicious satire of Humanist literary critics" counterattacks the *Bookman*'s humanist reviewers of *Farewell to Arms*. Her paragraph-at-a-time printing of and commentary on the discarded coda shows its extension of the story's imagery and commends Hemingway's "literary judgment and self-discipline" in omitting "the backstage machinery of personal experience that generated the fiction." Least interesting is Beegel's reprinting and analysis of the nine paragraphs that originally began the final chapter of *Death in the Afternoon*, material in which Hemingway remarks his experiences of disappointment and loss and his antagonism to Waldo Frank. Best is her chapter tracing the composition of "After the Storm" through its several versions and exhuming the story's fascinating historical background, the sinking of the *Valbanera* in a 1919 hurricane. Beegel reconstructs the story's composition, from a double-voiced frame-tale with hypocritical and detached narrators to imagined additions and an altered protagonist.

Hemingway and Nineteenth-Century Aestheticism (UMI) has its plodding segments, John Gaggin methodically outlining and then amplifying Hemingway's relationship to three salient features of the 19th-century aesthetic movement: aesthetic detachment, art-for-art's sake, and decadence. Nevertheless, Gaggin valuably documents the aesthetic inheritance to which Hemingway was considerably indebted. While this debt has been previously remarked, Gaggin persuasively shows that features often regarded as unique to Hemingway (valorization of professionalism, conflicting advocacy of aestheticism and activism, celebration of the formalism of athletic events) echo or extend values articulated and exemplified by aesthetic predecessors. Gaggin's weakest chapter, "Hemingway and Aesthetic Detachment," facilely equates Hemingway characters' disengaged stances or withdrawals to esthetes' contemplative stances. But the chapter on "Hemingway and Decadence" is excellent. Gaggin both elaborates on the history and antithetical meanings of decadence and engages with Hemingway texts to show that their fixation on deterioration and decay also reveals Hemingway's preoccupation with the androgyny and homosexuality so central to fin de siècle artists. Gaggin even reexamines Hemingway's male and female characters, finding a lack of "stereotypically masculine features" in the men and androgynous features in the women. Astutely noting Hemingway's "simultaneous resistance against and attraction to other themes of decadence," Gaggin concludes that "his characters are misplaced decadents, faced with the same hopeless challenges as their literary forebears but denied many of the compensatory charms of living out the final sweet moments of a dying culture."

Michael S. Reynolds's *The Sun Also Rises: A Novel of the Twenties* (Twayne) gives the novel a well-written overview, uncluttered with critical jargon or esoteric arguments and focused on central issues that have become part of the novel's critical heritage. Along with brief, format-required chapters on the novel's historical context and its critical reception, Reynolds divides his reading into five chapters that tend toward some repetition, discussions of money, work, religion in "Values," for example, overlapping discussions of image patterns and repeated motifs Reynolds remarks on in "Structural Unity." Drawing on manuscript materials for observations on the novel's composition, Reynolds acknowledges Hemingway's erratic planning of its structure, amply analyzes its ironies, and correctly sees it as "Jake's confession of guilt, his admission to the corruption of what values he had left to him." Yet Reynolds not only lets Jake off the hook—claiming that he "unconsciously misleads his reader" and insisting that he "is not an untrustworthy narrator"—but also denies change or potential for change to Brett. In his best chapter, "Signs, Motifs, and Themes," Reynolds explains many topical allusions, gives an Einsteinian answer to the novel's muddled chronology, and probes the $600 Jake has withdrawn from his bank account, first to show that profligate Jake is "spending more money than a single man in Paris needs to spend" and then to argue his thesis, that the novel documents "the careless attitude of the generation that carelessly spent its way into the whirlpool."

***b.* General Essays.** Of two broad essays on Hemingway (Fitzgerald got none), David Bromwich's "Hemingway's Valor"—despite the trite title—(*GrandS* 7:185–217) commands first mention. This intelligent, wide-ranging essay risks getting lost among book reviews, for it is part review of Lynn's biography and part analysis of *The Garden of Eden*, whose plot he compares briefly to Kipling's *The Light That Failed.* The essay also discusses Hemingway's aesthetic preoccupations and astutely compares Hemingway to Gertrude Stein and Henry James. Probing for the source of Hemingway's "hidden power" as an artist, Bromwich finds it inhering in his need "to serve as the witness of a privation. Whenever this pattern asserts control of his imagination, he is close to nihilism—that is, a liberty of action founded on a want of belief. There remains the anomaly that, for him, the action once taken, must be justified by a principle of morality." From this, Bromwich concludes that Hemingway "is probably the most striking instance in modern art of a man for whom the motives and the justification of action have suffered this kind of permanent division from each other." Robert Merrill's "EXTRA: Demoting Hemingway: Feminist Criticism and the Canon" (*AL* 60:255–68) takes exception to *AL*'s March 1987 "EXTRA," in which Lawrence Buell argues the virtues of feminist revisionism for American literature and parenthetically suggests that the potential for feminism to "foment reorderings in the pre-feminist canon" could bring about the beneficial demotion of Hemingway. Merrill points out the ideological shortcomings of Judith Fetterley's "resisting reader" essay on *A Farewell to Arms* and the erroneous cultural coding in Robert Scholes's reading of "Mr. and Mrs. Elliot" in his *Textual Power*. From these representative instances Merrill argues the pitfalls awaiting feminist revisionism—the elevation of texts on the basis of ideological codes and cultural biases and the demotion of texts of aesthetic excellence.

Three general essays of limited scope and achievement include two chapters from Bert Bender's *Sea-Brothers: The Tradition of American Sea Fiction from Moby-Dick to the Present* (Penn.), Peter L. Hays's "Hemingway, Nick Adams, and David Bourne: Sons and Writers" (*ArQ* 44, ii:28–38), and Howard L. Hannum's "The Case of Doctor Henry Adams" (*ArQ* 44, ii:39–57). In "Hemingway: Coming to the Stream" (pp. 167–75) Bender compares Hemingway with Thoreau, finding that although Hemingway grasped "a very dark image of life—violent and voracious—in the essential biological exchange with death," he also "had the consolation of having sucked the very marrow of life," allowing him both to insist "that a sufficient basis for affirming life exists in its 'genuine meanness,' " and to accept and celebrate "the bloody brotherhood in which all life is joined." In "Hemingway's Sea Men" (pp. 175–98) Bender finds a progression in Hemingway's three characters. Harry Morgan's Jack London-like "raw, animal vitality"—though at odds with an Eliot-derived *Waste Land* setting of impotence, hollowness, and artificiality—enables him to survive and celebrate the meanness of the life struggle. Thomas Hudson, Bender contends, undergoes spiritual regeneration because of his "awareness of his own 'meanness' as a participant in the complex violence of tenderness and love." Of Hemingway's "willful and aggressive parable," *The Old Man and the Sea*, Bender calls Santiago Ismael's sea-brother and finds him resisting full participation in "the voracious process of life," even though he ritually eats a piece of the marlin to affirm "his place in the violent brotherhood of life." Hays compares resemblances among Dr. Hemingway, Dr. Adams of the Nick Adams stories, and David Bourne's father. Despite Bourne's serious drinking, womanizing, and overt violence, Hays sees all three figures as unfortunate, law-stretching or law-breaking men with whom their sons have an ambivalent relationship. And Hannum methodically traces Hemingway's Dr. Adams through the Nick Adams stories, setting out to redeem his degraded-by-critics character, but acknowledging that his attempt "becomes the unworkable task of restoring balance to a scale that constantly tips against him."

c. Essays on Specific Works: Fitzgerald. Of the handful of items on Fitzgerald's works, *The Great Gatsby* garnered three. The one of merit is Joyce A. Rowe's "Closing the Circle: *The Great Gatsby*"

(*Equivocal Endings*, pp. 100–26, 151–57). Rowe reads the novel as a historically self-conscious consideration "of the contradictory nature of American idealism and the social cost of its attempt to subdue the facts of history to the faith of myth." Discussing Gatsby's vision of "aestheticized materialism" within an Emersonian framework, Rowe finds that Gatsby's self-deluding sham of heroic individualism thrives on guileless exploitation, ignores dualities, denies conflict, and maintains an "unblinking indifference to the ugly and criminal aspects of his own nature [, which] serves as the psychic counterpart to America's historical innocence about the sources of its own wealth." Remarking Gatsby's "imperial fantasy," Rowe finds "his amorally dissociated nature" indifferent to the consequences of his actions, and she contrasts Nick to Conrad's Marlowe of *Heart of Darkness*, Marlowe capable of trenchant epistemological questions and self-discovery, Nick morally shallow and blind to his repressed identification with Gatsby. Oddly, Rowe discounts facilely the compelling conclusion that Nick is a flawed moral guide. Nevertheless, she sees that in the novel "community as an informing social ideal exists only by negation," that attuned to social decency though Nick is, his awareness generates no positive vision, Nick remaining "committed to a self-sufficient solitude that mirrors Gatsby's own."

Andrew Dillon's "*The Great Gatsby*: The Vitality of Illusion" (*ArQ* 44, i:49–61) is an overwritten hymn to the gift of hope that Gatsby, "that knightlike vector of longing," represents to Nick, whom that gift has healed, enabling the once-lonely Nick to write his complex record, "a celebration, a Protestant's mass for the dead, of the vitality-bearer Gatsby, who has left both Nick and the reader little bits of his sacred energy." Dillon acknowledges the religious and Oedipal elements of Gatsby's character but reads Nick, "that balanced and honest self we hope we are," as hagiographer, ignoring tendentiousness in Nick's self-serving narrative. Edward J. Piacentino, "The Fatal Number '5' in *The Great Gatsby*" (*SDR* 26, iii:138–49), hunts down the 19 uses of the number five, finding that while Fitzgerald avoids assigning it traditional numerological meanings, his uses have "ominous and sinister implications," for they occur "most often in scenes and situations that delineate disillusioned aspirations and thwarted dreams, corruption and carelessness, and misfortune and violence."

Fitzgerald's last two novels received minor attention. Joanna E. Rapf, in "*The Last Tycoon* or 'A Nickel for the Movies'" (*LFQ* 16, ii:76–81), criticizes departures from the unfinished novel in the 1976 Sam Spiegel/Elia Kazan/Harold Pinter film: elimination of Cecilia Brady's narrative voice, overemphasis on a dark vision, and sense of defeat. Rapf also draws on her father's memories of experiences with Fitzgerald, claiming that conversations with Maurice Rapf, son of a vice-president at MGM and scriptwriter with Fitzgerald at Twentieth-Century Fox's Writers' Bungalow, led Fitzgerald to bring Stahr and Brimmer together at the Brady house in the novel. Udo Nattermann's "Nicole Diver's Monologue: A Close Examination of a Key Segment" (*MSE* [1986] 10:213–28) studies Nicole's 17-paragraph, 1,500-word, stream-of-consciousness monologue, disclosing its monetary and psychological subtlety, its phonological lyricism and structural significance, its archeological and thematic orientation, and its "sensitive and perceptive rendering of Nicole's inner condition," showing that the novel has characteristics of a psychological novel.

Robert Roulston's pair of essays on Fitzgerald's short fiction were all the attention the stories got this year. In "Fitzgerald's 'May Day': The Uses of Irresponsibility" (*MFS* 34:207–15) he discusses the story's flaws and achievements, both due to the discordant yoking of conventional plot contrivances and character traits found in Fitzgerald's early *Saturday Evening Post* stories to avant-garde themes and less-popular strategies favored by Mencken's *The Smart Set*. Roulston compares "May Day" to other early Fitzgerald stories and notes its naturalism and satire, "banality and vitality," "relentless cynicism," braidings of disparate narrative and modernistic angularities, and "lack of synthesis [, which] is part of the message." Like a "film run at high speed," the story "becomes a frenzied film clip of the birth of the Jazz Age," but is no "orgy of nihilism," despite Fitzgerald's "disgust directed at patricians and paupers, past and future, humanity and himself." In "Rummaging through F. Scott Fitzgerald's 'Trash': Early Stories in *The Saturday Evening Post*" (*JPC* 21, iv:151–63), Roulston rehashes the plots, background, and biographical sources of four stories Fitzgerald denigrated, commenting on the clichéd shortcomings of three stories—"Head and Shoulders," "Myra Meets His Family," and "The Camel's Back"—but justly admiring "Bernice Bobs Her Hair," finding in it "premonitions of Fitzgerald's best works."

***d.* Essays on Specific Works: Hemingway.** Seven essays shone low-wattage light on *The Sun Also Rises*. Linda W. Wagner-Martin, in

"Hemingway's Search for Heroes, Once Again" (*ArQ* 44, ii:58–68), strains the text first to find parallels between the biblical Jacob and Jake Barnes, then to establish comparisons between *The Song of Roland*'s titular hero and Jake. The literary analogues serve Wagner-Martin's efforts both at foregrounding Jake as a deeply religious man and at emphasizing the novel's conflict between religious (Jake, Romero) and nonreligious characters (Mike, Cohn, and Brett, the "alternative icon"). In "*The Sun Also Rises*: Good Manners Make Good Art" (*HN* 8, i:42–49) Lee Thorn finds that the "unrelieved litany of Cohn's unforgivable social sins is the connective tissue that runs throughout the novel." Equally unrelieved are Thorn's assertions that the novel's scenes and characters are preoccupied with etiquette, graceful behavior, manners, and social sensitivity, all of which presumably establish not only Hemingway's code and aesthetic, but also the novel's freedom from moral issues. Permit an unmannerly question, gentle reader: are Jake's mean-spirited behavior in Madrid and Brett's feeling good "deciding not to be a bitch" without moral dimension? "Love and Friendship/Man and Woman in *The Sun Also Rises*" (*ArQ* 44, ii:76–97) finds Sibbie O'Sullivan assembling some historical information on the New Woman, then arguing that in Brett Ashley Hemingway created "woman as Friend," not the Great American Bitch. This "story about the cautious belief in the survival of the two most basic components of any human relationship: love and friendship" centers on the friendship between "the New Woman and the shattered veteran," one based on "the honest assessment of each other's failings." This enables their reunion in Madrid, O'Sullivan unconvincingly writes, to exhibit the tenderness and caring necessary to mend their friendship's unraveled seams. In "The Importance of Count Mippipopolous: Creating the Code Hero" (*ArQ* 44, ii:69–75) Robert E. Fleming analyzes the ambiguity in Hemingway's first presentations of the Count's character, then argues his role as one of Hemingway's earliest code heroes, a man who likes quiet, insists on "getting good value for his money," is serene in watching others' frantic lives, and "maintains his self-respect, not allowing Brett to manipulate him as she does most of the men in her life."

Wolfgang E. H. Rudat unleashed three readings of *The Sun Also Rises*. In "Mike Campbell and 'These Literary Chaps': Palimpsestic Narrative in *The Sun Also Rises*" (*SNNTS* 20:302–15) Rudat infers from Brett's "radiance" on the morning after her first night with Romero that he's given her the sexual fulfillment she's long been without, that lack explaining her previous nymphomaniacal behavior. That observation somehow connects with Mike's sexual inadequacy and his role as a parodic Falstaff, Rudat finding two allusions to Falstaff in the text. In "He 'Just Lay There': Bill Gorton as Wounded Preacher in *The Sun Also Rises*" (*WascanaR* 23, i:22–30) Rudat sifts the Burguete banter between Jake and Bill to discover that their discussion of being unable to pedal an airplane reveals Bill's inability to "peddle" his genitals. A pedagogue but not a pederast, Bill is further exposed as impotent in some double entendre Rudat uncovers. In "Hemingway's Jake and Milton's Adam: Sexual Envy and Vicariousness in *The Sun Also Rises*" (*JEP* 9, i–ii:109–119) Rudat collapses several episodes to see Brett attempting psychological castration on Jake in the novel's closing scene and to hear Jake alluding to *Paradise Lost* when he throws his "misogynistic temper tantrum" against Brett earlier in the novel. Rudat unmasks Jake as a sadomasochist who eventually "exorcizes the need for *any* vicarious participation in other men's sexual affairs and becomes his own man when he fends off his own Eve's attempt to un-adam him also spiritually-psychologically."

Of three essays on *For Whom the Bell Tolls*, James L. Kastely's "Toward a Politically Responsible Ethical Criticism: Narrative in *The Political Unconscious* and *For Whom the Bell Tolls*" (*Style* 22: 535–58) is the important one, more for its critique of the shortcomings of Fredric Jameson's *The Political Unconscious* (the larger half of the essay) than for its analysis of the ethical issues that thwart critics who wish to pluck their political agenda from Hemingway's Spanish Civil War novel. Kastely musses up the procrustean bed of Jameson's schematic and hieratic theorizing, privileging as it does a single interpretive Marxist code. Kastely explains the necessity and legitimacy of ethical criticism that "makes ethical choice not the discovery of the appropriate rule, but the assumption of responsibility for calling a rule right." Turning to *For Whom the Bell Tolls*, Kastely explains that Robert Jordan's experiences point up the ethical responsibilities inherent in any political action, for while Jordan wishes to honor his political duties and specific mission, he learns that the practical realities of his duty impinge upon the guerrilla band: because his political acts have consequences for the people he has come among, he must also honor his ethical imperatives to them. Urging interpretive pluralism and ethical criticism that challenges Jameson, Kastely turns from *Bell Tolls* too soon, ignoring Jordan's cavalier dismissal of Maria's ethical claims upon him.

In "Knowledge as Power: Robert Jordan as Intellectual Hero" (*HN* 7, ii:131–46) Erik Nakjavani draws on Marx and Foucault's ideas for an abstract discussion of the relationship between knowledge and power, only to claim Jordan a "militant intellectual" who possesses or acquires various forms of knowledge—academic, experiential, ideological, and supernatural. As for Arturo Barea's 1941 criticism of a deep fissure in Hemingway's knowledge of Spain and its language—criticism that necessarily calls into question Jordan's intelligence as well—Nakjavani lamely asserts that Jordan is "impregnable to such criticism" and brushes away the issue with the observation that fictive reality is not Reality. The weakest of the essays on Hemingway's 1940 novel is Erik Arne Hansen's lengthy "Ernest Hemingway's The Fall of Troy in Spain" (*Dolphin* 16:54–87), a panoramic but pedestrian and index-carded discussion of the biographical, literary, and historical determinants of the novel, "a modern palmer's hymn to love, trust, and brotherhood."

Of three essays on Hemingway's recent posthumous novel, Ben Stoltzfus's "A Post-Lacanian Reading of Hemingway's *The Garden of Eden*" (*AJS* [1987] 5:381–95) warrants regard. After a Lacanian primer, Stoltzfus unwraps the latent content of the novel, connecting David Bourne's African story to the Riviera events and the ménage à trois, the story reenacting a primal scene that not only images Catherine's castration and incompleteness but also clarifies her role as neurotic woman and would-be father. And Stoltzfus triangulates semiotic diagrams to reveal Marita as a mother figure, she and David forming "the original and indissoluble mother and child" who achieve an incestuous "pre-Adamic state of fulfillment and bliss." Malcolm O. Magaw, in "The Fusion of History and Immediacy: Hemingway's Artist-Hero in *The Garden of Eden*" (*ClioI* [1987] 17, i:21–36) compares Robert Bourne to Jake Barnes and assigns Bourne greater importance because the war has neither desensitized him nor incapacitated him from writing historical fiction, be it the 1905 Tanganyika native rebellion or his aviation experiences in World War II. Claiming that Bourne balances "Eden, where imagination is fused with passion, and History, where intellection and design are infused with gravity," Magaw draws little from the actual text, making more of Bourne's historically indebted creativity than the novel readily allows. In "Life as Fiction: The Lure of Hemingway's *Garden*" (*SoR* 24:451–61) J. Gerald Kennedy is concerned with the link between Hemingway as fictionist and as autobiographer. Quoting from the unpublished manuscripts, he reads the published novel as Hemingway's "cumulative, self-exculpatory reflection on the hazards of love . . . and the travails of the literary life," a fiction that "explores the relation between the world of desire and the solitary space of writing."

Two essays tender revisionist readings of Catherine Barkley. The sound one, although hobbled by some dated dependency on "code hero" categories, is Sandra Whipple Spanier's "Catherine Barkley and the Hemingway Code: Ritual and Survival in *A Farewell to Arms*" (*Modern Critical Interpretations: "A Farewell to Arms,"* ed. Harold Bloom [Chelsea, 1987], pp. 131–48). Spanier argues that Catherine is a "code-hero" tutor to the uninitiated novice, Frederic Henry, teaching him "by example how to survive in a hostile and chaotic world in which an individual can gain at most a limited autonomy." A "synthesis of the priest's faith in an ideal of love" and service and of Rinaldi's cynical "impatience with platitude and illusion," Catherine takes control of the relationship with Henry, using him in a play she directs so as to "order her world and achieve some semblance of self-determination," contends Spanier, drawing on supporting manuscript materials and comparing her to Catherine Bourne. Ernest Lockridge, in "Faithful in Her Fashion: Catherine Barkley, The Invisible Hemingway Heroine" (*JNT* 18:170–78), also argues the "complex portrayal" of Catherine, "the most brilliant single embodiment of Hemingway's narrative technique of omission." To Lockridge, Catherine deliberately projects her dead fiancé onto Frederic Henry and constructs a therapeutic game of fantasy so as to remain faithful to her former lover, even though, when dying, "she remains torn between her lover of the mind and the father of her child." Lockridge contradictorily argues a sympathetic, intelligent, and ironic Catherine and also a manipulator who exploits Henry as a dupe in her therapeutic game.

Hemingway's short fiction continues to draw a large assembly of scholars, well over 20 articles seeing print this year. But not all deserve report here. Two divergent essays focused on Hemingway's first collection of stories. In "*In Our Time*: The Essential Hemingway" (*SHR* 22:305–20) James M. Cox quarrels with biographical readings of Hemingway's fiction and with reading this collection as the "biography" of Nick Adams. He argues its revolutionary qualities: its juxtaposition of "violently compressed" vignette-chapters and stories whose lack of attributive connections to those vignettes reveals a "radical spatial and temporal discontinuity" that creates "two disconnected times in alternating linear sequence." The significance of this, Cox maintains, is the volume's emphasis on an absence of connection that paradoxically possesses an uncanny presence, "a full sense of nothing strangely happening." Cox attends to "Big Two-Hearted River" and "Indian Camp" to emphasize "the nature of Hemingway's discontinuity" and vision of life as a trap in which, as Nick reflects, after crawling into his tent at the end of his first day in "Big Two-Hearted River," "Nothing could touch him," nothing being both something avoided and something welcomed. An ambitiously unsuccessful essay is Debra A. Moddelmog's "The Unifying Consciousness of a Divided Conscience: Nick Adams as Author of *In Our Time*" (*AL* 60:591–610). Grounding her argument in the ending monologue that Hemingway cut from "Big Two-Hearted River," Moddelmog reads the collection as a novel of Nick's authorship, Nick attempting "to come to terms through his fiction with his involvement in World War I and, more recently, with the problems of marriage and his fear of fatherhood." Nick's stories not only trace his psychological rather than actual history—fixated on loss, victimization, pain, and suffering—but also create experiences that conceal his current anxieties. For example, writes Moddelmog, Nick projects his own anxieties over marriage and paternity onto characters with similar anxieties and incapacities, such as "Mr. and Mrs. Elliot." Similarly, "Cross-Country Snow" links up with "Big Two-Hearted River," Nick's underlying anxiety over the duties of fatherhood and his attitudes toward Helen making up "the darker depths of the swamp he must one day fish." Ingenious though these inferences are, Moddelmog's circuitous methodology fails to skirt the biographical trap of psychologizing Hemingway, for Nick's psychological anxieties dwell in his creator, and Moddelmog's interpretations depend upon her unacknowledged knowledge of relevant Hemingway biography.

Two of the year's better essays on Hemingway's short fiction are by seasoned hands, Mark Spilka and Dewey Ganzel. In "Original Sin in 'The Last Good Country'; or, The Return of Catherine Barkley" (*The Modernists: Studies in a Literary Phenomenon*, eds. Lawrence B. Gamache and Ian S. MacNiven [Fairleigh Dickinson, 1987], pp. 210–33) Spilka combines manuscript, biographic, and textual criticism to register dissatisfaction with Scribners' editing, to clarify erroneous biographical assumptions, and to advance an androgynous reading of Nick Adams's character in Hemingway's story about "the frontier of childhood affections." Spilka includes two passages excised from the manuscript, showing that fastidious editing obscures a father-son relationship between Mr. Packard and Nick and that obtuse editing blurs the "innocent nature of physical love between brother and sister." The proof that at various times each of Hemingway's four sisters was his "favorite sister" leads Spilka both to claim that "Last Good Country" is Hemingway's "attempt to affirm the innocent closeness between brother and sister as the historic basis for responsible adult love" and to censure critics whose "failure in moral apprehension" has led them to find sexual undertones in the story's "barely sublimated incest." By comparing Littless with Catherine Barkley, Spilka finds that the model for Catherine draws less on Agnes von Kurowsky and Hemingway's first two wives than on his sisters, to whom this story pays a tribute. Ganzel's "A Geometry of His Own: Hemingway's 'Out of Season'" (*MFS* 34:171–83) records disparities between McAlmon's 1923 printing of the story in *Three Stories and Ten Poems* and Boni and Liveright's 1925 publication of it in *In Our Time*, the version since republished by Scribners. Ganzel identifies and discusses in detail three kinds of alterations by Boni and Liveright copyeditors: insertions of quotation marks to record dialogue, uniform expansion of the abbreviation "y.g." into "young gentleman," and substitution of the name Peduzzi for the ambiguous pronoun "he" in the story's opening paragraphs. By comparing "Season" to "My Old Man" and "Up in Michigan"—the three stories in McAlmon's publication—Ganzel cogently explains complex perspectives in this stylistically experimental story, whose "theme of anomie" would crop up in later fiction and whose "first use of a disjunctive point of view" here would be the technique of his best stories.

Two stories in Hemingway's so-called "marriage group" received annual genuflection. In "The Poor Kitty and the Padrone and the Tortoise-Shell Cat in 'Cat in the Rain'" (*HN* 8, i:26–36) Warren Bennett argues textually and contextually several points about the story which a manuscript fragment had originally titled "The Poor Kitty": that the kitty seen in the rainy garden and the tortoise-shell cat are different cats, that the wife (named Kitty in a manuscript fragment) is not pregnant, that the padrone is Hemingway's earliest code-hero, that the wife desires "a loving place with a 'padrone' incarnated in a man of her own generation" (not the insensitive, self-centered George), and that tortoise-shell cats of both genders are genetically sterile but resemble the exemplary padrone. James Barbour also takes up with the story in "Fugue State as Literary Device in 'Cat in the Rain' and 'Hills Like White Elephants'" (*ArQ* 44, ii: 98–106), but his vague definition of a fugue state left me with appreciation for neither this "literary device" nor the shopworn ideas it leverages from the story. In "Gender-Linked Miscommunication in 'Hills Like White Elephants'" (*HN* 8, i:2–12) Pamela Smiley differentiates the general traits of male- and female-language patterns to argue that the patterns yield two characterizations of Jig and two of the American man. Jig is "the nurturing, creative and affectionate Jig of female language, and the manipulative, shallow and hysterical Jig of male language"; likewise "he is a cold, hypocritical and powerful oppressor" and "a stoic, sensitive and intelligent victim." The categories are useful, but Smiley's rigidly binary approach restricts better possible characterizations, causes her to miss the sarcasm in Jig's "I don't care about me" (reading it as only sincere self-sacrifice or skillful social deference), and beguiles her into the cliché that finds a "sensitive portrayal of two strong personalities caught in a pattern of miscommunication due to gender-linked language patterns." In the first of two identically titled notes, Joseph R. Urgo, "Hemingway's 'Hills Like White Elephants'" (*Expl* 46, iii:35–37), finds that the railroad junction at which the story's couple waits "is not just the meeting of the Barcelona and Madrid lines, but the clash of male and female sources of power and authority in Hemingway's imagination," a clash that finds Jig subverting the man's cultural sources of authority—language, money, science, and reason. And in her note (*Expl* 46, iv:32–33) Laurie Passey argues that Anis del Toro, which Jig and the American drink while awaiting the train to Madrid, symbolizes their differing views of the child she's carrying, for anise, an herb whose seeds "aid in expelling gas from the alimentary canal" to relieve "a paroxysm of acute abdominal pain localized in a hollow organ" refers both to Jig's wish to relieve the pain and hollowness that would accompany abortion as well as to the American's wish "to eliminate the residual waste, the baby, from her body."

Three of Hemingway's war stories got looked at, but with little illumination. In "And the Wench Is Faith and Value" (*SSF* 24:393–98) Joseph J. Waldmeir squints for religious shadings in the numerous triplets of "In Another Country": bridges, wounded soldiers, photographs of restored hands, and shops and kinds of game. Equating the three wounded officers with the Holy Trinity, Waldmeir contends that the American narrator of the story rejects them as he rejects prewar theoretical values, his disillusionment with outworn values showing that like other stories of this period "prayer and religion overtly or symbolically play integral parts." Forrest Robinson also peers at this story in "Hemingway's Invisible Hero of 'In Another Country'" (*ELWIU* 15:237–44). Writing about his earlier hospital experience, the narrator is heroic because instead of merely looking out the window with the hand-injured major and resigning himself to the futility of recovery, he chooses the transcending method of healing found in writing, in "the creative act of giving a form and focus to his own condition of estrangement, as honestly and precisely as possible." In "'Old Man at the Bridge': The Making of a Short Story" (*HN* 7, ii:152–64) William Braasch Watson provides biographical details, analyzes the composition of the story from the field notes Hemingway jotted down (thinking to publish this as a dispatch), and compares the story and its compositional methods with the April 13, 1938, Dispatch 19, "Flight of Refugees." "Politics Over Art: Hemingway's 'Nobody Ever Dies'" (*SSF* 25:117–20) finds Stephen Cooper comparing "Nobody" with "The Revolutionist," whose ironic treatment of naive idealism "Nobody" lacks, primarily because Hemingway was "passionately devoted to the Loyalist cause in Spain." While the story tends toward propaganda, Cooper contends, it also contains "Hemingway's old skepticism toward ideologues and hints of his bitterness about the military inefficiency that contributed to the Loyalist defeat."

"Indian Camp" and "Big Two-Hearted River" continue to attract scholars and critics. In "Hemingway's Primitivism and 'Indian Camp'" (*TCL* 34:211–22) Hemingway biographer Jeffrey Meyers assails previous critics of the story, claiming that Hemingway's use of anthropological lore (he owned Frazer's *Golden Bough* and "fifty-seven books on Indians in his library") provides the only right explanation of why the Indian husband commits suicide: he cannot bear the intrusion of the white men who "violate the sacred confinement of the woman in childbed" and who "treat her brutally," defiling "his wife's purity, which is far worse than her screams." Consequently, "In an act of elemental nobility, he focuses the evil spirits on himself, associates his wife's blood with his own death-wound, and punishes himself for the violation of the taboo." Interesting lore, but Meyers fails to account for the discrepant behaviors of the husband's noble primitivism and Uncle George's smiling Indian's chumminess. He also fails to establish that turn-of-the-century Indian customs and traditions honored prehistoric peoples' mythologies and practices—the analogy his case rests on. Finally, the text is mum about when the husband slits his throat, but Meyers knows that the Indian kills himself "after his wife has survived the ordeal and given birth to a son." In an essay that deals briefly with Hemingway, "Negatives, Narrative and the Reader" (*Lang&S* [1987] 20:41–61), Bertrice Bartlett tallies up the 29 negatives in the first part of "Big Two-Hearted River" and the 20 of the second, noting both their infrequency "until the climactic paragraphs of both parts of the story" and that nine of the second part's negatives cluster "in the passage that constitutes the story's thematic climax." They reveal "Nick's mental struggle," their mingling with the repetition of the tragic swamp conferring "upon swamp-fishing a symbolic significance that the context suggests may be Nick's fear of his own psyche."

Some usually neglected stories attracted a handful of critics. In an essay that reads like a Kenneth Lynn throwaway, "Hemingway's Revenge and the Vulcan Myth" (*SSF* 25:73–76), Howard L. Hannum equates Grace Hemingway's painting of the blacksmith shop at Horton's Bay and her dismissal of misbehaving Ernest from Windermere in the summer of 1920 with Hemingway's likeness to Vulcan, chucked from Olympus by mother Hera. But Hemingway projects his Vulcan-self into Jim Gilmore, the blacksmith of "Up in Michigan" whose "near rape" of Liz, Hannum contends, exaggerates the moral issue over which Grace had expelled him, "exploding Grace's fevered image of something that had never taken place" and " 'punishing' Grace's unjust accusations." Tim Summerlin, in "Baseball and Hemingway's 'The Three-Day Blow' " (*Arete* [1987] 4, ii:99–102), finds "the dark *nada*" of *In Our Time* in Nick and Bill's references to Henry "Heinie" Zimmerman, still a heralded hero in September 1917—the time Summerlin dates the story's events—but soon a disgraced mortal, due to a bonehead play in that year's World Series and then, two years later at 32, to his permanent suspension from baseball for unspecified reasons. Joseph M. Flora's "Hemingway's 'The Strange Country' in the Context of *The Complete Short Stories*" (*SSF* 25:409–20) is a lengthy discussion of the unfinished narrative cut from the manuscript of *Islands in the Stream*. While acknowledging its incompleteness, Flora compares it to other Hemingway stories and finds a sense of closure in its focus on "the healing power of a woman," Helena able to share her past with Roger Davis and to elicit from him a similar sharing of his past and "most private pain," the "dark swamp" that he can fish, thanks "to the intelligent and sympathetic woman with whom he has embarked on a strange and uncertain journey." In "Crazy in Sheridan: Hemingway's 'Wine of Wyoming' Reconsidered" (*HN* 8, i:13–25) Lawrence H. Martin, Jr., tiresomely reviews the story's critical reception, biographical relevancies, and Hemingway's aesthetic principles before discussing the "failed hope, rejected optimism, [and] alienation" of "Wine," beneath whose surface "is a world surprisingly discordant and ungovernable." Although primarily a methodological and pedagogical argument for using short literary texts in English as a Second Language courses, Linda Gajdusek's "Toward Wider Use of Literature in ESL: Why and How" (*TESOLQ* 22:227–57) focuses on details from "Soldier's Home," explaining how they contribute to the story's theme: "The cost of lying to accommodate to social pressure is loss of integrity."

Last, if Hemingway's fiction seems exhausted, there's still his poetry, as George Monteiro shows in "Ernest Hemingway, Psalmist" (*JML* [1987] 14:83–95). He chronologically traces the composition of "Neothomist Poem" through its several manuscript and typescript versions, then examines a piece of manuscript fragment with the crammed-in title "The Lord Is My Shepherd I Shall Not Want/ him/ for/ long," which he dates as 1926 and convincingly suggests is the ur-text for the famous opening of *A Farewell to Arms*. But Monteiro tendentiously links the "Twenty-Third Psalm" to *Farewell* and to "A Clean Well-Lighted Place."

University of Montana

Part II

11. Literature to 1800

William J. Scheick

In a year that was not lackluster on the whole in its scholarly yield for the colonial period, two bright gems surfaced: James Axtell's ethnohistoric study of the encounter of Native American and European cultures, and Robert Lawson-Peebles's study of the encounter of European descriptive paradigms and the American landscape. Both are radiant examples of what scholarly wealth can be mined from the terrain of early American literature and culture.

i. Native Americans and the Colonial Imagination

How the vocabulary, metaphors, and self-image of the American colonists would have differed had there been no Native Americans is only one of James Axtell's fascinating explorations in *After Columbus: Essays on the Ethnohistory of Colonial North America* (Oxford), a shamanic book written with keen intelligence and passionate conviction. Axtell's quiver of perceptions includes pointed observations on the conscious motives of the settlers, on the European perception of the original occupants of the New World, on the Native American response to the seemingly magical power of the printed word, and on the vocabulary we use in discussing the encounter of the two cultures as a mental trap.

One disappointingly derivative reading of this encounter emerges in Gaile McGregor's sketchy *The Noble Savage in the New World Garden: Notes Toward a Syntactics of Place* (Bowling Green). In contrast, James Holstun's poorly written *A Rational Millennium: Puritan Utopias of Seventeenth-Century England and America* (Oxford, 1987) emphasizes an imaginative reading of this encounter in *The Christian Commonwealth*, in which John Eliot envisions his practical organization of Native American praying towns as a model for the progressive millennial reformation of civil government in England. Eliot figures as well, with Eleazar Wheelock and David Brainerd, in Margaret Connell Szasz's *Indian Education in the Ameri-*

can Colonies, 1607–1783 (New Mexico), which focuses on Native American attitudes toward the role of certain individuals who crossed the boundaries between the two cultures.

In "Some Thoughts on Colonial Historians and American Indians" (*WMQ* 46:94–119), James H. Merrell reinforces Axtell's observations by indicating that writers such as Dr. Alexander Hamilton knew what we have forgotten: that Native Americans were a usual feature of everyday early American life. And the degree to which this everyday presence pressed on the mind of one early visitor, whose response to Native Americans hardened over time, is noted by Karen Ordahl in " 'Brasse without but Golde within': The Writings of Captain John Smith" (*VC* 38, iii:66–75).

ii. Puritan Poetry

Not everyday experience, but a special interior struggle characterizes five studies of Anne Bradstreet's poetry. In *A Very Serious Thing: Women's Humor and American Culture* (Minnesota), Nancy A. Walker mentions in passing several times that Bradstreet's humor problematizes Puritan conventions of female self-definition and cultural restraint. That the endings of her verses reflect more than mere religious or literary conventions is argued in " 'To Finish What's Begun': Anne Bradstreet's Last Words" (*EAL* 23:175–89), Paula Kopacz's assessment of question-and-answer patterns, repetition, and framing as an expression of the poet's profound sense of eschatological closure. Another feature of this religious impulse interests Helena Maragou, whose "The Portrait of Alexander the Great in Anne Bradstreet's 'The Third Monarchy' " (*EAL* 23:70–81) indicates that this verse portrait displaces Puritan spiritual goals with an emphasis on desire for power and fame.

That Bradstreet's struggle with these religious concerns included considerations of gender, especially the treatment of women, is noted briefly in Paula Kopacz's " 'Men can doe best, and women know it well': Anne Bradstreet and Feminist Aesthetics" (*KPR* 2[1987]:21–28). According to Ivy Schweitzer in "Anne Bradstreet Wrestles with the Renaissance" (*EAL* 23:291–312), the poet's use of the conventional topos of (feigned) humility (a feature of an androcentric Renaissance tradition which allows women only a meek silent presence) is informed by her search for voice. Whereas in her elegies on Du Bartas and Sidney the poet reveals both the problems involved in this search for voice and the retreat from her desire to feminize the male center of the poetic tradition, in her elegy on Queen Elizabeth she finds authority for advancing a gynocentric view. This deconstruction of male authority, Timothy Sweet claims in "Gender, Genre, and Subjectivity in Anne Bradstreet's Early Elegies" (*EAL* 23:152–74), is evident in the poet's strategies of re-formation, which are often mistaken by critics as ungainly deformations in her verse. When she uses the convention of calling upon the muse (a traditional female presence as *object* in Renaissance poetry) Bradstreet actually reveals how gender is reified in poetic tradition, in which the authoritative writing *subject* is always male.

Another poet who owned a copy of Bradstreet's poems and who presented himself ambiguously as a writing subject figures in "Edward Taylor and the Impertinent Metaphor" (*AL* 60:337–58), in which Alan Leander MacGregor offers a bare application of Paul Ricoeur's theory of metaphor. The disparity of the two components of Taylor's metaphors, MacGregor explains, amounts to a semantic impertinence that replaces the collapse of the literal term and the confusion of rational sense with a new predicative meaning (another realm of knowledge); at the communal level this new meaning reduces the distance between the knower and the known. Metaphor, specifically as embodied in variations on the configuration of an emblematic arch (horizon, cage, human body, inverted barrel, God's bowels, rising dough, and crystal bowl), is featured as well in William J. Scheick's "Order and Disorder in Taylor's Poetry: Meditation 1.8" (*AmerP* 5, ii:2–11). The subtle underlying order imparted to the poem by these interrelated variations of image is authorially designed to intimate to the deity why the poet is worth divine attention; and this order contrasts with a deliberately crafted surface disorder, which is designed to reflect a proper humility at the same time as the poet makes a covert case for his merit. The aesthetic integrity of Taylor's meditation is threatened only when the surface of the poem becomes too transparently coherent as doctrinal discourse.

The degree to which Taylor's use of concrete signs (for example, images of burning lights) finds authority in Richard Baxter's instruction to materialize the abstract in meditations is remarked in Jerome D. DeNuccio's "Taylor's Preparatory Meditation 1.22" (*Expl* 46, ii: 9–11). And the still more substantial role of meditative tradition in Taylor's work is emphasized in Norman S. Grabo's good revision of his classic *Edward Taylor* (TUSAS 8). No longer claiming that Taylor was a mystic, Grabo now stresses how Taylor uses the mystical tradition to measure his failure to attain assurance, which failure becomes the main theme of his meditations. Grabo also discusses how the poet's management of rhyme, meter, and emblem varies the thematic structure of his meditations.

Taylor appears as well in an unimaginative survey of the traditions, themes, and sources of the tension between the temporal and the eternal in colonial verse: *American Poetry: The Puritans through Walt Whitman* (Twayne; pp. 1–34), by Alan Shucard. Relatedly, in "Some Colonial American Poetry and George Herbert" (*EAL* 23:28–51), John T. Shawcross reminds us of one influence on Puritan verse. Philip Pain, John Fiske, Urian Oakes, Jonathan Mitchell, and John Danforth (in contrast to Taylor) are indebted, albeit not blindly, to the "non-metaphysical" Herbert of uncomplicated lines, allusions, and language.

Shawcross also presents a variant version of a poem in "Another Printing of an Epitaph by John Saffin" (*EAL* 23:88–89). The secular world Saffin knew as a merchant enfolds with the spiritual concerns Shepard knew as a minister in "The Baroque Tendency in Early American Literature: The Achievement of Thomas Shepard II in His 1656 Almanac" (*AmerP* 5, iii:2–13), Calvin Israel's assessment of the combination of astrology and mythology, and of the persona's tongue-in-cheek integration of wit and sexual innuendo in Shepard's zodiac for Puritan New England. The man who was a schoolteacher in Charlestown while Shepard was minister of that parish is the subject of "The De-Thundered Textman: A Note on Benjamin Thompson's Epitaph for His Father" (*EAL* 23:82–87), in which Jerome D. DeNuccio rejects the view that this poem is extra-referential or self-consuming and asserts that it finally shifts away from audience to a focus on the departed subject and on itself as an encomium.

iii. Puritan Prose

Focusing on something departed characterizes Bradford's account of the Mayflower Compact, according to Mark L. Sargent in "The Conservative Covenant: The Rise of the Mayflower Compact in American Myth" (*NEQ* 61:231–51). Bradford saw this compact less as an ideological monument than as a plaintive reminder to a Pilgrim community which has gone astray; and so for him that document reflected not the democratic impulse identified by myth, but Bradford's desire to stop the spread of democratic impulses in the New World. If Bradford could not fix what went awry in his sphere of influence, John Cotton could at least attain rapprochement with an antagonist during the Antinomian crisis. In "'Revising what we have done amisse': John Cotton and John Wheelwright, 1640" (*WMQ* 45:733–50), Sargent Bush, Jr., documents how Cotton confessed to a modicum of guilt and, in turn, Wheelwright revised his views without admitting complete error. Tension of another kind, the numerous diverse attitudes informing the Puritan view of a life situated in the temporal but defined by the eternal, concerned the biographical subject of *Thomas Shepard* (TUSAS 519 [1987]), in which Thomas Werge also usefully notes this minister's reliance on dramatic-settings, dialogue, marriage and family motifs, and imagery of polarity and tactility.

A personal tension between a dedication to New England and a desire to live in England, the seat of real power, characterizes Michael G. Hall's *The Last American Puritan: The Life of Increase Mather* (Wesleyan), by far the most complete and fully researched life-and-times record of its subject to date. Perhaps marred by a lack of a probing bio-critical apparatus and by a curious interpretative timidity, Hall's well-written book not only revises certain factual matters but also suggests Increase's sensitivity to personal criticism, his attraction to secular power, his restlessness in New England, and his tendency to exploit the press. Mather's defense of capital punishment on the basis of scriptural precedent, civil authority, and the need for deterrence is remarked by Daniel A. Cohen, whose disappointing "In Defence of the Gallows: Justification of Capital Punishment in New England Execution Sermons, 1674–1825" (*AQ* 40:147–64) concludes that ministers not only condemned criminals but also implicitly vindicated judicial authority. Increase's more benign role in the publication of a popular book, which underwent various subsequent modifications for the sake of different audiences, is mentioned by Kathryn Zabelle Derounian in "The Publication, Promotion, and Distribution of Mary Rowlandson's Indian Captivity Narrative in the Seventeenth Century" (*EAL* 23:239–61).

The influence of an antagonist of Increase is documented by Philip F. Gura, whose "Going Mr. Stoddard's Way: William Williams on Church Privileges, 1693" (*WMQ* 45:489–98) suggests that since Stoddard's son-in-law agreed with his liturgical practices, Stoddardeanism was not isolated to the Connecticut Valley. Cotton Mather not only defended his father's version of providential design in their mutual press against Stoddard, but as David Levin reports in "Giants of the Earth: Science and the Occult in Cotton Mather's Letters to the Royal Society" (*WMQ* 45:751–70), Cotton's personal mingling of biblical scholarship, history, and scientific method imply his sanction of the use of rational investigation and conjecture to fathom the meaning of that design. The place of women in that design, according to Margaret Olofson Thickstun's *Fictions of the Feminine: Puritan Doctrine and the Representation of Women* (Cornell), troubled Cotton, who tended to discredit the redemptive value of motherhood and to emphasize merely its (sinful) biological function (even in the birth of Jesus). Thickstun, who could have benefited from an acquaintance with David Leverenz's *The Language of Puritan Feeling* (*ALS 1980*), notes that in English Puritan literary works male protagonists (representing the head, spirit, divinity) displace female characters (representing the body, flesh, humanity) from their traditional roles.

Another feature of this male image-making capacity is reflected in the Puritans' attempt to rewrite history, an effort that disturbed one of their antagonists, explains Daniel B. Shea in " 'Our Professed Old Adversary': Thomas Morton and the Naming of New England" (*EAL* 23:52–69). In his masque (*New English Canaan*) Morton is a Proteus figure who may be physically banished from the New World, but who re-creates himself by writing himself a Phoenix reclaiming that lost ground through the regenerative power of textual nomination (naming). Another visitor who was displeased by the Puritans appears in *John Josselyn, Colonial Traveler: A Critical Edition of "Two Voyages to New-England"* (New England), in which editor Paul J. Lindholdt emphasizes Josselyn's utilitarian interests, deliberate lack of sophistication, and royalist sympathies.

iv. The South

An author similarly capable of conveying the wonder of the New World landscape receives attention in three articles. Besides Karen Ordahl's general review of John Smith's life (noted above) and Nicholas Canny's attention to Smith's moral reformist emphasis on skill, character, and family (" 'To Establish a Common Wealthe': Captain John Smith as New World Colonist" [*VMHB* 96:213–22]), Alden T. Vaughan discloses that some of Smith's readers thought he was a braggart, buffoon, and liar ("John Smith Satirized: *The Legend of Captaine Jones*" [*WMQ* 45:712–32]). Stephen Innes's "Fulfilling John Smith's Vision: Work and Labor in Early America," in his edited collection *Work and Labor in Early America* (No. Car., pp. 3–47), observes how 17th-century British employment crises provided a context for Smith's view of the relationship between human freedom and the mastery of one's own labor in the New World.

The person who apparently directed, wrote, and edited almost all of the Georgian promotional literature from 1730 to 1732 is identified by Rodney M. Baine in "James Oglethorpe and the Early Promotional Literature for Georgia" (*WMQ* 45:100–106). An author of descriptive literature in Maryland is mentioned not only by James H. Merrell (noted above) but also by Robert Micklus, whose "The Delightful Instruction of Dr. Alexander Hamilton's *Itinerarium*" (*AL* 60:359–84) claims that this travel diary evidences two modes of perception, as defined by Foucault: the horizontal gaze of the natural historian, who focuses on external phenomena; the vertical gaze of the physician, who focuses on internal phenomena. This double gaze results in a precision of observation, by a generally unobtrusive narrator, that would have appealed to an 18th-century audience's expectation of empirical observation.

v. Edwards and the Great Awakening

An 18th-century intellect who pitted idealism against the demand of his time for empirical evidence received some attention, little of it new. M. X. Lesser's *Jonathan Edwards* (TUSAS 537) announces its intent "to trace Edwards's thought as a connected series of comments on the doctrine of divine sovereignty," but unfortunately only finally testifies to a failure of critical nerve. The obvious informs Helen Petter Westra's "Jonathan Edwards on 'Faithful and Successful Ministers'" (*EAL* 23:281–90), which observes that in his first ordination sermon (1736) Edwards jubilantly defines the role of the ministry, whereas in his last ordination sermon (1754) he reflects a pensiveness indicating that, as in his own case, one's ministry might not be efficacious.

Predictable too are most of the essays in *Jonathan Edwards and the American Experience*, Nathan O. Hatch and Harry S. Stout, eds. (Oxford). In "Jonathan Edwards and America," Henry F. May asserts that Edwards was more a Calvinist than an existentialist; in "The Spirit and the Word: Jonathan Edwards and Scriptural Exegesis,"

Stephen J. Stein notes that Edwards applied an expanded use of typology to explicate the Bible; in "History, Redemption, and the Millennium," John F. Wilson reports that Edwards's post-millennialism has New England roots; and in "Calvinism and Consciousness from Edwards to Beecher," James Hoopes explains that Edwards was an idealist rather than a Lockean empiricist. Such contributors as Norman Fiering (*ALS 1981*), Bruce Kuklick (*ALS 1985*), Harry Stout (*ALS 1986*), and Donald Weber (see below) present summaries of their longer works already in print. In " 'A Flood of Errors': Chauncy and Edwards in the Great Awakening," Amy Schrager Lang expands a little upon her previous work (*ALS 1987*) by arguing that in contrast with Chauncy, Edwards emphasized invisible signs (as the ground for sanctification) that language cannot express. (Incidentally, a synthesis of current scholarship on two of Edwards's contemporaries, who searched for a coherent religious vision, is provided by John Corrigan in *The Hidden Balance: Religious and Social Theories of Charles Chauncy and Jonathan Mayhew* [Cambridge, 1987]).

The visible signs of Edwards's language are considered in Wilson H. Kimnach's heavily indebted "Jonathan Edwards's Pursuit of Reality," which indicates that Edwardsean discourse relies principally on the power of specification (primarily simple imagery and repetition) to seize the attention of the audience. But the flight from specification informs David Laurence's abstract speculation that in Edwards's work there exists a constant "possibility that the life of the spirit will degenerate into a dreadful worship of impersonal force."

The generation and degeneration of Edwards's influence surfaces too in this collection: in "Jonathan Edwards and Nineteenth Century Theology," Mark A. Noll traces the longevity of interest in Edwards (whose mixed reception he also documents in "The Contested Legacy of Jonathan Edwards in Antebellum Calvinism: Theological Conflict and the Evolution of Thought in America" [*CRAS* 19:149–64]); in "Edwards, Franklin, and Cotton Mather: A Meditation on Character and Reputations," David Levin defensively complains that in contrast to Mather's less attractive traits and comments, those of Edwards have unfairly escaped critical attention; and in "Piety and Moralism: Edwards and the New Divinity," William Breitenbach argues that the New Divinity was faithful, with a few revisions, to Edwards's teachings.

Other discussions of Edwards's inheritance and bequeathal of tradition include "The Rhetoric of Grace in Jonathan Edwards' *Personal Narrative*" (*Man and Nature; L'Homme et la nature*, David H. Jory and Charles Stewart-Robinson, eds. [Academic, 1985], pp. 109–27), John Stephen Martin's review of concepts of spirituality and divine grace. In "The Melancholy Saint: Jonathan Edwards's Interpretation of David Brainerd as a Model of Evangelical Spirituality" (*HTR* 81:297–318), David L. Weddle reports on Edwards's misassessment of Brainerd's pathological depression (an obsessive self-interest and a glorification of death); the Brainerd model actually conflicts with Edwards's own view of religious experience (including a gracious melancholia) and became an exemplar of unsound spirituality for later evangelical tradition. Touching on how Edwardsean heritage extends beyond theology, Joan Dayan's *Fables of Mind: An Inquiry into Poe's Fiction* (Oxford, 1987) offers an unconvincing reading of the divine as a Lockean materialist whose surrender to God represents a collapse of relation and a cosmic negation. On the other hand, the best essay in many years on this heritage, James Duban's "From Emerson to Edwards: Henry Whitney Bellows and an 'Ideal' Metaphysics of Sovereignty" (*HTR* 81: 389–411) cogently challenges Perry Miller's famous Edwards-to-Emerson paradigm and identifies a major 19th-century effort to convert the Emersonian emphasis on autonomy into an Edwardsean idealism. Apparently Edwards was not only a dim ghost at Emerson's back door, but also a persistent presence on his front porch.

vi. Franklin, Jefferson, and the Revolutionary Period

The New Divinity, the inheritors of Edwardsean tradition, were not as politically remote as some previous studies have indicated. As Donald Weber insightfully reveals in *Rhetoric and History in Revolutionary New England* (Oxford), such ministers as Jonathan Edwards, Jr., Samuel Cooper, and Stephen West bound together religious language and Whig politics, thereby providing a ritualistic affirmation for their parishioners, who were unsettled by the times. The ambivalence of these ministers over the chaos of revolution and, as well, their liminal position (in Victor Turner's sense) concerning the seemingly uncertain course of history (where providential design was unclear) are, for Weber, reflected in their unpublished manuscripts, which reveal a certain anti-authoritarian incoherence and fragmentation that testify to an authorial struggle with narrative.

This time of upheaval was, in Franklin's view, an opportunity for protean re-creations. According to Joseph Fichtelberg's "The Complex Image: Text and Reader in *The Autobiography of Benjamin Franklin*" (*EAL* 23:202–16), Franklin understood that the process of reworking a book about to be made public was applicable to one's public identity, which is also an act of composition. Revision in his autobiography reveals a changing sense of audience: from ruminations with an intimate "you" to hortatory comments to fellow tradesmen who might profit from his example, to a documentary manner for the visionary community of the new republic. Franklin's self-fashioning is also of interest to John Updike, who, in his "Many Bens" (*NY* 64 [22 Feb]:105–108, 111–16), traces the influence of France, England, and Philadelphia in the successive selves Franklin assumed as if they were self-made artifacts.

That Franklin fashioned a persona in the *Autobiography*, a narrator who develops through three distinct stages from a personal to an institutionally detached spokesman, is a contention of Mark R. Patterson's interesting New Historicist *Authority, Autonomy, and Representation in American Literature, 1776–1865* (Princeton; pp. 3–33). Writing his own self, this narrator represents authority for the reader only through a subtle process of internalizing his own personal authority; he represents himself through the process of imitating, modifying, and exceeding others' authority over him.

The lifelong search for the authority of fame, expressed through an ongoing modification in his sense of identity as it shifts from an attraction to English culture to an acceptance of American prospects, is a theme of Ormond Seavey's *Becoming Benjamin Franklin: The "Autobiography" and the Life* (Penn State). Identifying mutations in tone and perspective similar to those remarked by Fichtelberg and Patterson, Seavey scrutinizes a Franklin who adopts Enlightenment notions to manage his readers rhetorically; first, to accept the narrator as their representative, and, second, to complete the narrator's goals. This narrator, Seavey reports, is like Franklin: a self-conscious, aloof Addisonian spectator who considers life to be like a book in which a pattern should be discernible. One pattern in the *Autobiography* that has influenced posterity, claims Robert Shulman in his Marxist *Social Criticism and Nineteenth-Century American Fiction* (Missouri, 1987), includes a promotion of the work ethic and a dependence on technology, both of which augment the capitalistic alienation of the (finally fragmented) individual from society and oneself.

Concerning influences on Franklin himself, Thomas J. Steele, S.J., suggests in "Orality and Literacy in Matter and Form: Benjamin Franklin's *Way to Wealth*," (*OT* 2[1987]:273–85) that Franklin selected only comparatively dismal proverbs on the human need for industry (to earn money) and for frugality (to keep money); these proverbs become a systematic ethic disguised by the illusion of oral tradition in his work. In this way Franklin subtly repudiates the culture of the Old World (the past) and at the same time employs its tradition to form a new literacy for the culture of the New World (the future). The effect of Puritan culture on *Poor Richard's Almanac* is mentioned in Paulo Warth Gick's "Benjamin Franklin and the Changing World of 18th Century American Society" (*IdD* 1–2[1986]: 29–36). Another influence is spotted by Dennis Barone in "A Note on the Influence of Lord Kames's Theory of Narrative on Benjamin Franklin's *A Narrative of the Late Massacres*, 1764" (*ANQ* 1:93–97). Barone claims that Franklin followed a Kamesian narrative progression whereby a reader is transformed into an eyewitness who accepts the account as sufficiently credible to warrant action.

Personal accounts appear in *The Papers of Benjamin Franklin, Volume 27: July 1 through October 31, 1778*, Claude A. Lopez, ed. (Yale). Challenges to previous attributions to Franklin emerge in A. Owen Aldridge's "The Attribution to Franklin of a Letter from China" (*EAL* 23:313–18) and in E. W. Pitcher's "The Essay on Conversation in *The Papers of Benjamin Franklin*: A Wrong Attribution" (*ANQ* 1:55–56), which assigns the work to Englishman Henry Baker. The enormous amount of 20th-century commentary on Franklin and his writings is superbly compiled and annotated in *Benjamin Franklin: A Reference Guide, 1907–1983* (Hall) by Melvin H. Buxbaum, who deserves our gratitude for this successful execution of a prodigious undertaking.

The themes, sources, associations, and reputation of a Pennsylvania contemporary of Franklin are enumerated by David S. Shields in "Henry Brooke and the Situation of the First Belletrists in British America" (*EAL* 23:4–27). Shields also describes the context of a New Jersey contemporary of Franklin, Lewis Morris, Jr., who penned a satire on the first "Princeton" commencement: "An Academic Satire: The College of New Jersey in 1748" (*PULC* 50:38–60). Morris's father, and future governor of New Jersey, interests Peter A. Davis in "Evidence of Collaboration in the Writing of Robert Hunter's *Androboros*" (*RECTR* 3:20–29).

The inner life—characterized by joy and sorrow as well as by a valuation of human existence—of a New England contemporary of Morris receives attention in Barbara E. Lacey's "The World of Hannah Heaton: The Autobiography of an Eighteenth-Century Connecticut Farm Woman" (*WMQ* 45:280–304). And another woman, the wife of the man who said that "there never was a democracy yet that did not commit suicide," appears in "The Abigail Industry" (*WMQ* 45:656–83), Edith B. Gelles's reminder that Abigail Adams was a private person wittily, spiritually, and emotionally devoted to maternal and uxorious domestic concerns.

National concerns weighed heavily on the mind of Adams's most famous political opponent, on whom a round of essays, most of them in French, is collected in *Voyage et tourisme en Bourgogne à l'époque de Jefferson*, Michel Baridon and Bernard Chevignard, eds. (Univ. de Bourgogne). Jefferson's fear that David Hume's *History of England* would perniciously influence uninformed youths in the new nation surfaces in "Jefferson vs. Hume" (*WMQ* 46:49–70), in which Douglas L. Wilson identifies Jefferson's sensitivity to Hume's apparent Tory orientation and his inadequate discussion of legal developments. Another book by Alexander Mackenzie, explains James P. Ronda in "Dreams and Discoveries: Exploring the American West, 1760–1815" (*WMQ* 46:145–64), encouraged Jefferson to create for Meriwether Lewis an unprecedented instance of directed exploration. But according to Robert Lawson-Peebles's excellent *Landscape and Written Expression in Revolutionary America* (Cambridge), Lewis's journal of his attempt to realize Jefferson's vision registers the inability of available strategies of descriptive language to report the reality of the American wilderness (also a linguistic frontier) and, instead, records the failure of the republican ideal of order. Underlying this failure is Jefferson's European heritage of the valuation of the written word as a model of order and the restriction of his imaginative appreciation of the American terrain to this gridlike European social and scientific verbal framework.

vii. The Early National Period

Jefferson is only one major figure in Lawson-Peebles's outstanding book, a rich excavation of early national cultural matter. J. Hector

St. John de Crèvecoeur, Philip Freneau, Benjamin Rush, Noah Webster, Hugh Henry Brackenridge, and Jedidiah Rush also appear; these writers projected their early national expectations in a European-engendered sense of novelty (for example, images of Eden) that displaced their real encounter with the facts of the American environment. Ultimately these writers became disillusioned and retreated from America, a withdrawal expressed in the very European images of malignity and negation they had initially sought to deny. Lawson-Peebles's assessment of the effect of inherited precedent imagery upon Americans' experience in the early republic corresponds to Sacvan Bercovitch's belief that the foundations of Puritan New England views were based on certain preceding literary and religious figures of speech that became historically factual through an ongoing dialectical interaction between imagination and culture (*ALS 1987*).

Eighteenth-century debates on the English origins of the language of the new nation interest Cynthia S. Jordan, whose "'Old Words' in 'New Circumstances': Language and Leadership in Post-Revolutionary America" (*AQ* 40:491–513) identifies the paradoxical tendency in the period to want to fix firmly the meanings of words and at the same time to unfix them from traditional meanings. The texts of the period, Jordan observes, reveal a self-conscious use of words that vary from context to context—a use of language which breaks from the past, interprets the present for the public good, and accommodates future reinterpretation. Webster's views, which figure in Lawson-Peebles's and Jordan's discussions, surface in "Noah Webster: The Language of Politics/The Politics of Language" (*EiP* 13:41–81), in which Charles Swann stresses that Webster privileged spoken (vulgar) over written (elitist) language, even though in politics he conservatively opposed a (Jeffersonian) direct democracy.

Using descriptive language imaginatively to project his understanding of the goals of America, particularly his hope for a continuity in ethics, one early national poet created multiple designs to frame New England life. In "Timothy Dwight 'Composes' a Landscape for New England" (*AQ* 40:359–77), Peter M. Briggs notes how these designs reflect Dwight's belief that order and variety could be harmoniously integrated in a coherent New World society (including upper and lower classes), provided that it reflected a breadth of social, moral, and aesthetic awareness. Multiple meanings certainly informed one popular cultural image in the verse, plays, fiction, almanacs, and cartoons of this time, explains Winifred Morgan in *An*

American Icon: Brother Jonathan and American Identity (Delaware). An inadvertently ambiguous caricature, Brother Jonathan served at once as a representation of patriotic native shrewdness and a criticism of naïvété.

Just as Dwight envisioned an integration of upper and lower social classes and just as the Brother Jonathan icon reflected the attitudes of both classes, the publishers of early national periodicals did not aim at one or the other social segment in particular. As David Paul Nord observes in "A Republican Literature: A Study of Magazine Reading and Readers in Late Eighteenth-Century New York" (*AQ* 40:42–64), these publishers sought an ideal republican audience, for whom information and knowledge would be the mainspring of the Republic as it had been for the Revolution itself.

A more personal revolution in a struggle for freedom is evident in *The Collected Works of Phillis Wheatley*, John C. Shields, ed. (Oxford), and *The Poems of Phillis Wheatley: A Revised and Expanded Edition*, Julian D. Mason, Jr., ed. (No. Car.). The delayed printing of the work of another poet is remarked in E. W. Pitcher's "On the Publication of James Elliot's *Poetical and Miscellaneous Works* (1798[?])" (*ANQ* 1:134–35). And a number of Elliot's and Wheatley's contemporaries who were publishers and editors are identified in *American Magazine Journalists, 1741–1850*, Sam G. Riley, ed. (Gale).

viii. Brown and Contemporaries

In his foreword to *Memoirs of Stephen Burroughs* (Northeastern), Philip F. Gura indicates that by the conclusion of the narrative (1798) Burroughs seems less the criminal than the victim of intolerant people; his behavior in fact seems rooted in two ideals of the new republic: reason and representation. Other ideals emerge in William J. Scheick's "Education, Class, and the French Revolution in Sarah Wood's *Julia*" (*SAF* 16:111–18), which traces Wood's argument in the late 1790s for an essentially Jeffersonian position on the role of education for both sexes in all social ranks; this point of view informs her final integration of common and aristocratic classes in her two protagonists. The more prevalent view of Wood as a conservative defender of class difference is reiterated by Anne Dalke, whose "Original Vice: The Political Implications of Incest in the Early American Novel" (*EAL* 23:188–201) also considers the writings of William

Hill Brown and Susanna Rowson to disclose in their work a recurrent pattern of unwitting incest; this pattern symbolizes their fear of the lack in early American culture of any hierarchical social stratification that would properly restrict the dangerous mobility of the classless early republic citizenry. However, this emphasis on incest is hardly unique to American fiction or to the 18th century, and a compelling alternative reading of the recurrence of this theme can be derived from John Boswell's disturbing *The Kindness of Strangers* (Pantheon).

Similar interest in the failure of a definitive social structure emerges as well in Patterson's *Authority, Autonomy, and Representation* (pp. 61–78), which considers Charles Brockden Brown's demonstrations of how paternal and societal institutional authority falters, thereby leaving American youth of the early republic vulnerable to dissembling, charismatic figures who capitalize on their audience's expectations. Since Brown's own authority as an author is absent from his romances, the reader is forced to look to himself or herself, even as (in Brown's opinion) Americans must look for the underlying motives of their culture not in their political representatives, but within themselves as the represented.

In looking to themselves, claims Beverly R. Voloshin in "*Edgar Huntly* on the Coherence of the Self" (*EAL* 23:262–80), Brown's readers, like his narrators, find narrative motives to be as elusive as is causality in the world; Brown de-centers the self in his works by raising questions (especially through the strategy of repetition) about the Lockean argument for a coherent personal identity. This conclusion is a mainstay, a stabilizing *repetition*, of Brown scholarship by now, and informs still another article which appeared this year in the same journal: "American Literature and the Nineteenth-Century Crisis in Epistemology: The Example of Charles Brockden Brown" (*EAL* 23:121–51). In this essay Roland Hagenbüchle states that Brown's loss of aesthetic coherence and narrative plausibility makes the reader insecure and thereby extenuates the Calvinistic heritage of a radical duality; in this way Brown questions the meaning of the world, the self, and language.

Whereas Hagenbüchle discerns Brown's departure from European aesthetics, Lawson-Peebles (*Landscape and Written Expression*, pp. 231–62) studies Brown's early infatuation with European literary models, his subsequent effort to approach the American terrain unmediated by these predecessors, and his final retreat (similar to his narrators) from the imaginative agrarian dream to a European definition of the pursuit of facts as a ground for social order. One of these European literary exemplars receives attention in "Profits of Altruism: Caleb Williams and Arthur Mervyn" (*ECS* 22:47–69), in which Dorothy J. Hale claims that Brown's protagonist is more successful and is a better Englishman than his Godwinian prototype could be; but this very altruistic success might be an expression of selfishness, which fact would then problematically suggest the inscrutable nature of moral and national identity.

No such vexing of the nature of virtue informs Michael Clark's limp thesis in "Charles Brockden Brown's *Wieland* and Robert Proud's *History of Pennsylvania*" (*SNNTS* 20:239–48): that this romance teaches the need for Quaker restraint in order to avoid the mania of excessive ambition. A far more negative message is decoded by Michael P. Sullivan, whose "Reconciliation and Subversion in *Edgar Huntley* [*sic*]" (*ATQ* 2:5–22) claims that by subverting conventional notions of benevolence, love, and marriage, Brown indicates not only that selfishness characterizes human behavior but also that human survival requires reconciliation with a necessarily corrupt social reality. Various kinds of subversion of convention are evident in the 11 stories by Brown edited by Alfred Weber in *Somnambulism and Other Stories* (Lang, 1987). And the nature of setting and structure is the concern of Tomasz Warchol's "Formal and Thematic Patterns in *Edgar Huntly*" (*BSUF* 28[1987]:16–24), which I have not seen.

ix. Miscellaneous Studies

Subversion of another kind might have improved Perry D. Westbrook's *A Literary History of New England* (Lehigh), something of a limited dictionary which unfortunately perpetuates the notion that New England is *the* source of our national literature and, even worse, provides capsule summaries of very outdated scholarship on the authors it deigns to include. Italian professor Marilla Battilana also attempts a sweeping survey in *The Colonial Roots of American Fiction: Notes Toward a New Theory* (Olschki), which inconclusively emphasizes the "uniquely American genre" of the captivity narrative and the "long hidden, or rejected, national tradition" of diary writing as the original foundations of contemporary American fiction. In these colonial antecedents and their contemporary successors, for instance, the journey motif transcends its background role in English literary tradition by becoming the real subject of the story. In the northern colonies, explains E. Jennifer Monaghan in "Literacy Instruction and Gender in Colonial New England" (*AQ* 40:18–41), women at home taught boys and girls how to read (basically for religious reasons), whereas men taught boys how to write. And colonial male attitudes concerning sports, Nancy L. Struna argues in "Puritans and Sport: The Irretrievable Tide of Change" (*The Sporting Image: Readings in American Sport History*, Paul J. Zingg, ed. [Univ. Press of Amer.], pp. 1–22), reflected the religious and political developments in their culture.

Writing on early American subjects was the topic of a forum, in which Philip F. Gura, Norman S. Grabo, David Levin, and Larzer Ziff pondered "The Study of Colonial American Literature, 1966–1987" (*WMQ* 45:305–51). Besides criticizing historians for believing that their reconstruction of truth is more successful than that of literary critics (Ziff), and chastising historians for abandoning intellectual heritage for demographic studies, and aesthetics for sociology (Grabo), the discussion also argued for a greater awareness by students of literature of the English roots of colonial American letters, of the possibility that early American writings evince less consistency than we wish to admit, and of our tendency to force connections between the major figures of this period and later authors (Gura).

Here I end, at fourth remove, with an act of interpretation of other critics interpreting their predecessors in the act of interpreting colonial writers, who were interpreting their experiences at firsthand physically but secondhand imaginatively. Even being close to our origins apparently provided no help for the epistemological dilemma implied in this conundrum, as John Smith painfully indicates in his *The General History of Virginia* (1624). In fact, Smith's record in this book of the "golden promises," the illusions characterizing the first American gold rush, reflects his own struggle with elusive colonial American origins, and it may serve as a fitting epigraph for our struggle today to explore and define colonial American literature: "no talke, no hope, no worke, but dig gold, wash gold, refine gold, laode gold, such a bruit of gold, that one mad fellow desired to be buried in the sands [to] make gold of his bones."

University of Texas at Austin

12. 19th-Century Literature

David J. Nordloh

Recovered and discovered writers, mostly women but a few men too, and innovative theoretical, historical, and genre issues continue to mark work on the 19th century. Utopianism and political issues were especially prominent, encouraged at least in part by the hundredth anniversary of Edward Bellamy's *Looking Backward.* A new edition of the correspondence of Stephen Crane and the final volumes of the letters of Henry Adams made a substantial addition to the base of published primary documents. There were new books on Irving, the Beechers, Gilman, Howells, and Norris, revised ones on Cooper and Freeman, a collection of essays devoted to Simms, and two collections devoted to Chopin. And there was a new literary history. Twenty-five years ago that event alone would have made several seasons; today it's barely a headline.

i. General Studies

Emory Elliott's introduction to the *CLHUS* notes that the history of the literature of the United States is "not one story but many different stories." The marked absence of pontifical assertion implicit in that remark indicates how different this enterprise is from the one undertaken by Robert Spiller and his colleagues some 40 years ago. Then the spirit of the writing was absolutist and definitive; now it is both argumentative and tentative; then essays presumed a canon and inventoried it; now they speculate about what the canon is, venture guesses about what it will become; then a comprehensive bibliography reinforced the whole; now there is no bibliography—and hardly a footnote; then, despite the number of contributors, the work was conceived of as a seamless and possibly eternal whole; now it is a collection of occasional essays.

At least the general sense of historical arrangement remains. Relevant to this chapter are part two, covering the period 1810–65, and part three, covering 1865–1910, under the associate editorship of Terence Martin and Martha Banta, respectively. An inventory of relevant chapter authors and titles signals the effort to mix the traditional and the new, and suggests the ongoing revaluations and realignments. In part two Michael J. Colacurcio's introductory essay, "Idealism and Independence" (pp. 207–26), is followed by Haskell Springer's "Washington Irving and the Knickerbocker Group" (pp. 229–39), H. Daniel Peck's "James Fenimore Cooper and the Writers of the Frontier" (240–61), G. R. Thompson's "Edgar Allan Poe and the Writers of the Old South" (pp. 262–77), Thomas Wortham's "William Cullen Bryant and the Fireside Poets" (pp. 278–88), Nina Baym's "The Rise of the Woman Author" (pp. 289–305), Neil Schmitz's "Forms of Regional Humor" (pp. 306–23), Claudia Johnson's "A New Nation's Drama" (pp. 324–41), and Carolyn Porter's "Social Discourse and Nonfictional Prose" (pp. 345–63). In part three Richard H. Brodhead's introductory "Literature and Culture" (pp. 467–81) is followed by Warner Berthoff's survey of philosophers, utopians, and social commentators in fiction and nonfiction, "Culture and Consciousness" (pp. 482–98); and that in turn by Eric J. Sundquist's "Realism and Regionalism" (pp. 501–24); Lee Clark Mitchell's "Naturalism and the Languages of Determinism" (pp. 525–45); Jack Salzman's discussion of Beadle, Alger, and other pulpists in "Literature for the Populace" (pp. 549–67); Werner Sollors's "Immigrants and Other Americans" (pp. 568–88); Cecelia Tichi's "Women Writers and the New Woman" (pp. 589–606); and John Carlos Rowe's "Henry Adams" (pp. 645–67), among the "Major Voices."

The canonical revision bubbling up in *CLHUS* also marks *American Literary Landscapes*, a gathering of seven essays originally presented in a 1985 colloquium at the University of Keele that focused on the relationship between literary texts and the "social, political and economic histories which are their enabling conditions." One essay relevant to this chapter is by now a reprint: Walter Benn Michaels's "Frank Norris, Josiah Royce and the Ontology of Corporations" (pp. 122–51) also appears in *Reconstructing Literary History* (1986). The two others are new. Brian Harding's "The Myth of the Myth of the Garden" (pp. 44–60) argues, in response to Henry Nash Smith's *Virgin Land*, that the overwhelming majority of 19th-century discussions saw farming not as pastoral and static but as a crucial and energized matter of commerce and growth. Christopher Mulvey's "Anglo-American Fictions: National Characteristics in

Nineteenth-Century Travel Literature" (pp. 61–77) continues the emphasis of his *Anglo-American Landscapes* (1983) in conceiving these works less as systematic and factually accurate accounts, more as "structuring fictions" devoted to asserting the superiority of one's native land.

The South as native land is the issue in Michael O'Brien's gathering of essays written over the past 15 years, *Rethinking the South: Essays in Intellectual History* (Johns Hopkins). O'Brien answers the objection that the South has not had an intellectual history by asserting that southern historians, "guardians of metaphysical innocence and practical hope," and southern novelists and poets, disciples of the "philosophical confusion of modernism," have broadcast confusing signals, particularly with respect to Romanticism, the heart of southern self-definition. He concludes that "the bleak side of Romanticism was given to the hands of the novelists and philosophers, the optimistic side to the historians." Though the discussion is often generalized and abstract, Hugh Legaré, Simms, Washington Allston, and Richard Henry Wilde are mentioned often, particularly in chapters on "The Lineaments of Southern Antebellum Romanticism," "Politics, Romanticism, and Hugh Legaré: The Fondness of Disappointed Love," and "Italy and the Southern Romantics." John Seelye makes a feisty foray into the same territory. His "If at First You Don't Secede, Try, Try Again: Southern Literature from Fenimore Cooper to Faulkner" (*PAAS* 98:51–68) argues in Seelye's usual confrontational and eccentric prose that "Again and again . . . we may trace Southern literary types and formulas to Northern originals, much as the ideology of nullification and secession were derived from New England's separatist ideals." Besides Cooper, his 19th-century examples include Simms, Stowe, Irving, Cable, and Chopin.

Bert Bender's *Sea-Brothers* employs a more traditional thematic strategy in examining the uses to which "the seaman's elemental existence" is put in American literature. A chapter on "The Voyage in American Sea Fiction after the *Pilgrim*, the *Acushnet*, and the *Beagle*" discusses the works of such major writers as Richard Henry Dana, Jr., Cooper, and Stephen Crane. Crane is also the subject of "The Experience of Brotherhood in 'The Open Boat,'" which treats as well the sea stories of other correspondents of his time, among them Richard Harding Davis and Frank Norris. Two other chapters—"From Sail to Steam: Sailor-Writers of the 1860s and 1870s" and "From Sail to Steam: Sailor-Writers of the 1880s and 1890s"—are the book's most useful contribution, both broadening the field of interest and justifying Bender's claim that "the sea's influence on American literature has been more profound and continuous than is presently accepted, exceeding even that of the inland frontier." Back on land Elizabeth I. Hanson offers interesting insights (but the annoyance of bad proofreading) in *The American Indian.* Cooper and Longfellow figure prominently in her first chapter, "Sources of Vision," a survey of the process of introduction of the Indian as a viable imaginative material into American fiction. And Sam S. Baskett goes abroad in "Beyond Native Grounds: American Literary Expatriation" (*CentR* 31[1987]:192–211), arguing that the myth of expatriation—the superiority of the Old World to the New or the greater clarity of vision of the New World when seen from the Old—is as pervasive as the myth of the American Adam to which it "has always been inevitably connected." The essay is a valuable overview of many of the specific discussions of the topic over the last 30 years, and includes Cooper and Irving among its examples.

Lorne Feinberg's *A Cuckoo in the Nest of Culture: Changing Perspectives on the Businessman in the American Novel, 1865–1914* (Garland) addresses a domestic rather than international cultural question. Proposing, à la Lucien Goldmann, that differences in genre and mode yield insights into the underlying values that separate social groups, the book surveys treatments of the businessman and business enterprise reflecting four different perspectives—defenders of gentility, professionals, the working class, and entrepreneurs. W. D. Howells figures most prominently throughout, and H. H. Boyesen, Charles Dudley Warner, David Graham Phillips, Winston Churchill, Edward Bellamy, Jack London, Frank Norris, Henry Blake Fuller, and Robert Herrick also have a say. Though more descriptive than conclusive, the survey does outline the tensions of morality, economic priority, and social transformation which marked the final quarter of the 19th century.

Several general studies deal with women writers and questions of women's culture. The most ambitious is *Patrons and Protégées,* a collection of essays undertaking to establish the reality of relationships stereotypically associating "the important male author and the aspiring lady writer." Eight of the nine essays are significant to this chapter: Mary G. De Jong, "Lines from a Partly Published Drama: The Romance of Frances Sargent Osgood and Edgar Allan Poe" (pp. 31–58); Joyce W. Warren, "Subversion versus Celebration: The

Aborted Friendship of Fanny Fern and Walt Whitman" (pp. 59–93); Shirley Marchalonis, "A Model for Mentors?: Lucy Larcom and John Greenleaf Whittier" (pp. 94–121); Raymond A. Mazurek, "'I have no Monarch in My Life': Feminism, Poetry, and Politics in Dickinson and Higginson" (pp. 122–40); Rita K. Gollin, "Subordinated Power: Mr. and Mrs. James T. Fields" (pp. 141–60); Cheryl B. Torsney, "The Traditions of Gender: Constance Fenimore Woolson and Henry James" (pp. 161–83); Lisa Pater Faranda, "A Social Necessity: The Friendship of Sherwood Bonner and Henry Wadsworth Longfellow" (pp. 184–211); and Joanne B. Karpinski, "When the Marriage of True Minds Admits Impediments: Charlotte Perkins Gilman and William Dean Howells" (pp. 212–34). The result is an uneven mix of history, biography, and aggressive critical perspective ("paternalism" occurs often), enacting the dilemma of contemporary enlightenment confronting its 19th-century equivalent.

In "The Female Bildungsroman in Nineteenth-Century America: Parameters of a Vision" (*JAC* 10, iv[1987]:69–75), Eve Kornfield and Susan Jackson test the subversive content of a subgenre of women's fiction. Their conclusion, too elaborately generalized from close examination only of Alcott's *Little Women* and Margaret Sidney's *Five Little Peppers and How They Grew*, is that this form of fiction created utopias within which heroines could find a freedom of development denied them in the male world outside. At least the argument is more accessible than that in Karen Sánchez-Eppler's "Bodily Bonds: The Intersecting Rhetorics of Feminism and Abolition" (*Representations* 24:28–59). William Lloyd Garrison, Lydia Maria Child, Stowe, Elizabeth Cady Stanton, and others share the stage with too many pages of notes continuing and qualifying the argument that "although the identifications of woman and slave, marriage and slavery, that characterize these texts may occasionally prove mutually empowering, they generally tend toward asymmetry and exploitation." Intersection of another kind is the topic of Zita Z. Dresner's "Sentiment and Humor: A Double-Pronged Attack on Women's Place in Nineteenth-Century America" (*StAH* n.s. 4[1985]:18–29), which argues that despite different methods the two forms of writing share a common perspective about "women's place." The strength of the essay is its survey of examples, from Ann Cora Mowatt, Caroline Kirkland, Ann Stephens, Frances Whitcher, Fanny Fern, and Gail Hamilton. In another essay concerned with humor and women's writing, "Limitations on the Comic Frame: Some Witty

American Women of the Nineteenth Century" (*QJS* 74:310–22), A. Cheree Carlson employs Kenneth Burke's notion of the comic frame to document the development of social attitudes. Her examination of works by Eliza Leslie, Whitcher, Phelps, Grace Greenwood, Gail Hamilton, Rose Terry Cooke, and Marietta Holley traces a shift in rhetorical mode from humor to satire to burlesque, and in content from debunking of the values of true womanhood, to bitterness about the difficulty of altering the social order, to diversion from present dangers as a means of avoiding the implications of the failure of the women's movement. Per Seyersted's "The American Girl from Howells to Chopin" (*ArAA* 13:183–92) is more obviously intended as a survey of the writers prominent later in the century, especially Howells, Freeman, Gilman, and Chopin. Seyersted concludes that the "portrayal of the young female" developed somewhat more fully among women writers than among the men.

Chief among the resources for research published during the year is *Humor in America*. Each of the 10 sections combines bibliographical essay and bibliographical inventory. Contributions dealing with 19th-century authors include Nancy Pogel and Paul P. Somers, Jr., "Literary Humor" (pp. 1–34); David E. E. Sloane, "Humor in Periodicals" (pp. 49–66); Zita Dresner, "Women's Humor" (pp. 137–61); Joseph Dorinson and Joseph Boskin, "Racial and Ethnic Humor" (pp. 164–93); and Stephen J. Whitfield, "Political Humor" (pp. 195–211). Steven E. Kagle's *Late Nineteenth-Century American Diary Literature* (*TUSAS* 524) is the third and final volume of his survey of the genre. Kagle is more interested in the kinds of histories reflected in the works than he is in a theory of diary. He discusses 26 diarists, major and minor, with an openness and lack of prejudice that make the book a comfortable introductory resource. There were also several additions to the continuing *DLB* industry—*American Magazine Journalists, 1741–1850*, ed. Sam G. Riley (*DLB* 73), the first of three volumes devoted to this group, and *American Short Story Writers Before 1880*, ed. Bobby Ellen Gimbel (*DLB* 74), the first of an as yet undetermined number. An unfortunate characteristic of the discussions of short story writers is a concentration on collections rather than on the original individual publications.

There were also two publications dealing with broadsides. Arthur Schrader's "Broadside Ballads of Boston, 1813: The Isaiah Thomas Collection" (*PAAS* 98:69–111) provides history and bibliography of a collection Thomas bought in 1813 and gave to the American Antiquarian Society in 1814. The broadsides themselves span the Revolution to the early stages of the War of 1812, and include political, military, and religious songs. William Moss's *Confederate Broadside Poems: An Annotated Descriptive Bibliography* (Meckler) describes the collection in the Z. Smith Reynolds Library at Wake Forest. Moss introduces the 228 entries with a thorough and useful survey of the literary and historical conditions surrounding their creation.

ii. Irving, Simms, Cooper, and Contemporaries

A book and three essays devoted wholly to Irving constitutes something of a modest revival. Jeffrey Rubin-Dorsky's *Adrift in the Old World: The Psychological Pilgrimage of Washington Irving* (Chicago) argues that past study of Irving has failed to place him in a full, active historical context. Rubin-Dorsky initiates the remedial process by setting out readings of the major work of the expatriate period, 1815–32, including *The Sketch Book* as a coherent whole, the separate stories "Rip Van Winkle" and "The Legend of Sleepy Hollow," *Bracebridge Hall*, *Tales of a Traveller*, and *The Alhambra*. Avoiding the more obvious biographical strategy that "historicizing" might seem to require, he opts instead for subtle psychological readings on the one side and broad cultural implications on the other. The energy and intensity of the effort are laudable and add depth to the Irving we already know: the "history of his search for order and literary sustenance in the Old World" proves to be, "in a wonderfully paradoxical fashion," a recapitulation of America's own effort to locate a national self in an age of unfathomable change.

The essays make less ambitious claims. Jane D. Eberwein's compact reading of "Transatlantic Contrasts in Irving's *Sketch Book*" (*CollL* 15:153–70) identifies the book's opposing views of English and American landscape, imagination, and character as a unifying device as compelling as the voice of Geoffrey Crayon, and yet indeterminate in their effect. Another treatment of Irving's use of the American scene, Hugh Egan's "The Second-Hand Wilderness: History and Art in Irving's *Astoria*" (*ATQ* 2:253–70), argues that the use of derivative materials freed the artist to present in that book "a bolder, more 'primary' vision of the frontier" than he was able to manage in *A Tour on the Prairies*, which had drawn on his own experience. Rather than dramatizing as *Tour* had done the shaping of an amoral wilderness into a coherent romantic history, *Astoria*, equally effective as conscious art, enacts the subversion of the unifying vision by "the stubbornly separate and limiting perceptions of experience." Donald A. Ringe's "Irving's 'Mountjoy': Philosophy in the Comic Mode" (*StAH* n.s. 3[1984–85]:290–97) describes Irving's philosophical sources and argues that the story, which breaks off abruptly, was not meant to continue: it had already made Irving's point—"the causes and consequences of, as well as the cure for, a disordered imagination."

Two other essays set Irving in a comparative context. John S. Hardt's "Doubts in the American Garden: Three Cases of Paradisal Skepticism" (*SSF* 25:249–59) treats "Rip Van Winkle," Poe's "The Fall of the House of Usher," and Hawthorne's "Young Goodman Brown" as parallel narratives on the return to a less-than-ideal rural setting; Hardt makes too much of Irving's not making much of the issue. And John Guthrie, in "Washington Irving's *Bracebridge Hall* and Annette von Droste-Hülshoff's *Bei uns zu Lande auf dem Lande*" (*MLR* 83:351–63), catalogues the significant features of a work the German writer took as a conscious model for a project she proved unable to complete.

The solid standard introduction to Cooper, Donald A. Ringe's *James Fenimore Cooper* (TUSAS 11), has been republished in an "updated edition." Ringe surveys developments in Cooper scholarship since the publication of the first edition of his book in 1962, including the ongoing edition of the writings at Clark University in which he is a participant, and enhances the already effective critical perspective of the original. His notion of Cooper's ever-developing search for the moral significance of the relationship of man and nature, however, remains compellingly the same. Cooper is the focus of a chapter in Mark R. Patterson's *Authority, Autonomy and Representation*, "Myth from the Perspective of History: James Fenimore Cooper and Paternal Authorities" (pp. 81–136). Patterson argues that Cooper responded to the literary and political dilemma of American democracy—how to influence a people suspicious of any kind of authority—by attempting to align history and myth and to combine traditional white power with native Indian authority.

Charles H. Adams in "Cooper's Sea Fiction and *The Red Rover*" (*SAF* 16, ii:155–68) reviews Cooper's uses of the "neutral ground," where human action must be based on an immanent or implicit sense of civilized order, and then offers a specific reading of the conflict of Stimson and Wilder in *The Red Rover* in that light. Adams's was the only essay not treating some aspect of the Leatherstocking novels. Lance Schachterle and Kent Ljungquist take Cooper's side in "Fenimore Cooper's Literary Defenses: Twain and the Text of *The Deerslayer*" (*SAR*, pp. 401–17), answering Twain's famous attack with an inventory of his distortions, manipulations, misreadings, and fabrications; in a spirit of fairness they also point out that Twain missed real errors in the reprinted edition of the novel he was using. Thomas S. Gladsky, "The Beau Ideal and Cooper's *The Pioneers*" (*SNNTS* 20:43–54), traces the concept, appropriated from Maria Edgeworth and Thomas Jefferson, from *Precaution* through *The Spy* to *The Pioneers*, where Oliver Effingham represents a triumph of both the idea and Cooper's skill in rendering it for purposes of cultural analysis. Much slighter is Reuben J. Ellis's "Cooper's Imps: A Way of Talking about Indians" (*MSE* 10[1986]:209–12), which counts the occurrences of devilish expressions and concludes that European-Americans could conceptualize about the indigenous peoples only in "already established metaphorical structures of language and thought." In "American Indians and German Indians: Perspectives of Doom in Cooper and May" (*WAL* 23:217–22) Martin Kuester draws especially on *The Last of the Mohicans* and Karl May's *Winnetou* (1893) to assert, unconvincingly, that differences in technical point of view in the novels permit Cooper to take various attitudes toward the Indians but May only one—an identification of the Indians' cause with his own which thus deprives them of their own history. Ruth Morse takes a densely argued comparative look at the same novel as well as at the Australian writer Katharine Susannah Prichard's *Coonardoo* (1828) and the English writer John Masters's *Bhowani Junction* (1954). "Impossible Dreams: Miscegenation and Building Nations" (*Southerly* 48:80–96) examines reduplication and character-splitting as devices for setting out cultural fantasies of both racial separation and racial equality. And Leonard W. Engel, "Sam Peckinpah's Heroes: Natty Bumppo and the Myth of the Rugged Individual Still Reign" (*LFQ* 16:22–30), advances a well-informed look at the same theme in different media. Comparing *The Prairie* and *The Deerslayer* to Peckinpah's western films, Engel notes the love-hate reaction of both artists to the struggle between wilderness and advancing civilization and their skill in embodying those tensions in "mythic moments" drawing on pastoral elegy and nostalgia. Female myth in the Leatherstocking novels and the intellectual relationship of father and daughter are the topics of "Susan

Fenimore Cooper and the Plain Daughters of America" (*AQ* 40: 131–46). Lucy B. Maddox notes James Fenimore Cooper's creation of an "American daughter-myth to complement the masculine hero-myth embodied in the figure of the childless man of the woods, Natty Bumppo," and sees Susan's writings as an attempt to justify that vision of the vulnerable daughter who through the father's violence survives moral and physical danger.

Simms, who of late has been the subject of only an essay or two a year, is represented by a collection of a dozen of them, and several more besides. *Long Years of Neglect: The Work and Reputation of William Gilmore Simms*, ed. John Caldwell Guilds (Arkansas), a festschrift in honor of the late Thomas Carey Eaves, presents an effective array of biographical and critical discussions. The editor's "'Long Years of Neglect': Atonement at Last?" (pp. 3–19) surveys Simms's reputation, with particular emphasis on the influence of William Peterfield Trent. The other essays are James B. Meriwether, "The Theme of Freedom in Simms's *Woodcraft*" (pp. 20–36); Anne M. Blythe, "William Gilmore Simms's *The Cassique of Kiawah* and the Principles of His Art" (pp. 37–59); Linda E. McDaniel, "American Gods and Devils in Simms's *Paddy McGann*" (pp. 60–75); Nicholas G. Meriwether, "Simms's *The Lily and the Totem*: History for the Purposes of Art" (pp. 76–105); James E. Kibler, Jr., "Perceiver and Perceived: External Landscape as Mirror and Metaphor in Simms's Poetry" (pp. 106–25); David Moltke-Hansen, "Ordered Progress: The Historical Philosophy of William Gilmore Simms" (pp. 126–47); Mary Ann Wimsatt, "The Evolution of Simms's Backwoods Humor" (pp. 148–65); Rayburn S. Moore, "Paul Hamilton Hayne and William Gilmore Simms: Friends, Colleagues, and Members of the Guild" (pp. 166–82); Miriam J. Shillingsburg, "Simms's Failed Lecture Tour of 1856: The Mind of the North" (pp. 183–201); John McCardell, "Biography and the Southern Mind: William Gilmore Simms" (pp. 202–16); and Louis D. Rubin, Jr., "Simms, Charleston, and the Profession of Letters" (pp. 217–34). In "Bald-Head Bill Bauldy: Simms' Unredeemed Captive" (*StAH* n.s. 3[1984–85]:321–29) Stephen E. Meats notes Simms's exploitation of the combination of southwestern humor and the fictional captivity narrative to express a number of the "most serious thematic concerns of his post-Civil War writings." And Charles H. Brichford offers up an exhaustive look at the uses of history in American fiction in "That National Story: Conflicting Versions and Conflicting Visions of the Revolution in Kennedy's *Horse-Shoe Robinson* and Simms's *The Partisan*" (*SLJ* 21, i:64–85). Brichford sees Simms's rewriting of history and his attack on Kennedy's novel as parts of a single-minded effort to protect "the elaborate fictional model of the South's past" he had labored to create.

There were only individual essays on other writers of the period. Hugh Egan, "'One of Them': The Voyage of Style in Dana's *Two Years before the Mast*" (*ATQ* 2:177–90) undertakes a close analysis of the tensions between the narrative of initiation and the language in which Dana expresses it, and concludes that Dana repudiates Boston gentility even as his style embraces it. The essay is particularly useful in breaking through the apparent sameness of early 19th-century historical prose. William W. Stowe describes how Virgil A. Stewart, author of a firsthand account of the capture of the notorious John A. Murrell in 1834, used his narrative account of the episode—an account hitherto ascribed to someone else—to transform himself from "shadowy witness" to "prototype thriller hero" ("Hard-Boiled Virgil: Early Nineteenth-Century Beginnings of a Popular Literary Formula," *The Sleuth and the Scholar*, pp. 79–90). And Michael John McDonough offers "James Kirke Paulding: A Bibliographic Survey" (*RALS* 15[1985]:145–61).

iii. Popular Writers of Midcentury

Harriet Beecher Stowe, Catharine Esther Beecher, and Isabella Beecher Hooker speak and are spoken about in Jeanne Boydston, Mary Kelley, and Anne Margolis's *The Limits of Sisterhood: The Beecher Sisters on Women's Rights and Woman's Sphere* (No. Car.). The volume offers some critical discussion by the authors, mostly introductory, with a valuable gathering of documents—mostly essays and letters by the three sisters but also several public statements about them—chosen to trace both the interrelationships of their lives and their participation in the evolution of ideas of womanhood.

Two essays dealing with Stowe took a narrower biographical tack. In "'Peaceable Fruits': The Ministry of Harriet Beecher Stowe" (*AQ* 40:307–32) Joan D. Hedrick proposes that Stowe's "immersion in a women's culture" led her to an "egalitarian vision" different from the pastoral model of her father and the male clerical establishment. But that vision, articulated in *Uncle Tom's Cabin* and *The Minister's Wooing*, was dismissed as sentimental by the Gilded Age; and since Stowe had not defined it systematically, she "had no formulated historical memory" of it and lapsed from it. The argument is provocative, the hard evidence elusive. In "'No Voice from England': Mrs. Stowe, Mr. Lincoln, and the British in the Civil War" (*NEQ* 61:3–24) Wendy F. Hamand recounts Stowe's highly successful efforts to employ her pen and her fame to establish the "moral superiority of the Union cause" among English readers. A third essay, Philip Fisher's "Democratic Social Space: Whitman, Melville, and the Promise of American Transparency" (*Representations* 24:60–101), contrasts *Uncle Tom's Cabin* to Melville's "Benito Cereno" in its reestablishment of unified social desires against the economic strain of slavery. Stowe's novel, Fisher concludes, repairs this fragmentation with "sentimental feeling, . . . the one universalizing, radical method for reconstructing a social world." Fisher ignores George Harris's argument for Liberia.

Louisa May Alcott was represented by two editorial enterprises. *A Double Life: Newly Discovered Thrillers of Louisa May Alcott*, ed. Madeleine B. Stern, with Joel Myerson and Daniel Shealy (Little, Brown), reprints five stories rife with desperate anguish and evil portent published anonymously in the Frank Leslie periodicals between 1863 and 1867. Stern's introduction (pp. 3–32) discusses origins, themes, and relationships to Alcott's other interests, but doesn't connect these items very clearly to similar items she collected in *Behind a Mask: The Unknown Thrillers of Louisa May Alcott* (1975). Editorial intervention is minimal and corrective. Myerson, Shealy, and Stern also prepared "A Calendar of the Letters of Louisa May Alcott" (*SAR*, pp. 361–99), supplementing their *Selected Letters* (1987).

Other women writers of the period received scanter attention, mostly single essays. D. G. Myers's "The Canonization of Susan Warner" (*NewC* 7, iv:73–78) attacks Jane Tompkins's advocacy of Warner's *Wide, Wide World* in her *Sensational Designs* (1985). Concerned that what will become canonical is not the novel but Tompkins's reading of it, Myers notes how Warner's religious novel has been critically transformed into an obsession with the "nature of power" and her message of salvation rewritten as submission. The essay is an attack writ small on the fundamentally ahistorical premises of the New Historicism. Susan K. Harris, "Inscribing and Defining: The Many Voices of Fanny Fern's *Ruth Hall*" (*Style* 22:612–27), presumes a writer conscious of the literary conventions of her time and deliberately manipulating them. Though *Ruth Hall* seems straightforwardly sentimental, Harris identifies it as subversive (the latest buzzword of gender-biased analysis): its apparent confusion in the portrayal of the heroine is actually "a split consciousness," contrasting an apparently silent, devoted woman with the real future awaiting her. Mary G. De Jong's biographical and critical introduction, with selected bibliography, of Lydia Howard Huntley Sigourney (*Legacy* 5, i:35–43), Shirley Marchalonis's like effort for Lucy Larcom (*Legacy* 5, i:45–52), and Patricia G. Holland's for Lydia Maria Child (*Legacy* 5, ii:45–53) form the most recent contributions to the "Legacy Profile" series. Sigourney was also the subject of Annie Finch's "The Sentimental Poetess in the World: Metaphor and Subjectivity in Lydia Sigourney's Nature Poetry" (*Legacy* 5, ii:3–18). In the course of surveying Sigourney's work, Finch also argues that 19th-century poetry by women, though mostly ignored now because of its sentimentality and failure to enact "a male model of poet as prophet or seer" intent on change, has its own model of self-effacement and of willingness to leave the world as it is.

The male writers of the period were not entirely ignored. Lawrence Buell edited *Henry Wadsworth Longfellow: Selected Poems* (Penguin) with an introduction defending Longfellow's stolid individualism and his commitment to a life of literature. In a thorough piece of literary detective work, Kent Ljungquist and Buford Jones, "The Identity of 'Outis': A Further Chapter in the Poe-Longfellow War" (*AL* 60:402–15), settle on Lawrence Labree, editor of the New York *Rover*, as Longfellow's defender against Poe's 1845 plagiarism charges. Fiction is the subject of Anne Dalke's "Economics, or the Bosom Serpent: Oliver Wendell Holmes' *Elsie Venner: A Romance of Destiny*" (*ATQ* 2:57–68). Dalke proposes that Holmes's fable on the unavoidable heredity of original/sexual sin is also an attack on the money-getting which threatens to displace everything else: Elsie "seeks affection in a world in which destiny is, immutably, economic." Discussion of Horatio Alger, Jr., mostly biographical and minor, was confined to the pages of *Newsboy* (published by the Horatio Alger Society). The exception was Eileen Mountjoy Cooper's "Horatio Alger, Jr. and Unitarianism" (25, iii[1986]:8–20), a review of family and personal relationships to the institution as well as attitudes expressed in the stories.

Michael Wentworth, "A Matter of Taste: Fitz-James O'Brien's 'The Diamond Lens' and Poe's Aesthetic of Beauty" (*ATQ* 2:271–84), forsakes text for influence. Wentworth insists on the debt of

O'Brien's 1858 story about a beautiful animalcule to Poe's blueprint for the perfect poem about the death of a beautiful woman. Richard L. Bushman, "The Book of Mormon in Early Mormon History" (*New Views of Mormon History*, pp. 3–18), connects the insistence on record-keeping in Mormon culture with the insistence expressed in the Book of Mormon itself on Joseph Smith's responsibility to translate it. And in a plodding, mechanical discussion, B. J. Rahn, "Seeley Regester: America's First Detective Novelist" (*The Sleuth and the Scholar*, pp. 47–61), argues that Regester (pseudonym for Metta Victoria Fuller Victor) and not Anna Katharine Green published the first detective novel in English.

iv. Humorists and Southern Writers

In "*Georgia Scenes*: The Satiric Artistry of Augustus Baldwin Longstreet" (*MissQ* 41, i[1987–88]:21–37) Keith Newlin offers a convincing if dull corrective to the notion of Longstreet's book as a collection of loosely connected sketches. Instead, he argues, it is unified by its alternation between episodes "portraying the cruelty inherent in encounters between common people" and those "satirizing the no less cruel behavior of the supposed social elite." The characters of Hall and Baldwin personify these dimensions, the former closer to the common world and eventually taking part in its violence, the latter more educated and distant and observing its manners.

Edward J. Piacentino makes extravagant claims for the stylistic skill of Mortimer Neal Thomson. "'A Series of Unpremeditated Literary Extravaganzas': Mortimer Thomson's *Doesticks: What He Says*" (*MarkhamR* 16[Fall–Winter 1986]:7–11) reviews the history and popularity of the series of newspaper letters collected into the book, then outlines and approves its comic strategies. Piacentino's "Doesticks' Assault on Slavery: Style and Technique in *The Great Auction Sale of Slaves, at Savannah, Georgia*" (*Phylon* 48[1987]: 196–203) praises "Doesticks' most unrestrained work of polemical satire, and his most unrelenting piece of propagandist protest." Piacentino also offers a slighter commentary on a lesser-known writer. In "Kittrell Warren's *Ups and Downs of Wife Hunting*: A Hybrid of Two Humorous Traditions" (*SoSt* 26[1987]:154–61) he identifies a Civil War pamphlet as a mixture of both southwestern and "more restrained and sophisticated" humor. Fritz Oehlschlaeger, "A Bibliography of Frontier Humor in the St. Louis *Daily Reveille*,

1844–46" (*StAH* n.s. 3[1984–85]:267–89), lists 163 items, the majority unascribed, from one of the principal outlets for southwestern humor.

"Writing Herstory: Mary Chesnut's Civil War" (*SoSt* 26[1987]: 18–27) advances an aggressively clever feminist reading. Clara Juncker claims that the diary form "allowed Chesnut to pen-etrate [*sic*] her adversaries" and fight the war on her own terms, "without any revealing stains on her own femininity." Even the gaps, erasures, and silences convey meaning: "its author could not or would not represent her woman's experience in language." The danger of reading so insistently, if not clear enough from this essay, is demonstrated in Melissa A. Mentzer's "A Note on Textual Concerns in the Journals of Mary Chesnut" (*ABSt* 4:53–56), which faults C. Vann Woodward for making an edition that incorporated earlier readings into Chesnut's 1880 text, for misidentifying the dates of those earlier readings, and for treating the different forms as versions rather than separate works.

Joel Chandler Harris was the subject of a dozen items, all but one of them in a special issue of the *Atlanta Historical Journal*, "Joel Chandler Harris: The Writer in His Time and Ours," guest-edited by Hugh T. Keenan (30, iii–iv[1986–87]). The contents include two bibliographical surveys, "The Works of Joel Chandler Harris: A Bibliography," by Bruce Bickley, Jr. (pp. 33–35), actually an odd and unsystematic list of books only, and Bickley and Keenan's "Joel Chandler Harris: An Annotated Secondary Bibliography" (pp. 141–48). The essays are Bickley's "Joel Chandler Harris and the Old and New South: Paradoxes of Perception" (pp. 9–31); Kenneth H. Thomas, Jr., "Roots and Environment: The Family Background" (pp. 37–56); Lee Pederson, "Rewriting Dialect Literature: 'The Wonderful Tar-Baby Story'" (pp. 57–70); Joseph M. Griska, Jr., "Joel Chandler Harris: 'Accidental Author' or 'Aggressive Businessman'?" (pp. 71–78); Eric L. Montenyohl, "Joel Chandler Harris and American Folklore" (pp. 79–88); Mary Louise Weaks, "A Meeting of Southerners: Joel Chandler Harris, Mark Twain, and George Washington Cable" (pp. 89–96); William R. Bell, "The Relationship of Joel Chandler Harris and Mark Twain" (pp. 97–111); and William Bradley Strickland, "Stereotypes and Subversion in *The Chronicles of Aunt Minervy Ann*" (pp. 129–39). The other item was Linda S. Chang, "Brer Rabbit's Angolan Cousin: Politics and the Adaptation of Folk Material" (*FForum* 19[1986]:36–50), comparing the different applications made of similar materials by Harris and the modern Angolan writer Manuel Pedro Pacavira.

Folklore is also the topic of one of the three essays dealing with George Washington Cable. Thomas J. Richardson's "George W. Cable's 'Jean ah Poquelin': Folklore and the New South" (*MissFR* 21[1987]:81–88) associates Cable's gradual decline as a writer of fiction with his ambivalence about the South, an ambivalence particularly reflected in the clash of judgment and sympathy in his treatment of Creoles in "Jean ah Poquelin." The other two essays offer different perspectives on the same work. Schölin Tipping's "'The Sinking Plantation-House': Cable's Narrative Method in *The Grandissimes*" (*EiP* 13:63–80) sets out two incompletely connected arguments. One is that Cable saw as destructive forces the Creole tendency to create pleasing fictions rather than acknowledge facts and to depend upon the institution of slavery; the other, that the shifting point of view, the various acts of irresponsibility, foolishness, and violence, and the images of decay and danger in *The Grandissimes* are marks of a society about to collapse. Charles Swann's "The Price of Charm: The Heroines of *The Grandissimes*" (*EiP* 13:81–88) is allusive rather than disconnected in remarking the ironic parallels between the subjugation of white women by men and that of blacks by whites.

Clara Juncker's "Grace King: Feminist, Southern Style" (*SoQ* 26, iii:15–30) reviews King's positions on women's questions, including her acknowledgment of cultural and biological limitations and her identification of solutions and alternatives. The essay is satisfactory as survey, though shaky in identifying its historical perspective, particularly when claiming of King that "Like numerous other nineteenth-century women writers, she hid her 'improper' anger and militancy behind a becoming imaginative veil." Juncker's "The Mother's Balcony: Grace King's Discourse of Femininity" (*NOR* 15, i:39–46), drawing on the work of Julia Kristeva and Hélène Cixous, reiterates this sense of the writer as subtle subversive: King, "trapped in patriarchal sign-systems" and mostly expressing a conventional view of southern culture, nonetheless employs a rhetoric that is distinctively feminine and creates a linguistic space—represented by the "mother's balcony" in *Balcony Stories*—where that rhetoric can be voiced. The only other essay dealing with King was Ahmed Nimeiri's "'Reconstruction, which was also war . .' : Realism and Allegory in Grace King's *The Pleasant Ways of St. Médard*"

(*MissQ* 41[1987–88]:39–54), an extravagant and unsubstantiated reading of the 1916 novel not as a picture of Reconstruction life or an effective rendering of personal experience but as a prototypical modernist text.

Ethel C. Simpson's "Ruth McEnery Stuart: The Innocent Grotesque" (*LaLit* 4, i[1987]:57–65) contrasts Stuart's accuracy in depicting southern life with her general sentimentality, optimism, and ignorance of the dark side, and compares her to Eudora Welty and Flannery O'Connor. Dorothy H. Brown's "Ruth McEnery Stuart: A Reassessment" (*XUS* 7, ii[1987]:23–36) responds with a view of Stuart's naturalness as a storyteller, understanding of human psychology, unstereotypical presentation of women characters, and insight into black-white relations.

Other southern writers were subjects of single essays. Alice Parker's "The Civil War Journal of Julia LeGrand Waitz (1861–1863)" (*NOR* 15, i:69–72) is mostly descriptive, emphasizing the writer as astute analyst of events, conditions, and issues. In "Mary Noailles Murfree's 'Special' Sense of Humor" (*StAH* n.s. 4, i–ii[1985]:30–38) Benjamin Franklin Fisher IV compares Murfree's uses of satire, irony, and violence with those of other southwestern humorists. His conclusion that she domesticates and tones down does not quite jibe with his finding that her villains are characterized by "rapaciousness and murderousness" rather than by "endearing roguishness." Rayburn S. Moore collects biographical and critical information bearing on Paul Hamilton Hayne's attitudes about Shakespeare in " 'A Soul That Took in All Humanity'—Hayne on Shakespeare" (*UMSE* n.s. 6:119–27). And in "Responding to the 'Airplant' Tradition: John Cooke's *My Lady Pokahontas*" (*SLJ* 21, i:54–63), A. Carl Bredahl compares that 1885 novel to Cooke's earlier *The Virginia Comedians* (1854) to assert on very tenuous grounds that the writer understood more clearly after the war the problem of the southern past, and so created a fiction that, unlike an airplant, had roots in real southern soil.

v. Post-Civil War Women Writers

"Rebecca Harding Davis (1831–1910): A Bibliography of Secondary Criticism" (*BB* 45:233–46) by Sharon M. Harris is both more and less useful than its title suggests. The first section adds to and corrects the record of *primary* items in Ruth M. Stemple's 1957 *BB* checklist; the second updates Stemple's record of secondary materials, in a somewhat unusual alphabetical rather than chronological-plus-alphabetical arrangement. In "Rebecca Harding Davis: A Continuing Misattribution" (*Legacy* 5, i:33–34) Harris identifies Fanny Aikin Kortright as the author of *Pro Aris et Focis* and explains the basis for the long-standing error.

Three essays on Jewett represent an interesting range of perspectives. Michael Holstein in "Writing as a Healing Art in Sarah Orne Jewett's *The Country of the Pointed Firs*" (*SAF* 16:39–49) offers a powerful elucidation of a work we thought we already knew well. Holstein sees as synthesizing Jewett's primary narrative, the biography of Dunnet's Landing, and her secondary one, the narrator's choice between objectivity or participation in the experience, by means of the evolution of the writer into a writer-healer, perfecting her role under the guidance of Elvira Todd. *Country of the Pointed Firs* is also the crucial text for Robin Magowan, whose chapter on "Jewett" (pp. 68–90) in *Narcissus and Orpheus: Pastoral in Sand, Fromentin, Jewett, Alain-Fournier and Dinesen* (Garland) is less successful. Magowan traces Jewett's debts in the pastoral tradition through Thérèse Blanc-Bentzon to George Sand and then offers comments about Jewett's strategies for exploiting the mode. Issues of genre in Jewett and the English writer Flora Thompson engage Sandra A. Zagarell in "Narrative of Community: The Identification of a Genre" (*Signs* 13:498–527). Defining a literary tradition in which the self is part of an "interdependent network of the community rather than . . . an individualistic unit," Zagarell proceeds to describe antecedents to and features of the genre, its differing function among male and female writers, and the cultural variations worked in Jewett's *Country of the Pointed Firs* and Thompson's *Lark Rise* (1939).

In the revised edition of *Mary Wilkins Freeman* (TUSAS 122) Perry D. Westbrook updates his 1965 biographical-critical introduction in light of more recent scholarship to enhance the view of Freeman as more than a regionalist. Susan Koppelman's "About 'Two Friends' and Mary Eleanor Wilkins Freeman" (*ALR* 21, i:43–57) adds to Freeman bibliography an item important for its lesbian perspective; Koppelman reprints the item and loosely speculates on the connection between its contents and Freeman's friendship with Mary Wales.

Not surprisingly, Charlotte Perkins Gilman received a significant amount of attention, including a book-length study. Polly Wynn Allen's *Building Domestic Liberty: Charlotte Perkins Gilman's Architectural Feminism* (Mass.) ties Gilman's concern with the difficulties of "middle-class domestic life" to her development of an "eclectic vision of alternative landscapes," ethical as well as physical environments more conducive to harmonious life. Allen concentrates on identifying other contemporary views of domestic landscape and Gilman's views of neighborhood design and world improvement, and emphasizes relevant social theory rather than literary art in the fiction. But those emphases do not diminish the book's value as background to the writer's literary strategies and achievements. The three essays about Gilman deal with "The Yellow Wallpaper." In "Who is Jane? The Intricate Feminism of Charlotte Perkins Gilman" (*ArQ* 44, iii:40–79) William Veeder applies to the story various psychological models of boundary- and object-relations, particularly those of Freud and Melanie Klein. It is not altogether clear that such a context is essential to Veeder's conclusion that "by denying any simple theory of female victimization and insisting upon the self-victimizing force of regressive inclinations and repressed desire, [Gilman] indicts marriage for fostering the infantile propensities that it should help wife and husband grow beyond." Eugenia C. DeLamotte's "Male and Female Mysteries in 'The Yellow Wallpaper'" (*Legacy* 5, i:3–14) construes the "medical mysteries" by which male doctors control women and the female mysteries which men cannot accommodate as Gilman's play against Gothic convention. Gloria A. Biamonte's "'. . . There is a story, if we could only find it': Charlotte Perkins Gilman's 'The Giant Wistaria'" (*Legacy* 5, ii:33–38) discusses a less well-known story published the year before "The Yellow Wallpaper" and containing the seeds of the latter's implicit "radical restructuring of society."

Alice James is the subject of Janet Varner Gunn's "The Autobiographical Occupation: Alice James's Diary and the Decoration of Space" (*ABSt* 4:37–45), an essay more theoretical than explicative. Referring to the means and effects of making "*living* rooms out of dead space" enunciated by Edith Wharton in *Decoration of Houses*, Gunn argues that for Wharton and James the autobiographical process was rehabilitative; for James in particular the making of the diary produced from an inert and indistinct past a present that was "smaller, sometimes miniaturized, but remarkably detailed and kinetic." A similar concern with the genre is addressed by Judy Nolte

Lensink in "Expanding the Boundaries of Criticism: The Diary as Female Autobiography" (*WS* 14[1987]:39–53). Lensink suggests tentatively and untheoretically that the privacy of the diary is more likely than other forms of writing to yield truth, and draws upon the 30-year diary of Emily Hawley Gillespie, an Iowa farm wife, for examples of strategies of revelation and secrecy, private and public personae.

Daniel E. Sutherland's "Some Thoughts Concerning the Love Life of Sherwood Bonner" (*SoSt*[1987]:115–27) accepts Ellen Kirk's *The Story of Margaret Kent* (1886) as equivalent to fact and thus proof that the lecture agent James Redpath was Bonner's principal romantic interest. That Bonner's correspondence is almost silent about Redpath, Sutherland thinks only "curious." Silence is very emphatically a consideration in Carol Holly's essay on Elizabeth Stuart Phelps, "Shaming the Self in 'The Angel over the Right Shoulder'" (*AL* 60:42–60). Extending comments about the story made by Judith Fetterley, Holly argues that its weak and sentimental ending represents an internalization of the prescriptions of a patriarchal culture and that the task of the modern "feminist reader" is to expose this "cycle of self-defeating behaviors and shame-based attitudes." The overassertiveness of the stance is particularly out of place in the pages of *American Literature*.

"Frances Miriam Whitcher: Social Satire in the Age of Gentility" (*WS* 15:99–116) by Linda A. Morris surveys Whitcher's various collections of sketches, particularly *The Widow Bedott Papers* (1880), as well as manuscript materials. Morris presents an unstrident view of a social commentator whose lack of political perspective led her to blame women themselves, not social or sexual constraint, for their shallowness; Whitcher's satire also put a strain on her social standing and her marriage. Mary Loeffelholz surveys the works of another lesser writer in "Subversion and Genre: The Postwar Fiction of Frances Dana Gage" (*Legacy* 5, ii:19–32). She describes Gage's combination of feminist analysis of class with temperance message, and concludes she did not go far enough: subversion, after all, "by its very nature courts recontainment within the very narrative and ideological structures it would hollow out." Beth Wynne Fisken, "Within the Limits of Alice Brown's 'Dooryards': Introspective Powers in *Tiverton Tales*" (*Legacy* 5, i:15–25), identifies yet another feminist alternative. Brown, she says, accepted the cult of domesticity but proceeded to stress its universality, its freedom from mere physical boundaries: "Her characters, meditating by their hearths, explore the uncharted territories of their own souls as poets, mystics, and inheritors." Two essays deal with Frances Hodgson Burnett. Claudia Marquis's "The Power of Speech: Life in *The Secret Garden*" (*AUMLA* 68[1987]:163–87) uses Freud and Lacan to locate the political significance embedded even in children's fiction; Burnett's particular political position is that motherhood is power. And M. Sarah Smedman, in "Springs of Hope: Recovery of Primordial Time in 'Mythic' Novels for Young Readers" (*ChildL* 16:91–107), compares the stable, pastoral world of Burnett's novel to the horrible modern life depicted in several more recent works.

vi. The Howells Generation: Realism and Utopianism

As Elsa Nettels puts it so succinctly in the first sentence of her introduction to *Language, Race, and Social Class in Howells's America* (Kentucky), "This study centers on William Dean Howells as a writer about language." Her chapters survey Howells's perspective on issues much discussed in his time—the nature of language, "correct" English, the implications of slang and vernacular, euphemism and exaggeration; his ideas about a peculiarly American language; and language matters addressed in his novels from *Their Wedding Journey* through *Leatherwood God.* The pace of the argument is sometimes plodding, and the issues not always as exciting as the title's reference to race and social class might suggest. And yet Nettels is fully sympathetic with Howells's agenda: his concern for the nuances as well as the crucial social effects of language, his work for democratic equality as a positive good, and his recognition that language constituted a barrier to that goal.

In "Howells on My Mind: Reflections on the Dean's Sesquicentennial" (*NEQ* 61:183–200) Jerry Herron pays curiously elusive tribute to Howells for having defined his cultural function in such a way as to assure his own lapse from fame: "The fact of his having been so conveniently forgotten allows us now to do more things with him. Howells remains, then, because we need him: ringmaster extraordinaire of our absence-seeking circus, a contented and successful nobody." Herron credits Howells with having recognized that the loss of belief in cultural or religious values demanded a replacement; replacement consisted for him in "service," performing and doing even when no end could be conceived or obtained. Herron makes most of

Howells's silences, particularly those moments in the creation of his fiction when he could not write. Marcia Jacobson's "The Mask of Fiction: William Dean Howells's Experiments in Autobiography" (*Biography* 10[1987]:55–67) is better tied to what Howells actually said and did. This examination of the autobiographical writing in light of the theories of Philippe Le Jeune and Shirley Neuman yields provocative assertions about Howells's formal and psychological responses to his awareness of the different selves existing within one personality. In an essay on *The Rise of Silas Lapham*, "Business Made Her Nervous: The Fall of Persis Lapham" (*ON* 12[1986]:419–38), Irene C. Gildman seeks to clarify the question of Silas's moral culpability for buying out his old business partner by examining his wife's credentials for making that judgment. In the process Goldman also illuminates Howells's general ambivalence about the moral superiority and the emotional weakness of women. Returning Howells's oft-quoted phrase about American realism to its original context, John Moore ("William Dean Howells and the Smiling Aspects of Life" [*JAmS* 22:255–58]) finds it "a far more profound indictment of Howells's moralism than any glib ritual invocation" has suggested.

Other fiction writers of the period received less attention. G. A. Cevasco and Richard Harmond print the author's own comments on the limitations of his badly received play in "Bret Harte to Robert Roosevelt on *Two Men of Sandy Bar*: A Newly Discovered Letter" (*ALR* 21, i:58–62). Veronica Brady's "The Return of the Repressed: J. B. O'Reilly and the Politics of Desire" (*Westerly* 33, ii:105–13) examines the American-published novel *Moondyne* (1880) and poetry of this Irish-born Australian convict and American newspaperman-man of letters. Her point: that O'Reilly's renditions of personal desire and isolation are more illuminating about western Australia than any other public writing of the time. Hamlin Garland was represented by two minor items. Kenneth M. Price argues unpersuasively in "Whitman's Influence on Hamlin Garland's *Rose of Dutcher's Coolly*" (*MStrR* 9, pt. 2:19–29) that Garland accepted the poet's candid and democratic notions of love relationships but did not sufficiently "internalize" them, and so created a novel at odds with itself. Price and Robert C. Leitz III print and annotate 12 letters written between 1886 and 1890 in "The Uncollected Letters of Hamlin Garland to Walt Whitman" (*WWR* 5, iii:1–13). And there was only one essay dealing with Harold Frederic. Richard S. Pressman's "*Seth's Brother's Wife*: Harold Frederic's Class Comedy" (*ALR* 21, i:29–42) defines the novel as comic rather than critical realism, thus basically conservative and in turn essentially preservative of the agrarian values it describes: "For Frederic, 'realism' is not so much a means of expressing protest over the loss of a tradition as it is a method of renewing that tradition."

Celebrating the centennial of America's best-known utopian fiction, *Looking Backward, 1988–1888: Essays on Edward Bellamy*, ed. Daphne Patai (Mass.), brings together nine original essays, including Patai's introductory "The Doubled Vision of Edward Bellamy" (pp. 3–20), which outlines the sources and innovations of Bellamy's socialism. The other contributions include Milton Cantor, "The Backward Look of Bellamy's Socialism" (pp. 21–36); Lee Cullen Khanna, "The Text as Tactic: *Looking Backward* and the Power of the Word" (pp. 37–50); Jean Pfaelzer, "Immanence, Indeterminance, and the Utopian Pun in *Looking Backward*" (pp. 51–67); Sylvia Strauss, "Gender, Class, and Race in Utopia" (pp. 68–90); Howard P. Segal, "Bellamy and Technology: Reconciling Centralization and Decentralization" (pp. 91–105); W. Warren Wagar, "Dreams of Reason: Bellamy, Wells, and the Positive Utopia" (pp. 106–25); Kenneth M. Roemer, "Getting 'Nowhere' beyond Statis: A Critique, a Method, and a Case" (pp. 126–46); and Franklin Rosemont, "Bellamy's Radicalism Reclaimed" (pp. 147–209), a disproportionately long attempt to fix Bellamy in the history of radical ideas and movements. The volume also provides a chronology by Sylvia Bowman and a modest bibliography prepared by Nancy Snell Griffith.

Both mass and thoroughness are the marks of Richard Toby Widdicombe's *Edward Bellamy: An Annotated Bibliography of Secondary Criticism* (Garland), which lists 2,310 items published between 1878 and October 1987, including books, articles, dissertations, chapters and subchapters, introductions and headnotes, and reviews. There are four different indexes, sections on sequels and ripostes to Bellamy's novels and on contemporary newspaper comment, and even a record of spurious and unlocated references. The annotation is factual and not interpretive.

The best of several separate essays focused on Bellamy was "Form and Reform in *Looking Backward*" (*ATQ* 2:69–82). Jane Gardiner is concerned with the ways literary form rather than ideology contributes to the novel's popularity and to Bellamy's purpose in writing "reform-propaganda" and not just "mere literary fantasy." She emphasizes particularly the interplay of "reflections and refractions," images of death and rebirth, and scenes of harmony and chaotic nightmare. Warren Sloat, "Looking Back at 'Looking Backward': We Have Seen the Future and It Didn't Work" (*NYTBR* Jan. 17:3, 34), takes a retrospective look at the implications of Bellamy's future world: "In too many places, history transmuted his tidy and inoffensive dream into a 20th-century nightmare." Janet Staiger, "Future Noir: Contemporary Representations of Visionary Cities" (*EW* 3, i:20–44) surveys literature—including *Looking Backward* and Bradford Peck's *The World a Department Store* (1900)—cinema, and television for models of the imaginative relationship between utopian ideas and the environments and architectures embodying them. Roger Neustadter, "Mechanization Takes Command: The Celebration of Technology in the Utopian Novels of Edward Bellamy, Chauncey Thomas, John Jacob Astor, and Charles Caryl" (*Extrapolation* 29:21–33), offers the works of these four writers as refutation of the commonplace that utopian fiction of the industrial age necessarily conceives technology as nightmare. David Ketterer's "'John Quill': The Women's Millennium" (*SFS* 15, i:82–87) advances an 1867 novel by Charles Heber Clark, writing under the pseudonym John Quill, as the "first SF utopia to focus on sex-role reversal."

vii. Fin de siècle: Crane, Norris, Bierce, Chopin, and Adams

The Correspondence of Stephen Crane, ed. Stanley Wertheim and Paul Sorrentino (Columbia), which prints letters both to and from, modestly but substantially replaces Stallman and Gilkes's earlier *Stephen Crane: Letters*, adding almost 400 items to their record—including 170 by Crane and 20 by Cora Crane—correcting their errors in text and dating, and relegating to an appendix because of serious doubt about their authoritativeness letters with no other source than Thomas Beer. The general introduction concentrates on the history of the letters, dealing with biography only in pointing out the unfortunate effect of taking Beer's work as fact. The letters are divided into sections preceded by brief introductions (though these divisions are not identified in the table of contents), and the annotation provides essential context. The format of the volumes could have used more thought, but in any case here is an edition that should make a difference. James W. Tuttleton takes the occasion of reviewing the *Correspondence* to offer a corrective to the popular images of Crane, in "'A Runaway Dog Like Me': Stephen Crane in His Letters" (*NewC* 6,x:49–58).

Stephen Crane is one of three writers (Virginia Woolf and Peter Matthiessen are the others) discussed in Deborah Schnitzer's chapter on "'Ocular Realism': The Impressionistic Effects of an 'Innocent Eye'" (*The Pictorial in Modernist Fiction*, pp. 7–62). Drawing heavily on the history of the development of Impressionism as an aesthetic, Schnitzer argues that earlier critics of Crane misunderstood or misapplied the term; and yet, she continues, some of Crane's work was impressionistic in the original sense of confining itself to the surface and to "the truths of the natural and factual vision." Another essay dealing with Crane and art, George Monteiro's "John Sloan's 'Cranes'" (*JML* 14:584–98) compares a group of sketches and paintings Sloan created between 1905 and 1916 to the Crane descriptions they parallel. Monteiro concludes both that Sloan knew Crane's work more fully than he admitted and that his treatment of similar subjects was "almost always softer, more humane" than Crane's. Donald B. Gibson's The Red Badge of Courage: *Redefining the Hero* (Twayne), meant as an elementary introduction, so oversimplifies the novel as a conflict between the perspectives of narrator and character as to do it serious injustice. Avoiding the recent battles over the text, Gibson uses R. W. Stallman's Signet Classic edition (1960) because it is "more thorough and detailed in its editing." Cinematic issues concern Richard Keenan, whose "The Sense of an Ending: Jan Kadar's Distortion of Stephen Crane's *The Blue Hotel*" (*LFQ* 16:265–68) finds fault with a film adaptation, and James A. Stevenson, whose "Beyond Stephen Crane: *Full Metal Jacket*" (*LFQ* 16:238–43) identifies Stanley Kubrick's 1987 film as a parody of *Red Badge*. Paul Sorrentino, "New Evidence on Stephen Crane at Syracuse" (*RALS* 15[1985]: 179–85), prints two statements written by college friends which bear on the period of the writing of *Maggie*.

The revival of interest in Frank Norris hits a peak with Barbara Hochman's *The Art of Frank Norris, Storyteller* (Missouri). Like Don Graham, whose lead she is following, Hochman wants to get behind Norris's current reputation as a "naive naturalist" (Graham's words) to the sources of his high repute in his own time. She examines the fiction "on the basis of recurrent motifs that resist incorporation into the pattern of meanings traditionally attributed to his work," principal among them language and storytelling, the problematics of self, and flux as an inevitable condition of life. The reconstructive effort is built firmly on the materials of Norris's own critical and philosophical speculations, and traces the increasing coherence of his engagement with the motifs through all of his fiction. Hugh J. Dawson, "A Trace of Scandal in Norris' Revision of *McTeague*" (*ELN* 25, iv:68–72), speculates that Norris revised the Owgooste Sieppe clothes-wetting catastrophe out of the novel because of censorship initiated by the notorious Mrs. Doubleday—this despite Norris's own denial of interference and the absence of clear proof. Joseph R. McElrath, Jr., "Ovid's Halcyone-Ceyx Myth in Frank Norris's *The Pit*" (*CML* 8:319–23), suggests that use of the myth in scenes involving Laura Jadwin and Sheldon emphasizes her fidelity to her husband and discourages the inference of adultery. McElrath's *Frank Norris and* The Wave: *A Bibliography* (Garland) should have been one long journal article rather than the essential 10-page list padded out into a book. Of various items on Norris appearing in the journal *Frank Norris Studies*, the more valuable are Benjamin S. Lawson, "The Presence of Joaquin Miller in *The Octopus*" (6:1–3), identifying Miller with the character Presley and remarking Norris's judgment that Miller had falsified the western experience; Richard Allan Davison, "Some Light on Gertrude Doggett Norris's 1894 Divorce Suit" (6:3–4); and Jesse S. Crisler's "Norris's 'Library'" (5:1–11), identifying 120 items with some association with Norris in various Bancroft Library collections.

The only essay dealing with Ambrose Bierce worth mentioning is Harriet Kramer Linkin's "Narrative Technique in 'An Occurrence at Owl Creek Bridge'" (*JNT* 18:137–52). Linkin emphasizes the process of reading the story for the first time rather than re-creating it after the fact, and points out the accumulating effect of conditional statements, shifts in perspective, contrasting levels of language, and dislocations of time.

Two collections of essays on *The Awakening* highlight study of Kate Chopin. *New Essays on* The Awakening, ed. Wendy Martin (Cambridge), features five substantial pieces. Martin's introduction (pp. 1–31) outlines Chopin's biography and the history of the novel's creation and reception, and establishes the general perspective taken by all the contributors that *The Awakening* is both innovative and flawed. Elaine Showalter's "Tradition and the Female Talent: *The Awakening* as a Solitary Book" (pp. 33–57) defines the novel as a transition from the traditional to the modern, approving but also punishing Edna's rebellion. Michael T. Gilmore, "Revolt against Nature: The Problematic Modernism of *The Awakening*" (pp. 59–87), conceives the novel as "premodernist" in challenging accepted ideas about nature and self, but also internally contradictory in conceiving nature as both objective and only socially constructed and the self as both accessible and inaccessible. Andrew Delbanco, "The Half-Life of Edna Pontellier" (pp. 89–107), comparing *The Awakening* to Frederick Douglass's *Narrative* and Charles Chesnutt's *The House Behind the Cedars*, sees it as acknowledging the power of a conservative regional tradition and sexual policy. Cristina Giorcelli, "Edna's Wisdom: A Transitional and Numinous Merging" (pp. 109–48), describes Edna Pontellier somewhat fuzzily as "steeped in ontological ambivalence," unsure and confident, hesitant and purposeful, and the novel as employing a cyclical structure which matches its thematic content. The other collection, *Approaches to Teaching Chopin's* The Awakening, ed. Barnard Koloski (MLA), features Koloski's introductory overview of novelist and novel and 21 essays, the longest of them seven pages. Each essay examines *The Awakening* in a cultural, gender, generic, thematic, historical, course-specific, narrative, mythic, or symbolic context (for example, "*The Awakening* as a Prototype of the Novel of Awakening," "*The Awakening* in an American Literature Survey Course," "A Reader-Response Approach").

The separately published items treating Chopin were of less consequence. Douglas Radcliff-Umstead's "Chopin's *The Awakening*: The Discovery of Eternity" (*ZAA* 36:62–67) reads like a bad report on a social science project, and concludes that suicide is not cowardly but "the source of everlasting beatitude for the brave soul." More successfully, Maria S. Suarez-Lafuente's "A Presupposition of Intertextuality in Clarín's *La Regenta* and Chopin's *The Awakening*" (*RR* 79:492–501) compares the two novels because of their common narrative lines and their mutual interest in imagery and the subtexts of language and idea (especially adultery). Those elements, however, are not well connected to each other or to Suarez-Lafuente's assertion that the novels end differently because of differences in geographical environment and social setting. In the only essay not dealing with the novel, "Kate Chopin's New Orleans Years" (*NOR* 15, i:53–60), Emily Toth, who is at work on a new biography of Chopin, nonetheless assembles information about the period crucial to its creation. If Toth has a point, it is that Daniel Rankin's *Kate Chopin and Her Creole Stories* (1932) drew the wrong picture: Chopin in New Orleans was mostly pregnant, mostly secluded, and mostly profoundly cut off from the female environment that had nurtured her.

The publication of *The Letters of Henry Adams: Volumes IV–VI, 1892–1918*, ed. J. C. Levenson et al. (Belknap), marks the conclusion of a magnificent enterprise. An introduction to volume 4 surveys the crucial events in the first three volumes, and section commentaries supplement the otherwise spare contextual discussion. The annotation is succinct and factual, the illustration more lavish. In all, the six volumes print 2,885 of a total of more than 4,700 known letters by Adams, 4,500 of them represented by manuscripts. The unprinted letters are identified in a calendar in volume 6, and the editors refer to making them available later in microform. The edition is so worth the having that I hesitate to complain about the absence of any kind of editorial record and about the near silence in the annotation about the other side of the correspondence.

In "Adams Stalking Jefferson" (*GrandS* 7, iv:140–53) Garry Wills examines Adams's treatment of and reaction to a political personality so different from his own, someone who made history rather than writing it. Wills credits Adams for being almost the only one to understand Jefferson, but he is also intrigued by the juxtaposition of the self-aware man weighing "Jefferson's peculiar lack of self-scrutiny." Michael Ann Holly, "Cultural History as a Work of Art: Jacob Burckhardt and Henry Adams" (*Style* 22:209–18), compares the "historiographic impulse that lies behind what appears to be the fanciful fabrication of culture" in Burckhardt's *Die Geschichte der Renaissance* (1860) and Adams's *Mont-Saint-Michel and Chartres*. Holly locates behind both Burckhardt's ironic nihilism and Adams's antimodernism the same mimetic impulse to re-create the past not in its facts but in the aesthetic structures favored by the cultures being described. Donald Hall, "Revaluation: Henry Adams's *History*" (*SR* 95[1987]:518–24), occasioned by the Library of America reprinting of the *History of the United States during the Administrations of Jefferson and Madison*, sets out fresh perspectives on Adams's style, his central insight in the *History* that "people do the opposite of what they say they do," and his delicate function as an apologist for his own family. Hall's incensed heavy-handedness is a striking contrast to Adams's bemused distance.

The *Education* was featured in three essays. In "The Objectivity of *The Education of Henry Adams*" (*Studies in Autobiography*, pp. 151–62) Thomas R. Smith is concerned with the tension between the obvious subject of the narrative and "the almost shieldlike carapace of supposed objectivity" of its third-person point of view, a tension sharpened by contrasts between the protagonist's immediate responses to events and the narrator's posterior ones. Barry Maine in "*The Education of Henry Adams*: 'Music for Ourselves Alone'" (*NEQ* 61:325–40) addresses questions of the reader implied by the text. Maine argues that the book's "failure of form" results from its having been directed so specifically to a small and uncharacteristic circle of readers. George Monteiro makes claims for influence in "Henry Adams' Jamesian Education" (*MR* 29:371–84), proposing that despite a generally negative response to much of Henry James's fiction, Adams did learn from the novelist about the crucial part played by knowledge of human nature in forming a coherent intellectual sense of things. Or possibly they were living in the same world?

Indiana University

13. Fiction: 1900 to the 1930s

Stephen L. Tanner

i. Willa Cather

Cather scholarship this year clearly displays a widening gap between traditional and recent theoretical approaches to her fiction. On the one hand are considerations of her spiritual or religious themes, her expression of regional life as encapsulating national and universal experience, her struggle with the tensions between agrarian values and modern technology, her treatment of art, the family, the relation of human beings to their environment, and so on. On the other hand are increasingly complex and challenging considerations of gender, sexuality, politics and power, subtexts, and indeterminacies in her fiction. The division is exemplified by the two most significant items appearing this year: a special Cather issue of *Literature and Belief* and Robert J. Nelson's *Willa Cather and France: In Search of the Lost Language* (Illinois).

Volume 8 of *Literature and Belief*, guest-edited by John J. Murphy, contains nine essays on religion in Cather, a review by David Stouck of five recent books on Cather (pp. 116–26), and a review by Lance Larsen of a new edition of *Life of Bishop Machebeuf* (pp. 127–29), the book she freely borrowed from in writing *Death Comes for the Archbishop*. Mildred R. Bennett, in "Cather and Religion" (pp. 5–13), provides the biographical facts about Cather's relation to churches, concluding that although she was always much interested in religion, she was an inquirer rather than a devout believer, "a deeply religious person" but not one who subscribed to creeds in any significant way. Bruce P. Baker II describes Cather's critique of one form of religion in "Before the Cruciform Tree: The Failure of Evangelical Protestantism" (pp. 14–26). After examining "Eric Hermannson's Soul," *The Song of the Lark*, and most extensively *One of Ours*, Baker concludes that on the whole Cather viewed evangelical Protestantism negatively and in its place posited "an ideal of true faith,

I am indebted to Shannon Toronto for research help in preparing this chapter.

real compassion, and honest devotion" based on her own artistic values and the qualities she admired in the truly devout. My essay, "Seeking and Finding in Cather's *My Mortal Enemy*" (pp. 27–38), argues that the primary problem in interpreting this novel is the evaluation of Myra's religious conversion, which I contend is neither genuinely admirable nor religious but more a matter of aesthetics than theology. In "The Integrating Vision of Bishop Latour in Willa Cather's *Death Comes for the Archbishop*" (pp. 39–57), Marilyn Arnold views the novel as a description of a man's perception expanding to encompass and integrate the physical and spiritual. Latour recognizes this integration in the Navajo attitude toward sacred land and objects. The vision of the novel thus creates "a model of religious tolerance, respect and even unity." And Latour's way of seeing, says Arnold, is a reflection of Cather's own perspective. In "The Missions of Latour and Paul: *Death Comes for the Archbishop* and the Early Church" (pp. 58–65), John J. Murphy points to parallels between the story of Latour building his church and early church history recounted in Acts and Paul's epistles.

The most unconventional essay in this collection is Susan J. Rosowski's boldly feminist "Willa Cather's Magnificat: Matriarchal Christianity in *Shadows on the Rock*" (pp. 66–75). Rosowski claims this novel is one of Cather's most radically feminine because in it she retells the Christian story of redemption, making it matriarchal. Cécile's story is identified with the life of Mary, and patriarchal institutions—even Jesus himself—are secondary to what Cécile represents: "Cather makes Cécile her redeemer." Merrill M. Skaggs, in "Death in C Major: Willa Cather's Perilous Journey Toward the Ordinary in *Lucy Gayheart*" (pp. 76–88), attempts to provide a positive way to view one of Cather's least admired novels by supplying a speculative biographical-psychological interpretation that sees the novel as one of forgiveness in which Cather reconciled herself to what she viewed as a betrayal by Isabelle McClung. The theme of religious quest is central to Jenny Hale Pulsipher's "Expatriation and Reconcilation: The Pilgrimage Tradition in *Sapphira and the Slave Girl*" (pp. 89–100). By making the concept of pilgrimage perhaps too inclusive and adaptable, Pulsipher argues for a "rich religious dimension" of the novel discernible in a cluster of pilgrimage patterns linked to the tradition represented by *Pilgrim's Progress.* Mae Blanch's "Joy and Terror: Figures of Grace in Cather and O'Connor Stories" (pp. 101–15) compares two stories by each author to make the point that although both writers treat grace in the traditional Christian sense, O'Connor was particularly concerned with our sinful nature and need for salvation, while Cather was interested in the spiritual enrichment of life that comes through grace. O'Connor wanted to shock readers into awareness of religious needs; Cather wanted to prompt awareness that if life becomes spiritually impoverished, art is thereby diminished.

Robert J. Nelson has two principal purposes in *Willa Cather and France* (Illinois). The first is to show that the mark of French language and culture on her work was persistent and profound. He ferrets out even the slightest hint of this French connection. The second is to treat her search for a "lost language"—that "prelapsarian moment of language in which signifier and signified were one," a kind of lost Eden that he says Derrida has taught us never existed. Thus he combines an exposition of Cather's ambiguous Francophilia with recent French critical and psychoanalytical theory in an attempt to probe more deeply her religion, sexuality, politics, and art. This deconstructive attempt emphasizes sexuality and is often overly ingenious and laden with unnecessary jargon. One of his main conclusions is that Cather retained "stereotypical surrogations of phallocentric strivings." He favors an approach that brings Cather out of her lesbian closet and her fiction "out of the cloister of suffocating piety about the plains and plain-living into which much traditional criticism [has] enclosed the novelist." He asserts that Cather's text is always "a countertext if not an antitext" and that despite her longing for confirmation of the logocentric vision she found "God and Reality and communion inaccessible." According to the acoustic metaphor that shapes his book, dissonance dominates over consonance in her fiction.

The *Columbia LHUS*, which like Nelson's book assumes the reader's familiarity with recent critical theory, devotes not a single full page to Cather. A few scattered paragraphs mention her exclusively in terms of sexual politics. The regional aspects of her fiction are discounted because regionalism is seen as an enclosure that kept women writers in their place. Cather and the other women writers of her generation were really mapping "the geography of their gender" rather than of their regions or the larger territories of human experience. It seems peculiar and lamentable that a writer of Cather's breadth and significance should receive in a history of American literature merely a few narrow and, for that matter, contradictory comments related to gender conflict. Her case points up the principal weakness of this book: it is long on theory and short on information.

Several articles this year examine Cather's search for a distinctively female vision or voice. Joan Wylie Hall's "Treacherous Texts: The Perils of Allusion in Cather's Early Stories" (*CLQ* 24:142–50) focuses on "The Treasure of Far Island" and "The Professor's Commencement" to point out Cather's distrust of devotion to the dominantly male literary tradition. Her protagonists reflect her own struggles with mostly male-inherited texts in her effort to achieve not simply recognition but an independent "woman's voice." She both relies on the male tradition and warns against overdependence on it. Ann Romines's "After the Christmas Tree: Willa Cather and Domestic Ritual" (*AL* 60:61–82) compares *My Ántonia* and *Shadows on the Rock* to show that although Cather began her career consciously avoiding the domestic concerns of previous female novelists, her attitude toward domestic ritual changed. The former novel represents ritual as "an androgynous cultural ideal of transcendence," while the latter "emphasizes domestic and female aspects of ritual." Thus, as she matured as an artist, she displayed an increased recognition of "women's culture" and developed "an aesthetic rooted in traditional women's experience." Susan A. Hallgarth makes a similar comparison between *My Ántonia* and *Shadows on the Rock* in "Archetypal Patterns in *Shadows on the Rock*" (*CLQ* 24:133–41). Like Romines, she perceives in the latter novel a more mature woman's voice and view. For Hallgarth, archetypes and symbols associated with Persephone and the Virgin Mary reveal the novel's nonpatriarchal values. "As the 'good daughter' in both Christian and classical terms, Cécile becomes a positive symbol of female artistic power." These essays by Romines and Hallgarth added to the one by Rosowski already mentioned make a case that *Shadows on the Rock*, formerly considered a secondary work, is in fact a major feminist text; but in each instance varying degrees of interpretive ingenuity are required to effect the transformation. Another attempt to trace Cather's quest for a distinctively female aesthetic is Mark Troy's "Secret Name: The Creative Realm of the Female Modernist" (*MSpr* 82:202–10), which suggests that Cather and the poet H.D. turned to ancient Egypt for metaphors providing values suitable to female artists. For example, Isis provides a model of an extremely powerful female to counter the patriarchal values that confine modern female artists to undesirable roles. The thesis is interesting, but particularly in the case of Cather, short on evidence. As Troy himself admits, Cather makes very few allusions to Egypt.

Scholarly interest in Cather has reached the point where even her minor or formerly disesteemed fiction receives attention. Sharon O'Brien's introduction to a new edition of *Alexander's Bridge* (NAL) focuses on gender and creativity in an attempt to show that the novel was not merely imitative and contrived but was a creative advance toward *O Pioneers!*. Playing rather fast and loose in detecting Cather's own feelings and ideas in the events and situations of the novel, O'Brien asserts that part of the novel's purpose is to deconstruct masculine aesthetics. She suggests we read the novel as an expression of Cather's inner self, her female preoccupation with the psychological dynamics of creativity. *Alexander's Bridge* is also the principal example in Cecelia Tichi's treatment of Cather in *Shifting Gears: Technology, Literature, Culture in Modernist America* (No. Car., 1987). The book's thesis is that American "gear-and-girder technology" had an important literary-cultural impact late in the 19th and early in the 20th centuries. It generated new literary forms suited to its perceptual values. Dos Passos, Hemingway, and Williams used the model of technology, and their work gained by it. Cather and Sherwood Anderson failed to recognize the opportunities and suffered artistically. The section devoted to Cather (pp. 173–80) uses *Alexander's Bridge* and "Behind the Singer Tower" to show Cather's alarmed distrust of engineering power. The bridge in her novel is not a structure of component parts but an organic symbol hearkening back to a waning holistic romantic worldview. Tichi finds this unfortunate and oddly suggests that the mechanistic component-part design in nature and culture would have enhanced Cather's art. Another example of attention given to a meagerly regarded work is Loretta Wasserman's "Willa Cather's 'The Old Beauty' Reconsidered" (*SAF* 16:217–27). Wasserman goes to Cather's early reviewing to find what she considers the germ of the story. Cather had written of the then famous actress Lily Langtry, who Wasserman believes is the model for Gabrielle of the story. Wasserman's interpretation, diverging from past critical comment, presents Gabrielle in a more favorable light: not as an object of satire but appearing rigid, old-fashioned, and irrelevant only because this is what naturally happens to one set apart by a gift—the artist.

A foreign response to Cather was furnished this year by a special literary issue of *WCPMN* (22, iii). The guest editor is Jean Tsien of Beijing, who in "Willa Cather's Reputation in China" (pp. 11–15) informs us that Cather was not widely known in China until the 1980s. Her fiction is now highly regarded there and more frequently translated than that of Hemingway, Faulkner, and Fitzgerald. The Chinese like her treatment of the family, agrarianism, the dangers of industrialization and wealth, and they are charmed by her simple, evocative style. The other five essays by Chinese writers are brief appreciative responses containing familiar critical insights and not a flicker of feminist or poststructuralist concerns.

Three final unrelated items deserve mention. Sharon O'Brien's "Becoming Noncanonical: The Case Against Willa Cather" (*AQ* 40: 110–26) examines Cather's fluctuating reputation (very high in the 1920s, lower in the 30s and 40s, recently ascending) as a way of revealing the social, political, and particularly gender issues involved in formulating the canon. Cather got caught in a generational and ideological shift in American culture. Leftist critics of the 30s were engaged "in a complex oedipal drama—seeking to replace an older generation of male critics and to repudiate a powerful maternal literary figure by defining her as limited." Moreover, academic critics, trying to compete with English literature, established an essentially masculine canon for American literature. Cather's stock is rising recently because canon formulation is being widely questioned. The argument is less than persuasive because it exaggerates the effects of antifeminism. The reputations of Faulkner and Fitzgerald, for example, manifest the same pattern of decline and rise; and renewed interest in Cather was well under way before "canon" became a buzzword. Narrative technique is the subject of Michael Leddy's "Observation and Narration in Willa Cather's *Obscure Destinies*" (*SAF* 16: 141–53). Leddy finds that the organization of this work involves narrative as well as thematic patterns. The three stories display variations on the possibilities of combining observations by characters with information from the narrator. The movement is toward less information from the narrator. Finally, in "New Letters from Willa Cather" (*WAL* 23:223–25), Mildred Bennett announces that 20 pages of holograph have been acquired by the Cather Center in Red Cloud. These are letters written by Cather as a teenager to a Mrs. Helen Stowell. Bennett describes them (Cather letters cannot be quoted), explains their discovery, and points out their relationship to the fiction.

ii. Edith Wharton and Ellen Glasgow

The most significant item of Wharton scholarship this year is clearly *The Letters of Edith Wharton* ed. R. W. B. Lewis and Nancy Lewis (Scribner's). The approximately 400 letters in this book were selected from about 4,000, and there are about that many more extant which deal mostly with routine business matters. The result is an interesting and readable collection demonstrating that Wharton belongs to the American company of prolific and eloquent letter writers. The principal features of this book include chronologies of the author's life and writings, about 50 photos of people and places, helpful and authoritative annotations, and an introduction analyzing Wharton's letter writing and describing its context. This collection serves as a complementary annex to R. W. B. Lewis's Pulitzer Prize winning biography of Wharton. The only other book devoted exclusively to Wharton this year is William Leach's *Edith Wharton* (Chelsea), a generously illustrated biography for "young adults." Part of an American Women of Achievement series, its strong feminist bias creates some distortion of events. Perhaps because of his targeted audience, Leach provides little insight into the complexity of Wharton's personality and his book is largely a superficial recital of events. Useful bibliographical information is provided this year by Alfred Bendixon's "Wharton Studies, 1986–1987: A Bibliographic Essay" (*EWhN* 5: 5–8, 10).

The few paragraphs of *CLHUS* devoted to Wharton reflect a general pattern of interest in Wharton this year. Cecelia Tichi suggests there that Wharton's treatment of sexual politics is more important than her treatment of the manners, mores, and hypocritical morality of old New York culture. Similarly, a number of articles on Wharton this year treat sexual politics in one form or another. In "Edith Wharton Reads the Bachelor Type: Her Critique of Modernism's Representative Man" (*AL* 60:575–90), Judith L. Sensibar uses *The Children* to argue that Wharton revised from a woman's point of view a central theme in modernism: "its romanticization of the erotic immaturity of the perennial bachelor." Sensibar has in mind the Prufrock figure found particularly in Eliot and James, the type of man who wants women to provide "a fantasy of unfulfilled desire to screen him from his homosexual panic." She argues that *The Children* is a subversive and demystifying "rereading" of James's "The Beast in the Jungle" intended to expose the negative consequences of valorizing the modernist's Representative Man. The claim is intriguing and argued with ingenuity, but the parallels suggested remain tenuous. Gwendolyn Morgan's purpose in "The Unsung Heroine—A Study of May Welland in *The Age of Innocence*" (Pat Browne, ed., *Heroines of Popular Culture* [Bowling Green, 1987], pp. 32–40) is revealed in her title. The narrative voice of the novel tempts us to accept Newland Archer's negative view of May when in reality she is intelligent, complex, loving, generous, self-sacrificing, and several other good things. May is certainly worth a sympathetic reexamination, but this essay is too much a programmatic demoting of male and promoting of female. In "Wharton Questions Motherhood" (Lyall H. Powers, ed. *Leon Edel and Literary Art*, UMI Research Press, pp. 161–69), Keiko Beppu finds Wharton far ahead of her time in questioning the "myth of motherhood" that on the one hand glorifies mothers as sacred and on the other subjugates them to the ideal of maternity and produces frustrated, repressed, disturbed, martyred women. In *The Children* and *The Mother's Recompense*, says Beppu, Wharton incisively criticized both traditional and modern motherhood. Jeanne Boydston argues a constrasting position in "'Grave Endearing Traditions': Edith Wharton and the Domestic Novel" (Alice Kessler-Harris and William McBain, eds. *Faith of a (Woman) Writer*, Greenwood, pp. 31–40). Boydston acknowledges that Wharton seemed antagonistic in her early writing to the tradition of 19th-century domestic literature that celebrated home and motherhood, but notes that Wharton's post-WWI perspective was closer to that tradition. The change has been attributed to old age, nostalgia, and the impact of the war, but Boydston claims that even the early work had an angle of vision close to the domestic tradition. She examines the presence and problem of "domesticity" in *The House of Mirth, The Custom of the Country*, and *The Age of Innocence*. Julie Olin-Ammentorp's "Edith Wharton's Challenge to Feminist Criticism" (*SAF* 16:237–44) is a salutary corrective to feminist interpretation pushed too far. According to Olin-Ammentorp, feminist criticism of Wharton, though valuable, displays limiting blind spots characteristic of feminist criticism in general. One weakness is in the treatment of men. Focusing on *The House of Mirth*, she argues that the social structures in Wharton's fiction cause male as well as female waste and notes that the actual wielders of power in this novel are often women. By failing to recognize historical situations and changing definitions of feminism, says Olin-Ammentorp, feminist critics expect

Wharton to be 50 years ahead of her time. They have shaped her to conform with their expectations and thus oversimplified her complexities. They respect part of her genius but detach it from the woman as a whole.

Dale M. Bauer's "Edith Wharton's 'Roman Fever': A Rune of History" (*CE* 50:681–93) is also concerned with sexual politics but attempts to link that subject with larger political realms. Combining feminism, leftist politics, and recent European critical theory, Bauer refuses to take at face value Wharton's statements about turning her back on politics and reads "Roman Fever" as an antireactionary thrust that gives the lie to the critical conception of her as apolitical or politically naive. She wishes to open "a new discourse on Wharton's politics." She finds "sexual violence" to be the principal concern of her late fiction. Wharton was "strictly in opposition to patriarchal powers that benefit from the disorder of civilization by insisting on their names as a conservative force." This is a highly provocative essay, but the concept of "sexual violence" is assumed more than explained and the leap from the context of this story to large issues of politics, particularly anti-Semitism, requires a generous reading. Bauer provides a significant study of *The House of Mirth* in her *Feminist Dialogics: A Theory of Failed Community* (SUNY, pp. 89–127). Using Bakhtin's social theory of utterance as a basis for a feminist subversion of the "normative discursive practices of patriarchal culture," she argues that Lily is totally determined by society, culture, economics, and language. In fact every "individual," says Bauer (the quotation marks are hers), is merely "a locus of social and cultural languages." Within this deterministic framework, Lily's role is not only given her by her culture, but society even dictates or circumscribes her oppositional voice so that any subversive "word" (meaning thought or action as well as word) reinforces the demands of society. Another blending of feminine concerns and politics, this time political economy, is Beverly R. Voloshin's "Exchange in Wharton's *The Custom of the Country*" (*PCP* 22[1987]:98–104). Voloshin, whose principal concern is commodities and consumption, views the action of the novel as "analogous to the dynamics of capitalism." Undine is a female capitalist who markets herself, and the plot suggests that the female who enters fully the "commodified world" sacrifices her personal freedom.

A major examination of the relation of politics, ideology, social forces, and literature in the context of realism is Amy Kaplan's *The*

Social Construction of American Realism (Chicago), a study of Howells, Dreiser, and Wharton. Threading her way between post-structuralist denial of referentiality on the one hand and reductive theories of "commodification" on the other, Kaplan applies a historical perspective that links the "textual production of reality" to the "discursive practices" of politics and ideology—"those unspoken collective understandings, conventions, stories, and cultural practices that uphold systems of social power." Her focus is realism's relation to social change, the representation of class difference, and the emergence of a mass culture. Her first chapter on Wharton (pp. 65–87) examines how she represented herself as a professional author writing at the intersection of the mass market, the tradition of women's literature, and a realistic movement in uneasy dialogue with modernism. Kaplan claims that Wharton challenges the paradigm of feminist criticism that locates women's writing in a separate sphere because her writing undermines boundaries between feminine-masculine, public-private, home-business. Even so, the conflict between her model of professional authority and a privatized feminine sphere remained unresolved. The second chapter on Wharton, devoted to *The House of Mirth* (pp. 88–103), is concerned with the "social production" of Lily, which takes place in a changing context of society viewed both as an elite group and as the impersonal network of civic, political, and cultural forces acting nearly imperceptibly but nonetheless potently.

David A. Godfrey uses a more traditional approach in " 'The Full and Elaborate Vocabulary of Evasion': The Language of Cowardice in Edith Wharton's Old New York" (*MQ* 30:27–44). He interprets *The Age of Innocence* to show Wharton's concern with the debilitating effects of "a language of cowardice" upon the relationships of her Old New Yorkers. This society created a vocabulary of evasion to preserve itself, but ironically the device contributed to that very society's demise by legitimizing a sheltered way of life. In the area of psychological criticism, Lev Raphael asserts that shame is the key to recognizing the unappreciated strengths and clarifying the weaknesses of Wharton's less-read novels. He furnishes three versions of essentially the same argument in "Kate Orme's Struggles with Shame in Edith Wharton's *Sanctuary*" (*MSE* 10[1986]:229–36); "Haunted by Shame: Edith Wharton's *The Touchstone*" (*JEP* 9:287–96); and "Shame in Edith Wharton's *The Mother's Recompense*" (*AI* 45:187–203). His method is to apply concepts of shame from recent psychological theory to characters in the novels as though they were case studies, the point being that we should value the novels more because what they reveal about shame is confirmed by recent psychological treatment of this emotion. Unfortunately, these articles display a procrustean tendency to accommodate interpretation to theory.

Wharton is considered in conjunction with Ellen Glasgow in Catherine E. Sanders's *Writing the Margins: Edith Wharton, Ellen Glasgow and the Literary Tradition of the Ruined Woman* (Harvard, 1987). Sanders notes how frequently these authors—perhaps because of their own "marginal" status as artists and women—use marginal protagonists, particularly "ruined women." The technique, as she attempts to illustrate using Wharton's *Old New York* and Glasgow's *They Stooped to Folly*, allowed them to present complex, moving, and satirical portraits of their societies. Sanders also examines how their early reading shaped the ways they chose to use writing as a tool for social criticism. She concludes with a demonstration of how echoes of *The Scarlet Letter* and *Tess of the d'Urbervilles* in *Summer* and *Barren Ground* illustrate the differing ways in which Wharton and Glasgow approached the literary tradition.

More of Glasgow's writing became conveniently available this year in Julius Rowen Raper, ed. *Ellen Glasgow's Reasonable Doubts: A Collection of Her Writings* (LSU). The book brings together shorter pieces—essays, interviews, reviews, a story, and a poem—hitherto uncollected. Raper describes it as a "profile of Glasgow's mind." The 33 items, of uneven quality, express Glasgow's views on feminist issues, the South, politics, science, and her literary friends and competitors. Of particular interest are the final two essays expounding her fundamental beliefs. Despite the appearance of Edgar E. MacDonald and Tonette Bond Inge's excellent *Ellen Glasgow: A Reference Guide* (Hall, 1986), Glasgow has recently received rather meager critical attention. A survey of Glasgow scholarship is provided in Frederick P. W. McDowell's "Ellen Glasgow: A Retrospective View" (*EGN* 24[1987]:7–11).

iii. Gertrude Stein

Surely the reputation of no other American writer has benefited so much from recent developments in critical theory as has Gertrude Stein's. Certain modes of feminist and poststructuralist criticism seem expressly designed for treating her writing, and Stein scholarship is ballooning. More books and articles appear this year on Stein than on any other writer included in this chapter. She is the only woman writer after 1910 to be specified by name in *CLHUS* chapter titles. Cecelia Tichi calls her the "matriarch of modernism," who exerted female consciousness and power by erecting structures of language defying critical penetration by patriarchy. Linda W. Wagner, in dust-jacket style, suggests that Stein might outdistance Hemingway and Fitzgerald and refers to her as "a model of experimentation," "years ahead of her time," an author of "astonishing" accomplishments.

Some of the best new scholarship is brought together in Shirley Neuman and Ira B. Nadel, eds., *Gertrude Stein and the Making of Literature* (Northeastern). The 13 essays come from three conferences held in 1984 and 1985 and represent several recent critical approaches—with feminism a constant—applied to a wide range of Stein's writing. An announced purpose of the book is to promote Stein and broaden her reception, an idle hope if the editors have in mind any sort of general audience, because many of these essays use specialized concepts and terminology to make very subtle points.

Stein admirers are often puzzled about why others fail to appreciate her genius. The first two essays of this collection, Charles Caramello's "Gertrude Stein as Exemplary Theorist" (pp. 1–7) and Marianne DeKoven's "Gertrude Stein and the Modernist Canon" (pp. 8–20), are examples of this sort of head-scratching. Caramello ponders why Stein has been ignored or attacked by a generation of modernists and not appreciated as a theorist. His answer is that she was a distinctively Anglo-American modernist and "an anti-theoretical theoretician." He appeals to us "postmoderns" to appreciate the element of theory in her work. DeKoven poses a similar question: Why if Stein is so central in modernism and postmodernism is she so generally perceived as marginal? Answer: she was a woman and a lesbian; moreover, being central to many divergent cultural phenomena she was marginal to any coherent tradition. Fitting between the male canonical tradition and the female margin, Stein "deconstructs" the notion of center and margin itself and gives feminists a position of strength in opposition to patriarchy.

Henry M. Sayre brings structural linguistics to bear on Stein's writing in "The Artist's Model: American Art and the Question of Looking like Gertrude Stein" (pp. 21–41) and determines that the postmodern concept of "difference" was the most profoundly influential aspect of her work. Ulla E. Dydo's "Gertrude Stein: Composition as Meditation" (pp. 42–60) is a thorough and illuminating exposition of Stein's method of composition. Meditation did not precede but *was* composing; it was not introspection but looking outward to capture the object: "the process of consciousness constructing speech." Marjorie Perloff argues in "(Im)Personating Gertrude Stein" (pp. 61–80) that the autobiographical texts are misread when viewed as simple communication with words used as means. For Stein words were always ends. Perloff's tendency to see even Stein's most accessible writing as problematical characterizes a current trend in criticism to emphasize the self-reflexivity of language and discount biography and referentiality. In "Gertrude Stein and Henry James" (pp. 81–97), Ira B. Nadel asks why Stein failed to acknowledge a personal indebtedness to James even though she proclaimed his prime importance in shaping American literary style. He answers using the theory of *tessera*, which is the notion that a follower enlarges and completes the work of a precursor. Stein believed she absorbed and superseded James and thus denied his influence to maintain her own integrity. Stephen Scobie's "The Allure of Multiplicity: Metaphor and Metonymy in Cubism and Gertrude Stein" (pp. 98–118) examines "metonymy" in its postmodern sense in relation to Stein and Cubism. This is a sophisticated and technical essay, self-consciously and rigorously resistant to oversimplification. It illustrates, explicitly as well as implicitly, how and why poststructuralists are attracted to Stein. Susan E. Hawkins's "Sneak Previews: Gertrude Stein's Syntax in *Tender Buttons*" (pp. 119–23) explains how Stein tried to free syntax from traditional restraints and linear reasoning by using the logic of syntax against itself.

The concept of "difference" is again the focus of attention in Neil Schmitz's loving defense of Stein and explanation of how her work must be read in order to be appreciated: "The Difference of Her Likeness: Gertrude Stein's *Stanzas in Meditation*" (pp. 124–49). Schmitz enthusiastically embraces Stein's manner and style and defends it against those who demand meaning, coherence, and conventional sense, which are the prejudiced strictures of patriarchal poetry. In "Masterpieces, Manifestoes and the Business of Living: Gertrude Stein Lecturing" (pp. 150–67), Alan R. Knight views Stein's 1933 lectures as manifestoes. Using Foucault, recent semiotic studies of avant-garde manifestoes, and specialized terminology, Knight attempts to define the generic characteristics of manifestoes and fit

Stein's lectures into the pattern. Knight ignores the paradox that manifestoes are intended to communicate and Stein and poststructuralism eschew the usual sense of communication. Shirley Neuman's " 'Would a Viper Have Stung Her If She Had Only Had One Name?' : *Doctor Faustus Lights the Lights*" (pp. 168–93) is an extended and intricate examination of the relationship between *Ida A Novel* and the opera *Doctor Faustus Lights the Lights.* Neuman tries to demonstrate what Stein had to learn by writing the opera: it enabled her to return to complete the novel. The essay by bpNichol (yes, that's the right spelling) blights the integrity of this book. "When the Time Came" (pp. 194–209) is idiosyncratic in style, tone, ideas, and spelling. A commentary on the first five pages of *Ida A Novel,* its arch cleverness (a sort of imitation of Stein) is difficult to take seriously. The final essay, Robert K. Martin's "*The Mother of Us All* and American History" (pp. 210–22), argues that this last major work, an opera, has not been properly appreciated because of a simplistic view of its barely disguised autobiography. It should be seen as part of Stein's last creative stage in which she moved beyond modernism "to an art that was both representational and firmly situated in historical space." She turned from formalist experiments to a literature of engagement, a struggle for emancipation—of language, of blacks, of women. The book concludes with three previously unpublished (at least in English) short pieces by Stein herself.

A very significant contribution to Stein scholarship this year is Bruce Kellner, ed., *A Gertrude Stein Companion: Content with the Example* (Greenwood). Designed primarily to introduce new readers to Stein, the book contains a variety of useful materials for any reader, including an extensively annotated list of Stein's published writings; an annotated bibliography of selected criticism; a collection of Stein quotations; and, perhaps most useful of all, a biographical dictionary of people with whom she was in some way associated. Kellner's advice in "How to Read Gertrude Stein" (pp. 1–15) is playfully daunting: read her chronologically, read all of her (about 9,000 pages), and "be prepared for impatience and somnolence and defeat." Additional instruction on how to read her is supplied by three Stein scholars. Marianne DeKoven's "Half in and Half Out of Doors: Gertrude Stein and Literary Tradition" (pp. 75–83) is another version of her argument in *Gertrude Stein and the Making of Literature*: Stein's middle position deconstructs "the hierarchical-idealist duality of center and margin itself." She views Stein as "a genuine (nonseparatist, non-self-excluding and therefore non-self-defeating) antidote to patriarchal cultural hegemony." Recent critical notions allow DeKoven to make what she will of Stein. She can normalize her when desirable, but if Stein's statements appear too conventional, DeKoven simply claims they actually subvert themselves. Ulla Dydo's "Reading the Hand Writing: The Manuscripts of Gertrude Stein" (pp. 84–95) suggests that the manuscript notebooks are a source of helpful information about Stein's process of writing and consequently a means of access to her published work. In an attempt to put to rest the notion that Stein wrote either "simply" to be understood or "obscurely" to mystify, Marjorie Perloff, in "Six Stein Styles in Search of a Reader" (pp. 96–108), delineates through close analysis of numerous examples six basic variations of Stein's style and insists that even the apparently simple autobiographical texts require "strenuous" reading for full appreciation.

One biography appeared this year: Ann La Farge's *Gertrude Stein* (Chelsea). This volume in an American Women of Achievement series designed for young readers, with photos on nearly every page, is brief and introductory. No attempt is made to probe beneath the surface of biographical events. The lesbian relationship is mentioned but not dwelt upon.

Janice L. Doane's *Silence and Narrative: The Early Novels of Gertrude Stein* (Greenwood, 1986) provides close readings of *Q.E.D.*, *Fernhurst*, *Three Lives*, and *The Making of Americans*. Doane draws upon Derrida and Foucault for her concept of silence and follows the pattern of much Stein criticism in equating Stein's obscurity with a feminist strategy: to subvert lucidity, coherence, unity, and meaning is to subvert patriarchy. Using ideas from contemporary theorists, particularly French feminists, Doane argues that Stein's exploitation of the subversive potential of silences provides access to "a shrewd analysis of the authority of patriarchal discourse."

Stein criticism is often demanding reading. Deborah Schnitzer's treatment of Stein and Cubism in *The Pictorial in Modernist Fiction: From Stephen Crane to Ernest Hemingway* (UMI Research Press, pp. 204–46) is particularly challenging. Focusing on *Tender Buttons* and using the discourse of current theory, she attempts to correct what she considers loose and inaccurate analogies formerly drawn between Stein's writing and Cubist painting. Probably few readers know art, literature, and current theory well enough to follow this technical argument comfortably. Another demanding article is Catherine N. Parke's "'Simple Through Complication': Gertrude Stein Thinking" (*AL* 60:554–74). This subtle and sometimes opaque explanation of Stein's theory of knowledge is directed to the thesis that Stein aimed for expression that was original and at the same time American and democratic. Elizabeth Fifer's "'In Conversation': Gertrude Stein's Speaker, Message, and Receiver in *Painted Lace and Other Pieces* (1914–1937)" (*MFS* 34:465–80) employs psychoanalytic insights from Lacan and Kristeva in a feminist interpretation that focuses on lesbian sexuality and multiple patterns of discourse. In *Painted Lace* Stein is in dialogue with readers, her lover, and various manifestations of her salon, both the sympathetic inner circle of friends and the judging outer circle of acquaintances. Lacan and feminist psychoanalysis also influence Christopher J. Knight's "Gertrude Stein's 'Melanctha' and Radical Heterosexuality" (*SSF* 25:295–300). Knight finds the central conflict in Jeff's failure to understand the "equivocacy" of Melanctha's character. Seeking an "essentialist" definition of character, he is blind to her "otherness." Knight presents the model of "radical heterosexuality" conceived by Jane Gallop, in which the genders meet not as opposites retaining their identities but as opposites intermingling. Finally, in an essay addressed to teachers of writing ("How to Write Like Gertrude Stein" in Louise Z. Smith, ed., *Audits of Meaning: A Festschrift in Honor of Ann E. Berthoff*, Boynton/Cook, pp. 229–37), Philip M. Keith recommends that Stein's writing methods be used in composition classes to teach that "reflexivity or even opacity of style" can entice readers to make meaning. I wonder if composition students, often already well able to keep readers guessing, really need encouragement in this direction.

iv. Theodore Dreiser and H. L. Mencken

Two collections of Dreiser's newspaper writings appeared this year, both edited by T. D. Nostwich. Volume one of *Journalism: Newspaper Writings, 1892–1895* (Penn.), part of the University of Pennsylvania Dreiser Edition, contains articles from seven newspapers in Chicago, St. Louis, Toledo, Cleveland, Pittsburgh, and New York. Dreiser never had his own by-line during these years, but he was talented enough to get good assignments as drama critic, special-feature writer, and investigative reporter, which provided raw material for his fiction and a large book on his newspaper days. Of the 106 articles in this collection, 59 had not been previously identified as Dreiser's, and only four had been reprinted elsewhere. *Theodore Dreiser's "Heard in the Corridors" Articles and Related Writings* (Iowa State) collects a group of Dreiser's short pieces done without by-line during 1892–1893. Ostensibly they were comments of local hotel guests, but most of these anecdotes and brief essays about individual persons were fabricated by Dreiser himself and constitute his earliest known creative work. Some are identified as his because they appear in his scrapbooks, the rest by internal evidence. Nostwich's useful introduction sketches Dreiser's newspaper career and explains the background for the pieces.

The convenient availability of the newspaper writings will aid the current trend of scholarship that focuses on Dreiser's relation to the social forces and mass culture of his time. That trend is represented this year by three significant items. Amy Kaplan's chapter "Theodore Dreiser's Promotion of Authorship" in *The Social Construction of American Realism* (pp. 104–39) reexamines Dreiser's apprenticeship to demonstrate how he carved a place for himself and constructed a social position for the realist by his newspaper articles, editing, free-lance articles, and autobiographical writing. He had to learn not only how to write but how to promote himself, and the tension between producing and marketing permeated his career. Kaplan claims no clear distinction exists between Dreiser's hackwork for the mass market and his realist art written to defy market conventions; both involved promotion of authorship in the market. Her chapter "The Sentimental Revolt of *Sister Carrie*" (pp. 140–60) counters the notion that sentimentalism entrapped his prose in popular conventions that blocked his achievement of realism. Rather than being just a vestige of convention, sentimentality in the novel is given new life—"recontextualized"—in an aesthetics of consumption. Kaplan tries to relate sentimentalism, realism, and the consumer ethos by explaining consumption as a compensation for social powerlessness and an expression of the desire for change. A similar interest in the relation of texts to their social environment informs Arun Mukherjee's *The Gospel of Wealth in the American Novel: The Rhetoric of Dreiser and Some of His Contemporaries* (Barnes and Noble, 1987). Mukherjee's primary assumption—increasingly familiar in current criticism—is that works of literature, seen as rhetorical utterance spoken in a context, help us understand how dominant groups seek legitimization by invoking consecrated symbols of authority. Read this way, literature helps to penetrate the mystifications that the social elite usually create around themselves. In the case of Dreiser's fiction, Mukherjee is interested in the way its rhetoric demystifies the discourse of the American businessman and his apologists. Attacking critics who identify Dreiser's own desires with those of his characters, Mukherjee presents Dreiser as a moral satirist challenging rather than championing the heroic mythology of American business. Susan L. Mizruchi's *The Power of Historical Knowledge* combines recent theory with Marxism to construct "a politically revisionary criticism." She fervently believes that criticism should produce political and social change. She wishes to expand our notion of what may be conceived as political in a novel to encompass all social relations, including the relationship between narrator and reader. As a gambit for skirting the way recent theory eliminates the relevance of authorial consciousness, she treats narrators as distinct from their authors in a way that supposedly reaffirms historical context and the possibility for political assertion. This involves some rhetorical sleight of hand abetted by jargon. The chapter on *An American Tragedy* examines the social-political effects of its deterministic vision and concludes that the novel deconstructs that vision, revealing it as a containment strategy "employed by the powerless to assuage their despair, and by social elites to maintain the status quo."

Additional biographical information is furnished by Thomas P. Riggio's " 'Down Hill': A Chapter in Dreiser's Story about Himself" (*DrS* 19, ii:2–21). Riggio introduces a hitherto unpublished autobiographical piece, written in the 1920s, which treats an 11-month period in 1903, a critical time of severe depression and poverty for Dreiser. A second part of the piece treating an "up hill" phase is to appear in a subsequent issue. Esther McCoy's "The Death of Dreiser" (*GrandS* 7:73–85) is a skillfully evocative memoir detailing aspects of Dreiser's death and funeral and the last years of his widow's life. McCoy was a close friend of Dreiser and did reading and research for him for 18 years.

Sister Carrie continues to be Dreiser's most frequently examined novel. In "A Star is Born: 'Celebrity' in *Sister Carrie*" (*DrS* 19, i:2–25), Philip L. Gerber presents the novel as perhaps the first to treat celebrity in any way near the present sense of the term. The novel adumbrates a phenomenon that is now a dominant aspect of our culture. Gerber informs us of Dreiser's own yearning for celebrity and of the example provided him by his brother Paul and Paul's Broadway acquaintances. The controversy over the 1981 University of Pennsylvania edition of the novel, which restored some 36,000 words cut from the holograph and typescript version of 1900 and eliminates the epilogue, continues in Stephen C. Brennan's "The Two Endings of *Sister Carrie*" (*SAF* 16, i:13–26). This significant essay persuasively makes a complex and subtle point. Brennan argues that while there are sound reasons for preferring the original ending, Dreiser changed it on his own initiative. The reasons were biographical, having to do with his relationship with his wife and a pattern of escape and entanglement he transferred to Carrie. He admired his wife and Ames (patterned after her) but ultimately feared that even such high-minded people would become only another snare of the spirit.

Previously unpublished writing by Mencken appeared this year in Carl Bode, ed., *The Editor, the Bluenose and the Prostitute: H. L. Mencken's History of the "Hatrack" Censorship Case* (Roberts Rinehart). This is Mencken's own history of the test case in which he sold the banned spring 1926 issue of *American Mercury* on the Boston Common to Reverend J. Frank Chase, secretary of the New England Watch and Ward Society. Bode's introduction explains Mencken's views on censorship and the context of the case. This is followed by the item that caused the ban: "Hatrack," Herbert Asbury's story of a churchgoing prostitute. Then comes Mencken's own account of the case from start to finish, a readable and detailed narrative written in 1937, focusing on press coverage of the incident and the ensuing legal battle.

Mencken continues to receive considerable bibliographical attention. *Menckeniana* regularly includes even brief mentions of him. Allison Bulsterbaum's *H. L. Mencken: A Research Guide* (Garland) is deliberately selective and makes no attempt to compete with or replace Betty Ader's *HLM: The Mencken Bibliography* or the supplements by Vincent Fitzpatrick. It aims to include the high points of primary and secondary Menckeniana. The introduction is a brief sketch of Mencken's life and work. An essay surveying Mencken scholarship might have been more appropriate for such a book. Mencken's attitude toward religion is informatively treated in two articles by D. G. Hart: "A Connoisseur of 'Rabble-Rousing,' 'Human Folly,' and 'Theological Pathology': H. L. Mencken on American Presbyterians" (*Amer. Presbyterians* 66:195–204) and "Mencken and Fundamentalism: Another Perspective" (*Menckeniana* 107:1–7). Hart illustrates that despite his pungent satirical statements about religion, Mencken admired certain religious persons such as Billy Sunday and J. Gresham Machen whose integrity appealed to him. Mencken objected to fundamentalism partly because of his hostility to democracy and egalitarianism and partly because of its Puritan element, which for him meant desiring and using power to interfere with and look down upon others. James Seaton approaches Mencken from a leftist perspective in "The Truth Value of Bourgeois Hedonism: On H. L. Mencken" (*JAC* 8, iii[1985]:53–57). Seaton claims that Mencken may be usefully considered a "bourgeois hedonist" as that term was used in Herbert Marcuse's 1938 essay "On Hedonism," and that such hedonism has much to offer contemporary culture. Mencken, despite his apparent reactionary elitism, when read carefully provides the kind of "imminent critique" advocated by the Marxism of the Frankfurt School.

Mencken scholarship continues to devote itself almost exclusively to biography. For example, the subjects in *Menckeniana* this year include his early schooling, his role in the Scopes trial, his relationship with Thomas Wolfe, his attitude toward Jews, and his feelings about New York City. Surely his writing itself warrants more study, particularly now when the essay genre is receiving considerable critical analysis.

v. Sherwood Anderson and John Dos Passos

The most significant addition to Anderson scholarship this year is Kenny J. Williams's *A Storyteller and a City: Sherwood Anderson's Chicago* (No. Ill.). Williams, a knowledgeable student of literature associated with Chicago, traces Anderson's relationship with this city, particularly as it is reflected in his fiction. Fitting Anderson's work into the context of the "Chicago School" near the turn of the century, Williams delineates the stages of Anderson's responses to urban life, from his liking for the urban business world to his keen awareness of its victims and disappointments and the discrepancy between the legendary and real city. Williams explains that Anderson came to recognize the inevitability of industrialism but did not accept without question a naturalistic view of life. For a time in his career he was a significant urban voice treating the phenomenon of the American city and the effects of urbanization. Anderson's attitude toward the technological aspects of industrial life is examined in

Cecelia Tichi's *Shifting Gears* (pp. 184–94). Focusing on *Poor White*, Tichi finds that Anderson, like Cather, was a nostalgic romantic in the gear-and-girder era, affirming the primacy of the writer's imagination as he attempted an exposé of the technological mind. *Poor White* is "an indictment of the pathology, sexual repression, and perversion of nature" he perceived in the technological imagination. In Tichi's estimation the novel is weakened by its worldview. The tension within Anderson between the urban and rural is also reflected in Leland Krauth's "Sherwood Anderson's Buck Fever; or, Frontier Humor Comes to Town" (*StAH* 3[1984–85]:298–308). When Anderson settled in Virginia in 1927, he bought and edited two country newspapers and wrote a column using the pseudonym Buck Fever. Krauth argues that Buck Fever has been neglected in the study of American humor. His significance lies in his ties to and departures from the southwestern humor tradition; he is a transitional stage in the movement from rustic to urban humor.

Additional and authoritative biographical information was supplied this year in two articles by Walter B. Rideout, whose biography of Anderson is forthcoming. " 'The Most Cultured Town in America': Sherwood Anderson and New Orleans (*SoR* 24:79–99) describes Anderson's two residences in New Orleans during the early 1920s as high points in his career when his third marriage was going well, he was enjoying local and national fame and stimulating friendships, and he was writing fluently. One unpleasant event of that period is treated in "The Break Between Sherwood Anderson and William Faulkner" (*WE* 13, ii:2–5). Rideout sifts through the existing information concerning this break and locates a reasonable cause in two particular quarrels between the two writers.

Winesburg, Ohio continues to receive the lion's share of critical attention. In "*Winesburg, Ohio*: The Apprenticeship of George Willard" (*Amerikastudien* 32[1987]:431–53), Monika Fludernik considers whether George is simply another of the book's grotesques or a developing artist. She demonstrates through an ambitious treatment of the book's major elements that he is a little of both. Fludernik also gives the book extensive treatment in " 'The Divine Accident of Life': Metaphoric Structure and Meaning in *Winesburg, Ohio*" (*Style* 22:116–35). Here, in "a structuralist version of close reading," she persuasively discerns a "complex web of crossreferential key images and leitmotifs." According to this reading, the book equates art with love and celebrates the former as a means of freeing the latter. Martin Bidney, in "Anderson and the Androgyne: 'Something More than Man or Woman'" (*SSF* 25:261–73), points out three passages in the book that he believes express the androgynous ideal. He would persuade us that all the characters are failed androgynes and that the androgyny myth is the book's generative core. Andreas Fischer's "Context-Free and Context-Sensitive Literature: Sherwood Anderson's *Winesburg, Ohio* and James Joyce's *Dubliners*" (Neil Forsyth, ed. *Reading Contexts*, Gunter Narr Verlag, pp. 13–31) uses close linguistic analysis of Anderson's "Hands" and Joyce's "The Sisters" to show that they illustrate two types of narrative technique: one informs the reader of the context, the other assumes a context or continuation of previous action.

Dos Passos scholarship was substantially augmented this year by four books. Donald Pizer's edition of *The Major Nonfictional Prose* (Wayne State) is a collection of reviews, travels accounts, argumentative reportage of various kinds, interviews, and addresses written from 1914 to 1971, most of them previously uncollected. Pizer used two criteria for selection: intrinsic quality and the amount of light shed on the author's life and beliefs. The unobtrusive annotation is useful and authoritative, and the book provides an extension of and balance to Dos Passos's nonfiction books, most of which were written after his shift to the right in the late 1930s. Barry Maine, ed., *Dos Passos: The Critical Heritage* (Routledge) consists of reviews, letters, and statements contemporary with the author's works and provides critical comment on 12 of Dos Passos's 40 books, primarily his best-known novels. The informative introduction, displaying an awareness of current theory, supplies a chronological description of Dos Passos's novels and a summary of their reception. David Sanders's *John Dos Passos: A Comprehensive Bibliography* (Garland, 1987) does indeed aim at being comprehensive in its annotated lists of primary and secondary materials. The information about the primary works includes even cost, binding, size, and number of copies in editions, but not all the specific information required by textual editors and book collectors. Sanders tried to include all items in all languages, and the book seems a thorough and reliable augmentation of previous bibliographies. Donald Pizer's *Dos Passos'* U.S.A.: *A Critical Study* (Virginia) is the first full-length study of this trilogy. The first chapter on the three works preceding *U.S.A.* lays out the emerging themes and techniques so important in the trilogy. The remaining four chapters are devoted to *U.S.A.*, from planning and composition to the function of its four narrative modes and their interrelatedness. Using manuscript evidence and hypotheses drawn from the nature of the modes, Pizer sketches a theory of composition of the novels. He is explicit and unapologetic about his traditional assumptions that the interdependence of themes and form and the relation of a literary work to its author and times are meaningful considerations in literary study. The readable clarity of this book indicates what is lost in much theory-oriented criticism, which, whatever its insights, is not comfortable reading.

The four-mode narration of *U.S.A.* receives a Marxist interpretation in Huck Gutman's "Alienation and Form in Dos Passos's *U.S.A.* Trilogy" (*PCL* 14:22–29). Taking a cue from a statement by Lukács concerning capitalistic alienation, Gutman argues that the four-part narrative form of *U.S.A.* "reifies the very alienation which is its central subject." Typical of modernists, Dos Passos compounds alienation when he attacks it using four modes of narration that themselves reflect alienation. Another kind of attempt to show that Dos Passos's fiction often implicitly contradicts what it overtly asserts is John Fichtelberg's "The Picaros of John Dos Passos" (*TCL* 34:434–52). Fichtelberg notes that although Dos Passos's novels are often characterized as reflecting anarchical individualism, many of the individualists fail to thrive. Fichtelberg finds Dos Passos portraying his world in the dark manner he discovered in Pío Baroja's 1904 trilogy *The Struggle for Life*, and the irony and paradox he found in Baroja fits with the reversals of the picaresque tale. This is an informative essay, but the emphasis on picaros is a little misleading because the term is so broadly and accommodatingly applied. A Dos Passos-Spain connection is also the subject of Townsend Ludington's "Spain and the Hemingway-Dos Passos Relationship" (*AL* 60:270–73). Ludington, a Dos Passos biographer, presents a letter describing a bullfight that Dos Passos wrote to a French woman in 1919 from Madrid. Ludington uses it to make this point: part of the reason the two authors ended their friendship (in addition to their bitter disagreement about the Spanish Civil War) was that Dos Passos had visited Spain first. Hemingway always wanted to be the authority on things. Moreover, the letter shows Dos Passos's lack of respect for the ritual of the bullfight, which was so important to Hemingway.

vi. Jack London and Sinclair Lewis

A milestone in London scholarship is Earle Labor et al., eds., *The Letters of Jack London* in three volumes (Stanford). A decade in the making, these handsomely produced and scrupulously edited volumes constitute the first large, comprehensive collection of London's letters, more than doubling the number previously in print. The editors provide full and informative annotation, useful chronologies and indexes, and 112 photos, facsimiles of letters, drawings, and maps. These volumes are sure to become a standard source of biographical information. Another significant contribution to London biography is Clarice Stasz's *American Dreamers: Charmian and Jack London* (St. Martin's). Using Nancy Milford's *Zelda* as inspiration, Stasz wishes to depict another talented woman who sacrificed her own potential for achievement in the service of a famous spouse's creativity. This desire to put another unheralded American feminist on the map gives the book its markedly sympathetic slant. Allowing for this slant and some questionable attempts at psychoanalysis, the book is a readable source of information about the Londons and the literary scene in California at the turn of the century.

The growing interest in film studies recently has prompted a number of essays on the film versions of London's fiction. A substantial essay based on thorough research in primary sources is Robert S. Birchard's "Jack London and the Movies" in the new journal *Film History* (1[1987]:15–38). Making ample use of unpublished correspondence, Birchard narrates in detail the tangled story of London's business dealings with the emerging film industry around 1913. A good deal of legal squabbling about film rights and arrangements characterized this period before precedents for such things were clearly established. London's unflagging energy involved him in the world of drama as well as the movies. In "Portrait of a Professional: The Plays of Jack London" (*ALR* 20, ii:65–84), Keith Newlin's purpose is threefold: (1) to examine the available information about what plays London actually authored (some dispute here); (2) to examine the genesis of the plays for what it reveals about London as a writer; and (3) to show that with one exception the plays were conscious attempts at realistic drama and thus valuable early examples of American dramatic realism. London's reading of Jung near the end of his life has prompted several articles in the last few years. This subject is treated once again in Jeanne C. Reesman's "The Problem of Knowledge in Jack London's 'The Water Baby'" (*WAL* 23: 201–15). Focusing on a single example from the late South Seas stories, Reesman argues that the reading of Jung in the summer of 1916 resulted in stories reflecting a new and more sophisticated sense of the ambiguity of knowledge, a recognition of the value of ancient, unconscious, collective knowledge of the self to balance modern self-consciousness. The stories of the North are the subject of Jacqueline Tavernier-Courbin's "Social Myth as Parody in Jack London's Northern Tales" (*Thalia* 9, ii[1987]:3–14). Her thesis is that in these tales London parodied traditional myths and archetypes of Western culture by ironically transposing them to the primitive Klondike environment. She provides examples of three types: social comedies, social tragedies, and historical and religious parodies. Interpreting the stories with a feminist awareness, she claims that seen as parodies they deserve more respect from critics.

The novels of Sinclair Lewis received very little attention this year. Perhaps they don't wear well with time, or they hold little attraction for recent critical approaches. The only article on *Main Street* is done from a social science rather than literary perspective. Hans-Jürgen Grabbe's "The Ideal Type of the Small Town: *Main Street* in a Social Science Context" (*Amst* 32[1987]:181–91) uses the theoretical framework of Max Weber to make the commonplace point that the novel is the equal of and sometimes preferable to the "reality" of social science constructs in revealing the nature of small towns. Sanford E. Marovitz's "Ambivalences and Anxieties: Character Reversals in Sinclair Lewis' *Mantrap*" (*SAF* 16:229–44) examines a little-known and regarded novel done in 1926 when Lewis was at the height of his career. Marovitz poses the usual question applied to such works: is it better-crafted than is generally assumed? The affirmative reply is predictable, but its grounds are revealing: the novel deserves more appreciation because it fits the pattern of Lewis's social satire, his penchant for caricature. This is characteristic of Lewis criticism, which frequently implies that his aesthetic achievement rarely transcended social caricature. Thomas Wolfe recognized this limitation, according to Frank W. Shelton's "Thomas Wolfe and Sinclair Lewis" (*TWN* 12:7–12). After reviewing the familiar facts about the Lewis-Wolfe relationship, Shelton delineates the parallels between *Babbitt* and *Welcome to Our City*, a play Wolfe wrote the year the novel was published. Shelton explains that after this play Wolfe came to realize he was not essentially a satirist and to recognize the limits of Lewis's vision of America's heartland. Though continuing to admire Lewis's work, he took a different direction.

Michele A. Vaccariello's "Tutoring Sinclair Lewis: A Personal Account" (*SDR* 26, ii:35–56) furnishes more biographical information. Edited by Martin Bucco, this is the first printing of Vaccariello's diary entries on teaching Lewis Italian in the summer of 1949. Vaccariello was a professor at Williams College. Lewis was living at the time on a farm nearby. He is quoted on such subjects as proverbs, hypocrisy, snobbery, complexes, Faulkner, DeVoto, Mary Hemingway, and Garbo and is portrayed as sensible and friendly. Also in the category of biography is "Fragments from a Marriage: Letters of Sinclair Lewis to Grace Heggar Lewis" (*Missouri Rev.* 11:71–98), in which Speer Morgan and William Holtz provide annotation for a selection of Lewis's letters (spanning 1913–44) to his first wife.

vii. General Studies and Additional Authors

Two sections of Marcus Cunliffe, ed., *American Literature Since 1900* (Peter Bedrick, 1987) include discussion of the authors treated in this chapter. Malcolm Bradbury's "The American Risorgimento: The United States and the Coming of the New Arts" (pp. 1–27) highlights Dreiser and Stein in explaining that the blossoming of American fiction in the 1920s resulted from a blending of American naturalism and European influences by way of Stein. Dennis Welland's "The Language of American Fiction Between the Wars" (pp. 29–51) is a descriptive survey shaped by the general thesis that the fiction of the period oscillates between detached social observation and imaginative rendering of sensitively apprehended experience, between capturing American society at large and capturing the buried life of the individual. " 'The Amazing Hotel World' of James, Dreiser, and Wharton" (*Leon Edel and Literary Art*, pp. 151–60) by Joseph A. Ward informs us that the three writers found the new phenomenon of luxury hotels fascinating, culturally significant, and morally barbarous. In different ways and for different reasons all three were repelled by life centered in such hotels. John Rohrkemper's "The Great War, the Midwest, and Modernism: Cather, Dos Passos, and Hemingway" (*MMisc* 16:19–29) uses *One of Ours, Three Soldiers*, and *In Our Time* to show how these writers explored the striking contrast between the Midwest and war-ravaged Europe while at the same time experimenting with the modernist technique of juxtaposition. Two articles provide useful background information for students of the immigrant novels of this period. Guy A. Szuberla's "*Dom, Namai, Hein*: Images of the New Immigrant's Home" (Jack Salzman, ed. *Prospects: An Annual of American Cultural Studies*, Cambridge, 1985, pp. 139–68) treats "the lingering ambiguities of the new immigrant experience—the paradoxical act of finding and losing home and identity in America." His approach compares promotional literature used to attract immigrants to America with fiction portraying the actual immigrant experience. Authors treated: Sienkiewicz, Sinclair, Cather, Rölvaag, and Mlakar. A counterargument to the usual view that wind and solitude drove the women of the Great Plains settlement to despondency if not madness is offered by Peg Wherry in "At Home on the Range: Reactions of Pioneer Women to the Kansas Landscape" (*KanQ* 18[1986]:71–79). After sifting through letters and diaries of the time and region, she concludes that these documents show no signs that the women were particularly alienated from or repelled by their environment.

Moving from general studies to individual authors, we begin with Upton Sinclair, whose fiction receives its first extensive treatment in R. N. Mookerjee's *Art for Social Justice: The Major Novels of Upton Sinclair* (Scarecrow). The novels considered in this attempt at a reevaluation of Sinclair are *The Jungle, King Coal, Oil!, Boston*, and *Dragon's Teeth*. Applying the criterion of social purpose rather than artistic excellence, Mookerjee considers the novels in their own terms as aiming to promote social justice. He highlights Sinclair's role as forerunner of the "new journalism" and as a writer treating contemporary events based on a socialist analysis of society. The analysis of plot, character, and historical context is sound but pedestrian and fails to justify his concluding claims for Sinclair's literary achievement. James R. Barrett's introduction and notes to a new edition of *The Jungle* (Illinois) are intended to accomplish four purposes: (1) link scenes and characters with actual people and events; (2) provide historical context by supplying further information on subjects treated; (3) refer readers to relevant literature; and (4) translate Lithuanian phrases. Sinclair's unsuccessful campaign for the governorship of California in 1934 is treated in two articles by Greg Mitchell. "How Media Politics Was Born" (*Amer. Heritage* 39, vi:34–41) argues that modern media politics emerged when the Republicans were forced to use new methods to defeat Sinclair. The methods included the use of media experts from outside the party apparatus, the manipulation of the print media to promote a wholly negative campaign, and the first use of motion pictures in a campaign. The role of motion pictures is detailed in "How Hollywood Fixed an Election" (*Amer. Film* Nov.:26–31). Louis B. Mayer, who happened to be vice chairman of the state Republican party at the time, is the major figure in the story. He concocted a smear campaign and pressured employees to contribute money and theaters to run the campaign films, which were added to the Metronome Newsreels.

Carl Van Vechten, perhaps the leading dilettante of his age, has hitherto attracted little critical attention, but a selection of his letters appeared this year and recent interest in the Harlem Renaissance prompted two substantial articles on his novel *Nigger Heaven*. Bruce Kellner, ed., *Letters of Carl Van Vechten* (Yale) is a very selective collection. Kellner, who himself received 800 letters from Van Vechten, included only letters that he found "amusing or informative as signposts along the cultural avenues." The book is illustrated by Van Vechten's photographs of his friends and correspondents. Charles Scruggs's "Crab Antics and Jacob's Ladder: Aaron Douglas's Two Views of *Nigger Heaven*" (Victor A. Kramer, ed., *The Harlem Renaissance Re-Examined*, AMS Press, 1987, pp. 149–81) uses two advertising illustrations for the novel done by Aaron Douglas, one for a white audience, the other for a black, as the basis for two interpretations of the novel. The main argument is that Van Vechten did not limit himself to the underside of Afro-American life, as some allege, but functioned as "a sociologist, a myth-maker, and a satirist" and consequently provided large themes for black novelists who followed, whatever their attitude toward his novel. In "Carl Van Vechten Presents the New Negro" (*The Harlem Renaissance Re-Examined*, pp. 107–27), Leon Coleman tries to sort out the controversial role of *Nigger Heaven* in the Harlem Renaissance and the development of the New Negro (the urban blacks of the 20s seeking a new identity). Van Vechten's activities in behalf of the movement included writing about black arts and artists, helping individuals get published, and promoting social contacts between the races. Coleman judges these efforts to be important and positive. Some of these activities are mentioned in Eleanor Perényi's brief recollection of her first meeting in "Carl Van Vechten" (*YR* 77:537–43).

Several writers of popular fiction during this period have benefited from the growing scholarly interest in popular culture during the last decade. William Sydney Porter (O. Henry) is the subject of two books. Trueman E. O'Quinn and Jenny Lind Porter, eds., *Time to Write: How William Sidney Porter Became O. Henry* (Eakin, 1986) contains an essay by each editor and 12 O. Henry stories written while he was in prison. The essays are written by two enthusiasts (who spell the middle name with an "i") interested in even trivial details about Porter's trial, imprisonment, and fiction. Karen Charmaine Blansfield's *Cheap Rooms and Restless Hearts: A Study of Formula in the Urban Tales of William Sydney Porter.* (Bowling Green) focuses on the New York stories, which constitute about 100 of the 272 he wrote. By delineating plot patterns and character types, she defines Porter's formula and defends the value of formula artists.

Despite his extraordinary popularity, Edgar Rice Burroughs has received relatively little serious and sustained study, but some recent items are worth mention. In *Edgar Rice Burroughs* (TUSAS 499, 1986), Erling B. Holtsmark, a scholar of classics, provides a sympathetic but judicious overview emphasizing myth elements. *Burroughs Dictionary* (Univ. Press, 1987) by George T. McWhorter, curator of the Burroughs Memorial Collection at the University of Louisville Library, is an alphabetical list of proper names, words, phrases, and concepts contained in Burroughs's published works. Michael Orth's "Utopia in the Pulps: The Apocalyptic Pastoralism of Edgar Rice Burroughs" (*Extrapolation* 27[1986]:221–33) argues that apocalypse (destruction of a bad order) and pastoralism (restoration of an old order) are important elements of utopian thinking in Burroughs's fiction and part of its enduring popular appeal. In "The Time and Place of Edgar Rice Burroughs's Early Martian Trilogy" (*Extrapolation* 27[1986]:208–20), Benjamin S. Lawson relates the novels to the time and circumstances when they were written (about 1912) to show how the fantasy was shaped by the contemporary social-historical context. John Newsinger's "Reader He rescued Her: Women in the Tarzan Stories" (*Foundation* 39[1987]:41–49) is an attempt, prompted by feminist criticism, to reexamine the portrayal of masculine identity in the Tarzan series. Predictably, Newsinger discovers throughout the stories "benevolent patriarchy," "racist discourse," and a fascination with threats to the lives and virtues of white women, but fails to penetrate much beyond the obvious.

In the growing body of scholarship devoted to western and detective fiction, Zane Grey receives extensive treatment in Cynthia S. Hamilton's *Western and Hard-Boiled Detective Fiction in America: From High Noon to Midnight* (Iowa, 1987, pp. 71–93). In attempting to combine broad perspective with close analysis, this biographical-critical chapter sometimes appears discontinuous, shifting abruptly from biographical facts to Grey's treatment of lawlessness, property and power, the role of women, the gunfighter syndrome, and gold fever. The main theme is that Grey's fiction is recorded daydream. He recast both personal and western experience to fit romantic and mythic patterns; consequently, his work did not mature. Moreover, he wanted to claim contradictory virtues: tough adventure hero and idealistic romantic; imaginative writer and educator; inspired author of literature and practical writer of popular fiction. A contrasting view of the sophistication of his style is presented by Arthur Kimball in "Silent Walls: 'Nature' in Grey's *The Vanishing American*" (*SDR* 26, i:78–90). Kimball discerns a subtle level of irony and complexity in Grey's descriptions of nature, particularly in the purple prose used to describe sunsets. The argument is highly suggestive but not entirely convincing.

James M. Cain's distinctive contribution to the writing of crime fiction is examined in Richard Bradbury's "Sexuality, Guilt and Detection: Tensions between History and Suspense" (Brian Docherty, ed., *American Crime Fiction: Studies in the Genre*, [St. Martin's], pp. 88–99). That contribution lies in Cain's rejection of the dominant paradigm for the crime novel: gradual, reasoned detection. He wrote from the criminal's perspective. This makes the examination of motivation immediate and convincing, but there is no informing intelligence within the text to return the reader to a sense of rational order and explanation. In "Collecting Mystery Fiction: James M. Cain" (*ArmD* 21:262–66), Otto Penzler claims that Cain's influence on other American writers follows closely after that of Hemingway and Hammett. Penzler's lists and descriptions of Cain's novels and their film versions and current prices for first editions are designed primarily for book collectors.

Finally, the following items related to lesser-known authors warrant at least brief mention. Ernst Schürer and Philip Jenkins, eds., *B. Traven: Life and Work* (Penn. State, 1987) is a collection of 30 essays covering all aspects of the author's life and writing. In addition, Traven's best-known novel is treated in relation to the American Dream in K. Payne's "Americans and Indians: Cultural Commentary in B. Traven's *The Treasure of the Sierra Madre*" (*DQR* 18:46–58). Edward J. Piacentino's *T. S. Stribling: Pioneer Realist in Modern Southern Literature* (Univ. Press) examines six of the seven novels by this forgotten writer, who during the 1920s and 1930s treated the southern town with the kind of iconoclastic critical realism popularized by Sinclair Lewis. The work of Ruth Suckow, a lesser-known but talented midwestern writer, became more readily available, with an introduction by Clarence A. Andrews, in *A Ruth Suckow Omnibus* (Iowa). Selections from Louis Bromfield's farm books, some of his best but out-of-print writing, appeared in Charles E. Little, ed., *Louis Bromfield at Malabar: Writings on Farming and Country Life* (Johns Hopkins). A flicker of interest in John P. Marquand is represented by Terry Teachout's "Justice to John P. Marquand" (*Commentary* October 1987:54–59).

Brigham Young University

14. Fiction: The 1930s to the 1960s

Gary Scharnhorst

The sheer bulk of scholarship devoted to this period as measured in column-inches of the *MLA Bibliography* diminished slightly this year, even though there was no corresponding contraction in the number or variety of works discussed. Among the writers included in this chapter, such perennial favorites as John Steinbeck, Flannery O'Connor, and Vladimir Nabokov continued to inspire and provoke the most interest. Indeed, Steinbeck was the subject of an early crop of commentary as scholars and critics began to gear up for next year's semicentennial of the publication of *The Grapes of Wrath.*

I inherit the task of compiling this chapter from Virginia Spencer Carr, who has executed it admirably the past two years. Lest my remarks at any point seem too smug: R. R. Bowker observed in 1885 that, of all people, bibliographers have "most occasion to realize the imperfections of human endeavor. Completeness is an *ignis fatuus* that eludes even the closest pursuit and the most painstaking endeavor."

i. Proletarians

***a.* John Steinbeck.** In *Looking for Steinbeck's Ghost* (Okla.), Jackson J. Benson, author of *The True Adventures of John Steinbeck Writer* (*ALS 1983*, p. 260), recounts his own adventures in Steinbeck's footsteps. Benson muses sympathetically but by no means uncritically on the literary biographer's task in this lively and engaging anecdotal history of the 15 years he spent researching, writing, revising, and shepherding his manuscript through publication. He explains how he was forced to delete some details from his earlier book when members of Steinbeck's family threatened legal action. After describing his problems with a bevy of editors and lawyers at Viking, he admits that "even now, years later, I don't feel about the book as I once did." Benson's volume belongs to an honorable subgenre of biographers' memoirs which includes A. J. A. Symons's *The Quest for Corvo* and Richard Holmes's *Shelley: The Quest.* In *Conversations with John Steinbeck* (Miss.), Thomas Fensch collects 25 feature articles published between 1935 and 1972 which were based at least in part on personal interviews with the author, as well as a written questionnaire prepared by an enterprising M.A. candidate to which Steinbeck supplied answers in 1938. These pieces are like a series of quaint snapshots pasted in the family album. We recognize the subject, to be sure, but we wonder how he looked during the months and years between exposures. In *Staging Steinbeck* (Cassell), Peter Whitebrook reprints the journal he kept between September 1986 and September 1987 as he dramatized *The Grapes of Wrath* for production at the Edinburgh Festival Fringe. Lamentably, the best part of the book is its alliterative title. The journal is pretentious ("I have the idea of the play opening in the executive office of a New York bank") as well as self-indulgent ("Mid-afternoon. Deconstructing Rose of Sharon and Connie. Phone rings").

Steinbeck is well represented in the journals this year by two comparative studies. In "The Depression's 'Graveyard Ghosts': A Shared Motif in *Waiting for Nothing* and *The Grapes of Wrath*" (*IFR* 15, i:21–22), John Ditsky notes that Tom Kromer used the same simile in 1935 that Steinbeck used four years later "to express the lowered vitality of the dispossessed." In "The Emergence of Class Consciousness in *Germinal* and *The Grapes of Wrath*" (*Comparatist* 12:44–57), William J. Beck and Edward Erickson discuss the conflict of labor and capital depicted in Zola's and Steinbeck's novels from a Marxist perspective in a fairly predictable way. Douglas L. Rathgeb's "Kazan as Auteur: The Undiscovered *East of Eden*" (*LEQ* 16, i:31–38) will also spark interest among Steinbeckians, if only for its problematical assertion that Elia Kazan "is as much the author of *East of Eden*, the film, as Steinbeck is of *East of Eden*, the novel." The Steinbeck Society issued *John Steinbeck on Writing*, ed. Tetsumaro Hayashi, a selection of the author's "candid remarks and confessions on the craft of writing" organized topically, and *Steinbeck's "The Red Pony": Essays in Criticism*, ed. Hayashi and Thomas J. Moore. The latter pamphlet contains a fine introduction by Warren French (pp. ix–xiv) and four provocative articles on the story-cycle: Thomas M. Mammaro's "Eric Erikson Meets John Steinbeck: Psychosocial Development in 'The Gift'" (pp. 1–9) relates the circumstances of the story's composition to Erikson's theory of the "eight stages" of human experience; Robert S. Hughes, Jr.'s "The Black Cypress and the Green Tub: Death and Procreation in Steinbeck's 'The Promise' " (pp. 9–16) explicates this story in light of a specific pattern of imagery; Roy S. Simmonds's "The Place and Importance of 'The Great Mountains' in *The Red Pony* Cycle" (pp. 17–26) both questions whether Steinbeck deliberately planned "a fully integrated cycle of stories tracing the progress of Jody Tiflin's maturation" and defends the inclusion of this tale on the basis of the "thematic and philosophic depth" it gives the whole; and Mimi R. Gladstein's " 'The Leader of the People': A Boy Becomes a 'Mensch' " (pp. 27–37) compares this text to Hemingway's Nick Adams stories.

The *Steinbeck Quarterly* exceeds its usual high standards this year. In "The First-Person Narrator in 'Johnny Bear': A Writer's Mind and Conscience" (21:6–13), Charlotte Byrd argues convincingly that in this early story Steinbeck "anticipated the animosity with which an audience receives unwanted truths about human nature." In "The Neglected Rib: Women in *East of Eden*" (21:13–23), Beth Everest and Judy Wedeles defend Steinbeck from the charge of sexual stereotyping in the novel. Such figures as Liza Hamilton and Faye, they suggest, "move beyond the stereotype to join seemingly disconnected story lines and to act as foils and counterparts to the more dominant male characters." The argument, however, rests on the paradoxical premises that the novel transcends character-types in its idealization of mothers and its "grimly realistic portrayal" of prostitutes. In "John Steinbeck's Use of the Bible: A Descriptive Bibliography of the Critical Tradition" (21:24–39), John H. Timmerman follows up his recent *John Steinbeck's Fiction* (*ALS 1986*, p. 263) by listing the most important essays on Steinbeck's biblical allusions, particularly in *The Grapes of Wrath* and *East of Eden.* Timmerman briefly summarizes Steinbeck's ambivalent religious attitudes: "Jesus was for him one of the great heroes—on the order of Zeus, perhaps." Richard A. Davison's "Hemingway, Steinbeck, and the Art of the Short Story" (21: 73–84) plows scorched earth and turns up nary a seedling—Steinbeck "fluctuated from outright worship of Hemingway's art to a grudging admiration for Hemingway's genius"—though the essay does contain brief analyses of "Flight" and "The Chrysanthemums." More entertaining and informative is Robert E. Morsberger's "*Pipe Dream*, or Not So Sweet Thursday" (21:85–96), a composition and production history of Steinbeck's failed big-budget Broadway musical. Finally, in "Struggle for Survival: Parallel Theme and Techniques in Steinbeck's 'Flight' and Norris's *McTeague*" (21:96–103), Elaine Ware contends that Steinbeck modeled Pepe's escape into nature on the final chapters of Norris's novel. The speculation is neither fatuous nor forced—Steinbeck no doubt knew Norris's story. However, like the most elementary of source criticism, the parallels do not significantly enhance our understanding of either work.

***b.* Mary McCarthy, James Agee, and Others.** Carol Gelderman's long-awaited *Mary McCarthy: A Life* (St. Martin's) is a remarkably readable biography of an underrated critic and novelist. Though Gelderman enlisted McCarthy's cooperation in the project, the book is no authorized hagiography. It chronicles in detail McCarthy's "eventful love life," her disastrous marriage to Edmund Wilson, and even her defamatory remarks about Lillian Hellman on national television in 1980 as well as the litigation that ensued. While this is not the definitive biography—after all, McCarthy died only in October 1989—Gelderman's volume will be an indispensable source to future biographers. It is based on a wealth of unpublished correspondence and interviews with literally dozens of McCarthy's friends and associates over the years, including Elizabeth Hardwick, Dwight Macdonald, and Arthur Schlesinger, Jr. Whereas Gelderman discusses McCarthy's criticism (both social and literary) with insight and skill, she reviews the fiction more perfunctorily, largely by summarizing composition and reception histories of such novels as *The Groves of Academe* and *The Group*. McCarthy's reportage from Vietnam in 1967 and 1968 is briefly discussed in Virginia Elwood-Akers's *Women War Correspondents in the Vietnam War, 1961–1975* (Scarecrow).

In "Agee" (*New Yorker*, 18 July 1988, pp. 72–82), John Hersey reminisces fondly about his colleague on the staff of *Time* in the 1940s. "His was the consciousness of a moralist," Hersey writes, "one in whom anger against wrong and injustice burned hotly, but also one in whom conviction was forever being shaken by doubt." Hersey's memoir adds depth and color to Lawrence Bergreen's portrait of the artist in *James Agee: A Life* (*ALS 1984*, p. 268). In "Unimagined Existence and the Fiction of the Real: Postmodernist Realism in *Let Us Now Praise Famous Men*" (*Representations* 24:156–76), T. V. Reed defines Agee's "self-conscious, ironic, politically engaged mode of writing that takes reality more seriously than did the realists and aesthetic form more seriously than did the modernists." Similarly, in "As Close As You Can Get: Torment, Speech, and Listening in *Let*

Us Now Praise Famous Men" (*MissQ* 41:147–60), Michael Staub explores moments in James Agee's text "which highlight the crucial interrelationships of Agee's own torment with his efforts to make his readers listen attentively to three Alabama tenant-farmer families." Staub concludes that Agee's work derives its power from "its fierce insistence on the sacred indescribability of each life and condemnation of a society that permits the spiritual crippling and subjugation of human beings bound by extreme poverty." Staub also places Tillie Olsen's only novel in the tradition of Depression-era literature "that counseled middle-class Americans to *listen* to impoverished minorities" in "The Struggle for 'Selfness' Through Speech in Olsen's *Yonnondio: From the Thirties*" (*SAF* 16:131–39). Ironically, Olsen's novel was not published until 1974; that is, it "became a silenced text that could not be fully articulated." Nelson Algren is remembered by Bettina Drew in "Drifting into a Career" (*MissR* 11, iii:224–66), an excerpt from a forthcoming biography of Algren which focuses on his experiences in Louisiana and Texas early in the Depression. Burns Ellison, Algren's friend and student, discusses the writer in "The First Annual Nelson Algren Memorial Poker Game" (*IowaR* 18:61–97). The eight novels James T. Farrell set in the vicinity of Washington Park in south Chicago comprise a single sequence cohering around two recurrent experiences in Charles Fanning's "Death and Revery in James T. Farrell's O'Neill-O'Flaherty Novels," an essay in *The Incarnate Imagination* (Bowling Green), ed. Ingrid H. Shafer. In "*Jews Without Money* as a Work of Art" (*SAJL* 7:67–79), Richard Tuerk effectively discredits the notion that Mike Gold's novel is a roman à clef. Gold largely invented his narrator's "proletarian roots," Tuerk explains, and he heavily revised for the book a series of sketches of East Side life he had first published in *Masses* over a decade before.

Another pair of long-silent and unjustly neglected writers from the 1930s also were the subjects of individual essays this year. In "Williamsburg in Wonderland: Daniel Fuchs's 'Triplicate'" (*SAJL* 7:80–89), Gabriel Miller attempts to resurrect an obscure novelist from the footnotes to which he has been consigned. Fuchs's novella, first published in 1979, is "his most significant fiction since the thirties" and represents a breakthrough from his more despairing early stories, according to Miller. In a similar vein, Henry Roth, who published *Call It Sleep* in 1934 and then lapsed into a literary silence so complete that it makes Melville after 1857 seem loquacious, finally published a second book in 1987 at the urging of an Italian professor of American literature. Unfortunately, *Shifting Landscape: A Composite, 1925–1987, Henry Roth*, ed. Mario Materassi (Philadelphia: Jewish Publication Soc., 1987) consists of the sort of stuff Woody Allen satirized in "The Metterling Lists." As Donna Rifkind remarks in "Call It Irresponsible" (*NewC* 6, ii:75–76), Roth's collection is "an unmistakable bomb," a collection "composed entirely of false starts, notes, scribbles, second-rate stories, transcribed interviews, endless explanations of and meditations on writer's block—everything, in short, except actual literary achievement." She blames the fiasco not on Roth but on perverse "hangers-on" who "pant for some literature to publish."

ii. Southerners

***a.* Robert Penn Warren, the Agrarians, and Others.** The major Warren publication this year is John Burt's *Robert Penn Warren and American Idealism* (Yale), a critical study with a deceptively simple thesis. Warren is both attracted by romantic idealism and the force of "higher laws" in art and politics and repelled by the seductive appeal of such pretty ideas on this moonstruck and dream-visited planet—that is, according to Burt, Warren's method "is a simultaneous evasion and experience of primary truth. Warren attempts, through his alternations of confrontation and retreat, to apprehend a possessing truth without, in turn, becoming possessed by it." Burt aptly compares Warren to Hawthorne in this respect, for both writers seek "a neutral territory where the dangers inherent in both alternatives may be avoided while the aims of both alternatives may be achieved." Thus Warren's novel *Night Rider* is both inspired by Agrarian concerns and critical of the Agrarians themselves; *All the King's Men* illustrates "how the hunger for justice, when thwarted, turns to means that ultimately place justice out of reach"; and *World Enough and Time* proves "how those best instincts which make one worthy to have been one's self lead inevitably into self-repeal and self-destruction." In "The Power of Filiation in *All the King's Men*," a chapter in *Modern American Fiction: Form and Function* (LSU, pp. 156–69), ed. Thomas Daniel Young, James H. Justus reminds us of the importance of the narrator's voice in Warren's novel—Jack Burden "tells us finally more about himself and his difficult moral education than he does about Willie Stark." Justus concludes that Warren was more interested in dramatizing the anxieties of the "divided self" than in fictionalizing the protofascist politics of Huey Long. Warren also published revised versions of his memoir of R. F. Warren (see *ALS 1987*, p. 259) and of his well-known elegy "Mortmain" (in *Portrait of a Father* [Kentucky]). Warren and Cleanth Brooks's anecdotal history "The Origin of the *Southern Review*," first delivered in Baton Rouge in 1985, reaches print this year in *The* Southern Review *and Modern Literature* (LSU), ed. Lewis P. Simpson, James Olney, and Jo Gulledge. Of lesser interest is Walter Sullivan's *Allen Tate: A Recollection* (LSU), a reminiscence of Sullivan's own 35-year friendship with Tate so gorged with gossip, so steeped in the history of critical and academic tempests, that it opens with a glossary of "names mentioned herein." Among the literati of the period who appear in cameo roles are Warren, Caroline Gordon ("Novelist and first wife of Allen Tate"), Jean Stafford ("Novelist, short story writer, and first wife of Robert Lowell"), Flannery O'Connor, Katherine Anne Porter, Andrew Lytle, and Peter Taylor ("Fiction writer; winner of a Pulitzer Prize").

Fortunately, Taylor appears to better advantage this year in several other publications. James Curry Robison's *Peter Taylor: A Study of the Short Fiction* (Twayne) is a quite serviceable volume, with synopses and brief analyses of 26 of Taylor's 57 published stories. Robison belabors no thesis; rather, he strides from tale to tale as bravely as Eliza glides across the ice floes. His critical pronouncements are perceptive, especially as they compare and contrast Taylor with the Agrarians to whom he (literally) went to school. Robison reprints reminiscences of Taylor by Warren and Tate and a swatch of contemporary reviews of his work. The volume also contains three interviews with Taylor, one conducted by Robison and published here for the first time. In two *Southern Review* articles overlooked last year, David Robinson corrects the critical devaluations of Taylor as a minor or regional writer. In "Tennessee, Taylor, the Critics, and Time" (23:281–94), Robinson proves that Taylor's neglected 1958 story "Venus, Cupid, Folly and Time" is one of his "most precise social dissections" and "most enthralling psychological analyses," a "work with the critical force and artistic sympathy which marks fiction of major stature." In "Summons from the Past" (23:754–59), Robinson reviews Taylor's novel *A Summons to Memphis* and fairly predicts that, after Faulkner, Taylor and Welty will "prove the most durable" of modern southern writers. The 120 miles between Nashville and Memphis, he writes, "have in recent years become Peter Taylor's Yoknapatawpha." Stuart Wright's *Peter Taylor: A Descriptive Bibliography 1934–1987* (Virginia) is an invaluable reference tool, with complete listings of Taylor's publications, interviews, translations of his works, even his dust jacket blurbs and sound recordings. In "A Psychoanalytic Appreciation of Peter Taylor's 'A Spinster's Tale'" (*JEP* 9:309–16), Maureen Andrews adopts a Freudian perspective to emphasize the protagonist's sexual fears; in the course of the story, Andrews writes, she "discovers that it is mortally dangerous to be a woman." Ironically, in "Determined Failure, Self-Styled Success: Two Views of Betsy in Peter Taylor's 'Spinster's Tale'" (*SSF* 25:49–54), Roland and Gargi Sodowsky illustrate how the protagonist of Taylor's story may seem either "trapped by the forces of parent-child relationships and sexual fears" or "as choosing and controlling the unsocial direction of her life," depending on the "Freudian" or "Adlerian" point of view of the reader. These "disparate interpretations," the authors suggest, demonstrate "the profundity of Taylor's characterization." However, their analysis may simply demonstrate Taylor's immaturity as an artist when he completed the story—he was, after all, an undergraduate at Kenyon College at the time—or the difficulties of reading it coherently in psychoanalytical terms.

b. **Flannery O'Connor, Eudora Welty, and Others.** Scholarship on Flannery O'Connor continues to be a growth industry this year with no less than two new books, parts of six others, and several major articles in press. Suzanne Morrow Paulson's *Flannery O'Connor* is a first-rate addition to Twayne's Studies in Short Fiction series. Paulson discusses all of O'Connor's stories except those rewritten for her novels, but her analysis is never superficial, and her method never reductive. She organizes her commentary thematically, a plan which enables her to discuss O'Connor's art and her attitudes on such topical issues as race before she turns to matters of critical and religious dogma. Her remarks on "Parker's Back," in particular, should begin to spur interest in this late, relatively neglected tale. As she suggests, it "rather than the usually anthologized 'A Good Man Is Hard to Find,' should be the starting point" for readers new to O'Connor. In all, Paulson emphasizes O'Connor's "modern consciousness" rather than her Catholicism. Similarly, Martha E. Cook, in "Flannery O'Connor's *Wise Blood*: Forms of Entrapment," another chapter in *Modern*

American Fiction (LSU, pp. 198–212), explains how the imagery, parallel events, and doubling of characters in the novel serve the author's artistic (as distinct from proselytic) purpose. Clayton Koelb analyzes O'Connor's "The River" according to the theories of reader-response, albeit without the daunting jargon, in his *Inventions of Reading* (pp. 188–202). The story is, he avers, "arguably one of the most elegant constructions of the verbal imagination to be written since the death of Franz Kafka," for its reader is repeatedly forced "to rethink the relation between tenor and vehicle." Mary Jane Schenck disputes the author's own interpretation of her work in "Deconstructed Meaning in Two Short Stories by Flannery O'Connor," in *Ambiguities in Literature and Film* (Florida State, pp. 125–35), ed. Hans P. Braendlin. As Schenck explains, at the conclusion of both "A Good Man Is Hard to Find" and "The River," the "reader is left with a vision of destruction of human life both literal and figurative that is absurd rather than tragic." In "Compromising Positions: Systemic Linguistics and the Locally Managed Semiotics of Dialogue," an essay in *Functions of Style* (Pinter), ed. David Birch and Michael O'Toole, Michael Toolan examines "the lexico-grammatical dynamics" of a brief conversation in O'Connor's "Greenleaf."

Whereas Paulson et al. reject out of hand the idea promulgated by Robert Drake over 20 years ago that O'Connor told but "one story" of religious trial and faith in all her fiction, most O'Connor criticism continues to smack of Christian apology. Indeed, Arthur F. Kinney in "Flannery O'Connor and the Art of the Holy" (*VQR* 64: 215–30) cites Drake with approval and rehearses the more familiar, polemical, and traditional approach to her work. O'Connor was "an incarnational writer," he claims, whose "basic theme, first and always, is the separation of nature and grace." Marion Montgomery, in "Eric Voegelin as Prophetic Philosopher" (*SoQ* 24:115–33), ponders the influence of Voegelin, a self-described "Pre-Reformation Christian," on O'Connor, who reviewed three volumes of his *Order and History* for her diocesan paper. David Jauss, in "Flannery O'Connor's Inverted Saint's Legend" (*SSF* 25:76–78), suggests that the bus trip in *Everything that Rises Must Converge* is the satirical progress of an ironic St. Julian Hospitator. Edward Strickland examines the quest motif in O'Connor's "most explicitly Catholic" story in "The Penitential Quest in 'The Artificial Nigger'" (*SSF* 25:453–59). Jill P. Baumgaertner even claims O'Connor as the ally of fundamental Protestants against "liberal theology," in *Flannery O'Connor: A*

Proper Scaring (Harold Shaw). Similarly, Ralph C. Wood's discussion of O'Connor in *The Comedy of Redemption* (Notre Dame, pp. 80–132) focuses on her "Christian faith and comic vision." Her fiction, according to Wood, "affords a fitting comic subject for theological analysis," especially of the Augustinian variety. Unfortunately, his judgments are more biographical and theological than literary, as when he describes O'Connor as "a strange mixture of pre- and post-Vatican II Catholicism." He reduces O'Connor to little more than a didacticist whose fictional "criminals and egotists" are "almost without exception" made "into reluctant recipients of grace." To his credit, however, Wood singles out O'Connor's late story "Revelation" for special praise, ordaining it "quintessentially comic." Larue Love Sloan underscores the significance of the metaphor of sight in this same tale in "The Rhetoric of the Seer: Eye Imagery in Flannery O'Connor's 'Revelation' " (*SSF* 25:135–45). "Throughout the story," Sloan suggests, "eyes, glances, gazes, and visions form a subtle chain that inevitably leads to the final epiphany, that final blast of vision" which gives the work its title. In "Space and the Movement Through Space in *Everything That Rises Must Converge*: A Consideration of Flannery O'Connor's Imaginative Vision" (*SLJ* 20, ii:81–98), Shannon Russell asserts that, in the several stories of this collection, "space and motion operate as vehicles for the revelation of the reality of the divine in life." According to William M. Burke in "Protagonists and Antagonists in the Fiction of Flannery O'Connor" (*SLJ* 20, ii:99–111), O'Connor's "religious perspective is more complex than generally acknowledged"—but this analysis still presumes that she was primarily a religious writer. Leo Schneiderman covertly responds to this school of scholarship in *Literary Mind* (pp. 84–101) by insisting O'Connor was a flawed artist with a weak ego ideal, her fiction "the work of an angry spirit" that repeatedly betrays "hatred of the mother figure." Lamentably, Schneiderman's analysis is no less reductive than the traditional religio-allegorical reading of O'Connor's fiction it purports to correct.

Welty scholars are well served by the publication of *The Welty Collection* (Miss.), a 250-page guide to the Welty manuscripts and other documents at the Mississippi Department of Archives and History. Editor Suzanne Marrs supplies useful introductions to chapters on Welty's story manuscripts, photographs, and correspondence. The *Eudora Welty Newsletter* this year is, as usual, a valuable clearinghouse of bibliographical data. Welty's fiction, especially her novels, also attracts more than its usual spate of admirers. According to B. H. Carson's "Eudora Welty's Dance with Darkness: *The Robber Bridegroom*" (*SLJ* 22:51–68), this early novel replicates in its form the movement from a fairy tale and a child's world "to a philosophically, psychologically, and historically corrected outlook." Like Michael Kreyling in his *Eudora Welty's Achievement of Order* (*ALS 1980*, p. 287), Ellen L. Walker and Gerda Seaman find in "*The Robber Bridegroom* as a Capitalist Fable" (*SoQ* 26:57–68) a "comic retelling" of the central experience in American culture—"the transformation of the forest to the market place." In " 'Coming Through': The Black Initiate in *Delta Wedding*" (*MissQ* 41:541–51), Barbara Ladd underscores the changes which occur to black figures in this novel, particularly Pinchy. "Welty seems determined to claim for her black characters," Ladd concludes, "the same impulse to love and separateness as well as the same power to change the community that she claims for her white characters." J. S. Leonard discusses the novel's submerged pattern of "male violence and female accommodation" in "*Delta Wedding*: Eudora Welty's Plunge into Freudian Symbolism" (*WVUPP* 34:110–17). According to Patricia S. Yeager's Lacanian analysis in "The Case of the Dangling Signifier: Phallic Imagery in Eudora Welty's 'Moon Lake,'" a chapter in *Faith of a (Woman) Writer* (Greenwood, pp. 253–71), ed. Alice Kessler-Harris and William McBrien, Welty deconstructs "phallocentrism" by way of exploring in this story "the ways in which the dominant sex/gender system erases woman's past and endangers her future." B. H. Carson's "In the Heart of Clay: Eudora Welty's *The Ponder Heart*" (*AL* 59: 609–25) revises the critical estimate of Edna Earle's role in this novel; she emerges not as the "proponent of the old, orderly, rational ways but as the life-engaged, dynamic balancer of reason and feeling." In "The Harmonies of *Losing Battles*," in *Modern American Fiction* (pp. 184–97), Peggy Whitman Prenshaw celebrates Welty's blend of voices and motifs in the novel. Floyd C. Watkins's admirable essay "Death and the Mountains in *The Optimist's Daughter*" (*ELWIU* 15:77–85) probes the autobiographical and familial sources of this story, one of Welty's few fictions set outside Mississippi, and silhouettes its spiritual topography—"its symbolic use of high place."

Several other southern women writers also received critical notice this year. Curiously, Carson McCullers's stock seems to be on the wane these days, though her work may still inspire an exceptional essay. McCullers's story "Wunderkind" is "vastly more" than a "thinly-veiled autobiographical record" of the author's training in piano, writes Alice Hall Petry in "Carson McCullers's Precocious 'Wunderkind'" (*SoQ* 26:31–39). Rather, it is "a remarkable rendering of an adolescent's turmoil over her growing awareness of her sexual passion for her music teacher." Janice Fuller explains in "The Conventions of Counterpoint and Fugue in *The Heart Is a Lonely Hunter*" (*MissQ* 41:55–67) that McCullers used musical conventions in the form of this novel, even developing "a number of separate voices or melodic lines." Unfortunately, Fuller's essay largely reiterates C. Michael Smith's analysis of the novel from a decade ago (see *ALS 1979*, p. 263).

Darlene Harbour Unrue's *Understanding Katherine Anne Porter* (So. Car.), the latest issue in the Understanding Contemporary American Literature series, is a solid introduction to Porter's life and work. Also the author of *Truth and Vision in Katherine Anne Porter's Fiction* (*ALS 1985*, p. 262), Unrue organizes the initial chapters of the study by setting, with individual sections devoted to Porter's fiction set in Mexico, the Old South, the rural Southwest, and New England–Greenwich Village, followed by entire chapters on "Pale Horse, Pale Rider" and "The Leaning Tower," *Ship of Fools*, and Porter's non-fiction. While the volume breaks no new ground, advances no new thesis, and generally slights her religious imagery, it is an excellent overview of Porter's career, a crisply written survey well-grounded in recent scholarship. Willene and George Hendrick's book on Porter in the Twayne series also reappears this year in a revised and updated edition (TUSAS 90). Kaye Gibbons explains in "Planes of Language and Time" (*KR* 10:74–79) how the "forces of memory and time" eddy beneath the "calm narrative surfaces" of the Miranda stories. Mary Titus's "'Mingled Sweetness and Corruption': Katherine Anne Porter's 'The Fig Tree' and 'The Grave'" (*SoAR* 53: 111–25) analyzes these stories as "explorations of the sexual terror and guilt originating in [Porter's] most painful childhood experience: her mother's death after childbirth" when she was not yet two years old. In "Literary Criticism, Katherine Anne Porter's Consciousness, and the Silver Dove" (*SSF* 25:109–15), George Cheatham decries the "antiformalism" of Georges Poulet and the Geneva school, illustrating his reservations by referring to the silver coffin-screw which Miranda and Paul discover in "The Grave." The dove "unquestionably symbolizes the resurrection of man's immortal soul through the power of the Holy Spirit," he asserts, implying that the "antiformalists" acquainted with Porter's agnosticism would overlook this point and thus misread the story. In effect, Cheatham draws a line in the sand after the train has left the station. Joel Williamson's "How Black Was Rhett Butler?", in *The Evolution of Southern Culture* (Georgia), ed. Numan V. Bartley, taps a number of neglected biographical sources in its sketch of Margaret Mitchell's life, though the speculation that Mitchell flirted with a miscegenation theme and portrayed the scalawag Cap'n Butler as a biracial type simply ignores the symbolic shorthand of fair and dark characters available to American romancers since Cooper and Poe.

Marjorie Kinnan Rawlings is the subject of two books this year, the fiftieth anniversary of the publication of *The Yearling*. Elizabeth Silverthorne's *Marjorie Kinnan Rawlings: Sojourner at Cross Creek* (Overlook), the first full-blown biography of the author, is episodic and reverent, full of dates and place-names, the stuff of which informational footnotes are made. It contains virtually no critical commentary on Rawlings's fiction except in the letters of Maxwell Perkins to Rawlings which Silverthorne excerpts. In *Invasion of Privacy* (Florida), Patricia Nassif Acton, a law professor, reviews the celebrated suit filed against Rawlings by a litigious Florida neighbor after the publication of her autobiographical best-seller *Cross Creek* in 1942. Based in large part on the trial transcript, the narrative is as fresh and absorbing as a legal brief.

***c.* Thomas Wolfe and Erskine Caldwell.** In *Thomas Wolfe and His Editors* (Okla.), a volume overlooked last year, Leslie Field attempts to "dispel the myth" that "Wolfe's posthumous publications were written by his last editor, Edward C. Aswell. Internal evidence and newly discovered letters prove that Wolfe was the writer, Aswell the editor." Field admirably summarizes the major battles in the war regarding Wolfe's authorship of the three late books waged principally between John Halberstadt and Richard Kennedy early in the 1980s (see *ALS 1980*, pp. 288–89; *ALS 1981*, p. 267; *ALS 1982*, p. 264; *ALS 1983*, pp. 276–77). Field also offers a concise documentary history of Wolfe's plans for the "mess" of manuscript left at his death and he examines Aswell's editorial "discards" as he ordered and shaped the manuscript. Field persuasively supports his argument for the authenticity of the posthumous fiction with a series of "Cameo Test Cases," a close comparison of various manuscript and typescript versions of key episodes with the texts as they were finally printed in

The Web and the Rock, You Can't Go Home Again, and *The Hills Beyond.* In the conclusion to his monograph, he quotes at length from the correspondence of Aswell and Elizabeth Nowell, Wolfe's agent. According to Field, these letters corroborate the other evidence that Aswell did not write Wolfe's posthumous books. The correspondence to which he refers, letters Aswell and Nowell exchanged between 1949 and 1958, was edited by their respective daughters Mary Aswell Doll and Clara Stites and published this year as *In the Shadow of the Giant: Thomas Wolfe* (Ohio). Whereas Field believes these letters demonstrate that Aswell wished merely "to edit Wolfe to capture exactly what he wanted to render," Doll and Stites claim that "some of Aswell's statements about what Wolfe wrote were really about what Aswell himself had written in the name of posthumous editing." Not even the principal scholars, it seems, quite agree about what these letters prove. For his part, in "Thomas Wolfe and His Biographers" (*Review* 10:203–9), Kennedy describes David Donald's *Look Homeward: A Life of Thomas Wolfe* (*ALS 1987*, p. 269) as "the first really adequate biography of Wolfe that has emerged"—no small praise from the author of *The Window of Memory: The Literary Career of Thomas Wolfe.* Nevertheless, Kennedy disputes Donald's harsh assessment of Aswell's editorial "interference" in the preparation of the posthumous books. And so the controversy, while no longer aboil, still simmers.

Wolfe inspired only a few rather specialized studies in the journals this year. Richard Walser discusses Wolfe's fascination with rail travel in "Thomas Wolfe's Train as Symbol" (*SLJ* 21, i:3–14), for example. By far the most important Wolfe criticism this year appears in the *Thomas Wolfe Review,* which includes such insightful essays as Duane Schneider's "Imagination and Fantasy in the Works of Thomas Wolfe" (12, i:2–6), Daphne H. O'Brien's " 'The Banquet of Life': Hunger and Plenty in *Look Homeward, Angel*" (12, ii:23–32), and Karen L. Whitlow's "Thomas Wolfe and the 'Incommunicable Prison' " (12, ii:38–49). Wolfe's influence on other writers is chronicled in Diana Orendi Hinze's "William Faulkner and Thomas Wolfe" (12, i:25–32), Morton I. Teicher's "Ray Bradbury and Thomas Wolfe" (12, ii:17–19), and John S. Phillipson's "Herman Wouk and Thomas Wolfe" (12, ii:33–37); his relations with several of his contemporaries are explored in Frank W. Shelton's "Thomas Wolfe and Sinclair Lewis" (12, i:7–12), James D. Boyer's "Thomas Wolfe's Quarrel with the Lost Generation" (12, i:33–38), and Thomas A. Underwood's "Thomas Wolfe and H. L. Mencken" (*Menckeniana* 106:1–4).

Conversations with Erskine Caldwell (Miss.), ed. Edwin T. Arnold for the Literary Conversations Series, reprints in 300-plus pages 31 selected interviews with the author between 1929 and 1987 and a previously unpublished interview conducted for this volume a year before Caldwell's death. Ironically, Caldwell, who disdained academic criticism, seems most forthcoming in the interviews with the editors of such academic journals as *Studies in the Novel*, the *Georgia Review*, the *Arizona Quarterly*, and the *Mississippi Quarterly*.

iii. Expatriates and Émigrés

***a.* Vladimir Nabokov.** Nabokov's fiction has spawned a particularly rich harvest of scholarship this year, with two new books, parts of three others, and several major articles in press. Despite Nabokov's antipathy to Freud and his disciples, in *Freud and Nabokov* (Nebraska) Geoffrey Green considers Nabokov's comments about fiction in his introductions, interviews, and essays as a text which illumines certain psychoanalytical principles. Green wisely resists the temptation to psychoanalyze Nabokov on the basis of his writings; Leo Schneiderman succumbs to this temptation in *Literary Mind* (pp. 63–83)—for example, he declares that "Nabokov uses aestheticism in the service of affect diffusion, creating a fantasy world in which conflicts are resolved mechanically rather than psychologically." Charles Kinbote would be proud. Brian Stonehill devotes a chapter of *Self-Conscious Novel* to "Nabobov's Imitations of Mortality" (pp. 73–114). Solipsism was "not merely a manner but the very matter of his fiction," reflexivity "the essence of [his] fictional technique," Stonehill writes. Paradoxically, however, Nabokov's novels "have the effect of educating and persuading the reader of the ubiquitous presence of death in the world." Elizabeth Deeds Ermarth approaches the same paradox from a theoretical perspective in "Conspicuous Construction; or, Kristeva, Nabokov, and The Anti-Realist Critique" (*Novel* 21:330–39). Ermarth finds "no abyss between representation and reflexion" and argues that Nabokov's emphasis on the semiotic powers in language is "consistent with social and moral function." Leona Toker suggests in "Ambiguities in Vladimir Nabokov's *Invitation to a Be-*

heading," in *Ambiguities in Literature and Film* (Florida State, pp. 95–103), that the novelist employed a "pervasive ambiguity" as a structural principle, so remarkable an idea it will be greeted with a shrug. Toker's "Nabokov's 'Torpid Smoke'" (*StTCL* 12:239–48) contends, rather awkwardly, that this story was a "safety valve" for "urgent material" the author "kept out" of *Invitation to a Beheading* and *The Gift.* David Field suggests in "Sacred Dangers: Nabokov's Distorted Reflection in 'Signs and Symbols'" (*SSF* 25:285–93) that this story proves "how artistic imagination can become distorted and turn to insanity, preventing any communication," a risk the author recognized even in his own case. Janet Gazari underscores the resemblances between solving a chess problem and reading a text—both activities "restructure and improve a finite stretch of time"—in "Chess Problems and Narrative Time in *Speak, Memory*" (*Biography* 10:151–62). In "The Narrator in Nabokov's *Pnin*" (*RLT* 22:169–81), Corrinne Hales maintains that the novel is less about a bumbling professor of Russian than it is about his erstwhile biographer: "The aesthetic energy of this novel goes right through Pnin and focuses on the narrator." The Book of the Month Club(!) has issued a facsimile first edition of *Lolita* this year, the thirtieth anniversary of its publication, with an introduction by Erica Jong also printed in the *New York Times Book Review* (5 June 1988, pp. 3, 46–47). Stephen Jan Parker compiles a list of the books in Nabokov's home in Montreux, Switzerland, in "Nabokov in the Margins: The Montreux Books" (*JML* 14:5–16).

As usual, this year some tenacious source-hunters stalk Nabokov into the dense forest of his allusions and report spotting him through the trees. In *Find What the Sailor Has Hidden: Vladimir Nabokov's* Pale Fire (Wesleyan), Priscilla Meyer inventories various mythological, historical, and literary analogues to the novel and analyzes some of its base elements. The volume reprints revised versions of a number of Meyer's earlier essays, including a symphonic trio from 1988. Meyer's "*Pale Fire* as Cultural Astrolabe: The Sagas of the North" (*RusR* 47:61–74) compares the novel to such Scandinavian myths as the *Eddas.* In "Igor, Ossian, and Kinbote: Nabokov's Nonfiction as Reference Library" (*SlavR* 47:68–75), Meyer explains how the novel refracts details in Nabokov's translation of *The Song of Igor's Campaign.* Meyer exhaustively catalogs the novelist's myriad references to the Bard in "Reflections of Shakespeare: Vladimir Nabokov's *Pale*

Fire" (*RLT* 22:145–68). Meyer even turns up a real (or "real") V. Botkin who wrote an introduction to a 19th-century Russian translation of Shakespeare's plays. In all, Meyer's monumental study is one of the most important contributions to Nabokov scholarship in recent years. Similarly, Maaja A. Stewart, in "Nabokov's *Pale Fire* and Boswell's Johnson" (*TSLL* 30:230–45), traces "the numerous allusions to Boswell's *Life of Johnson* in *Pale Fire*" which "underline an unexpected similarity between Nabokov's oddly matched pair of men and the historical odd match between Boswell and Johnson." Lois Feuer discusses the Shakespearean background of another Nabokov novel in "The Unnatural Mirror: *Bend Sinister* and *Hamlet*" (*Crit* 30:3–12), though Feuer prudently qualifies her thesis: the correspondence between the works is "thematic rather than literal." In "Humbert Humbert's Use of Catullus 58 in *Lolita*" (*TCL* 34:1–15), Gary R. Dyer argues convincingly that Nabokov's narrator invokes the same classical source five times in the novel to emphasize "the immortality he wants" for Dolores Haze. Bob Grossmith examines "Nabokov and Self-Divestment: A Gnostic Source" (*ELN* 25:73–78) "the relevance of gnostic mythology to metaphors of dying" in "Terra Incognita," *Bend Sinister*, and *Invitation to a Beheading*. *The Nabokovian* this year also contains no less than five source-identifications. Sam Schuman suggests in "*Laughter in the Dark* and *Othello*" (20:17–18) that yet another Nabokov novel is in some ways "a grotesque reflection" of yet another Shakespeare play; Emily Emery opines in "The Ripples of Chekhov in *The Real Life of Sebastian Knight*" (20:24–29) that the novel "contains a sufficiently complete paradigm" of *Seagull*; in "Beautiful Soup: Psychiatric Testing in *Pnin*" (20:36–44), Gennadii Barabtarlo reports that Nabokov ridiculed in chapter 4 of the novel some tests actually administered by Freudians; A. Katherine Dewey speculates in "The Sixteenth-Century 'Blue Cloak' in Vladimir Nabokov's *Laughter in the Dark*" (21:29–31) that the author used the color blue in his translation-revision of this novel "to recreate Brueghel's sixteenth-century painting *The Proverbs*"; and Paul R. Jackson proposes in "*Pale Fire* and Poe's Past" (21:32–33) that Shade lifts the title of his first collection of verse, *Dim Gulf*, from the second stanza of Poe's "To One in Paradise."

***b.* Anaïs Nin, Henry Miller, and Others.** For whatever reason, only Nin's diaries attract much critical attention nowadays. Her fiction seems to have lost the audience it once enjoyed. *Anais*, the official organ of the Anais Nin Foundation, this year contains three reviews of *Henry and June* (see *ALS 1987*, p. 272), a collection of previously suppressed passages from Nin's diary for 1931–32 regarding her intimacies with the Millers. In "Dropping Another Veil" (6:27–32), Philip K. Jason compares the new volume to the original, expurgated edition of the diary published in 1966. In "Economics and the Need for Revenge" (6:33–35), Meryle Secrest criticizes Nin as a "kept woman for decades" who exploited men, particularly her husband Hugh Guiler. A financier, Guiler subsidized Miller, if only indirectly through Nin's agency, for years—a painful truth that gives new meaning to the phrase "Left Bank." Karin Struck's "Logbook of a Liberation" (6:36–42) underscores the value of the diaries as a record of Nin's literary no less than her sexual development. Anna Balakilan focuses on the feminist implications of volume 3 of Nin's "Early Diaries," covering the period 1923–27, in "A Tale of Two People" (6: 58–66), and Doris Niemeyer discusses the therapeutic purposes to which Nin put her diaries in "How to Be a Woman and/or an Artist" (6:67–74). *Anais* for 1988 also publishes unedited excerpts from Nin's diary for 1933 describing her relationship with Antonin Artaud (6: 3–26); an interview with Nin in 1969 (6:86–92); and an unedited letter Miller wrote her in 1932 about her prose poem "Mona" (6: 93–103). *The Durrell-Miller Letters, 1935–80* (New Directions), ed. Ian S. MacNiven, approximately doubles the published correspondence between the two writers, though even these 500 pages contain only about a fifth of the million words they exchanged. In "A Mediterranean Encounter: George Seferis and Henry Miller" (*StHum* 14:79–94), George Thaniel chronicles another of Miller's friendships from the 1930s. Michael Woolf argues in "Beyond Ideology: Kate Millett and the Case for Henry Miller," an essay in *Perspectives on Pornography* (St. Martin's, pp. 113–28), ed. Gary Day and Clive Bloom, that despite her professed antipathy for Miller in *Sexual Politics*, Millet in *Sita* and *Flying* "reveals a profound sympathy for many of Miller's attitudes and narrative strategies."

Two other expatriate writers also attract critical attention this year. Largely through the herculean efforts of Sandra Whipple Spanier, Kay Boyle is finally receiving the acclaim long due her. The author of *Kay Boyle: Artist and Activist* (*ALS 1986*, p. 264), Spanier this year edits *Life Being the Best and Other Stories* (New

Directions), a collection of Boyle's best short fiction from the thirties, and a Kay Boyle special issue of *Twentieth Century Literature.* Spanier contributes biographical and critical introductions to both book and journal (34:245–57). The special issue also contains a panoply of testimonials about Boyle by such noted figures as Malcolm Cowley, Herbert Gold, Jessica Mitford, Howard Nemerov, Studs Terkel, and George Wickes, as well as six new critical essays. In "Revolution, the Woman, and the Word: Kay Boyle" (34:322–33), Suzanne Clark describes Boyle, a signatory of the *transition* manifesto in 1929 calling for "the Revolution of the Word," as a "revolutionary of lyric language." Clark's essay focuses on the "shattering of syntax" and linear discontinuities in three of Boyle's early stories. Deborah Denenholz Morse discusses one of Boyle's autobiographical novels of the thirties as a "female version of the Künstlerroman"—though one "less overtly polemical" than many similar works—in "*My Next Bride*: Kay Boyle's Text of the Female Artist" (34:334–46). In "Sexual Politics in Kay Boyle's *Death of a Man*" (34:347–62), Burton Hatlen deftly deflects the assertions of contemporary reviewers that this novel was pro-Nazi. Rather, Hatlen contends, Boyle's work subtly depicts "the destructive effects of patriarchy" and the will to power. As Ian S. MacNiven demonstrates in "Kay Boyle's High Country: *His Human Majesty*" (34:363–374), Boyle modeled the hero of her fifth war novel upon her husband, the diplomat Joseph Franckenstein, and addressed in it "a passionate concern: the defeat of xenophobia and the affirmation of love and fidelity." In "Tails, You Lose: Kay Boyle's War Fiction" (34:375–83), Edward M. Uehling deconstructs "Army of Occupation" and "The Lost" to illustrate Boyle's "fascination with the possibilities and failures of language." According to Elizabeth S. Bell's "Call Forth a Good Day: The Nonfiction of Kay Boyle" (34:384–91), Boyle's essays "reveal the connections that unite her work and chronicle the growth of her artistic vision." Spanier also contributes "Kay Boyle: In a Woman's Voice" to *Faith of a (Woman) Writer* (Greenwood, pp. 59–70) and emphasizes again Boyle's candidacy for rediscovery by modern readers. In yet another chapter in the same volume ("Two Women: The Transformations," pp. 71–81), Alison Rieke avers that in Nora Flood and Robin Vote, the paired heroines of *Nightwood*, Djuna Barnes depicted "subtly transformed modern version[s] of the female character in *The Blithedale Romance* and *The Bostonians*." Barnes is also the subject of a first-rate biographical sketch, based on unpublished correspondence, in *Writing for Their Lives* (Women's Press) by Gillian Hanscombe and Virginia L. Smyers.

iv. Westerners

Though the quantity of scholarship published this year on western authors of the period was rather modest, its quality was consistently high. David Roberts's *Jean Stafford: A Biography* (Little, Brown) is on the whole a remarkable work, a sympathetic portrait of a tortured writer who failed to realize her early promise. Roberts skillfully interweaves threads of biographical narrative with perceptive analysis of Stafford's fiction and journalism, including a number of aborted manuscripts left among her papers. "Stafford's life was beset by almost constant unhappiness," he concludes, but a "happier" author "might have written even less." Still, some 10 or 12 of Stafford's short stories are "near masterpieces," *Boston Adventure* "remains a remarkably original psychological novel," and *The Mountain Lion* is arguably her finest novel. Roberts's treatment of Stafford's marriage to A. J. Liebling is excerpted in the *American Scholar* ("Jean and Joe," 57:373–91). In "Grafting Onto Her Roots: Jean Stafford's 'Woden's Day'" (*WAL* 23:129–39), William Leary discusses the first chapter of the novel Stafford was writing at her death. Some of Leary's details (for example, the date Stafford contracted to write the novel) are at odds with Roberts's book, but his analysis of the autobiographical moorings of Stafford's story is solid and respectable.

A number of other western writers of the period earned kudos this year, two of them in the Western Writers Series (Boise State). Richard W. Etulain's *Ernest Haycox* (WWS 86) is a handy introduction to the work of this neglected regionalist, known today if at all for his story "Stage to Lordsburg," which John Ford adapted in the 1939 movie *Stagecoach*. James Ruppert's *D'Arcy McNickle* (WWS 83) cogently summarizes the literary and other achievements of the "grandfather of Modern Native American Literature and Modern Native American Ethnohistory." Ruppert reads McNickle's novels *The Surrounded*, *Runner in the Sun*, and *Wind from an Enemy Sky* against the backdrop of his ethnohistorical study *They Came Here First* in "Politics and Culture in the Fiction of D'Arcy McNickle" (*RMR* 42:185–95). Edward Abbey is the subject of four provocative articles in this last year of his life. John A. Murray in "The Hill

Beyond the City: Elements of the Jeremiad in Edward Abbey's 'Down the River with Henry Thoreau'" (*WAL* 22:301–6) weighs the natural-religious implications of Abbey's essay and concludes it contains the essential elements of the Puritan jeremiad, at least if *Walden* is valorized as holy writ. Similarly, Jay Dougherty in "'Once more, and once again': Edward Abbey's Cyclical View of Past and Present in *Good News*" (*Crit* 29:223–32) notes Abbey's shift to a dystopian perspective in this late novel, which ironically inverts several strands of western mythology. David E. Gamble explores the metaphysical labyrinth of Abbey's *Desert Solitaire* in "Into the Maze with Edward Abbey" (*SDR* 26, i:66–77). Bill McKibben appreciatively reviews two new collections of Abbey's prose, *One Life at a Time, Please* (Holt) and *The Best of Edward Abbey* (Sierra Club), in "The Desert Anarchist" (*NYRB*, 18 August 1988, pp. 42–44). Bert Bender in *Sea-Brothers* (pp. 160–66) places *Lightship*, a novel by the Pacific sailor Archie Binns, in the tradition of American sea writing originated by Cooper, Dana, and Melville.

Jon Wallace suggests in "The Implied Author as Protagonist: A Reading of *Little Big Man*" (*WAL* 22:291–99) that Thomas Berger opposes transcultural language codes in the novel and subverts the voices of both Jack Crabb and Ralph Fielding Snell to underscore Crabb's uneasy relation to his culture. In "Focus and Frame in Wright Morris's *The Works of Love*" (*WAL* 23:99–112), Joseph J. Wydeven eloquently explains how the novelist shaped his narrative method "through an imaginative fusion of his dual preoccupations as fiction writer and photographer." Richard H. Corning attempts, with mixed success, the critical reclamation of H. L. Davis's last novel in "Unity and Point of View in *The Distant Music*" (*WAL* 23:113–20). Thomas W. Ford emphasizes the significance of auditory motifs in "A. B. Guthrie's *Fair Land, Fair Land*: A Requiem" (*WAL* 23:17–30). The twenty-fifth anniversary issue of the *South Dakota Review* reprints John Milton's interviews over the years with Frank Waters, Walter Van Tilburg Clark, Harvey Fergusson, and Wallace Stegner under the general title "Approaches to Region/Place" (26, iv:33–75). Finally, Ann Ronald, one of the most prolific and perceptive analysts of the literature of the American West, illustrates "how easily a western tale [specifically Clark's 'Hook'] may be misinterpreted" to prove a larger point: that "too many critics and reviewers callously dismiss western American fiction." Ronald's complaint has merit; in our haste to revise the canon, we should not ignore nature-based literature. Or, as Ronald concludes, "We need brave critics—men and women who will take on the task of assessing more fully and re-evaluating more fairly the ranges of western short fiction." Hear, hear!

v. Easterners

Writers as different as Conrad Aiken and Shirley Jackson enjoyed modest critical revivals in 1988. Aiken is, in fact, the subject of two new books: Harry Marten's *The Art of Knowing: The Poetry and Prose of Conrad Aiken* (Missouri), a selective treatment of Aiken's novels and narrative poems that proposes simply to "illuminate his search to comprehend and express the possibilities of human knowing"; and Edward Butscher's overwritten *Conrad Aiken: Poet of White Horse Vale* (Georgia), the first volume of a projected two-volume biography. Neither Marten nor Butscher try to exaggerate Aiken's achievements; that is, he remains a minor writer and flawed artist whose failures were less those of intention than of execution. In "Voyaging Around the Great Circle: Freud and Aiken" (*L&P* 34:26–33), Catharine F. Seigel summarizes Freud's influence on Aiken's "working philosophy," particularly in his novels *Blue Voyage* and *Great Circle*. Jackson's stock, like shares in a rediscovered and re-opened mine, began to rise again this year. As Lynette Carpenter declares in "Domestic Comedy, Black Comedy, and Real Life: Shirley Jackson, a Woman Writer," yet another essay in *Faith of a (Woman) Writer* (Greenwood, pp. 143–48), feminist critics especially "should be able to appreciate the variety of Jackson's writings and the range of her experiences," including her so-called "matriarchal comedy." Anne LeCroy takes up the critical cudgels, as if in response to the challenge, in "The Different Humor of Shirley Jackson: *Life Among the Savages* and *Raising Demons*" (*SAH* n.s. 4:62–73). Fritz Oehlschlaeger develops an allied reading of Jackson's most famous story in "The Stoning of Mistress Hutchinson: Meaning and Context in 'The Lottery'" (*ELWIU* 15:259–65). The story, Oehlschlaeger convincingly argues, depicts "a society in which authority is male, potential resistance female," and the patriarchy controls fertility and female sexuality.

Best known as the author of *Robert Lowell: A Biography* (*ALS 1982*, pp. 339–40), Ian Hamilton surfaces in 1988 with the account of his abortive attempt in 1986 to issue an unauthorized life of J. D. Salinger, who successfully sued to enjoin its publication in its original form. Hamilton responds with *In Search of J. D. Salinger* (Random House), a "substantially new" exercise, albeit one both remarkably self-serving and dull. As Bruce Bawer notes in "Salinger redux" (*NewC* 6, x:92–96), "the two stories told side by side in this book—that of Salinger's life, and that of Hamilton's researches"—do not dovetail "in any significant way." Hamilton, who seems to consider American copyright laws a bloody nuisance, misses a prime opportunity to justify, if possible, the ways of the "publishing scoundrel" (as James's Miss Juliana calls the type). Its defensive tone notwithstanding, Hamilton's book satisfactorily silhouettes the life of the most notorious recluse in America since Howard Hughes. However, Warren French's Twayne book on Salinger, which appears this year in a substantially new edition entitled *J. D. Salinger, Revisited* (TUSAS 542), is still the standard critical study. Moreover, Alan Nadel avers in "Rhetoric, Sanity, and the Cold War: The Significance of Holden Caulfield's Testimony" (*CentR* 32:351–71) that the text of *Catcher in the Rye* betrays the dynamics of the McCarthy era, what Fredric Jameson terms the "political unconscious," in its censure of "phonies." The argument, however provocative, tends to ignore the long composition history of the novel. Though a religious skeptic, Peter De Vries is not spared Ralph C. Wood's solemn judgment in *The Comedy of Redemption* (Notre Dame, pp. 230–79). According to Wood, "the salient fact about De Vries's fiction is its near obsession with characters who cannot rest at ease in the Babylon of their secularism" and who "keep backsliding out of their unbelief, stumbling into Zion, lapsing into faith." Robert Emmet Long turns his sights on another of the *New Yorker* coterie in *James Thurber*, yet another volume in Ungar's Literature and Life series flawed only by the absence of any of Thurber's quirky drawings.

The Bellow critical industry has scaled back its production this year, though the *Saul Bellow Journal* continues its exemplary service as a single-author review. Dolly Smith in "Move Over, Menander" (7, i:3–14) discusses the theory of comedy Bellow advanced in *The Last Analysis* and refined in *Humboldt's Gift*. Burton R. Pollin lists his "conspicuous and functional" allusions to Poe in "Poe and Bellow: A Literary Connection" (7, i:15–26). In "Bellow's Canadian Beginnings" (7, i:27–34), Michael Greenstein ponders the role Bellow's native country plays in his novels. Kathleen King, in "Bellow the Allegory King" (7, i:44–50); Ellen Pifer, in "Beyond History and Geography" (7, ii:16–34); and Ellen Schur in "Eugene Henderson's

Many Selves" (7, ii:49–57) each weighs the quest motif in *Henderson the Rain King*. Thomas Loe's "Modern Allegory and the Form of *Seize the Day*" (7, i:57–66); Robert Birindelli's "Tamkin's Folly: Myths Old and New in *Seize the Day*" (7, ii:35–48); and Gerhard Bach's "'Howling Like a Wolf from the City Window': The Cinematic Realization of *Seize the Day*" each considers a formal aspect of Bellow's 1956 novella. Two other essays in the annual volume redress the relative neglect of Bellow's short stories. Walter Shear's "'Leaving the Yellow House': Hattie's Will" (7, i:51–56) examines one of Bellow's few female protagonists, and Ann Weinstein's "Ijah, 'Our Cousins' Keeper': Bellow's Paradigm of Man" (7, ii:58–70) identifies the attitudes expressed by the narrator of "Cousin" with those of the author. Margaret Morganroth Gullette's glib gerontological analysis of Bellow's fiction in *Safe at Last in the Middle Years* (pp. 120–45) is neither insightful nor particularly well-written ("Tommy Wilhelm is Bellow's worst loser" and "Herzog is not-Henderson"). David D. Anderson's "Saul Bellow and the Midwestern Tradition: Beginnings" (*MMisc* 16:59–68) is less about Bellow than it is a brief history of the Chicago Renaissance. Patrick W. Shaw's "History and the Picaresque Tradition in Saul Bellow's *The Adventures of Augie March*" (*ClioI* 16: 203–19) is by far the best essay on Bellow this year; according to Shaw, Bellow exploited the satiric mode of the picaresque in part by portraying a *picaro* who maintains a "peculiar silence" about postwar history. Surprisingly, apart from a special memorial issue of *Studies in American Jewish Literature* (7, ii), Malamud receives scant notice, though Lawrence Jay Dessner in "The Playfulness of Bernard Malamud's 'The Magic Barrel'" (*ELWIU* 15:87–101) resolves some of the critical problems associated with this story by insisting upon its "incessant irony."

The critics Lionel Trilling, Edmund Wilson, and Malcolm Cowley also attracted attention in a variety of venues this year. Stephen L. Tanner's *Lionel Trilling* (*TUSAS* 523) is a splendid introduction to the career of one of the most prominent literary intellectuals of his generation. In "Lionel Trilling and the Agency of Terror" (*PR* 54: 18–35), Lewis P. Simpson compares Trilling to Allen Tate in his effort to align the dual roles of critic and aspiring artist. Mark Krupnick in "Lionel Trilling and the Politics of Style," in *American Literary Landscapes* (St. Martin's), ed. Ian F. A. Bell and D. K. Adams, traces Trilling's changing ideas about literary style as a moral counterweight to leftist ideology. James W. Tuttleton qualifies Wilson's reputation as "a major sympathetic spokesman" for the Modernist movement in "The Vexations of Modernism: Edmund Wilson's *Axel's Castle*" (*ASch* 57:263–72). A new quarterly, *Horns of Plenty: Malcolm Cowley and His Generation* (Chicago), fills a critical niche once occupied by the now-defunct *Lost Generation Journal.* The first issues contain Adam Gussow's first-rate essay on Cowley's culture-criticism, "'Whatever Roots We Had in the Soil': Malcolm Cowley and the American Scholar" (1, i:5–15, 19–24); an exchange by Nicholas Natanson and Henry Dan Piper on Cowley and the Moscow Purge Trials of the late 1930s (1, ii:14–27); and Robert B. Heilman's "Cowley as a University Professor" (1, iii:12–23), a reminiscence of the controversy surrounding Cowley's temporary appointment to the faculty of the University of Washington in 1950.

vi. Iconoclasts and Detectives

Most fads are fleeting, but the Beats go on. Arthur and Kit Knight this year edit *Kerouac and the Beats: A Primary Source Book* (Paragon), a collection of interviews, letters, and other documents culled from their fanzine *unspeakable visions of the individual.* Martin Green reviews it and the larger implications of Kerouac's career in "The Loneliest Writer in America" (*LitR* 32:123–28). Green bluntly diagnoses Kerouac's problem: While the public at large failed to treat him seriously as a writer, he became something of a cult figure in the counterculture. Richard Hill reminisces about Kerouac's last months in Florida in "Kerouac at the End of the Road" (*NYTBR*, 29 May 1988, pp. 1, 11). John Guzlowski redirects the eschatological and scatological focus of recent Burroughs criticism to "more mundane issues" in a brilliant essay, "The Family in the Fiction of William Burroughs" (*MQ* 30:11–26). As Guzlowski explains, Burroughs depicts the family institution as one of the control systems that "can only be thrown off at the price of our humanity," a gloomy prospect that makes him "one of the most pessimistic writers" of a somber century.

Scholarly interest in Nathanael West seems to have gone west this year, with only three essays on the docket. In "The Apocalyptic Vision in Nathanael West's *Miss Lonelyhearts*" (*Apocalyptic Visions*, pp. 111–19), Walter Poznar finds an unrelenting nihilism and a "corrosive satire" in perhaps "the most tragic novel in modern American fiction," a "bleak indictment of human nature" partly relieved by the author's own "sorrow for mankind." In an allied note, "Nathanael West, Paul Valéry, and the Detonated Society" (*ELN* 25:66–73), Robert Wexelblatt discusses West's interest in the ideas of Spengler and Valéry, from whom he learned "not just to write about a civilization in decline, but about a culture of lonelyhearts columns and movie premieres." In fact, according to Blake Allmendinger's "The Death of a Mute Mythology: From Silent Movies to Talkies in *The Day of the Locust*" (*LFQ* 16, ii:107–11), West showed in his last novel how talking pictures "pervert the dreams of his characters and harm them irreparably."

The year also occasioned a resurgence of critical interest in detective fiction of the period, with a collection of essays and several vagrant articles in press. Most of the pieces in *American Crime Fiction* (Macmillan), ed. Brian Docherty, are germane and valuable. In "Camera Eye/Private Eye" (pp. 23–38), Peter Humm weighs the significance of the camera-eye device which appears repeatedly on both sides of the Atlantic in fiction, journalism, and films of the 30s and 40s, in works as diverse as Agee and Evans's *Let Us Now Praise Famous Men*, Hammett's *Red Harvest*, and Chandler's filmscript of *The Lady in the Lake*. Gary Day deconstructs Hammett's early fiction in "Investigating the Investigator: Hammett's Continental Op" (pp. 39–53), an essay which proves in effect that every reader of these stories is utterly befuddled—or if he isn't he should be. Christopher Bentley hypothesizes in "Radical Anger: Dashiell Hammett's *Red Harvest*" (pp. 54–70) that Hammett's leftist politics are most evident in his earliest fiction, especially in his first novel—a point John Cawelti elaborated as early as 1976 in *Adventure, Mystery, and Romance*. Stephen Knight's structural approach to Chandler's fiction in "'A Hard Cheerfulness': An Introduction to Raymond Chandler" (pp. 71–87) and Odette L'Henry Evans's "Toward a Semiotic Reading of Mickey Spillane" (pp. 100–14) reveal little that is new. For example, according to Evans, "the heroic actants, Mike Hammer, Tiger Mann, Cat Fallon and others, are defined according to their semiotic function, in relation to their direct opposites, the villains." (One hardly wonders what Spillane would say about the French *sémiotique*. After all, he once declared that "Mike Hammer doesn't drink cognac because I can't spell it.") Richard Bradbury's "Sexuality, Guilt and Detection: Tension between History and Suspense" (pp. 88–99) is an excellent analysis of James M. Cain's contribution to the hard-boiled style of crime fiction. Leroy L. Panek contends with conviction and at length in "The Naked Truth" (*ArmD* 21:362–76) that the hard-boiled school derives from the idiom of the streets, an American vernacular inseparable from the realistic characters and situations that distinguish the genre from its more formal or classical models. On a more specific topic, Richard Harp outlines Chandler's metaphorical use of tobacco as part of the "nastiness" of urban experience and an index "to the integrity and social status of his characters" in "Tobacco and Raymond Chandler" (*Clues* 9:95–104). Finally, two fine essays about cinematic adaptations of detective stories appear this year. Leslie H. Abramson's "Two Birds of a Feather: Hammett's and Huston's *The Maltese Falcon*" (*LFQ* 16, ii:112–18) demonstrates that in both the novel and film "facility as a storyteller is directly connected with power over the world." And in "*The Big Sleep*: Production History and Authorship" (*CRevAS* 19:1–21), Peter Lev describes in remarkable detail the group authorship of a well-known Hollywood film, a collaboration that certainly includes the work of Chandler as author of the original text and Faulkner as principal screenwriter.

University of New Mexico

15. Fiction: The 1960s to the Present

Jerome Klinkowitz

Half the business undertaken in the criticism and scholarship of contemporary literature seems devoted to defining and characterizing the subject. These efforts are proportional to the period's duration; whereas 20 years ago current fiction could be studied with an innocence of larger claims, by 1988 few analyses can be ventured without at least implying that any text is part of a larger theoretical agenda. Each new novel or collection of short stories would carry the burden of announcing a new aesthetic epoch, given the apparent difference of such new work and failure to have any established cultural category in which to fit it. Hence the great variety of names used to describe our era, all with their own competing aesthetic strategies. To date, none has been able to claim authority over the other, but by locating a style of fiction within the era's signal historical event one new work takes a great step toward establishing what today's most characteristic fiction may in fact be.

i. General Studies

The event which more than any other dominates the political, sociological, cultural, and now aesthetic history of our time is the Vietnam war. While previous studies have treated it as a special area, Thomas Myers's *Walking Point: American Narratives of Vietnam* (Oxford) reaches far beyond its topicality of subject to become one of the most astute analyses of not just fiction about the war but of the larger transformation that has come to characterize the style of writing other critics have labored to call postmodern, poststructural, innovative, or antitraditional. To Myers's credit he works inductively, letting theory emerge from the material rather than the other way around; but because this strategy works so well, with the body of existing Vietnam war fiction virtually creating the aesthics of Derrida, Foucault, and Bakhtin in native terms, *Walking Point* stands as one of the best self-contained treatments of what distinguishes postmodern American fiction.

The antitraditional nature of the war itself made it necessary for novelists to reinvent their forms of description. In so doing, these writers tell us something about the larger developments at hand. "If the buried structures of culture are made visible by war," Myers advises, "so are the aesthetic strategies of the text in which they reside." And so when journalist David Halberstam is driven to fiction as a form of "compensatory history," John Del Vecchio reveals the "discursive formations" underlying force and ideology, Tim O'Brien rewrites his culture's "prime narratives" as a way of demystifying their content, Michael Herr creates a new linguistic space for action, and the characters in *Going After Cacciato* sustain themselves in the freer realm of dialogic play, a new form of fiction is invented to handle the transformed reality of a war without identifiable lines of progress or achieveable goals. Experience and creation, Myers finds, join together to form a cooperative process. The brilliance of his study is not just that it traces this mode in the Vietnam war novel, but correlates it to the theoretical developments that explain why postmodern literary art is something different from its epochal precedessor.

Myers's study becomes one of the era's most important because, while beginning with a narrow subject, he applies the full range of aesthetic and cultural intelligence to it, until a structure emerges that can define our period's most characteristic fiction. Sadly, just the opposite happens in Linda Hutcheon's *A Poetics of Postmodernism: History, Theory, Fiction* (Routledge). Here the announced topic is nothing smaller than the literary philosophy of our age and the current fiction it shapes. Like most of her colleagues, Hutcheon believes that "postmodern teaches that all cultural practices have an ideological subtext which determines the conditions of the very possibility of their production of meaning"; therefore to the extent that fiction makes reference to the world, such history is problematized—yielding not a product but a relativized production, and not a history but a historiography. As a theory, her approach has obvious merit; but in practice it forces her to seize upon a very narrow style of work, which she calls "historiographic metafiction," and disclaim the true innovations as involuted late modernism. E. L. Doctorow's *Ragtime* does serve as a vivid example of Hutcheon's thesis, but she regards it as the only valid style for our age (while dismissing out of hand the major achievements of Ronald Sukenick, Raymond Federman,

Steve Katz, and others whom the profession regards as key innovators). At its worst, *A Poetics of Postmodernism* shows a scholar succumbing to that most fatal of critical attractions: being swept away by the sudden and unexpected popularity of a genuinely serious novel, until its presence becomes an idée fixe that drives out intelligent consideration of any other style of work, no matter how much it might complement and deepen the original thesis. One positive contribution, however, is Hutcheon's continual reminder that to question is not to deny, that to problematize is not to annihilate, that to interrogate history is not to discard it.

A much larger and more responsible view is found in Matei Calinescu's *Five Faces of Modernity: Modernism, Avant-Garde, Decadence, Kitsch, Postmodernism* (Duke, 1987), where the key figures are identified as Sukenick and Federman and the crucial issue is considered to be not just history but all reference in general. The central question here is "decidability"—if things are undecidable, then one accepts the label of postmodernism for fiction, while if one believes this issue was dealt with sufficiently by the great modernist experiments, then one does not. Calinescu's Eurocentric prejudice shows itself in claiming this issue was best treated by Beckett, Nabokov, and Borges, none of whom considered themselves postmodernists but whose coattails were grabbed by lesser American writers in order to dignify their own work. Just as Hutcheon restricts her essential source work to just one piece of criticism—Larry McCaffery's 1974 dissertation minimally revised as *The Metafictional Muse* (1982)—as a way of reducing all nonhistoriographic fiction to self-reflection, so does Calinescu rely overbearingly on Brian McHale's reductive contrast of epistemology (modernism) with ontology (postmodernism), the "how do we know" being replaced with "what is to be known." Because these two philosophical terms share a family relationship, Calinescu feels comfortable to conclude that postmodernism is simply one more face of modernity. But he is able to construct his thesis without disqualifying the greater body of postmodern fiction as illegitimate, as does Hutcheon.

General editor Emory Elliott's *Columbia Literary History of the United States* (Columbia), to be successful, would have to be a dispassionate authority on these subjects. Unfortunately, there is a great unevenness to the section's several essays treating current fiction, largely attributable to the personal agendas some contributors wish to advance. In "Culture, Power, and Society" (pp. 1023–44) Charles

Molesworth willfully misreads Donald Barthelme and John Barth as "metafictionists" (a very specific term that in fact applies to only a small portion of a few others' works), decrying them as "playful stylists" and regarding style itself as "fashion or mere stylishness." Molesworth's own choice is for a literature that focuses the imagination on modes of political and social power, and no matter that the literature of our day has chosen a radically different approach to ends that Molesworth cannot perceive (Ishmael Reed's comment is quite apposite: "You go after the cop on the beat, I'll go after the Pope, and we'll see who causes a true revolution"). For "The New Philosophy" (pp. 1045–59) Gerald L. Bruns claims everything we have had these past years is simply an echo of Nietzsche (akin to those modernist critics who say the writers of our day have done nothing beyond rehearsing *Finnegans Wake*). Bruns protects his thesis by scarcely mentioning Barthes, Derrida, or Foucault, and handles Deconstruction in a quick paragraph on Jonathan Culler. Catharine R. Stimpson tries to discuss "Literature as Radical Statement" (pp. 1060–76) by running through a hodgepodge of themes while asking the most fleeting questions (and never answering them) about why protest literature seems (but is not) restricted to the 1960s and how such statements can be made when the era's fiction claims to be nonrepresentational. Balancing these unhelpful chapters are Malcolm Bradbury's "Neorealist Fiction" (pp. 1126–41) and Raymond Federman's "Self-Reflexive Fiction" (pp. 1142–57). The two pieces are complementary in a way that escapes those of the other contributors, for Bradbury treats realism with a sharp awareness of Federman's antirealistic subject, and vice versa. The former knows that language is the empire of signs, and that realistic fiction of this period "found itself amidst the failing empire . . . bearing its burden of slippage, its lexical crisis, its sense of the displaced relation between the sign and what it sought to signify." Hence neorealism is problematic and draws its energy from that struggle. Federman cites the long history of self-consciousness in debate with realism, but counters that self-reflexiveness is something quite different, establishing a special relation between author and text that involves the reader in the interplay between them. Far better than do Molesworth and Stimpson, Federman relates this style of fiction to the day's social and political issues, concentrating not on theme but on the formal properties shared by aesthetic and historical developments. These two essays, however, cannot carry the book, and there is a disappointment to Larry McCaffery's "The Fictions of the Present" (pp. 1161–77) that skits facilely from trend to trend, reading like a chat column from the *New York Times Book Review* (which seems to be the sole resource for the author's judgments), and even more to Henry M. Sayre's "The Avant-Garde and Experimental Writing" (pp. 1178–99) which confuses avant-gardism with modernism and hence has trouble accounting for innovations that set themselves against the modernist mode. The answer eluding Sayre is, of course, postmodernism, a consideration the vast majority of Elliott's contributors would prefer to ignore.

When critics not only admit their specific interests but fashion them into genuine visions, the results can be gratifying (and especially useful as they supplement and in part correct the bland reductionism of the *Columbia Literary History*). But how different this year's two such leading critics are. In *After the Avant-Garde: Essays on Art and Culture* (Penn. State) Robert Boyers measures good versus bad in innovative fiction by examining the "obsessions" and "resistances" within such works. But here Boyers follows the anti-postmodernist approach of considering all innovations as metafiction, in this case by disregarding those who would replace referential realism with a new veracity of the written page in favor of William H. Gass, whose work advocates "formal complexity or nuances of verbal texture" rather than exercising an "ability to satisfy easy moral imperatives." Boyers' ultimate authority is Tolstoy, but citations of this master provide not a theory but just an emotional disposition to write a certain way; because Boyers considers Tolstoy's dictums as unquestionable, readers will find no investigations of postmodern problematics here. Opposed to Boyers is Ihab Hassan, whose two related essays on quest set out from these very problematics that conservative critics would pretend do not exist. "Spirit of Quest: The Place of Adventure in Contemporary American Letters" (*MQR* 27:17–37) and "Quest for the Subject: The Self in Literature" (*ConL* 29:420–37) are developed from Hassan's initial chapter on the subject discussed in *ALS 1987* (p. 287). In a quest, a person invites risk, reminding us that any such projection of a self is a fiction more durable than those of any literary theory and more likely to yield lasting insights about human conduct and aspirations. The first essay asks "what kind of symbolic option does this genre provide at the present time," and answers that just as the historic experience of America, in its need for finding otherness in the wilderness, "proved singularly congenial to the spirit of quest," so do contemporary circumstances provide a "wound from which history, planetized history, flows," and thus novelists from Norman Mailer to James Dickey compel themselves to discover the "radical lack" underlying "all life as perceived by *human beings*," the something that is always buried and lost to us. Doing so is an "extreme enactment of our fate in the universe," plucking the "nerve of existence" in a way that generates the artistic act. Hassan's second essay particularizes this "textualization of the autobiographical self" as an encounter with an imagined life, a subjectivity other than the author's own. Within this *other* is an uncertainty only our power can resolve; such resolution allows the fiction writer to feel at one with the world rather than contaminated by it (which is in fact a circumstance in which he or she contaminates the world instead). The great opportunity postmodern times offer is that of making the self's creative identity apparent—no longer just a provisional definition, but the creation of a text whose virtual conative powers are evident in its very mode of being, as the postmodern fiction Boyers would discount as merely narcissitic metafiction, a trivialization that ignores the most developed philosophies of our era. (My own *Rosenberg/Barthes/Hassan: The Postmodern Habit of Thought* [Georgia] presents a full study of how Hassan's vision draws on the aesthetics of postmodern fiction.)

Three more particularized studies, ranging from conservative to moderate and radical, consider how self-consciousness of form operates. In *The Self-Conscious Novel: Artifice in Fiction from Joyce to Pynchon* (Penn.) Brian Stonehill follows Alan Wilde's awkward and ultimately unsatisfactory compromise in claiming that "the best self-conscious fiction may 'render the highest kind of justice to the visible universe' *and* at the same time 'not only mean but be.'" The result, as with Wilde's *Middle Grounds* (*ALS 1987*, pp. 284–85), is only to remove the opposition by so weakening both sides that neither retains any integrity as art. Stonehill prefers reading stories that he can care about in terms of their subject matter while still appreciating their fictive form; therefore his treatment of American postmodernists is preceded by (and to a large extent based on) his interpretations of Joyce and Nabokov. Thus what he admires in the work of William Gaddis is the use of "self-conscious devices in order to repudiate the esthetic premises of self-consciousness itself," just as Pynchon's *Gravity's Rainbow* offers the reader "two antithetical perspectives on everything that happens in its pages . . . either as related *caus*ally, or as related *casu*ally." This approach, generated by Stonehill's desire to hedge each bet, climaxes with his reading of Barth's *LETTERS* as a dramatization of "the conceptual principles of its own composition"—which is, of course, the standard interpretation of this novel from the beginning, and should serve as the starting point for an analysis of how self-consciousness works in fiction rather than as the ultimate summation. "If Modernism represented a concern for the medium, often foregrounded as translucent or opaque before the subject itself," Stonehill concludes, "then perhaps Postmodernism suggests a mediation that has been prepared for and enacted by self-consciousness."

Stephen-Paul Martin would disagree, insisting that postmodernism makes a radical departure from modernist practice, and his *Open Form and the Feminine Imagination: The Politics of Reading in Twentieth-Century Innovative Writing* (Maisonneuve Press) insists that in this new style of work we are encouraged "to learn from ourselves in the act of reading, and not to pretend that we are learning from our identification with unreal characters." Words in fiction only appear to describe the world, but in fact combine to form a separate system of meaning "that alters what we perceive and leads us to think about it in a preconceived way." Fictions which remind us that they have no inherent authority thus transform a previously male-based style of narrative art into something approximating the feminine imagination, with key practitioners being Clarence Major, Ronald Sukenick, and Teresa Cha. Fictions by Harry Mathews and Raymond Federman are central to Welch Everman's complementary thesis in *Who Says This? The Authority of the Author, the Discourse, and the Reader* (So. Ill.). As opposed to the "docufiction" appeal to history's authority in the parajournalistic works of Norman Mailer, Jay Cantor, and Jack Kerouac, Federman seizes such paradox directly as a theme as well as technique, forcing himself to write about the unwritable features of his autobiography in a way which by necessity yields fiction. When Mathews devises a form that produces its own content, the transition is complete.

One inescapable truth about the postmodern is that its fiction writers have proven themselves as able and frequent critics. Many have PhDs, and nearly all have extensive university teaching experience coupled with the regular occupation of drafting reviews, essays, and even critical books. These talents are exploited by two especially valuable projects, editor Heide Ziegler's *Facing Texts: Encounters Between Contemporary Writers and Critics* (Duke) and the special number, *Novelist as Critic*, of *The Review of Contemporary Fiction* 8, iii. Ziegler's text pairs critical essays, autobiographical statements, or critically pointed fictions by Stanley Elkin, Donald Barthelme, Robert Coover, Guy Davenport, Susan Sontag, Walter Abish, William H. Gass, John Hawkes, Joseph McElroy, and John Barth with critical commentaries by mostly European critics. Only the responses to Barthelme and McElroy are noticeably weak or off-base; Marc Chénetier's piece on Coover explores brilliantly the consequences of both mythmaking and demystification, while Christopher Butler becomes one of the extremely few critics equal to Walter Abish's work, explaining how its fragmented surface is only apparently disruptive and in fact both identifies and encourages moral responses in the reader (based on his or her reading prejudices which Abish's techniques uncover). The volume's most important essays form its two-part conclusion, John Barth's defense of the imagination as virtually unlimitable and Manfred Pütz's astute observation that while the human imagination on its own terms may be without limits, history certainly imposes some very real ones that Barth's fiction should not be allowed to sidestep. The fictionist's tactic is "to put to shame that which *is* by producing countless alternatives of that which is not"; as a larger strategy, however, it faces two ambiguities, for both its components (words) and its end product (make-believe) are arbitrary, whereas history is real, making the limitations of the imagination more substantial than Barth would initially suggest. Pütz's commentary identifies one of the key issues in dealing with postmodern fiction and ably rounds out this volume's larger implied thesis: how moral concerns and the issue of history recur even in a fiction from which one would think they would have been banished.

The *Novelist as Critic* issue of *RCF* 8, iii, contains a wide range of interesting essays, including an icy-eyed glance at the new fiction industry being worked by young graduates who barely distinguish an MFA from an MBA (David Foster Wallace's "Fictional Futures and the Conspicuously Young," pp. 36–53) and Keith Abbott's appreciative analysis of a former colleague's command of metaphor ("Shadows and Marble: Richard Brautigan," pp. 117–25). But the volume's truly important essays are facing pieces by John Barth ("Postmodernism Revisited," pp. 16–24) and Gilbert Sorrentino ("Writing and Writers: *Disjecta Membra*," pp. 25–35). In Ziegler's collection Manfred Pütz had objected rightly to Barth's antihistorical slipperiness; for his own position, Barth was limited to the forum of a reprinted essay, but his original contribution to editor John O'Brien's magazine shows him in a hardly more favorable light, dodging the issues of contrasting periods of aesthetics by insisting that not all historically important fiction writers are good (and that not all good writers are historically important). Sorrentino much more frankly reminds us that the style of postmodern writing dismissed as exotic, weird, or skewed in fact is sequestered "because otherwise we would be faced with the intolerable proposition that the reality such writing offers is, indeed, our own, but that we cannot, though we live in the middle of it, recognize it." Far from ignoring history, such writing "shakes our precarious sense of ourselves, so it is much safer to pretend that it is but the excrescence of a strange mind sifting through its own invented detritus." Narrowing his topic to a specific technique, Sorrentino proceeds to show how one approach, using the form of the list, allows the writer to avoid the combinative processes of language and subvert any prejudicial tendency to select in advance of truly artistic demands.

On a more mundane but necessarily practical note, James L. W. West III rounds out this year's shelf of general studies with *American Authors and the Literary Marketplace Since 1900* (Johns Hopkins). Ever since Richard Kostelanetz published *The End of Intelligent Writing* in 1974, scholars of the contemporary have been warned that marketplace factors must be considered for their determining force over any work of literary art. West's analysis is especially acute for its sense of metaphor—that the publishing industry has changed just like the National Basketball Association, from a loose confederation of family-owned businesses (who cared for their properties, be they William Faulkner or Elgin Baylor) to a new style of enterprise more concerned with entertainment values than solid quality. Especially helpful is his understanding of the special relationship among editors, agents, and publishers which often leaves the author with the least important status in the industry.

ii. Isaac Bashevis Singer, Philip Roth, and other Jewish-Americans

A tendency to study only major figures has been balanced by a fresh interest in critical theory, the best of which shows forth in L. S. Dembo's *The Monological Jew* (Wisconsin). Notions drawn from Buber and Bakhtin supplement the thesis that "committed only to words and performance or manipulation, not to communication, the Monological Jew is an exile from all facets of his life—a self-absorbed loner compelled to endure *distance from,* never *relation to,* others. That is to say, he inhabits not only a literal diaspora but a psychological one as well." This view allows Dembo to read Bruce Jay Friedman's *Stern* not as an exploration of social and economic causes, but as a drama in which "the characters are what they speak . . . an index to the linguistic mastery of their creator." Edward Lewis Wallant's *The Tenants of Moonbloom* offers further experimentation with voice, here seen in contrast to the holocaust-death tone of *The Pawnbroker.* The Bakhtinian carnivalization of language reaches full development in the work of Leo Rosten and is celebrated in Neil Klugman's carnivalization of himself in Philip Roth's *Goodbye, Columbus,* a dialogical gesture that can be traced to the example of Isaac Bashevis Singer.

Singer himself is given paralinguistic treatment by Marilyn R. Chandler in "Death by the Word: Victims of Language in *Enemies, A Love Story*" (*SAJL* 7, i:105–17), in which the postmodern distortions of language serve as a reminder of how "the letter kills" when it is divorced from life. A similarly fresh reading of Roth's reaction to the Jewish tradition is found in James E. Young's *Writing and Rewriting the Holocaust* (Indiana), a brightly conceived study of not just the Holocaust details in literature but how narrative understanding shapes them. The traditional role of the Holocaust in Jewish-American self-knowledge is mocked in Roth's fiction; rebelling against the "martyrological ikon of Anne Frank" as the only available memory, his protagonists seek to reauthenticate their selves in some other way than dying for being Jewish—ultimately the present-day Czech underground provides an example, where one can suffer not as a Jew but as a writer. An admirable collection of original essays distinguishes editors Asher Z. Milbauer and Donald G. Watson's *Reading Philip Roth* (St. Martin's). The best is Watson's "Fiction, Show Business, and the Land of Opportunity: Roth in the Early Seventies" (pp. 105–25), which shows that the author of *The Breast, Our Gang,* and *The Great American Novel* is not a Barthesean *bricoleur* or a Barthian satirist of myth but rather one who glories in the comic inventiveness of farce, aspiring to a carnivalization encouraged by Bakhtin (leading to an emphasis of the "direct material aspect" of images opposed to a classical ideal). Rounding out the year's work on Roth is the author's own *The Facts: A Novelist's Autobiography* (Farrar), something more than a memoir because it includes the very Bakhtinian device of incorporating letters to and from his characters. Roth's confession of his own desire to step beyond the unruffled style of Henry James and flirt with mimicry and comic destruction completes the picture, which some of this year's critics will insist makes the analogy with Bakhtin complete.

The single truly contemporary essay in editor Lewis Fried's *Handbook of American-Jewish Literature* (Greenwood), "Images of America in American-Jewish Fiction" (pp. 315–56), finds Sanford E. Marovitz drawing welcome attention to the Runyonesque speech and urban interaction of Grace Paley's characters. A serious flaw results, however, when E. L. Doctorow is identified as the period's key experimenter, simply because of his topical diversity. A sharper eye would note that Paley's variations of voice and structure are far more innovative, as is the work of a whole group of writers Marovitz seems not to realize are Jewish-Americans: Steve Katz, Ronald Sukenick, and especially Raymond Federman (who is identified elsewhere in Fried's volume as a major source of study among German Americanists).

iii. Walker Percy, William Styron, and other Southerners

As usual, Walker Percy draws the greatest share of attention, some of it first-rate but too often tending toward fulsome praise. Linda Whitney Hobson is taken with the man's reputation but does not know where to place it other than among leather-bound classics; her *Understanding Walker Percy* (So. Car.), as a volume in Matthew J. Bruccoli's series meant to train critics of the future, provides a poor introduction to literary judgment, given as it is to such deep praise for the most superficial of reasons (usually thematic pretention and gestures toward moral issues). Her book itself is awkwardly written, another sign that Percy's unexamined reputation is itself expected to carry the day. For Hobson it all comes down to Percy's brooding fear of disaster, his "existential Catholicism" placing man in a concrete situation while at the same time demanding a transcendence of "everydayness." In a Kierkegaardian sense, faith engenders a will that makes quest possible, but from here Hobson simply turns to a rehearsal of the most familiar of Percy's themes: the temptation of easy, false escapes, the irony provided by distance, and the special nature of the religious sphere. A more cogently pointed approach to similar issues is found in Ann Jerome Croce's "The Making of Post-Modern Man: Modernism and the Southern Tradition in the Fiction of Walker Percy" (*Crit* 29:213–21), where only the experience of modernism is seen to allow a return to old southern values (thanks to modernism's commitment to probing for the truth). Also of interest is "Walker Percy and Gabriel Marcel: The Dialectical Self in *The Moviegoer*" (*Renascence* 40:279–87), Preston Browning's able proof that a certain coaxing must accompany man's search for being as the motive force in Percy's first novel; the philosopher's conviction that there can be no selfhood apart from interpersonal communion thus encourages a more dialectical sense of self, one to which Percy subscribes. On a more specialized level, Lewis A. Lawson considers the special facets of medical and psychoanalytic knowledge in "Will Barrett Under the Telescope" (*SLJ* 20, ii:16–41), while Stephen R. Yarbrough draws on the literary theories of Stanley Fish and James M. Cox to show the extent to which "the story being read and the story of the reader's reading are in some sense the same story," as one's reading reenacts the story, the example here being that of mankind's fall as analyzed in "Walker Percy's *Lancelot* and the Critic's Original Sin" (*TSLL* 30:272–94).

Sophie's Choice is given an insightful reading by Ralph Tutt in "Stingo's Complaint: Styron and the Politics of Self-Parody" (*MFS* 34: 575–86). Self-conscious about writing a serious work of conventional realism in postmodern times, the author is seen to protect himself from ridicule by constructing an elaborate parodic structure as a virtual inside joke on the more experimental efforts of Norman Mailer and Philip Roth. But rather than stay with Styron, a greater number of this year's critics have focused attention on less commonly studied writers. George Garrett's *Understanding Mary Lee Settle* (So. Car.) is a professionally based study, heavily biographical, of her career and concentrating more on Settle's struggles and triumphs with publishers and reputation than with the materials of her fiction. There is a central evenness to Settle's work that Garrett finds consistent with her personal observation that "I long for the simple semiboredom which seems to drive other women to extremes of anger and denial." Garrett himself is the subject of R. H. W. Dillard's *George Garrett* (So. Car.), but here the unfortunate coziness of Matthew J. Bruccoli's series becomes uncritical as well, Dillard delivering an unabashed puff of a writer who would merit praise for little other than being "ruggedly independent of contemporary fads." Dillard dotes on his subject's interview repartee and is satisfied that his work is a noble response to a "Christian fallen world." More interesting is Garrett's understanding that "discovery and understanding are so difficult to come by in a world in which truth and illusion are so inextricably intertwined." Like the weakest of southern criticism, these statements are expected to hold up by themselves, a de facto proof of the writer's importance. When applied to Walker Percy, they seem unchallengeable; but Garrett is no Walker Percy, and just as Percy's work would benefit from more specific and less culturally fulsome analysis, so too might the fiction of this lesser writer tell another story entirely when subjected to more rigorous study. Closer analysis does take place in "Researching Her Salvation: The Fiction of Gail Godwin" (*HC* 25, ii:1–9), John Alexander Allen's treatment of "the dignity of uniqueness" in Godwin's characters (who achieve such status even when ambiguous "or just disappointingly dull"). Such an approach, sufficiently close to the text yet broad enough to situate the writer's achievement, would have improved Vereen M. Bell's *The Achievement of Cormac McCarthy* (LSU), a work that aspires to explore the author's "prevailing gothic and nihilistic mood" in which "meaning does not prevail over narrative texture" but gets bogged down in tediously close readings (to no apparent point) and demurs from taking any theoretical overview. How much attention structure can achieve is shown by Joyce M. Pair in "Growing Up Female: The Creative Pattern of Sylvia Wilkinson" (*SLJ* 19, ii:47–53), in which the travails of adolescence provide a "spectrum of possibilities for female gender identification" and, in Wilkinson's hands, trace the female hero's search for a literary self.

Two general studies remind one of both the brilliance and delusion possible in southern literary studies. In "Politics and Literature: The Southern Case" (*VQR* 64:189–201) Richard H. King questions how it is possible to have a history without politics, as much southern literature has. An early essay by Walker Percy suggests that the rule of "Snopses" made any truly public zone of affairs impossible for decent people, something King ascribes to the larger tradition of "family romance" in which "political action and speech would naturally be seen as expressions of inauthenticity, not freedom." Younger writers, however, such as Jayne Anne Phillips, Bobbie Ann Mason, and Ellen Gilchrist have written about the civil rights movement, and their interests, along with those of black writers, may signal an eventual embrace of the political novel. A far different picture is painted by Paul Binding in *Separate Country: A Literary Journey*

Through the American South (Miss.). A British book from 1979 now in a second edition, Binding's survey covers six months of travel through the American South in 1978, now updated with notes on the authors' subsequent publications. Here one encounters all of the stereotypes created by southern literary critics, to the point that they become the only features this British visitor can discern. Ever on the lookout for confirmation of what his studies have taught him, Binding rhapsodizes on the most inconsequential of manners, as long as they are sufficiently regional—such as David Madden cooking crayfish in his Louisiana backyard. It therefore seems no accident that when Binding determines to visit all of the region's creditable writers, every one of them turns out to be white.

iv. The Mannerists: John Updike and John Cheever

A major study of each author makes 1988 a worthwhile year for Updike and Cheever scholarship. Judie Newman's heavily thematic *John Updike* (St. Martin's) follows his career's development from its earlier attention to the functioning of social groups and the world of work, through the midpoint novels devoted to aesthetics and religion, to the nature of "imagination interrogating its own status" in the more anomalous novels *The Coup* and *The Witches of Eastwick*. Newman is especially adept at bringing other texts to bear upon Updike's, be they Whyte, Fromm, and Marcuse for the earlier novels or Kierkegaard for the middle works. Less satisfactory is her study of the most recent work, which consists largely of plot summary, although her interpretation of *Roger's Version* and S. as castings of *The Scarlet Letter* (from the husband's and adulteress's points of view) bears further investigation.

The major work on Cheever is Scott Donaldson's ample and fascinating *John Cheever: A Biography* (Random House). There are interesting early parallels with the life of F. Scott Fitzgerald, and a further thread of personal autobiography in Cheever's drawing of talent from his mother's side of the family while mythologizing his paternal ancestors. From the author's first story onward, Donaldson feels comfortable relating published plots to personal experience—something the materialism of a fiction of manners not only allows but encourages. Most valuable is the specific research Donaldson undertakes on Cheever's professional life, from his residencies at Yaddo to his travels abroad and self-styled squire's life at home. Most admirable is his ability to deal straightforwardly with the author's alcoholic degeneration and late recovery—facing the facts squarely and showing how they influenced his work, all without romanticizing the abyss of sickness and glory of recovery (as other critics have tried to do for the similar life of Cheever's friend Raymond Carver, as a way of adding moral stature to his fiction).

The shorter works this year are devoted to Updike, and bear lesser interest. Margaret M. Gullette's *Safe at Last in the Middle Years: The Invention of the Midlife Progress Novel* (Calif.) does little more than restate the author's most obvious themes. A more structural use of theme distinguishes Kerry Ahearn's "Family and Adultery: Images and Ideas in Updike's Rabbit Novels" (*TCL* 34, i:62–83); marriage and community, two strong themes in Updike's work, meet in the situation of adultery, a "tense balance" which encourages the author to gather masses of imagery appropriate to each pole in an attempt to subvert conventional moral associations. "Updike's Witches," Donald J. Greiner's contribution to editor Dorothy M. Joiner's *Selected Essays*, pp. 20–25, argues that *The Witches of Eastwick* is less an attack on feminism than it is a conventional exercise in crafting a black humor novel (along the lines developed by Barth, Hawkes, Heller, and Pynchon), a variation on the author's conventional mode of social observation and religious concern—the emphasis now being on "comic distortion as an indication that anything is possible." A freshly current view distinguishes T. M. McNally and Dean Stover's "An Interview with John Updike" (*Hayden's Ferry Review* No. 3:102–16), thanks to Updike's candid comments on minimalist fiction, which include his suggestion that broken homes and unstable geographies have made it much harder for young writers to generate traditional warmth, empathy, and caring. Updike does however admire Raymond Carver's "polished texture" and Frederick Barthelme's "glazed hardness" as an alternative to exhausted experiments of the 1960s.

v. Realists Old and New: Truman Capote, E. L. Doctorow, John Gardner, and Others

A Flaubertian sense of "Holly Golightly, c'est moi" pervades Gerald Clarke's *Capote: A Biography* (Simon & Schuster). The implied thesis is that from an initial attractiveness, due most likely to the models he chose for his own writing and conduct, Capote degenerated into a fascination with what most people would wish to avoid. Being a captive of his own reflection eventually took its toll in his prose as well; other narrative voices than his own self-absorption would have helped, Clarke believes.

E. L. Doctorow figures prominently in Linda Hutcheon's *A Poetics of Postmodernism*, considered in section *i.* above, and also fills the pages of editors Herwig Friedl and Dieter Schultz's *E. L. Doctorow: A Democracy of Perception* (Die Blaue Eule). Chief among these papers presented at the University of Heidelberg is Sam B. Girgus's "In His Own Voice: E. L. Doctorow's *The Book of Daniel*" (pp. 75–90), in which the novel's many levels of meaning are shown to force new technical explorations of narrative voice.

A broad range of realists, whose many variations of mimesis create an interesting field for exploration, have prompted an uncommonly large number of excellent studies this year. James Dickey's first novel is ever surprising in its inability to be critically exhausted. In "Dickey, Dante, and the Demonic: Reassessing *Deliverance*" (*AL* 60:611–24) Peggy Goodman Endel shows how in its wealth of tunnels and funnels the novel becomes a birth canal, but also allows for a rectum though which the darkest visions may be expelled. Bert Bender's *Sea Brothers* places Peter Matthiessen in the tradition of Melville and Crane, with *Far Tortuga* drawing on the bare essence of reality through the sun's constant presence and man's pursuit of "the ungraspable phantom of life." William Dowie provides a solid and comprehensive analysis in "A Final Glory: The Novels of James Salter" (*CE* 50:74–88), arguing that his canon places him in the tradition of Emerson. A helpful corrective to the insulting misreading of an exceptionally sensitive writer is found in " 'Macho Mistake': The Misrepresentation of Jim Harrison's Fiction" (*Crit* 29:233–44) by William H. Roberson. A prolific but not yet widely studied novelist gets comprehensive treatment from Donald J. Greiner in *Domestic Particulars: The Novels of Frederick Busch* (So. Car.). Busch favors the traditional staples of formal realism, giving his "domestic morality" a quality lacking in the more minimal fictions of Carver and Beattie (who celebrate "diminishing control"); his special talent is to open up small lives with prose sounding like Dylan Thomas's poetry. Samuel Coale is similarly responsive to another realist in *Paul Theroux* (TUSAS 520), where the clash of cultures observed in travel invites self-renewal and rebirth in a consciousness feasting on close detail and eager to contrast cultural ideas with specifics of reality. Coale explores Theroux's advice that "there is a way in which all the books are in a chain," one that the critic finds to be deepening and widening in a trail of multidimensionality. One drawback is an overdose of uncritical praise which adds little to Coale's argument. Garrison Keillor shows signs of becoming a subject for serious study in Peter A. Scholl's excellent survey of his work (pp. 326–38) in *DLB: Yearbook 1987* (Gale), where he is seen celebrating oddities rather than satirizing them and evoking the true evanescence of home as "the ideal American place to come from," an attitude refined from an ironic awareness preventing any easy surrender to nostalgia. Minimalism is given less comprehensive treatment than in recent years, but noteworthy are Norman German and Jack Bedell's "Physical and Social Laws in Ray Carver's 'Popular Mechanics' " (*Crit* 29:257–60), which posits a technical equivalent to the snap-on, snap-off relationships in Carver's fiction, and author Frederick Barthelme's self-analysis in "On Being Wrong: Convicted Minimalist Spills Beans" (*NYTBR* 3 April: 1, 25–27), where the style's moral poverty is refuted by an appeal to more serious grapplings with major problems in realism (such as an overbearing emphasis on ideas and the conventionality of characterization).

Minimalism in fiction has sparked serious debate and responsible study. Moral fiction hasn't, and the two studies that address it this year are seriously flawed. In *The Novels of John Gardner* (LSU) Leonard Butts notes that the author's characters are themselves artistic creators, dedicating their lives to a search for meaning and their art to a quest for vision. Gardner's fiction evolves toward an intense selection and ordering by imagination, testing the strength of central values and the experiences framing them. His protagonists are challenged to overcome the fallacy of pastoral retreat and are urged to reenter the action and celebrate existence. All this becomes "moral fiction" when the reader absorbs the writer's power. Butts's problem is that he accepts all of this at Gardner's word, never pausing to test it against contemporary theory or competing fictions; the most annoying feature of moral fiction is its authors' smug claim that their own importance is virtually guaranteed by nothing other than their professed commitment, and a failure to examine this work as closely as we customarily do other styles of work severely weakens credibility in regard to long-term impact and success. Especially harmful is Thomas E. Kennedy's approach in *Andre Dubus: A Study of the Short Fiction* (Twayne). Rather than analyze the author's strengths, Kennedy prefers to make blanket condemnations, none of them supported, of William H. Gass's work and the general tenor of postmodern innovative fiction (nearly all of which is beyond Dubus's interest). Dubus's work itself is misread as a reactionary rejection of form as once advanced by Poe and Sterne; but there is no attention to what technical achievements the author makes instead—just a thematic reading of love as a spiritual state versus spiritual hunger, women's challenge to define themselves versus others' definitions of them, and a general movement toward wholeness in the successive works of fiction. Dubus himself is a much better writer than this, and as a graduate of the University of Iowa Writers Workshop when its faculty included Kurt Vonnegut, Robert Coover, José Donoso, and Robert Scholes is especially interested in style and form. But since these writers are the enemy to Kennedy, his subject must survive without them, no matter how central are their ideas to his work.

How Vietnam war fiction transcends realism is established in Thomas Myers's *Walking Point*, discussed in *i.* above. More specific studies are available in editor William J. Searle's *Search and Clear: Critical Responses to Selected Literature and Films of the Vietnam War* (Bowling Green); "Words and Fragments: Narrative Style in Vietnam War Novels" (pp. 58–61) by Nancy Anisfield outlines three forms of fragmentation—time jumps, fantasy mixed with reality, and intensely isolated incidents within the psychic dislocation of an unstructured war—which set the stage for a nervous energy most specifically suggested in the rhythms of language that carry these books. Dean McWilliams's closer study, "Time in O'Brien's *Going After Cacciato*" (*Crit* 29:245–56), identifies three narrative lines and relates their sequences of time as a way of explaining the chaos of memory and the pursuit of fantasy.

vi. Experimental Realists: Grace Paley, Max Apple, and Thomas McGuane

Grace Paley's special status, lying just between postmodern experiment and traditional realism, is faced squarely and revealingly by Minako Baba in "Faith Darwin as Writer-Heroine: A Study of Grace Paley's Short Stories" (*SAJL* 7, i:40–54). Tracing this central character through three volumes (and three decades) of Paley's work, Baba finds that a general movement from self toward family and then community has now resolved itself in a candid treatment of artistic self-apparency. A similar multidimensionality of interest is found by Jon Wallace in "The Language Plot in Thomas McGuane's *Ninety-Two in the Shade*" (*Crit* 29:111–20). The novel foregrounds language throughout as a means of dramatizing how difficult it is to express a personal identity within the common codes of communication. But rather than stating this theme abstractly, McGuane interweaves it with a more conventional struggle between protagonist and antagonist, with the result that the narrative language shifts and transforms itself so often as to become virtually a subject itself.

Paley and McGuane are realists whose experiment tends toward language and other self-consciously technical devices. Max Apple shows how myth and ritual can serve as equally experimental devices—not just as John Gardner's moral grounding of authority, but as something quite the opposite, a reminder that all myths are imaginative fabrications that work best when both author and reader share an awareness of the artifice at hand. In Allan Vorda's "An Interview with Max Apple" (*MQR* 27, i:69–78) the author admits a special fondness for the fiction of Paley and Doctorow, but places most trust in the fantastic impulses that seize upon the more familiar objects of life (such as gasoline stations, subject of a crucial Apple story) and show how truly remarkable they are—a tendency that allies his fictionist's eye with the best essay techniques. His larger works tend to be mock epics, combining historical personages, not as Doctorow does for a resonance of language and imagery, but for the mythic import of these figures on our lives (where they have indeed met and worked together in forming a national popular consciousness).

vii. Early Innovators: Joseph Heller, Kurt Vonnegut, and Jerzy Kosinski

Good insights into Joseph Heller's *Catch-22* are still to be found, this year chiefly in David Marr's *American Worlds Since Emerson* (Mass.). "Emersonian privatism, moralism, and anti-politicism are major elements in American social character," Marr believes, and he incorporates postmodernism into this scheme by reading it not in the style of fiction writers and literary theorists but as the architects do, as a conservative adjustment to the past as an historical site locating "the best civilization has to offer." How other postmodern writers fill this definition would be puzzling, but Heller's work fits right in with its investigation of "the problematic other" (which is unknowable yet thoroughly believeable). *Catch-22* expresses this paradox by making

Yossarian's perceiving mind act very much like the war machine's mentality, leaving the final question to be very Emersonian indeed: how can the excluded other be recognized as Human, which makes the problem of other minds the problem of my own.

Work on Kurt Vonnegut proves strong and steady. Lawrence R. Broer's *Sanity Plea: Schizophrenia in the Novels of Kurt Vonnegut* (UMI) takes a broader approach than its subtitle suggests. Not a reductive psychoanalytic critic like Josephine Hendin, Broer discovers how the creative tensions in Vonnegut's novels force the reader into a debate as to what sanity is, enfranchising artists as agents of change with regard to these terms and others. Psychic and social trauma are perfectly fused, as are the themes and techniques the fiction employs. Broer's finest work is with the later novels, many of which have complicated earlier theses on Vonnegut's development. Here we see *Deadeye Dick* meld Vonnegut's artist-priest identity with that of Rudy Waltz, as the story of regeneration through artistic creation dispels false illusions even as it yields valid hopes; *Galápagos* furthers this style of "autobiographical psychodrama" by revealing how human beings, and not nature, write the fictions of existence; finally, with *Bluebeard* readers can see an artist emerge from false instruction (the artist as moralistic illustrator of grandly external pageants) to find the important realities inside himself—which is itself the richest reading of Vonnegut's masterpiece and key point of development, *Slaughterhouse-Five*. Agreeing with Broer that Vonnegut's vision is positive is William H. E. Meyer, Jr., whose "Kurt Vonnegut: The Man with Nothing to Say" (*Crit* 29:95–109) allies the author with the major figures in the American literary canon, to the point that Vonnegut, like Thoreau, can succeed as a "word-smith" in a "hypervisual realm" where matching saying with seeing often seems an impossible and thankless task. My own essay with Edward Jamosky, "Kurt Vonnegut's Three *Mother Nights*" (*MFS* 34:216–20), shows Vonnegut complicating and enriching the essentially textual nature of his third novel by enfolding it in successive introductory envelopes, each of which changes the author's relation to his work and his protagonist's role in the action. Editor William Rodney Allen's *Conversations with Kurt Vonnegut* (Miss.) collects most important such pieces dating back to 1969 and provides a helpful index; especially interesting is the original interview conducted by Allen and Paul Smith that concludes the book, where Vonnegut talks about his experiences with colleagues at the University of Iowa Writers Workshop, sources for *Bluebeard,* and how sincere individual voices get a hearing in America.

The biggest year yet for Jerzy Kosinski studies has yielded two major books and several important essays. No such work can now be undertaken without facing the plagiarism scandal that rocked the field and knocked Kosinski's own career off course in 1982. The author himself came out of it this year with a novel, *The Hermit of 69th Street* (Holt), the plot of which tells just such a story, and nearly all of the critical work this year addresses the same issue—to the point that Kosinski himself may come out the hero for his troubles. In *Words in Search of Victims: The Achievement of Jerzy Kosinski* (Kent State), Paul R. Lilly, Jr., bases his interpretation on two autobiographical considerations: that all Kosinski's work is about the art of writing fiction (not metafictionally but from the narrow rhetorical stance of his own perception as imposed on the narrative vision), and that this vision itself is expressed by rejecting his native tongue (Polish) in favor of the English he learned as an abstract and intellectually controlled exercise. Lilly's study is especially distinguished by his treatment of the plagiarism issue which focused immense attention on the author's allegedly illicit fabrication of not just his novels but of his life story (as reported to a generation of interviewers and literary reporters) as well (see *ALS 1983*, pp. 311–12). Also commendable is Lilly's critical candor with the author's later and much lesser works; rather than rationalize or defend them, Lilly shows how their own weakness causes Kosinski to lose the formerly tight control over his words (and over his readers), and that now—with plot becoming a much stronger force than before—the readers of Kosinski's words can control *him.* As Lilly focuses on words and language, Barbara Tepa Lupack highlights Kosinski's game-playing strategies in *Plays of Passion, Games of Chance: Jerzy Kosinski and his Fiction* (Wyndham Hall). Lupack locates her interpretation within two complementary histories: that of the 20th-century novel, which has seen the steady effacement of both the active protagonist and the consequential plot, and of Kosinski's own struggle against social and political totalitarianism. She agrees with Lilly that Kosinski's later novels are of a texture different from his earlier work, but believes that this change is inevitable given the nature of his heroes, whose individualistic qualities abstract them from confining societies and eventually leave them without any worthy opponents (the fate of Fabian in *Passion Play* and Domestoy in *Pinball*), factors which necessarily decrease the quality of the game. Herbert B. Rothschild, Jr., reflects both Lilly's and Lupack's understanding in "Jerzy Kosinski's *Being There: Coriolanus* in Postmodern Dress" (*ConL* 29:49–63). "Like his art, Kosinski's life discovers a powerful tension between the private and the political," Rothschild argues, and establishes *Being There* as the author's most profoundly political novel and a key to his essentially political view of life. Thomas S. Gladsky takes much the same tack in "Jerzy Kosinski's East European Self" (*Crit* 29:121–32), suggesting that Slavic heroes, customs, and themes are found throughout his work and present the picture of the author's "own struggle to come to terms with his Polish past—a struggle which, as a common thread in all the novels, offers a way to understand Kosinski's artistic growth," a pattern comprising rejection, accommodation, and eventually reconciliation of old and new world selves." That Kosinski's public image remains an important part of his fictionist's pose and even of the work's texture is established by Stephen Schiff's "The Kosinski Conundrum" (*Vanity Fair* 51, vi:114–19, 166–70).

viii. John Barth, John Hawkes, and Thomas Pynchon

Although things are relatively quiet on the John Hawkes front of late, Barth and Pynchon continue to generate a large quantity of work. Broadest in its view is Elaine B. Safer's *The Contemporary American Comic Epic: The Novels of Barth, Pynchon, Gaddis, and Kesey* (Wayne State). These writers disappoint readerly expectations as a way of creating an absurdist vision, taking Cotton Mather's unified and meaningful universe, flavoring it with Whitman's edenic world, and systematically destroying all of the illusions such visions promise. Here Barth and Pynchon are the key figures, *The Sot Weed Factor* and *Giles Goat-Boy* being sharply antiedenic, while *V.* and *Gravity's Rainbow* darkly satirize any quest for meaning, yielding the absurdist ramifications of apocalypse in the contemporary world (of lesser interest are readings of *The Recognitions* as distress over materialism and of *Sometimes a Great Notion* as an "encyclopedic spectrum of expectations and hopes that fail"). One regret is that Safer's style is so heavily professorial, favoring references and allusions over the reading experience itself—something that critics like Tom LeClair and Larry McCaffery are able to capture so well.

Bradford Morrow's "John Hawkes: An Interview" (*Conjunctions* No. 12:89–105) captures the author of *Whistlejacket* explaining how his linguistic fascination with the word *corgi* stimulates the theme of obscenity, while the plot itself is drawn from a Peter Greenaway film, *The Draughtsman's Contract.* Of special note are Hawkes's revelation that he does not know very much about American life, and the lively dinner conversation with Robert and Pilar Coover included as a slice of realism.

Barth, as usual, finds his way into both wide-reaching and closely studied work, his fiction offering perhaps the purest example of modernist themes and techniques turned back upon themselves to suggest the dawn of postmodernism. In *Labyrinths of Language: Symbolic Landscape and Narrative Design in Modern Fiction* (Johns Hopkins) Wendy B. Faris appreciates *Lost in the Funhouse* for its artistic initiation, a narrative of forking paths between literary concerns and the more inviting temptations of sex; in the end, Barth's narrator is condemned to solitude, as intellectual activity overextends itself. Gabriella Bedetti adds that Barth can experiment with sexual roles in storytelling, reversing the customary structure of masculine telling and feminine listening. In "Women's Sense of the Ludicrous in John Barth's 'Dunyazadiad' " (*StAH* n.s. 4, i–ii:74–81) this transformation draws on the expensive paradox (rather than dualist irony) of woman's humor. Subservience to the father characterizes all of Barth's fiction until *LETTERS*, argues Douglas B. Johnstone in "John Barth and the Healing of the Self" (*Mosaic* 21, i:67–78); his latest novels, however, shift the view outside the fiction and, by refracting his theme among his characters, disarms its psychologically wounding force. Parenthood itself is finally resolved as an issue in *Sabbatical.* Loretta M. Lampkin's "An Interview with John Barth" (*ConL* 29: 485–97) concentrates on *Lost in the Funhouse*, but in the process uncovers Barth's allegiance to Faulkner (whose Yoknapatawpha inspired Barth to write about his own native Dorchester County, Maryland) and *Finnegans Wake* as an example "of narrative form becoming the grounding metaphor" for his more technically complex work.

A refreshingly novel view of Pynchon is provided by David Seed, whose *The Fictional Labyrinths of Thomas Pynchon* (Iowa) deals with the author's generative concerns and the reader's dealings with them. Seed's originality lies in his studies of Pynchon's reading and with his nonfiction writing, both of which focus on "the precarious nature of legality in a place where no creditable legal institutions exist." Early models include Jack Kerouac's free flow of narrative and colleague Richard Fariña's uncommitted life-style, the two of which keep Pynchon's own work from bogging down in intellectualism.

A double issue of *Pynchon Notes* (nos. 18–19) covers the full canon, with thematic attention from Hanjo Berressem in "V. in Love: From the 'Other Scene' to the 'New Scene'" (pp. 5–28) and the technique of *assemblage* being explained in terms of its sources by Michael W. Vella in "Pynchon, *V.*, and the French Surrealists" (pp. 29–38). Derrida's contribution to reading Pynchon's style of fiction is explored by Alec McHoul's "Telegrammatology Part 1: *Lot 49* and the Post-Ethical" (pp. 39–54), while the French distinctions between story (diegesis) and narrative (discourse) are employed by James Perrin Warren in "Ritual Reluctance: The Poetics of Discontinuity in *Gravity's Rainbow*" (pp. 55–65), where paraliptic absences imply the only chance for "a kinder universe." Rounded out by pieces on trickster narrators and "ecological ghost stories" plus a section of reviews, *PNotes* remains the most trustworthy repository for the finest Pynchon scholarship. Elsewhere, *Gravity's Rainbow* is the generalist reader's touchpoint for familiarity with Pynchon. How much that novel offers is detailed by Stephen Weisenburger in *A* Gravity's Rainbow *Companion* (Georgia); with references to history, philosophy, science, mechanics, jokes, puns, slang, and cultural fragments (especially good are the materials from Britain's wartime verbal ambience), Weisenburger not only graphs the extent of the book's pertinence but implies the encyclopedic nature of its vision. Yet *Gravity's Rainbow* is no simple encyclopedia, for Weisenburger is also able to offer a careful structure for its temporal development. An attempt to construe Pynchon as a humanist in the manner of Joyce is found in Susan Swartzlander's "The Tests of Reality: The Use of History in *Ulysses* and *Gravity's Rainbow*" (*Crit* 29:133–43). More conscious of peculiarly postmodern techniques is Kathryn Hume, whose "Views from Above, Views from Below: The Perspectival Subtext in *Gravity's Rainbow*" (*AL* 60:625–42) shows how a "glimpse of the sacred" is allowed through the successive encodings of implied levels of reality by the novel's various characters. Similar critical tools allow Gregory T. Polletta to establish how Pynchon's novel is a production rather than just a product; "Textuality, Actuality, and Contextuality: The Example of *Gravity's Rainbow*" (*SPELL* 4:83–101) is especially good for showing how the novel itself replicates the immense production of World War II's massive military machine.

ix. Ronald Sukenick, Raymond Federman, Gilbert Sorrentino, and Stanley Elkin

Sukenick and Federman have seemed paired since birth, to the extent that insiders refer to their canon as authored by "Sukefedermanick." Typically, their autobiographies appear together this year in *Contemporary Authors, Autobiography Series* (Gale) 8:63–81 and 283–95. But both in terms of subject matter and form, these essays show how different are the two writers' approaches. Sukenick sees fiction as self-invention, and therefore there is little of the historically autobiographical in this piece. Instead, he generates a self-identity by recounting struggles with literary and theoretical issues; the most stridently argued point is his disaffection for the term "experimental," unless by that identification the critic means the way all human beings fabricate their existence from childhood on. Federman's autobiography seems at first glance more conventional, with reams of material on his family in prewar Paris and how the Holocaust brought all that to an end. Equally rich details fill Federman's postwar narrative, which brings him to the United States and an academic career. However, the central event of his life—its own near extinction, while all other members of his family were lost to the Nazi genocide—is an ungraphable absence, an emptiness that can never be filled, and must instead be surrounded by the self-constructed text his remaining life has become—whether searching for forgotten and historically effaced memories in the ruins of Europe, or creating a new life out of nothing in an America of open possibilities. Yet Federman's effort is to come to terms with a problematic history that Sukenick's fiction, born in the U.S.A., prides itself in never having to face. In Sukefedermanick's novels, the old and new worlds meet, their complementarity giving a more complete picture of postmodern fiction than would either by itself. No wonder that their writings feed off each other and form the terms of an ongoing dialectic that has powered innovative fiction for the past two decades.

Critical references to Sukenick are brief this year, but Richard Kostelanetz fits his work into the larger context in "Late 60s Experimental Fiction" (*NWR* 26, i:125–31), while Stephen Cole and others at Colorado State University propose a wide-ranging series of questions in "Is Realism 'State Fiction'?: A Conversation with Curtis White and Ronald Sukenick" (*Colorado Review* [Fort Collins] 15, ii:1–12). Politics in the novel is made by the audience rather than the author, Sukenick advises, citing the different ways Jack Kerouac's *On the Road* has been received in successive decades. The greatest danger in realism becoming commodified opinion comes from publishers, he argues; when Michael Korda quips that "Some people sell shoes, some people sell books. What's the difference?," Sukenick responds by calling his publishing house "Simon & Shoestore."

Raymond Federman's fiction generates three important pieces of critical work: Welch Everman's *Who Says This?* (discussed in section i. above), Zoltan Abádi-Nagy's articulate "An Interview with Raymond Federman" (*MFS* 34:157–70), and Marcel Cornis-Pop's brilliant "Narrative (Dis)articulation and the *Voice in the Closet* Complex in Raymond Federman's Fictions" (*Crit* 29:77–93). To Everman's understanding of Federman's exploitative tension between an unwritable history and the urge to report oneself in fiction, Cornis-Pop adds an appreciation of how "the multiplication of voices and story framed in this fiction speaks of an effort to bridge the central void 'between the function of memory and that of thinking, between being-then and being-now or if you prefer being and non-being.'" Federman's rush of words spans that hollow space and reduces it to a writing surface, upon which his personal narrative is inscribed. To Abádi-Nagy, Federman admits that there is no sense in denying that reality exists, but insists that fiction must always challenge reality's impostures. Our relationship with reality has changed, and therefore the novelist must find tools newer than traditional mimesis to express this truth.

Stanley Elkin's work interests two leading critics frequently drawn to postmodern issues. In "MS or 'The Imp of Ossibility': Making Sense of the Trite and the Trivial in the Work of Stanley Elkin and Gilbert Sorrentino" collected in editor Rob Kroes's *High Brow Meets Low Brow* (Free Univ. Press, pp. 157–71), Marc Chénetier finds both writers interested in challenging "impossible sentences" that have no apparent meaning. The act of their fiction-making draws new meaning from stale material or else "transcends paralysing trivialities" in order to produce shimmering new meanings (which are in fact based on nothing but the writer's action). "Ego and Appetite in Stanley Elkin's Fiction" (*LitR* 32, i:111–18) is Arthur M. Saltzman's able critique of the author's "richly metaphorical, relentlessly clever, unmistakably poetic narrative voice" which "enters our concerns through the ear." What drives this aural technique is narrative obsession for metaphor, the vehicle for which is often chosen for sound as much as sense.

x. Women

This year's work points out an interesting feature in studies of fiction where concerns of women are foremost: unless the subject is self-consciously given over to genre, such as in mass market romance, science fiction, or crime detection, the scholar's interest is almost always thematic. This dominance of theme over form or technique characterizes Sandra M. Gilbert and Susan Gubar's *No Man's Land: The Place of the Woman Writer in the Twentieth Century; Volume 1: The War of the Words* (Yale). For Gilbert and Gubar, words are important for *what* they mean rather than *how*, and it is on this thematic basis that their choices for a canon are made. For postmodern fiction, this slant throws interpretations off center, such as Hubert Selby's *Last Exit to Brooklyn* becoming simply a nightmare of rape and degradation rather than a tour de force of language (as Gilbert Sorrentino has pointed out in *Something Said*), while the feminine linguistic power of Ursula Le Guin's heroines is reduced to little more than a plot device. Similar readings of Philip Roth, John Barth, and Woody Allen draw these radically unalike authors together in what Gilbert and Gubar consider a valorization of female power—even though the breast of Roth's narrative and the sperm of Barth's "Night-Sea Journey" have only the most superficially topical of connections. Their response to the rich, multiform fiction of William H. Gass is that he disregards women's lack of "genital drive," while Pynchon's *V.* is reduced to dreams of male vengeance. Certainly there are major problems in how sexuality is handled in our culture; but to conflate Thomas Pynchon's *V.* with Larry Flynt's *Hustler* only distracts from the seriousness with which such true abominations as the latter should be faulted.

More helpful is the collection of papers from a 1982 Hofstra University conference only now getting into print: editors Alice Kessler-Harris and William McBrien's *Faith of a (Woman) Writer* (Greenwood). Especially noteworthy is Elaine Showalter's "Joyce Carol Oates's 'The Dead' and Feminist Criticism" (pp. 13–19), a reading that finds Oates in dialogue with the male tradition in a way that shows how when women writers move away from typically feminine themes, they become regarded as male. Showalter's achievement is to maintain her feminist viewpoint even in the face of such challenges, which demand and receive more than a simply thematic interpretation.

All major subgenres have attracted women writers, and there are productive womanly ways to read them. For science fiction, one turns to Joanne Blum's *Transcending Genre: The Male/Female Double in Women's Fiction* (UMI), a study given to the constraints of genre and how to overcome them. Women science fiction writers in particular have found that fantasy offers room for transcending limits; Ursula Le Guin's *The Left Hand of Darkness*, Dorothy Bryant's *The Kin of Ata Are Waiting for You*, and James Tiptree, Jr.'s *Star Songs of an Old Primate* all show how a male character-narrator's experiences of an alien culture can be transformative of his views; in this way an acknowledgment of gender can be helpful in overcoming the divisiveness of our own perceptions.

Two books are devoted to women and detective fiction. Kathleen Gregory Klein's *The Woman Detective: Gender and Genre* (Illinois) notes that as "detection" has given way to an emphasis on "crime" in postwar fiction, so too have plot and adventure receded in favor of psychological motivation and a stronger interest in character development. Within these changes the woman detective has emerged, but largely as a parodistic figure, surrounded as she almost inevitably is by men and their definitions. In *Sisters in Crime: Feminism and the Crime Novel* (Continuum) Maureen T. Reddy sees a more active role for women, as their presence as active forces in such fiction inverts structures and stereotypes to reveal an underclass as powerless (to the benefit of those who do hold power); having a woman in control forces readers to reconsider their customary reading strategies in order to make the new narrative understandable.

Finally, in a study supposedly focused on narrower issues, Jan Cohn brings the debate back to Gilbert and Gubar's terms, but with a contrary judgment. Her *Romance and the Erotics of Property: Mass-Market Fiction for Women* (Duke) follows Janice A. Radway in its skepticism of Gilbert and Gubar's thematic polemics. Her own thesis is more formally developmental: that the subgenre of popular romance develops from the situation of the captivating hero coming to inherited wealth and continues through the injured and/or depropertied hero now on his own (until a woman supports him). Along the way, a structure develops that gives women characters more to do, and this action has consequences on the fiction's shape as well as theme. Certain givens in contemporary romance, such as women's socioeconomic inferiority, their powerlessness, and the potential for emotional victimization, are overcome by feminist writers. Erotic content, however, is more than simply stimulation or essentialist sexuality; we must remember, according to Foucault, that sexuality is a fairly recent historical construction and is more of a fresh contemporary problem than a limiting, inherited tradition. Hope is seen in that such sexuality promotes a new role model: the heroine who can frankly enjoy sex, rather than be used by it.

xi. Science Fiction and Horror

Kingsley Widmer's *Counterings: Utopian Dialectics in Contemporary Contexts* (UMI) is built on the premise that utopia is best defined by its opposites. Such an interpretation misreads Kurt Vonnegut's *Player Piano* as thematically dystopian in a journalistic sense, whereas the author is in fact using journalistic conventions as a style of anthropological subtext. In the transformative American 1960s, Raymond Mungo (who was strongly influenced by a Vonnegut beyond Widmer's reading) is written off as a parasitic loser, with no thought to his structural subversion. Most deplorable is Widmer's uncalled for attack on writers of what he calls "femtopianism." One is shocked that Widmer's appraisal made its way past UMI's editors and readers: "But perhaps what these women really need is a good . . . writer" (the elipses are his own). But when the author dismisses Marge Piercy's work and prefers Margaret Atwood's "because it could have been written by a man," one wonders how such offensive and unfounded comments could make their way into print.

Far superior is Bernard Selinger's *Le Guin and Identity in Contemporary Fiction*, also from UMI. Selinger provides, from a theoretical and psychoanalytic viewpoint, a refutation of Jungian readings of feminism in Le Guin's work, seeing much more than a binary opposition of discourses. Open to experiencing very early ego states, Le Guin's type of artist has no strong sense of identity but rather creates various configurations of the self. Her central concern is this puzzle of identity as formed by or against language. The question becomes how to balance sameness and distinctiveness, symbiosis and separateness (or autism). From Derrida she takes names as pure signifiers, with naming as the father principle; Kristeva reminds her that true naming, however, arises out of a space prior to the sign, a notion that corresponds with Bettelheim's observation that the autistic child separates its self from a reality no longer trustworthy. It is in the psychotic state that one transcends the standardizing effects of language.

In *Peter Beagle* (Starmont Reader's Guide 44) Kenneth J. Zahorski conducts a full scholarly investigation of the fiction itself, including Beagle's early and largely unknown stories, and extending through his popular novels to the less accessible screenplays. There is some distractingly uncritical biography, but what survives is an accurate analysis of the author's transforming love within the confines of tyrannical time.

Stephen King seems to be everywhere, even in criticism, and Joseph Reino's *Stephen King: The First Decade,* Carrie *to* Pet Sematary (TUSAS 531) will help readers learn how King begins as a master of formulaic self-mutilation. Essential to his talent is the attractiveness of horror, and of horror writing itself. Private nightmares are often drawn from family traumas, the root of an irresistible appeal. Reino's readings are heavily thematic, with the only technical analyses consisting of irony and reversals. However, there may be no more to King's narrative art than this.

xii. Native American Fiction and the West

As usual, a narrowly select number of Native American fictionists continue to interest critics and scholars, to the exclusion of younger talents. But the work done is strong, especially the overview provided by Roberta Orlandini in "Variations on a Theme: Traditions and Temporal Structure in the Novels of James Welch" (*SDR* 26, iii:37–52). Welch's first two novels rather traditionally show Native Americans "trying to invest with meaning their empty existence in small town western America." His difference from other Native American fiction writers, especially from Momaday and Silko, is that Welch is ironic toward his heritage, showing how those who respect it are even more cut off from the world. With *Fools Crow,* however, he uses a new language and tone to view ethnic tradition in a brighter, more positive way.

Complementary pieces on Leslie Marmon Silko's major work appear in the same issue of *ArQ* 44. In "Healing the Witchery: Medicine in Silko's *Ceremony*" (pp. 86–94) B. A. St. Andrews cites the power of language in forming identity on a cosmic level and the perspective of health within a holistic dimension. James Ruppert's "The Reader's Lessons in *Ceremony*" (pp. 78–85) shows how an understanding of how stories can ward off illness, evil, and death is just as essential for the reader to understand as it is for the novel's characters. The reader's experience is thus structured in a way that compels an understanding of the Laguna people, just as the Lagunas are compelled within this tale to understand the workings of the larger contemporary American culture.

A similar allegiance to contemporary theory is found in Jon Wallace's "The Implied Author as Protagonist: A Reading of *Little Big Man*" (*WAL* 22:291–99), in which by listening to the "other voice" of Jack Crabb in Thomas Berger's novel one discovers a second story, told in terms of style rather than plot and much richer in self-consciously linguistic action. A newly dystopian vision is explored by Jay Dougherty in " 'Once more, and once again': Edward Abbey's Cyclical View of Past and Present in *Good News*" (*Crit* 29:223–32), a cyclical vision that nevertheless still embraces possibility.

University of Northern Iowa

16. Poetry: 1900 to the 1940s

Melody M. Zajdel

It has been a busy year in modernist studies. Several new additions of selected and collected poems were issued, most notably *The Collected Poetry of Robinson Jeffers. Volume 1, 1920–1928* (Stanford), ed. Tim Hunt, the first of four volumes; *Selected Poems of John Gould Fletcher* (Arkansas), ed. Lucas Carpenter and Leighton Rudolph, the first in a six-volume series; and *H.D.: Selected Poems* (New Directions), ed. Louis L. Martz. Additionally, two new biographies from the University of Georgia Press provide the first full-length treatments of both Adelaide Crapsey (*Alone in the Dawn: The Life of Adelaide Crapsey* by Karen Alkalay-Gut) and Conrad Aiken (*Conrad Aiken: Poet of White Horse Vale* by Edward Butscher). Gender studies remain a major area of investigation, as evidenced by the number of books and special journal issues with this focus. This year, disputes have arisen around not only individual authors and readings, but around literary critical methodology and theory. This is most apparent in the criticism on Stevens, who continues to be the writer generating the most book-length studies (four) and dissertations (three). It is also clear in the books of general interest written this year.

i. General

Emory Elliott's *Columbia Literary History of the United States* (Columbia), Albert Gelpi's *A Coherent Splendor: The American Poetic Renaissance, 1910–1950* (Cambridge, 1987), and Sandra Gilbert and Susan Gubar's *No Man's Land. Volume 2: Sexchanges* (Yale), all contribute to the ongoing redefinition and critique of modernism.

Disclaiming an attempt to "constitute a new consensus" (p. xi) about American literature, Elliott has eschewed a monolithic authorial voice by appointing associate editors and individual critics to produce essays reflecting current information, issues, and approaches. The result is what David Minter, the associate editor of "Part Four, 1910–1945," calls the "contested terrain" in modernist studies (p. 926). Individual essays on Frost, William Carlos Williams and Wallace Stevens, and Ezra Pound and T. S. Eliot, by Jay Parini, J. Hillis Miller, and A. Walton Litz, respectively, are good introductions to the writers, their reputations, and current issues surrounding them. Parini summarizes Frost's career, but makes the point that Frost did not " 'develop' from book to book" (p. 943) as other major modernists, and hence has had a lesser reputation. Miller juxtaposes Williams and Stevens, stressing their fundamental differences in order to expand the boundaries of modernism. But in addition to these essays on established figures, two other essays call for fundamental revisions of the period and reevaluations of writers. Elaine Showalter's "Women Writers Between the Wars" looks at the "frustration, fragmentation, and silencing" (p. 835) of women writers in the 1920s and 1930s. Showalter explains how femininity and minority status were linked by critics, then examines the strategies Wylie, Moore, and Millay used to break the constraints of sexual and literary double standards. Cary Nelson's "The Diversity of American Poetry" asks that writers usually deemed insignificant be reevaluated and that critics and historians "recover . . . some of the social and literary context that is often ignored" (p. 913). Nelson wants the canon to include women, minorities, popular forms, and "poetry of significant historical interest" (p. 914), cognizant all the while that any canon-making is ideological and that modernism is not "a single coherent development" (p. 926). His call for criteria beyond the solely aesthetic and his very choice of words run counter to the thesis and title of Gelpi's new book.

A Coherent Splendor, the companion piece to Gelpi's earlier *The Tenth Muse* (Cambridge, 1975), looks at modernism as an outgrowth of and reaction to 19th-century American romanticism. Gelpi poses a basic ideological dialectic in modernism between Symbolisme and Imagism. In monograph-length chapters he places the major figures of modernism within his dialectical schema. Gelpi's two poles represent the psychological split at the base of modernist thought: Symbolistes seek to objectify their subjective reality, while Imagists seek to subjectively express their experience of an objective world. Gelpi sees Stevens, Eliot, Tate, and Crane as influenced by Symbolisme, and Pound, Williams, and H.D. as quintessential Imagists. His chapters on each poet are comprehensive, with insightful close readings, although his determination to make all writers fit his paradigm of dichotomous approaches to the psychology of the imagination is sometimes confining. Two chapters bracket the six main essays, helping to define modernism by showing contemporary writers who were modern but not modernist (Frost and Ransom) and writers who were philosophically opposed to modernism (Winters and Jeffers). His chapters on Stevens, H.D., and Williams are particularly interesting. He does some fine side-by-side readings of texts by Williams and Stevens and explores the issue of gender and creativity quite well in both Williams and H.D.

No Man's Land. Volume 2: Sexchanges is the second volume of Gilbert and Gubar's encompassing trilogy redefining modernism. It continues to investigate how "men's hostility . . . and women's anxiety" (p. xii) regarding female autonomy is intrinsic to our understanding of the modes and motives of modernism. This volume explores three phases of the writing from the 1880s to the 1930s. Part I, "Feminism and Fantasy," examines "the repudiation or revision of the Victorian ideology of femininity," while Part II, "Feminization and Its Discontents," looks at the "antiutopian skepticism" of Edith Wharton and Willa Cather (p. xii). It is, however, Part III, "Reinventing Gender," which is most relevant to readers of this chapter. In the three chapters of Part III, Gilbert and Gubar show "the virtually apocalyptic engendering of the new" in poets like H.D., Stein, Lowell, and Renée Vivien (p. xii). In "'She Meant What I Said': Lesbian Double Talk," they discuss the literary strategies that Stein, Vivien, Lowell, and H.D. use to "represent . . . alienation from . . . literary inheritance" (p. 218). Whether with a fantasy partner, like Sappho, or a real one, these women make an aesthetic of mutuality and authorize their writing via a collaborative rhetoric. The study of H.D.'s Sapphic fragments and Stein's *Autobiography of Alice B. Toklas* are exceptionally useful here. In "Soldier's Heart: Literary Men, Literary Women and the Great War," Gilbert and Gubar show how the war was experienced differently by the two genders. Their best points concern H.D., who has as her muse both the war and the dead soldier as she writes *Trilogy*, a work that is "a vision of patriarchy defied and denied" (p. 304). Their final chapter on "Cross-Dressing and Re-dressing" does less direct reading of poetic texts than the previous two chapters, but it raises fundamental issues of critical methodology. This chapter truly needs to be read opposite Frank Lentricchia's comments in *Ariel and the Police* (Wisconsin) on essentialist feminism. In this chapter Gilbert and Gubar demonstrate their awareness of poststructuralist theories of sexuality, textuality, and subjectivity and make direct and cogent arguments for why it is not their preference. In response to critics like Lentricchia, their statement that "male-authored philosophic and psychoanalytic attempts to 'desexualize' the subject can be seen in this context as attempts to defuse feminist militancy" (p. 372) is particularly noteworthy. I look forward to next year's volume, which promises in-depth studies of H.D., Millay, and Moore. This text is one of the most significant this year.

Two other books deserve brief mention. For some reason, *Coming to Light* (Michigan, 1985), ed. Diane Middlebrook and Marilyn Yalom, was not noted in 1985–87. This excellent collection of 16 essays shapes itself around two central themes: (1) how women writers have claimed for themselves a place in a hostile tradition and (2) how they have used uniquely female experience in their poetry. It contains now well-known articles on revisionist feminist mythmaking (Alicia Ostriker), H.D. (Albert Gelpi), Bogan (Mary DeShazer), H.D. and Rich (Susan S. Friedman), Moore and Bishop (David Kalstone), and Loy (Carolyn Burke). Most of the articles appeared in journals in 1983–84; still, as a collection this is exemplary. The second volume is Gillian Hanscombe's and Virginia Smyer's *Writing For Their Lives* (Northeastern, 1987). Given recent biographies and criticism, there is not much new material here. Still, it is a useful book for nonspecialists (particularly students) in demonstrating the connectedness for feminist modernists of their lives and works. It clearly shows how female patronage assisted women writers and how many writers (e.g., H.D., Stein, Lowell, Loy, Moore, and Harriet Monroe) made both their lives and works "a challenge to . . . 'heterosexism'" (p. xv). Discussions of women's networkings around periodicals and small publishing companies are especially noteworthy.

ii. Stevens

The four books on Stevens this year illustrate what makes him so attractive to critics and so central to current debates. *Wallace Stevens and the Critical Schools* (Arkansas), by Melita Schaum, is as much a study of critical theories' ideological infighting over the last 70 years as it is a study of Stevens; or as Schaum notes, "The history of controversy surrounding Wallace Stevens's placement in the American literary canon affords a remarkable diagram of the agonistic process of critical appropriation" (p. 183). Schaum does an excellent job of delineating this process, defining four phases in Stevens criticism. The early critics of the 1910s and 1920s pitted humanist interpretations against traditional aesthetic criticism. In the 1930s New Critics focused on the "autotelic nature of the art work, and the uniquely qualitative nature of the aesthetic experience" (p. 60). Using methodology different from (although an outgrowth of) the earlier two, these critics produced fruitful discussions of Stevens's shorter poems but failed to explain the lack of closure and resolution in his later works. A third group, postmodernist critics like Riddell, Vendler, and Miller, generated "two central paradigms for Stevens' later poetry—the decreative and the deconstructive" (p. 103), while the more recent critics of the 1980s have placed Stevens in the center of debates on canon formation and the redefinition of modernism. Schaum's book is excellent at showing that Stevens's complexity, his historical placement, and the sustained critical interest in his writings make him an exemplum of the critical enterprise's process of change. Although the focus is on the critics, Schaum's arguments send us back to Stevens's poems in order to assess this interpretive evolution.

A more polemical book is Frank Lentricchia's *Ariel and the Police: Michel Foucault, William James, Wallace Stevens* (Wisconsin). Concerned with what he sees as "determinism" (the police) in literary criticism, Lentricchia critiques three approaches: New Historicism (linked to Foucault), neopragmatism (linked to William James), and essentialist feminism (linked to Sandra Gilbert). Lentricchia calls his book "a dialogue with Marxism precisely on the issue of the personal subject which it dismisses" (23). Using Stevens's personal conflicts over his masculinity and the role of an artist in our culture, Lentricchia looks at how current critical schools either help, or fail to help, explain such a struggle. His first chapter, "Anatomy of a Jar," explores how Stevens's work has defied single readings and establishes the mode of the book's argument as a dialogue to avoid the appropriation obvious in some readings. The next two chapters look intently at the theories of Foucault and James, applied to reading Stevens. The final section, "Writing After Hours," has two parts. The first, "Patriarchy Against Itself," shows Stevens's struggle to resolve the conflict between masculine, capitalist values and feminized poetry. It includes, as I discussed last year, his attack on Gilbert and Gubar's essentialist feminism. Part two, "Penelope's Poetry—The Later Wallace Stevens," reclaims a personal subject in poetry and shows Stevens's reshaping of the modern personal lyric form. The image of the poet for Stevens becomes Penelope, not Ulysses. While a number of Lentricchia's points on Stevens's internalization of and resistance to cultural attitudes regarding gender and poetry are good, his final comments, particularly his discussion of Gilbert, are not well founded. Stevens's internalized feminine is possible only at the expense of actual females in his world. Gilbert and Gubar are not ignorant or blind to the complexity of current thoughts on gender and language. Nonetheless, Lentricchia has stirred up some lively arguments and the ensuing discussions should be interesting to chronicle next year.

The last two books are considerably tamer. Robert Rehder's *The Poetry of Wallace Stevens* (St. Martin's) is a chronological survey of Stevens's major poems, focusing on commonly recognized themes and taking the dialectic between imagination and reality as its central thesis. It is strongest in its readings of individual poems, such as "The Man with a Blue Guitar," "Notes Toward a Supreme Fiction," and "An Ordinary Evening in New Haven." Neither controversial nor new in approach or readings, Rehder's book is a solid introduction for nonspecialists. Conversely, Eleanor Cook's *Poetry, Word-Play and Word-War in Wallace Stevens* (Princeton) is definitely for scholars. Cook looks in detail at "the play of rhetoric and dialectic against each other" in Stevens's major poems (p. xi). Arguing a developmental progression in Stevens's thinking and poetic strategies, her individual examples and interpretations of Stevens's grammatical play, punning, riddling, use of synecdoche and metaphor, and his thwarting of readers' expectations are often fascinating. Cook balances on the edge of too much detail (she acknowledges this danger), but in the end the cumulative effect of her readings compels us to agree with her: "Once we have heard what Stevens does with some language, we cannot read it in the same way again" (p. 5), and reading Stevens "teaches us to read contemporary poetry" (p. xii). Particularly strong are her discussions of allusion, echoes, and dislocations, and her close readings of "Esthetique du Mal," "Notes Toward a Supreme Fiction," and "An Ordinary Evening in New Haven." Throughout her book, Cook demonstrates how Stevens disrupts the usual relationship of language and reader, while also showing how he alternately belongs and responds to a literary tradition including Milton, Keats, Whitman, Emerson, and Eliot.

The articles on Stevens this year cluster around three main topics: the status and method of Stevens criticism, women and Stevens, and Stevens's relation to other artists and philosophers. Helen Vendler and Roy Harvey Pearce include chapters on Stevens in their books on the nature of literary criticism. Vendler's "The Hunting of Wallace Stevens: Critical Approaches," in *The Music of What Happens* (Harvard), reviews the status of Stevens criticism in 1986, when books by Bates, Lensing, and Richardson appeared. Vendler's major notation is that the opening of the Huntington Library collection has made possible new "investigations of Stevens through his life and reading" (p. 89), reinforcing the trend toward contextual studies. Her essay adds another facet to Schaum's discussion of current trends. Pearce's essay, "The Cry and the Occasion: Rereading Stevens," in *Gesta Humanorum,* fits more interestingly next to Lentricchia and Cook. Pearce first positions himself in relation to New Historicism, by reaffirming himself as an old-style historical/contextual critic. Then, he seeks out the unique historical situations which gave rise to some of Stevens's poems. Within his analysis of occasions, Pearce, like Cook, demands that we refine our sense of allusion. His connections of "the readymade" to "Anecdote of the Jar," of a walk in Ybor City to "The Emperor of Ice Cream," and of Henry James's meditation of a mountain in *The American Scene* to "Chocorua to Its Neighbor" are insightful.

An impressive special issue of the *Wallace Stevens Journal* (12,ii, Fall 1988), ed. Melita Schaum, includes several excellent essays on Stevens and women. In some ways the essays by Wagner, Brogan, Steinman, and O'Hara are enhanced by reading in conjunction with Lentricchia. Daniel T. O'Hara's "Lava-Writing: A Status Report on Stevens and Feminism, 1988" (pp. 173–80), examines the critical furor raised by Lentricchia's critique of essentialist feminism, meanwhile calling for less focus on sociocultural study and a return to more formal, aesthetic analyses. Lisa Steinman's "The House of Fathers: Stevens and Emerson" (pp. 162–72) explores how gender issues "impinge on both Emerson's and Stevens's consideration of the poets' social role." Steinman concurs with critics like Lentricchia that Stevens internalized and resisted the feminization (and concurrently, trivialization) of poetry, then goes further to consider what Stevens's final stance means for gender-conscious readers. Jacqueline Vaught Brogan raises some questions about the feminine voice in Stevens's poetry and self, in " 'Sister of the Minotaur': Sexism and Stevens" (pp. 102–18). Although conflicted, Stevens came, according to Brogan, "as close as it was possible for a person in his time and circumstances to cure himself of the 'infection in the sentence' that the dominant, phallocentric structures in our culture inevitably breed" (102). Finally, C. Roland Wagner, in "Wallace Stevens: The Concealed Self" (pp. 83–101), examines Stevens's biography and works to understand "the nurturing female others of his mind" (p. 83). Such an analysis allows Wagner to question if and why Stevens converted to Catholicism, concluding Stevens's spirituality becomes a quest for the unattainable Other, a quest paralleling his interaction with the feminine throughout his life. The other three essays in the issue continue the engendering of Stevens by arguing that Stevens's modes of expression are "related to . . . l'ecriture feminine'" (Mary Doyle Springer, "The Feminine Principle in Stevens' Poetry: Esthétique du Mal," p. 125); that by making the rabbi a prototype of the poet Stevens makes Wisdom take on the characteristics of the feminine in his poems (Rosamund Rosenmeier, "Getting Wisdom: The Rabbi's Devotion to *Weisheit* and Its Implications for Feminists," pp. 138–49); and that the difference between the Muse for poets like Rich and Stevens is illustrative of gender issues in poetry (Maria Irene Ramalho de Sousa Santos, "The Woman in the Poem: Wallace Stevens, Ramón Fernández, and Adrienne Rich," pp. 150–61).

Stevens's kinship with earlier philosophers and artists is the topic of four other essays. Paul Kenneth Naylor looks at the term "idea," comparing how both Stevens and Husserl employ it. His essay, "'The Idea of It': Wallace Stevens and Edmund Husserl" (*WSJour* 12, ii: 12–55) does not claim influence, but discusses each to elucidate the other's meaning. D. L. MacDonald, "The Return of the Dead in 'Large Red Man Reading,'" looks at the ancestry or echoes for the title poem, suggesting that it, "both allegorizes and exemplifies . . . *Apophrades*" (*WSJour* 12, i:21–34). MacDonald shows how Stevens uses the metaphor of the family romance to discuss "relations between text and voice and between writer and reader" (p. 21). Rosemary M. Nielsen and Robert H. Solomon take a semiotic approach to the study of geometric shapes and spaces in Stevens, Horace, and Whitman to show "technological significance adheres to the earliest structuring figures in the poems" along with "religious resonances" ("Structuring 'Praiseworthy Space': Building from Horace to Wallace Stevens," *Mosaic* 21, ii–iii:1–12). Finally, Betty Buchsbaum, in "Contours of Desire: The Place of Cézanne in Wallace Stevens' Poetics and Late Practice," examines how both artists use the motif of mountain landscapes to "penetrate to, and celebrate, a capacious being-in-world" (*Criticism* 30, iii:303–24).

iii. Moore

In two special issues of journals, *The William Carlos Williams Review* (14, i, Spring 1988) and *Sagetrieb* (6, iii, Winter 1987), Theodora Rapp Graham and Celeste Goodridge, respectively, continue the study of Moore begun in her centenary year. The majority of this year's criticism focuses on comparing and contrasting Moore to Williams or other modernist poets and to reexamining her literary place, her feminist voice, and selected individual poems.

The comparisons and contrasts of Moore to Williams in the Spring 1988 issue of *WCWR* are helpful in assessing what is typically modernist and what is uniquely feminist about Moore. In tandem pieces, John M. Slatin and Rachel DuPlessis explore how gender issues separate Williams and Moore. Slatin's " 'Something Inescapably Typical': Questions About Gender in the Late Work of Williams and Moore" (pp. 86–103) focuses on Moore's response to Williams after the 1920s, and particularly her dislike for the characters of Corydon, Phyllis, and C. in *Paterson.* While both Williams and Moore seek public roles and voices as poets, Moore's gender automatically marginalizes her. That marginality is implicit in her choice of forms (prose) and vehicles (popular magazines) for the public woman poet. Given Williams's representation of women, Slatin shows how Moore came to realize that Williams's works contain "a deeply seated and unconscious contempt for the predicament of a woman trying desperately to make poetry" (p. 101). Small wonder she disagrees with and disapproves of the late poems of Williams. DuPlessis's "No Moore of the Same: The Feminist Poetics of Marianne Moore" (pp. 6–32) explores the system that Moore creates, since she has no ready-made place, being a woman, in the poetic tradition. DuPlessis investigates the four tropes Moore used to "define . . . access to authority and vocation" (p. 11): vocative poetry, plural or shared authority, the authority of otherness, and the fusion of genders in an androgynous voice. Both these essays are helpful additions to not only the ongoing assessment of Moore, but of modernism newly gendered.

Other essays contrast Williams and Moore by looking at specific elements in their writing. Marie Borroff uses two poems by Moore and two by Williams to show how the "experience of reading" them is essentially different ("Questions of Design in Williams and Moore," *WCWR* 14, i:104–15). Rather than use or modify an established form, Moore creates unique templates for her poems. Borroff provides an excellent study of the devices and effects of design when reading Moore and Williams, noting that the template approach "adds an intellectual component . . . not present in . . . Williams" (p. 108). Janet Sullivan, in "Encountering the Unicorn: William Carlos Williams and Marianne Moore" (*Sagetrieb* 6, iii:147–61), shows the difference in first person narrative in Moore and Williams by comparing "Sea Unicorns and Land Unicorns" to Book 5 of *Paterson.* She concludes that Williams's "I" is already known, a Subject, while Moore's "is constantly being hedged about and disguised" (p. 148), seeking to find itself and to remain independent. Eleanor Berry chooses to investigate how the typewriter, as image and tool, is used similarly by the two poets to generate movement and to avoid the rigid versification of earlier poets ("Machine Technology and Technique in the Poetry of Moore and Williams," *WCWR* 14, i:50–68). And last, William Doreski, "Extra-Literary Voices in Williams and Moore" (*WCWR* 14, i:39–49), looks at rhetorical strategies that both poets use to broaden the lyric form: nonpoetic language, syntax, and voices. The results are radically changed modern lyrics.

Other artists besides Williams influenced and were influenced by Moore. In two separate articles, Bonnie Costello discusses Moore in relation to Emerson ("Marianne Moore's Wild Decorum," *APR* 16, ii:43–54) and to Longinus and Hazlitt ("Marianne Moore and the Sublime," *Sagetrieb* 6, iii:5–13). While looking at Moore's classical elements in the first essay, Costello argues that there are parallels between Emerson's "transparent eyeball" and transcendental vision and Moore's poetic of apprehension. In the second essay Costello links the notion of the sublime to Moore's theory of gusto. For Moore, "the sublime is a drama of consciousness thrown off balance by an object which exceeds its mastery" (p. 9). Moore's conscious and careful restraint in choosing not to dominate objects is central to her poetics. Celeste Goodridge, in "Towards a Poetics of Disclosure: Marianne Moore and Henry James" (*Sagetrieb* 6, iii:31–43), looks at the connections between her title's authors. After noting how the two writers were connected by mutual friends, Goodridge establishes Moore's view of James as a "characteristic American" (p. 32) and their mutual belief that things are only "known through partial disclosure," an idea Moore represents in her image of the octopus. Cleo McNelly Kearns reverses the usual assumption of Eliot's influence on his contemporaries to show how Moore influenced him, in "Consanguinities: T. S. Eliot and Marianne Moore" (*Sagetrieb* 6, iii:45–56).

Kearns examines "Virginia Britannica" and "Little Gidding," maintaining that Moore's sense of detachment and balance prompted Eliot to change his style and stance between *The Waste Land* and "Little Gidding." While her assertion that Eliot's stylistic change was "undertaken quite deliberately under Moore's aegis" seems stronger than her support, Kearns's essay is interesting in its contrasting of the two poets. In "Moore's 'New York' and Sandburg's 'Chicago': How Modern Can a City Be?" (*WCWR* 14, i:33–38), Charles Molesworth examines how distinctively both poets use the image of a modern city. Although both detail city life, Molesworth points out that Moore uses her descriptions as metonymy not as personification, hence is able to allude to larger issues. Elizabeth Bishop is compared to Moore by Margaret Holley, who looks at how each represents women in their poetry ("Portraits of Ladies in Marianne Moore and Elizabeth Bishop," *Sagetrieb* 6, iii:15–30). Holley delineates four stereotypes of women: the ornamental, the maternal, the temperamental, and the artistic, and examines how each representation functions in the two poets. Although the women evaluate the first three differently, Moore and Bishop are surprisingly similar in their treatments of women as both the subject and object of art. Finally, Rosanne Wasserman, in "Marianne Moore and the New York School: O'Hara, Ashbery, Koch" (*Sagetrieb* 6, iii:67–77), notes Moore's influence on the postmodernists in the article's title. The range of comparisons and contrasts between Moore and other writers helps to extend our sense of her literary place.

More general articles on her place in modernism were done by Charles Altieri and Alan Nadel. Altieri, in "Powers of a Genuine Place" (*SHR* 22, iii:205–22), looks at the difficulty inherent in being a woman poet and shows how Moore was able to "criticize male versions of . . . [modernist values] and propose alternatives still faithful to constructivist commitments" (p. 206). Like Kearns above, Altieri focuses on how Moore rejects a prevailing notion of impersonality in order to present a variety of perspectives and voices (to establish a shared authority). Nadel, in "Marianne Moore and the Art of Delineation" (*Sagetrieb* 6, iii:169–80), looks at how her treatment of objects is different from that of contemporaries like Williams, Stevens, and Pound. Nadel argues that by rejecting an overriding or superimposed cosmology, Moore must turn to rhetorical forms to make connections between objects. Two other useful essays are Vicki Graham's "Whetted to Brilliance" (*Sagetrieb* 6, iii:127–45) and Jeanne

Heuving's "Gender in Marianne Moore's Art: Can'ts and Refusals" (*Sagetrieb* 6, iii:117–26). Graham analyzes "Those Various Scalpels" to illustrate how Moore dissolves dichotomies like subject-object and mind-body when portraying women in poetry. Moore shifts from a notion of opposition to one of alliance, "developing the woman's subjectivity in tandem with her own" (p. 129). Heuving also argues that Moore rejects the subject-object duality as a part of her feminine experience of reality. She argues that because Moore realizes the marginality of women and the woman poet's inability, therefore, to serve as a cultural representative, she must acknowledge the reality of the other as other. In doing so, Moore undermines a basic patriarchal hierarchy and paradigm.

Moore's feminist attitudes are investigated in several essays about "Marriage." Lynn Keller and Christanne Miller, in " 'The Tooth of Disputation': Marianne Moore's 'Marriage' " (*Sagetrieb* 6, iii:99–115), show Moore rejects simplistic resolutions to problems and opposites and therefore uses multiple voices in her poetry. Sabine Sielke shows the affiliation between Moore and Adrienne Rich around the problem of voice ("Snapshots of Marriage, Snares of Mimicry, Snarls of Motherhood: Marianne Moore and Adrienne Rich," *Sagetrieb* 6, iii:79–97). Sielke has an excellent discussion of both the intertextuality of the poets' works and their use of mimicry to challenge "tradition and canonicity" (p. 83). She also charts their movement from using mimicry to a more maternal discourse. Less theoretically, David Bergman's reading of "Marriage" points out Moore's personal feminism, noting that Moore did not work to reconcile the roles of wife and poet, finding them mutually exclusive. Nonetheless, her feminism led to her method of representing animals, led to her stylistic rebellion, and led to her ambivalence and interest in such institutions as marriage ("Marianne Moore and the Problem of 'Marriage,' " *AL* 60:241–54).

iv. Williams, Frost

The criticism on Williams this year was restricted to two primary areas: the comparisons with Moore cited above and examinations of Williams's relationship to the visual arts.

William Carlos Williams, the Arts, and Literary Tradition by Peter Schmidt (LSU) was this year's only book. Schmidt looks at how Williams used his understanding of Precisionism, Cubism, and

Dada to "renew specifically *literary* traditions and modes," not just to imitate painting techniques. Rather than solely drawing parallels between visual works and Williams's poems, Schmidt shows how an understanding of Precisionist techniques and ideas led Williams to renew the pastoral lyric form; how Cubism led to revisions of the sublime ode; and how Dada led to experiments in fiction, to reconsiderations of Emerson's and Whitman's notions of originality, and to a new epic form. His section on the differences between Cubist and Dadaist collages provides an interesting framework in which to read *Paterson.* Books 1–4, taken as a complete unit, illustrate admirably the Dadaist mode of decomposition. The addition of Book 5 changes the ending and requires a reinvestigation that suggests the new unit is more Cubist in inclination. In the end, an appreciation of Williams's later poetry requires a synthesis of all three theories. Schmidt does an admirable job of not merely citing parallels between the visual and literary arts, but of illustrating how aesthetic theories usually associated with visual media explain and prompt Williams's revision of literary topics and forms.

Peter Halter, Terence Diggory, and Michael North look at how Kandinsky, Brueghel, and Demuth help to explain Williams's poetics. In "Expression in Color: The Theory of Wassily Kandinsky and the Poetry of William Carlos Williams" (in *Poetry and Epistemology: Turning Points in the History of Poetic Knowledge,* ed. Roland Hagenbüchle and Laura Skandera [Pustet 1986], pp. 232–48), Halter delineates the similarities between Kandinsky and Williams, applying Kandinsky's three modes of Impression, Improvisation, and Composition to various stages of Williams's career, and examining how both artists use color to represent the expressive dimensions of the world around them. In "The Reader in Williams and Brueghel: *Paterson* 5 and *The Adoration of the Kings*" (*Criticism* 30:349–72), Terence Diggory explains how understanding the role of the father in Brueghel's picture is analogous to understanding the role of the reader in Williams's poem. Both father and reader maintain a complex relation of "intimacy and distance, equality and difference" with the subject of the works, without which the painting and poem lose much of their potential meaning (p. 350). Michael North's "The Sign of Five: Williams's 'The Great Figure' and Its Background" (*Criticism* 30:325–48), investigates how both Demuth and Williams defy simple representation in their art, each using techniques unique to their separate forms: "just as Williams uses syntactical and visual techniques to collapse subject and object . . . so Demuth uses both linguistic and visual" (p. 343).

A final essay on Williams, while not alluding to other media, discusses, as did Diggory, the active nature of Williams's poetry. Eniko Bollobas, in "Measures of Attention: On the Grammetrics of Lineation in William Carlos Williams' Poetry" (*Poetry and Epistemology*, 262–77), discusses how sentence-level linguistic strategies make poetry "not function as a value-creating activity but as participation in the process of discovery" in Williams's early poems (p. 266). In addition to critical essays, a number of previously unpublished materials, particularly letters, appeared in the Fall 1988 issue of *The William Carlos Williams Review* (14, ii). Surprisingly, given the number of books out in the last two to three years, there was only one dissertation on Williams in 1988.

Two books on Frost were published this year. *The Brain of Robert Frost: A Cognitive Approach to Literature*, by Norman Holland (Routledge), uses readings of Frost to discuss the application of recent research on the brain and cognition to literary study. Holland critiques semiotic and deconstructive critics for relying on a "simple text-active model" of reading and argues for a psychoanalytic model which privileges an interactive feedback model. All Holland's observations on how people interpret texts and all of his data reinforce his commitment to a specific form of reader-response criticism: readers create literary experiences to reinforce their identity themes, hence meaning is interactive, not "in" a text. Holland's chapter on six college professors reading Frost's "The Mill" shows the variety of responses possible even within a community of critics. The book tells us less about Frost, however, than about Holland's theory of reading.

George Monteiro's *Robert Frost and the New England Renaissance* (Kentucky) looks at Frost more directly and academically. Monteiro places Frost's poems "within contexts provided by the poems and essays of his New England precursors": Dickinson, Longfellow, Emerson, and Thoreau. In Dickinson, whom he read in the 1890s, Frost found congenial images, languages, and themes. From Longfellow, Frost derived his theme and imagery of choice, or what Monteiro calls his two-path tradition. Thoreau's *Walden* parallels Frost's attitude toward nature and man's relationship to his world. Finally, Emerson's didacticism, symbols, and philosophy parallel Frost's. All of these precursors are linked to Frost by a major design strategy: the curve or a circle. The most interesting part of the book is part II on Thoreau, where Monteiro does side-by-side readings of *Walden* and poems like "The Oven Bird" and "Birches." Occasionally the book alludes to a general New England tradition that Frost would know without establishing direct influences. Still, the recognition of an American historical tradition for Frost's writing is useful.

Four other essays look at influences on Frost, or precursors to whom he makes allusion. Ron Thomas's "Thoreau, William James, and Frost's 'Quest of The Purple-Fringed': A Contextual Reading" (*AL* 60:433–50) establishes botanical, historical, textual, and biographical contexts for Frost's poem. Thomas shows what the orchard in the poem represents to Thoreau and Frost, how James's theory of cognitive fringe is assumed by Frost, and how the poem can be read as an artifact representing Frost's sense of self in 1901. J. Gerald Janzen and Robert F. Fleissner examine biblical allusions in Frost. In "Reassessing Frost's Fair Impression and His Mistrust" (*R&L* 20, iii: 71–87), Janzen looks at the Hebraic, versus Classical, influence on Frost. Janzen uses "Happiness Makes Up in Height for What It Lacks in Length" to look at the motifs and themes affiliated with Frost's Old Testament religious stance. Frost's use of the apple tree, bird song, and weather within the context of an Edenic setting all lead Janzen to see Frost as "a poet of Joban faith." Fleissner, in "Frost as Ironist: 'After Apple-Picking' and the Preautumnal Fall" (*SCR* 21, i:50–57), also points to the image of fruit-gathering as symbolic of an Edenic past and points to Frost's use of this lost paradise image as implying both a Romantic notion of innocence and a moral problem of grace lost. One last influence on Frost is noted in Ronald Bieganowski's "Robert Frost's *A Boy's Will* and Henri Bergson's *Creative Evolution*" (*SCR* 21, i:9–26). Bieganowski uses Frost's annotations in his copy of Bergson to show how the two men's concepts of remembrance and recollection are similar. Bieganowski equates Frost's "remembering something he did not know he knew" with Bergson's interval of duration most interestingly.

Reassessments of Frost's modernism and literary stature continue to be prominent in this year's criticism. Wallace Martin considers the negative effects biographical readings of Frost have had on his literary reputation in "Frost's Thanatography" (*Post-Structuralist Readings of English Poetry*, ed. Richard Machin and Christopher Norris, Cambridge, 1987, 395–405). Martin notes that "For an understanding of Frost's literary corpus, thanatography is as necessary as biography" (p. 405). "Frost and Modernism," by Robert Kern (*AL* 60:1–16), cites Frost's use of everyday language and sonal experiments (such as his development of sentence-sounds) as characteristically modern. Kern notes that, perhaps most modernly, Frost had to "define himself, and thus to participate in the collective effort . . . 'to rethink the nature of an English poem.'" In "Education by Poetry: Robert Frost's Departure from the Modern Critical Tradition" (*SCR* 21, i:27–37), Joan D. Peters reverses the assessment process to question how Frost is distinct from typical modernists. Her answer is his belief in the didactic function of poetry. Her Frost is committed to writing poems which help a reader learn how to think, not just to emotionally respond. Frost's distance from mainstream modernists is also pointed out in Peter Strong's "Robert Frost's 'Nighthawks'/Edward Hopper's 'Desert Place'" (*CLQ* 24, i:27–35). Strong makes a point that both Hopper and Frost have been slow to receive their due recognition because of their conservatism. The essay points out their similarities in "temperament and outlook," suggesting they are problematic inclusions to some definitions of modernism. E. D. Lloyd-Kimbrel compares and contrasts Frost's "Directive" to Eliot's "Little Gidding," in "A Condition of Complete Simplicity: Poetic Return and Frost's 'Directive'" (*Worcester Rev.* 10, i:32–41). Both poets share a "mutual concern with a return to source and the search for some kind of affirmation," but they are different in the roles given to their narrators. Frost's narrative voice is a guide, an initiated "I," who maintains an almost ironic distance from the reader. Eliot's narrator is a fellow traveler who, by the end of "Little Gidding" has become one with the reader, "we" not "I." This idea of Frost's narrative voice being instructive is similar to Peters's point earlier.

Three individual readings are worth noting, too. "Robert Frost's 'The Census-Taker' and the Problem of Wilderness" by William Doreski (*TCL* 34, i:30–39) looks at the humanist philosophy that distinguishes Frost. Doreski shows how the speaker of Frost's poem establishes the human value in nature, recognizing "civilization is not the fact of inhabitation but the fact of consciousness" (p. 37). Walter Jost ("'The Lurking Frost': Poetic and Rhetoric in 'Two Tramps in Mud Time'," *AL* 60:226–40) and Darrel Abel ("'Against and With' in Robert Frost's Poetry," *CLQ* 24,iv:205–11) both look at how opposition functions in Frost. Both argue that Frost's fundamentally ambiguous and ambivalent vision shifts the emphasis of his poems from a rhetoric and structure of either-or oppositions to one of balance. Reading "Two Tramps in Mud Time," Jost is able to illustrate that "the very act of splitting wood becomes emblematic of the possibility of discriminating without dividing" (p. 232). Abel, in the other essay, reveals Frost's skill in posing dilemmas which have no single or simple resolution.

v. H.D.

Agenda's special issue for H.D.'s centenary (25, iii–iv, Autumn/Winter 1987/1988), guest-edited by Diane Collecott, provides previously unavailable H.D. pieces, reminiscences, and strong critical essays. One of the strongest is Susan Stanford Friedman's "Exile in the American Grain: H.D.'s Diaspora" (pp. 27–50). Friedman sees H.D.'s expatriatism as representative of her marginality. As an American and a woman, H.D. necessarily had to create a new poetics. Friedman sees her alienation as "fundamental to the psychodynamics of her creativity" (p. 33). Particularly interesting is her reading of *Paint It To-Day,* in which H.D. explores "the connection between the expatriate flight from home and alienation from a conventional feminine destiny." One distinctly feminine element in H.D.'s evolving poetics is her response to World War I, as Gary Burnett develops in his "H.D.'s Responses to the First World War" (pp. 54–63). Rejecting the aesthetic of destruction which modernism seems to adopt after the war, H.D. shapes a poetics based on a belief in the "absolute presence [of beauty] and on its place within a Palimpsest or matrix of all times" (p. 63).

Two of *Agenda*'s essays focus on a reconsideration of H.D.'s early Imagist poetry. In "H.D., 'Imagist'" (pp. 77–96), A. D. Moody reexamines the speakers of the poems in *Sea Garden* in light of H.D.'s comments in "Notes on Thought and Vision." Moody shows that the personae of the poems are actively engaged in discovering identity, not simply describing scenes. Moody argues that "the sort of artist they posit is one engaged in the making of a self, or of a psyche." The poet of these early poems is actually engaged in the same activity as the poet of H.D.'s epic *Helen in Egypt.* Zara Bruzzi, "H.D. and the Eleusian Landscape of English Modernism" (pp. 97–112), argues that *Sea Garden* and *The God* should be read together as "the first Modernist long poem" (p. 99). She also sees these poems as chronicling a psyche's quest for wholeness and androgyny. Bruzzi delineates H.D.'s indebtedness for theme and symbols to Balzac's *Seraphitas* and *The Homeric Hymns* and examines her use of Greece as both setting and symbol. A third essay, by Eileen Gregory, "A Myth of Margins" (pp. 113–23), also reads H.D.'s poetry, early to last, as a quest for self. Like Bruzzi, she examines H.D.'s use of Greek settings, in particular pursuing an investigation of the image of deep falling which she links to "a maternal origin of desire" and " 'virginal' wholeness."

Two noted critics reexamine *Trilogy*. Alicia Ostriker, in "The Open Poetics of H.D." (pp. 145–54), looks at H.D.'s musical strategies and form, arguing that H.D.'s technique in *Trilogy* is "a formal correlative of the poem's premise that order, beauty and meaning remain permanently present in our shattered world but not permanently obvious." Cyrena Pondrom, in "*Trilogy* and *Four Quartets*" (pp. 155–65), sees the two poems as contexts and counterparts to one another. She focuses on the image of the Lady in "Tribute to the Angels," showing how this vision of H.D.'s refutes the masculine and patriarchal images of Deity in Eliot. She makes a vital distinction between the visions of H.D. and Eliot: "God is outside or inaccessible to Eliot, approached through an enigmatic female, and inside H.D., where she is discovered through images of female self-affirmation" (p. 164).

"The Forging of H.D." by Gloria Fromm (*Poetry* 153:160–72) argues against the biographical approach of some feminist criticism. Fromm accuses some critics of using H.D. to "rearrange the past . . . to accommodate present political views and social goals" and suggests that studies of H.D. the person/persona dominate H.D. criticism to the detriment of valuing her poetry. The essay raises a critical question about how much is appropriated by various critical approaches. Still, after the essays in *Agenda*, many of which effectively use biography for context, this essay is less than totally persuasive.

A few other essays should be noted as helpful this year. Paul Smith's "An End to Torment: H.D.'s Metonymic Course" (in *Faith of a (Woman) Writer*, ed. Alice Kessler-Harris and William McBrien (Greenwood, pp. 273–78) suggests that H.D.'s use of metonymy in *End to Torment* is a feminist strategy to represent Lacan's realm of desire and stands in opposition to the metaphor, a strategy Smith cites as a dominant linguistic mode of patriarchy. Although interesting, the argument is more suggested than developed. Both Gary Burnett, "H.D. and Lawrence: Two Allusions" (*HDN* 1, i:32–35), and David Roessel, "H.D. and Lawrence: Two More Allusions" (*HDN* 1, ii:46–50), show the intertextual connections between the two authors in both their fiction and poetry, again pointing to the conscious dialogue H.D. maintained with her male contemporaries. Additional articles in *HDN* provide biographical background and reminiscences, contexts, and updates of bibliographies and library collections. Continuing graduate student interest is evidenced in two dissertations this year.

vi. Adams, Crapsey, Loy, Millay, Miller, Wylie

Leonie Adams's death this year generated two essays in *The New Criterion* (7, ii), which may be the start of a reevaluation of her career and works. Wallace Fowlie reminisces about Adams as a colleague and teacher ("Remembering Leonie Adams," pp. 16–20), while Bruce Bawer laments that she is overlooked, omitted, and underappreciated by current critics ("Leonie Adams, Poet," pp. 21–26). Bawer notes her affinities with the Metaphysical poets and suggests that her reputation may have suffered because of critical attitudes toward the limitation of the lyric form. His assessment encourages further criticism on Adams: "Adams's poetry is notable at once for its extremely narrow range . . . and for the impressive (if not quite perfect) command that Adams exercises" (p. 22).

Karen Alkalay-Gut's biography of Adelaide Crapsey, *Alone in the Dawn* (Georgia), charts the problems attendant on a woman, without financial or emotional independence from family, fulfilling her goal as poet. Alkaly-Gut's final chapter, "The Urn," provides the most comprehensive look at Crapsey's theory of poetry and her poetry I've ever seen.

Jean Gould's "Edna St. Vincent Millay—Saint of the Modern Sonnet" (*Faith of a (Woman) Writer*, 129–42) combines biographical contexts with reassessment. Gould praises Millay as the finest practitioner of the modern sonnet form, looking at the alterations she makes in language and feeling. She locates the source of Millay's inspiration in her love for Arthur Davison Ficke. Gould's is one of several works this year which suggest that a re-evaluation of forms (such as lyric or sonnet) is necessary for cogent re-evaluations of women poets.

Anna Shannon Elfenbein and Terence Allan Hoagwood continue with this call for reassessment by arguing that readers and critics have failed to see Wylie's "Wild Peaches" as a conscious and ironic revision of the traditional pastoral love-idyll ("'Wild Peaches': Landscapes of Desire and Deprivation," *WS* 15:387–97). They make a convincing case that Wylie's four-sonnet sequence is a protest against conventional amatory poetry which "enacts formally, narratively, and emotively . . . a story of suppression, constraint, conflict, and violence between the sexes" (p. 388).

Understanding feminine use of satire and irony is also urged by Zita Dresner in "Heterodite Humor," (*JAC* 10, iii:33–38). Dresner examines how Alice Duer Miller's *Are Women People?* and *Women Are People!* use satiric verse to comment on male-female roles and suffrage. Dresner also notes the usefulness of feminine community, in the form of the Heterodoxy Club, for the development of this type of verse challenge to social and intellectual norms.

Melita Schaum looks at Mina Loy and reappraises the "female autobiographical epic," showing that women's forms and themes in modernist poetry are poetic responses "very much *in* [their] time" ("'Moon-flowers Out of Muck': Mina Loy and the Female Autobiographical Epic," (*MSE* 10, iv:254–76). Schaum argues effectively that female epics in the 1920s and 1930s are a subgenre undervalued because they offer "resistance to the constrictions of culture and canon," speaking instead from particular economic, political, and gender experiences (p. 256). Her reading of *Anglo-Mongrels and the Rose* is fascinating.

vii. Tate, Ransom, Jeffers, MacLeish

The editors of the *Southern Review* have produced a book looking at the founding, philosophy, and historic place of the journal, in celebration of its fiftieth anniversary, The Southern Review *and Modern Literature 1935–1985* (*LSU*). Containing an essay on the journal's origin, by Cleanth Brooks and Robert Penn Warren, and a transcription of the 1935 Baton Rouge conference on southern literature, the book reemphasizes the importance of the *Southern Review* in studies of American modernism and New Criticism. Not the least important point is its attraction of writers such as Ransom and Tate.

The complex relationship between New Criticism and Ransom is made clearer in Kieran Quinlan's essay on T. S. Eliot's and John Crowe Ransom's philosophical and religious differences and the resultant effect of these differences on their poetry and criticism ("Sacred Eliot, Secular Ransom: Dead Opposites," *KR* 10, iv:1–14). Particularly good is the discussion of the more secular Ransom's critique of Eliot in *The New Criticism* and his late affinity for the views of Wallace Stevens.

The two essays on Tate are studies in the limitations of his fiction and poetry. C. Barry Chabot examines the end of Tate's Agrarian phase by reading *The Fathers* and the character of George Posey as Tate's illustrations that "tradition cannot be reclaimed through individual acts of will" ("Allen Tate and the Limits of Tradition," *SoQ* 26, iii:50–66). George Core reviews Tate's career, seeing in both his poetry and prose a failed search for authority and sustained voice. Committed to being a man of letters, there is nonetheless an imbalance between the quality and quantity of Tate's criticism and poetry. Core's final assessment is that Tate "never experienced the sustained burst of creativity that makes a major joet" ("Mr. Tate and the Limits of Poetry," *VQR* 62, i:105–14).

William Everson's *The Excesses of God* (Stanford) investigates Robinson Jeffers in light of Rudolf Otto's *The Idea of the Holy.* Everson ignores the philosophical content and formal poetic elements of Jeffers in order to show Jeffers's mysticism and religious attitude. Everson calls the book "a venture in classification: an attempt to determine the character of a writer" (p. 167). Since his subject is Jeffers's disposition, much of Everson's discussion is a personal meditation on how Jeffers fits in a religious tradition of awesome wonder at God and creation. Although Everson provides numerous passages of Jeffers for the reader, there is little concrete or academic explication offered. He does point out an interesting reason for Jeffers's unpopularity: since he discovers early and retains his religious stance, Jeffers runs into "a very grave aesthetic charge: the failure to change" (p. 50). A slightly variant reason for critical disfavor is offered in Scott B. Stevens's "Robinson Jeffers: Recovering a Spiritual Legacy" (*RJN* 72:23–29). Stevens also calls Jeffers a mystic and notes that "it was his continual repudiation of the humanistic aesthetic that disturbed critics."

Three other essays provide other reappraisals of Jeffers. Paula Huston, "The Beauty of Vultures: The Relevance of Robinson Jeffers' Poetry in the Modern Age" (*RJN* 71:18–22), argues that Jeffers's stark philosophy and confrontation with death in his poems are part of his "concept of creative destruction" and help him to develop a sense of perspective and peace in an inhuman world. Jean Kellogg Dickie, "Robinson Jeffers and the Quality of Things" (*RJN* 71:23–29), praises his realism while also noting "the metaphysical and abstract qualities of these same things" (p. 23). She also compares him to two painters (Fernand Léger and John Muir) and another poet

(Robert Frost), who have similar senses of the connectedness between appearance and moral reality. Patrick D. Murphy shows how a similar attitude may link Jeffers to Ursula K. LeGuin ("Robinson Jeffers's Influence on Ursula K. LeGuin," *RJN* 72:20–22). In particular, he looks at the symbol of the stone in LeGuin's *Always Coming Home*, seeing it represent for her as well as Jeffers an "ancient lasting world in which we participate."

On a more practical note, Tim Hunt looks at how multiple versions of Jeffers's typescripts present problems for the Jeffers scholar. As he shows in his analysis of typescripts of "To the Rock That Will Be a Cornerstone of the House," "we have been left, in most cases, with two versions of poems, each textually inadequate" ("A Typescript Is a Typescript Is a Typescript (Or Is It?)," *RJN* 74:5).

Finally, *Pembroke Magazine* published a special volume (no. 7) on Archibald MacLeish. The majority of the articles are appreciative memoirs of MacLeish as public servant, teacher, dramatist, and poet. Five essays are especially noteworthy. Barry Wallenstein's "Poetry and Experience: A Re-evaluation" (pp. 57–64) examines *Poetry and Opinion* and *Poetry and Experience* to determine MacLeish's attitude toward art and criticism. A public man, MacLeish is Arnoldian in his linking of aesthetic and moral judgments. Sanford J. Smoller continues the investigation of MacLeish as a sociopolitical poet. He sees *The Hamlet of Archibald MacLeish* as a turning point after which MacLeish is able to move beyond individuals to a larger social awareness; Smoller links him to the muckrakers and Whitman ("Escape from the Shadow of Hamlet: Archibald MacLeish's Social and Political Writings," pp. 11–17). Philip Gardner, "'Rediscovery Would Have Its Fitness': Archibald MacLeish's Poetry" (pp. 132–46), sees MacLeish from 1928 to 1948 trying to present his image of America and the American experience. Gardner identifies motifs of search and discovery as essential to MacLeish's American vision and traces his evolution from *Conquistador* to *Colloquy for the States*. Two final pieces are transcripts of talks by and with MacLeish. "MacLeish Speaks to the Players" (pp. 78–87) discusses the role of Sarah in *J.B.* and explains the final conflict between justice and love at the end of the play. MacLeish makes the fascinating distinction that "the point is not that Job *gets* it all back. The point is that he *takes* it back." Stanley Koehler's "Conversation with A. MacLeish" (pp. 95–108) includes comments by MacLeish on the role of women, his contemporaries, his definition of modern, and the role of myth in poetry.

viii. Robinson, Masters, Lindsay, Sandburg, Crane, Cummings

Edwin Arlington Robinson (Chelsea), ed. Harold Bloom, is part of the Modern Critical Views series. This volume contains nine essays in addition to Bloom's introduction. Several (Bloom, Winters, Waggoner) study Robinson's links to Emerson. Pearce and Miles look at Robinson's themes of failure and nostalgia, while Donoghue and Starr look at his use of myths. A very interesting case of poetic affiliation is reflected in Howe's and Dickey's essays. Howe argues that Robinson's lyrics influenced Dickey, Lowell, and Wright. This belief is reinforced by Dickey's appreciative essays on Robinson. In all, this is a strong collection of essays.

K. Narayana Chandran looks at myth differently in Masters's *Spoon River* ("Revolt from the Grave," *MQ* 29:438–47). Chandran sees the anthology as reversing "all the premises of the country town myth . . . to build a counter-myth of an abhorrent small town community." Spoon River becomes a community that has failed its citizens, a part of the American dream and mythology that has failed. Vachel Lindsay, meanwhile, strives throughout his career to establish the validity of American myths, dreams, and heroes. Stanley Wertheim shows that Lindsay is part of the bardic tradition, a writer of public poetry where "form is subordinated to social utility and mass appeal is more important than aesthetics" ("Vachel Lindsay's American Dream," *CLQ* 37, iii:13–24). His discussion of Lindsay's use of Lincoln, Bryan, and Altgeld as American heroes is good.

Work on Sandburg this year consists of a biography (North Callahan's *Carl Sandburg: His Life and Works*, Penn. State) and a memoir (Helga Sandburg's "Eyeing the World with All Delight," *JISHS* 81, ii:82–94). Callahan's "Chapter 7: The Poetry" (pp. 80–103) presents a synopsis of the critical responses to Sandburg's poetry, but does almost no appraising or reading of the poems themselves. Sandburg's reminiscence is personal and likewise not critically instructive.

Hart Crane scholarship is most active this year on the graduate school level. Crane is the subject of three dissertations, a number matched only by those on Wallace Stevens. The only critical essay published this year is James Longenbach's "Hart Crane and T. S. Eliot: Poets in the Sacred Grove" (*DQ* 23, 1:82–103). Longenbach argues that Crane's critical reputation has been a victim of debates between the New Humanists and the New Critics. *The Bridge* is, according to Longenbach, more consistent, more logical, and more originally visionary than *The Waste Land.* Longenbach asks that the relationship between the two poets be revised in light of their chronologies, without the critical biases of their own time.

A final two essays on E. E. Cummings focus on his awareness and use of language as a political tool. Philip Gerber ("E. E. Cummings's Season of the Censor," *ConL* 29, ii:177–200) shows how Cummings's fear of censorship led him to avoid sexually explicit language and to develop imagery and euphemisms to discuss erotic themes and ideas in his poems. Kristiaan Versluys ("'the season 'tis, my lovely lambs': E. E. Cummings' Quarrel with the Language of Politics," *American Literature in Belgium*, ed. Gilbert Debusscher [Rodopi], 77–88) examines Cummings's poem, showing how his use of ironic language and persona mock uncritical readers who, like the persona, are taken in by rhetoric. Versluys convincingly demonstrates that the poet's voice "works as in interlinear gloss . . . an implicit running commentary laying bare what the speaker would like to cover up."

Montana State University

17. Poetry: The 1940s to the Present

Richard J. Calhoun

The critical mills still grind out informative articles on Robert Lowell, John Ashbery, A. R. Ammons, W. S. Merwin, Elizabeth Bishop. This is not unexpected. The reexamination of Sylvia Plath continues unabated. Because of the power of the last poems, she is becoming more and more accepted as a major poet. There are surprises, such as a lean critical year for James Merrill and Galway Kinnell after significant work last year. The major surprise is the abundance of work on Anne Sexton. Her admirers are attempting to make her much more than a confessional poet. For the middle generation poets, who still provoke much interest, this is the year of John Berryman. The cultural balance between two friends and rivals—Lowell and Berryman—is being readjusted. Lowell is the major poet, but Berryman has gained.

i. Overview

The overview this year is the chapter on recent poetry in the *Columbia Literary History of the United States* (Columbia), ed. Emory Elliott, the first multiauthored history of American literature since the *Literary History of the United States* 40 years ago. When I purchased *LHUS* as a graduate student to help me pass my Ph.D. orals, I hardly needed much help on contemporary poetry since it was seldom taught and rarely asked about. In my one-volume first edition there was only one 23-page chapter, written by F. O. Matthiesen, simply designated "poetry," but a more descriptive title might have been "Eliot and company." William Carlos Williams and E. E. Cummings were brusquely noticed. A postmodernist revolt was not even dreamed. In *CLHUS* the chapter on contemporary poetry is scarcely longer, again titled "Poetry"; but it exhibits the good sense of one of the most knowledgeable writers on contemporary poetry, a former editor of this chapter, James Breslin.

Breslin begins "Poetry" (pp. 1079–1101) with the poets we knew in the 50s as the "middle-generation," three of whom had achieved literary fame by then—John Berryman, Randall Jarrell, and Robert Lowell. The complacency of F. O. Matthiessen about the homogeneity of modern poetry lasted another 10 years as evidenced by a quotation from an essay Delmore Schwartz wrote in 1958, "The Present State of Poetry," documenting that poet's view of how genteel and complacent modern poetry had become. Schwartz seemed unaware that all hell was about to break loose. Breslin finds this same complacency in the early poetry of the next generation of poets after the middle generation—James Merrill, W. S. Merwin, Adrienne Rich, Peter Viereck, Richard Wilbur. At first, they regarded themselves as "New Formalists" completing the modernist revolution, not realizing that by returning to tradition they were undermining modernism. Completely overlooked by Delmore Schwartz in 1958 were private underground movements like Charles Olson's "Projective Verse" manifesto and the work of his students at Black Mountain, who desired changes in a Western writing that had become too gentrified, civilized, and logical. Then there was the much more public revolt by the Beat Poets, who had the advantage of being political and physiological as well as mystical. Soon to become publicly known were the confessional poets—Berryman, Lowell, W. D. Snodgrass, Sylvia Plath, and Anne Sexton—who shed the New Critical doctrine of a poetic mask and soon found that opening up the self in their poetry also required the opening up of form. Unlike the Beats, they had a lasting effect on contemporary poetry. Somewhat later, influenced by all of these movements but turning introspectively toward the deep images of the subconscious were the "deep image poets"—Robert Bly, W. S. Merwin, Louis Simpson, and James Wright.

Breslin's essay, which I have paraphrased in part, is orthodox, traditional—well said. It is scrupulous as literary history, more descriptive than evaluative. Verification of what is important is determined more by space allowed than by judgments made. The "deep image poets" are obviously important in Breslin's scheme of things as are the New York School—John Ashbery, Kenneth Koch, Frank O'Hara—the poets who have produced the most boldly experimental poetry of the period. Breslin's narrative finds confessionalism dominant in the 60s; deep image surrealism commanding in the 70s; the autobiographical lyric, new language poetry, and a new formalism attracting attention without dominance in the 80s. Like Matthiessen's account 40 years before, this is both a consensus and an establishment view, to be expected in standard histories. Breslin's essay is not only a good synopsis of the frame of mind of criticism in 1988 but a reminder that there is a criticism by omission. He omits some good poets who fall through the cracks between acknowledged schools of poetry. Richard Wilbur is only a name; and James Dickey is not remembered at all, two poets thought in the 50s and 60s to be writing some of our best poetry. Karl Shapiro, whom we thought a leader against the Eliot establishment, is only a name; and Howard Nemerov, recently Library of Congress consultant and poet laureate, is not mentioned in this history. Any glimpse of future directions is foreshortened because the history ends with John Ashbery, not reaching far into the 70s or venturing into the poets of the 80s at all. Nevertheless, for what it does include this is a valuable essay.

The second most inclusive overview of contemporary American poetry this year is Richard Jackson's *The Dismantling of Time in Contemporary Poetry* (Alabama). That contemporary poets have been preoccupied and have had problems with time is hardly news. A study of how six significant poets—Robert Penn Warren, John Hollander, James Wright, Denise Levertov, John Ashbery, and Charles Simic, dismantle time and then restructure it to serve their poetry is different, because, except for Warren, the poets are new. Jackson is most instructive on Hollander and Simic; least so on Warren and Ashbery. He observes that in their respective restructurings of time Simic uses a mythological context; Robert Penn Warren turns to philosophy; Ashbery, with his language sophistication, moves to deconstructionism; Denise Levertov goes to political and social forces. None of these poets manages to re-create the past; the best they can do is to restructure their experience of it. Jackson has written a difficult but often rewarding study based on a careful reading of all the proper influences on time-obsessed modern writers—Heidegger, Kierkegaard, Husserl, and Bergson. Disappointingly, there is no concluding chapter to determine the importance of what he has shown about individual poets to contemporary poetry.

For general interest and background only, I would call attention to James L. W. West's *American Authors and the Literary Marketplace Since 1900* (Penn.), a study of the tensions between art as craft and publishing as business. West has brought up to the 20th century

William Charvat's definitive research on literary publishing in America in the 19th century.

Burton Raffel's *The Art of Translating Poetry* (Penn. State) is an excellent study of the difficulties of bridging gaps between languages and literary traditions through translations. What interests me is that under types of translations he includes the "imitative," important to many contemporary poets, including Robert Lowell, his exemplar of this kind of work. It is useful to be reminded that "imitations" were in vogue in the 1960s.

Ronald E. McFarland's *The Villannelle: The Evolution of a Poetic Form* (Idaho) traces the form from its origin in 16th-century Italian poetry to its use by James Merrill today. His book is also an anthology, including 33 contemporary villanelles to demonstrate that the form is alive and well in this century. I merely record Helen Vendler's *The Music of What Happens: Poems, Poets, Critics* (Harvard), reprints of her previously published book reviews, in order to observe from her early work this important critic's lack of sympathy for experimental or open form poets and her doubts about Anne Sexton or Sylvia Plath as not judgments recently arrived at. Otherwise, she has had a sustained interest in the poetry of A. R. Ammons.

Gregory Woods, *Articulate Flesh: Male Homo-eroticism and Modern Poetry* (Yale), contends that homoeroticism is central to the male tradition in poetry. He identifies and discusses homoerotic themes that have been used by modern poets. He writes on D. H. Lawrence, Hart Crane, W. H. Auden, but only on Thom Gunn and Allen Ginsberg among recent poets. What he says about Ginsberg is less new even than what he says about Auden, for instance. To make his point more convincingly, Woods needs more on contemporary poets.

One of the most interesting recent books is Norman Finkelstein's *The Utopian Moment in Contemporary American Poetry* (Bucknell), written from a Marxist perspective. The term "utopian moment" has different meanings in his book, but his most useful definition is "something that moves above and beyond the ideology of a particular age." He divides poets that can be connected with this concept into those who use "interiorizing and exteriorizing discourses." Among contemporary poets, he discusses Zukofsky, Oppen, the New York School of Ashbery and O'Hara as "poets of process," the San Francisco Renaissance with insightful treatment of Jack Spicer. His final chapter deals with contemporary poet William Bronk, who has produced some of the clearest examples of utopian moments in his preoccupation with "the theme of the self in time."

I should call attention to one festschrift of note, Vereen Bell and Laurence Lerner, eds., *On Modern Poetry: Essays Presented to Donald Davie* (Vanderbilt), for its essays by Robert von Hallberg and Helen Vendler. There is no overall theme.

Not everything this year is devoted to thematics. Robert Frank and Henry Sayre's *The Line in Postmodern Poetry* (Illinois) contains speculations about current possibilities for the free verse line from "leading authorities on postmodern poetry." The right questions are asked—whether the poem organically or historical and cultural forces determine the poetic line; whether free verse is still viable or become merely a part of the poet's repertoire of effects; whether an ascendancy of free verse is part of our culture's acquiescence to a loss of authority. Only one essay is devoted to an analysis of the practice of a single contemporary poet and deserves mention here, Mary Ann Caw's "Strong-Line Poetry: Ashbery's Dark Edging and the Lines of Self" (pp. 51–59). The other essays are theoretical and technical. Even more theoretical and technical than these is Joseph Riddel's "The Anomalies of Literary (Post) Modernism" (*ArQ* 44:81–118). I can mention here only Riddel's close reading of Charles Olson as central in theory and poetry to postmodernism as Eliot was to modernism. There is a detailed analysis of Olson's "The Kingfishers" as an exemplar of postmodernism.

The last two years I have found articles in the *New York Quarterly* series on "The Present State of American Poetry" useful for an overview. In "On Maintaining Artistic Integrity Within a Decadent System" (*NYQ* 35:115–21), the ninth in the series, H. L. Nix agrees that the American poetry system is now "largely decadent" but denies that only poetry written outside the system can be good. He disagrees with previous contributors who seemed to imply that criticism must reverse the system by making the alternative poetry "good" and establishment poetry "bad." Poets must not let the establishment tell them what to think. Rather than overthrow the system they must simply not be corrupted by it. The tenth in the series, Will Inman, "Time for New Synthesis" (*NYQ* 36:109–19), calls for a break with all "narrow ilks and faiths and causes" and for writing only from an individual perspective by poets who will "refuse to substitute jargon for organic spiritual metamorphosis." He warns against "deadly MFA programs" and names the few little magazines that encourage new voices. The problem is that the individual voices are just the poets who are omitted from histories and overall assessments of poetry. The two contributions this year suggest that this series has run out of steam.

ii. The Middle Generation and Contemporaries

***a.* Roethke.** Nineteen eighty-eight was a lean year for Roethke criticism. There is Wittgenstein applied to Roethke in Daniel James Sundahl's "Theodore Roethke's 'The Lost Son' Solipsism and the Private Language Problem" (*EAS* 17:41–61). Sundahl contributes to the current downplaying of confessional poetry in a rereading of Roethke's "The Lost Son." He focuses on the problem of solipsism and private language as contrasted with non-egocentricism in public language. The elementary error critics have made is not separating the persona from the poet himself. " 'The Lost Son' is half visual experience and half thinking." Sundahl draws on Wittgenstein's interest in the sensational properties of seeing and noticing and the consequent question of whether they are the same as thinking. The reader of Roethke's poem should be aware that when the solipsist becomes aware of his "I," he simultaneously becomes aware of all that is not his "I." Sundahl's conclusion is that "Roethke offers here a Wittgenstein version . . . It is the negative 'not-I' replaced by the positive 'I-Thou.' " The case that Sundahl makes is worth making, and his careful reading of all six sections of the poem is worth having; but jargon makes the reading almost unbearable. John Rohrkemper revisits Theodore Roethke's posthumously published poems of the "North American Sequence" (*CP* 21:i, 28–37) as the poems in which Roethke was most able "to disassociate his poetry from his pathology, to transform childhood trauma into a meditative vision of life's wholeness." The memories that made this possible were "rooted most firmly in his birthplace, Saginaw, Michigan," revisited as "a child's Eden." Eden ended when Roethke was 14, with an argument between his father and his uncle resulting in the selling of the greenhouse and with the death of his father from cancer. The difficulty for Roethke became how to summon those images for his poetry. One method was mining the memory through dream, "by symbiotically linking memory, dream, psychosis, and perhaps therapy," with Roethke even thinking of himself as "an Aeolian harp, through which an ill wind, a necessarily destructive gale, must blow." He found life increasingly difficult, but he was able to gain control of his creative life by "associating the dream state with his illness and memory with the creative shaping power of the artist." He began the "North American Sequence" determined to use memory not as dream or psychosis but as meditation, influenced by Whitman and the catalog of American sounds that memory unlocked.

***b.* Lowell, Berryman.** Katharine Wallingford's *Robert Lowell's Language of the Self* (No. Car.) is a step away from the usual stress on the confessional, sensational, and pathological in Lowell to a consideration of his poetry as serious self-examination using methods in common with psychotherapy, particularly with Freudian analysis. Wallingford admits that Lowell did not get around to serious reading of Freud until the early 1950s and that he was never actually under Freudian analysis. Wallingford contends that Lowell's later poetry makes use of such analytical techniques as "free association, repetition or 'working-through,' deliberate concentration on the relation between the poet and the 'other' to whom he addresses himself, and the use of memory to probe the past." For Lowell all this was just an extension of his Puritan heritage of conducting the search for truth within the self. This approach to Lowell is not new since Alan Williamson had used some of it before in *Pity the Monsters* (*ALS 1974*, pp. 360–61), even corresponding with Lowell about it. What is of value in this new study is that the method leads to useful readings of individual poems. The division of the book into chapters on association, repetition, relation, memory causes some difficulties in contending with any sense of Lowell's development.

Jeffrey Myers continues to be one of our most understanding critics of troubled writers. His latest book is a collection of interviews with and memoirs of Lowell. I am reminded of a similar volume some years ago on Randall Jarrell, of which Lowell was one of the editors—Robert Lowell, Peter Taylor, and Robert Penn Warren, eds., *Randall Jarrell, 1964–65* (Farrar). Though all items are reprints, Myers's book, like Lowell's on Jarrell, is a valuable resource from those who knew Lowell well enough to exhibit other sides to his personality than the near monster emerging from Ian Hamilton's biography. Myers believes that his collection discloses "a sophisticated, urbane, learned and allusive mind." The value of the book is its inclusiveness; interviews of every possible kind; memories before and after Lowell's death, including the *Harvard Advocate* memorial issue; impressions favorable and unfavorable. The most penetrating of these items,

Myers acknowledges, are those by his poet and critic peers—Seamus Heaney, Stanley Kunitz, Robert Fitzgerald, Helen Vendler. The value of the collection is enhanced by what is new—Myers's own incisive comments in his introduction on the value of what he has included.

The main distinction of Philip Hobsbaum, *A Reader's Guide to Robert Lowell* (Thames), is that it makes a case for neglected works, *The Mills of the Kavanaughs* (1951) and *Imitations* (1961), and the disappointment is that it adds little new on the more acclaimed books. Hobsbaum is especially informative on Lowell's sources. This is an eccentric book, in which a critic does not like the books most critics do and likes those most do not like without bothering to make enough of a case for his own unorthodox views.

Among the middle-generation poets this is a year for John Berryman, with three books published in 1988. The first of these is a memoir, *John Berryman and the Thirties* (Mass.), by E. M. Halliday, who was closely associated with Berryman from 1933 to 1943, when both were in their twenties. It is based on Berryman's letters to Halliday as well as reminiscences. Halliday justifies his memoir because during these years, long before the day of confessional poetry, Berryman was less revealing in his poetry of his personal life. He is able to document the influence of the young Bhain Campbell, who died at the age of 29, on Berryman's poetic consciousness. The memoir is not without revelations of the dark side of Berryman's personality, but its charm is that it gives us a lighter, more zestful Berryman. The fame and the accompanying alcoholism and disintegration Halliday missed, as he and Berryman by then had long gone their separate ways.

The subtitle of the book edited by Harry Thomas, *Reflections on the Poetry*, is more descriptive than the actual title *Berryman's Understanding* (Northeastern). It is a collection of interviews, memories, and comments on the poetry, all previously published. Thomas especially values the essays by John Bayley, Denis Donoghue, and William Wasserstrom on the *Dream Songs* as providing insights into the relationship of the persona, Henry, and the poet, Berryman. These are valuable essays, as is Robert Pinsky's discussion of Berryman's language, excerpted from his book, *The Situation of Poetry*. I would single out William Meredith's "In Loving Memory of the Late Author of the Dream Song" as addendum to Halliday's account. It is not policy to discuss previously printed essays, but I can recommend this as the best collection of essays on the man and on the poetry.

The third book is a short one, Stephen Matterson's *Berryman and*

Lowell: The Art of Losing (Barnes and Noble). *The Art of Losing* is a comparison of two poets from mother-dominated families who had difficulties with father figures. Both succeeded for a time by being concerned with loss and losing as themes in their poems while also pursuing order in whatever form they could find it. Their concern with loss leads them to a search for an appropriate poetics, "a rhetoric of destitution" Lowell called it. Matterson discusses the strategies each poet employed, most successfully for Lowell in *Life Studies* and for Berryman in *Dream Songs.* Afterward both poets lost control of the poetics they had found. Berryman abandoned memory in his poetry; Lowell became helplessly possessed by it.

There is actually a fourth book out on Berryman, not criticism, but an important volume of primary material, Richard J. Kelly's *We Dream of Honour: John Berryman's Letters to His Mother* (Norton). Berryman was a prolific letter writer. This selection of 228 of some 7,000 letters demonstrates his skill in prose, wittily and engagingly discussing literary as well as personal matters. It reveals much about his personal life and a bit less about his poetry. The edition is well edited and finely glossed. There should be obvious comparisons with two other recent publications of interest, Randall Jarrell's letters in 1986, and Delmore Schwartz's in 1985.

This Berryman year also includes an article by Paul Mariani, " 'My Heavy Daughter': John Berryman and the Making of *The Dream Songs*" (*KR* n.s. 10, iii:1–30), an excerpt from his forthcoming life of John Berryman in which Mariani charts Berryman's life during 1962, the year he made his major effort in completing *The Dream Songs.* It is an account of a man progressively living a life in disorder and of a poet desperately trying to find order. Berryman taught unhappily at Minnesota during the academic year and maniacally that summer at Bread Loaf, often drinking a quart of gin and writing in the afternoon, reflecting on the death of Faulkner. On Labor Day he listed all the themes he could find for his new poems: "Freedom, Law, Death (plenty of that), paranoia, terror . . . Love and (in Henry's case) Lust and finally the imponderables. . . ." These themes, Mariani finds, "interknit like the constituents of a DNA molecule." Through his persona, Berryman discovered his equivalent of the voice Whitman used to communicate to his reader in "Song of Myself," "a distinctive and unstopped human voice laughing and weeping in the same, shuddering breath." The poems he wrote scarred over the wound he had felt from his father's suicide. As the New Year approached, Berryman came back to his obsession with his father's ghost. He still could not understand what this ghost was saying. I am impressed with Mariani's work, not just with what he says, but with how well he says it. I anticipate the longer work.

Jeffrey Alan Triggs, "Dream Songs and Nightmare Songs: The Balance of Style in the Later Poems of John Berryman" (*SDR* 26: ii, 57–70), finds the strength of Berryman's poetry not in his poses, or in his "losing," but in his style. In his last poems, living on the cutting edge, Berryman managed a style requiring a perilous balance he could not maintain—a balance between the grotesque and elegant, literary and colloquial styles, elegant wit and clownish lust, objective statement and anguished confession, Berryman's voice and Henry's. This is an interesting essay, but the point sometimes is obscured by explicatory detail. By the time he wrote *His Toy, His Dream, His Rest*, Berryman had lost the balance that Henry's voice had allowed. In Triggs's judgment except for the success of *Dream Songs* Berryman was otherwise a brilliant but flawed poet.

c. **Contemporaries.** This year Karl Shapiro received notice only in Robert Richman's recapitulation in a review-essay of *New and Selected Poems*, 1940–1986, "The Trials of a Poet (*NewC*: 6, vii, 74–81). I mention this as the kind of reexamination that is timely. Richman competently provides "an outline of the twists and turns" of Shapiro's career from the early influence of an Auden who had abandoned the "deliberate difficulty of modernism" through his first anti-intellectual essay, *Essay on Rime*, celebrating Whitman, Lawrence, and Williams; his discovery of his Jewish identity in *Recapitulations* and *Poems of a Jew*; his attack on modernism in *In Defense of Ignorance*; his own final turn from his master Auden to his own ironic version of Beat poetry in *The Bourgeoise Poet*; his decision to distance himself from counterculture in *To Abolish Children*; then his coming full circle back to Auden in his most recent poems, as evidenced by "At Auden's Grave." This is a good brief survey of the contours of the career of a poet whose war poetry along with Randall Jarrell's is the poetry we read immediately postwar—and whose attacks on Eliot were as influential as any antimodernist prose written then. Shapiro is remembered in the *Columbia History* only as a member of the "Middle Generation of Poets," the only one whose work is not discussed.

Richard Wilbur's "A Late Aubade" comes under attack in Nancy

K. Barnard, "Wilbur's 'A Late Aubade' " (*Expl* 46:iv, 37–39). Barnard takes a stance against the critical consensus that Wilbur's poem is "a love lyric" and "charming." Rather, his picture of the way a woman's mind works is trivializing and the suggestion insulting that if she must be up at all, she could bring in a snack of cheese and wine for her lover. Wilbur has obviously treated his subject too lightly for feminist tastes today.

Howard Nemerov's stint at the Library of Congress did not produce a bounty of critical articles on his poetry. The item that appeared this year, Ejner J. Jensen's "Howard Nemerov and the Tryanny of Shakespeare," (*CentR* 32:ii, 130–49), is an attempt to apply Harold Bloom's "the anxiety of influence" to Nemerov by demonstrating how "considerable" and "self-conscious" his debt to Shakespeare has been. This influence pervades his two major concerns, "how thought emerged from a world of things" and "the relation between perception and reality." Jensen reexamines several Nemerov poems to show how often he alludes to and uses Shakespeare and, consequently, must struggle with the influence or "tyranny of Shakespeare," as genius and guide. Nemerov is concerned that meaning sought by the mind will be meaning imposed by the mind. Jensen is especially instructive about the influence of *Hamlet*, which for Nemerov presents a "paradigm of the function of great art."

iii. The Poetry of Women

***a.* Bishop, Rich, Levertov.** Robert Dale Parker's *The Unbeliever: The Poetry of Elizabeth Bishop* (Illinois) continues the evaluation of Bishop's poetry that has been taking place in the decade since her death. Parker connects her poetry to her own troubled family background, to her concern with gender, and to an anxiety about creativity common among writers of her own time. He wants to do for Bishop's reputation "something akin to what Lionel Trilling did for Robert Frost," reveal "the terror behind the apparently light-hearted imagery." He finds in her poetry an anxiety "about sexuality, politics, the burdens of imagination, the fate of the self." In exploring Bishop's struggles with these anxieties Parker finds three stages in her poetic career—poems of wish, poems of where, and poems of retrospect. Each of these stages is dominated by her attitude of an unbeliever. This is a good study, worth reading for its overview of this important poet and for some new insights into major poems, though it may not quite establish a canon of terrifying poems. Perhaps the greatest value lies in the explications of her less-examined poems. Thomas J. Travisano, *Elizabeth Bishop: Her Artistic Development* (Virginia), attempts to locate Bishop's rightful place among her contemporaries—Lowell, Berryman, Jarrell, who admired her work. He discloses the span of her 30-year career from *North and South* (1946) through *Geography III* (1976). He divides Bishop's career into three phases, "Prisons," the exploration of imaginary worlds; "Travel," actual places and people; and "History," exploration of private and public experience with a new openness. He convincingly demonstrates a movement from introspective poems to more public poems as she found an accessible voice. Finally, Bishop's "Anaphora" is revisited in Chanita Goodblatt's "Bishop's 'Anaphora'" *Expl* (46:iii, 40). This is an attempt to show how Bishop uses Satan's plunge from Heaven as an image of the day's route from sunrise to sunset and as a metaphor for "man's fall out of the celestial grace." Mention of Bishop's use of anaphora throughout the poem and discussion of the use of "classic poetic form," two 14-line stanzas, are also included in an explication that is not quite concerted. Brian C. Avery, "Bishop's 'The Colder the Air'" (Expl 46: iv, 35–37), finds the key to the description of the woman's femininity not so much the reference to her as "huntress," but the suggestion that she is a thermometer, with the colder setting preferable. In her role as the Diana goddess she will not rule forever. The clock marking time will return to supremacy with the changing seasons. Victoria Harrison, "Recording a Life: Elizabeth Bishop's letters to Ilse and Kit Barker" (*ConL* 29:498–517), discusses Bishop's correspondence with English friends to whom she could reveal much about both her "exile" in Brazil and the early days in Nova Scotia, two places essential to her poetry.

Volumes in the Poetry and Critics series appear irregularly. The latest is Craig Werner's *Adrienne Rich: The Poet and Her Critics* (ALA), an annotated bibliography in essay form. A contributor to *ALS* can hardly fault the potential value of this format. I am pleased that this particular volume departs from the usual form a bit more than previous volumes by a focus on the poetry and not just on criticism. Werner also devotes more time to his overview of Rich, on such subjects of her poetry as patriarchy, lesbianism, political radicalism. He even offers a thesis of his own, with some support from other critics. Rich is "not simply a feminist Whitman." She has other poetic ancestors, including Yeats, Dickinson, and a sometimes kindred spirit in James Baldwin—and even a consistent target to attack—T. S. Eliot. Werner blocks out in Rich's poetry "the complexity of evasion," "the suspicion of structure," "the acceptance of processes," "embodied anger," and a final "return to the world." This book is factual and critical, managing to discuss a good many poems, making it worth a look although it is not well written enough to be pleasurable reading.

Harry Marten's *Understanding Denise Levertov* is another entry in the Understanding Poets series, published by the University of South Carolina Press. He makes a case for Levertov's importance through attempting to show that she offered an alternative to modernism both in England and in America during four decades. She has also consistently viewed the obligation of a writer as being, "to take personal and active responsibility for his words" while also knowing that the poet's special task is "to clarify . . . not answers but the existence and nature of questions." Levertov was personal before being personal was the fashion because she believed that "in order to know the world one must know oneself" and that the private consciousness and the public consciousness of the poet are interconnected. Marten's study is especially valuable for demonstrating how extensive Levertov's range is: she is seldom purely lyrical but rather combines "the lyric together with the narrative, the visionary with the reportorial, the mythical with the everyday, intense intimacies and public proclamations." It is difficult to cover so much—15 books—in 200 small-size pages, and many of Marten's explications are minimal. Still the selection of poems for illustration is solid. Marten concludes that Levertov's most recent work reveals "a new spirituality," an awareness that "there are forces larger than man which the poet can experience through the imagination." Denise Lynch's explicatory comment, "Levertov's 'An English Field in the Nuclear Age'" (*Expl* 46:4, 40–41), is another example of an attempt to cram too much into too little space. The point is made that the immediacy of this poem comes from "its balancing the subjectivity of nature with the equivalent subjectivity of mind." But Lynch also attempts to show that this poem illustrates Levertov's "organic form," a belief that "verisimilitude is elusive" and that vision must be "wrought," a task similar to "that of smelting ore in steel production." She also came to think that religious undertones overlap the private and public "dimensions of poetry." Timothy Viator, "Levertov's 'Pleasures'" (*NConL* 18, iv:2–3), attempts to show how the visual appearance of Levertov's poem and the arrangement of images (the pleasures of form) reinforce the subject (the pleasures from renewal in nature).

***b.* Sexton, Plath.** Any neglect of Anne Sexton has been redressed by a banner crop of critical reexaminations in 1988. Diana Hume George has followed up her gender biography *Oedipus Anne* (reviewed last year) with a collection of 16 essays she judges the best written on Sexton in the 70s, after Sexton's death, and in the 80s, after the publication of the *Complete Poems.* George's collection is called *Sexton: Selected Criticism* (Illinois). Added to the previously published items are new essays: Heather Cam's persuasive "'Daddy,' Sylvia Plath's Debt to Anne Sexton" (pp. 223–26); Steven E. Colburn's "The Troubled Life of the Artist" (pp. 283–302), the kind of analysis needed to rebuild Sexton's reputation through demonstrating her concerns go beyond mere confessionalism to an interest in the creative process; Stephanie Demetrakopoulos's "Goddess Manifestations as Stages in Feminine Metaphysics in the Poetry and Life of Anne Sexton" (pp. 117–44), an overelaborate analysis of the mother-daughter poems as important contributions to feminist literature; two articles by Dianne Wood Middlebrook, a chapter, "Anne Sexton at the Radcliffe Institute" (pp. 192–208) from her forthcoming biography, and "Seduction in Anne Sexton's Unpublished Play *Mercy Street*" (pp. 19–28), a biopsychoanalytical study of conflicting attitudes toward seduction and incest in her poetry; Alicia Ostriker's "Anne Sexton and the Seduction of the Audience" (pp. 3–18), the most interesting of the new pieces, an analysis of the relationship between the "you" Sexton addresses and the "I," Sexton's voice as it establishes intimacy with the reader. We are even treated to a student-reader response, Kim Krynock's "Not That It Was Beautiful" (pp. 312–16), an 80s response to a 60s poet who committed suicide in the 70s. The new essays do not equal in quantity or quality the best of the previously published ones, which include William Shurr's minority view argument for the sustained quality of the last poetry in "Mysticism and Suicide: Anne Sexton's Last Poetry" (pp. 171–96) and Estella Lauter's reading of "The Jesus Papers" (pp. 145–64), a discussion of the religious quest in Sexton's poetry. There are more good reprints than I can mention other than to say the editor has had a good eye for selecting what is valuable for making a case for Sexton. George also includes a brief overview of Sexton's canon, indicating how the inclusion of her poetry in the 60s among confessional poetry called attention to her works as a follower of Lowell. But it has kept readers from noticing that she explored far beyond the personal boundaries of confessional poetry. This is a valuable collection and the most important contribution so far to the Sexton revival.

Francis Bixler's *Original Essays on the Poetry of Anne Sexton* (Central Ark.) contributes 13 essays to the critical canon. Diane Wood Middlebrook's essay ("Anne Sexton and Robert Lowell" pp. 5–22) draws once more on her research for her biography to reveal how encouraging Anne Sexton's personal poetry was to Lowell at a time his new direction toward the personal was under attack by Allen Tate and other old friends. Lowell's reception of her poetry was restrained by his conviction that only Emily Dickinson and Elizabeth Bishop were "major as poets." Other women poets were "minor." Nevertheless, Lowell encouraged her to think of her writing as a craft, and he helped see that her writing got the attention it deserved. There is a commendable section of essays on the importance of Sexton's formalist perception of poetry as craft. Michael Burns's "Confession as Sacrament" (pp. 130–38) finds this concern evident in several of her early confessional poems. Lynette McGrath's "Anne Sexton's Poetic Connections: Death, God, and Form" (pp. 138–68) examines the connection between theme and the turn to open forms in Sexton's later poetry. Caroline King Barnard Hall, "Transformations: A Magic Mirror" (pp. 107–29), focuses on Sexton's use of transformations as a method of mirroring the ugly and beastly in herself and others. Another grouping of essays contains Jenny Goodman's "Anne Sexton's *Live or Die*: The Poem as the Opposite of Suicide" (pp. 71–80), an attempt to account for Sexton's poetics in relation to her confessional and suicidal tendencies. Brenda Ameter's "'Put Your Ear Down to Your Soul and Listen Hard': Anne Sexton's Theory and Practice of Archetypal Poetry" pp. (81–91) finds in her poetics a concept of archetypal poetry, a mode leading beyond the personal. Francis Bixler, "Anne Sexton's 'Motherly' Poetics" (pp. 92–106), focuses on the mother-daughter poems to show the importance to Sexton of creating an intimacy between speaker and reader. Three essays are concerned with the quest in Sexton's poetry. Diana Hume George, "Anne Sexton's Island God" (pp. 169–83), goes to Squirrel Island, where Sexton's family spent their summers, connecting her search for a God she could not believe in to her search there for her father and her grandfathers. Margaret Scarborough's "Anne Sexton's

Other World Journey" (pp. 184–202) explores her quest to comprehend fully what it is to be a woman. In another essay, "Journey Into the Sun: The Religious Pilgrimage of Anne Sexton" (pp. 203–42), Francis Bixler attempts to show that in her late poetry Sexton sought to maintain a balance between traditional Christian values and the new sense of selfhood she had defined in her poetry. In "'I Have Been Her Kind': Anne Sexton's Communal Voice" (pp. 22–45) Kay Ellen Merriman Capo finds a functional unity between voice and character in some of the more effective poems. Ann Marie Seward Barry's attempt, "In Praise of Anne Sexton's *The Book of Folly*: A Study of the Woman/Victim/Poet" (pp. 46–70), struggles to demonstrate a relationship between this book and Erasmus's work. This essay reinforces the impression that the essays are uneven in their accomplishments, but that the book as a whole contributes toward the rehabilitation of the reputation of the poet.

Richard E. Morton's *Anne Sexton's Poetry* (Edwin Mellen) is a further attempt to repair her reputation by correcting the view that Sexton was a talented amateur without much awareness of literary tradition and that her life was of more interest than her poetry. Morton sees her as a professional whose writing of poetry had a healing effect, who often wrote in the tradition of the conversion narrative. This thesis is rather surprising in the face of evidence that Sexton was hardly doctrinal, but Morton sees this kind of narrative as a great tradition in American literature useful as the narrative of a search for grace. He admits that it is a genre that can be only loosely defined, and he proves his point by rather loosely seeing Sexton's poetry in terms of it. Morton is also not quite able to explain how the posthumous volumes, *45 Mercy Street* (1976) and *Words for Dr. Y* (1978), ignore the "pilgrimage towards grace," and yet include powerful poems.

The most inclusive and most valuable volume of all may be Steven E. Colburn's *Anne Sexton: Telling the Tale* (Michigan). He follows the format of the series and tells the tale by including everything—memoirs, reviews, and essays, adding a chronology and a bibliography. All the Sexton specialists are included as well as major critics, Helen Vendler, Steven Axelrod, Ralph J. Mills, M. L. Rosenthal. The selections are arranged to reveal the first critical reactions to her work, then probe the period of experimentation that followed *Live or Die*, with her only foray into drama, *Mercy Street*. The final section is intended to find in Sexton's later work a return to experimenting with form and an "increasing concern with religious belief, her elaboration of a personal cosmology, and her use of eschatological content, language and tone." The collection concludes with two opposing views of the *Complete Poems*—Helen Vendler's negative case, "Malevolent Flippancy" (pp. 437–46), and Diane Wood Middlebrook's positive case, "Poet of Weird Abundance" (pp. 447–70). The point intended is that no critical consensus exists. But I would add that what has been published this year makes it easier to make a case for Sexton. Catherine Georgoudaki makes a modest contribution with ("Sexton's Poems [Spoon Images]" *Expl* 46:iii, 48–49), associating spoon images with Sexton's female persona's "physical, sexual, and mental qualities and attitudes." Three poems are examined, "Horse," "Barefoot," and "Song for a Lady," the last associating spoons with sexual love.

Last year Linda Wagner-Martin published her biography of Sylvia Plath. This year she has edited the first collection of reviews and essays on Plath, *Sylvia Plath: The Critical Heritage* (Routledge). The book has a limitation: the selections are entirely contemporaneous with the works they comment on. Nothing indicates current critical perspectives on these works. On the other hand, Wagner-Martin includes selections on everything that has been published, through the *Collected Poems* (1981) and the *Journals* (1982). Since there are 83 extracts in all, it is impossible to comment on all of them. Of special interest is the selection of comments on Plath by women writers and feminist critics. Many of these selections are not readily available elsewhere. This is not the usual gathering of scholarly and critical essays. William Pritchard poses the question that this collection is assumed to answer: is Sylvia Plath only "An Interesting Minor Poet"? (pp. 262–68). Pritchard confides that he has long endorsed this judgment. The best reasons for dissatisfaction with that judgment, the powerful last poems, are examined by Marjorie Perloff, "Sylvia Plath's *Collected Poems*" (pp. 293–303). But even her judgment is tentative, dependent on a better text than Ted Hughes has apparently permitted.

It is this case for these last poems that is the strength of Pamela J. Annas's *A Disturbance in Mirrors* (Greenwood). She makes it by stressing Plath's powerful, disturbing use of mirror images throughout her poetry but particularly in these last poems. From the isolation seen in the last poems that use the mirror image came a device for locating the place where self and world meet. At its most powerful this image can reflect an existential situation where the self seems to exist in a "circus hall of mirrors, where it is distorted, disguised, or shattered into slivers of reflection." When the self and world no longer meet, are no longer mirrored, there is loss of self—death. The power of the last poems comes from her continuing struggle to be whole in the face of this existential situation. A key to Plath's emerging feminist views is her lone radio play, *Three Women. A Disturbance in Mirrors* is perhaps the best book so far on Plath.

Mary G. De Jong's "Sylvia Plath and Sheila Ballantyne's *Imaginary Crimes*" (*SAF* 16, i:27–38) compares and contrasts the narrator-protagonist in that work with the speaker in Sylvia Plath's "Daddy." The protagonists are daughters plagued with "identity formation," sharing a need for a form of patricide. The effectiveness of both works comes in part from breaking a taboo against women writing narratives that detail what life with Dad is all about. DeJong believes that unleashing parricidal furies is part of the cure for daughters with fathers who block their "self-definition." She may not throw much new light on Plath's poem, but she may help explain reader response to this poem as well as the creative ambiguity which created it. I enjoyed Garry M. Leonard's "The Necessary Strategy of Renunciation: The Triumph of Emily Dickinson and the Fall of Sylvia Plath" (*UDR* 19, i:79–88) because it explores an important theme, renunciation, and clearly distinguishes the two women poets' attitudes toward it. Emily Dickinson realizes the dangers of writing to her role as a woman, and she withdraws from the exalted state of womanhood as defined by church, family, and society. She accepted a perception of herself as insignificant in order to explore the quality and parameters of her own mind. Sylvia Plath publicly strove to establish her identity within her culture, hoping that "some outward event or force will redeem her." She begins "Daddy" with an attempt at renunciation but ends "asking to be rescued."

The *Centennial Review* (vol. 32) has an issue (summer) mostly devoted to Sylvia Plath. Susan Van Dyne's "Rekindling the Past in Sylvia Plath's 'Burning the Letters'" (pp. 250–65) is another account of her artistic breakthrough in the summer and fall of 1962. She sought "to dismantle and dispose" of Ted Hughes's poetry as an obstacle to her own creativity "by finding a voice for her pain" in poems about a male aggressor and also an object for her rage through writing over sheets she had used in typing Ted's poems. Van Dyne makes clear that Sylvia experienced not just cold misery but creative rage. Of minor interest is Mary Kurtzman, "Plath's 'Ariel' and Tarot" (pp. 286–95), detailing her interest in Tarot cards and suggesting that her arrangement, though not Ted Hughes's, of the poems in *Ariel* was in Tarot order. Knowledge of Tarot also makes it possible to see "Ariel," written on her thirtieth birthday, as a "rebirth poem, not a suicide poem." Edward Klienschmidt, "Shed, Unfinished Lives: Plath and Keats" (pp. 279–95), compares the enthusiasms for horse-back riding of Keats and Plath, just before their respective deaths. More substantial and different is Leonard M. Scigaj's "The Painterly Plath that Nobody Knows" (pp. 330–49). Scigaj seeks to correct the current imbalance from basing her reputation on the last poems and ignoring the earlier. The early poetry has become the unknown Plath. To show the value of what has been ignored, he focuses on the 10 meditations she wrote on paintings from 1956 through 1959. I am not sure that Scigav will gain many converts, but it is important to have these poems intelligently read. He makes use of the transcript of Plath's 1961 BBC interview and a notebook she kept while auditing a modern art course while teaching at Smith during the spring of 1958. The influence of formalism on her critical ideas is supported by examination of her notes and underlinings in Cleanth Brooks's *The Well Wrought Urn* and Brooks and Warren, *Understanding Poetry*, two books any English major of her generation could hardly have missed.

c. Forché, Glück. There is only one small item on Carolyn Forché this year, David Montenegro's "Carolyn Forché: An Interview" (*APR* 17, vi:35–40). Forché comments on her current work, *The Angel of History*, as comprising six voices that grew from several reams of fragments she only recently recognized as a "form" rather than as separate pieces. She talks about influences from her childhood in Detroit and her adult experiences in Central America, South America, and South Africa. As a political writer she has been attempting to react to a "censorship by neglect and omission." This is a short interview but worth reading as testimony.

Louise Glück rarely makes these pages. There is this year an article by Burton Raffel, "The Poetry of Louise Glück (*LitR* 31:262–73), intended to correct that situation. Raffel, surprisingly, finds the book that won literary awards, *The Triumph of Achilles*, a "severe falling off." To prove that she is "one of the most interesting poets working today," Rafael offers a critique of her first four collections of poetry.

He regards *Firstborn* as good technically as the first works of Robert Lowell and Anne Sexton. In this book are themes that she was to use later in her poetry—the poet as outsider; push and pull between parent and child; irony in the face of pretension; a longing for a peace expected in childhood but not found. In her third book, *Descending Figures*, she becomes open about her debt to T. S. Eliot and William Carlos Williams. Raffel regards the influence of Eliot as bad for her poetry. He concludes that she may have lost her way in *The Triumph of Achilles*, but she is too fine a poet not to find it again.

iv. Beats, Open Form, Nature: Surrealism, Realism, Metaphysics

***a.* Snyder, Olson.** David A. Carpenter's "Gary Snyder's Inhumanism, From Riprap to Axe Handles" (*SDR* 26:110–38) labors to claim Gary Snyder as the poet who has become the contemporary spokesman for Robinson Jeffers's inhumanism. Snyder's direction has been to reject the heritage of Western civilization for "non-Christian myths" and to live a new way in order to "hatch a new myth." As an influence study this tends to ignore obvious differences. Its value is to stress Snyder's attempt to reawaken "humans to responsibility for their biological world and reintegration of the human with the inhuman in life-style and consciousness."

George Butterick offers a detailed analysis of "The Kingfishers" in "Charles Olson's 'The Kingfishers' and the Poetic of Change" (*AmerP* 6, ii:28–69). He adequately supports the view that this was Olson's "first grand poem" and a work in preparation for the *Maximus Poems*. Photocopies of manuscript pages are included.

***b.* Bly, Wright.** William V. Davis's *Understanding Robert Bly* (South Carolina) is a standard introductory survey in this series. It is hardly news to say that Bly has been influential and controversial. More should be said of his deep image poetry (much of it very good), especially of his relationship to the other "deep image poets" and of their importance to postmodernism, and even of his political poetry (most of it much less good). The overview is even briefer than in a Twayne volume, the bibliography, slimmer. Davis does contribute a good brief discussion on the importance of the depth psychology of Carl Jung to Bly. But that is about all.

Robert M. Randolph, "The Possibilities of Creativity: Nicholas Berdyayev and Robert Bly" (*MQ* 19:321–32), is as much about Berdyayev as it is about Bly. The point about Bly is that he "seems to be trying to do what Berdyaev says is impossible—to transcend the symbolic nature of art to the extent of producing forms of being—to, as Berdyayev might see it, create the Kingdom of God." The primary evidence seems to be the common influence of Jakob Boehme on both writers and Bly's 1963 essay, "A Wrong Turning in American Poetry," rather than Bly's poetry.

This seems the year for comprehensive studies of the unorthodox, open form, or deep image poets, rather than of the orthodox establishment. My first impression of Kevin Stein's *James Wright: The Poetry of a Grown Man* (Ohio) was that it has one of the sillier titles I had seen recently. The book is an attempt to find unity in Wright's poetry by stressing personal and aesthetic development rather than the diffuseness others have found. Stein shows that Wright's poetry moves from nagging doubt and depression to "a poetry of affirmation and integration." He is in the Emersonian tradition, attempting to use language for self-definition, equating the struggle with language with the struggle with the self. His language alters only as the "self redefines its values and goals." Wright's brand of romanticism was concerned with perfecting both a way of writing and a way of living that will overcome the separation of the individual from the natural world and from spiritual values. Stein discerns three stages in Wright's career: containment from the experiential world through retaining traditional religious values; vulnerability through entering the world of experience; integration through accepting in the human experience of the natural world such dualities as beauty and terror. He attempts to relate this movement toward integration to similar transformations in the poetry of W. S. Merwin, Galway Kinnell, Robert Bly, and Louis Simpson.

The *American Poetry Review* in "James Wright and the Slender Woman" (17, iii:29–33) prints Robert Bly on James Wright and the "Mysterious Hidden Woman" who began to appear in Wright's poetry soon after Bly met him. She represented the same spirit that Juan Jiménez and Lorca had also written about. Wright was also influenced by this figure's appearances in Chinese, German, Taoist, Provençal, and Arabic poems. Bly mentions poems in which her influence appears and finds absurd attempts by critics to reduce what is a simple way of seeing the soul in poetry to a "deep image." This is hardly archetypal criticism, but it is interesting testimony from one who knows.

c. Duncan, Rexroth. The year of Robert Duncan's death is marked by the first book-length study of his work, Mark Andrew Johnson's *Robert Duncan* (Twayne). This is a reasonably good introductory survey, given added importance because it is the first book on a neglected poet. Duncan is depicted as one of those poets outside the mainstream who have taken risks, but not much space is devoted to spelling out exactly what risks were taken. As is inbred into this series, there is more attention given to explications of selected poems than to situating Duncan in relation to movements like modernism or postmodernism or even to individual fellow poets. The kinship established is with Whitman, not unimportant to a poet who wrote, "Speaking of a thing I call upon its name, and the Name takes over from me the story I would tell." James Breslin in his brief treatment of Duncan in *CLHUS* (pp. 1091–93) is better at identifying the major risk taken by Duncan—a commitment so strong to "recording the shifting energies of the moments that, as a matter of policy, he refuses to revise." Johnson does provide some discussion of this strength and resulting weakness in his chapter on the poetics, but I would wish for a better evaluation of a career now ended. I cannot help noting that time had passed since the preparation of this book in 1985 (the last references) and its publication in 1988, before Duncan's death.

Duncan's death is commemorated by a special issue of the *H.D. Newsletter* (2, i) since Duncan was an H.D. enthusiast and influenced this magazine by his own *H.D. Book*, which appeared in little magazines from 1964 to 1981. There are several brief and deeply felt tributes and a bibliography of the publication of the *H.D. Book*. The fall issue of *American Poetry* (vol. 6) also offers obituary tributes to Duncan from critics and fellow poets. There is an influence study, Christopher Beach, "Objectivist Romantic: Ezra Pound and the Poetic Constellations of Robert Duncan" (pp. 3–24); a brief reexamination of "Often I am Permitted to Return to a Meadow," by Donald Gutierrez (pp. 25–30); a transcription of comments on Ezra Pound and Williams by Duncan from a tape made by James Laughlin (pp. 31–38); and a Duncan checklist (pp. 88–89). The question about Duncan's reputation is—will this interest continue into next year?

Lee Bartlett's *Kenneth Rexroth* (WWS 84) is a gracefully written account of the man and of the writer that says so much that it seems longer than a mere 50-page pamphlet. Within these limitations Bartlett manages to include a biographical sketch that is informative, a brief discussion of Rexroth's longer poems, an estimate of his volumes of shorter poems, and even add an account of his criticism on poetry and other poets. He concludes with a candid appraisal of Rexroth's reputation as "extremely problematic." Rexroth is a poet who has received only brief notice from major critics. Bartlett's case for recognizing Rexroth is that he has been "a singular voice in mid-century American writing . . . a formal innovator, animated aesthetician, and committed social thinker." He admits that much of Rexroth's work is of "the second intensity," but contends that some individual poems, such as "The Dragon and the Unicorn," "When We with Sappho," and "Toward an Organic Philosophy" as well as some of his Laurentian critical essays are "a major legacy." Bartlett may not convince that this is "a major legacy," but he does make a case for remembering some of the poetry of this poet now mentioned only as the mentor of the younger San Francisco poets.

d. **Berry, Simpson, Stafford.** Wendell Berry's existence as a poet is not evidenced by the *Columbia LHUS*; and David Perkins's brief mention in his *A History of Modern Poetry*, reviewed last year, scales the achievement of Berry's poetry to his view of nature from the smallness of his 12-acre farm, from which he writes quiet pastoral verse showing his belief that rural life can save us—a modern-day agrarian.

It is good to have an article, Jeffrey Alan Triggs, "Moving the Dark to Wholeness: The Elegies of Wendell Berry" (*LitR* 31:279–92), on the poetry Berry has written since he returned in 1964 to that farm. Before his retreat he had written lyrics typical of his generation of poets, "emphasizing paradox and irony . . . to protect his sensibility from the hostile environment." With *The Broken Ground* (1964) farming provided the central metaphor of new life-and-death cycle. Triggs makes an especially good case for the quality of the elegiac verse Berry has been able to write there—characterized by naturalness and simplicity appropriate for ordinary events and real people. But Berry's poetic gaze "rises from the particular toward the universal." His song of death is a song of life, an attitude "offering neither glibness of orthodoxy nor glibness of despair." This article makes no claim for major status, but it does convince that Berry can effectively use the life around him to write some good poems. In "Wendell Berry: The Mad Farmer and Wilderness" (*KR* n.s. 8, ii:40–52) David E. Gamble identifies a new wrinkle in Berry's use of the farmer, transforming the farmer from the "enemy of wilderness to its most devoted guardian." Everything in his farmer's rural world depends on harmony with the natural cycles of life that are "wild, beyond his control." Since the cycles of life are associated with farming, it must be practiced as a religious rite. The ideal relationship between agriculture and wilderness is designated in the series of poems, "The Mad Farmer," where Berryman uses a voice reminiscent of Nietzsche's philosophical "madman." The concern for profit becomes a call for the restored health of the land. For relief from a diet of critical articles, I could recommend for its comic seriousness Richard Moore's "Why Wendell Berry Ought to Reconsider His Decision Not to Buy a Computer" (*NER* 2: 112–14) an exchange with Wendell Berry on all aspects, comic and technological, as to whether a poet ought to use a computer in the production of his poetry. Berry is all for anti-progress, for horses rather than tractors in farming and pencils in creative composition and typing by one's wife rather than surrender to technological determinism.

Louis Simpson has written a long essay, "The Poet's Theme" (*HudR*:91–143), that is interesting as a major modern poet's view of the themes and drama in poetry but disappointing because, as he admits, "I have avoided speaking of living poets." Indirectly, he indicates some of his preferences: "It will be clear that I think highly of the writings of Denise Levertov. It is not likely that I will appreciate the writings of Amy Clampitt." Hank Lazer continues his contributions to contemporary poetry by an edited volume, *On Louis Simpson: Depths Beyond Happiness* (Michigan), in Donald Hall's "Under Discussion" series. As is customary for this format we have a large collection of reviews from Simpson's first publication to the last, a selection of previously printed essays, and a conclusion. Lazer's introduction provides an overview of all the previously published material. Simpson's early work received notice in quantity (Lazer counts 11 reviews of *The Arrivistes*, 1949) and in quality (reviews by Randall Jarrell, John Ciardi, Paul Engle, Louise Bogan). He points out that about the time Simpson was being located along with Robert Bly, James Wright, and William Stafford in the camp of deep imagists, Simpson was actually "moving off, independently, in his own direction as a poet, increasingly exploring the possibilities of narrative and of a poetry more and more drawn to the 'common life.'" With this new direction his poetry received "diminished attention." He was now outside the enthusiasms of critics like Helen Vendler, Harold Bloom, and Charles Altieri, who turned enthusiastically to championing the work of John Ashbery, better suited to the realm of new theory, peculiarly to deconstruction. Lazer's introduction is a good assessment of the importance of Simpson as well as an account of how his "narratives of common life" put him outside the mainstream of poetry, at least in the eyes of influential major critics, but they have still received good critical notices. None of these achievements is acknowledged in the *Columbia Literary History,* where Simpson is only a name among the Bly-led "deep image" school of poets.

William Stafford is interviewed about his craft, in "Craft Interview with William Stafford" (*NYQ* 35:17–32). The format in this, the thirty-fourth in the series, is limited to questions about techniques and influences. Stafford comments respectively on place in his poetry, on the poet as explorer, on the "physicality" of his metaphors, and, in some detail, on the poem "Traveling Through the Dark." He admits that he has been attracted to "edges" with regret for having to leave what he has loved. He finds the present state of poetry to be a mixed bag. There is a second brief, limited interview, Claire Cooperstein, "Postmark: Lake Oswego: A Mail Interview with William Stafford" (*NWR* 26:iii:25–32). Stafford discusses his attempt in the early poetry to get away from the "self-centeredness" of much contemporary poetry by turning to a way of looking at the world in the tale of American Indians and exemplified in the lessons of the Zen masters of the Orient. Here again much of the interview is devoted to technique, to comments on Stafford's unusual pairings of subject and predicate, to the closures of his poems, and to his intentions in his "Father" poems. This interview does call attention to the work of a poet who has not recently received the regard his work merits.

***e.* Dickey, Kinnell, Merwin.** There is a book out on James Dickey this year, Robert Kirschten's *James Dickey and the Gentle Ecstasy of Earth: A Reading of the Poems* (LSU). Kirschten draws on the Chicago Neo-Aristotelian critic Ronald Crane's "multiple working hypotheses" to explore a complexity in Dickey's poetry that recent critics have failed to see. Three of the hypotheses that he finds behind Dickey's poetics I can accept—mysticism, romanticism, and primitivism. These have been discussed before and support a case for Dickey's importance to postmodernism. The fourth is unexpected: Neoplatonism. Kirschten's case for Dickey is that through his mysticism Dickey is able to unify such opposites as man and nature, life and death. His romanticism permits him to reintroduce the great emotional topics of the nature poets and to make a reentrance to nature.

His primitivism allows him to explore "the ritual component in human experience." His Neoplatonism "reanimates the classical commonplace of motion and music in a method that gracefully recaptures lost love or unifies disparate cultures through song." Kirschten's tolerance of Dickey's excesses is expressed in a baseball metaphor. He may strike out too often; but he is basically a home run hitter, a poet whose vision and poetic achievement when he connects rank him with Hart Crane, Robert Penn Warren, and Theodore Roethke. *The James Dickey Newsletter* guarantees mention of Dickey each year. This year there is another interview (Ronald Baughman, ed., "James Dickey at Drury College," *JDN* 5:i, 16–28), undertaken on November 26, 1973, at the apex of Dickey's popularity, after the success of *Deliverance*, the novel and the movie, and is more about the movie and fame than about poetry. Jim Varn, "Primordial Reunions: Motion in James Dickey's Early Poetry" (*JDN* 5, i:4–14), discusses the guilt for one's existence, for one's birth, that Dickey believes can be overcome only by "a unity often with the larger more primal forces that have been buried as a result of materialistic concerns." Varn discusses the symbols for the realm in which the synthesis can take place—water, wind, Dionysus, Orpheus, and the hunt.

Granville Taylor's "From Irony to Lyricism: Galway Kinnell's True Voice" (*C&L* 37:45–54) attempts to relate Kinnell to Christianity and to show how in his poetry he has moved from irony to lyricism and from pessimism to "affirmation and joy." Kinnell early attempted to reconcile Christian theology to human mortality and suffering but surrendered his effort for a natural theology "that views the world as sacramental and emphasizes immanence over transcendence." Pessimism and irony were necessary as long as Kinnell fought the wrong battle of arguing against his own religious upbringing. The central problem was always death. He found his true voice when he accepted his romanticism, seeing poetry or music as harmonizing death with life. He also sees the world as "sacramental," as "the vehicle for grace." His later poetry demonstrates that "the sacred dimension can be found in contexts which are not explicitly Christian and even explicitly Christian." There is nothing exactly new here, but any approach showing development and change in Kinnell is valuable, since so many have failed to see it.

The interview of note this year is David Elliott's "An Interview with W. S. Merwin" (*ConL* 29:1–25), recorded in 1984 in Hawaii, where Merwin was at work on two projects: a history of the island of

Kahoolawe and translations of poems by the 13th-century Zen master, Dogen. Merwin's main preoccupation is with myth, which he finds "a coherent sense of experience," and he now regards language as "the "articulation of myth." The anger and suffering that inspired his earliest poetry almost caused him to quit writing. His interest in "deep image" poetry was a concern with the place from which all images come, something like "the imagination as distinguished from fancy by Coleridge." He has utilized surrealist devices but dislikes the term. Language poets are "boring, decadent, unoriginal" because they forget what myth has reminded him of, that "there must be no urgency in poetry—of all arts." He does not like simply naming things because it "inhibits the relation between the observer and the thing observed." He pessimistically finds much modern poetry mired in "listlessness," "preaching," "frivolity," "fluff." This is an informative interview, revealing Merwin's current preoccupation without the overall comprehensiveness of a *Paris Review* effort.

Michael Clifton, "Breaking the Glass: A Pattern of Visionary Imagery in W. S. Merwin" (*ChiR* 36, i:65–83), constructs a "visionary" schema concerned with altered states of consciousness and then compares works of Blake, Poe, and Huxley with poems of Merwin in order to describe better the unconscious as subject and to determine whether the attitude toward that subject is positive or negative. Merwin's progress is from a negative view to a positive, as he comes to terms with both the unconscious and with death. Beginning with "The Lice," Merwin introduces concepts from Zen. Clifton notes that Merwin compares the act of writing a poem to a diver staring at his own reflection as he dives. He concludes his essay with a detailed look at glass, light, and flower images in poems about significant deaths—Merwin's mother's, his brother's, and meditations on his own. Having specified his fears, Merwin comes to terms with them, "breaking the glass to reach the golden light behind."

***f.* Others.** John Burt's *Robert Penn Warren and American Idealism* (Yale) is a comprehensive study of Warren as poet, novelist, and literary critic, proposing to find all these endeavors unified by not just common themes but by a concept of inwardness, a romantic faith in the private sensibility as capable of imaginative power in both the arts and in politics. But Warren was also antiromantic with an awareness of the negative consequences of such power. His long-term regard for Jefferson came from his seeing this dual vision in Jefferson as the political idealist and the half-mad interlocutor of *Brother to Dragons*. In Warren's own works this duality is evidenced in a direct approach to experiences and an indirect withdrawal under the cover of irony. The conflict that interests Warren is "between those who sacrifice the integrity and autonomy of the self by rejecting the idea of internal authority and those who, adopting internal authority, commit themselves to destruction." This book is a complex, difficult, and, perhaps, profound work, revealing more about the novels than the poetry, but worth recommending here for what it has to say about *Brother to Dragons* and his elegies.

Floyd C. Watkins in "The Body of This Death in Robert Penn Warren's Later Poems" (*KR* 10:31–41) turns to that portion of Warren's work that belongs in this chapter, his later poems. Watkins begins with some personal accounts of his discussions with Warren about his religious beliefs. Warren told him that he "cannot believe but he has a great yearning." To Watkins the very late poems in the last separate volume of poems, *Rumor Verified*, seem to progress toward "acceptance and possible belief in divine being after skepticism." Not one of the 10 collections of poems before the last volume focuses on "death, time, eternity." Earlier characters and personae vacillate between doubt and faith. Warren's latest poems are meditations on a strong possibility of immortality and God. But the best poems still preserve an ambivalence about the finality of death or a belief in God. There are even two conflicting strains of images in the poems, reflecting either doubt or a glimpse of whatever afterlife there may be. Watkins concludes with an application of what Warren said in his introduction to Hemingway's *A Farewell to Arms* to his own recent poems: "If it does not offer a religious solution, it is nevertheless conditioned by a religious problem." Watkins may not succeed in finding religious faith in God in Warren's late poetry; what he does show is that some of the power in these poems comes from Warren's modern perspective of entertaining both faith and doubt.

I enjoyed Dave Barney's interview "Happy Men in Desert Places: An Interview with Donald Hall" (*SHR* 22:225–37). He makes the point that he does not believe it is possible for Hall to exhaust the genre of poems about the farm and farm folk because his style changes, permitting him to see his subject matter in a new way. He gains variety through writing about the same subject in different genres. It is also impossible for him to separate his professional from his personal life. His poetry is similar to Frost's in that they both have written about New England, but he writes in free verse and Frost in blank verse. Hall's own response to poetry is in terms of sound and shape rather than content. It is good to hear from a New England resident poet who has demonstrated the variety of a man of letters.

There has recently been much theological concern with William Everson (Brother Antoninus), most of which does not have enough literary concern to be discussed here. Lee Bartlett has written *William Everson: The Life of Brother Antoninus* (New Directions), which does earn mention since it is the first book-length autobiography of a poet important to the San Francisco movement and an advocate of Robinson Jeffers. It reveals the surprising fullness and variety of Everson's life. Bartlett wisely does not discuss Everson's theology in detail. He approaches the poetry because it is largely autobiographical, but he does not attempt the currently popular literary biography.

v. Eastern and New Establishment

***a.* Ashbery.** A major advocate, Charles Altieri, has written a significant article on John Ashbery—"John Ashbery and the Challenge of Post Modernism in the Visual Arts" (*CritI* 14:805–30). He turns to Ashbery to find an answer to a question about contemporary poetry that he believes crucial right now: "Can it continue to elaborate new dimensions of late fifties postmodernism . . . against the formalist versions of modernism that then dominated the art world and the poetry workshops? Or does the age demand new sensibility . . . in post-structuralism?" Both 20th-century modes, modernism and postmodernism, suffered from flaws: the first from "excessive metaphysics lacking psychological/ethical standards" and the latter for revolutionary "political gestures." He disagrees with Helen Vendler's suggestion that we do not seek new lyrical subjects but rather a rehashing of the old because this view ignores "the new needs of culture and the poet's news not found in the old." Altieri turns to a "schematic account of two aspects of Ashbery's contemporaneity—the verbal transformation of a painterly relation between transparency and depth and the use of that relation to define a distinctive model of our capacity to negotiate certain emotional investments basic to bourgeois life." This is a long and complex essay dealing with modernism, postmodernism, the artistic techniques of Jasper Johns, and the poetics of Ashbery. Modernism to Altieri "projects . . . a principle of testimony as its means for redefining Western art's traditional claims to offering a distinctive form of truth . . . [T]he more we see about seeing, the more we realize our vulnerabilities and sympathies cannot be stated." He believes that Ashbery's recent poetry offers an ethic: "proposing and testing of an attitude that the poem can lead us to try in life." Ashbery's poems "compose an overall ethos which extends a responsiveness to the imperfections of language into willingness to subordinate the demands of the ego's imaginary life to the contingencies that love must accept and thrive on." The rest of the article is an exploration of Ashbery's practical ethos, based partly on the way painters redefine the nature of the subject, "the aspectual sense of human agency . . . adapted to language." Wallace Stevens offered the richest positive model of the shifts required to begin reflecting on this aspectual self. Ashbery has demonstrated a new way of fleshing out the psychological and interpersonal implications of Stevens's aspectual ontology by writing a poetry that "speaks at once of timely wisdom and a profoundly contemporary philosophical reflection."

David Fink's "The Poetry of David Shapiro and Ann Lauterbach: After Ashbery" (*APR* 17, i:27–32) compares both poets with their forerunner and is as much about Ashbery as it is about his followers. Ashbery's obscurity is the result of his "decentered quality . . . the doing/ undoing oscillation." He is not deliberately trying to be obscure but to be exploratory by an attempt to "illustrate opacity." David Shapiro wrote his dissertation on Ashbery, and Ashbery has praised his poems. Shapiro is "friendly to theory and uses many traditional forms." Ashbery is ironic, skeptical of traditional form, and distrustful of theory. They use ordinary language differently. Shapiro may have a subject expressed as a cliché in his title, but the poem does not use clichés. Ashbery can achieve poetic effects by stringing clichés together. Lauterbach also does not use clichés, but she also likes abstractions. Her subject matter is more easily identifiable, with less of the Ashbery doing/undoing. This is a minor Ashbery article, but it does suggest how the influence of the master has been received by younger poets.

A poet, James Applewhite, has written the best article on the obvious subject "Painting, Poetry, Abstraction and Ashbery" (*SoR* 24: 272–90). It begins with a general discussion of the semblances of painting and poetry in the 20th century as well as some historical background on "abstract" and "abstraction." Although T. S. Eliot thought that style without subject matter would destroy the medium of poetry, Applewhite believes that poetry has moved in that direction since the 50s. Ashbery has a "painterliness of vision . . . a tendency toward spatialized linguistic structures," creating "verbal geometries in place of natural ones." Applewhite's judgment is mixed: Ashbery's mode of response is "to a world trivialized in its commonplace conceptualization and unknowable in its terrain." On the other hand, in Ashbery's poetry "the possibility of style as its own self-subsistent self-justification is approached more closely and successfully than was possible before the abstract art of modernism and, in particular, the painting of the abstract expressionists." Like Ashbery, Applewhite is a poet who understands painting and can consequently recognize the true experimental nature of much of the former's poetry.

***b.* Ammons.** Nathan A. Scott, Jr., "The Poetry of Ammons" (*SoR* 24:717–43), finds A. R. Ammons to be "a poet of the Sublime in the tradition of Emerson and Whitman." He sees the world as "an affair of reciprocity, what Stevens calls the 'candor' in things." But Ammons can also find room in his poetry for "the absurdity of the world." He does not like heights, the "search after eternity in the high heavens." Rather he is searching for what he calls "saliences," a dialectic between absence and presence, a concern which Scott, a professor of religion, relates to Martin Heidegger. Ammons is known for his commitment to using the open form in long poems. But Scott notes that he has recently returned to a "short, hard lyric," in which Scott finds a deep religious sensibility. To Scott, Ammons is rightly praised as "'the central poet' of our generation." This is a useful essay on a southern poet who has become part of the eastern establishment, though some critics might have disagreements.

In his minuscule mention in the *CLHUS* James Breslin sees Ammons as resisting "any yearning for rest, for synthesis, for completion," quoting from "Corson's Inlet": "I see narrow orders, limited tightness, but will/ not run to that easy victory." Thomas Dilworth explicates a classroom favorite in "Ammons's 'Coon Song'" (*Expl* 47, i:40–44). His emphasis is fashionable, showing how the poem "seems to deconstruct itself by denying its opening narrative description." Not only does Ammons refuse to satisfy his reader's "voyeuristic expectation," but he also shifts to nonsense to show that what we have accepted as real is "built on airy nothing." Dilworth identifies the two choices the speaker presents to the reader as "Platonic idealism" and "Aristotelian realism." Leaving the choice to the reader liberates the poet from "literary bondage."

c. Merrill. Timothy Materer, "Death and Alchemical Transformation in James Merrill's 'The Changing Light at Sandover'" (*ConL* 29:82–104), contends that this narrative of friendships over 30 years is one of the "great contemporary explorations of the unconscious mind." It resembles a "modern psychological novel" but is also "a virtual anthology of archetypal images." For Merrill to be appreciated his unconscious must be related to Carl Jung's "most dancing Gnostic and alchemical speculating." In spite of critics' negative responses to Merrill's Ouija board revelations, he is on a serious quest as a major poet not for the Jungian "God" but rather for some means of reconciling with the death of friends. Five friends, two of them dead, make up a "supernatural seminar"—Merrill, David Jackson, Maria Mitsotaki, W. H. Auden, a peacock (a bird of great importance to alchemy). The discussion of alchemy is obscure and often seems meandering, and Materer's intention seems a bit ambitious, to prove not only that Merrill's occultism enriches "the humanity of his poetry but also to authenticate him as a worthy successor to Yeats. Ruth Thompson provides us with an explication of Merrill's poem "Bronze" (*Expl.* 47, i:48–50). The poem seeks a tension between the immutability of art and the sorrow of the personal since the alloy bronze symbolizes both the timelessness of art and the permanence of personal loss. The loss of his own childhood is represented through a bronze bust of Merrill at six. The other loss is of a relationship with his friend, David Jackson. The two bronze statues they see in Florence help them to realize that they must go separate ways, alone.

One never quite gets everything he wants to include. Copies are missing from libraries; a few books and magazines are not sent or arrive too late. The preliminary *PMLA* bibliography, as helpful as it is, never includes everything. Still editors and publishers are generally cooperative, and nearly all of a considerable amount of criticism is covered. Anything not noted this year for any of the reasons mentioned above will, I hope, be accounted for next year if it is significant enough.

Clemson University

18. Drama

Walter J. Meserve

One of the more interesting volumes I read this past year was *Variety Obituaries*, vol. 1, 1905–1928 (Garland). From these excerpted death notices, I had hoped to find information on those American playwrights who left play titles and little else for historians. Unfortunately, I discovered very few references to playwrights, but I was appalled at the mayhem surrounding the death scenes of actors—murder, suicide, drunkenness, violence of all kinds. Acting was seldom a happy profession in the 19th and early 20th centuries. I was particularly struck by the last words of an actor, rejected by his love, who took his life with a pistol and left this note: "Send my body to Chicago." A touch of drama or pathos, this notice is typical of the revealing information that this volume holds for historians or simply those numerous and sane people who like to read obituaries.

Perhaps of greater interest, 1988 marked the centennial anniversary of the birth of Eugene O'Neill, an event celebrated around the scholarly world. One of the most distinctive celebrations was the Nanjing-Shanghai Eugene O'Neill Festival held in June. More than a dozen Americans attended this conference, which drew scholars from three continents. Eight O'Neill plays were produced, including the first production in China of *Long Day's Journey Into Night*. Other celebrations of O'Neill's career occurred in America and Europe. Certain entrepreneurial and vocal scholars sought to enhance their résumés during 1988 not by significant writing but by listing the number of O'Neill conferences at which they spoke. It should also be noted that a number of publishers and editors of journals contributed to the O'Neill Centennial Celebration.

i. Reference Works and Anthologies

Contemporary Dramatists (St. James) appeared in a fourth edition, ed. D. L. Kirkpatrick with a brief preface by Ruby Cohn who wrote about a diminishing audience for a drama that will endure if only in spite of the efforts of modern playwrights. For each of the 300 entries there are the basic facts concerning playwrights and plays, published or produced, plus an assessment by a recognized critic and a comment by the playwright. There are many names that will be long forgotten in 50 years, but each edition of *Contemporary Dramatists* is a valuable resource. Eugène Van Erven wanted to write a history of *Radical People's Theatre* (Indiana), but he lacks historical knowledge of his topic and encumbers himself with debatable theses: that all art is political, for example, or that radical theater groups in the United States, France, Great Britain, West Germany, and Italy share essential characteristics and ideological objectives and that prior to the 1920s and 1930s American drama was "of a notoriously poor quality." Chapter four deals with "Revolutionary Voices in the American Political Theatre" (pp. 24–63) and includes reviews of the plays and summary comments on the progress of the San Francisco Mime Troup, el Teatro Campesino, and the Bread and Puppet Theater. Van Erven's conclusions relative to these contemporary groups are effectively argued and revealing, particularly the idea that a radical theater cannot remain pure in a capitalistic society. The volume ends with a chronology of the theater groups, a good set of notes, and a brief bibliography.

I am not a fan of David Savran's book on the Wooster Group because I find the group's activities blatantly representative of the abusively self-conscious and self-indulgent performance that severely limits audiences for contemporary theater and increasingly identifies the theater as an arena for immature and arrogant theater people to applaud each other's grotesque and meaningless antics. This year, however, Savran has edited a volume well worth space on your library shelf: *In Their Own Words* (*TCG*). It is a collection of well-executed interviews—and Savran is extremely adept in the art of the interview—in which one acquires a clear sense of the playwrights' attitudes toward dramatic literature, American theater, and cultural and political forces as well as factual information on these writers' early experiences, training, influences, and goals. There are also pictures of each playwright. Chosen for their vital and distinctive voices in American theater, everyone accepted the invitation to be interviewed except Sam Shepard: Lee Breuer, Christopher Durang, Richard Foreman, Maria Irene Fornes, Charles Fuller, John Guare, Joan Holden, David Hwang, David Mamet, Emily Mann, Richard Nelson, Marsha Norman, David Rabe, Wallace Shawn, Stephen Sondheim, Megan Terry, Luis Valdez, Michael Weller, August Wilson, and Lanford Wilson.

It might be well to mention as resource material three other interviews published this year. The best was Jackson R. Bryer's "An Interview With Robert Anderson" (*SAD* 3:100–21). Much of the interview deals with *Tea and Sympathy*, but one learns more as Anderson explains his interest in relationships between men and women, family relationships. Taking his A.B., M.A., and Ph.D. from Harvard, Anderson wrote his master's thesis on Maxwell Anderson; he enjoys the work of Philip Barry, Robert Sherwood, and S. N. Behrman but not O'Neill, and he does not like most plays written today. Susan Harris Smith had greater difficulty in "An Interview With Charles Gordone" (*SAD* 3:122–32), a man who calls himself "a playwright of color who does not write black plays." Gordone also confesses that he does not enjoy going to the theater very much these days. In "An Interview With Jean-Claude Van Itallie" (*SAD* 3:134–46) Alexis Greene elicited background information about a three-quarter Jewish person who confesses to being a Buddhist, but most of the interview pertained to a discussion of Van Itallie's plays—*Paradise Ghetto* and *Struck Dumb*—as well as his close relationship with Joe Chaikin.

With all of the problems professors encounter in securing an adequate anthology for a course in American drama before O'Neill, it would be nice to announce the appearance of that perfect collection. Alas! that is not to be. There are abundant choices for the contemporary period, however, and Brooks McNamara offers another—*Plays from the Contemporary American Theater* (Mentor): David Rabe, *Streamers*; John Guare, *Marco Polo Sings a Solo*; Arthur Kopit, *Wings*; Christopher Durang, *Sister Mary Ignatius Explains It All for You*; Beth Henley, *Crimes of the Heart*; A. R. Gurney, *The Dining Room*; Tina Howe, *Painting Churches*; and August Wilson, *Ma Rainey's Black Bottom*. It seems hardly appropriate to publish *Famous American Plays of the 1980s* (Dell) before the decade is over, but Robert Marx has selected and introduced Sam Shepard's *Fool for Love*, Jules Feiffer's *Grown Up*, Wallace Shawn's *Aunt Dan and Lemon*, Stephen Sondheim and James Lapine's *Sunday in the Park with George*, and August Wilson's *Ma Rainey's Black Bottom*.

ii. Drama and Theater in the 19th Century

Published research in 19th-century American drama and theater is particularly gratifying this year in terms of number, approach, and quality. *Minnesota Theatre from Old Fort Snelling to the Guthrie* (Pogo Press) by Frank M. Whiting mixes history and memory. Although Whiting's interest is in theater since 1933, he has uncovered a lot of information about the various early stock and road companies, their managers and actors, who played in Minnesota from 1821 to 1883. It was a far busier time in America than historians usually acknowledge, and Whiting entitled his pages on theater during the mid-century decade "The Booming Fifties." The theater became big business from 1883 to 1933, and the years from 1933 to 1963 are called a "coming of age." After describing the advance of theater in several colleges and universities, Whiting provides a personal perspective on Minnesota theater, allowing nearly a quarter of his book for the Guthrie. These pages on people, plays, events, and accomplishments are well illustrated with beautiful colored pictures but also interlaced with personal observations on people whose subsequent careers have not always proved worthy of his praise for their early work.

Susan G. Davis writes about *Parades and Power: Street Theatre in Nineteenth Century Philadelphia* (Calif.) from the point of view of a cultural historian. Davis's research is excellent as she shows how traditional street theater in Philadelphia from the early part of the century through the 1860s can be of value to the historian as evidence of public concern, a strengthened economy, or public commitment. The discussion of activities ranges through burlesque militia parades, Christmas maskings, charivari processions, workers' parades, mock funerals, and such folk traditions as the career of Colonel Pluck. In a convincing and interesting manner Davis shows how processions and mimes reflect social criticism, political protocol, and personal satire of known individuals. Looking at more traditional theatrical ventures during the third quarter of the 19th century, Peter A. Davis argues with more logic than actual evidence that the Panic of '73 served as a catalyst to change the stock system to the combination company and to promote variety theater. His essay is entitled "From Stock to Combination: The Panic of '73 and Its Effect on the American Theatre Industry" (*THStud* 8:1–9). Eugene H. Jones is more interested in sociology than drama in *Native Americans as Shown on the Stage, 1753–1916* (Scarecrow). In tracing the American Indians, Jones lists or refers specifically to more than 200 plays and provides pertinent quotations to illustrate his interests. Clearly Jones has studied the plays carefully, but his work is marred by a limited knowledge of basic scholarship on American drama and theater and an apparent lack of interest in recent reference works.

The Brief Career of Eliza Poe (Fairleigh Dickinson) by Geddeth Smith provides some fascinating footnotes for the historian of American drama and theater and would undoubtedly meet the approval of Mrs. Poe's more famous son. Considering her very brief life—1787 to 1811—and the fact that she acted nearly 300 roles on the American stage, it is interesting to me to read the names of a number of American plays in which she performed: *The Battle of Bunker Hill, Oberon; or, The Siege of Mexico,* and *Bethlem Gabor,* by John Daly Burk; James Workman's *Liberty in Louisiana*; Williams Dunlap's *Glory of Columbia*; William Ioor's *The Battle of Eutaw Springs*; and Williams C. White's *The Poor Lodger.* Two notes on actors of this general period include Clifford Ashby's discovery in the journal of an early playgoer that a Negro may have appeared on the Boston stage in 1794 in a role that "fitted his character with great propriety" ("A Black Actor on the Eighteenth Century Boston Stage?" *ThS* 28 [November 1987]:101–02) and Rosemarie K. Bank's "Actor Training at the Mid-Point in Nineteenth-Century American Repertory" (*ThStud* 8:157–62).

The papers from a conference sponsored by Warren Kliewer's East Lynne Company in April 1985 analyzed *The Drews and the Barrymores: A Dynasty of Actors.* Published in *Performing Arts Resources,* vol. 13, these papers included the text of a little-known play by Maurice Barrymore entitled *Nadjezda,* a modern tragedy in a prologue and three acts (pp. 92–161). James Katsilibas-Davis provides an excellent "Introduction" (pp. 87–91) in which he traces the unfortunate stage history of *Nadjezda.* Other essays in the volume are by Don B. Wilmeth, "American Acting Dynasties" (pp. 1–15), Mary Ann Jensen, "From Strolling Players to Steven Spielberg: 200 Years of a Theatrical Family" (pp. 17–28), C. Lee Jenner, "The Duchess of Arch Street: An Overview of Mrs. John Drew's Managerial Career" (pp. 29–43), James Katsilibas-Davis, "The Unbroken Chain: Tradition in Style" (pp. 45–55), and William Roerick, "Remembering Ethel Barrymore and Others" (pp. 57–64). The volume includes an excellent chart (p. 16) and a good selection of pictures (pp. 65–75).

The Age and Stage of George L. Fox (Univ. Press of New England) by Laurence Senelick is a far more valuable book than one might think from its title. An actor and superb mime, Fox reached his greatest success with *Humpty Dumpty,* the first American pantomime in two acts. Written by a minor but popular dramatist, Clifton W. Tayleur, the pantomime opened on March 10, 1867, at the Olympic Theatre in New York and ran for 62 weeks. Because there is relatively little information on Fox, Senelick emphasized the "Age and Stage" and created a fascinating picture of American theater during the third quarter of the century. Basically concerned with theater activity rather than American drama, he found little to say about playwrights, and his generalizations concerning American drama are open to question, but he is accurate and compelling in his understanding of American theater of the 1850s and 1860s and of the American public which all actors and playwrights must please. The "public," he wrote, "divided against itself sought in the theatre nothing but amusement, the hearty laugh or the urgent tug of the heart strings, escape from the pressing problems of everyday life" (p. 37). This book is an excellent resource for students of mid-19th-century American drama and theater.

Although James H. Dorman's essay on "Shaping the Popular Image of Post-Reconstruction American Blacks: The 'Coon Song' Phenomenon of the Gilded Age" (*AQ* 40:450–71) is not directly concerned with American drama, it touches upon an aspect of popular culture that historians of American drama and theater must understand. Dorman documents the use of "coon songs" in popular entertainments from the pre-Civil War stereotypes of Jim Crow and Zip Coon through the minstrel shows of the Gilded Age as well as vaudeville and variety theater. Sketching the frenzied activity that accompanied the exploitation of the Comstock Lode, George Moss chronicles the "Silver Frolic: Popular Entertainment in Virginia City, Nevada, 1859–1863" (*JPC* 22, ii:1–31). Among other amusements, Moss allows a few paragraphs on the theater and focuses briefly on Mark Twain's role as a drama critic for the *Enterprise*. In "Art for Awe's Sake" (*Theater* 19, ii:32–34) Gabrielle Cody compares Peter Brook's production of the *Mahabharata* with Buffalo Bill's late 19th-century *Wild West Show*. Aside from claiming some obvious parallels, however, she fails to develop a convincing argument and shows a need to delve more deeply into the spectacles of 19th-century theater around the world.

Maintaining his scholarly interest in early American drama, Peter A. Davis finds "Evidence of Collaboration in the Writing of Robert Hunter's *Androboros*" (*RECTR* 3, i:20–29). Davis's solid scholarship is to be encouraged. Karen S. Langlois tries to awaken interest in an early 20th-century woman playwright—"Mary Austin and the New Theatre: The 1911 Production of *The Arrow Maker*" (*THStud* 8:71–87). Feminist theater historians and critics should be aware of Mary Austin's career. Although more interested in romance than race in *The Arrow Maker*, Austin provided a good and modern portrayal of the American Indian. I must also mention Patricia Marks's essay on "*The Scarecrow*, Percy Mackaye's Adaptation of 'Feathertop'" (*NHR*: 14:13–15). Historians and critics, regardless of gender interests, should discover the great wealth of drama and the theatrical endeavors that make the years between James Herne's *Margaret Fleming* (1890) and O'Neill's appearance at the Provincetown (1916) one of the most interesting and least understood periods in the history of American drama.

iii. The Centennial Celebration of Eugene O'Neill

America's only playwright to receive the Nobel Prize in Literature, Eugene O'Neill was remembered and feted in many gatherings around the world during 1988, while he and his works were subjected to an alarming array of critical opinions, astute as well as wayward and self-serving. Most admired among the celebrants is Travis Bogard whose authoritative studies of the playwright and his work have provided a firm basis for younger scholars who have discovered that they really do "like O'Neill." The Library of America has now published the *Complete Plays*, 50 plays arranged in the order in which O'Neill wrote them, and edited by Bogard who has supplied concise and perceptive notes for each play, including an unpublished draft of *More Stately Mansions* and a biographical commentary focused on O'Neill's problems as a writer who was tormented by his haunted past as well as a continuing life of physical and spiritual ailments. This three-volume set is a great improvement over the Random House edition of 1941—in number of plays, obviously, but also in the editorial plan and the clarifying commentary.

This is the place to note that Bogard's *Contour in Time: The Plays of Eugene O'Neill* (Oxford), a standard text for the appreciation of O'Neill's plays since its publication in 1972, has been revised for the centennial event. More of Eugene O'Neill's plays appeared in *Eugene O'Neill: The Unfinished Plays* (Ungar), edited by another notable O'Neill scholar, Virginia Floyd. Essentially, these "plays" are the long scenarios, a consistent aspect of O'Neill's writing process before beginning a play, of three stories he did not complete before his death—"The Visit of Malatesta," "The Long Conquest," and "Blind Alley Guy."

There is also *The Unknown O'Neill: Unpublished or Unfamiliar Writings of Eugene O'Neill* (Yale), ed. Travis Bogard. I found this a fascinating collection of plays, fiction, poetry, criticism, and tributes to others—all prefaced by sensible and sensitive notes that help clarify the reader's understanding of O'Neill's work. In the theater section Bogard includes *The Personal Equation*; the scenario for *The Reckoning*; *The Guilty One*, which appears to be as much the work of Agnes Bolton as O'Neill; Act IV of *The Ole Davil*, which should be read with *Anna Christie*; *The Ancient Mariner*, forever identified as "the cracked test tube" in the laboratory of the Provincetown Players; and *Marco Millions*, before O'Neill picked up his blue pencil. There is also a sad and pathetic poem entitled "To a Stolen Moment," plus examples of O'Neill's sensible if idealistic criticism—"Are the Actors to Blame?" 1925—and tributes to George Pierce Baker, Maxwell Anderson's *Winterset*, and even Carlotta's dog, Silverdene Emblem O'Neill. Bogard teamed up with Jackson R. Bryer to edit *Selected Letters of Eugene O'Neill* (Yale). Prefacing the letters with an exceptionally appropriate and well-written introduction, the editors divide their entries into eight chronological periods, choosing letters that reveal the "qualities of the external man." I was particularly interested in a letter to Macgowan written on August 23, 1926: "All I ask . . . is new actors, new directors and a new theatre for my new plays to be worked by and with!!! Surely a simple matter! . . . I stand for the playwright's side of it in this theatre." He was, indeed, an idealist with a sense of humor, and it may be best that he has not lived to see how directors have taken over the theater and how playwrights have eagerly abased themselves to the new god. From these letters one can like O'Neill for himself—as he revealed himself in his last letter to Carlotta (July 22, 1952), "who for twenty-three years has endured my rotten nerves, my lack of stability, my cussedness in general." The American theater needs a little more honest "cussedness."

Two other books take quite different approaches to the study of Eugene O'Neill and his plays. With a self-serving touch of Irish blarney and a coy style of writing, Edward L. Shaughnessy has created a volume entitled *Eugene O'Neill in Ireland* (Greenwood), a purposefully ambiguous title because O'Neill never went to Ireland. His plays, however, have been produced there, and a number of Irish critics, responding to questionnaires from Shaughnessy, ventured opinions on the playwright, his work, and, among other things, why O'Neill never visited Old Ireland. Shaughnessy would like to show O'Neill's Irish heritage, and he incorporates references to Dion Boucicault, James O'Neill, and the Abbey Players along with the reactions of St. John Ervine and Andrew E. Malone. In the second section of this two-part volume Shaughnessy reprints essays by Irish critics such as Christopher Murray. In "O'Neill and 'The Ultimate Wound': An Essay on Tragedy" (pp. 182–93) Murray contends that O'Neill's need for a culture in which to express his sense of tragedy found an Irish voice that continues to be heard in Ireland. Almost in spite of its poetic thesis, *Eugene O'Neill in Ireland* contributes well to O'Neill scholarship.

My essay this year might well be devoted to books and essays on O'Neill, but that approach does not interest me. O'Neill scholars, however, should look carefully into *Perspectives on O'Neill: New Essays* (University of Victoria) ed. Shyamal Bagchee and *Critical Approaches to O'Neill* (AMS) ed. John Stroupe. For students who want carefully researched information about the first performances of 22 of O'Neill's plays—theaters, actors, directors, designers, manuscript notes, and critical responses—look at Ronald H. Wainscot's *Staging O'Neill: The Experimental Years, 1920–1934* (Yale). This is a monumental work, accomplished with the highest of standards.

Inevitably, the number of essays on Eugene O'Neill increased this year. The editors of *Modern Drama* devoted an issue (no. 1) to the efforts of O'Neill devotees. *The Eugene O'Neill Newsletter* continued to publish its cluster of brief essays, including observations by some of the best-known O'Neill scholars. With a centennial salute the editor of the *Newsletter* (vol. 12) selected the spring issue to print papers from 1984 and 1986 O'Neill conferences at Suffolk University in Boston: Travis Bogard on a teenage O'Neill as an epistolary swain, Paul D. Voelker on life and art in O'Neill's first play, Gary Jay Williams on O'Neill's debut in Provincetown, Marc Maufort on craftsmanship in the Glencain one-acts, Thomas P. Adler on John M. Synge's *Riders to the Sea* and *Anna Christie*, and Susan Tuck on *All God's Children* and William Faulkner's *Light in August*. In general, the three issues of the *Eugene O'Neill Newsletter* this year contain essays reflecting a rich abundance of attitudes and approaches destined to haunt, and perhaps clarify, the efforts of one who recognized his own "cussedness."

Other scholarship on O'Neill this year can easily be divided between essays or books focused upon a single play and those emphasizing a theory or concept. In both instances the issue is frequently of only passing interest. Take Ann Massa's essay on "Intention and Effect in *The Hairy Ape*" (*MD* 31:41–51). Discussing the possible aesthetic gap between the playwright's intention and the effect produced by the director, Massa uses the Peter Stein production in German at Britain's National Theatre to suggest the potential absurdity. O'Neill knew this potential and feared it. In "O'Neill's *Hairy Ape* and the Reversal of Hegelian Dialectics" (*MD* 31:35–40) Hubert Zapf accepts dramas as "intelligent experiments" and argues that *The Hairy Ape* shows O'Neill reversing the Hegelian-Marxist dialectic. Laurin R. Porter selects the year 1912 to explain "*The Iceman Cometh* As Crossroad in O'Neill's Long Journey" (*MD* 31:52–62). The year is projected as a vital bridging mechanism between O'Neill's historical and autobiographical plays. Gary Vena's *O'Neill's* The Iceman Cometh, *Reconstructing the Premiere* (UMI Research Press) may have a limited audience, but it is a model for the kind of scholarship it illustrates. Tracing the origins of the play, O'Neill's relationship with the Theatre Guild and all of the details of lighting, costuming, casting, and rehearsing, Vena reconstructs the production and relates everything to the text of the play. It is, indeed, a scholarly presentation, one of the best in this series.

In "The Play of the Misbegotten" (*MD* 31:81–90) Robert Ready tries to interpret the theatricality of *A Moon for the Misbegotten* but provides only a slight and artificial reading. Basing some of his ideas on a book by Kerby Miller entitled *Emigrants and Exiles*, John Henry Raleigh develops some interesting if not wholly original ideas relative to "Communal, Familial, and Personal Memories in O'Neill's *Long Day's Journey Into Night* (*MD* 31:63–72). John H. Ashington makes some comparisons between Shakespeare's *Antony and Cleopatra* and *Long Day's Journey Into Night* in "Shakespeherian Rags" (*MD* 31:73–80). By editing *More Stately Mansions: The Unexpurgated Edition* (Oxford), Martha Bowen provides much more reading for O'Neill scholars.

One of the more thought-provoking theoretical essays on the work of Eugene O'Neill is entitled "O'Neill and the Tragedy of Culture" (*MD* 31:1–15) by Ernest G. Griffin, who suggests some ideas linking T. S. Eliot, O'Neill, and Matthew Arnold. In the best part of the essay Griffin uses Arnold's *Culture and Anarchy* to show O'Neill's work in a philosophical light reflecting our Western cultural heritage.

Linda Ben-Zvi rephrases ideas from several past critics in discussing "Freedom and Fixity in the Plays of Eugene O'Neill" (*MD* 31:16–27). Normand Berlin doubts his own thesis and strains to make it work in "The Beckettian O'Neill" (*MD* 31:28–34). Charles Lock, on the other hand, takes an intelligent look at American theater in "Maurice Browne and the Chicago Little Theatre" (*MD* 31:106–16) and wonders why people should assume that O'Neill's work is "the origin of American drama." To prove his point, Lock discusses the work of Maurice Browne and the 55 previously unproduced plays, some of them American, which illustrate the falseness of the assumption by American critics. It is a point worth remembering.

iv. Susan Glaspell, Clifford Odets, Lynn Riggs, and Lillian Hellman

A motley crew, grouped by convenience. Few scholars have paid much attention to Lynn Riggs. Phyllis Cole Braunlich's *Haunted by Home: The Life and Letters of Lynn Riggs* (Okla.) may stimulate some interest. Thanks to the increased feminist criticism, Susan Glaspell seems to be getting a more just assessment. She should have received it long ago simply on the merits of her work, but the shadow of Eugene O'Neill was apparently too intimidating. Two essays this year, unfortunately, offer nothing of substance and evidently indicate mainly that Glaspell's plays have become a "popular" topic which the superficial entrepreneur in scholarship may use to entice similar-minded editors. In "On the Edge: The Plays of Susan Glaspell" (*MD* 31:91–105) Christine Dymkowski discusses Glaspell's plays as dramatizing the "limits of experience" and argues that the dramatist has been denied her place in the history of American drama because she was a woman. In an apt example of forced and inconsequential analysis Philip C. Kolin writes of "Therapists in Susan Glaspell's *Suppressed Desires* and David Rabe's *In the Boom Boom Room*" (*NConL* 18, v:2–3). Glaspell deserves better.

The Time Is Ripe—The 1940 Journal of Clifford Odets (Grove), intro. William Gibson, with a preface by Walt Odets, the dramatist's son, is a very self-conscious attempt by a very youthful dramatist to pass his experiences on to future generations. The year 1940 was important for Odets, and he had an itching desire to tell the "truth of life today." And thus it emerges from his "confessions"—from statements like "everywhere there is graft and corruption" (1/13/40) to "ate alone at the saloon on Fifty-sixth Street, stopped in a book shop and bought more books" (12/6/40). Consistent with his view of himself as a man of "good heart" and "strong ego," Odets filled his journal with his observations on women, money, the good life and an "abnormal fixation on the orgasm as an end in itself" (10/2/40). "Here I am now . . . my birthday, witless, torpid, swimming for my life" (7/18/40). There is very little about playwriting in his journal, only comments about plays Odets is going to write. Just as Odets feels terribly sorry for himself, one can feel sorry for him—for the man who confessed to writing "this journal" for the purpose of "forgetting myself" (10/3/40), for the man who felt not only the need to pose but the need to explain that he was doing it. No doubt the journal is revealing, but I do not believe that it enlightens the reader in any good way or helps him understand Odets's plays.

Two books were published this year on Lillian Hellman, plus the paperback publication of *Lillian Hellman: The Image, The Woman* (Ballantine) by William Wright, the journeyman reporter. Peter Feibleman—*Lilly: Reminiscences of Lillian Hellman* (Morrow)—is a writer who enjoyed Hellman's friendship for 43 years and inherited her house on Martha's Vineyard upon her death. His book is filled with gossip and trivia, a lot of name-dropping, a good amount about Feibleman and the crude, boring, and vulgar woman he adored. "Lillian's sexuality was at the root of her being" (p. 346); "The two of us, lewd and bawdy and loud" (p. 395). There are also some interesting stories, about William Faulkner and Dashiel Hammett, for example, and some good comments on play plotting (p. 229), but Hellman's work as a playwright is not a strong part of this book, which shows a partiality for praise and sentiment. Hellman was, we are told, a "good fisherman." Perhaps that is sufficient compensation, if one can believe it, for her consistently less than appealing behavior.

In *Lillian Hellman* (St. Martin's) Carl Rollyson is charmed by the "Nasty Old Lillian." Presumably, this is a thoroughly researched study, mainly employing interviews, but the bibliography is padded, the footnotes inadequate and lacking page references, and the book filled with quotations for which there are no sources indicated. It is a long book, beginning with a listed cast of characters numbering more than a hundred, in which trivial observations and obvious gossip take up most of the space. Rollyson does include interesting anecdotes relating to Hellman's plays, information on the writing of *The Little*

Foxes, and commentary on the political and social interest in her plays. Basically, however, although he does not resolve any of her misstatements, he becomes a true apologizer for her lies and her conduct—everyone knew that she was a liar—and defends her as truthful in terms of "artistic and biographical truth." Both of these books exhibit the "nasty" Lillian Hellman for purposes that appear to be completely commercial.

v. Arthur Miller, Tennessee Williams, and Edward Albee

In his essay on "Arthur Miller: Public Issues, Present Tensions" for the special issue of *SLitI* (21:97–106) Robert A. Martin distinguishes between the early and the late plays, editorially divided into the two volumes of Miller's collected plays. Whereas the plays in volume one reflect both public and present tensions with an emphasis upon social relationships, the issues and tensions of the later plays are overshadowed by an introspective and existential angst. For Miller, Martin argues, it becomes not so much what is right or wrong but what is real. After studying the interplay of male and female in Miller's best plays, Priscilla S. McKinney contends that the importance that Miller attaches to the female may be understood as "the unconscious feminine expression of the protagonist's masculine nature" as described by Jung in terms of the anima and animus. Her essay is entitled "Jung's 'Anima' in Arthur Miller's Plays" (*SAD* 3:41–63). With reference to Miller's major plays, McKinney believes that Miller deliberately assigned the role of 'anima,' the feminine personification of man's consciousness, to his female characters to hide his Jungian methods. Although assumptions of this kind may be dangerous, the author's argument is clearly presented. Leah Hadomi suggests an interesting approach in "Fantasy and Reality: Dramatic Rhythm in *Death of a Salesman*" (*MD* 31:157–74). Harold Bloom's editions of *All My Sons* (Chelsea) and *Death of a Salesman* (Chelsea) show the disturbing effects of "fast-food" publishing. The same may be said of Bloom's editions of Tennessee Williams's *Glass Menagerie* (Chelsea) and *A Streetcar Named Desire* (Chelsea). There is nothing new in any of these volumes.

Tennessee Williams still attracts book-length studies as well as essays. In addition to Judith Thompson's derivative study of *Tennessee Williams' Plays: Memory, Myth and Symbol* (Peter Lang) there is Dennis Vannatta's *Tennessee Williams: A Study of the Short Fiction* (Twayne, Short Fiction series, no. 4). I mention the Vannatta volume because a number of Williams's stories served as prototypes for plays: "Twenty-Seven Wagons Full of Cotton," "Portrait of a Girl in Glass," "The Angel in the Alcove," and "Three Players of a Summer Game." Jordan Y. Miller discusses Williams's private tensions in "The Three Halves of Tennessee Williams' World" (*SLitI* 21:83–95). His vehicle is *Camino Real*, which dramatizes Williams's divided world of the good, the dark, and—the third part—the forbidding dry square of *Camino Real*, which is the middle ground.

Thomas Bonner, Jr., found 17 production photographs of Williams's plays produced in New Orleans theaters from 1949 to 1987—"On Stage in New Orleans: A Photo Essay of Tennessee Williams's Plays" (*SAD* 3:79–98). They may be of interest to some, I suppose, but they lack the purpose of, say, W. Kenneth Holditch's 1985 essay in the *Southern Quarterly* on "The Last Frontier of Bohemia: Tennessee Williams in New Orleans, 1938–1983." Two rather slight additions to Williams scholarship appear in *Notes on Mississippi Writers*: K. Balachandran's "Tennessee Williams in India: Stagings and Scholarship" (20, i:17–27) and John H. Jones's "The Missing Link: The Father in *The Glass Menagerie*" (20, i:29–38). It would appear that the intense interest in Williams's work artificially stimulated by his death and consciously created by the ever-watchful hearse-chasing scholars has somewhat subsided.

Conversations with Edward Albee (Miss.), ed. Philip C. Kolin, includes a brief chronology of Albee's activities and 27 interviews from 1961 to 1986. The purpose of this volume, as stated by the editor, is to show Albee as playwright, man of the theater, art collector, cultural ambassador, critic, and teacher. It also reveals Albee as arrogant, arch, friendly, fatuous, intelligent, and superficial, and quotes him as saying that he makes two drafts of a play and never changes the second one. Having been interviewed 125 times over the past 25 years, Albee manages many faces; he is much in the public eye. But this year few scholars could find much to say about his plays. Two essayists tried to suggest possible sources for his work. In "Albee's Titles" (*Expl* 46, ii:46–47) Scott Giantvalley points out that such titles as *Lady from Dubuque* and *Man Who Had Three Arms* appeared in phrases from letters to the editor of the *New York Times* by people who did not care for *Who's Afraid of Virginia Woolf?* I should also note here Giantvalley's *Edward Albee: A Reference Guide* (Hall, 1987), which did not get into last year's essay. Jeane Luere has discovered a similar plot to that in Albee's best-known play in a short story by Elizabeth Taylor, "A British Parallel for Edward Albee's Imaginary Child: 'A Dedicated Man' and *Who's Afraid of Virginia Woolf?*" (*SAD* 3:65–78).

vi. Contemporary Playwrights in Alphabetical Order

The current and not very exciting New York production of *Born Yesterday*—at least Judy Holiday was not 47 years old when she played the female lead in 1946—reminds us that Garson Kanin along with Sidney Howard and the ageless George Abbott are still part of the New York theatrical scene. The Dramatists Guild shows some generational comparisons in "Playwriting in Two Perspectives: Garson Kanin and Tina Howe" (*DGQ* 24, vi:10–27). The inveterate comparativist and wandering commentator, Thomas P. Adler, decides that public policies and private beliefs cannot be separated—"Public Faces, Private Graces: Apocalypse Postponed in Arthur Kopit's *End of the World*" (*SLitI* 21, ii:107–18). In "Mitch and Murray in David Mamet's *Glengarry Glen Ross*" (*NConL* 18, ii:3–5) Philip C. Kolin complicates a slight observation by suggesting that the characters in the play represent both corporate America as well as sweatshop workers while being victims of the business world. The title of Pascale Hubert-Leibler's "Dominance and Anguish: The Teacher-Student Relationship in the Plays of David Mamet" (*MD* 31:557–70) suggests a sympathetic theme for a member of the academy.

Marsha Norman has reached a certain status level in academic scholarship with Irmgard H. Wolfe's "Marsha Norman: A Classified Bibliography" (*SAD* 3:148–75). Wolfe lists Norman's six plays, various interviews, criticism, reviews (by far the largest section in the essay), as well as biographical information. The single addition to Norman's criticism section this year is shared with Beth Henley, "Orality and Identity in *'night, Mother* and *Crimes of the Heart*" (*SAD* 3:23–39) by Laura Morrow. She asserts that both plays present women who are identified through habits of eating, drinking, smoking, and speaking which reveal traits of acquisitiveness or aggression. It seems a bit tricky because one must first accept Morrow's psychological theories.

David Rabe appears to be getting more than his share of critical attention, but such close study may be due to the enthusiasm of a single critic, Philip C. Kolin, who also coedits *Studies in American Drama.* A fragment from a cycle of plays that Rabe began several years ago was published as "Oddo's Response to the Queen Regarding the Question of Whether or Not Lamar Lies" (*SAD* 3:1–7). For the uninitiated, the fragment is an exercise in frustration in which truth and falsehood are perceptively clothed in confusion and only ill-mannered characters are identifiable. In "David Rabe, *Goose and Tomtom*" (*WLT* 62:128–29) Philip Kolin tries without success to place this new work in the Rabe canon. *David Rabe: A Stage History and a Primary and Secondary Bibliography* (Garland) may seem premature to some readers, but Kolin has done a thorough and scholarly job. Of the three parts in this volume, the first includes a short biography, a summary of Rabe's journalistic endeavors for the *New Haven Register* (1969–70), and a carefully researched stage history of Rabe's plays (1959–87). Part two is a primary bibliography of 177 items, and the third part is a secondary bibliography of 1,318 items. The Boswells obviously still live, but do the Johnsons?

Sam Shepard, A Casebook (Garland) is an anthology of 12 essays, commissioned, collected, and introduced by Kimball King to show the range, complexity, and achievement of this singular dramatist. All of the authors are enthusiastic in a manner reminiscent of the Albee fetish of 25 years ago. Although the complexity of Shepard's plays is more than evident, there is little indication of his range other than a belief in the significance of every word he ever wrote. Patrick J. Fennell's "Shepard's Lost Sheep" (pp. 3–20) considers his unpublished work from 1969 to 1979. Albert E. Wilhelm in "*Icarus's Mother*: Creative Transformations of a Myth" (pp. 21–30) has a problem because Shepard never mentions the Naucrate myth. Elizabeth Proctor emphasizes incongruity in situation and dialogue in "Offbeat Humor and Comic Mystery in Shepard's Plays: *La Turista, The Unseen Hand, The Mad Dog Blues,* and *Forensic and the Navigator* (pp. 31–51). Doris Auerbach asks "Who was *Icarus's Mother?* The Powerless Mother Figures in the Plays of Sam Shepard" (pp. 53–64) and provides a generic description. Christopher Brookhouse concentrates on Shepard's habit of speaking to the audience in "Story Itself" (pp. 65–72). "Notes on *Buried Child*" (pp. 73–80) is simply a rehearsal of Jane Ann Crum's problems as a producer of the play. Bruce J. Mann, in "Character Behavior and the Fantastic in Sam Shepard's *Buried Child*" (pp. 81–94), takes the easy way out and concludes that Shepard's characters are unexplainable. Ron Mottram feels that the disturbing contradictions in Shepard's view of the American condition may be explained as "Exhaustion of the American Soul: Sam Shepard's *A Lie of the Mind*" (pp. 95–106). Leonard Wilcox uses Freud's *Interpretation of Dreams* to explain "Language and Desire: The Object in Shepard's *Red Cross*" (pp. 107–20). Phyllis R. Randall praises Shepard's use of language in "Adapting to Reality's Language in Shepard's *Curse of the Starving Class*" (pp. 121–34). Ann Wilson has yet another essay on language and Freud, "Great Expectations: Language and the Problem of Presence in Sam Shepard's Plays" (pp. 135–53). On an off-beat subject but one of the most original essays in the volume, Tommy Thompson writes of Shepard's work as a musician with the Red Clay Ramblers: "Working for Sam" (pp. 155–58). One would never choose this volume as a good example of a casebook.

Although she is the author of a book-length study of Shepard, Linda Hart questions the greatness of a dramatist who is anti-women, arbitrarily violent, and resentful of any criticism. In "Sam Shepard's Pornographic Visions" (*SLitI* 21, ii:69–82) she criticizes Shepard's "Peep-show mentality," his pornographic imagination, and the "authoritarian violence" he directs against women. In some anger, she sees Shepard as oblivious to the issues he portrays and wonders about the politics of an artist who writes as he does. Finally, there is Lanford Wilson whose interests in comedy Martin J. Jacobi compares to those "smiling aspects" of humanity presented by William Dean Howells in both his novels and his plays. The essay, in which Jacobi comments on Wilson's dual themes in comedy, is entitled "The Comic Vision of Lanford Wilson" (*SLitI* 21, ii:119–34).

vii. Black Drama and Theater

In *Drumbeats, Masks and Metaphor* (1983) Geneviève Fabre argued that American blacks must decide whether they want to write only for blacks and have a minority drama or write universal plays and be part of world theater. Three books published this year on black American theater consciously or unconsciously react to that declaration. *Contemporary Black American Playwrights and Their Plays*

(Greenwood), ed. Bernard L. Peterson, Jr., is a biographical dictionary and dramatic index listing more than 700 playwrights who have written at least one play that has either been produced—although frequently in quite obscure places—or published since 1950. The number of playwrights listed suggests the inclusive character of this dictionary in which information varies from extremely slight to substantial. Of the playwrights listed, only two-thirds were actually contacted, and only 200 responded to the questionnaire, facts which lead one to wonder about the reliability of this work. It is a record of black playwriting, however, padded though it may be, and it describes an activity freely practiced in America. The Dramatists Guild boasts more than 8,000 members, and that is only the tip of the great mass of people, whatever their race, who write plays.

Elizabeth Brown-Guillory's *Their Place on the Stage: Black Women Playwrights in America* (Greenwood) provides an historical overview of black women playwrights and a detailed discussion of the plays of Alice Childress, Lorraine Hansberry, and Ntozake Shange. Emphasizing the structure and struggle in the plays of black women playwrights who promote the black family and the African rituals which are basic to African-American plays, Brown-Guillory tries to reach beyond the theater. Moreover, she believes that no white dramatist can interpret black life. Basically, her book is about black American women, not simply as playwrights in the American theater, but as propagandists for black African culture.

The most valuable book of the three is *The Development of Black Theater in America: From Shadows to Selves* (LSU) by Leslie Catherine Sanders. Sanders understands the history of black theater as the process of creating a black stage reality where black figures can be themselves and playwrights can employ only those European theatrical conventions that are appropriate to black interests and audiences. Although Sanders believes that white people are the main readers of black literature, she feels strongly that black writers should address blacks and that a national Negro theater providing drama meaningful to black audiences is an eventual necessity. She approaches this "process of creating a black stage" through a careful analysis of the works of five black playwrights. In the efforts of the first two—Willis Richardson and Randolph Edmonds—blacks laid claim to the theater. As Sanders analyzes the works of Langston Hughes, LeRoi Jones, and Ed Bullins, she shows how each playwright built upon the work of the earlier playwrights. Sanders's concept is clearly stated and her arguments are solidly expressed and sensitive to the feelings of all playwrights. She is particularly effective in her thorough discussion of the plays of Langston Hughes.

viii. Mélange

I include here a variety of essays that attracted my attention. Seth L. Wolitz provided some interesting background on a character that most of us discovered in *Fiddler on the Roof.* In "The Americanization of Tevye, or Boarding the Jewish *Mayflower*" (*AQ* 40:514–36) Wolitz writes about Tevye's appearance in several Jewish works as he became an archetype in American cultural history. In "Judy Grahn's Gynopoetics: The Queen of Swords" (*SLitI* 21, ii:47–67) Sue-Ellen Case defines Grahn's "voice" as that of the lesbian feminist, distinct from other feminist advocates and a constant challenge for the critic. In a well-ordered and convincing argument, Tom W. Boyd explains that "Clowns, Innocent Outsiders in the Sanctuary: A Phenomenology of Sacred Folly" (*JPC* 22:101–09) play out "their spectacle in order to undress us and reveal us to ourselves." They operate outside the norm, invite us to explore, and, by their eventual fall, remind us of our limits. In two panel discussions sponsored by the Dramatists Guild the 14 participants reveal some of the problems facing "The Playwright-Director Relationship" (*DGQ* 25, iii:6–18). And on the theater front, Ron Jenkins—"Penn and Teller" (*Theater* 19, iii:72–76)—argues that their show is an attempt to prepare audiences to deal with those con artists, such as advertising agencies and Ollie North, who try to run their daily lives. Linda Henderson, in "*Serious Money* and Critical Cost: Language and the Material World" (*Theater* 19, iii:87–88), indicts both Frank Rich and Joe Papp for their part in destroying *Serious Money.* Marc Robinson discusses "Dual Nationals: Squat, Squat/Love and Robbie McCauley" (*Theater* 19, ii:46–53) to point out the isolation from American society and the romantic character the three shows share. W. D. King is convincing in the distinction he suggests between "Good and 'B-a-d-d-d' Storytelling: John O'Neal's Junebug Jabbo Jones" (*Theater* 20, i:73–83), as performed on college campuses, and Garrison Keillor's storytelling on "A Prairie Home Companion."

ix. The Critics

"The critics, my dear Jonathan, are the very pests of society," so said Andrew Quoz; and many would agree that opinions on this matter have changed very little since Washington Irving endeared himself to playwrights so many years ago. In setting up the special issue of *Studies in the Literary Imagination* (vol. 21) on "Public Issues, Private Tensions: Contemporary American Drama," Mathew C. Roudané solicited the views of three well-known critics. Herbert Blau expressed his opinions in "Hysteria, Crabs, Gospel and Random Access: Ring Around the Audience" (*SLitI* 21, ii:7–21). After some preliminary wry remarks about theatricality becoming the "end-all of performance," Blau concentrated upon the audience as a "body of thought and power" and, with his usual acumen bolstered by uncustomary clarity, he disagreed with Walt Whitman that to have great poets there must be great audiences. It is a good thought, perhaps a desperate one. Martin Esslin took the opportunity to condemn American drama "as mainly a purveyor of entertainment" (p. 2), lacking spiritual insight, imagination, depth of thought, and daring—for, essentially, not being more like English and European drama which, presumably, always had these qualities. He had fun with his title, too—" 'Dead! And Never Called Me Mother!': The Missing Dimension in American Drama" (*SLitI* 21, ii:23–33)—although it would seem that if American dramatists did anything superbly, it was to imitate the sensational English melodrama of the 19th century. That could hardly be a "missing dimension."

Gerald Weales paid more attention to his assignment and argued convincingly that, although "Of Course, It's Only My Private Opinion" (*SLitI* 21, ii:35–45), the public issue intrudes into the private tension. Indeed, everything is public; "Privacy is an illusion." Weales sees the private plot within the public plot and feels that such plays demand much of their audiences which frequently disappoint the playwright. For more of Weales's opinions on the Broadway offerings this season read "American Theater Watch, 1987–8" (*GaR* 42:592–604). From a different point of view C. W. E. Bigsby addressed the question: "Whatever happened to American drama?" In "The Absent Voice: Drama and the Critic" (*SAD* 3:9–21) he explains why the theater is meaningful, even vital, to him and why modern American drama in particular rewards attention. It is an interesting, if completely unplanned, response to Esslin's observations by an English scholar and critic of considerable stature.

The world of criticism heaves and gasps in awkward fashion sometimes and emits a variety of sounds ranging from the sedate to the bizarre. Modern criticism reveals yet another of its many-faceted approaches in Jill Dolan's *The Feminist Spectator as Critic* (UMI Research Press). After describing herself as a white, middle-class, female, Jewish lesbian, Dolan explains that her "spectator" is different from the spectator of the traditional past. Her stated objective in this book is "to conduct a feminist inquiry into representation as a form of cultural analysis," "to uncover ideological meanings that perpetuate cultural assumptions oppressive to women." Such a thesis appears admirable, but the book marches quickly off in a slightly oblique direction to the demanding rhythm of a distinctive drummer. In an extremely self-conscious manner, Dolan rejects both liberal feminism and the cultural feminist to wave a banner in support of "Materialist Feminism" and a defense of lesbianism and lesbian theater. The X-rated portion of her argument, which appears in a chapter entitled "The Dynamics of Desire" (pp. 4–81), is little more than an excuse to describe and attempt to justify lesbian performance as a legitimate part of modern theater and lesbian sexuality as a legitimate perspective for the "feminist spectator as critic" as well as an appropriate alternative to the "white middle class, heterosexual male spectator."

This is my sixteenth essay on "Drama" for *ALS*—1966–73, 1981–88—and my last. In all of these essays and from my own prejudiced point of view I have tried to encourage the study of American dramatic literature. It has been something of a mission, I admit, and there are clearly recognizable roadblocks to the ideal scholarship I envision. Students of American literature are reluctant to see any value in plays written before Eugene O'Neill went to Provincetown where, on the sand dunes of Cape Cod, William Archer later discovered the beginnings of an American drama and announced his discovery to a world of literary scholars who have seldom questioned his presumption. Students of theater are mainly concerned with what is happening "right now" on the stages of America. If they are interested in theater history, they attach no importance to dramatists and have little knowledge of textual analysis. (In his monumental *Annals of the New York Stage* George C. D. Odell seldom mentions the author of a play.) Students of popular culture and folklore are beginning to find drama and theater exciting, but their prejudices run to spectacles and oddities. It is unfortunate that few cultural historians have learned the inestimable value of drama and theater. I have answers for all of these students, but mainly I would suggest that the study of American drama belongs in several disciplines. It is literature (good and bad); it can become a performance art; it reveals a great deal about people during any period of history. Roadblocks? "Au valeureux coeur rien impossible!"

Graduate School, City University of New York

19. Black Literature

R. Baxter Miller

The criticism and theory of Black American literature seeks a conscience as much as a method. Until the early 1960s literary history had held almost complete sway in African-American critical study. For the most part, the once-New Critics had been completely bypassed. With the arrival of the often more popular and populist black aestheticians of the late sixties and early seventies, the criticism of the field took on a more Marxist bent, delightfully bold and engaged. While so psychologically liberating, however, the method often was neither very textual nor discursively honed. Since 1978–79 the masterful structuralism of a Robert Stepto has given way to the variant versions of post-structuralism as practiced by the well-promoted Henry Louis Gates and Houston Baker. Concurrently, we have had the historical and racial feminism of Barbara Christian as well as the Marxist and postmodern feminism of Hazel Carby.

But we still have not had a substantial core of practical works about nearly any period other than the Harlem Renaissance and about any genre other than fiction or narrative. While other fields could afford the luxury of advancing naturally into theoretical superstructures and interdisciplinary paradigms of experimentation, the move for us has proved to be a sometimes unfortunate process of leapfrogging over the very basic homework yet unresearched. Where, for example, are the collected works and letters of Zora Hurston and Langston Hughes? I have designed a scheme to move from general commentary to that of a more focused and specific kind. Hence, I shall consider first a few general studies of scholarship and theory, including some critical reflection on the topic of women and feminism. Then I shall look chronologically at the various assessments of 12 or so writers who have been the primary subjects of discussions in this past year. What I intend to close with is some coherent state-

My colleague, Professor La Vinia Jennings, has aided me substantially in bibliographic searches and in providing critical insights—particularly in dealing with the works of Richard Wright and Toni Morrison.

ment about the way in which we are now engaged in reshaping the canon of African-American literature.

What I would suggest is that an invisible ideology informs the process of critical reception regardless of gender, that since the mid-seventies any hint of racial nationalism is socially forbidden. This rather elfish inquiry prompts a natural curiosity about who is marketing our theoretical and critical canon for whose approved consumption. It is practical, I think, to point to so many neglected areas of useful scholarship.

i. General Criticism and Theory

Despite a current trend heavily favoring critical and theoretical work, a few studies have generally been historically oriented. Probably the strongest of them has been Bernard Bell's *The Afro-American Novel and Its Tradition* (Mass., 1987). The author assumes the social boundaries of black America and proposes that they are as important as social and cultural change in the shaping of the form and content of the Afro-American novel. Consequently, he asserts that the black novel is more than a branch of the Euro-American one, for the former draws upon oral tradition as well. Bell raises the following questions: How are the "historical and cultural roots" that produce consciousness and aesthetic choices in the Afro-American novel different from those of Euro-America? And how have these differences shaped the double-consciousness in black American fiction? The study covers more than 150 novels by possibly a hundred novelists or more, giving close attention to 41. His very definition of the genre invalidates the prospects of a more rigidly defined formalism, structuralism, or post-structuralism: "The phrase Afro-American novel, for example, refers to any extended prose narrative written by an American of African ancestry that illuminates *the experience of black Americans* in a formal, imaginatively distinctive manner—thematically, structurally, or stylistically—*and whose intrinsic linguistic properties do not wholly explain its interpretation, reception, and reputation*" [my emphasis].

Though the methodology as practiced is somewhat of a historical throwback to Hugh Gloster's *Negro Voices in American Fiction* (No. Car., 1948), Robert Bone's so culturally flawed *Negro Novel in America* (Yale 1958), and Arthur P. Davis's extremely informative *From the Dark Tower* (1974), the book is clearly the best literary history of this generation. The study is well-researched and exhaustive, especially for the early years of narrative. Quite good for its comprehensiveness, the volume manages a rather humorous distinction between Euro-American and Afro-American readings of history, hence appropriating enough of a deconstructionist theory to give Bell a bit of a new angle. While tracing the plot and theme of the various works, Bell broadly considers major movements such as social and critical realism. His book, in addition, is one of first literary histories by a black male ever to be so painstaking in its efforts to enfranchise the historical struggle of black feminism. Though one may look elsewhere for boldly original insights, particularly for newly polished astuteness about symbolic form and value, this work will likely prove of vital help to graduate students who are about to take comprehensive exams in American and African-American fiction.

A more rudimentary book, *Self-Discovery and Authority in Afro-American Narrative* (Harvard 1987), by Valerie Smith, might be equally useful for undergraduates who need help with plot summary and theme. The work takes up the subjects of form and ideology in three slave narratives, including privilege and evasion in *The Autobiography of an Ex-Colored Man,* alienation and creativity in the fiction of Richard Wright, the invisible autobiographer of Ralph Ellison, and Toni Morrison's narratives of community. Smith argues that slave narratives, as well as the narrators of selected novels by black Americans in the 20th century, affirm the psychological legitimacy of personal and narrative autonomy.

Her introductory remarks show a critical astuteness probably rewritten into the text later. By fictionalizing life, Smith says, protagonists authenticate it. She places her reading of the slave narrators Equiano, Douglass, and Jacobs in the context of the economic and political production shaping their ends. In the subsequent treatment of more modern narratives, such as those by James Weldon Johnson and Ralph Ellison, she explains the way that they "invoke and subvert the form of this most American of genres." Finally, she intends to demonstrate the way that Wright's Bigger Thomas [*Native Son*] and Toni Morrison's Milkman [Macon Dead III, *Song of Solomon*] must be comprehended within the structural context of voice and narration. The ambitious approach is so admirable, but the effort still requires a focused authority and view in the critical voice that speaks it.

Smith's study does have a historical advantage over another one,

Conscientious Sorcerers: The Black Post Modernist Fiction of LeRoi Jones/Amiri Baraka, Ishmael Reed, and Samuel R. Delany (Greenwood 1987), by Robert Elliot Fox. While Baraka had the greatest influence on sociopolitical creativity, the author proposes, Delany's vision is ultimately more radical. Delany is the most "profoundly imaginative and intellectual of the three," but Reed is the most experimental and colloquial. While Reed is the most spontaneous in expression, Baraka is the most chameleon-like and demagogic. Delany has opened up new territories of black writing by imagining "realms of pure possibility." His visionary reach, therefore, frees his works from the burdensome problem and responsibility of African-American history. This encoded conservatism of an aesthetic, I would add, privileges an apparently ahistorical method (Delany) and a racially integrationist and multiethnic posture (Reed) over a historically intellectual standing (Baraka). But precisely this kind of (mis)reading—or failing to read—our accountability to historical consequence gets the protagonist in *Dutchman* killed.

Alden L. Nielsen's *Reading Race: White American Poets and the Racial Discourse in the Twentieth Century* (Georgia) is far more astute in decoding the ideological consciousness informing aesthetic structures of value. In the mid-19th century, he says, Herman Melville wrote the clearest disruption in white discourse, which would be expressed by James Baldwin a century later as "the real terror that engulfs the white world [and] is now a visceral terror. . . . It's the terror of being described by those they've been describing so long." Nielsen pursues the trace of the idea through the poets of transition and some more recent authors, all of whom inscribe poetically the racial "other." What Nielsen finds is that exoticism persists within the traditional structure and imagery of American verse in every decade of this century regardless of political persuasion. In writers as varied as Conrad, Lindsay, Eliot, Crane, and Stevens, Africa is the dark continent inhabited by primitives and "ruled over by death." In learning to read the American canon, in other words, we learn to read the hidden trace of racial preference; we fashionably adapt to the socialization of being [racist] Americans. For African-Americans today, there is no really indigenous need to retrace that hackneyed ground of seeing oneself through the ethnocentric eyes of the "other," as was true for Sterling Brown and others in the late thirties. But Nielsen has gone far beyond even his ablest predecessors by keeping with the spiritual revolution in deconstructionist theory more than with the linguistic dramatics of it. In short, he examines the way that the existence (or *being*) of race inscribes itself so covertly within American textuality. In doing so, he provides one of the most refreshingly brilliant studies in our literary history.

This is exactly the kind of brilliantly original and developed book that Houston A. Baker, Jr., envisions in his current work, *Afro-American Poetics* (Wisconsin 1988), the second volume in his trilogy that began with *Modernism and the Harlem Renaissance* (Chicago 1987) and that is scheduled to end with *Workings of the Spirit: The Poetics of Afro-American Women's Writing.* Quite honestly, Baker asserts that few moralists do not discover in their lives evidence of their own assumed rightness. Similarly, he proposes, few critics do not find in their own work evidence of their own "stunning fidelity to the 'spirit' of their subject." He proposes *Afro-American Poetics* as a kind of intellectual biography in which he takes his publishing career as a synecdoche for the struggles of the Afro-American intelligentsia. The book, he claims, is his own narrative for "confronting the disappearance of culture and the self announced by post-modernism." His subtopics are the art of Jean Toomer's *Cane*, the poetry of Countee Cullen, and the reflections on Amiri "Imamu" Baraka [who dropped the middle name], the criticism of Larry Neal, and the reflections of Hoyt Fuller.

While the first two of these writers are most problematic in terms of racial identity, I think, the subsequent ones are more culturally nationalistic. Baker suggests his early scholarly work as a sign of a possibly symbolic journey from the first group, with its integrationist ideology of literary art, to the second group with its post-1960 aesthetic. What this highly suggestive synecdoche does conceal is the way that his own interim studies between *The Journey Back* (Chicago 1980) and those today have—through a post-structuralist revision and reorientation—returned quite literally toward European conceptions, forms, and terminologies. But quite commendably Baker continues to rediscover and inscribe his own soul-searching. So aware of the determinacy of language, he concedes that some interpretive postures are privileged in a scholarly will to power. His critical discourse itself suggests a privileged rebirth into blackness on the African-American side, yet a mellowed maturation into Euro-American and liberal idealism on the other. While directly regretting his own younger moments of critical polemic over the possibility of expository theory as well as history, he intends to close with humility: "We offer . . . a much belated apology." Ultimately he invokes the liberal diction of "Goodwill," a favorite term of Booker T. Washington.

Baker has some very intelligent defenders. Michael Awkward, for example, proposes to defend him and Henry Louis Gates against the "attack" by Joyce Joyce. Awkward's inquiry focuses on the way that "blackness" dictates the practice of critical interpretation. To him, Baker and Gates appropriate post-structuralism to "allow Afrocentric reading [undefined] to pursue its full potential [undefined and undescribed]." In allying Baker and Gates with Mary Jacobus, as opposed to Elaine Showalter, who is a far more "reductionist" feminist, Awkward inscribes a highly intelligent posture of critical theory. But beneath this guise of radical liberalism, the position proves quite reactionary. Though he is quite open-minded, for example, in calling with Adrienne Rich for a "re-vision" of texts, he might have considered something else possibly even more provocative: Who, for example, produces contemporary and theoretical discourse for whose consumption and whose academic advancement? Though Marx would allow for this kind of question, Locke and others—including the founders of the Enlightenment and the Western logic of the ad hominem fallacy—would preclude any inquiry of the kind.

Perhaps the most original article in the *College Language Association Journal*, meanwhile, was on "The Characterization of Native Americans in the Antebellum Slave Narrative." Focusing on the autobiographies of Henry Bibb, Solomon Northup, and Josiah Henson, as well as Austin Steward, the Shawnee becomes not only a metaphor but a sign of racial brotherhood expressed against white racism. The essay details the way that the slaves themselves struggle against internalizing the values of "other" races and nations, including the stereotypes of Native Americans as drunkards as well as barbarians. We look in vain for a perspicacity of literary technique and metaphor; we want for some idea of whether the texts she studies are actually any good. But asking good literary history to do so is probably demanding that an apple become an orange.

At least one issue of the *Langston Hughes Review* did attempt to achieve a reasonable compromise. The special issues dedicated to Therman B. O'Daniel, founding editor of *CLAJ* and of the *Review* itself, was a rare treat. Black American critics—except in the pages of *ALS* and in those of similarly admirable forums of intellectual democracy—are usually invisible. Burney J. Hollis (This Was a Man! A Tribute . . . *LHRev* 5, ii[1986]:1–4) dates O'Daniel's achievement as a literary historian. As editor of the *Journal* from 1957 to 1982, says Hollis, O'Daniel exerted a prominent influence on the quantity and quality of African-American literary scholarship.

O'Daniel was equally visionary and distinguished while assisting in the founding of the Langston Hughes Society. In his role as the originating editor of the *Review*, he was unusually helpful; sometime earlier he had favored pioneering in books of black writers through his *Langston Hughes, Black Genius: A Critical Evaluation* (Morrow 1971) and *James Baldwin: A Critical Evaluation* (Howard). As the second scholar to join the Middle Atlantic Writers Association, marking an imaginative resurgence of literary Africana in Baltimore, in 1984 he received the award for Distinguished Literary Criticism. R. Baxter Miller ("'One Prime Obligation': The Example of Therman B. O'Daniel" *LHRev* [1986]5, ii:5–10) reads the work and life of the scholar as signifying a problem in black American critical theory, including a tension between traditionally classic and populist aesthetics and the inseparability of literary form from morality.

Whatever the authors the scholar focused upon, what bound them together in O'Daniel's thought was morality. In trying to resolve the dilemma of segregated and integrated worlds, O'Daniel focused much of his critical attention during the past 20 years on writers who emerged during the 1950s. Intuitively he recognized the degree to which the African-American and European-American called upon somewhat different forms to portray the black experience either as catastrophe or humor. What he revealed indirectly through his work, is the limit of the high style to inscribe absolutely a standard of "either human value or great art." After essays on Blyden Jackson, Charles T. Davis, and George E. Kent, this one continues Miller's inquiry dating from 1984 into the black American imperative to resolve theoretical dualism.

ii. Women and Feminist Criticism

Women studies has inspired a realignment of African-American literature. For convenience of discussion, I refer to "women" as the theme of the critical discourse; "Feminism" I define as the self-conscious theory of empowering Woman as a self-determining voice within the body of her own language.

In "Through Their Sister's Eyes: The Representations of Black Men in the Novels of Toni Morrison, Alice Walker, and Toni Cade Bambara," (*DAI* 48, 8:2009A), Komla Messan Nubukpo achieves an unusually candid and balanced view that does somewhat displace black woman as her own writing subject. While Toni Morrison focuses on the psychological integration of black men in the North, Walker stresses the black Southern male's marginal attempts to both assert his manhood and meet his human obligations. Morrison's view, on the other hand, allows for individual expression of males, while her fictional world creates a Manichean perspective weighted with the burden of gender. Toni Cade Bambara, who has favored racial unity over any gendered division, believes that the fulfillment of black men will have to accompany the acknowledged contributions of black women. Like Alice Walker, Bambara reads the racial commonalty of expression but does not allow individual choices to undermine communal cohesiveness. While each of these women proposes to know men better than they know themselves, the men would probably disagree. What the author superbly achieves beneath this delightfully rare humor is the awareness that each of us inscribes our privileged myth of gender, class, and race in our own image. In other words, we almost always risk a psychological rebellion against—yet inevitable complicity with—the very critical and theoretical orders we condemn.

The impressive majority of "womanist" criticism is quite historically objective. Sandra Y. Govan, for example, has edited a fine special issue of the *Langston Hughes Review*, so astutely inviting talented scholars to fill in significant gaps of neglected writers in the Harlem Renaissance. Women are especially subjects for five of the seven articles. T. J. Bryan (6, ii[1987]:11–21) takes Helene Johnson as a rather standard exemplar of the misled talent (*Obsidian II* 3, ii:1–8). Bryan blames Dean Kelly Miller of Howard University, who, in the *Crisis* of 1915, favored the disenfranchisement of women and encouraged them to write a kind of 20th-century poetry now out of favor. In many instances, she says, Johnson's poems are "ladylike," treating the standard subjects of love and nature, though other of her works are more innovative. Through urban speech and experimental forms, Johnson initiated a new phase in black female poetry. Bryan persists in her usual theme that "black" males such as William Stanley Braithwaite and Alain Locke had foisted an outdated ideal for black womanhood upon their female contemporaries.

What she might have added, without any inclination to blame both black women and men as victims, is that the women involved did have their own freedom of choice. Black patriarchy could not control their wills. Indeed, the same patriarchy that confined them favored in many ways the genteel Countee Cullen and Jessie Fauset over the folk Langston Hughes and Zora Hurston. So it is that gender makes even more sense when we place it within the biases of social class and the consequent production of a pervasively ideological conservatism. Johnson's polite warning against "bitterness," for instance, parallels the male diction of Booker T. Washington, who was in part her intellectual progenitor. In the Bryan essays, we still need a feel for the flavor and tone of these women's aesthetic world and the individualized voices of their communal language.

Govan's own article "Gwendolyn Bennett" (*LHRev* [1987]13, 1: 70–74) is an interesting inquiry into the constant tension between the public and private lives of the poet. Of particular note is her quite revealing aside to Langston Hughes: "I don't like the idea of your being styled a bus-boy gone poet, [*sic*] I know some of what you feel, although I have not reached the famous state *yet* [my emphasis]." Later, she would cite one of his favorite tropes from Robert Frost: "One always chooses the wrong thing. Two roads diverged in a wood and I . . . I took the one less traveled by and that has made all the difference." Then we realize that Bennett's engagement to Alfred Jackson, her future husband who was then a medical student at Howard University, would cause a minor scandal on that campus of then so strict a patriarchal autocracy. To Bennett, I believe, Frost's road was the complex sign of a creative woman's imagined yet unfulfilled self.

"The Female as Harlem Sage: The 'Aunt Viney Sketches' of Oliva Ward Bush Banks," by Bernice F. Guillaume (*LHRev* [1987]6, 2:1–9, takes more of a purely factual approach to literary genre and tradition. The author, an interdisciplinary scholar in American studies, documents that Oliva Ward Bush Banks (1869–1944) [and–without formal mention–Guillaume's literal ancestor] completed skits of folk comedy similar to those by Langston Hughes on Simple. As one of the first 20th-century characters of Afro-American dialect, Viney conveys ethnic pride and self-confidence. This article reminds us about how the literary indebtedness of a particular form belongs to more than any one person.

What we do find now and then in even the most brilliant and

self-reflexive feminist criticism is a displacement of the racially holistic text. Perhaps the most rewarding and sustained of all these general studies of gender, for instance, is Hazel V. Carby's *Reconstructing Womanhood: The Emergence of the Afro-American Woman Novelist* (Oxford 1987). The author, a Marxist feminist of international persuasion, charts a mission worthy of a distinguished series in literary scholarship. She proposes to rethink black feminist theory in terms of the women's era, slaves and mistresses, narratives of slave and free women before Emancipation, work of Frances Ellen Watkins Harper, black feminist thought after Emancipation, magazine fiction of Pauline Elizabeth Hopkins, and black cultural politics. First, Carby proposes that black women had to confront "the dominant domestic ideologies and literary conventions of womanhood" in order to be published, and, second, that her historical account questions those strands of contemporary feminist historiography and literary criticism that seek to establish the existence of an American sisterhood between black and white women; finally, she states that though Afro-American cultural and literacy history commonly assumes the late 19th and early 20th centuries to be the times of great men, such as that of Washington and Du Bois, the view marginalizes the political contributions of black women. These were, in fact, the years for the first flowering of autonomous organizations by women and a period of intensely intellectual production. Carby, bolstered by a look at the work of Harper and Hopkins, as well as at the political writings of Anna Julia Cooper and Ida B. Wells, seeks to reconstruct the traditional view of the period. Writing in the midst of a new "black women's renaissance," she wants to reestablish the existence of a "perhaps more politically resonant renaissance" of rethinking the cultural politics of black women." This study is incredibly ambitious and vital. While it does bite off a bit too much—so much that nearly every subtopic merits a book of its own—the volume is quite provocative. Once more we need *the feel* of these women speaking in their own metaphors and in their own voices.

Were the writings and writers themselves any good? By whose design, if any, must gender completely displace race as a valid way for reading American history? Why? Does anyone consciously *produce* this displacement, or is the apparent product only a coincidentally natural order of historical enlightenment? Finally, what has all of this to do with colonial regimes by the West, particularly the British legacy in South Africa? What, then, is this complex connection between gender and the patriarchal power still writing itself out in Western history, including the destinies not only of women but of entire peoples?

To demonstrate what I mean, consider two highly intriguing examples of a quite diverse persuasion. For the sake of contrast, I shall consider them here broadly rather than in the more individually organized sections on Toni Morrison and Alice Walker below. Wendy Wall's "Lettered Bodies and Corporeal Texts in *The Colored Purple*" (*SAF* Spring 16, 1:83–87) is simply brilliant and ingenious. Through the narration of rape, wife-beating, genital mutilation, and facial disfigurement, *The Color Purple* tells many instances in which the *human body* [female] [my italics] must submit to the forces of patriarchal authority. But, in the course of the narrative, Celie learns to reshape the marks of oppression and to define herself through letters. These forms of "operating" as a "second body" mediate between her and the power structure so as to give her a voice. Her letters signify the secrecy open to violent intrusion. The work symbolically enacts the current rift between *Anglo-American feminism* (my italics) positing the powerlessness of female fragmentation and *Franco-American feminism* (my italics), asserting disjunction and disunity as desirable conditions. In the latter view, this marginalized or "partitioned" woman is better able to disrupt "fixities within the [whose?] culture."

The article is delightfully postmodernist, showing once more a polished and inadvertent complicity with the very Western patriarchy it only so apparently condemns. For example, the very epistolary form of *The Color Purple* places it quite traditionally within the bourgeois rise of the English novel with Samuel Richardson and Henry Fielding; the use of epigraphs implies nicely a kind of convenient structuralism, or a reading of textual and verbal relations, ultimately directing us away from any truly proposed radical difference of woman's body to a more formalistic or verbal design. Our aloof destination is, in other words, quite subconsciously toward a reanointment of the sacredness of lettered texts—hence back to the "future" of "formalism." It is the last of these, I think, that finally displaces woman's very human body with "literate" and idealized form (letters). What is missing from this view is quite literally African-American feminism. The same is true for the tradition of the black female novel and for black critics in general. Wall's scintillating reading so impresses itself on the body of first world thought that it renders the very conception of this vision powerless and invisible. We read here, in other words, a confined and self-subverting radicalism marking a failure to write black woman's own body so as to make it not only a [white] feminist trope but a [black] material force in American history.

What are these African-American women supposed to do other than be? The very question disrupts our easiness because black woman's body is not only an intertextual sign but a reference to the sociopolitical power inscribing itself in "English" texts. The consequent disfigurement marks her racial body in ways apparently not so easily seen or ignored. Through African-American women writers, we read at least *three* bodies simultaneously: the body of gendered text, the body of racial community and struggle as translated into the writing consciousness, and the body of American history.

Carolyn Denard's "The Convergence of Feminism and Ethnicity in the Fiction of Toni Morrison" (Nellie Y. McKay, *Critical Essays on Toni Morrison*; [Hall], 171–79) proposes a more complexly varied sisterhood than does Wall. While feminism is more political for [some] white women, she says, it is more cultural for [most or some] black women. Morrison develops primarily women characters who combine feminism and ethnicity and who are not self-centered but group-centered. In contrast, Morrison portrays but does not condone characters such as Jadine (*Tar Baby*) and Sula (*Sula*). Morrison suggests that their cultural detachments result in existential emptiness. When the woman in yellow (*Tar Baby*) sees Jadine and spits, I extrapolate, the symbolic action underscores a structural irony. And though it is certainly dubious to make absolute distinctions between racial groups of women, at least Denard makes an astute effort to free Morrison's world from the traditionally reductive ideology of individualism. The last of these has been widely praised in MLA sessions and elsewhere since the mid-seventies. Somewhere between Walls and Denard exists the kind of sensitively brilliant methodology we require, but both scholars may need to hear the unique voices of black women writers and to facilitate a criticism allowing for culturally gendered intonations to speak for themselves.

iii. Individual Writers

***a.* Frederick Douglass.** Recent criticism on the work of Frederick Douglass demonstrates once more the way that scholarship makes for the conscious reading of the literary text and the subconscious reading into it of our own self-interested signs of interpretation. To John Burt, in "Learning to Write: The Narratives of Frederick Douglass (*WHR* 42, 4:330–44), literacy enables Douglass to cross between the two identities of "selfhood" and "citizenship." In the three narratives written between 1845 and 1892, Douglass fashions the democratic identity in which the individual can interact with other people in the public world.

While I believe a basic tendency is to appropriate this writing as an expression of democratic individualism, a more challenging prospect would mean reading the work as an ironic enactment of American codes of ideological value. The work of Douglass signifies our communal failure in having once promoted institutionalized slavery. To say that the drafts of Douglass's autobiography represent only varied states of the literate self or of the American government is to be structurally reductive. These narratives, on the contrary, suggest a real need to redress a capitalistic imbalance regarding the relative worth of property and humans. *My Bondage and My Freedom,* the 1855 revision of the 1845 narrative, represents for David Leverenz (*Criticism* 29, 3[1987]:341–70) a "shift in Douglass' assessment of American manhood." Though Douglass associates this state initially with freedom, he interprets it later as dominance, fear of humiliation, and dignified self-control. This redefinition also led to his feminism, after which he demonstrates a more refined linguistic command.

What Leverenz prefers to overlook, however, is the way that the autobiographical narrator and voice become far more insufferably detached and bourgeois, even regarding the temporary refusal by Douglass in later life to acknowledge racial discrimination against his own daughter at school. But Leverenz does show quite positively the way that feminism now influences our reading of even black male writers.

***b.* Jessie Fauset.** Even today Jessie Fauset is still misunderstood. But she is an invaluable link in revealing the ideological bond between gender and class as well as that between black women and men. While Fauset claimed that a member of the black bourgeoisie was primarily similar to every other (white) American (Margaret Perry "The Santa Claus Myth: The *Crisis* Short Stories of Jessie Redmond Fauset," *LHRev* 6, ii[1987]:44–49), she was an important writer in the Harlem Renaissance. Her overriding theme was that the "handicap" of color burdened and limited her art. Usually she wrote "dreamy, bloodless stories about beautiful, intelligent people who were searching for the American dream of love, freedom[,] and a home." Without a true dimension of verisimilitude, and with strained and elevated dialogue, she presented weak plots about implausible situations. So determined to prove that Afro-Americans were comparable to Euro-Americans, she created fairy tales of black life. But she was an informal mentor to someone like Langston Hughes, whose class ideology differed markedly from her own. She helped, I think, imprint a diverse color on American culture. Whatever her bourgeois inclinations, she achieved an intellectual authority and genuine dignity unrivaled perhaps by even Hurston.

What Fauset also succeeded in having—as was almost inexplicably more true with Du Bois than with Hurston—was a genuine love for children. Violet Harris ("Jessie Fauset's Transference of the 'New Negro' Philosophy to Children's Literature," *LHRev* 6, ii[1987]:36–43) writes that Fauset merits distinction for *The Brownie's Book*, an example of emancipating literature for children, a publication that first appeared in *The Crisis*. As the Du Bois's agent, Fauset had many objectives for making black children realize the normality of their experience. She intended, for example, to provide them with role models of success and to teach them a chivalric code of interracial cooperation. She hoped to transform their pain into communal love as well as to instruct them on the value of life; she hoped to make them professionally responsible regarding public sacrifice. With ideology as a post-1960s factor, she has never received her critical due; with her Phi Beta Kappa key figuratively in hand, she never made the claims to the masses as Hurston did. But she was a serious thinker, particularly regarding the fictional representation of woman's dilemma of self and marriage. I find it difficult to imagine a Harlem Renaissance without her nurture as well as her guidance. Her work merits more serious study.

***c.* Zora Neale Hurston.** Now that Zora Hurston is so firmly entrenched as the symbolic mother of black female writing, too many scholars are still examining her in the hackneyed terms and concepts of oral tradition. Others continue to read her opus rather superficially for stock devices (quilt, shawl, etc.) of female writing. Now while some readers even reaffirm some dubious superstructures of Freudian psychology, critics elsewhere propose that her voice has the posture of feminist empowerment and liberation.

But how, exactly, is it hers? Klaus Benesch, in "Oral Narrative and Literary Text: Afro-American Folklore in *Their Eyes Were Watching God*" (*Callaloo* 11, iii:627–35), observes the merger of literary and oral style, indicating the protagonist Janie Crawford's "blackness" in celebrating speech as a "natural [?], artistic gift." In most instances writers focus almost exclusively on the aesthetic forms or social dynamics. For instance, a quite able article, "The Anthropological Narrator of Hurston's *Their Eyes Were Watching God* (*SAF* 16, ii:169–80), by John D. Kalb, observes the way that Janie Crawford creates her own vision of the world, hence internalizing and externalizing her private experience. He writes that Janie selects and arranges the material of her narrative as an authentic recorder, spectator, and ethnographer of her culture. Afro-American life is the absent dimension.

d. **Jean Toomer.** Sometimes when scholars do look culturally at American literary history, they read comfortably the voice of a writer who happened to be black. For instance, critics almost never have known exactly what to do with Jean Toomer, a brief interloper into the Harlem Renaissance. Without ever escaping the margins of traditional American history, he was an anomaly and sometimes even a quack more than the genius he wanted to be. *The Lives of Jean Toomer: A Hunger for Wholeness* (LSU 1987), by Cynthia Earl Kerman and Richard Eldridge, provides a very informative narrative of this author (1894–1967), arrived on the American literary scene in 1923 with the publication of *Cane*, a highly experimental collection of prose and poetry.

What Toomer needed for lasting greatness, I think, was a powerfully synthetic voice; what he refused to see was that difference must be faced before it can be dissolved; that delighting in cultural diversity could in the long run facilitate a human family on more honest grounds. Only momentarily in *Cane* does he ever represent the artist's profound tension in dramatic fiction. Eldridge and Kerman give us the textual evidence needed to read the anxiety in his literary world and to redeem our own.

e. **Langston Hughes.** The true excellence of Arnold Rampersad's biography of Langston Hughes (*The Life of Langston Hughes*, 2 vols. (Oxford 1986) is that it inevitably looks beyond the same Harlem that Toomer almost never wanted to claim. While Rampersad's narrative voice depends primarily upon some brilliant detective work and superb detail, extending even to medical records, the comprehensive facts can signify only the true essence of the artist who in his own way was so uniquely mysterious and privately guarded, so publicly acclaimed and protective of his national as well as his international reputation. Of the three narrative voices present in different dimensions, one is that of Langston Hughes, who speaks in the form of correspondences and essays on behalf of himself. Then there are the mixed narratives of the friends and acquaintances who speak posthumously through interviews about him. Beyond all the rest of the voices is that of the well-versed literary historian who most trusts his own story.

The first volume of the *Life*, published in 1986 with great acclaim, won the Anisfileld-Wolf award in Race Relations while earning a listing by the *New York Times Book Review* as one of the best books of the year. This volume chronicled the poet's life from his birth through the advent of World War II. Now the second narrative charts Hughes's development from his status as black America's most original and beloved poet in 1940–41 to his death in 1967. Hughes, who was by then the dean of Afro-American writers, had become a renowned artist. His fiction, plays, and poems had sewn seeds of influence throughout the Caribbean and Africa as well as in the Americas. Having contributed steadily to the war effort in the United States, while consistently attacking racial segregation at home, he would come under surveillance by the FBI as early as 1940. Besieged by right-wing bigotry in the fifties and sixties (as he had been in the thirties) he was a verbal artist committed to black life.

I can word the fascinating implication of Rampersad's work another way: Langston Hughes was unwilling for the human limits of the biographical self to tarnish the artistic character living on in the work, making him one of the few modern poets of any persuasion or race to have a true voice or signature. In his art he was out to sell not an artifact of form but a varied literary soul embodied through these very forms. To him, the modernist disjunctives between "me" and "it," between, for example, the bearer of soul in "The Negro Speaks of Rivers" and the larger Soul informing his literary world was largely nonexistent. Whatever the varied reading of the work itself, Rampersad has written an original biography that will be definitive for a very long time. A primary reason is what we rarely associate with fine biographies at all—the painstaking and almost coincidental discovery of neglected texts, hence facilitating fresh readings of artistic theory and practice that will go far beyond this one book.

Subconsciously, Hughes had understood the mutual bond between the historical world and his own creative one. What Faith Berry (*Langston Hughes: Before and Beyond Harlem* 1983) had displayed several years before Rampersad's work was often the *literary sense* expressed in her subtitle; Richard Barksdale's *Langston Hughes: The Poet and His Critics* (1977) looks as well for the voice and vision of the artistic Hughes behind the cultured forms. Rampersad's brilliant research gives new factual weight to this deference of history and triumph of art.

En route to his definitive narrative, Rampersad had considered "Langston Hughes and His Critics on the Left" (*LHRev* [1986]5, ii: 34–40). Radicalism, he proposed, left an unhealed wound on Hughes's reputation. The "virtual surrender" before Senator Joseph McCarthy's Permanent Subcommittee on Investigations as well as the apparently political decisions to omit political undesirables such as W. E. B. Du Bois and Paul Robeson from a few writings in later life discomforted Hughes. Between 1926 and 1940 he owed very little to the left, which generally provided his published work with only an inferior criticism marred by reductive intolerance. What the left misunderstood as his "petty bourgeois ambivalence" was actually his continued effort to mediate between historical racism and the communal love of blacks. Whereas only Hughes could have written "The Negro Speaks of Rivers," any writer with appropriate range and adroitness might have managed "Good Morning Revolution."

What Hughes tried to do, I think, was negotiate an independent voice between the position of institutionalized European power and racism on the one hand and the prospects of African-American self-redemptive love on the other. Hughes sought, in other words, to balance the dialectic between the humane self and deterministic history. This effort moved him beyond many capitalists who exploit the ideas of the Enlightenment only ostensibly to seek this human self and many Marxists who propose a certitude of social determinism only to empower themselves as media for achieving the end.

With the exception of Hurston, Hughes is the only African-American writer to have an entire periodical dedicated to his own work, his literary circle, and to black folk tradition. Thanks to the highly able George H. Bass, who was Hughes's secretary and is now the executor of the estate, the issues have displayed brilliant planning of unusually high quality. At the forefront has been Faith Berry, a pioneering biographer and editor of his collected work. In "Saunders Redding as Literary Critic of Langston Hughes" (*LHRev* 5, ii[1986]: 24–28), she reports that the scholar was a regular reviewer for the Baltimore-based *Afro-American* from 1944 through 1966. Indeed, Redding assessed nearly all of the books that Hughes had published. While the paths of the two creative men of so different a calling never crossed at Lincoln University in Pennsylvania, from whence Redding would transfer to Brown University, and Hughes would receive his degree in 1929, the two men met in Hampton, Virginia, in 1943. Redding is one of the most persistent and important voices on Langston Hughes.

This article would prove to be an informative precursor of Berry's excellently edited issue (Spring 1987) containing 10 fine articles that reassess the international range of Hughes scholarship near the close of the eighties. Here Myriam Díaz-Diocaretz offers a provocative revision of the way we read women in Hughes. Alberta K. Johnson, for example, is the most complex representation of Hughes's poetic world, for here the first-person narrator empowers herself as a speaking subject. Madam's figure is neither matriarchal, the "seductive dark-eyed whore," nor a "kinder" mistress; it is that of a working woman. Clearly the author's tone is feminist-Marxist. Though the essay bogs down into a dehumanized structuralism, it is one of the most balanced and perceptive studies of its kind.

Elsewhere, Ugo Rubeo documents the way that Hughes and Richard Wright became in post-World War II Italy the focus of a few intellectuals, particularly of Stefania Piccinato, who was destined to emerge as the leading Italian expert on Hughes's work. All of this was news to us. True to his fine reputation, Michel Fabre, possibly the dean of Afro-American Studies in France, observes the often undocumented role of Wright's founding there of Présence Africaine. Subsequently, Fabre pioneers the observation that the presence of Hughes in Africa and his "persistent struggle to make certain that black American writers would be present on the shelves of USIS libraries abroad" made him the most popular of African-American writers in French-speaking Africa and the Antilles.

A final essay by Amritjit Singh, "Beyond the Mountain: Langston Hughes on Race/Class and Art," is a brilliant application of contemporary theory to the writer's work. Hughes reminds us, says Singh, that a total understanding of a work's cultural background ("difference") is not necessarily a prerequisite to artistic meaning ("equality"). Hughes had the creative power to recognize and reveal a rhetorical duality of a "different" environment permeated by a still very human self. This admirable article tends to modify the often inflexible principles of a narrow structuralism so as to recognize with balance both the needs of culture and those of myth.

So much of Faith Berry's success actually goes back to Marvin E. Lewis, who wrote the foreword to the *LHRev* 5, i (1986):vii–viii. Lewis places the published presentations of Dellitta L. Martin-Ogunsola, Carolyn Hodges, and Richard L. Jackson within the context of a continuing discussion of Hughes internationally.

Whereas Martin-Ogunsola focuses on the common myth in the musical structure of Hughes and Negritude, poets such as Nicholás Guillén, Jacques Roumain, Leon Damas, and Richard Jackson offer a complementary reading of Hughes, who was a spiritual inspiration to Latin American poets. Yet where black writers have promoted the poet's impact on developing countries, literary scholars in Germany have assumed the responsibility themselves. What makes the Hodges essay on German scholarship so interesting is her subconscious implication that our very conceptualization of race and nation exists *within* Indo-European language, particularly English (High German) and German, and that to reassess the importance of writers like Hughes means conceiving an aesthetic beyond the self-enclosure of Indo-European language. By extension, we would have to re-view the linguistic derivatives of Latin and, hence, the literary consciousness inherited from the Roman Empire. The problem, in other words, is that English and German irreducibly encode the consciousness and values of the European colonizer—indeed, a conception of the very world and universe. Someday a literary linguist will likely follow this concept to a significant discovery about the way that our inherited language subconsciously binds the blue horizon (Hurston) of our thought.

Today for the first time Steven C. Tracy's *Langston Hughes and the Blues* (Illinois) provides a solid and sustained revision of knowledge that most of us could have researched over the past 60 years. But the integrationist paradigm or bifurcation of black African oral and European written forms began to be received with great enthusiasm near the close of the seventies. Tracy "traces" the influence of the oral blues tradition on Hughes's blues poems, thereby demonstrating how Hughes merged Afro-American oral and written traditions by exploiting conventions and goals of both to achieve a poetry that is intellectually stimulating, sociopolitically responsible, and aesthetically pleasing as folk poetry and literature. While the last two terms are not mutually exclusive, Tracy looks at the topics of folklore and the Harlem Renaissance as they prove instrumental in defining and creating the blues. In a spin-off, "'Midnight Ruffles of Cat-Gut Lace': The Boogie Poems of Langston Hughes" (*CLAJ* 32, i:55–68), he observes that Hughes accomplishes jazz improvisations of styles and riffs. His method imposes a musical superstructure that minimizes the dialogue between verbal and musical designs in the poetry itself. Tracy also might consider the significant qualities of historical consciousness within the context of black literary scholarship. But the job is solidly competent.

***f.* Richard Wright.** Though the deadline for this 1988 edition of *ALS* postpones our assessment of *Richard Wright: Myths and Realities*, ed. Trotman James (Garland), until next year's report, other work on Wright pigeonholes his literary art into one or two readily established superstructures of ideology. Probably the most obvious exception is Keneth Kinnamon's *Richard Wright Bibliography* (Greenwood). This significant book is an annotated list of 13,117 items printed from 1933 to 1982. It is exhaustive for books, articles, reviews, notes, news items, publisher catalogs and promotional materials, and includes dissertations, theses, encyclopedias, biographical dictionaries, handbooks, and study guides. For a test, I examined annotations of scholars such as Michel Fabre, Kinnamon himself, Trudier Harris, Houston A. Baker, Henry Louis Gates, R. Baxter Miller, and Jerry W. Ward. The inclusions are impeccably thorough. In fact, Miller, who then had not written even a single article on Wright, has nine entries for passing commentary alone. Kinnamon's great tome of nearly a thousand pages—I wince at the years of work involved—is surely an academic fetish mitigating against qualitative selection; his compilation favors the annotation of content over originality for the works reviewed. We need to look elsewhere for the literary forms as well as for the techniques and theories of original expression by and of Wright; far more emphasis here goes to biography and sources. But every serious library needs this relentlessly industrious and comprehensive book.

More typical now are studies, such as that by Alan W. Frances ("Misogyny and Appropriation in Wright's *Native Son*," *MFS* 34:413–23), that shrewdly displace the psychological struggle of the black male in America. In looking beyond the conflict with white racism, says Frances, Bigger's fear of expropriation sets in motion his effort to appropriate and dehumanize women who are reduced to objects of male status conflict. While this view of Wright's literary sexism has become somewhat standard during the past decade or so, the critical posture of the essay may be either transparently progressive or deceptively reactionary.

Nearly every Wright critic has missed the epiphany of Bessie Mears, who exclaims something like "I *see* [my italics] it all now. I *see* everything you [Bigger, the *native son* and synecdoche of America] ever tried to do to me." Perhaps Bigger is as much a murdering chauvinist as might be this so noble country of which he is only a sign. Blaming only Bigger helps us to identify completely with the society that sent him to the electric chair, and Wright's brilliantly ironic reading of us continues unabated into another generation.

Similarly, critics have constantly overlooked the way that Sarah in "Long Black Song" offers a nurturing alternative to patriarchal and linear time. Indeed, she sets into remarkable relief the male competition and acquisitiveness fostering so boyishly a mating feud, the synecdoche for war. The "woman-hating" Wright—who never forgave the "female" sensitivity in himself because fate and society had literally paralyzed his mother—was curiously a precursor of African-American feminism.

Jack Moore's "Black Power Revisited: In Search of Richard Wright," (*MissQ* 61:161–86) is a close examination of the impact of Wright's three-month stay in West Africa in 1953 and the formation of *Black Power* (1954). A prose work of factual and accurate recording, the book shows Wright playing the role of outsider in his ancestral land. Wright reshapes his perceptions of Africa to conform to the role he "feels" is his.

g. Ralph Ellison. Several years ago Darwin T. Turner suggested in these pages that the epoch of Wright had become supplanted by the age of Ellison. What Turner may have been so tactfully implying was that a new age of enthusiastic integration—primarily on the part of Afro-Americanists who hungered so desperately for being in on the mainstream—was displacing the equally militant black nationalism of the sixties. The temperament of African-American literary criticism in the eighties would, consequently, be closer to that of the twenties and fifties than to that of the sixties. Time has borne out this impeccable wisdom.

Since the late seventies, many critics have looked back to Ellison's *Invisible Man* as a textual sign of cultural blending and integrationist possibility. But now they find themselves locked into a need to make fresh insights about the technique of a brilliant novel that has often been recovered for ideological reasons. Hence, the current scholarship says little that is provocatively new about the text itself, particularly in the way that a reading might lead to cultural insight about understanding racial "others" on their own terms. Even the best of the Ellison criticism now tells us what is rather perfunctorily expected. Norman German looks once more at the routinely examined "Battle Royal" chapter (*CLAJ* 31:394–99). Though many critics believe, he says, that the "experimental attitude" of *Invisible Man* is apolitical, Ellison's vision of social reality would be senseless without politics. Moreover [as Kimberly W. Benston once told us], images of the mask aid in defining the novel's reality.

John S. Wright, on the contrary, reads the text against the backdrop of European traditions rather than in light of the African symbolism implied by German's mask metaphor. Wright, a maturing African-American of fine repute on Ellison, decodes the narrator as a bourgeois hero of a bildungsroman, yet one who has been displaced into the picaresque. Throughout the narrator's "education," his errors cause him increasing pain. Ellison's protagonist becomes, therefore, a mock-heroic counterpart to Lord Ragland's traditional hero (*The Hero: A Study in Tradition, Myth, and Drama*).

John F. Callahan, an Ellisonian in good standing ("Frequencies of Eloquence: The Performance and Composition of *Invisible Man*," in *New Essays on* Invisible Man, ed. Robert G. O'Malley [Cambridge]), provides one of the most synthetic and provocative views. To him, the narrator of *Invisible Man* is a failed orator because he inconsistently fluctuates between the spoken and written word. In the "Prologue" the "hero" comments from behind a hostile mask; in the "Epilogue" he converses in an intimately democratic eloquence. Callahan's underlying paradigm, I fear, suggests a liberal advancement from racial "bitterness" (a posture forbidden by Booker T. Washington in American history) to the principle (Bledsoe, in *Invisible Man*) of a democratic fraternity of literate men. But the problem is that bitterness itself is a metaphor blaming the victim. So it is that Callahan's critical voice reaches back through the ideological accommodation of Booker T. Washington to re-speak the unintentionally ironic code of the admirably idealistic Thomas Jefferson, who was an owner of slaves and who slept with one.

***h.* Alice Childress.** Without the popularity of an Ellison, Alice Childress has still not received her earned acclaim during any of the last three generations. While her fine dramas are at last receiving some useful overviews, they require even far more serious and insightful reading of text and trope as well as of dramatic strategies. One possibility, for example, is to look at the way she adapts the Aristotelian design of dramatic reversal to a play structured on the slow revelation of black female consciousness.

Elizabeth Brown-Guillory (Houston) is doing much of the pioneering research in this regard. In an interview with Childress (*Sage* 4[1987]:66–68), the dramatist attributes her success as an artist to female self-empowerment. Her grandmother, Eliza, activated her imagination and exposed her to art, community, and other cultures. Her teacher, Miss Thomas, inspired her to read incessantly, and the testimonials of so many troubled church women taught her to be a writer. She discusses the play as her favorite literary form and her instinctual process of writing in it by trial and error. Finally, she acknowledges African-American theater as a positive influence. Concurrently, Brown-Guillory distinguishes Childress's work by placing the African-American female writer within cultural tradition. With Lorraine Hansberry and Ntozake Shange, she writes, Alice Childress has played a crucial role in dispelling the myths of "the contented slave," "the tragic mulatto," "the exotic primitive," and other black stereotypes that black male and white playwrights have promulgated, replacing trite models with more diversified ones. These playwrights frequently include portraits of "the black male in search of his manhood" (Childress's John Nevins in *Trouble in Mind* and Teddy in *Mojo*); "the black male as a walking wounded" (Hansberry's Hannibal in *The Drinking Gourd*); and the evolving black woman (Shange's *For Colored Girls Who Have Considered Suicide*). In each, these women depict positive images of black men who ultimately rise above impotence, and black women who reject male oppression. Sometimes it would be helpful to go down a step or two in order to analyze the individuating strategies in language and structure that empower Childress's uniquely gifted dramatic voice, though Brown-Guillory's pioneering literary history is far preferable to benign neglect.

i. **Toni Morrison.** An interview with Toni Morrison—who *is* surely a writer of her own and of universal kind—reads like an article. It is awful for Sula to put away her grandmother, as she speaks from a black communal view; the act violates the cultural mandate to protect the helpless and the needy. What makes the deed so unforgivable is that it shows an insensitivity to community. While critics "devoted to the Western heroic tradition of individualism" read Sula as triumphantly alone, the black community reads her as being lost. If Sula is pathological in that sense, she is so as a communal rather than an individual voice. While she is not inherently evil, the townspeople "use" her as if she were. To Morrison, revealing a "message" means thwarting the readers in their expectations of a happy end and having them see all of their prospects collapse. Tragic Epiphany (my terminology) of the sort supersedes any need for tidy ends.

What we might have left in fiction, I would add, would be endings without either narrative or rhetorical closure. Morrison's own efforts at unraveled finishes are neither the ones of the intrusive narrator evolved from the fiction of Fielding, Sterne, and Richardson—then on through those of Dickens to Ida B. Wells and Ishmael Reed—nor those of artistic activists such as Sonia Sanchez or Amiri Baraka. The failure to show (*and* tell) her closure or endings at once—while artfully concealing the rhetoric of the telling—is possibly the major flaw in her fictions.

But here we see why Morrison is not only an outstanding writer but a gifted thinker as well. In one instance she succinctly poses the most fundamental problem of gender and race: How can we assume and accept biological difference without inherently codifying values of both superiority and inferiority—exalting one human being over another? Then she suggests the profound degree to which this dilemma influences the choices of narrative posture for female writers who, like her and Paule Marshall, rank among the most sensitive readers of black male consciousness. Finally, she brilliantly reads the socially strategic cycle by which patriarchal hegemony turns white women and blacks against each other.

With Morrison, as has been true with Gwendolyn Brooks, sexuality is organic more than self-consciously imposed for political advantage. What Morrison draws upon includes her remarkable synthesis of human psychology and historicity. This she couples with a suspicious feel for commercial exploitation of the black woman artist. She is naturally suspicious about a hierarchy of power and even the very women that it empowers. Though in this way she has learned the lessons of Richard Wright, she has imaginatively rewritten and liberated them. A comparative book on the two of them remains unwritten. But Morrison has converted all the skills of Wright, this figurative father, to the needs of her own black feminist time and that of Paule Marshall as well as Alice Walker. The two interviews discussed above, taken together, are landmarks in the struggle for American equality of gender and race, including the appreciation of diversity on its own grounds.

The criticism on Morrison and her work proves outstanding for both quantity and quality. Its impact on the mainstream scholarship of Afro-American literature will probably be significant, for we can hardly read Morrison's complexly psychological and mythic texts (*Beloved*) without rethinking the questions of morality and guilt in American culture. Neither race nor gender spares us from the responsibility of her carefully narrated reckonings within fictional art.

One example will suffice to demonstrate the ingenuity of contemporary discourse to repress from itself this so powerful reckoning. Gerry Brenner's "*Song of Solomon:* Morrison's Rejection of Rank's Monomyth and Feminism" (*SAF* 15[1987]:24–34) is an intelligently written assessment. But it pigeonholes Morrison's brilliant narrative within the reductive monomyth of Otto Rank, who maps the "standard saga of the hero." While the nine-point plan proposed would suit nearly any major mythic work, it hardly reveals the uniqueness of Morrison. To misread the tone of her voice and ending, as Brenner probably does, would be to portray Milkman as ultimately irresponsible and Guitar as unredeemably psychopathic. What is more likely is that the former inscribes the triumph of cultural blues (or laughing to keep from crying) even as the latter (Guitar-lost-Blues) perverts his potential for human love (black music) into self-destructive violence.

Critical Essays on Toni Morrison, ed. Nellie Y. McKay (Hall), achieves significantly more self-honest balance, though some of the essays are shortsighted. Perhaps most of them would do better to detail the black poetic discourse distinguishing Morrison's literary art. An informative article by Anne Adams (190–214), for instance, documents that Morrison is the most widely read and criticized black female writer in West Germany. Academic critics reading the work in the "American" language, with literary critics encountering her novels in German translation, provide themes and motifs that "elucidate the social, cultural, and historical dimensions" as well as those that allow for Afro-American experience. Michael Awkward ("Roadblocks and Relatives: Critical Revision in Toni Morrison's *The Bluest Eye*, McKay:57–68) writes from a structural and post-structural extreme rather than from a historical one. To him, Morrison's depiction of incest in the novel revises Ellison's conception and portrait of this process as "material and tribal gain." I call this examination "structural" because it takes up "portrait" as the European standard for measuring human space primarily in geographical or pictorial form (Western modernism) rather than in temporal form (Aboriginal World and Western romanticism); I define as "post-structural" what refers to "material" (capitalist commerce) as well as to "tribal gain" or cultural regression—hence implying the mutual processes of Neo-Marxism and devolution. What the two movements of structuralism and post-structuralism have in common is the mission to minimize the narrating consciousness of the theorist or critic who proposes to have some considerable skill at negative capability.

The invisible "actor" in this critical and theoretical drama is history. While sometimes the current discourse in theory seeks to deceive us into believing that the relationships between *Invisible Man* and *The Bluest Eye* are purely linguistic and figurative, racial history is clearly an a priori reason for mentioning the two novels together. What goes unmentioned is the critical and historical consciousness bonding them; it is no natural order of the scientifically inevitable. Awkward shows unwittingly the way that both structuralism and post-structuralism pretend that history does not exist, yet both inscribe so secretly, and at once, this same ineffaceable history. In Morrison's *Song of Solomon*, for instance, the narrator reads the way that the name engraved "Sonny's Shop" can never be scraped away from Macon Dead's (Milkman's father's) work window any more than the hidden resonances of *Michigami* (Michigan) will ever fail to signify those Native Americans still inscribing their voices through the very name. Often contemporary scholarship misunderstands Morrison's own "great spirit" figured as the "Song of Solomon."

***j.* Ernest J. Gaines, Amiri Baraka, and Alice Walker.** What Baraka once called so subjectively the bourgeois efforts to empower Ishmael Reed as the major black male writer from the mid-seventies through the early eighties seems now to be waning. Except for an interview and essay on Baraka himself and for Nat Hentoff's "Finding Malcolm X" (*YR* 76[1987]:181–83), Gaines is about the only African-American male writer critically resurrected from the sixties and seventies. In an interview with Marcia Gaudet and Carl Wooton, "Talking with Ernest J. Gaines" (*Callaloo* 11, ii:229–43), the author says that black writers had no influence on him as an author because they were not a part of his school curriculum. Toomer's *Cane* might have been a factor under other circumstances insofar as he admires *Cane*'s structure. His migration from Louisiana to Vallejo, California, affected the fiction in which old women often parallel those from his childhood. While defending his allegedly too sympathetic treatment of black male characters, he discusses his work in progress. Though he probably reads "black writer" too literally, I suspect—as being an individual author rather than a cultural sign—he has striven nearly all of his career to achieve a southern folk voice. His roots, in other words, resemble those of Henry Dumas (Quincy Troupe, "For the Griot from Sweet Home: Henry Dumas," *BALF* 22, ii:379–83).

The reemergence of scholarship on Dumas, who like Baraka was born in 1934, along with the ascendancy of a solid yet scattered body of theory and criticism on Alice Walker (b. 1944), is now eclipsing the historical importance of Baraka. What is indeed so fascinating about our specialization is that it rewrites itself with the appearance of any newly accepted work, revealing only periodically a mastery of political and intellectual history. Baraka criticism today, saying virtually the same thing that it did a decade ago, suggests either that his creativity and artistic vision are static or that his critics are instead. Perhaps the contemporary scene partakes a little of both possibilities.

A fine interview with Elaine I. Duval ("Reasserting and Raising Our History," *Obsidian II* 22:1–19) indicates his own inertia of theory. Here aligning himself with Marxism, he views the role of the black artist in the eighties as virtually unchanged from that in preceding decades: black artists must be cultural revolutionaries who raise the level of human consciousness. Maurice O'Sullivan writes something unusually new ("Dutchman's Demons: Lula and Lilith," *NMAL* 10 [1986]:4–5) by researching the biblical sources.

It would be far more chic to decode Alice Walker's autobiographical narrative *Meridian* as Alan Nadel does ("Reading the Body: Alice Walker's *Meridian* and the Archeology of Self," *MFS* 34, 1:55–68). To him, Walker treats narrative as archaeology and the body as inscribed site. Establishing a connection between Meridian's body and the body politic, she exemplifies this archaeological approach to narrative in her synchronic examination of Meridian's life, ancestry, and maternal history. Presumably, the theoretical construct supersedes the artistic word. The reading, in other words, takes precedence over the author's signature or way of seeing. Particularly Walker's critics are more likely to assume a theory that ignores or effaces her racial mark. Often readers seem to base a critical assessment on only a work or two—for instance, on *The Color Purple* alone—leaving us to believe that even a (European) feminist method is now somewhat disfiguring Walker's (racial) text as well as her past. Though Alice Walker is much written about, she is still an invisible woman who merits far more serious homework.

At least two outstanding articles almost enable us to reread Walker's fictional world in light of the early Baraka's. In *The Color Purple*, according to Lauren Berlant ("Race, Gender, and Nation," *CritI* 14:831–59), Walker uses the myths of origin as well as political discourse to create an Afro-American nation, and she employs the mythic spirit of American capitalism to produce an Afro-American utopia. Of equal curiosity is J. Charles Washington's "Positive Black Male Images in Alice Walker's Fiction" (*Obsidian II* 3, i:23–48) that refutes somewhat effectively the charge that Walker hates black men. Celie of *The Color Purple* is unable to permanently despise the black men who abuse her. To Washington, "Love and Trouble," "Really," "Doesn't Crime Pay," and "To Hell with Dying" all contain positive images.

Several rather elfish inquiries come to mind. For example, could Celie forgive her tormentors, yet still contribute to negative portraits? Second, in what way does the Judaeo-Christian impulse of unconditional forgiveness, as is true in the *Life and Times of Frederick Douglass*, violate the principles of poetic justice? Third, what has Washington so unwittingly encoded in this 1989 work by taking most of his examples from 1973? For what few scholars of any persuasion have asked since then is whether Walker successfully depicts a love of her ancestral community and a love of herself.

iv. Blue Horizons: New Directions

With the timely emergence of African-American feminism, we have had a brilliant realignment of authors and their literary worlds. But for now the substantial gaps in our critical concerns are only shifting or reversing. We are displacing the focus of a few marginal male texts and authors with a few female works and pioneers. But we have yet truly to expand the *space* of the black American literary canon. What was already established by 1960 has only turned around a bit.

For the most part, 15 to 25 scholars still produce the great bulk of sustained work. We shall, figuratively speaking, have to water a sufficient pool of African-Americanists to cover both the new voices and those previously canonized. This new consortium, so attuned to the principles of critical theory and cultural value, would produce the many practical works still needed. In other words, we may well retrace our critical steps of the last decade while taking care soon to fill a scholarly void. There we leapfrogged so impatiently from literary history to post-structuralism.

Now we can assess the way that this new alignment has helped reveal that Langston Hughes, except for Countee Cullen, was possibly the only significant writer of the Harlem Renaissance born in the 20th century. Once Hurston and Fauset take their rightful places beside him, we can largely reread that period as one for which temperament and vision were rooted in the late 19th century. If and when Cullen and Claude McKay are ever published about in America again, the reassessments would appear in this new light. The scarcity of groundbreaking works about the Renaissance signifies the numerous opportunities for specialization. We still require sustained studies on individual writers of all persuasions and periods, especially on those from times other than the Renaissance; on the immediate postwar world of Richard Wright, Margaret Walker, and Gwendolyn Brooks; and on the writers of the Renaissance itself. Except for one or two exceptions, fresh studies are woefully lacking. The importance of Margaret Danner and her writers' workshop at Boone House still needs a thoughtful volume.

Scholars have almost always had fertile ground for definitive contributions on any genre other than that of narrative and fiction. Seminal volumes on the dramas of William Branch and Loften Mitchell remain to be written, while the modern poets Carolyn Rodgers and Sterling Plump have disappeared from the new canon.

Sonia Sanchez and the militant women of the sixties are equally invisible. While the new realignments have created ideological and textual gaps of their own, they facilitate new ways of interpreting black literary traditions. Alice Childress, James Baldwin, and Maya Angelou, in addition to Paule Marshall, were all born within eight years of each other; so it is that the apparently earlier vacuum between the time of Wright and that of Baldwin now disappears. We have instead a rich diversity of forms and gender, allowing broadly for drama, fiction, and autobiography as well as for the contemplative essay. Toni Morrison is restored to her rightful place of chronology beside Henry Dumas and Amiri Baraka, as well as Ishmael Reed; the narrative experimentation of allegory, of the delightful blend of social realism and surrealism, of expressionism, and, finally, of even the multiethnic fable reveal a formal continuity in the varied writings of reappraised peers. What was missing from the historical puzzle was the writings of black women, whose work would be published later than that of the men. And, of course, there was Henry Dumas.

In 1989 we rediscover the want of original books that assess the achievements of so many invisible men. Of Morrison's generation, Hal Bennett (b. 1930), Ernest J. Gaines (b. 1933), and Al Young (b. 1939), all of whom are now in their fifties, still merit serious research. Some talented scholar, like James Coleman, charts new ground on the fiction of John Edgar Wideman (b. 1941) and John A. McCluskey, Jr. (b. 1944), as well as that of the remarkable David Bradley (b. 1950).

Given the proliferation of some 260 writings about the classic works of African-American men, as well as the wide range of publications by contemporary black women, the most challenging and provocative questions are still taboo. Eventually some courageous thinker will, I hope, pose the kind of inquiry so forbidden by poststructuralism: Should we have an intellectual center and viewpoint for racial and gendered studies? If so, which shall we privilege? Do we privilege some position automatically, even if it is a theoretical indifference that empowers the status quo indirectly? Does an accompanying inquiry of whether to favor a fragmentation or proliferation of ideas about either freedom or race emerge from a blindly studied acceptance of nihilism? Are critical and theoretical detachments about texts such as *Mumbo Jumbo* and *The Color Purple* the luxury of the academically empowered, of the inherently protected and privileged? How do the fictions of African-American men and women speak to each other within an expanded and mutually liberated space? In what way can an orientation toward a pluralistic feminism serve as a tool for mediation and communication between genders, allowing for both male and female bodies to express themselves freely beyond a hierarchy of power?

To redress the most crucial issues of African-American criticism and theory—and, indeed, American literary scholarship in general—means finally to grapple with the academic marketplace for what method now sells. In some way a departure from the black nationalism of the sixties marks a conscious move toward greater sophistication of method and experimentation. But it is also a chameleon adaptability mandated in part by the contemporary reception of critical and theoretic texts. Despite even a move toward theoretical Marxism, practical Marxism proves rather curiously and humorously absent from this report. The posture of the work reviewed is, indeed, often purely theoretical, for we ignore the way that our own critical acts are both the shapers and shapes of the very real history beyond our theoretical words. The learnedly feigned detachment underlying so many of our positions is largely illusory; the natural symbiosis between black literary art and American politics will almost never really go away.

One figurative voice or silent player in this critical discourse is the racial integration of American literary scholarship since 1970. The widening opportunity of opened doors has left African-Americanists to ponder whether they might still follow the old-line literary history of Saunders Redding and Hugh Gloster (black aesthetics is no longer a *practical* option) or forge ahead with some varied philosophies of literary form by Kenneth Burke, Simone de Beauvoir, and Julia Kristeva. The remarkably conscientious and folk analytic of Norman Harris as well as that of Trudier Harris (no family ties), like the more self-consciously linguistic constructs of Henry Gates and Hazel Carby, pose diverse paths toward the interpretation of text and race.

The second figurative voice underlying most of the literary scholarship for 1988 belongs to Booker T. Washington. The hidden expression signifies that of the academic entrepreneur who subtly disclaims any professional interest in the theoretical commodity or productivity to be sold. This hidden inscription of viewpoint and value privileges the early accommodation of both W. E. B. Du Bois and Martin Luther King, Jr., though many inevitable doubts troubled each thinker separately in later life, prompting consequent revisions on the fly. For both men came to question the very language and intellectual systems through which they had sought to write a higher freedom; both had looked for new turns of language rather than for those they had inherited. Perhaps one day new studies of Paule Marshall and David Bradley will advance beyond what often has deteriorated into commercial production, by academic capitalists, of post-structuralism. Perhaps, the criticism and theory of black literature conscientiously reshapes itself even as we write.

University of Tennessee

20. Themes, Topics, Criticism

Michael J. Hoffman

Because 1988 witnessed its usual proliferation of potentially relevant books for this chapter, I am forced once again to summarize most of those I treat and to choose carefully for fuller treatment the books I think will be most useful to *ALS* readers. I am retaining the same categories I have used for the past few years, with a separate section for gender studies but also integrating, where appropriate, books on gender-related issues into other sections. The most interesting events of general importance during 1988 were the publication of the *Columbia History of American Literature*, to which I shall devote a large amount of space, and the exposure of Paul de Man's equivocal past, to which I shall also devote some space. Otherwise, there was little to distinguish 1988 from most of the years preceding it.

i. American Literature

In *America in Theory* (Oxford), ed. Leslie Berlowitz, Denis Donoghue, and Louis Menand, the theory referred to is not contemporary critical theory but the theory of "America" that underlies all statements about American ideals, goals, and activities. The contents of this book, given originally as conference papers, attempt to express this theory in such areas as the law, domestic policies and politics, and foreign policy. The quality of the essays is high, and the distinguished contributors include John Patrick Diggins on "Theory and the American Founding," Deborah L. Rhode on "Gender Equality and Constitutional Traditions," John Brademas on "Scholarship and Public Duty," McGeorge Bundy on "Presidents and Nuclear Weapons and Truth," and an eloquent Epilogue by E. L. Doctorow called "A Citizen Reads the Constitution." This stimulating book's basic concern is to explore how the American Constitution expresses American ideals as they manifest themselves in American life.

Art Berman's *From the New Criticism to Deconstruction: The Re-*

ception of Structuralism and Post-Structuralism (Illinois) discusses the contexts of American literary study that led to the strong reception of such French imports as structuralism and deconstruction. These contexts include the British empiricist tradition and the New Criticism that was an outgrowth of it. Berman sees "four criteria [emerging] for an ideal American critical theory . . . in the 1960s." These are (1) "an alliance with some form of empiricist science," e.g., linguistics; (2) "the maintenance of a free, autonomous, creative, Cartesian and Romantic entity of self"; (3) the fact that "theory must account not only for literary language, but for all language"; and (4) that "critical theory requires support on the political 'left' " (2–3). This carefully constructed study deals with all the significant figures on either side of the Atlantic.

F. O. Matthiessen and the Politics of Criticism (Wisconsin), by William E. Cain, is part of The Wisconsin Project on American Writers. It reads its subject's work from the perspective of a politically committed criticism much like Matthiessen's own, mixing well the biographical, social, political, and institutional contexts that characterized Matthiessen's work. In the process Cain lucidly summarizes and analyzes a great deal of Matthiessen's writing, in particular his masterpiece *American Renaissance*, subjecting it to a severe political analysis and occasionally taking it to task for its emphasis on canonicity. Cain is concerned with the ways we study literature, and I enjoyed his acute comments on the School of American Studies, of which Matthiessen was one of the founders.

The American City: Literary and Cultural Perspectives (Vision Press), ed. Graham Clarke, is a collection of essays on the American city, all produced by faculty members of the University of Kent at Canterbury. The editor's brief introduction presents an overview of the attitudes toward the city expressed by American writers, and the opening essay by Christine Bolt states the themes more elaborately, discussing the ambivalence toward urban life that has been a part of American cultural expression for the past two centuries. The essays—which vary in quality—are all about specific urban locales, with about half centering on New York City and others on Washington D.C., Los Angeles, New Orleans, and Chicago. The focus of each essay is primarily thematic and historical, with the subject matter usually derived from specific literary authors.

The prolific Robert Coles, known primarily for his works on psychiatry and children, has collected his literary essays in *That Red*

Wheelbarrow: Selected Essays (Iowa). These essays, collected from the past two decades, have appeared in such literary outlets as the *New York Review of Books* and the *American Poetry Review*. The range of reference is wide, from the 19th century in a number of national literatures to 20th-century poets and novelists. Two authors have been a major focus for Coles: William Carlos Williams (subject of seven essays) and Flannery O'Connor (subject of five). Coles's introduction is explicit about the genuine debt he owes to Williams, another physician. Coles's writing is elegant, literate, and broadly humanistic.

L. S. Dembo's *The Monological Jew: A Literary Study* (Wisconsin) is a collection of essays not originally intended as a unified book. Nonetheless, the author does follow certain themes with some consistency. Although the title suggests Bakhtin, a more prominent presence is that of Martin Buber, and his theory of the I/Thou predominates. It is not monologue in Bakhtin's unidirectional ideological sense, but the contrast between self-centered monologue and relational dialogue that is this book's thematic center. There are elegant essays on Richard Stern, Henry Roth, Philip Roth, and Abraham Cahan, with such witty titles as "The Tenants of Moonbloooo-oo" and "Carnivalizing the Logos." Dembo also writes on the monologic anti-Semitism of Pound and Hemingway.

Most important to American literature was the *Columbia Literary History of the United States* (Columbia), ed. Emory Elliott, published 40 years after the previous *LHUS*, which was edited by the late Robert Spiller. Let me begin this extended discussion on a personal note. When I began graduate study in 1959 I spent the summer previous to the start of classes reading both Baugh's *Literary History of England* and Spiller's *LHUS* because I thought one had to know all that information before one *began* graduate study (it was also the case that both gentlemen were members of the English department where I took my doctorate). Whatever such a story tells about my own compulsiveness, it also indicates that I am one of a rare breed who has read all the way through the *LHUS* of 1948 and the one of 1988. What I shall attempt in the following paragraphs is not so much to compare the two editions head to head as to suggest how well I think each fulfilled what its generation saw as its need for a literary history of the United States. Much scholarship and a number of critical movements have intervened in the 40 years that separate the two books, but one thing that each editorial board makes explicit is that literary histories must be written anew every few generations to reflect contemporary concerns and recent scholarship.

It is also the case that the new *LHUS* has made what can only be a conscious attempt to imitate the structure of its predecessor. It is of approximately the same length and is overseen by a board of editors, with an editor-in-chief. Each is divided into sections which contain chapters, 81 in the former, 61 in the latter. The chapters are written by individual authors, with some authors contributing more than one chapter. Structural similarities include a physical presence that seems solid and authoritative, as if to say that herein reposes the collective scholarly wisdom on this country's literature. It is from within this set of apparent similarities that one must begin to talk about the ways in which the two enterprises diverge.

The tone of Spiller's introduction is more authoritative than Elliott's, reflecting a scholarly consensus which no doubt reflected that of a nation that had just won a lengthy world war over a commonly accepted enemy. The 1948 *LHUS* speaks of "the vast historical changes which [literature] reflects" (viii). It speaks of "American literature as the record and analysis of a series of cultural waves beating in from across the Atlantic to our shores in a continuous series and changing their form and nature and sometimes their direction as they sweep over the New World" (xx). It finally speaks of itself as telling "the story of the importation into our New World of European ideas and shapes for the imagination" (xxi). In its calm authority the 1948 *LHUS* sees American literature as the reflection of history, the record of culture, and the importer of European ideas.

Forty years later the new *LHUS* expresses no such collective assurances. It expresses much more unease about literature's reflection of history, or indeed what history may turn out to mean. It sees the course of American literature as much less progressive and much more multidimensional, even paradoxical in its various expressions. It compares itself to its predecessor in the following telling paragraph: "The *Literary History of the United States* of 1948 reflects the culture that produced a style that many critics of architecture have labeled 'modern': streamlined, uniform, and confident in its aim of useful service. By contrast, the present project is modestly postmodern; it acknowledges diversity, complexity, and contradiction by making them structural principles, and it forgoes closure as well as consensus. Designed to be explored like a library or an art gallery, this book is composed of corridors to be entered through many portals intended to give the reader the paradoxical experience of seeing both the harmony and the discontinuity of materials" (xiii). The contrast between uniformity and discontinuity sets the extremes by which the two histories can be compared, although not always as comfortably as one might wish, for the current *LHUS* seems to suggest that it is free from the kinds of ideology which characterized its predecessor, even though it substitutes for it an ideology of nonideology that has serious consequences.

There is no point in arguing with the assumptions on which each *LHUS* is constructed. Clearly they reflect shared scholarly beliefs that are endemic to each historical moment. Most of us cannot any longer accept the view of history in the 1948 *LHUS* that was once not so controversial. I do not wish to quarrel with the new *LHUS*'s desire to reflect the diversity of American literature along gender and ethnic lines that were not high in most people's consciousness in 1948 or to contest the theory of history that reflects the intercession of Foucault, Braudel, phenomenology, structuralism, poststructuralism, Marxism, or feminism in American scholarship. What is important is how well each of the two histories met the needs of their particular time. In that regard I should like to tip my hand early by saying that I think the nod goes to Spiller—even though I shall mostly use Elliott as my own reference work from now on, with the following caveats.

The major intention of the new *LHUS* is to be a history of theme rather than fact, because what constitutes historical "fact" is ambiguous and even the nature of theme can be arbitrary. Certain themes do run throughout the new *LHUS*, although less from a coordinated effort than from the fact that different chapters deal with some of the same thematic material. For instance, there are chapters on ethnic minority contributions in both the 19th and 20th centuries. What is missing, however, because of the conscious decision to decentralize the book's authority, is that only occasionally are there discussions in other chapters of ethnic materials where they might well be relevant; and this only on the accidental decision of a particular chapter author. The ideology of nonauthoritarian editorship causes problems and creates opportunities for the right chapter authors. I should like to go into this in more detail.

For some of the *CLHUS* authors the opportunity to write with only minimal editorial constraints has allowed them to write chapters that emerge as something close to the current definitive statement on their subject. As examples, I nominate Richard Brodhead's "Literature and Culture" 1865–1910, Wendy Steiner's "The Diversity of American Fiction," 1910–45, and Cary Nelson's "The Diversity of American Poetry," of the same period. But in the hands of others the same freedom has resulted in either solid but conventional treatment, such as Lawrence Buell's chapter on "The Transcendentalists," or the brilliant, but quirky eccentricity of Michael J. Colacurcio's "Idealism and Independence," 1810–65.

More significant problems emerge from the ideology of editorial nonauthoritarianism, which I think manifests itself in the confusion between what is authoritative and what is authoritarian. For one thing, there are not enough dates in this book. It is as if the presence of a date makes too definitive a statement. One would certainly grant that history is more than simply the presence of dates, and one would not like to see the *CLHUS* degenerate into mere chronology, but history has to be anchored in something when it becomes a form of discourse, and dates and facts can in fact be documented. On the other hand, there are frequently problems with the dates that do appear, because from chapter to chapter one frequently finds the kind of contradictions that no work of scholarship should tolerate, that an editor who had read the manuscript through from beginning to end would have discovered. Here is where I think the dominant editorial ideology got the book in trouble.

Let me give some examples, at the risk of seeming petty. On page 505 it is said that William Dean Howells "set out for New England in 1860 at age twenty-nine." He was born in 1837. Poe's *Eureka* is dated 1849 (p. 385). It was published the year before. On page 523 David Graham Phillips's *Susan Lenox* is dated 1917. Just ten pages later, in the following chapter, it is dated 1908. The former is correct. Susan Warner's *The Wide, Wide World* is dated 1850 on page 299 and 1855 on page 562. On page 326 the play, *The Blockheads: or, The Affrighted Officers*, is attributed to Mercy Otis Warren: on page 149 a different writer claims that the same play is "often attributed to Warren but [is] almost certainly by another hand, probably male and military. . . ." Which scholar are we to believe? Jack London's *Martin Eden* was published in 1909 on page 847 but in 1908 on page 541. Gertrude Stein is said on page 773 to have been born in the Midwest and to have sprung "out of the country's heartland." She was born in Pennsylvania. Her *Three Lives* was supposedly completed in 1904 (p. 878). It was actually completed in 1906. On page 1130 it is claimed that Stein died in 1945. She in fact died in July of the following year.

I could multiply these examples, as could anyone who had also read the book through from cover to cover; but I think I have made the point. In the apparent interest of not appearing coercive, the editors of this volume have allowed themselves to be simply careless. As a result, for many readers the volume will seem much less authoritative than it should have been. History without scholarly authority is severely compromised, particularly in a volume that will be consulted by scholars and teachers for precisely the kind of factual accuracy one had every right to expect from so magisterial a book. The *CLHUS* does represent much of what is new in our approaches to American literature. It has the vitality of a new generation of scholars, and it does reflect the diversity of American literature and culture much better than any other previous work of its kind. Its coverage has a kind of completeness that is enviable (although I wonder why there is not a chapter on the latest works of American literary theory). Still, it should have been better, and its flaws seem attributable to a basic misconception of what might best represent an ethic of theoretical diversity. Sloppy scholarship represents only itself.

I turn next to Allen Guttmann's *A Whole New Ball Game: An Interpretation of American Sports* (No. Car.), which is a sociological study of sports in American culture. It is topically organized, and although it contains lots of statistics, it takes a strong moral position about the uses and abuses of sport in our society, and it is particularly good in tracing the development of the American sports mania. Using a Weberian analysis, Guttmann "discovers certain characteristics of modern sports: secularism . . . equality . . . bureaucratization . . . specialization . . . rationalization . . . quantification . . . the obsession with records . . ." (5–6). Guttmann follows these characteristics throughout his book, writing cultural as well as social history, and seeking to be "attentive to the interactions of such sociologically relevant factors as ideology, class, ethnicity, race and gender as they have impeded, furthered, modified, and distorted American sports" (11). The author traces the history of sport from the games Puritans played to those Cavalier sports that were played on horseback in the colony of Virginia. He naturally pays a great deal of attention to baseball, agreeing with Jacques Barzun that to know American culture requires one to know baseball as our national game. The book is studded with suggestive insights, such as the statement that "Alexander Cartwright's inspired invention [of baseball] eased the difficult transition from an agrarian to an urban-industrial society" (55) and "The ideal of fair play, in its Victorian and Edwardian heyday, was a *class* ideal. . . . In the realm of sports, as in other realms, the ruling class makes up the rules" (57). Among the remaining chapters are ones on basketball ("Muscular Christianity and the Point Spread"), organized play for children, black athletes, women's sports, and "The Anomaly of Intercollegiate Athletics." For any halfway enthusiastic sports fan this book offers pleasure and stimulation.

Lois Hughson's *From Biography to History: The Historical Imagination and American Fiction, 1880–1940* (Virginia) is a lively book, much of whose contents will be discussed elsewhere. It is Hughson's thesis that during the heart of the realist period American writers of fiction shifted their paradigm from biography to history, a shift that brought about changes in both fictional and historical narrative. The book takes most of its early lessons from Henry Adams's historical, biographical, and fictional works and then demonstrates how the change in perspective affected James, Howells, Dreiser, and Dos Passos. Overall, this book constitutes one of the interesting recent discussions of realism and naturalism.

The subject of volume 63 of the *Dictionary of Literary Biography* is *Modern American Critics 1920–1955* (Gale), ed. Gregory S. Jay. The book contains solid biographical/critical essays about 25 prominent American critics, including all the well-known ones from that period—e.g., Eliot, Pound, Matthiessen, Babbitt, Cleanth Brooks, and Van Wyck Brooks. The essays are written for the most part by established middle-generation scholars, and the standards are high. This book is a useful reference tool; aside from very good essays, there is extensive bibliographical material and a number of charming photographs. It is especially useful for scholars who might wish to work up some of these critics without having to read a full volume about them.

One of 1988's fascinating books is *The Selected Correspondence of Kenneth Burke and Malcolm Cowley, 1915–1981* (Viking), ed. Paul Jay, a volume that contains not only personal glimpses of two important literary figures, but is a history of American literary concerns during much of this century. The book is divided into four roughly equivalent chronological sections, each of them introduced by the editor. There is also a helpful preface and a minimal amount of other apparatus, including only such footnotes as are necessary.

This book is leisurely, pleasurable to read, and the epistolary style of both men reflects how we know them from their other books.

I have somewhat mixed feelings about Alfred Kazin's latest book, *A Writer's America: Landscape in Literature* (Knopf), a study of the pervasiveness of landscape in American literature from the 18th century to the present. Glossy, handsome, and slick, the book has the appearance and tone of a coffee table volume, and it contains a number of interesting and relevant photographs. The style is that of a popular literary history, but the scholarship, while unobtrusive, seems to be first-rate. There is little here, however, that is new or of much theoretical interest. Rather, the work is descriptive, enthusiastic, and wise, more perhaps a contribution to wisdom literature than to American literary scholarship. For fresh insights into the American landscape there are other places to go—e.g., Barbara Novak. I must say, also, that I was annoyed that a number of the photographs and drawings were not dated.

Gerald J. Kennedy and Daniel Mark Fogel have edited a festschrift in honor of Lewis P. Simpson, *American Letters and the Historical Consciousness* (LSU). The long list of distinguished senior scholars focuses on a variety of historical themes that range in American literary history from the 18th century to Ernest Gaines. Contributors include Eugene and Elizabeth Fox Genovese, Sacvan Bercovitch, Louis D. Rubin, Jr., Daniel Aaron, Cleanth Brooks, and Daniel Hoffman. I particularly recommend Bercovitch's "The Modernity of American Puritan Rhetoric," J. A. Leo Lemay's "Robert Beverley's *History and Present State of Virginia*, and the Emerging American Political Ideology," and Daniel Hoffman's "History as Myth, Myth as History, in Faulkner's Fiction."

Vincent B. Leitch's *American Literary Criticism: From the Thirties to the Eighties* (Columbia) is an excellent descriptive and analytical history of its subject. Leitch organizes his vast field into themes and movements, with 13 chapters on such topics as "Marxist Criticism in the 1930s," "The 'New Criticism,' " "The Chicago School," "Reader-Response Criticism," "Deconstructive Criticism," "Feminist Criticism," and "Black Aesthetics." This is not only a good history of criticism, it also presents an excellent overview of changes that American literary study has undergone during the last five decades. The author places critical movements in historical context, and he examines events outside literature for how they lend urgency to certain kinds of critical developments. In the areas I know best the summaries seem accurate and the analyses acute. The book could certainly be read as a narrative history, but I suspect that it will prove more useful as a reference work.

Perhaps my favorite book in this section is by historian Lawrence W. Levine, *Highbrow/Lowbrow: The Emergence of Cultural Hierarchy in America* (Harvard), a study of how the concept of culture evolved in 19th-century American life. Originally given in 1986 as Harvard's William E. Massey Sr., Lectures in the History of American Civilization, this book ranges throughout the arts to show how what were apparently open and popular forms early in the last century evolved into more exclusive and often closed forms by the beginning of our own. Levine discusses opera, concert bands and orchestras, and museums, but because I have limited space I shall simply focus on his fascinating discussion of Shakespeare.

Levine warns us in his "Prologue" that "one of the central arguments of this book is that because the primary categories of culture have been the products of ideologies which were always subject to modifications and transformations, the perimeters of our cultural divisions have been permeable and shifting rather than fixed and immutable. To accept this thesis is to accept a picture of the American cultural past and present that departs considerably from the images most of us have learned to accept, which is never an easy thing to do" (8). The dominant ideology of America in the early part of the previous century found the works of Shakespeare to be a strong part of the common (what we would call today the "popular") culture. "Shakespeare was presented as part of the same milieu inhabited by magicians, dancers, singers, acrobats, minstrels, and comics" (23). Furthermore, the structure of the theater was not the same as ours, with its tripartite seating arrangement that divided the audience into different social classes depending on their ability to pay a certain price for a ticket. The audience did not obey the same rules of decorum as we do in our darkened theater, where even a stray cough seems disruptive. It is therefore clear to Levine "that an understanding of the American theater in our own time is not adequate grounding for a comprehension of American theater in the nineteenth century" (26).

One major problem in understanding the difference in our contemporary relationship to Shakespeare lies in our using the word "popular" to call anything mediocre if it has a widespread audience.

Shakespeare was popular in the 19th-century use of the word in being accessible to everyone in the culture, in being a familiar part of the common cultural environment. Shakespeare remains "widely known, respected, or quoted . . . ," but he is "no longer [our] familiar, no longer part of [our] culture, no longer at home in [our] theaters or on the movie and television screens that [have] become the twentieth-century equivalents of the stage" (31). He has become part of "polite" culture, "the possession of the educated portions of society who disseminated his plays for the enlightenment of the average folk who were to swallow him not for their entertainment but for their education" (31). Levine presents a series of images of Shakespeare as part of 19th-century popular culture, then shows how a cultural transition, which he calls "The Sacralization of Culture," gave rise to a hierarchical culture, designed to reinforce social structures and keep certain groups—many of them immigrant and working class—in their place. The book is well documented, well written, and deeply though unobtrusively informed by theory.

Brief mention goes to a collection of essays by Andrew Lytle, the southern man of letters and editor of the *Sewanee Review*—*Southerners and Europeans: Essays in a Time of Disorder* (LSU). The book was edited by Lewis Simpson and contains a useful foreword that discusses Lytle's career. Most of the essays are on southern topics, with a particularly interesting discussion of Lytle's best-known novel, *The Velvet Horn*, as well as literary portraits of prominent southern writers whom Lytle knew: John Crowe Ransom, Allen Tate, Caroline Gordon, and Flannery O'Connor. A second section includes essays on major European works of fiction, such as *War and Peace* and *Madame Bovary*.

In *Patrons and Protégées: Gender, Friendship, and Writing in Nineteenth-Century America* (Rutgers), Shirley Marchalonis has edited an interesting collection of essays about literary relationships between men and women. These relationships include Ralph Waldo Emerson and Margaret Fuller, Fanny Fern and Walt Whitman, Emily Dickinson and Thomas Wentworth Higginson, Henry James and Constance Fenimore Wilson, and William Dean Howells and Charlotte Perkins Gilman. The essays mix biography, criticism, and influence study, and they explore how gender determined the interaction between the two writers. While little new material is uncovered, the overall point of view brings about a number of fresh insights.

David Marr's *American Worlds Since Emerson* (Mass.) proposes the centrality of the Emersonian tradition in American life and culture. It follows the establishment of this tradition in Emerson's lifetime, along with the opposition raised to it by such contemporaries as Melville. Marr traces the influence of Emerson through Whitman, William James, Robinson Jeffers, R. P. Blackmur, Joseph Heller, and Ralph Ellison. Although covering ground that has been trod before, this well-written book ranges widely through political theory, history, and politics, as well as literature. Marr's insights are filtered through such thinkers as Stanley Cavell and Richard Rorty.

Leo Marx's long, distinguished career in American Studies is summed up in a collection of essays entitled *The Pilot and the Passenger: Essays on Literature, Technology, and Culture in the United States* (Oxford). In an introduction, Marx discusses his career and its central concerns. The book's first section deals with major American authors, the second with more general topics in American culture, the third with American criticism. Some of these essays, such as those on *Huckleberry Finn* or on "The Machine in the Garden," have become staples of the classic tradition in American Studies.

In *An American Icon: Brother Jonathan and American Identity* (Delaware), Winifred Morgan discusses the iconic Yankee figure as it appeared in a number of cultural arenas, including the stage, cartoons, verse, anecdotes, and literature. The book is a straightforward historical study of these images and their cultural importance. The documentation seems thorough, and there is a wealth of examples, including many reproductions of Brother Jonathan cartoons from the late 18th century to the Civil War.

Daniel T. O'Hara's *Lionel Trilling: The Work of Liberation* (Wisconsin) is another excellent volume in The Wisconsin Project on American Writers. O'Hara takes Trilling seriously, treating his life as a unified, self-fashioned creation, in which Trilling emerges as a patriarch of the ethical approach to literature. The succession of chapter titles (without their subtitles) gives a good sense of how the author has organized his study: "Sacred Mourning," "Spectral Politics," "Worldly Messiah," "Subversive Patriarchy," "Normal Mysticism," and "Infectious Apocalypse." Readers will recognize the summative aptness of these categories as they relate to Trilling's life and work.

Brief mention goes to The Southern Review *and Modern Litera-*

ture (LSU), ed. Lewis P. Simpson, James Olney, and Jo Gulledge, an eccentric book that celebrates 50 (though discontinuous) years of a distinguished literary review. The first section discusses the original *Southern Review* (1935–42), with retrospective pieces by Robert Heilman, Cleanth Brooks, and Robert Penn Warren, along with the publication of a 1935 conference proceeding on "Literature and Reading in the South and Southwest." There is even a short piece by Governor Huey Long. The second section discusses "The Cultural Context of the *Southern Review*," with emphasis on the most recent series of the journal (1965–). The final section is entitled "T. S. Eliot, the South, and the Definition of Modernism." The book brings together various articles and symposia, and the contents seem disparate. Lewis Simpson's introduction does, however, contain a lot of interesting information.

One of the better books in this section is Nancy A. Walker, *A Very Serious Thing: Women's Humor and American Culture* (Minnesota), part of that press's American Culture series. "The tradition of women's humor in America," Walker claims, "developed along different lines than did the standard canon of (primarily) male humor. Its subject matter, themes, and even its forms have been influenced by women's quite different relationship to authority, decision-making, and social change . . . women writers have developed forms suited to their own lives and needs: the domestic saga, the skit, and humorous fantasy" (12). The focus on domestic affairs changes not only the subject matter of women's humor, but the premise underlying it. "The world they inhabit is not of their making, and often not much to their liking, so their tactics must be those of survivors rather than those of saviors" (36). The circumstances of most women's lives cause their humor to develop a "we-they" dialectic, the product of a group consciousness. "Women's humor, like that of minorities, is usually expressed within the group, rather than in mixed company—orally, in groups composed only of women, and in print, in publications intended primarily for other women" (105).

Walker ranges from such 19th-century subjects as Frances Whitcher and "Fanny Fern" to the current century's Dorothy Parker and Erma Bombeck. Writing about gendered humor is a sensitive matter, but Walker has a light touch and does not allow herself to be overly theoretical or thesis-ridden. This is not only a good book about humor, it has a lot to say about American culture.

Walker has also edited with Zita Dresner *Redressing the Balance:*

American Women's Literary Humor from Colonial Times to the 1980s (Miss.). This excellent collection ranges from Anne Bradstreet to Cyra McFadden and Fran Liebowitz. It represents the 19th and early 20th centuries especially well, and it has an excellent introduction for those who do not have the time to read *A Very Serious Thing*. The editors strike a good balance between well-known and obscure writers, and they rescue a number of authors from undeserved oblivion.

American Authors and the Literary Marketplace since 1900 (Penn.), by James L. W. West III, studies how the publishing industry affects the ways books are written. It provides a fascinating account of relations among authors, agents, editors, and publishers; it explains the complex matter of subsidiary rights and their effect on writers; it demonstrates how the economics of publishing can determine what writers produce. The book is full of good insights for developing a critical understanding of such matters as genre. Here, for example, is an account of American publishing in the later 19th century: "In truth, conditions were not ideal for book publishing in the United States during the mid- to late nineteenth century. They were almost perfectly suited, however, for newspaper and periodical publishing, which tends to flourish in countries that are large, politically active, and economically vigorous. The newspaper and magazine industries took the lead in American publishing; the book industry followed behind, both economically and philosophically. . . . Faced with this kind of conservatism, American authors learned to look to magazines and newspapers for steady income and wide exposure" (42–43). With periodicals providing the primary outlets for publishing either short fiction or serialized novels, it is no wonder that the period witnessed the flourishing of shorter forms and novels with neatly segmented chapters designed to fit the available space in magazines. In our own age almost precisely the opposite situation has dominated, with almost no novels being serialized and with few commercially viable outlets for short fiction.

I finish this section with notice of a solid work of traditional literary history, Perry D. Westbrook's *A Literary History of New England* (Lehigh). The book is organized in a series of relatively brief chapters, each of them about a few authors. While the coverage is thorough, the book contains little that is new. I found Westbrook's discussion of the Transcendentalists to be helpful and the book to be well written and erudite. Most students will use it as a reference work, but it makes one realize that we are overdue for a serious scholarly revaluation of New England as a literary region, perhaps done by a team of scholars much like the history of southern literature that was edited by Louis Rubin and others (*ALS 1985*).

ii. Gender Studies

This field continues to show productivity that befits a discipline which has reached a level of high maturity. A number of books that I might have included in this section I have reviewed in sections more in line with their topicality. Even so, I include here almost a dozen such books, and I could have included more.

Jan Cohn's *Romance and the Erotics of Property: Mass Market Fiction for Women* (Duke) studies the conventions of popular fiction that is designed primarily for an audience of women. Unlike other recent books on similar themes, Cohn does not use a lot of statistics but instead takes a few prominent novels as basic models for women's fiction in the late 19th and early 20th centuries and examines how mass-market writers made calculated use of them. The three principal models are *Pride and Prejudice*, *Jane Eyre*, and *Gone With the Wind*, each of them famous as love stories, but it is Cohn's thesis that "power, not love, lies at the heart of the fictions of popular romance. . . . In heavily coded structures these stories redistribute not only the power relations that exist within marriage, within the patriarchal family, but through and beyond that threaten existing gender relations in the broadest areas of power in patriarchal society itself" (3). The author organizes her study thematically, exploring how the conventions established by the more classic works of fiction were exploited by popular novelists in the late 19th century, most of them unfamiliar today, in such categories as "The Romance Hero," "The Victorian Popular Romance," "Women's Work," "The Erotics of Property," and "Romance and Sexual Politics." A well-argued, thoughtful book.

Michel Foucault's theories of power and their application to the contemporary debate on feminism are the subject of essays in *Feminism & Foucault: Reflections on Resistance* (Northeastern), ed. Irene Diamond and Lee Quinby. The authors, who come from a variety of disciplinary backgrounds, engage in a dialogue between Foucault and feminism on a number of issues, including questions of femininity, authority, epistemology, sexuality, power, and language. Most of the authors are younger academics, and the level of discourse is high.

The most extraordinary book in this section is Jane Gallop's *Thinking Through the Body* (Columbia), a collection of essays she published between 1977 and 1986, all of them revised substantially. On the cover of the book is an enlarged closeup photograph of the author giving birth to her son, explicitly showing the boy's little head emerging from the mother's vagina and looking like a fat penis with a nose. The book includes an essay that discusses book jackets, and I have no doubt that the author wishes to invite the kind of descriptive analysis in which I have briefly engaged in the previous sentence. Like many exhibitionists, Gallop intends her shock tactics to have significance beyond outraging the audience. These essays attempt to define the interplay of mind and body, presupposing no such legitimate distinction as the mind-body split. Gallop's style blends theory and autobiography; she is personal at times when traditional rhetoric says one ought not to be, and she pushes back the boundaries of scholarly discourse (and "good taste") through such devices as puns, slang, and continuously personal verbal gesturing. Influenced by Lacan and French Lacanian feminists such as Luce Irigaray, Gallop discusses *The Hite Report* in "Snatches of Conversation" (yes, the pun is intentional), female genitalia in "Lip Service," and a variety of other topics in such essays as "A Good Lay" and "The Prick of the Object." Although much of what she writes is more clever than profound, Gallop is someone whose work should not be ignored. It is a challenge to academic pomposity.

An interesting, though somewhat quirky book is *Writing a Women's Life* (Norton), by Caroline Heilbrun, which is more a mediation on women's lives and marriage than on biography. "In this book," says the author, "I want to examine how women's lives have been contrived, and how they may be written to make clear, evident, out in the open, those events, decisions, and relationships that have been invisible outside of women's fictions . . ." (18). It is how women's lives are fashioned, not only in fiction, but in reality, that is the subject of the book, and it is the model that fiction provides for both fictional lives and those lived in this world that concerns Heilbrun. "What matters is that lives do not serve as models; only stories do that . . . . We live our lives through texts. They may be read, or chanted, or experienced electronically, or come to us, like the murmurings of our mothers, telling us what conventions demand. Whatever their form or medium, these stories have formed us all: they are what we must use to make new fictions, new narratives" (37).

Heilbrun is concerned that so many women write with such diffidence about themselves, even though in private communications, such as letters and diaries, they express the same intense ambitions for their lives as do their male counterparts. This diffidence often reflects a belief that there is an objective tone that is standard in literature, but Heilbrun disagrees. "There is no 'objective' or universal tone in literature, for however long we have been told there is. There is only the white, middle-class, male tone" (40). The lives on which Heilbrun focuses include Colette, Virginia and Leonard Woolf, the Brontës, George Eliot, George Sand, Vera Brittain and Winifred Holtby, and Heilbrun herself (or Amanda Cross in her mystery writer persona). The book is thoughtful, provocative, and a bit disjointed.

In *Herself Beheld: The Literature of the Looking Glass* (Cornell) Jenijoy La Belle studies the gaze that women give themselves in works of literature. "My subject is the confrontation between a woman and her reflection in a mirror" (1). Not merely narcissism or vanity, this confrontation is an act of self-definition that one discovers continually in the literature of the past few centuries. La Belle focuses on this confrontation in many well-known authors, including Nathaniel Hawthorne, Sylvia Plath, D. H. Lawrence, George Eliot, and the Brontës. There are good sociological insights throughout the book and interesting reflections on the nature of male and female egos.

Brief mention goes to a good collection edited by Toril Moi, *French Feminist Thought: A Reader* (Basil Blackwell). This brief book brings together full-length essays by many leading French feminists from Simone de Beauvoir to Julia Kristeva, Luce Irigaray, and Sarah Kofman, a number of which appear in English for the first time. The disciplines represented go beyond literature to philosophy, history, and psychoanalysis, with an emphasis on sexual difference and the definition of gender.

Elizabeth V. Spelman's *Inessential Woman: Problems of Exclusion in Feminist Thought* (Beacon Press) is a provocative study of how feminist theory has focused primarily on white, middle-class, heterosexual women while creating a unitary image of "women." In the process, Spelman argues, it has relegated to the margins such individuals as lesbians, women of color, Jewish women, non-Western women, and poor women. Spelman detects this white middle-class bias in such well-known authors as Simone de Beauvoir, Nancy Chodorow, and Betty Friedan. She detects a false homogeneity in the notion of "sisterhood," and she believes it will take an extraordinary effort for feminist thought to extend its margins far enough to be truly inclusive. This well-written, tightly argued book should incite some controversy.

I received Catharine R. Stimpson's new book, *Where the Meanings Are* (Methuen) too late to do more than skim it, but I should like to mention it here. A collection of essays published or presented between 1970 and 1987, it is on a variety of topics that range from theoretical discussions of women's studies to essays on female authors and lesbian writing, to essays on the importance of the humanities and on cultural criticism. Stimpson has emerged not only as an important author of literary and feminist studies, but also as a voice of conscience in the profession, because of her early work in establishing *Signs*, and also through her work on the MLA Commission for Academic Freedom. Some of these essays are already widely quoted; e.g., "Zero Degree Deviancy: The Lesbian Novel in English."

A more casually wrought book is Janet Todd's *Feminist Literary History* (Routledge), which surveys feminist literary history since around the time of Kate Millett. Todd favors the American approach to the subject, contrasting Elaine Showalter and Gilbert and Gubar favorably with such French critics as Luce Irigaray and Helène Cixous. Todd is a good explainer and high-level popularizer; but she dilutes her effects with a somewhat loose chattiness that undermines her persuasiveness. As a result, while the book is easy to read and contains much that is useful, it ultimately lacks coherence.

Brief mention goes to Chris Weedon, *Feminist Practice & Poststructuralist Theory* (Basil Blackwell). Weedon brings many leading poststructuralists, particularly Foucault, into her argument as she suggests that patriarchal power has become widespread throughout all social institutions and practices. Weedon believes that successful feminist theory will arise from such an understanding. She is a good summarizer.

One of the more interesting books in this section is Patricia Yeager's *Honey-Mad Women: Emancipatory Strategies in Women's Writing* (Columbia). Yeager presents women writers as not merely the victims of patriarchal culture but as actively devising a literary countertradition that enables women to express their own desires in their own voices. She adapts the South American myth about the honey-mad woman reported in Claude Lévi-Strauss's *From Honey to Ashes* as her central metaphor. "Lévi-Strauss suggests that it is woman's capacity to act out her hunger, to go stir crazy, sweet crazy, to eat too much honey, that provokes the need, in cultures where this tale is repeatedly told, for imposed social order . . . this systematic control of women's minds and bodies never quite works, since woman remains, like honey itself, both natural and unnatural, 'raw' and 'cooked'. . . . Thus the honey-mad woman's consumption of honey is especially threatening to her culture because it reminds other members of her society that classificatory systems do not work . . ." (27). Women thus have the potential to become a subversive force, and it is this force that Yaeger sees as central to women writers who are not merely victims. She traces this subversive process from Emily Brontë through Kate Chopin to Elizabeth Bishop, and she enlists in her argument such theorists as Mikhail Bakhtin, Michel Foucault, and Jürgen Habermas. Women's writings are for Yaeger not merely texts, they are "works" that do the work of establishing a culture. I found her argument quite persuasive.

iii. Modernism

There has continued to be much activity in this area, not only in studies of classic modernism, but also in the increasing literature on postmodernism. Jonathan Arac's multidisciplinary collection, *After Foucault: Humanist Knowledge, Postmodern Challenges* (Rutgers), measures Michel Foucault's impact on a developing theory of post-modernity. The essays cover politics, history, psychoanalysis, and feminism; their quality is high, and the distinguished discussants include Edward Said, David Couzens Hoy, Paul Bové, Daniel T. O'Hara, and Sheldon Wolin.

I give brief mention to Norman F. Cantor's *Twentieth-Century Culture: Modernism to Deconstruction* (Peter Lang) only to say that it is the most opinionated book I have read this year. A very comprehensive survey, it reads unfortunately like a set of lecture notes (which I suspect it largely is) that are overly formulaic and summary. Cantor seems to disapprove of much of what has occurred in this century, and his tone is that of someone preparing for the barbarians to invade. A waste of erudition.

Brief mention also to a much better book by the late Terrence Des

Pres, author of *The Survivor*, one of the best books on the Holocaust. In *Praises & Dispraises: Poetry and Politics, the 20th Century* (Viking), Des Pres examines the interactive roles of poetry and politics, describing the latter as an inescapable form of reality. He believes that poetry must transcend the private by engaging with the political. The five poets on whom he concentrates did precisely that: Yeats, Brecht, Breyten Breytenbach (South Africa), Adrienne Rich, and Thomas McGrath. Des Pres admires their ability to use the political as a form of cultural renewal.

In *Form and Society in Modern Literature* (No. Ill.), Thomas C. Foster interprets classic modernist works by balancing a concern for literary form with a focus on the written work as a product of social forces. For him literature is a form of action: "If one defines Modernism as a characteristic action or process rather than a characteristic product, then one can begin to overcome certain misunderstandings based on the appearance of the poem or the novel or whatever. . . . If literature is a total historical process—that is, if it is a movement within and through history, society, and culture as well as other literature—then we are not free of Modernism but instead still are living through it" (17). To see the work of literature as an outgrowth of society is obviously not a new idea, and Foster's apparatus plays less of a role than he thinks, given his fairly straightforward readings of *The Waste Land*, *Ulysses*, *Go Down, Moses*, and Yeats's later poetry.

Gillian Hanscombe and Virginia L. Smyers's *Writing for Their Lives: The Modernist Women 1910–1940* (Northeastern) is a narrative about the interaction of such important female modernists as Djuna Barnes, Gertrude Stein, Dorothy Richardson, H.D., Marianne Moore, and Mina Loy. While less scholarly than Benstock's *Women of the Left Bank*, this pleasant mix of biography and interpretation is a good introduction to the topic, and it reads like a novel. The thesis is simple. "It's because women writers are anomalous that the lives and writings of 'self-indulgent,' unpoliticised, literary innovators are of particular interest," say the authors. "H.D., Richardson, Stein and the rest discovered—and recorded the discovery—that changing literature means changing lives; and that, equally and simultaneously, changing lives means changing literature" (13).

Richard Kearney's *The Wake of Imagination: Toward a Postmodern Culture* (Minnesota) meditates on the mounting threat we feel about the waning power of the imagination. "One of the greatest paradoxes of contemporary culture is that at a time when the image reigns supreme the very notion of a creative human imagination seems under mounting threat. . . . We are at an impasse where the very rapport between *imagination* and *reality* seems not only inverted but subverted altogether. And this very undecidability lends weight to the deepening suspicion that we may well be assisting at a wake of imagination" (3). Kearney's approach is historical, but it is history with some irony, because he believes that in the postmodern period "history as continuity becomes history as collage" (20). It is the opportunity to view history through the fragments put together in a kind of *bricolage* (Lévi-Strauss) that constitutes our peculiar task in understanding our present situation. "Postmodernism might thus be seen not just as a moment of apocalyptic paralysis but as an occasion to reflect upon the inner breakdown of modernity, to . . . explore the causes of our contemporary dislocation" (26). Kearney believes the postmodern sense of dislocation affords us a unique opportunity: "Postmodernism would thus refuse to view itself as a mere *afterword* to modernity. . . . In this respect, the task of a postmodern imagination might be to envision the end of modernity as a possibility of rebeginning" (27). In the rest of the book Kearney presents a history of the imagination as it was conceived from biblical times to the present day. Dividing his book into "Premodern Narratives," "Modern Narratives," and "Postmodern Narratives," he finishes by studying a number of contemporary French thinkers as well as a series of international novels and films.

James F. Knapp's *Literary Modernism and the Transformation of Work* (Northwestern) believes that modernism was shaped by how work was transformed through modern revolutions in science, technology, and management. The author is particularly concerned with the scientific management theories of Frederick Taylor and with the extent of "modernism's engagement with the most basic assumptions on which management theorists such as Taylor attempted to persuade the business community and the public at large" (16). Knapp's writers include Pound, Lawrence, Joyce, and William Carlos Williams, whose works he examines from within the following set of assumptions: "A literary text may thus engage with a movement such as scientific management in three ways: it may take social and economic change as its explicit content; it may understand its own work as *analogous* to other kinds of work within society (e.g., the poet as 'craftsman'); or, most fundamentally, it may render visible those general discursive patterns which in any given era have been appropriated to shape the possibilities of knowledge and of human interaction" (22). Knapp's primary topic is the third of these, and he challenges the dominant "interpretation which holds that modernist form necessarily signifies a rejection of historical consciousness and an escape into myth" (46). I found the early theoretical sections to be the most interesting parts of this book.

Brief mention goes to an interesting collection edited by J. D. McClatchy, *Poets on Painters: Essays on the Art of Painting by Twentieth-Century Poets* (Calif.). Some of these poets were either collectors or critics of painting; others were individuals with a sensitivity to the plastic arts. In either case, the essays are informative not only because of what they say about the paintings themselves but because of what they reveal about the commentator's assumptions. From early in the century we can read Pound on Vorticism, Stein on "Pictures" (from *Lectures in America*), and Williams on "Painting in the American Grain." More recent poets include Robert Duncan ("An Art of Wondering"), Guy Davenport ("Balthus"), John Ashbery ("Respect for Things as They Are"), and Mark Strand ("Crossing the Tracks to Hopper's World"). The book also contains excellent reproductions of paintings that are discussed in the essays.

In *Universal Abandon? The Politics of Postmodernism* (Minnesota), Andrew Ross has edited essays that originally appeared in an issue of *Social Text*. These pieces, most of them written by younger academics interested in social and cultural issues, focus on areas in the postmodernist debate such as politics, economics, feminism, psychology, and art. The quality is uneven, but collectively this book is a good introduction to the issues.

iv. The Profession Examines Itself

An important spinoff from the study of theory is the increasing tendency for humane letters to examine itself, its premises, and its activities. I begin with David Bleich, who deals with a number of dyads in *The Double Perspective: Language, Literacy, and Social Relations* (Oxford): male/female, mind/body, societies/individuals, orality/literacy, and his own double perspective as professor of both English and Education. His writing reflects not so much a Marxist perspective as that of a 1960s academic liberal who believes that the traditional classroom has ignored issues of class, race, and gender in the name of objectivity. He uses recent critical theory in discussing such matters as literacy and gender, and he opts for an educational system that tries to balance the individual's relationship with language among the community, and the social and political orders. Some of Bleich's chapter titles indicate his concerns: "Gender Interests in Language and Literature," "Reauthorizing Classroom Membership," "Mutuality Between Student and Teacher," "Collaboration Among Students," "Literacy and Citizenship." A thought-provoking book.

The Vocation of a Teacher: Rhetorical Occasions, 1967–1988 (Chicago) collects many speeches and a few essays by Wayne C. Booth on subjects related to his teaching. Booth, who has also held administrative positions, understands the academic enterprise very well, and he knows the importance of matching rhetoric to occasion. As a result, these talks seem not only clever and well written; they are also appropriate to their subject matter and audience. They include occasions for persuading teachers and students about academic values, large lectures given to undergraduates, ceremonial speeches on formal occasions, and a journal in which Booth examines himself and his pedagogical commitments. The book is full of wise and often urgent reflections.

Pierre Bourdieu's *Homo Academicus* (Stanford), trans. Peter Collier, provides a good model for a similar study of American higher education. This sociological/anthropological examination of French academic life and its faculty discusses the social classes from which faculty members derive, the nature and amount of their publications, the ways in which power is manifested and used in that culture. The study and its conclusions are based on much factual evidence in the form of statistical summaries, charts, and graphs; the observations and judgments are trenchant and to the point. While American and French academic cultures differ in regard to their governing hierarchies and the issues of centralization versus federalization, we could learn a lot about how we function if someone were to commission such a study of the humanities and social sciences in American higher education.

Literature, Language, and Politics (Georgia), ed. Betty Jean Craige, brings together a series of talks given at a 1987 MLA Symposium on "Politics and the Discipline." The overall point of view is opposed to the conservative agenda of such writers as Allan Bloom, E. D. Hirsch, and former Secretary of Education William Bennett.

Most of the essayists believe that Reagan's America put at peril much of what was recently gained through academic theoretical consciousness. The writers and their topics are Paul Lauter, "The Two Criticisms: Structure, Lingo, and Power in the Discourse of Academic Humanists"; Henry Louis Gates, Jr., "On the Rhetoric of Racism in the Profession"; Annette Kolodny, "Dancing Between Left and Right: Feminism and the Academic Minefield in the 1980s"; Ana Celia Zentella, "Language Politics in the U.S.A.: The English-Only Movement"; Ellen Messer-Davidow, "The Right Moves: Conservatism and Higher Education"; Catharine R. Stimpson, "Politics and Academic Research"; and Gerald Graff, "Teach the Conflicts: An Alternative to Educational Fundamentalism."

Betty Jean Craige proposes an alternative to Allan Bloom's *The Closing of the American Mind* in her own polemic, *Reconnection: Dualism to Holism in Literary Study* (Georgia). Craige wishes to develop an alternative to "Cartesian dualism, which provided for the objectification of knowledge and, consequently, academic specialization in a body of knowledge" (1). Before discussing contemporary academic life, Craige summarizes Cartesianism since the Scientific Revolution, talking on the way about science and higher education, the rise of American universities, and the canon. She wishes to replace dualism with holism, in which "a model of interaction and connectedness replaces that of opposition, a concept of network replaces that of vertical hierarchy, and a 'top-down' approach to learning (that is, looking at the system first) replaces reductionism. When systems thinkers come to dominate the academy, eventually 'integrative' fields may replace disciplinary departments" (92). Craige believes that we are at the end of the paradigm that created separate disciplinary units, which is why we have been examining ourselves so busily in recent years. "The entire culture," she writes, "is in a period of massive, fundamental change, and it needs intelligent cross-disciplinary thinkers to ponder the effects of our technology and of our laws" (114–15). Craige ends by proposing practical steps for reorganizing the curriculum. I found these disappointing, which may mean that up to this point theory has outstripped our ability to implement it.

A more polyphonic, though basically conservative point of view is represented in *Teaching Literature: What Is Needed Now* (Harvard), ed. James Engell and David Perkins, a series of essays by well-known scholars on ways to continue the study of literature amid theoretical ferment. The scholars, from both sides of the critical revolution, include Hugh Kenner, Nathan A. Scott, Jr., Helen Vendler, Barbara Johnson, J. Hillis Miller, and David Perkins. While the essays tend frequently to be defensive, this tone is missing from the best of them, notably those by Johnson and Miller, who see the new intellectual developments as presenting an opportunity rather than posing a threat.

Brief mention goes to Northrop Frye's *On Education* (Michigan), a collection of his talks and occasional pieces on educational topics, most of them previously unpublished. There are sections on education in Canada, Frye's home country; on the period of student unrest two decades ago; and one on relating research to teaching in the humanities. While the essays cover a variety of topics, the book has one overarching message: one learns to think primarily through the educated use of language.

The most challenging book in this section is Jerome J. McGann's *Social Values and Poetic Acts: The Historical Judgment of Literary Work* (Harvard), which calls for a criticism that is engaged with historical, social, and political contexts. "The purpose of this book," writes the author, "is to argue that poetic discourse has other obligations than to speak for the orders of the state . . . ; indeed, to argue that poetic discourse . . . has special resources for carrying out this critical and antithetical role . . ." (x). The fourth volume in a series that attempts to devise principles for a literary historical study of "Euro-American" writing, this book marshals evidence from Plato to contemporary poetry, showing itself thoroughly versed in contemporary theory. But McGann engages with theorists primarily to challenge them, believing that revitalizing literary studies goes beyond an obsession with theory that he believes has become "a social and institutional problem." "The chief problems," McGann states, "facing literary studies today do not seem to me theoretical ones; they seem, rather, social, institutional, and methodological" (x).

McGann is strongly influenced by Paul De Man's assertion that there is no commensurability between language and meaning, a claim that informs most of the readings in this book. He believes further that "what happens in the histories of reading is that the full and dynamic reality of the works is dismembered by the uses to which they are put by their later readers . . . one of the chief functions of criticism is to re-member the works which have been torn and distorted by those losses" (6). Because of space limitations, I shall quote just a few memorable passages. In discussing "what carries Socrates into dialectics and away from rhetoric," McGann suggests that "the point of the latter is to establish a certain view or perspective, whereas the aim of the former is to interrogate perspectives" (27). And in concluding McGann states: "Poems are not mirrors and they are not lamps, they are social acts—readings and writings which promote, deploy, and finally celebrate those processes of loss which make up the very essence of human living" (246). While the book's structure is occasionally clumsy, the issues are very well defined and discussed.

Another stimulating look at the humanities is William R. Paulson's *The Noise of Culture: Literary Texts in a World of Information* (Cornell), which ingeniously adapts information theory to literary study. Reflecting on literature's apparent marginality when compared to the status of science, Paulson asserts "the assumptions that underlie the central arguments of this book: first, that literature is a noisy transmission channel that assumes its noise so as to become something other than a transmission channel, and second, that literature, so constituted, functions as the noise of culture, as a perturbation or source of variety in the circulation and production of discourses and ideas" (ix). That literary study teaches us to hear this noise makes its marginality crucial to our culture. "Science attempts to use a transparent language, the meaning of whose statements depends on universally accepted procedures and definitions. In literary culture, meaning cannot be separated from the particular language game being played by author and reader" (4). Paulson devotes his book "to what [Michel] Serres would call passages between science and literature, in particular to the group of related passages offered by the theories of information, self-organization, and autonomous systems" (37). Once the noise of culture is understood as being important to the organization of knowledge, literature's apparent marginality to "truth" becomes one of its assets. Paulson applies his insights convincingly to a series of texts in a number of languages.

v. Theory of Narrative

I begin this section with Wayne Booth's latest book on the subject. *The Company We Keep: An Ethics of Fiction* (Calif.) seeks a way of putting ethical concerns at the center of our study of fictional texts. By ethos Booth refers to the core of being or the center of character; an ethical effect for him is therefore not the same as a marketplace definition that finds an ethical approach to literature to be primarily judgmental. This large book is always an easy pleasure to read; it wears its extensive erudition easily and discusses texts from throughout the long history of the novel. But perhaps Booth covers too much ground, and at too leisurely a pace, because this compendious discussion does not have the concentrated power of *A Rhetoric of Fiction*, and it defies easy summary or quotation. With the valedictory quality of a lifelong teacher, Booth is comfortable in the rhetoric of the lecture hall, the classroom, or conference platform. But in an age of critical readjustments, I found that this book left me with little to argue for or against, and not much to apply to the novels I read. Maybe I expected too much.

Perhaps the most satisfying work on narrative was by anthropologist Clifford Geertz, *Works and Lives: The Anthropologist as Author* (Stanford), a book that does for anthropology what Hayden White does for history in his *Metahistory*. Geertz focuses on the ethnographic writings of Claude Lévi-Strauss, Edward E. Evans-Pritchard, Bronislaw Malinowski, and Ruth Benedict, bringing to his analysis questions of critical theory as well as a sensitivity to the problems of narrative. It is not so much that ethnographers fictionalize their writings as that in telling their experiences they face the same kinds of problems as novelists. Ethnographers need "to convince us that what they say is a result of their having actually penetrated (or, if you prefer, been penetrated by) another form of life, having, one way or another, truly 'been there.' And that, persuading us that this offstage miracle has occurred, is where the writing comes in" (4–5). Geertz discusses Foucault's "What Is an Author?" and Barthes's "Authors and Writers," using the latter's distinction to much advantage. "(1) How is the 'author-function' . . . made manifest in the text? (2) Just what is it . . . that the author authors? The first question, call it that of signature, is a matter of the construction of a writerly identity. The second, call it that of discourse, is a matter of developing a way of putting things . . ." (8–9). Ethnographers have to "construct . . . texts ostensibly scientific out of experiences broadly biographical" (10), a process that leaves them vulnerable, no matter what strategy they choose, to accusations of their being too distant or too manipulative, and so they switch back and forth between being authors and being writers. Students of narrative can learn a great deal from this book.

A very good attempt to explore the similarities between psychoanalytic writing and fiction is Daniel Gunn's *Psychoanalysis and Fiction: An Exploration of Literary and Psychoanalytic Borders* (Cambridge). Gunn draws his examples primarily from 20th-century French writers. Like many recent theorists, he finds analogies in the binary relationships of author/reader and analyst/analysand. Writers frequently force readers to deal with narrative problems by writing them "in" or writing them "out" of the text. On the other hand, readers can experience many reactions to texts, including resistance, equivocation, and ambivalence. Gunn, a practicing analyst and novelist, is fully abreast of current theory. Though a student of Lacan, he is not rigidly Lacanian.

Essentials of the Theory of Fiction, ed. Michael Hoffman and Patrick Murphy (Duke), is the only collection of essays currently in print that is completely devoted to the theory of narrative. The contributors range from Henry James to Rachel Blau DuPlessis, and the collection mixes familiar essays with recent material, while attempting to avoid trendiness and jargon. Although the essays are published in the order they were written, the book has two indexes, one that lists the essays in chronological order, and a second that organizes them into such categories as narrative, point of view, and structure. An introduction discusses most of the thematic categories, and each selection is preceded by a brief essay (one page or less) that discusses the author's and the essay's place in the history of issues related to narrative.

Robert Newsom, in *A Likely Story: Probability and Play in Fiction* (Rutgers), discusses what role predictability or probability plays in how we interpret works of fiction. He traces philosophical concepts of probability since Aristotle, asking how fiction relates to the empirical world and how actions in books relate to actions in the world. Newsom is concerned with how readers respond to fictional narrative, and with how we talk about such matters as believability and coincidence. Why do we trouble ourselves with such questions when we know that the characters in books are all made up? *A Likely Story* is organized historically and provides a good addendum to such classics as Ian Watt's *The Rise of the Novel.*

I include in this section Wendy Steiner's *Pictures of Romance: Form Against Context in Painting and Literature* (Chicago) because it explores historical and theoretical interrelationships between narrative painting and literary narrative. Painting before the Renaissance used narrative conventions in both individual canvases and in series of paintings that represented a story (usually biblical). Renaissance conventions did away with the idea that paintings could incorporate a temporal dimension by assuming that reality had to be represented in a frozen moment in time. "In assenting to the restrictions of [this] perceptual model, visual artists split picture from narrative, space from time, and cohesion from sequence in an attempt to insure adequacy to reality . . . to equate reality and its representation, realism, with atemporality is to destroy the logical basis of realism—the concept of identity as a repetition traversing time" (42–43). Steiner follows the historical development of this concept, equating it with analogous literary tendencies represented in such writers as Keats and Hawthorne (particularly in *The Marble Faun*) and in other representatives of the "romance" tradition.

For Steiner the breakdown of this paradigm at the end of the 19th century is represented in the work of such protomodernists as Seurat, who began moving toward a form of narrativity that was fully developed by Picasso and Joyce. Even a subsequent movement like Pop Art played with narrative as part of its conventions. Steiner further sees "twentieth-century art . . . as a systematic emptying out of the value structures in painting" (172), because "non-representationality severely reduced the work's ability to transmit value in terms of a referential context" (172). This well-written book is one of the best works I know in showing how the various 20th-century arts developed shared aims and methods.

Brief mention goes to Jennifer A. Wicke, *Advertising Fictions: Literature, Advertisement, and Social Reading* (Columbia), which poses a dialectical interplay between reading advertisements and reading fictions. Wicke suggests that conventions of advertising writing as well as the social reading of advertisements influenced Charles Dickens, Henry James, and James Joyce. *Ulysses* provides her with an ideal site for her kind of reading, but Wicke also convincingly demonstrates how James used advertising conventions in *The Bostonians* and *The American Scene.* An interesting work of cultural criticism.

I conclude this section with James E. Young's *Writing and Rewriting the Holocaust: Narrative and the Consequences of Interpretation* (Indiana), a well-written, thoroughly researched, and compendious study. The author believes we can know the Holocaust only through its various texts, and he examines diaries, poetry, novels, autobiographies, and histories. To develop a narrative understanding of what happened during the Holocaust may be impossible, but it is also necessary to seek it. That is why there is writing and rewriting, for it is only through such repetitions that narrative can trace a story coherent enough for our understanding. This powerful study deals well with the dilemmas posed by this intractable subject, and it develops a structure for further work in this area by presenting one of the most complete bibliographies I have seen on Holocaust literature.

vi. Literary Theory

In what follows I shall be treating perhaps one-fourth of the books I considered among the general theoretical works published during 1988. In making these Draconian selections I have written about those books I think are most likely to have an impact as well as those by and about major theorists. Many of the latter will receive only brief mention.

Roland Barthes, *The Semiotic Challenge* (Hill and Wang), trans. Richard Howard, is a collection of essays on semiotic topics that Barthes published between 1963 and 1973. There are pieces on Ferdinand de Saussure, advertising, urbanism, medicine, and the Bible, as well as a long essay entitled "The Old Rhetoric: an aide-mémoire," which ranks in importance with Barthes's *Elements of Semiology.* Barthes's excellent brief introduction gives us a vivid idea of his semiotics. Here are a few lines from his definition of a "text":

> it is not an esthetic product, it is a signifying practice;
> it is not a structure, it is a structuration;
> it is not an object, it is a work and a game;
> it is not a group of closed signs, endowed with a meaning to be rediscovered, it is a volume of traces in displacement (7).

Another important French poststructuralist, Jean Baudrillard, is beginning to be translated into English. *Jean Baudrillard: Selected Writings* (Stanford), ed. and introd. Mark Poster, contains single chapters from a series of his books along with a good introduction. Baudrillard is an expert on the roles of communication and the media in society, and he is one of those rare French thinkers who seems to understand American culture. The early essays, which are the most accessible, are full of good insights and examples, whereas the later ones get more abstract and polemical. Baudrillard likes sweeping generalizations, and he does not always define his terms. As an example, here is his definition of a "code," which he describes well without defining it: "The code is totalitarian; no one escapes it: our individual flights do not negate the fact that each day we participate in its collective elaboration. Not believing in the code requires at least that we believe that others sufficiently believe in it so that we can enter the game, even if only ironically. Even actions that resist the code are carried out in relation to a society that conforms to it" (19).

Another important Marxist thinker, active earlier than Baudrillard, is the philosopher Ernst Bloch, a collection of whose works, *The Utopian Function of Art and Literature: Selected Essays*, trans. Jack Zipes and Frank Mecklenburg, was published by the MIT Press as part of their Studies in Contemporary German Social Thought. Bloch is a figure much referred to in contemporary Marxist discourse. This collection contains essays on aesthetics, poetry, fairy tales, the detective novel, architecture, opera, and painting, all of them written within a Marxist ideology and vocabulary.

Paul de Man's case has been discussed so much recently that there is little need for me to rehash most of the notorious information or repeat old arguments. I should like to mention two recent collections that will give readers access to both the primary materials written by de Man and some of the many essays written by literary and other scholars trying to make some ethical sense of the situation. *De Man's Wartime Journalism, 1939–1943* (Nebraska), ed. Werner Hamacher, Neil Hertz, and Thomas Keenan, reprints all the extant essays that de Man wrote as a very young man for five journals in Brussels during the German occupation of Belgium. There are essays in both French and Flemish, and all are republished by a photo-reproduction process that has resulted in an oversized book. The articles in French are published without translation. Those in Flemish are reproduced along with an English translation. Most of the essays are on literary or cultural topics and do not appear to contain offensive material, although they were published in papers controlled by the occupying authorities, particularly, it appears, *Le Soir*. It is in the latter journal that the most blatantly anti-Semitic piece appeared on March 4, 1941: "Les Juifs dans la littérature Actuelle," which talks among other things about the expulsion of Jews from Europe.

Those who wish to be informed at first hand should consult this volume along with a companion that was published in 1989, *On Paul de Man's Wartime Journalism* (Nebraska), another oversize book edited by the same individuals. This volume contains discussions by many scholars, including some highly distinguished theorists who were friends of de Man, such as Jacques Derrida and J. Hillis Miller, as well as long-time critical antagonists such as Jeffrey Mehlman. These serious attempts to deal with the horrible skeleton in de Man's closet are riveting to read, for they confront the significance of what texts can mean in more desperate ways than an essay on, say, *Moby-Dick* or "Ode on a Grecian Urn." I must confess that, while deploring what the 22-year-old de Man wrote, I am sympathetic with those who argue that one should not attempt to throw out the whole deconstructionist enterprise—or de Man's other writings—as a sham because of de Man's equivocal past. Such an attitude not only smacks of book burning, it also gives people an easy opportunity to dismiss what they have either not understood before or have been unwilling to accept.

I agree with Christopher Norris's belief that Paul de Man will remain an influential and important theorist whose presence will have to be taken account of by anyone interested in theory—much, I believe, like the analogous case of Ezra Pound. Norris expresses his opinion in *Paul de Man: Deconstruction and the Critique of Aesthetic Ideology* (Routledge), which contains the best discussion of de Man's theoretical writings I have read, along with an excellent essay appended as a "Postscript on de Man's Early Writings in *Le Soir*." Norris is a gifted and intelligent summarizer, and his discussions render many matters clear that are murky in the original. He describes the various stages of de Man's critical career, and he measures the work in the context of other critics and theorists.

I extend a similar compliment to Norris's *Derrida* (Harvard, 1987), which is probably the clearest exegesis I have seen of that writer. Norris's philosophic erudition is a great asset, for Derrida is primarily a philosopher whose discourse needs to be read within the philosophical tradition from Plato to the present. Norris has in fact organized his book around the dialogue in which Derrida has engaged other philosophers, such as Plato, Hegel, Rousseau, Kant, Austin, Nietzsche, as well as Freud and Saussure. Norris explains why Derrida has met with such resistance from both theorists and philosophers, and he neither overvalues nor dismisses him. This is a good book for either the relative newcomer to Derrida or for one who has read a great deal of him.

I have reviewed four books that are either by or about Michel Foucault. The first is *Michel Foucault: Politics, Philosophy, Culture: Interviews and Other Writings, 1977–1984* (Routledge), ed. and introd. Lawrence D. Kritzman. Most of the texts in this volume are interviews, a form to which Foucault was increasingly exposed as he became more of an international celebrity. He responded well to the interview situation, and he seems to have taken pleasure in being a good explainer who made the interview an instructive form of discourse. Those who know a bit about Foucault's work will get a lot out of reading these texts. *The Final Foucault* (MIT), ed. James Bernauer and David Rasmussen, originally an issue of *Philosophy and Social Criticism* (1987), contains an interview with Foucault as well as a series of essays by a number of well-known scholars. Most interesting, perhaps, is Thomas Flynn's discussion of the last lectures Foucault gave at the Collège de France during the four months before he died. They were on "the practice of truth-telling . . . in the ancient Greek and Roman worlds" (102). One hopes these lectures are in complete enough condition to be published. The book also contains a thorough bibliography of Foucault's writings and a useful biographical chronology. *Technologies of the Self: A Seminar with Michel Foucault* (Mass.), ed. Luther H. Martin, Huck Gutman, Patrick H. Hutton, contains an interview with Foucault and two essays that Foucault presented as papers shortly before his death: "Technologies of the Self" and "The Political Technology of Individuals." The book also contains commentary by various scholars on the subject matter of the essays. Finally, there is a kind of memorial volume by Gilles Deleuze, *Foucault* (Minnesota), trans. Seán Hand. This is a very French kind of meditation: abstract, philosophical, with a minimum of specific quotations and examples. Nonetheless, Deleuze gets inside Foucault and his work as well as anyone has. He establishes Foucault as, first, an archivist and, then, a cartographer, discussing these concepts in terms of *The Archaeology of Knowledge* and *Discipline and Punish.* In the second section Deleuze meditates on Foucault's theories of historical strata and the nature of thought, power, and subjectivation.

Roman Jakobson's *Language in Literature* (Harvard) collects the late linguist's essays on artistic matters. One's image of the many-tongued Jakobson as being primarily a master of linguistic technicalities is shattered by this book's extraordinary range of subjects, which include meditations on Futurism and Dada, on Shakespeare, Baudelaire, Yeats, Pushkin, and Blake, all written in technically exact, lucid English, and composed over almost three-quarters of a century. Perhaps the most important essay contains Jakobson's frequently discussed distinction between metaphor and metonymy, with the unlikely title of "Two Aspects of Language and Two Types of Aphasic Disturbances."

Fredric Jameson's shorter pieces are collected in two volumes entitled *The Ideologies of Theory: Essays 1971–1986* (Minnesota), with a Foreword by Neil Larsen. The first volume, *Situations of Theory*, contains polemical discussions about the role of theory and the nature of interpretation. It deals with issues like "The Ideology of the Text," and it polemicizes directly with the work of such writers as Jacques Lacan, Kenneth Burke, Alain Robbe-Grillet, and Alasdair MacIntyre. Larsen's foreword does a good job of positioning Jameson among the leading Marxist theorists. The second volume, *Syntax of History*, deals more with actual historical discussion, placing Marxist analysis within definite chronological contexts in such essays as "The Politics of Theory: Ideological Positions in the Postmodernism Debate," "Marxism and Historicism," and the by now classic essay on "Periodizing the 60s." In many ways Jameson's ideas are more accessible through these essays than through such formidable texts as *The Political Unconscious.*

Words about Words About Words: Theory, Criticism, and the Literary Text (Johns Hopkins) collects the essays Murray Krieger has published since 1981. They are organized into three sections: "Theory and Institutions: Critical Movements and Academic Structures," "Critical Positions: Self-definition and Other Definitions," and "Reconsideration of Special Texts for Special Purposes." Krieger's preface is helpful in situating the changing theoretical concerns that influenced the essays. Krieger is an eloquent spokesperson for a broadly humanistic point of view impatient with the belief that language has no meaning or that history is inexorably determined. Unlike many theorists, he has had a chance to put his ideas to work in two theoretical enterprises: he has been founding director of both the School of Criticism and Theory, now located at Dartmouth, and the recently opened University of California Humanities Research Institute, located at Irvine. His opening address when the latter was founded eloquently describes the warring of critical schools that he hopes will bring about a creative ferment in the humanities.

Frank Lentricchia's *Ariel and the Police: Michel Foucault, William James, Wallace Stevens* (Wisconsin) is a lively, personal, even playful book that seeks a place for the self in contemporary criticism.

The title comes from a statement in Wallace Stevens's letters, with the two characters intended to represent different poles of being: Ariel regeneration and restoration, the police the coercive, controlling power that represses regeneration. Lentricchia blames the New Criticism for moving the self from a privileged center in the reading process—despite the ironic fact that it democratized reading—by encouraging the belief that literary language is itself privileged and that there is nothing outside the text. In fact, there is always something outside the text; otherwise, we could not read it. Lentricchia, who writes from a class-based, Marxist position, also uses feminist criticism to read Stevens from within a gendered perspective. His chapter on Foucault is crucial for understanding the book's theoretical perspective, but Lentricchia, while skeptical of theories, is also critical of both the New Historicism and its related "anti-theory" movement. He finds James's disciplined pragmatism the most useful way to be both theoretically sophisticated and empirically responsive. Lentricchia's ambivalence about the lyric is indicative of the complex train of thought in this stimulating, somewhat loosely structured book. "High-modernist lyricism is the creation of radical privacy in the belief that feeling cannot be entrusted to social context" (222); but earlier he says, "The anecdotal lyric is (at best) a marginal and eccentric literary form, but its eccentricity may bring all the way forward what is most typical about literary form—its resistance to formalist desire for closure: there is always something outside the text" (7).

A developing area of literary activity is the hermeneutics of legal texts. To a certain extent legal scholars accept the idea of undecidable texts, whereas literary theory seeks to explain the nature of linguistic ambiguity. *Interpreting Law and Literature: A Hermeneutic Reader* (Northwestern), ed. Sanford Levinson and Steven Mailloux, brings together essays that interpret both kinds of texts and discuss each field's theories of interpretation. Contributors include legal and literary scholars, including Stanley Fish, Gerald Graff, Walter Benn Michaels, and David Couzens Hoy. Some of the most interesting essays are E. D. Hirsch's "Counterfactuals in Interpretation," Kenneth S. Abraham's "Statutory Interpretation and Literary Theory: Some Common Concerns of an Unlikely Pair," Clare Dalton's "An Essay in the Deconstruction of Contract Doctrine," and James Boyd White's "Judicial Criticism." I think we can look for a lot more work here in the next few years.

Three books by and about Jean-François Lyotard have come to my attention. *The Differend: Phrases in Dispute* (Minnesota), trans. Georges Van Den Abbeele, is organized by discussions of a series of terms or phrases, each argument within the term presented in numbered sequence as in, say, Wittgenstein. By "differend," Lyotard means "a case of conflict, between (at least) two parties, that cannot be equitably resolved for lack of a rule of judgment applicable to both arguments" (xi). He analyzes a series of major problematic terms in relation to how differentness gives rise to the kind of dispute described above. These include the Differend; The Referent, The Name; Presentation; Result; Obligation; Genre, Norm; and The Sign of History. In each case Lyotard uses other writers as intermediaries for reading the key term. These include Kant, Aristotle, Plato, Gertrude Stein.

A more accessible work is *Peregrinations: Law, Form, Event* (Columbia), the 1986 Wellek Library Lectures. David Carroll helped Lyotard turn these into English. They constitute an intellectual autobiography in which Lyotard reviews his career and the concerns expressed in his writing, analyzing them with an ironic, critical eye. The lecture titles "Clouds," "Touches," and "Gaps" indicate some of this irony, as does the following quotation: "As a pretender to being a philosopher and a writer, I confess I have no chance of avoiding being a shammer. There is no genuine thinking without a sense of indignity. The only way of recovering a bit is by arguing how ineluctable it is for thinking to be situated here and now and to be confronted with only one situation at once" (6). Through such ironic self-examination, Lyotard establishes a model for avoiding dogmatism and self-importance. The volume also contains an essay entitled "A Memorial for Marxism" and a bibliography of Lyotard's writings. Interested readers might also consult Geoffrey Bennington, *Lyotard: Writing the Event* (Columbia), a solid, brief summation and analysis that certainly helped me to make more sense of *Le Differend.*

Michael J. Shapiro's *The Politics of Representation: Writing Practices in Biography, Photography, and Policy Analysis* (Wisconsin) analyzes political dimensions in the forms of representation. The author claims that "representations do not imitate reality but are the practices through which things take on meaning and value; to the extent that a representation is regarded as realistic, it is because it is so familiar it operates transparently" (xi). He further states that "this book issues a plea for treating the language of inquiry less as an occasion for clarity and precision than as an opportunity for disruption and transgression, for writing peculiarly in order to disclose that what has made for intelligibility and coherence in our analyses is not the intelligible world but our intelligibility-producing practices" (xii–xiii). His chapters study the ideology of the political analyst, reading biography, the case of "Guatemala," and "The Political Rhetoric of Photography." Foucault's influence is central to this fascinating analysis.

The Ethics of Criticism (Cornell), by Tobin Siebers, explores the proposition that although poststructuralism sees discourse as primarily linguistic, criticism nonetheless always has an ethical base. "*The Ethics of Criticism* focuses . . . on the means by which literary criticism affects the relation between literature and human life. Its area of interest does not extend to all literary criticism, but rather emphasizes a particular line of theoretical development that many see as the main path of what is now called critical theory" (2). The shift from the human to the linguistic resulting from structuralism makes criticism problematic. "The substitution of language for the self produces its own distinct moral dilemma because it has created a view of human consciousness in which ethical reflection is always destined to fail. The character of language promoted by theory today makes extremely difficult the type of consciousness necessary to moral reflection" (10). Beneath all the apparent concern for language, however, is a hidden ethos which insists that "literature is a human activity, and the character of criticism must remain as resolutely human. The power of marginality in the modern world is an inescapable fact, but this power is purchased at an enormous expense by modern critics. It places criticism in the margins of life. It expels literature as an undervalued and flawed manner of thinking, if it gives literature the status of thought at all" (12–13). Siebers tests this idea through reading Freud, Lacan, Lévi-Strauss, Derrida, de Man (before the revelation of his early journalism), Nietzsche, and René Girard. This well-written, densely textured book constantly challenges the apparently cold detachment of so much modern theory.

Barbara Herrnstein Smith's new book, *Contingencies of Value: Alternative Perspectives for Critical Theory* (Harvard), also deals with evaluative questions, but from a different perspective. Smith is concerned with our basis for making evaluative judgments about literature. She finds that such values reside neither in the object of perception, nor completely within the perceiving consciousness, but rather in transaction between the two. She can thus take a skeptical position without declining into pure relativism. What Smith thinks we do "when we make an explicit value judgment of a literary work is (a) articulating an estimate of how well that work will serve certain implicitly defined functions (b) for a specific implicitly defined audience, (c) who are conceived of as experiencing the work under certain implicitly defined conditions" (13). Smith believes we have gone too far in trying to escape from making value judgments—perhaps from fear of moral absolutism—and that we must now find ways to return evaluative standards to literary discourse. "The issues that attend the concept of literary value and the activities that constitute literary evaluation are a central part of the network of problems and phenomena that constitute the domain of literary theory, and therefore they must be permitted and encouraged to return from their present exile" (16). After discussing the history of evaluation and its exile from academic life, Smith examines various historical attempts at defining evaluative standards, from Hume and Kant to the present. Her knowledge of philosophy is invaluable, and although she does not develop a genuine system of evaluation—an "undoable" task—she explores the subject as well as anyone has in recent years, making the subject respectable for the first time since Northrop Frye's *Anatomy of Criticism* suggested that evaluation was not the critic's proper task.

vii. Conclusion

When I began writing this chapter I assumed that 1988 was another run-of-the-mill year in literary studies, but on completing the task I realize that it was more interesting than most. The vast number of books that are being published on literary topics and theories suggest an enterprise that is less in crisis than we tend to think; or, if I am wrong, we are at least using that "crisis" to generate a lot of interesting prose. I look forward to reviewing the 1989 crop of books which promises to be even more interesting, with new books by Bloom, Culler, Derrida, Fish, and Graff, the publication of books in the emerging field of gay studies, and the extraordinary explosion of books in women's studies, gender studies, and feminist criticism.

University of California, Davis

21. Foreign Scholarship

i. East European Contributions

F. Lyra

Over the past two years Soviet scholarship of American literature was largely circumscribed by "correlation" and its various near-synonyms such as "interaction," "influence," "connection," "dialogue," "relation." All these terms reflect a state of mind that seeks affiliation rather than confrontation, distinction through reception rather than exclusion, catholicity rather than particularity or imperious uniqueness, though a few of the publications are not entirely free of the last attribute (for instance, D. M. Urnov's essay or N. A. Anastas'ev's book). Marx, Engels, Lenin, and the resolutions of the latest party congress are still invoked occasionally to sanction a critic's literary opinion, and most Soviet scholars continue to study American letters as a reflection of social reality, but social conflicts are seldom viewed exclusively in terms of class struggle. Socialist realism has yet to be relegated to the dustbin of literary history; it is increasingly superseded by the rhetoric of humanism, especially in reference to authors who for ideological reasons were either ignored or in various degrees deprecated in the past, as was the case with Thornton Wilder and William Faulkner. Critical realism and realism, tinged with shades of communist ideology, remain the basic standards among many Soviet literary scholars and critics analyzing and commenting on American literature.

With few exceptions, Soviet criticism of American literature this year consists of discussions of individual authors or even works. The list is impressively long, but only a few studies reveal fresh insights. As in the past, several Soviet contributions were beyond reach for comment—some will be mentioned in the course of the review—while a few of last year's became available. Regretfully, my efforts to enlist cooperation of Americanists from countries outside the Soviet Union and Poland have produced only promises of participation.

***a.* Pre-20th-Century Literature.** The earliest writer discussed was William Cullen Bryant. Significantly, Valentina A. Libman's American literature in Russian translation (see *ALS 1977*) does not reveal a single study about Bryant in the Soviet Union. For this reason alone, E. P. Khanzhina's "Put' cheloveka v filosofskoi lirike U. K. Braianta" (K probleme purytanskoi tradytsii) [Man's Progress in W. C. Bryant's Philosophical Lyrics: On the Problem of Puritan Tradition] (*Traditsii i vzaimodestviya*, pp. 45–57) amounts to a literary event, the more so that from Khanzhina's study Bryant emerges as a more religious poet than from American biographies and criticism. But Khanzhina finds Bryant's poems on death in the Christian spirit less interesting than those treating death from the point of view of man in the natural world (e.g., "June," a poem praised by Poe). Khanzhina draws forth the rich texture of Bryant's poetry. Philosophically, she assigns him a niche between the "providentialism of the Puritans and romantic symbolism." She points to his complex view of man, but she is particularly interested in his changing views of death, discussing poems on death that are hardly ever mentioned by critics. Thus, apart from commenting on the canonical pieces, e.g., "The Prairies," "Monument Mountain," "A Hymn of the Sea," "Hymn to Death," Khanzhina briefly deals with "The Future Life," "The Past," "The Twenty-Seventh of March," "The Life That Is." She gives a close reading of "To a Waterfowl," but one almost feels grateful to her for excluding "Thanatopsis."

Poe specialists will appreciate Reet Sool's "Edgar Allan Poe in Estonian (Notes on Critical Reception and Method)" (*Uchenie Zapiski Tartuskogo Universiteta* 792:77–86), though he confines his study to a discussion of only three Estonian versions of "The Raven," trans. G. Kajak in 1915 (a free translation based on K. Belmont's Russian version of 1892), Johannes Aavik (1929), and Ants Oras (1930). "It is a curious fact," observes Sool, "that through the translations of Aavik and Oras, Poe, whose vocabulary is not large for a poet writing in English and in whose poems neologisms are especially rare, was destined to become a vehicle for linguistic innovation in the Estonian language."

V. A. Milovidov's "Ob elementakh naturalizma v novellistike E. Po" [On Naturalistic Elements in Poe's Stories] appeared in *Khudozhestvennoe osmyslenie i deistvitel'nost'* [Artistic Understanding and Reality] (Moscow) which I was unable to get. As a result, I cannot comment on a piece by A. F. Golovenchenko, "*Roman o Blaitdeile* N. Gotorna" [N. Hawthorne's *The Blithedale Romance*], that appeared in the same collection, either. It may be a contribution of good quality, judging from his "Istoriya i sovremennost' (*Angliiskie zapisnye knizhki* i *Nash staryi dom* N. Gotorna)" [History and Contemporaneity: N. Hawthorne's *The English Notebooks* and *Our Old Home*] published in another collection, *Pisatel' i obshchestvo* (pp. 9–20). To control the complex contents of *The Notebooks*, Golovenchenko divides it into three categories: "autobiographical, historical-cultural and publicist," and complements the description with copious footnotes that show Hawthorne's books in a wide context and background. The article is of great cognitive value to the Soviet student of American literature, but it has little to offer the American scholar. In "Istorizm kak esteticheskii printsip v proizvedeniakh N. Gotorna kontsa 40-kh godov" [Historicity as an Aesthetic Principle in N. Hawthorne's Work of the End of the Forties] (*Traditsii i vzaimodeistviya*, pp. 57–69), O. N. Berezovskaya analyzes "Main Street" and *The Scarlet Letter* to argue that individual freedom is the central theme in Hawthorne's philosophy and history of New England. She draws an interesting comparison between Hawthorne's and Bancroft's views of New England history, saying that in contrast to Bancroft, Hawthorne did not mix the political, civic, and spiritual concepts of freedom. To Berezovskaya, *Main Street* and *The Scarlet Letter* demonstrate the process of the loss of freedom.

In view of the Soviet scholars' negligible interest in Emerson, any publication on him deserves notice, as does V. G. Prozorov's "K probleme politicheskikh vzglyadov R. U. Emersona" [On the Problem of Emerson's Political Views] (*Pisatel' i obshchestvo*, pp. 58–64). Prozorov handles the topic with admirable restraint, concentrating on "Politics" and drawing on "Wealth," "Man the Reformer," "New England Reformers," "The Young American," "The American Scholar," and "Self-Reliance," but he has omitted *Lectures on the Times*. In a spirit of understanding, the Soviet scholar comments on Emerson's contradictory views, the paradoxes, the nature of his beliefs, only mildly censuring him for his philosophy of individualism. Following Daniel Aaron's lead, Prozorov explains that the "logic" and "system" of Emerson's were those of a "yes-no" thinker, critic-apologist of his generation. He also interprets Emerson's vision of America which was that of a poet—"a symbolic image of a peculiar Utopia," not that of an ideologue. Prozorov concludes his all-too-short study with a somewhat facile generalization by stating that Emerson was not unique in his dual attitude toward his country as a critic and as a believer in an ideal democracy in America. "It is typically characteristic of the majority of 19th-century American writers from J. F. Cooper to W. Whitman and M. Twain."

***b.* 20th-Century Literature.** I should like to open this section by drawing attention to Igor' Vinogradov's article "Pered litsom neba i zemli" [In the Face of Heaven and Earth] (*Literaturnaya ucheba* 1: 73–96), which contains a censorious exposure of the state of present-day literary life in the Soviet Union, especially the stale condition of Soviet literary criticism. Vinogradov calls for a return to the standards of "real criticism" as practiced by A. N. Dobrolyubov and D. I. Pisarev in the second half of the 19th century. Vinogradov's publication provoked several responses in subsequent issues of the periodical, among them one by A. Mulyarchik, a familiar name to the readers of *ALS*—"Kritika v 'normalnykh usloviyakh'" [Criticism in 'Normal Conditions'] (*Literaturnaya ucheba* 4:83–87). Mulyarchik, however, dodges taking a stand on the main issues raised by Vinogradov. Instead, he uses the occasion to demonstrate that Vinogradov's call for "a union of literary criticism and reality" does not apply to the American literary situation at the turn of the 19th and 20th centuries, which produced only muckrakers but no critical school comparable to the "real criticism" movement in Russia. American criticism, says Mulyarchik, was concerned with "self-determination" and with catching up with literary Europe. He mentions Van Wyck Brooks, but does not recognize his attempt at establishing what Russia's "real critics" were after. It is to Mulyarchik's credit that in elucidating the main concern of American criticism of that period, he presents an outline of James G. Huneker's role in American literary life. He seems to be the first Soviet scholar to see Huneker's work in positive terms. Even more noteworthy is his appreciation of Edmund Wilson, whom he considers Huneker's "continuator." Mulyarchik's high regard for Wilson, however, is grounded in the American writer's temporary love affair with Marxism and the Soviet Union in his earlier career. Mulyarchik overlooks Wilson's complex and highly ambivalent attitude toward either in his later life. In writing positively about Huneker, Wilson, and later critics (including Malcolm Cowley and Alfred Kazin), Mulyarchik for once has no ideological ax to grind. As a matter of fact, he praises contemporary American critics as "preservers of the cultural core" of American society that is presently "exposed to ideological, ethnic, political currents and tornadoes."

In "Ideinaya bor'ba v SSHA i khudozhestvennaya literatura" [The

Ideological Struggle in the United States and Artistic Literature] (*Problemy amerikanistiki* 6:275–99), however, Mulyarchik returns to conservative thinking to launder in Marxist soap and water the works of a score of novelists published during the 1980s, discussing them in the framework of "conservatism," "neoconservatism," "traditional liberalism," "New leftism," "New patriotism," "Neoliberalism." These ideological tags do not prevent him from discriminating the novelists aesthetically. He even uses the attribute "spiritual" to characterize "the creative concept" underlying the works of Anne Tyler, John Gardner, John Updike, and John Irving.

With the growing appreciation of universally recognized writers, both domestic and foreign, whose work does not conform to orthodox Marxist ideology, Soviet critics justify their reception in the Soviet Union by resorting to the accommodating concept of humanism. It may take a long time before an American writer's humanistic values are officially appreciated, for his work to be found worthy of translation and critical recognition. Such was the case with Faulkner. Though three of his stories—"That Evening Sun," "Artist at Home," and "Victory" had been translated in 1934–36, respectively, his first book in Russian, *The Hamlet*, came out only in 1964. But except for two modest books by Yu. V. Palievskaya (1970) and A. K. Savarenok (see *ALS 1979*), there have been no comprehensive studies of his work until this year: *Chelovek vystoit. Realizm Folknera* [Man Will Prevail: Faulkner's Realism] (Moscow: Khudozhestvennaya Literatura) which its author, A. N. Nikolyukin, says was already written in 1973–75, yet he chooses not to disclose the reason(s) for its publication only now, nor does he answer the question he himself has posed concerning the causes of the slow reception of Faulkner's work in the Soviet Union. As if to compensate for the scorn Soviet critics showered on Faulkner in the past, Nikolyukin produced a book that verges on hagiography; he has been seduced by Faulkner's Nobel Prize acceptance rhetoric about man. Nikolyukin has practically nothing to criticize in Faulkner's works—at least he acknowledges his contradictions seeing them as marks of the humanistic ethos. He lets Faulkner support his interpretations by resorting to his public interviews and letters (Nikolyukin edited a selected collection of them, along with speeches and articles; Moscow: Reduta, 1985). Apparently with an eye on the conservative literary establishment, Nikolyukin takes liberty with some of Faulkner's references to communism and the Soviet Union to make him appear more sympathetic toward either than he was in reality. "In Paris in 1925 with youthful enthusiasm he [Faulkner] contended that 'in England and America there should be a revolution similar to the one which was in Russia.'" Nikolyukin has lifted Faulkner's words out of context; Faulkner was writing to his mother with indignation at the American government's indifference to the dismal plight of the French farmers, saying the French were "heroic," and continues: "In England and America there would have been a revolution as there was in Russia" (Joseph Blotner, *Faulkner: A Biography*, p. 469). Being familiar with Blotner's biography and with Faulkner's paraliterary writings and interviews, Nikolyukin certainly knows Faulkner's real attitude toward communism and his native country, yet he manipulates Faulkner's opinions to the point of distortion. Referring to his "Address to the National Commission for UNESCO delivered on October 2, 1959," Nikolyukin imputes to him having stated "That in the end communism will prevail over capitalism" (p. 7). What Faulkner actually said was this: "Mr. Khrushchev says that Communism, the police state, will bury the free ones. He is a smart gentleman, he knows that this is nonsense, since freedom, man's dim concept of and belief in the human spirit is the cause of all troubles in his own country. But if he means that communism will bury capitalism, he is correct. That funeral will occur about ten minutes after the police bury gambling. Because simple man, the human race, will bury both of them. That will be when we have expended the last grain, dram, and iota of our natural resources. But man himself will not be in that grave" (*Essays, Speeches, and Public Letters*, 1965, p. 167). Elsewhere, however, Nikolyukin comes closer to truth when he writes that Faulkner was far from being a communist, that he had little sympathy with this ideological system. Faulkner was too sensitive an artist to think about human society in terms of class structure. It is therefore wrong to say, as does Nikolyukin, that Faulkner hated the bourgeoisie; moreover, Nikolyukin idealizes Faulkner's attitude toward people of the lower classes; for having an individualistic conception of man, he treated each character as a unique, complex human being irrespective of the character's social status. But Nikolyukin misreads Faulkner when interpreting, for instance, Sutpen's failure exclusively in terms of individualism, which he identifies mistakenly with Emerson's principle of self-reliance. "Indeed, no one has subjected the concept of ethical individualism to such crushing criticism as Faulkner. After *Absalom, Absalom!* it is difficult to talk seriously in America about the fruitfulness of Self-Reliance as a cornerstone of humanism, which was so obvious until recently" (p. 127).

From the pages of *Man Will Prevail* Faulkner emerges as America's greatest 20th-century writer, in which opinion he is not alone, of course, though many critics would object to Nikolyukin's argument justifying his artistic stature. Predictably, the arguments are thoroughly circumscribed by the doctrine of realism which Nikolyukin has made the fundamental basis for evaluating his art. He does not deny Faulkner's affiliation with modernism, but he demonstrates how Faulkner overcame modernism ideologically and artistically. He was as if doomed to become a realist, since only realists have the capability to believe in man, and, of course, they hold the exclusive right to truth and great art. It is this article of belief that Vinogradov questions in the above-mentioned article.

This is not to deny the value of Nikolyukin's book. It is, above all, a good guide for Soviet readers; there is no need to question the interpretations as he backs them up with the writer's numerous comments. In reading his work, Nikolyukin does not fall back on Faulkner alone. He devotes a separate chapter to Faulkner and Hemingway (pp. 232–59), taking the occasion to discuss briefly their artistic, ideological differences. Presenting *A Fable* in a chapter entitled "The Concept of Humanism" (pp. 261–77), he compares it with Dostoyevsky's *The Brothers Karamazov* and Bulgakov's *The Master and Margarita*, with special attention to the problems of good and evil, and passingly about the writers' affinities and differences.

Soviet scholars' reading of individual 20th-century authors and books is so diverse thematically that the best way to review them is chronologically, admitting some overlapping. Thus approached, Robert Herrick emerges as the earliest among them. His work is the subject of E. I. Mikhailina's useful article, "Kapitalistichekii gorod v chigagogskikh romanakh Roberta Kherikka" [The Capitalist City in Robert Herrick's Chicago Novels] (*Pisatel' i obshchestvo*, pp. 72–77), in which she examines the "Chicago trilogy"—*The Web of Life*, *The Common Lot*, and *The Memoirs of an American Citizen* and Herrick's use of "the poetics of contrast." V. I. Samokhvalova contributes to the abundant Soviet criticism on Upton Sinclair with "O nekotorykh zhanrovykh osobennostyakh romana E. Sinklera *Boston*" [On Some Genre Peculiarities of Upton Sinclair's *Boston*] (*Pisatel' i obshchestvo*, pp. 145–51), describing the work as "Sinclair's most tendentious novel" about the working class, and calls attention to its artistic complexity. "Like no other novel, *Boston* expresses the democratic and socialist aspirations of the author"; because of these qualities "bourgois literary scholarship chose to ignore it"; but Samokhvalova failed to add that so did Soviet scholarship. In the same collection of articles I. E. Lunina makes a valiant attempt at raising the artistic status of Jack London's *The Little Lady of the Big House*, "Nekotorye aspekty poznego mirovozzreniya Dzheka Londona i roman *Malen'kaya khozyaika bol'shogo doma*" [Some Aspects of the Late Worldview of Jack London and the Novel *The Little Lady of the Big House*] (pp. 122–28). Granting the sentimentality of the novel, Lunina points to the "philosophical reflections" contained in the work which "help to better understand the writer's worldview." Despite London's spiritual and literary crisis after 1909, "he continued to search for answers to many questions that agitated his whole life."

Since many Soviet scholars insist that the thirties were the most important decade in 20th-century American literature, the paucity of studies devoted to works of that period must seem a glaring discrepancy between word and practice. This year's bibliographical research produced only one item connected with the literature of the thirties, unavailable to me. It is E. Burin's "Zagadka Margaret Mitchel" [The Enigma of Margaret Mitchell] (*Nauka i zhizn'* 9:97–108).

There seems to be no end to the study of World War II literature. In "Antivoennaya poeziya Dzh. Chiardi i R. Dzharrella" [The Antiwar Poetry of J. Ciardi and R. Jarrell] (*Pisatel' i obshchestvo*, pp. 93–101), E. N. Kalacheva is less interested in the artistic quality of their poems than in how "serious they were engaged on behalf of the future without war." Ciardi and other American poets "did not entirely understand the goals of the Second World War"; but she appreciates his poetic achievement. Jarrell appears to her a better war poet as he wrote about his war experiences with more seriousness and less ambiguity than Ciardi. O. E. Osovskii's contribution, "Sootnoshenie 'realizm–naturalizm' v amerikanskom voennom romane XX v" [The Correlation "Realism-Naturalism" in the American War Novel of the 20th Century] (*Pisatel' i obshchestvo*, pp. 136–44), announces a general theme, but it deals mostly with the same subject matter. In traditional Soviet literary thought naturalism to be appreciated must serve realism. Osovskii therefore argues tautologically when maintaining that naturalistic elements in the war novels contribute to their realistic value. He takes note of the American writers' intensification of naturalistic features in the course of the 20th century, especially in the depiction of "details, characters, and events." The ways in which American war novel writers apply naturalistic elements runs predictably along ideological lines: apologists of militarism use naturalistic features differently from novelists critical of militarism. Osovskii accepts naturalism as a separate current only historically; he denies its existence as "a state" in contemporary American literature. In contrast to Donald Pizer, he declines to regard Mailer, Joyce Carol Oates, and others as naturalistic writers. The war is also the subject of N. A. Kubanev's "Tema vtoroi mirovoi voiny v literature SSHA" [The World War II Theme in American Literature] (*Mezhliteraturnye svyazi i problema realizma* [Gorkii], pp. 35–45), but the book could not be located.

Critical attention to Carson McCullers's work has not been intense but quite steady since the early sixties. This year Tiina Tarik examines McCullers's best-known novella in "Human Relations in Carson McCuller's Novella 'The Ballad of the Sad Cafe' (Aspect of Genre)" (*Uchenie Zapiski Tartuskogo Universiteta,* 828:107–15). She neatly analyzes the work as yet another aspect of the writer's "pattern of love" and shows how her "theory of love" is acted out by the chief protagonists. But Tiina Tarik fails to substantiate the parenthetical subtitle.

Among more recent writers, William Styron has been favored by several critics. In "Funktsiya snov v tvorchestve Uilyama Staironа" [The Function of Dreams in William Styron's Works] (*Uchenie Zapiski Tartuskogo Universiteta,* 792:88–97), L. Tsekhanovskaya regards *Lie Down in Darkness, Set This House on Fire,* and *The Confessions of Nat Turner,* touching upon the influence of neo-Freudianism (a movement characteristic of capitalism) and the tendency of southern writers to depict reality in symbolic terms; but she does not explore them, confining herself to tracing types of dreams of various protagonists, especially Ellen Loftis (*Lie Down in Darkness*). She finds Jean-Paul Sartre's existential psychoanalysis in the description of Cass Kinsolving (*Set This House on Fire*) and Nat Turner. On the whole, however, L. Tsekhanovskaya approves of dreams as a writer's legitimate method to reveal the inner world of modern characters. "Dreams carry a touch of poeticality so characteristic of southern writers' prose." In another article Tsekhanovskaya looks at "the hero-rebel in Styron's work" (*Uchenie Zapiski Tartuskogo*

Universiteta 828:97–103). *Sophie's Choice* received an excellent interpretation by E. A. Stetsenko in "Roman U. Stairona *Vybor Sofi* kak sposob osmysleniya istorii" [W. Styron's Novel *Sophie's Choice* as a Way of Understanding History] (*Vzaimodeistvie formy*, pp. 149–68)—remarkable for balanced insight and temperate tone so contrasting with the novel's vociferously controversial reception in Poland shortly after its publication. Stetsenko reads it as a complex exploration of the nature of truth. He also studies the components of the lyric-epic structure of the narration and its various forms that Styron uses to better deal with the problem of evil in its historical, psychological, and philosophical aspects.

Robert Penn Warren and Thornton Wilder are latecomers in the Soviet Union; the former made his debut in Russian only in 1967 with *All the King's Men*, the latter two years later with *The Skin of Our Teeth*. While critical interest in Warren has been fairly intensive, Wilder, for long considered a decadent reactionary, came to be appreciated only in the early eighties. A few Soviet scholars like L. N. Tatarinova and T. E. Nekryach have even become specialists in Warren. In " '*Vsya korolevskaya rat*' R. P. Uorrena. Na perekrestkakh dramy i romana" [R. P. Warren's *All the King's Men*: On the Border of Drama and Novel] (*Vzaimodeistvie formy*, pp. 119–48), Nekryach argues convincingly against those who read the work only as a political novel. Warren managed to synthesize the epic, lyric, and elements of poetic drama. Nekryach is looking for an answer to why *Proud Flesh* as a drama was inadequate artistically to serve the author's epic purpose. Want of the above-mentioned *Mezhliteraturnye svyazi i problema realizma* accounts for the absence of comment on M. K. Bronich's contribution entitled elaborately "Traditsiya 'yuzhnoi shkoly' i roman R. P. Uorrena 'Pribezhishche' (K voprosu kontseptsii mira v tvorchestve Uorrena) [The Southern School Tradition and R. P. Warren's Novel: On the Question of Worldview in Warren's Work] (pp. 35–45).

Wilder's *The Ides of March* is the subject of V. K. Kukhalashvili's "*Martovskie idy* Torntona Uaildera: Obraz istoricheskii i obraz khudozhestvennyi prozy" [*The Ides of March*: The Historical and the Artistic Image of Prose] (*Vzaimodeistvie formy*, pp. 93–118). This is the best study of a work of Wilder's published so far in the Soviet Union, giving full justice to the philosophical and artistic complexity of the novel. After Kukhalashvili, any Soviet critic will run the risk of ridicule should he/she apply orthodox Marxist criteria in evaluating *The Ides of March.* As a matter of fact, Kukhalashvili tactfully points out a few erroneous Soviet interpretations of the novel, disposing of them with unequivocal arguments inherent in the text. *The Ides of March* also received a close reading by R. F. Yashen'kina, "O formakh vyrazheniya avtorskoi pozytsii v istoriko-khudozhestvennom povestvovanii" [On Forms of Expressing the Author's Position in Historical-Artistic Narration] (*Traditsii i vzaimodeistviya,* pp. 118–30). She provides an interesting comparison with *Boski Juliusz* [The Divine Julius] by Jacek Bochenski, a Polish writer. The previous year O. N. Rodina published "Formirovanie literaturno-kriticheskikh vzglyadov T. Uaildera (Nachal'nyi etap) [The Formation of T. Wilder's Literary-Critical Views: The Initial Stage] (*Pisatel' i obshchestvo,* pp. 78–82) in which she integrates Wilder's literary views contained in *The American Characteristics and Other Essays* with his artistic biography. I. V. Nikolaeva's "O nekotorykh osobennostyakh psikhologizma Torntona Uaildera" [On Some Peculiarities of Thornton Wilder's Psychologism] (*Vestnik Kievskogo Universiteta. Romano-Germanskiya Filologiya* 22:116–19) was not available for comment.

Wilder's *The Ides of March* call up Gore Vidal's *Julian,* which inspired Yu. V. Stulov to write "V poiskakh spravedlivosti (Roman G. Vidala *Julian*) [In Search of Justice: G. Vidal's Novel *Julian*] (*Pisatel' i obshchestvo,* pp. 65–71). Appreciating *Julian* as historical fiction, Stulov reads it above all as a political novel of "a liberal democrat" who is critical of America's contemporary political scene: "Julian's views, so close to G. Vidal's heart, are typically liberal ideals of a moderate democrat . . . . The writer was unable to work faithfully in the dialectic of the historical process."

In the collection of articles *Traditsii i vzaimodeistviya v zarubezhnoi literature XIX–XX vekov* [Traditions and Interrelations in Foreign Literature of the 19th and 20th Centuries] (Perm': Permskii Gosudarstvennyi Universitet) ed. R. F. Yashen'kina, four Soviet authors present their interpretations of as many 20th-century American writers: Waldo Frank, Katherine Anne Porter, John Gardner, and Alice Walker, of whom only Gardner has received noticeable attention among Soviet critics. Waldo Frank is absent in Valentina A. Libman's bibliography, as is Alice Walker, while Katherine Anne Porter figures there only in three reviews of her work, the first as early as 1941 (*Pale Horse, Pale Rider*). Under these circumstances, and given the exigencies of space, it is understandable that the scholars are eager to say as much as possible about their work in general, the astringent titles of the articles notwithstanding. Thus O. B. Metlina—"Ideinokhudozhestvennoe svoeobrazie romana Uoldo Frenka '*Prazdnik*' i negrityanskaya tema v literature SSHA 1920–kh godov" [Ideo-Artistic Originality of Waldo Frank's Novel *Holiday* and the Black Theme in American Literature of the Twenties] (pp. 85–96)—takes the occasion to discuss Frank's *Holiday*, which appeared in Russian in 1926, to provide a survey of white writers' books about blacks in the twenties. She briefly describes several other books of Frank's and the Harlem Renaissance to draw a perspective on this novel. A comparison of Metlina's reading of *Holiday* with that of Yevgeni Lann's in 1928 reveals the critical distance in the perception of the novel on the part of Soviet critics at the threshold of socialist realism and the post-socialist-realism era. And yet, either out of ignorance of Frank's biography or in a willful gesture to Marxism, Metlina lapses into ideological backwaters when passing judgment on Frank's novels of the thirties: "In the novels *The Death and Birth of David Markland* (1934) and *The Bridegroom Cometh* (1939) Frank attempts to present an artistic-philosophical interpretation of the process of birth of revolutionary consciousness."

I. V. Shikhova initiates the Russian reader to Porter's work by discussing dominant themes in her stories, " 'Yuzhnaya traditsiya' v novellakh K. A. Porter [The Southern Tradition in K. A. Porter's Stories] (pp. 97–105). In "Filossofskaya problematika romanov Dzhona Gardnera" [Philosophical Problems in John Gardner's Novels] (pp. 141–48) E. F. Osipova discusses *Resurrection, Sunlight Dialogues, October Light*, and *Freddy's Book*. Finally, I. N. Klepatskaya writes about Alice Walker's *The Color Purple* as a Feminist Novel in the Context of Afro-American fiction—"Roman E. Uoker *Tsvet Bagryanyi*: Tradytsii sovremennoi literatury SSHA" [Alice Walker's Novel *The Color Purple*: Traditions in Contemporary Black American Literature] (pp. 148–56).

Voronchenko sacrifices analysis for a general treatment of the theme "Stachechnaya bor'ba sel'kokhozaistvennykh robochikh meksikanskogo proiskhozhdeniya v 60–70-e gody i poyavlenie teatra amerikanskikh chicanos" [Strike-Struggle of Farmhands of Mexican Origin in the 60s and 70s and the Appearance of the American Chicano Theater] (*Pisatel' i obshchestvo*, pp. 52–57).

c. **Nonfiction prose.** On the whole, Soviet critics have not viewed New Journalism favorably, but Piret Tergen and Hilja Koop in "New Developments in American Nonfiction in the 1960s" (*Uchenie Zapiski Tartuskogo Universiteta* vyp. 828:116–25) offer a balanced view of the genre and describe its three basic types represented by Tom Wolfe's *The Kandy-Kolored Tangerine-Flake Streamline Baby*, Truman Capote's *In Cold Blood*, and Norman Mailer's *The Armies of the Night* with its characteristic subtitle *History as a Novel, The Novel as History*, over which scholars tripped, for they read it as "The Novel as History, History as the Novel."

New Journalism is also the subject of *Contemporary American Nonfiction* (Lublin: Uniwersytet M. Curie-Sklodowskiej) by the Polish scholar Jerzy Durczak. He raises the semantic issue concerning the name of the genre to justify, convincingly, the use of the term "literary nonfiction." Durczak might have enriched the onomastic survey by linking the various terms with authors and critics who have used them. The baffling semantic confusion provides sufficient cause to side with Jack Newfield who favors the use of the qualifiers "good" or "bad" only; or agree with E. L. Doctorow's argument that there are no longer any differences between fiction and nonfiction—there is only narrative; or to settle simply with John Hellmann's "new fiction" which, incidentally, slipped Durczak's attention. He brings order into the confusion and refines the taxonomy by introducing two types of literary nonfiction, "the personal" and "the impersonal." In his study he concentrates on the former, choosing Tom Wolfe, Norman Mailer, and Hunter E. Thompson as representative of as many varieties of personal nonfiction—each gets a chapter. The schematic composition of *Contemporary American Literary Nonfiction* belies rich contents that make his book a valuable contribution not only to the study of the three authors but to New Journalism in general. Its usefulness is further augmented by the sporadic comparative references to Polish practitioners of the genre and criticism.

d. **Drama.** Eugene O'Neill's hundredth birthday was commemorated by two books: S. M. Pinaev, *Yudzhin Gladston O'Nil (K 100-letiyu so dnya rozhdeniya)* [Eugene Gladstone O'Neill: On the Hundredth Anniversary of His Birth] (Moscow: Znanie), which I was unable to obtain for review, and Peter Egri, *The Birth of American Tragedy* (Budapest: Tankonyvkiado)—undoubtedly the best work in American literary scholarship published in Eastern Europe this year. Egri commands great authority in the study of American drama, based on his earlier contributions. As a matter of fact, *The Birth of American Tragedy* concludes a unique scholarly tetralogy of the highest order. The preceding studies were *A költészet valosaga* [The Reality of Poetry] (1975) dealing with the poetic nature of O'Neill's drama; *Töésvonolak* [Fault Lines] (1983) analyzes American drama within the framework of European drama at the turn of the century; *Chekhov and O'Neill* (1986) examines the typological convergence between the two dramatists and "the integration of the short story pattern in the dramatic texture." In the present study Egri analyzes "the genetic and generic conditions of the birth of American tragedy from an axiological point of view," starting with a detailed analysis of Thomas Godfrey's *The Prince of Parthia* to trace "the shadow of Shakespeare across the Atlantic" and succinctly describes the Shakespearean tradition in early American tragedy, placing it within the context of an outline of American social and literary history which he views as a process of growing opposites until they reached a stage of contradictions "charged with intrinsic tensions" providing the proper conditions of the appearance of a truly American tragedy (p. 20). These kinds of generalizations come dangerously close to historiographical triteness; among them one is relegated to a footnote referring to Whitman and Poe that is particularly tantalizing: "When the attitudes underlying Whitman's and Poe's achievements had turned against one another, the great moment of American drama arrived. This happened when Eugene O'Neill entered the stage" (p. 184). But Egri easily avoids the pitfall in the second chapter providing a thorough survey of the controversial issue of the causes that promoted O'Neill's achievement and the reasons that explained it. He discusses them in terms of "continuity" (pp. 22–26), " 'Miracle' " (pp. 26–28), "Theatrical Developments" (pp. 28–30), "Psychology" (pp. 30–33), and "Civilization and Alienation" (pp. 33–37). Egri has constructed his discourse proper around O'Neill's individual plays, which are interpreted around a cluster of themes and ideas, with "alienation" as the key concept. Thus, for instance, chapter 3 deals with *The Personal Equation* read in terms of "The Politics of Alienation" and the following themes: "Radicalism at the Crossroads," "The Patterns of the Well-made Melodrama and the Attraction of Naturalistic Tragedy," "Epic Milieu and Episode Structure" (pp. 38–47). Such an approach highlights O'Neill's mosaic pattern, "which is the mold and matrix of this achievement, the epic, the lyric, and the tragic are perfectly fused; alienation is revealed and rejected; and American tragedy is born at a universal level" (p. 181). In chapter 4, "The Sociology and Metaphysic of Alienation," Egri analyzes *The Hairy Ape* (pp. 48–71); in the long fifth chapter, "Alienation and Dramatic Form: The Novel, the Lyric, and the Short Story in the Drama," Egri structures the exposition into seven subchapters, each devoted to a play: *Strange Interlude* (pp. 72–85), *Mourning Becomes Electra* (pp. 85–99), *A Tale of Possessors Self-Dispossessed* (pp. 99–115), *A Touch of the Poet* (pp. 115–22), *More Stately Mansions* (pp. 122–400), *The Calms of Capricorn* (pp. 140–50). The last chapter, "Alienation and Tragedy," is devoted to *Long Day's Journey into Night* (pp. 154–81).

By any standards Egri's book is an impressive success. It integrates in-depth analysis of O'Neill's works with his poetics of the drama, his concern with human values that he was testing against the conditions of the changing social and political reality and his own life. Egri proves that O'Neill's unequal and divers achievement is best understood when approached typologically rather than chronologically.

In the Soviet Union, apart from Pinaev's work, V. M. Paverman published a substantial article on Edward Albee's famous play—not Paverman's first contribution on the playwright. In "Kharaktery i konflikt v p'ese Edvarda Olbi 'Ne boyus' Virdzhinii Vulf' " [Characters and Conflict in Edward Albee's Play "Who's Afraid of Virginia Woolf?"] (*Problemy kharaktera v literature zarubezhnykh stran*) [Problems of Characters in the Literature of Foreign Countries] (Sverdlovsk: Sverdlovskii Gosudarstvennyi Pedagogicheskii Institut, pp. 88–100) he surveys Albee's social, political, and aesthetic views, stressing his ideological discrepancies and contradictions that condition the duality of his poetics. With occasional inclinations toward anti-drama, his play reveals affinities with Ibsen, Chekhov, and Brecht. Paverman's chief aim, however, is to trace the ideological and aesthetic direction Albee takes in the play, which he analyzes on various levels to conclude that in Albee's artistic career the play "is a step backward from his realistic achievement of such works as *The Zoo Story* and *The Death of Bessie Smith.*

V. L. Nechesov has reminded us of Barry Stavis's work in "Antimakkartiskaya drama B. Stevisa 'Chelovek, kotoryi nikogda ne umret' " [B. Stavis's Anti-McCarthy Play "The Man Who Never Died"] (*Pisatel' i obshchestvo*, pp. 102–8). An interview with Arthur Miller, conducted by Eimuntas Nekroshyus (*Litva Literaturnaya* 6:177–79), proved disappointing. Prompted by Nekroshyus, Miller briskly discussed the situation of the artist in America, glasnost, minority cultures, the artist as "dualist," ecology—and least of all his work.

University of Warsaw

ii. French Contributions

Michel Gresset

I would like to begin with two remarks, the first of which is about translations. This will not surprise those who know I have created a Maurice Edgar Coindreau Prize for the best American book in French translation every year. The Prize for 1988 went to François Hirsch for his translation of Cormac McCarthy's *Blood Meridian.* The jury's surprise was complete when they heard that this was Hirsch's first translation from the English but that he had been Milan Kundera's French translator for years—under a pseudonym! Translations usually remain unlisted and uncommented in these reviews because they are not literally *about* American literature; yet for the general public on this side of the Atlantic, they *make* American literature, and although specialists almost always use the texts in their original versions, it might be illuminating to interview translators, as they are by definition the first readers of original works abroad and, as such, not necessarily dumb or mute. One good example is Philippe Mikriammos, one of the translators of the complete *Cantos* of Ezra Pound (Paris: Flammarion, 1986), now at work on the translation of the Tytell biography.

The second remark is only a reminder: with the highly specific French system of national competitive examinations held each year in each discipline with a syllabus set for students all over the country, there usually crops up a number of articles, even occasionally a special issue, devoted to the study of the subjects and authors assigned. Thus, 1988 was a year highlighting Mark Twain's *Pudd'nhead Wilson* (hereinafter abbreviated as *PW*), William Faulkner's *The Wild Palms* (*TWP*), and Grace Paley's *The Little Disturbances of Man* (*TLDM*).

A new literary handbook came out in 1988 under a remarkably

ecumenical title: *Les Littératures de langue anglaise depuis 1945: Grande-Bretagne, Etats-Unis, Commonwealth*, by Denise Coussy, Evelyne Labbé, and M. and G. Fabre (Paris, Nathan). We owe the American part, unfortunately limited to a neat third (or 120 pages), to the ever-active duet formed by Michel and Geneviève Fabre. The former wrote the first two chapters on fiction and on poetry, and the latter wrote the third and last on contemporary American drama. As each author is hardly ever given more than one page, what is new is no more or less than what is made clear by the title: the stress is on the contemporary.

***a.* About Books and the Book Industry.** A special mention must be made of University Paris VII's *Cahiers Charles V* [*CCV*], no. 10, entitled *Le Livre aujourd'hui (Grande-Bretagne, Irlande, Etats-Unis)* (*The Book Industry Today in Great Britain, Ireland, and the United States*), which breaks new ground here by being entirely devoted to the many dramatic changes occurring in the English language book trade. Two contributions in English are on American topics: one, by Véronique Cauquil, is the self-explanatory "The Selling of an Author [by himself]: John Irving" (*CCV* 10:91–100), and the other is my own interview of Herbert Lottman, writer and Paris correspondent of *Publishers Weekly* (*CCV* 10:189–99). The other contributions, by members of the CIRNA (Centre interdisciplinaire de recherches nord-américaines) like myself, are in French: Simone Chambon and Jean-Paul Rospars write at length about the existence of censorship (yes, even now, in 1988) in the United States (*CCV* 10:101–43), and Claire Bruyère, after raising the problem of the author in "Où en est l'auteur?" regrets that "the death of the author" has not led to the symbolic "birth" of the reader in a country in which the act of reading has become an exception: "to save reading has become a national priority in the U.S.—but it is only incidentally for cultural reasons" (*CCV* 10:37–69). No. 1 of *A Descriptive Catalogue of French Periodicals of English and American Studies* has been published by Publications de la Recherche, Université Paul Valéry, (Montpellier).

***b.* 19th-Century Literature.** It is hardly necessary for me (who began my research at the University of Virginia, under the same auspices and at the same time as Claude Richard) to echo Marc Chénetier's liminary words on our colleague's untimely death in *ALS 1987*. I will simply use the proceedings of the third conference on science fiction held in Nice in April 1987 on "Edgar Poe et la raison visionnaire" and published (poorly edited) as nos. 15–16 of *Métaphores* to stress the fact that Claude Richard's and Henri Justin's contributions stand out as the most serious ones (by far) in this collection. (Among no fewer than 25 articles on Poe, also outstanding is Mireille Gouaux's thoroughly convincing analysis of the intertextual link between Jules Verne's *Le Sphinx des glaces* and *The Adventures of Arthur Gordon Pym* [*Métaphores* 15–16:111–16].) Justin's contribution, "Vortex: Raison et Vertige" (*Métaphores* 15–16:179–87), shows that in "A Descent into the Maelstrom" Poe takes *contradiction* (or "perversity") as his founding principle: the tale's vortex, or "still center" (a version of Justin's perfectly relevant notion of an "infinite center"), illustrates the idea that, with Poe, the teller of the tale turns the poet's *vision* into his *reason*—which is exactly what happens in *Eureka*. Richard's "La Physique de Poe" (Poe's Physics, *Métaphores* 15–16:205–13) is a late and remarkable, albeit difficult, contribution to the study of Poe's debt to the Greek atomists, particularly Epicurus via Lucretius: "Atomistics is the science in whose contradictory foundation Poe's physics finds its inspiration." To one familiar with Poe's notion of the "perverse" and with the text of *Eureka*, Richard writes, this cannot come as a real surprise. Richard and Justin agree that in *Eureka* lies the consummation of both Poe's art and Poe's system.

Very different are two earlier contributions to Poe studies, both published in 1987. One is by Philippe Rousseau under the title "Six exemples chez Poe de fantasmes sur la femme," published by the Centre de recherches anglo-américaines of University Paris X in *Tropismes* no. 3, pp. 85–104. This is a number devoted to "Le Fantasme." The other is Ann Lecercle-Sweet's analysis of "The Oval Portrait" in *Les Forteresses vides de l'oncle Toby: Etudes sur la représentation dans les pays anglo-saxons* (Paris: Les Belles Lettres, 1987), pp. 47–62. What is under focus is the text as anamorphosis, the oval portrait functioning like the head of Medusa, i.e., like a female sex organ—a provocative though quite convincing reading in which Freud and Lacan are used as the tools of analysis. However, Ann Radcliffe's *The Mysteries of Udolpho*, a book quoted right at the beginning of the tale, is also shown to have been used by Poe as the main framing device of his tale. The only question not raised in the article is that of the possibility of irony on Poe's part—often a question by-passed by psychoanalysis.

There is irony in the fact that, although he is currently seen as "a sort of American Yeats," Thoreau, especially in "Life Against Principle," was possessed of the same moralizing itch as his fellow Transcendentalists—all inheritors of Calvinism. This is shown by Yves Carlet in his "Un demi-siècle de moralisme bostonien: unitariens et transcendentalistes," *Morales et moralités aux Etats-Unis* [*MMEU*] (Aix: Université de Provence, Actes du GRENA), 69–83. The title of the volume is misleading since some of the contributions are not about society or even about culture, but about literature; so are Etienne de Planchard's self-explanatory "G. W. Cable: un moraliste américain chez les créoles" (*MMEU*:33–45) and Michèle Bonnet's "Le Dessin dans le tapis: les jeux optiques de l'anamorphose dans *The Turn of the Screw*" (*MMEU*:9–32).

After reading an earlier study by Christian Fournier of the Leatherstocking tales as a cycle (unpublished M.A. thesis, Paris VII, 1981), two students of Ecole normale supérieure were given a chance to publish part of their stimulatingly fresh work on language and ideology in Fenimore Cooper's *The Prairie* in the second half of *RFEA* 37, bearing the slightly pretentious title "Les Aventuriers du language." After a brief introduction nicely entitled "Des mots sur la prairie" ("Words on the Prairie") (*RFEA* 37:235–37), in which the Cooper revival is found to have been too much concerned with the documentary or the aesthetic (particularly the landscapes), comes François Brunet's "Linguisters in the Prairie" (*RFEA* 37:238–66)—a good article, couched in clear French (in spite of its English title), though obviously too long (and with all quotations newly translated—a most unnecessary trouble when it is clear to me that all such quotations should be kept in the original, especially when they are meant to draw the attention to the importance of the language); it deals with the prairie as "an analogue of the motley, confused linguistic and cultural reality of America," in which overdetermined characters communicate mostly through Leatherstocking the "linguister," i.e., the only one to be able to establish communication with and between everybody through *translation.* The other contribution, by Eric Fassin, is entitled "Théorie du language et idéologie dans *La Prairie*" (*RFEA* 37:267–82)—a title leaving an erroneous impression of pretentiousness. After finding that the dilemma of Cooper's characters was to long for a nature unspoilt by man as they strove all the while to transform it, Fassin succeeds in establishing a rather obvious relationship between Cooper and his successors, Melville and Poe, as "critics of signs"; he also establishes a much less obvious, though rather more stimulating one between Cooper's *The Prairie* and Rabelais' *Quart Livre*. Both authors seek for an ideal use of language; although they fall short of being critics of language (particularly of its capacity of representation), they often stage linguistic quarrels. Most of all—runs the rather sweeping conclusion—they both belong to a *renaissance* in which a language (French, American) becomes the means through which 16th-century France and 19th-century America emerge as the subjects of literary discourse.

In the first number of still another publication in the field of American studies, University Paris IV's *Americana* (a number entirely devoted to the three works of American literature on the syllabus of the Agrégation for 1988), Jean Rouberol, working from the evidence of the author's "literary caesarean" which consisted in the separation of the book from *Those Extraordinary Twins*, examines *PW* from the point of view of his title: "*PW* ou la tragédie des erreurs" (*Americana* 1:43–49). He concludes, somewhat disappointingly (after Leslie Fiedler's own glib regret), that the caesarean left us with only half a masterpiece. Rouberol's article follows American expatriate Peggy Castex's two contributions on the book's language, both clearly meant for the students' use: " 'Pears, Is and Sounds. . . : Remarks on Black Speech and Black Identity in Mark Twain's *PW*" (*Americana* 1:9–21) and "Negro Dialect in Mark Twain's *PW*" (*Americana* 1:23–42). This aspect does not bother Jean-Claude Dupas who, in "*PW* et approximations," analyzes the half we have in terms of "the approximation of the fundamental conflict between the hierarchy of races and equality between men which organizes the novel and is taken in a system of symmetries" (*Fabula* 10:127–38).

c. 20th-Century Fiction Through the Fifties. Faulkner (whose *New Orleans Sketches* and *Mayday* were published this year, only a few months after *Elmer* and *Father Abraham* [1987], all in my translations), takes the lion's share again, though not, this time, because he is perhaps, along with Poe, the most "French" of all American writers (and because *TWP* has always been a favorite with French readers), but for a far more matter-of-fact reason: this novel was on the Agrégation syllabus in 1988. Hence a flowering of articles, many by non-Faulknerians writing without being aware of (and apparently without caring about) what has already been written on their subject. Thus a set of six articles published in *Americana* falls short of being the remarkable contribution to the critical literature on the novel that it might have been. The first article, by Jeanne-Marie Santraud, one of the two editors of the journal (neither has picked up an embarrassing "Harry *Mel*bourne" on p. 93), is a harmless paraphrase of the dual structure of the novel. The article is aptly (un)titled "William Faulkner, *TWP*" (*Americana* 1:51–57).

The second contribution is much more ambitious and not quite so harmless. Not that Marc Saporta does not write gracefully (he signs "novelist" after his name), and sometimes usefully: his *Histoire du roman américain* (1970) had some merits. But in this instance, he is (deliberately, too) the polar opposite of a scholar. As in a special issue of *L'Arc* he edited in 1983, he would indeed be a novelist with an enormous and no doubt sincere passion for Faulkner (rather than for Faulkner's work), but this passion is somewhat flawed by an overriding interest in "Faulkner's Loves: some psychobiographical elements in *TWP*"—a brief article (*Americana* 1:59–66) curiously followed by two "annexes": "Le Dossier d'Helen Baird" [The Helen Baird File] (*Americana* 1:67–83), and "Le Dossier des *Palmiers sauvages*" [The *TWP* File] (*Americana* 1:85–97). The paradoxical truth about what Saporta writes on Faulkner is that it is of interest only to the very few who have a vested interest in the originals of Faulkner's characters in Faulkner's life. As these are necessarily familiar with Carvel Collins's pioneering work on the biographical circumstances of Faulkner's early production (a work that Saporta knows well, even if it is scholarly), there is hardly anything new in such derivative writing. There is even less in the view that *TWP* marked "the end of the major work, the magnificent conclusion of the saga" (*Americana* 1:87). No serious critic will now share such a belatedly Cowleyan view of the work as a "saga," nor so grossly overlook *The Hamlet* and *Go Down, Moses*, not to speak of *Requiem for a Nun*, *The Mansion*, and *The Reivers*.

Next (*Americana* 1:99–107) comes Giliane Morell's contribution, Lacanian as usual, on the "double birth" or the "dissymmetry" of the two male protagonists' plights. Interestingly enough, this notion is at odds with Alain Geoffroy's more strictly Freudian interpretation of the novel. Geoffroy's title, "The Fluidity of Time: The Effect of a Time Structure in *TWP*" (*Americana* 1:109–26), is both awkward and misleading; his article bears on no less than the meaning of the (unconscious?—so does one read on p. 120) structure of the novel, which he sees as "inverted" and thus comparable to a musical canon like J. S. Bach's *Musical Offering*. The blemish of this article lies with the critics quoted: Backman, Howe, Vickery, but none after that—particularly not Joseph Moldenhauer's decisive article on the unity of the novel. The last but one article, by Béatrice Rossi-Bouchrara, is the least useful of all, as, although curiously (and glibly) entitled "Sens du désir, désir des sens" (*Americana* 1:135–51), it relies on the notion of "folie" (madness) in Faulkner's work without the least definition (nor much evidence) to start from. No wonder the author asks at the end: "What is this madness we have been talking about?" The last contribution, "Faulkners's Time/Space in *TWP*" (*Americana* 1:153–63), by non-Americanist Patrick Hubner, is an honest (though hardly new) proposal that the now almost 50-year-old Sartrian idea of a "metaphysics of time" in Faulkner's work be balanced with the need for a "poetics of space." Another occasional contribution on this novel by one who is not a Faulknerian was Colette Gerbaud's "Les Femmes, ou le grand dérangement dans *TWP* de William Faulkner" in *L'Image de la femme dans les littératures de langue anglaise* (University of Reims), pp. 95–105. In spite of a definitely unpromising "Acadian" title, this is a typical example of literature read as prophecy, the question at the end being whether mankind's future lies in women (a view shared by Grace Paley). However, what a woman [not a feminist] who has long been working on Faulkner can do with this novel is better shown in Monique Pruvot's "*TWP* : les ailes du faucon" (*Fabula* 10:138–58). This is a superb portrait of Charlotte, the titular falcon and the doomed Idealist according to Faulkner.

By far the most important French publication on Faulkner's novel, however, and the only one to properly emphasize its stunning literary qualities, was the 120-page monograph hewn by François Pitavy out of his chapter on Faulkner's eleventh novel in his unpublished dissertation, "William Faulkner romancier: 1929–1939" (Sorbonne, 1978). Although a highly economical one, *Oublier Jerusalem*: The Wild Palms *de William Faulkner* (Paris: Didier Erudition) is a thorough, well-done job. To the original four chapters of his doctoral dissertation, Pitavy has added a first one on biography and a sixth on "The Portrait of the Artist" (which he also published as "Mémoire, langage: le portrait de l'artiste dans *The Wild Palms* de William Faulkner" in *EA* 41:56–73). Other chapters are devoted to the very special history of the text (and of the title), to the highly important question of Faulkner's deviations from the norms in genre (tragedy vs comedy) and in mode (the meaning of the different narrative strategies in "Wild Palms" and in "Old Man"), to the themes proper ("Point Counter Point"), and to the "Structures." The conclusion rightly emphasizes the "extraordinary intensity" of this novel, truly a unique achievement in Faulkner's production.

I also would like to draw attention to an article on *Absalom, Absalom!* published in *Multiple Worlds, Multiple Words: Essays in Honor of Irène Simon* (University of Liège, 1987), pp. 193–202, in which Pierre Michel's contention is that "the whole novel emanates from Quentin's consciousness and that it is written, or told, from his vantage point in Cambridge." Faulkner, Michel argues rather convincingly, does not assign a voice (Quentin's), but rather "extracts" that voice and gives it full control over the narrational perspective. "Memory," Michel writes cogently, "becomes a creative act analogous to Faulkner's imaginative act as a novelist."

Since they were both left out of *ALS 1987*, two titles should be reviewed here. *Tropismes* 3 (University of Paris X-Nanterre) has two articles, in French, on *As I Lay Dying*: mine is entitled "La mise en scène du fantasme dans *As I Lay Dying*" and argues that the novel "stages" the Rite of the Mother, while André Bleikasten's is the self-explanatory "Mourning Becomes the Bundrens: Fantasmes de deuil dans *As I Lay Dying*" [Fantasies of Mourning in *As I Lay Dying*]. Under the title "William Faulkner: Ontologie du discours," *Delta* 25 consists of a whole chapter from my own doctoral dissertation that had to be left out of my book *Faulkner ou la fascination* (Klincksieck, Paris, 1982), now translated as *Fascination: Faulkner's Fiction, 1919–1936* (Duke University Press, 1989). The 110 pages are divided into three very unequal parts: the first is concerned with the year 1935 and with the writing of *Pylon* as a deadly experience inducing a re-evaluation of the goals of writing. Part two is concerned with the question whether the drama performed in/by Faulkner's work is Puritan (i.e., Baudelairean) or purist (Mallarmean). Part three, entitled "The Two Poles of Faulknerian Idealism," follows the "diffusion" of Keats's "Ode" through the novels, particularly *Light in August*, and then takes the pair Father/Son (or Realist/Idealist) through *The Sound and the Fury*, *Absalom, Absalom!*, "Lion," *The Wild Palms*, and *Go Down, Moses*, concluding with a comparison of the aims assigned to literary discourse by both William Faulkner and Saint-John Perse in their acceptance speeches of the Nobel Prize for Literature.

The collection of essays published by Presses Universitaires de Reims under the title *L'Image de la femme dans les littératures de langue anglaise* also carries a study of Fitzgerald's women in the stories, in which Elizabeth Boulot could hardly do better than quote the writer admitting that he had been "tagged" with writing about young love, but that he would be "either a miracle man or a hack if [he] could go on turning out an identical product for three decades . . ." (p. 91).

RFEA 37 has articles on Vladimir Nabokov and J. D. Salinger. Along with an American article on Ring Lardner's "playlets," the essays tend to show that there is (even) more linguistic awareness in these writers than was thought. In "Productivité d'un titre double, figure d'une figure divisée" (*RFEA* 37:215–25), Danièle Roth-Souton brings a rather top-heavy analytical discourse to bear on the title *Bend Sinister*. And in "Signe et production du sens dans 'Pretty Mouth and Green My Eyes'" (*RFEA* 37:226–37), François Happe shows that no less than with the rest of *Nine Stories* by Salinger, the close study of narration and dialogue in this one proves that "intertextuality and metaphor are the crevices in the discourse through which ideology pours in." In no. 36 of *RFEA*, a number I edited on the topic "Les Lieux de la vie américaine" ["The Topology of American Life"], two articles were devoted to the South as a literary locus. One, by Paul Carmignani, examined the island and the (Indian) mound as two essential *topoi* in the history of American literature from Mark Twain via Erskine Caldwell's "Maud Island" in *Men and Women* to Shelby Foote in both his novel *Follow Me Down* and his collection of stories *Jordan County*, and to William Humphrey in the story "The Last of the Caddoes" from the collection *A Time and a Place* (*RFEA* 36:292–301). The other, by Marielle Rigaud, read *Absalom, Absalom!*, *Other Voices, Other Rooms* and *The Ballad of the Sad Café* for "spaces of intrusion" and places of interior exile (*RFEA* 36:302–10).

d. 20th-Century Fiction: Contemporary. *Caliban* no. 25, in spite of its deludingly collective title "Le Roman juif américain d'aujourd'hui" (The Jewish-American Novel Today), is only a collection of stray contributions fronted by Leslie Fiedler's inevitable (latest?) article (on the American-ness of I. B. Singer, "the American Jewish Writer"), here paired with a simple reading of the narrative in Singer's "*The Penitent* ou l'exil et le royaume" by Maurice Abiteboul in *Caliban* (Université de Toulouse, 25:13–23). This pair is followed by another on the late Bernard Malamud. In "Bricolage textuel: le Robinson juif de Bernard Malamud" (*Caliban* 25:25–37), Marcienne Rocard writes on *God's Grace* as a "hypertext" based on two "hypotexts" (these notions are borrowed from Gérard Genette): Genesis and *Robinson Crusoe*; Martine Chard-Hutchinson's topic is everyday life's little miracles as seen by Malamud (*Caliban* 25:39–45). Homage was inevitably due to Saul Bellow, although the same impatience with his recent production is perceptible here as in the United States. This is what Claude Lévy starts from in " 'More Die of Heartbreak': une relation d'emprise"—a study of *The Dean's December* as a parodic and even autoparodic text woven out of all sorts of citations and repetitions (*Caliban* 25:47–61), while in "A propos du 'Roi Rumkowski': note sur l'écriture majoritaire de Bellow" (*Caliban* 25:111–17), the late Hélène Rozenberg-Zoltowska takes issue with those who, like Rachel Ertel in her *Le Roman juif américain: une écriture minoritaire* (Paris: Payot, 1980), and Gilles Deleuze and Félix Guattari in *Kafka: pour une littérature mineure* (Paris: Minuit, 1975), consider Jewish-American writers to be a minority. Ellen Epstein-Levy considers Joseph Heller's *God Knows* as "Parody and Patricide" (*Caliban* 25:63–76), Marie Anne Clabé wonders whether Erica Jong's *Fanny Hackabout-Jones* is a Jewish novel (*Caliban* 25:77–85), and Lazare Bitoun briefly introduces the subject of his dissertation, the work of "Edward Lewis Wallant" (*Caliban* 25:103–09). Considering that six out of the 10 contributors are women, however, Judith Stora-Sandor probably hits the mark best with her lively review of *feminine* Jewish humor: "L'humour juif au féminin" (*Caliban* 25:87–101), in which once more Grace Paley takes the lion's share, because "her humour is not limited to her ethnic group." The issue comes to a finale with a serious interview of Grace Paley by Noëlle Batt and Marcienne Rocard (*Caliban* 25:119–37). What a pity, though, that this issue was not planned in terms of the changing (rather than the selfsame) Jewish-American scene: what about younger Jewish writers like Philip Roth, Jerome Charyn—or Cynthia Ozick?

On Grace Paley (because *TLDM* was on the syllabus of the Agrégation this year) there are no less than three sets of contributions. To begin with, no. 14 of *Delta* (May 1982) was reissued as

Prétextes: Grace Paley: Entretiens—Critiques (Montpellier: University Paul Valéry), with the addition of the author's "Of Poetry and Women and the World" from *The Writer in Our World—A Tri-Quarterly Symposium* (1986), of Claude Richard's pellucid "Temps de la vie, temps du récit dans 'Good Bye and Good Luck' " (*Prétextes* 67–76), and of Marc Chénetier's short "Une belle voix pour écrire" (*Prétextes* 93–98). Next, no. 5 (1987) of *Théorie, Littérature, enseignement* [*TLe*] (University Paris VIII) has a "Dossier Grace Paley" containing three articles besides a student's rather awkward attempt at interviewing the writer. In a brief series of remarks entitled "Amazing Grace: du familier au mythe" (*TLe* 5:175–80), Pierre Gault finds a correspondence between Paley's main theme, "the heroism of repetitive everyday life," and her fondness for ellipsis and juxtaposition rather than for causal relations. In "Des enfants et des singes ou la passion d'Eddie Teitelbaum" (*TLe* 5:181–90), Claude Richard has written a luminous analysis of the tragic (which is neither a genre nor simply a mood) which he sees in Paley, particularly in "In Time Which Made a Monkey of Us All"/—one of the writer's favorite stories. And in the longest of the three articles, "Grace Paley: une herméneutique du quotidien" (*TLe* 5:191–208), Noëlle Batt bravely asserts that it is the task of academic criticism to elucidate the pleasure taken at a book by the lay reader (or even by the reviewer). After showing that "the strategy of narration and of focalization" in most of Paley's stories usually implies a character-narrator who is basically *resistant*, she resorts to Bakhtin (whom she quotes at length). What he calls "stylization" she sees occurring through "ironic reversal" in her stories: her example in "Good Bye and Good Luck" is thoroughly convincing.

Americana 1 (University Paris IV) also has four articles on Paley. In "Grace Paley: Les Voix d'une histoire" (*Americana* 1:165–76)—an article in which he has deliberately kept an oral quality (quoting Paley's wonderful "nobody is not part of their time")—P.-Y. Pétillon replaces the writer in the history of Jewish immigration in New York and of subsequent Jewish literary production; she calls her a "second-and-a-half generation" writer—between Saul Bellow and Philip Roth, Bernard Malamud and Jerome Charyn. Next in *Americana* 1:177–92 comes an incredibly ill-edited hodgepodge of linguistic and/or referential remarks on the text of *TLDM* (written, one supposes, to ease the way of Agrégation students into the text), without even a reference to Claude Richard's translation of the text. Colette Gerbaud's "Diaspora et vie quotidienne au féminin dans *TLDM*" (*Americana* 1:193–212) is unusually and unnecessarily long, as it dutifully repeats what students should but usually do not know about Jewish immigration to the United States, and curiously assumes the existence of a dual contradiction between Judaism on the one hand, and feminism (p. 192) and anarchism (p. 197) on the other. "Grace Paley's Voices" (*Americana* 1:213–15), by Thomas Cousineau, is negligible: it only confirms that with Paley the notion of "voice" is a must.

As usual, busy Marc Chénetier is omnipresent in his field of election, contemporary American fictionists—preferably, I might add, those among them who, like him, have an inextinguishable taste for the play of language. I even find a self-portrait *malgré lui* in the way he seems to frown upon those who do not like Coover's fiction (clearly an unforgivable sin according to Chénetier): "one wishes [Coover's] detractors had had the decency to pay some attention to the exuberant pyrotechnics of his language and to compare its ebullience and pleasure-provoking zest to the dullness of our general critical discourse," he writes about *Aesop's Forest* in "Ideas of Order at Delphi." (Elsewhere one reads of "the tedium and formal congealment of academic speech." Shouldn't he know that the medium is the message, though?) This long article, whose title is rather obviously a parody of Wallace Stevens's splendid poem "The Idea of Order at Key West," was published in *Facing Texts* (Heide Ziegler, ed., Duke University Press), pp. 84–108. It is certainly Chénetier's most revealing article this year, as it shows him to be, somewhat like Coover, "maximal in his various toyings with dramatic excess and linguistic saturation." One is treated with even more of both—and of the " 'post-Modernists' delight in repetition and plagiarism" (Chénetier's own, apparently irresistible imps seem to be alliteration and name-dropping)—in his self-explanatory "MS or 'The Imp of Ossibility': Making Sense of the Trite and the Trivial in the Work of Stanley Elkin and Gilbert Sorrentino," published in *High Brow Meets Low Brow*, ed. Rob Kroes (Free University Press), pp. 157–71. The next three titles are in French. "Drôles de genres: remarques sur l'hybridation générique dans la fiction américaine contemporaine," published in Jean Bessière, ed., *Hybrides romanesques: Fiction 1960–1985* (Paris: Presses Universitaires de France), pp. 15–36, briefly covers a work that is already well-known, especially in France: Nabokov's *Pale Fire*; then taken up are Sorrentino's *Mulligan Stew*, Guy Davenport's four books, and Coover's productions.

The latter's second novel, *The Universal Baseball Association,* certainly entitled Chénetier to contribute "Football et baseball chez Robert Coover: ontologie, rituel et histoire" for *Le Sport en Grande-Bretagne et aux Etats-Unis: Faits, signes et métaphores,* ed. John Atherton and Richard Sibley (Presses Universitaires de Nancy), pp. 93–102. The same collection also contains Pierre Gault's whimsical piece on tennis and literature: "Propos sur le tennis: divertissement de circonstance" (pp. 103–11). Gault is both cautious and clever with his topic. Starting from Barthes's well-known analysis of Le Tour de France, he analyzes Theodor Saretsky's *Sex as Sublimation for Tennis: From the Secret Writings of Freud,* J. P. Donleavy's *De Alfonce Tennis,* the part played by tennis in *Lolita,* and the final (tennis) scene in Michelangelo Antonioni's *Blow-Up.* In "Sport in American Poetry, or Moore Beats Williams to First Base," Taffy Martin, a French-based American, compares the two poets' approaches to sport and shows that Williams's "The Crowd at the Ball Game" remains a "romantically bucolic" poem while Marianne Moore's "Baseball and Writing" is "irreverently unromantic."

MMEU has a piece entitled " 'What Makes Iago Evil?' Figures du Mal dans l'oeuvre de Joan Didion" (pp. 47–67) in which Sylvie Mathé, after finding "a Gothic fascination with evil" in the writer's work, analyzes the "figures" it takes: that of the desert (not only geographical but ontological) is seem by her as "the 'existential' wasteland of post-modernism" (which ties in nicely with what Jean Baudrillard has written about the desert in *Amérique.*)

Delta comes in once more at this point (although for the last but one time, since, following Claude Richard's last wish, publication will be discontinued after no. 27 [February 1989]) with an issue devoted to Robert Steiner's four novels, *Bathers, Passion, Dread, Matinee*—an untranslated extract of which is to be found here, as well as a piece by the author entitled "E/nil: The Catastrophe of Jackson Pollock," the latter with a translation into French by Nancy Blake. The first three contributors are American; the latter two are French and have written in French on the two novels translated so far. *Bathers* (superbly rendered into French by Philippe Jaworski under the title *Plage*), and *Passion* (*Passion,* by Nancy Blake). Denise Becker and Deborah Elliot have written on " 'I' ou l'être du langage" (" 'I' or the Being of Language") after Lacan and Blanchot (*Delta* 27:71–82), while Marc Pérez is miraculously luminous on "Simulacre et Métafiction dans *Passion*" (*Delta* 27:83–97).

e. Poetry. Apart from a one-page presentation of William Bronk's "In Navaho Country" by Alain Suberchicot in *RFEA* 38, the crop of articles is almost nil this year, but two volumes of translated poetry have appeared. The first one is a bilingual choice of *Poèmes* by Wallace Stevens (Delta)—a late but noteworthy first in France, where for some unknown reason the work of this major American poet had been published only in anthologies. Nancy Blake has written a brief abstract introduction in which the implicit comparison is with Mallarmé; and, with the collaboration (what kind?) of Hedi Kaddour, she has translated 50 poems. However, one is soon led to the conclusion that the pair should not have endeavored so many. Against a few felicitous individual lines, how many total renderings appear to be flatly literal, to which must be added a few gross grammatical mistakes like the use of "puisque" to translate "as" when it means "quand." Certainly these are among the most difficult poems in the English language as they so powerfully *compel* instead of *inviting*. But one would have been happy with 10 real translations, i.e., rythmic re-creations like the 18 poems published in 1989 by Bernard Noël as *Description sans domicile*—not versions that make one yearn for the text on the other page.

The other collection of poems, also bilingual, is Galway Kinnell's *Poèmes choisis/Selected Poems* (Aubier). Selected by whom? By Jacqueline Ollier, the author of the four-page introduction and the only translator of the 48 poems selected (some of which are long ones)? One would like to know if the poet himself was consulted. As for the translations, one feels that in this case being literal may well be the mask under which is hidden the modesty of the translator, who seldom dares to change anything in the original rhythm, so that one might paraphrase Kinnell and ask, "Is it simply that [translation]/does not have to be metered and rhymed?" The French versions could hardly do without the presence of the text on the left page. Bilingual editions are an ordeal in a sense—but in another they are a comfort, since one can always rely on the presence on the left page of the original version of whatever is *not* on the right one.

f. Theater. Georges-Michel Sarotte has written a charming literary curio (Grasset) to which he has given the properly ambiguous title *La Romanesque* (The Novelistic [Element] / The Romantic One), in which he imagines Blanche DuBois as she is taken away from Stanley and Stella's to the lunatic asylum at the end of *A Streetcar*

Named Desire. Her reminiscence, narrated in the first person, is framed by a narrative in the present tense involving a male double, Franck Rigault, who is also a patient in the psychiatric clinic.

The only critical study of the American theater that I could read was published by Colette Gerbaud in no. 8 of *Coup de théâtre* under the title "Le(s) Temps de la mémoire dans deux pièces en un acte d'Arthur Miller: *A Memory of Two Mondays* and *A View from the Bridge*" (pp. 11–21). In this dyptich, Miller aimed at contrasting the "romantic" and the "mythic" visions of past and present.

g. Ethnic Literature. While Michel Fabre's *AFRAM Newsletter* (nos. 26, 27) continues to make available a wealth of news of all kinds, and while he has had the sad task of writing several obituary articles after the death of James Baldwin on November 30, 1987, it is now Geneviève Fabre who takes the lead with the publication of the proceedings of an international conference on "Hispanic Cultures and Identities in the U.S." (organized by CIRNA at University Paris VII in 1986), under the title *European Perspectives on Hispanic Literature of the United States* (Arte Publico Press). Besides 11 contributions by Chicano and other non-French participants, the volume contains quite a few non-French participants and a substantial introduction by Geneviève Fabre, "Blueprints in the Development of a New Poetics" (pp. 5–21), "Ricardo Sanchez: the Poetics of Liberation" by Yves-Charles Grandjeat (pp. 33–43), and Marcienne Rocard's deceptively titled (as she deals not with sociology, but with literary utterance) "The Chicana: A Marginal Woman" (pp. 130–39).

Another plentiful collection of essays on a current issue is *Multilinguisme et multiculturalisme en Amérique du Nord: Survivance, transferts, métamorphoses* [*MMAN*] (University of Bordeaux). (The title is misleading; the first issue, that of multilinguism, is not really raised—unless it is seen as springing from the mere juxtaposition of contributions.) The 14 papers are French, and in French. They range from two contributions on Indian writers, Elisabeth Béranger on Anna Lee Walters's *The Sun Is Not Merciful* (*MMAN* pp. 9–19) and Bernadette Rigal-Cellard on Paula Gunn Allen's *The Woman Who Owned the Shadows* (*MMAN* pp. 33–42); two on Jewish writers, Ginette Castro on Esther Broner's *A Weave of Women* (*MMAN* pp. 43–58) and Suzanne Duruty on Cynthia Ozick's *Trust* (*MMAN* pp. 59–69); three on Italian-Americans: Jean Béranger on John Fante's

Arturo Bandini novels (*MMAN* pp. 71–80), Nicole Bensoussan on Mario Puzo's *The Godfather* (*MMAN* pp. 81–90), and Robert Rougé on Jerre Mangione's *Reunion in Sicily* (*MMAN* pp. 91–101). That there should be more contributions on Chicano literature than on anything else is no surprise. Christian Lerat writes on Miguel Mendez's remarkable short story "Tata Casehua" (*MMAN* pp. 21–32); Serge Ricard on the "avatars of Chicanismo" from José Antonio de Villareal's *Pocho* to his *Clemente Chacon* (*MMAN*:103–13); Jean Cazemajou searches John Rechy's *The City of Night* as a paradigm of "the long quest of a Chicano in the 'electric' night of contemporary America" (*MMAN* pp. 115–26), and Yves-Charles Grandjeat studies Gary Soto's ambiguous relationship with Chicano literature (*MMAN* pp. 127–37). (Serge Ricard also contributed a brief study of ethnic space in the writings of Rolando Hinojosa in *RFEA* 36:274–79.) Evelyne Andouard-Labarthe's may well be the only essay in the collection to deal with the problem of the two languages in "Alurista et les hiéroglyphes du bilinguisme" (*MMAN*:139–50). The last two contributions are on odd topics: one, by Nicole Ollier, is on Greek-American Nanos Valaoritis (*MMAN* pp. 151–61), and the other, by Jean-Michel Lacroix, takes off from the tremendous success of the magazine *Vice Versa*—or "Les Métamorphoses des Italo-québecois de Montréal" ([*MMAN*] pp. 163–78). Grandjeat signs a final essay for all of the contributors. In *RFEA* 38, a number devoted to American Indians, Bernadette Rigal-Cellard plot-summarizes two novels by James Welch, author of *Winter in the Blood* and *The Death of Jim Loney* (*RFEA* 38:377–85).

Just as I began with a collection of essays on the book industry, I would like to finish with another on an even more vital subject—the real. *Les Fictions du réel dans le monde anglo-américain de 1960 à 1980* (Tours) are the proceedings of a conference organized by GRAAT (Tours: Groupes de Recherche anglo-américaines de l'Université François-Rabelais,) in 1987. Two articles concern us here. The first is Gérard Cordesse's "Binarité, Linéarité, multiplicité dans 'Calliope Music,' *The Floating Opera*" (pp. 73–82), in which John Barth's division of one page in two columns like two threads of the same text is seen not only as a criticism of causality, but more radically as an "epistemological lesson." Claude Cohen-Safir has endeavored more (perhaps too much) in "Sous-réalité et sur-fiction" (pp.

93–104), in which he reviews first *Lolita* under the heading "L'Amérique-Fiction," then Vonnegut's *Slaughterhouse-Five* and Barth's *Letters* as maximalist books, with D. M. Thomas's *The White Hotel* seducing America in 1981, and perhaps marking the end of the era of representation.

Université Paris VII

iii. German Contributions

Rolf Meyn

The 1988 harvest presents the usual picture. Colonial literature is sadly underrepresented, and most German publications again center on the 20th century. This, however, does not mean that the scholarly output on the 19th century is lacking in quality. Joint endeavors and monographs are more balanced than in previous years, and in contrast to 1987 there are more publications dealing with binational authors and themes.

One personal statement: I find it increasingly difficult to obtain review copies. Since both our university library and our department library suffer from severe budget cuts, I fear that henceforth some significant publications will not be discussed in my review or, if so, only belatedly.

***a.* Literary Criticism and Theory: Comparative Studies.** One of the highlights of the 1988 scholarly turnout was Hartmut Heuermann's *Mythos, Literatur, Gesellschaft. Mythokritische Analysen zur Geschichte des amerikanischen Romans* (München: Fink). It consists of a theoretical framework and an analysis of 12 American nineteenth- and twentieth-century novels within that structure. Although the interpretations are stimulating, it must be said that the first part of the book accounts for its quality. Heuermann begins with a phenomenology of mythic manifestations. Mythos (which is more comprehensive than myth and, unlike it, cannot be told) is defined and explained with the help of dichotomies (e.g., language vs. mythos, ideology vs. mythos, history vs. mythos, logos vs. mythos, and, finally, mythogenesis vs. mythopoesis). Of special interest is Heuermann's claim that ideologies, even if they incorporate highly differentiated and intellectualized ways of thinking, receive the energies necessary for their sociological accomplishments from myths. Real myths, he insists, always contain a collective experience. Yet the difference between mythical partaking and perception—in other words, the mythos-logos dichotomy—results from mental and cultural evolution, which in turn triggers the process of demythization. To this day, however, mythos and logos are battling each other. Heuermann is certain that in American popular culture myths still have a decisive impact on the creation of concepts of reality. Masterworks and classics are also caught in the process of mythification. But it is impossible to say how myths constitute a text since there is no typical structure. Heuermann discovers seven approaches to mythos. He calls his respective models "Freudian," Marxist, psychohistorical, functionalistic, semiological, structuralistic, and, finally, archetypal/poetological (Northrop Frye). Though his book is a plea for what he calls "mythocritical literary studies," he is well aware that mythos, whatever its form, is a mixed blessing since it is principally a regressive phenomenon, determined by forms of thinking and acting that should be historically overcome. Mythos is hostile to time and history, and many writers who resort to it obviously want to avoid the responsibilities of history. Mythos is, furthermore, "ethically blind" because it can embody any value system and expand boundlessly, thereby usurping all levels of culture. Moral insight is often suppressed by mythic coercion.

Heuermann illustrates his findings with many examples from American cultural history and literature. He also refers frequently to the novels he discusses in the second part of his book: Cooper's Leather-Stocking Tales, Alger's *Ragged Dick*, Melville's *Billy Budd*, Wister's *The Virginian*, Thomas Dixon's *The Clansman*, Faulkner's *The Bear*, Ray Bradbury's *Fahrenheit 451*, Bellow's *Henderson the Rain King*, Updike's *The Centaur*, Mario Puzo's *The Godfather*, Margaret Atwood's *Surfacing*, and John Barth's *Chimera*. These 12 works are good choices since all contain a wealth of different myths. Though some of the book's interpretations leave questions open, Heuermann incorporates an admirable amount of information. More scholars should become aware of his underlying thesis, namely, that the problem of mythos and myth is not an esoteric matter that concerns only literary critics, but that it extends into cultural history, philosophy, popular art, politics, and everyday life.

Another truly comparative study dealing with an Austrian-

American writer who has been in vogue for several years is Günter Schnitzler's *Erfahrung und Bild. Die dichterische Wirklichkeit des Charles Sealsfield (Karl Postl)* (Freiburg: Rombach). Schnitzler begins with the impact of the Bible on Sealsfield's work. He thinks that the biblical influence mainly found expression in "catholic ideas"—the Virgin Mary, for example, appears in many forms in this writer's works. Schnitzler claims that Sealsfield interpreted Mexico in his novels *Virey* and *South and North* in biblical terms. To him, the country was ruled by Pharisees and false prophets, personified as defenders of despotic Spanish rule, but also as revolutionary leaders. Schnitzler also notes frequent allusions to such painters as Turner, Caravaggio, Rosa, Hogarth, and Cruikshank. All these artists, he holds, were responsible for Sealsfield's use of colors and the interplay of light and darkness. One of the most interesting chapters compares Sealsfield and Thomas Cole. Schnitzler cogently shows that the Austrian-American writer could not have created many of his poetical landscapes without an intimate knowledge of the chief representative of the Hudson River School. Another poetic and biblical theme Schnitzler discovers in both artists is the expulsion from Paradise, a theme he relates to Sealsfield's attitude toward America in general: the Austrian-American writer found America to be a paradise during the years he tried to make his adopted country a home. Later, however, when he wrote about America from memory in his Swiss exile, it became a lost paradise because it had not fulfilled his political expectations.

This leads to the second part of the *habilitationsschrift*, mainly concerned with Sealsfield's relationship with the United States. According to Schnitzler, Sealsfield considered the westward movement a part of a supranational process, as Zschokke and Herder had already outlined it. For them, the development of civilization went west, from ancient Egypt and Greece to Rome and Central Europe and across the Atlantic. This explains why Sealsfield supported the westward movement in the United States, for which the ship became the appropriate symbol in his works. In contrast to most scholars, Schnitzler thinks that Sealsfield's attitude toward the United States was far more critical than was apparent on first sight, despite his hatred of restorative Europe. Schnitzler even surmises that if Sealsfield had any future form of American government in mind, it could only be an enlightened monarchy. To clarify his political views, Schnitzler compares Sealsfield to his contemporary Alexis de Tocqueville. Since Sealsfield had published some of his works earlier than Tocqueville's *Democracy in America*, Schnitzler is sure that the latter was influenced by the former. Both writers saw the United States as a mercantile nation, both feared the pressure of majority groups, and both looked toward Europe, hoping for spiritual guidance from an America that had already put some distance between herself and the Old World on her way to enlightenment and democracy. Schnitzler, like almost every Sealsfield critic, is puzzled by the author's attitude toward slavery, which he justified in terms of economic necessity in the South. Yet Schnitzler emphasizes that Sealsfield was a contradictory writer anyway: he glorified Andrew Jackson, but at the same time criticized his reckless policy of Indian removal. He also sensed that in the end the United States would be dominated too much by money and materialism. Schnitzler has written a stimulating and provocative book. Whether it will be the final word on Sealsfield remains to be seen. I, for one, doubt that he was as critical of the United States as Schnitzler wants us to see him.

Quite a different theme, but also comparative, is assessed in Gertrud Lehnert-Rodiek's dissertation *Zeitreisen. Untersuchungen zu einem Motiv der erzählenden Literatur des 19. und 20. Jahrhunderts* (Rheinbach-Merzbach: Clasen 1987). The literary motif of "time travel" as the author emphasizes, has rarely been explored. She discusses more than 120 novels and stories containing time travels in various forms, belonging to utopian, dystopian, apocalyptic, science fiction, fantastic, or satiric literature. The scope is truly impressive, ranging from classic literature to rather trivial works and covering examples from American, English, German, and French literature. Lehnert-Rodiek concludes that the time travel motif is often used to simply initiate different plot constructions but that most of the texts have one thing in common: they are escapist. Only rarely is time travel undertaken for scientific reasons. Usually the time traveler wants to flee from his/her own time. As a rule, the traveler wants to get away because of social and political conditions, dissatisfaction with a mediocre life, or to become a hero or heroine in remote times. The escapist character is strongest in trivial science fiction texts. As a rule, time travels complicate plots and start adventures; they are rarely more than marginal to the story. Lehnert-Rodiek by no means neglects the "long sleep motif" that one finds in so many sagas and fairy tales and is closely related to the religious metaphors of death and resurrection. Consequently, "Rip Van Winkle" and the great utopian novels of the 18th, 19th, and 20th centuries by Sebastian Mercier, Edward Bellamy, William Morris, H. G. Wells, and others are analyzed at some length. The author differentiates between "normal" time traveling and "two-track" time traveling, i.e., texts in which the protagonists are able to move back and forth from past or future. Twain's *A Connecticut Yankee* is pointed out as one of the first examples; more influential for modern science fiction, Lehnert-Rodiek holds, was Wells's *The Time Machine*. After this work, many "time machines" appeared in science fiction, and they often depicted fantastic future worlds that were explained (pseudo-) scientifically. Whether time travel is just part of an ordinary adventure or part of a spiritual or mental adventure or even a means to manipulate history—in all cases it is rooted in the wish to control the threatening mystery of time. Lehnert-Rodiek's dissertation is in many respects a pioneer study. But the reader is simply overwhelmed by the mass of texts. Less material would have given the author a better chance to deal more thoroughly with many important works.

The theoretical basis of women's studies covers an ever-growing portion of theoretical debates in German scholarship, as a special issue of *Amerikastudien/American Studies* testifies. Renate Hof in her introductory essay "Einleitung: Feministische Wissenschaft—A New Feminine Mystique?" (*Amst* 33:135–48) calls for a stronger emphasis on the study of social and economic power structures that determine the lives of women now as ever. Evelyne Keitel's "Weiblichkeit und Poststrukturalismus—Perspektiven einer feministischen Literaturwissenschaft" (pp. 149–66) is a critical analysis of poststructuralist theories (mainly those of Lacan and Kristeva) and their usefulness for a feminist approach. Keitel concludes that in poststructuralism the static concept of feminine subjectivity is replaced by a dynamic definition of feminine "decentralization," which is open and in flux. This entails a change in the textual understanding of literature under feminist perspectives. Elisabeth Bronfen also takes resort to Lacan and his "return to Freud" in her "Wandering in Mind or Body: Death, Narration, and Gender in Djuna Barnes' Novel *Nightwood*" (pp. 167–77). Bronfen warns against the danger of reducing Barnes once more to a cult personality, "to a counter-myth in feminist couleur." Barnes, she insists, critically exposed a woman's search for self-identity as being totally dependent on roles assigned to her by Western culture. Jochen Barkhausen takes up a woman writer who is slowly gaining recognition in German scholarship. His "Zur Begründung eines feministischen Realismus: Lisa Althers Roman *Original Sins*" (pp. 179–91) is a plea in favor of Alther's unjustly ignored second novel. *Original Sins*, Barkhausen convincingly argues, is nothing less than a fascinatingly fictionalized social history of the protest generation of the sixties and seventies from a feminist perspective.

In contrast to Barkhausen, Ruth Nestvold-Mack in her " 'Lies Will Flow from My Lips'—On the Relationship Between Women's Writing and Women's Experience" (pp. 193–206) is far more encompassing. After discussing such different novels as Wharton's *The House of Mirth*, Oates's *Marya: A Life* and *Bellefleur*, Bellow's *Humboldt's Gift*, French's *The Women's Room*, and Alther's *Kinflicks*, Nestvold-Mack concludes that though gender neutrality is a myth, self-centeredness is common to women's and men's fiction. Also, the supposedly "authentic" representation of women's experience in autobiographical novels largely results from literary conventions also used by male authors, dating back to the 18th century. Andrea Beck's "Reflexion über die Beziehung von Kunst, Traum und Alltagsrealität in Grace Paleys Erzählwerk" (pp. 207–14) is devoted to a writer who steadily gains ground in German scholarship. Beck thinks that despite the self-reflexiveness and plotlessness of Paley's stories, there prevails a "rearranged reality" that could be even called utopian as far as its aesthetic structure is concerned.

b. **Literary History.** A joint endeavor—the fruit of a conference of the Austrian Association of American Studies, held in the Orwell year of 1984 on the general topic of "Utopian Thought in the USA"—was a major contribution in 1988. Arno Heller, Walter Hölbling, and Waldemar Zacharasiewicz, eds., *Utopian Thought in American Literature. Untersuchungen zur literarischen Utopie und Dystopie in den USA* (Tübingen: Narr) is devoted mainly to individual works of authors after 1945. But there are so many allusions to utopian and dystopian literature from Thomas More and Jonathan Swift onward that the book can be discussed in this section. Michael Draxlbauer's "Utopia 'Re-Membered': Nathaniel Hawthorne's Brook Farm Romance" (pp. 43–68) is the only essay focusing on the 19th century. After painstaking studies of Hawthorne's diaries, letters, and forewords, Draxlbauer argues astutely that *The Blithedale Romance*

(1852) is not a personal, anti-utopian, and satirical evaluation of the Brook Farm experiment, as many critics have claimed, but an "experimental text about the texture of an American romance."

The other essays, however, are concerned mainly with social changes reflected in recent utopian and dystopian literature, especially ecology and feminism. Thus Uwe Böker in his "Naturbegriff, ökologisches Bewußtsein und utopisches Denken: Zum Verständnis von E. Callenbachs *Ecotopia* (1975)" (pp. 69–84) discovers in this novel a denial of the Protestant work ethic and an attempt to outline the empirical foundations of an ecological system, the origins of which are found in the preservation-of-the-wilderness ideas of the 19th century. For Böker, Callenbach was not always successful in avoiding a male perspective, though in his eyes women were clearly better fitted to a life in harmony with the biosphere. Heinz Tschachler assesses a writer who in Germany is far less known than Callenbach. In "Apologie für die Apokalypse oder wie auch die Ökologie das Abendland nicht vor dem Untergang retten kann: Ein Beitrag zu Edward Abbeys utopischem Roman *Good News* (1980)" (pp. 85–110), Tschachler singles out a novel that combines conventions of the literary western with those of dystopian satire. For Tschachler, Abbey attacks in *Good News* the engineering mentality that turns the Southwest into an industrial part of the sunbelt. The novel's military usurpers of power represent a conservative America responsible for an ecological apocalypse that is well under way. Yet there is still hope. The rebels, still living close to nature, will overthrow tyranny and help to recapture what Tschachler calls an "ethical relationship" between man and nature, a subject in its own right. Gudrun Grabber treats a similar theme, albeit in poetry, in her contribution "Der lyrische Dialog mit der Natur: A. R. Ammons' ökologische Vision" (pp. 111–30). Her close analysis of eight of Ammons's poems reveals this poet as a "unique voice in lyrical ecological vision" who enters a subtle philosophical dialogue with nature. Hans Ulrich Seeber's "Tradition und Innovation in Ursula Le Guins *The Dispossessed*" (pp. 147–69) is the book's most extensive essay. Seeber begins with a glance at the classic utopias of More, Campanella, and others, which in his opinion were replaced by counterworlds in the guise of pastoral antitheses in the works of 19th-century writers such as Morris and Hudson. From then on, positive utopian concepts were credible only if they pronounced an ecological balance between man and nature and expressed a vision of anarchic freedom instead of the totalitarian coercion of the classic utopias. Ursula Le Guin's *The Dispossessed* is, as Seeber lucidly shows, deeply influenced by the anarchist Peter Kropotkin and an interesting contribution to the postmodern discussion of utopian and dystopian writing.

Arno Heller in his "Die literarische Utopie mit einer exemplarischen Erörterung von Margaret Atwoods *The Handmaid's Tale*" (pp. 185–204) also dives into the history of utopian writing to prove that dystopian literature is always marked by a basic distrust of utopian dreams and by the conviction that a causal link exists between rational ideality and structural violence. *The Handmaid's Tale*, Heller tells us, is a dystopian story of the victimization of women and men in a predatory, manipulative, and patriarchal civilization. Yet the novel is also a conservative plea for the status quo, for family life, consumerist attitudes, everyday trivialities, and restricted freedom. Bernd Schäbler's "Wirklichkeit, Möglichkeit und die Utopie. Die Verflechtung von Melancholie und Utopie bei B. F. Skinner, Richard Brautigan und Ronald Sukenick" (pp. 205–22) concludes this stimulating collection, which is another proof of the vogue utopian and dystopian literature has enjoyed in recent years. Schäbler surmises that Albrecht Dürer's "Melancholia I" and Robert Burton's "Anatomy of Melancholy" are the first signs of an increasing tension between man's desire to explore reality and escapist utopian dreams. This split is particularly dealt with in novels. Schäbler illustrates this by analyzing Skinner's *Walden Two*, Brautigan's *In Watermelon Sugar*, and Sukenick's *Out*. The last two postmodern novels, he claims, are paradigmatic, since their protagonists are inactive, unheroic, and figure in texts that are mixtures of utopian visions and melancholy self-reflections.

An important part of literary history comes under scrutiny in Fritz Fleischmann and Deborah Lucas Schneider, eds., *Women's Studies and Literature. Neun Beitrage aus der Erlanger Amerikanistik* (Erlangen: Palm & Enke 1987). Helga Oppermann's "'Daughters of His Manhood': Patriarchal Femininity and the Masculine Systems, with an Afterthought on Woman's History" (pp. 14–38) goes far back into the chivalric tradition to show that "the notion of the household as a necessary counterweight to deeds and activities in the larger world" has often been "part of the ideal of patriarchal femininity," especially in the 19th century. In her "Afterthought on Woman's History," Oppermann argues that women, like words, too often have become mere signs, manipulated by men. Fritz Fleischmann in "Margaret Fuller, the Eternal Feminine, and the 'Liberties of the Republic'" (pp. 39–57) focuses on *Woman in the Nineteenth Century* (1845) and holds that Fuller rejected the idea that woman is a victim of history. In her opinion, gender had to be disconnected from power or domination. Though the cold intellect might be more masculine than feminine, and "the especial genius of woman" more intuitive, examples could be found where these distinctions were totally blurred. Deborah Lucas Schneider in a well-argued study, "Henry Adams' *Esther*: Woman as Artist and Woman as Artist's Model" (pp. 58–81), sees this novel as an essential addition to *The Education of Henry Adams* since *Esther* offers an explanation why Adams omitted women and his own marriage from an autobiography meant to be a major summing up of the country's cultural history. *Esther*, Schneider thinks, has to be read as an autobiographical novel, a portrait of Adams's wife, Clover, whom he wished he had never married.

Hans-Joachim Lang turns to the 20th century in "Mary Antin und das Vermächtnis von Emma Lazarus" (pp. 83–130), an attempt to reevaluate the author of *The Promised Land* (1912). In Lang's opinion, Antin was not the ecstatic assimilationist many critics claimed her to be. Susanne Opfermann's "'The mystical male force which rules the universe': Katherine Anne Porters *Ship of Fools*" (pp. 131–55) tackles Porter's novel from a strictly feminist point of view. Opfermann cogently relates the threatening world situation—strikes, economic crises, revolutions—to nationalistic, fascist, and racist views, and these in turn to male chauvinism, thereby pointing out that their differences are only minor. In other words, male chauvinism shares some basic structures with racism and nationalism. The suppression and exploitation of women ultimately explains the subjugation and even the extermination of ethnic minorities and dissident groups. Birgit Fromkorth in "Lisa Alther's *Kinflicks*" (pp. 156–78) scrutinizes a feminist novel, which combines elements of the picaresque and the bildungsroman. Alther, Fromkorth insists, was not able to develop a concept of a woman's new identity, as the fate of her protagonist Ginny Babcock proved, but definitely propagated a radical break with old patterns of behavior.

The last two essays are concerned with Margaret Atwood. In her "Paper Heads and Zero at the Bone: Margaret Atwood's Unclaimed Territory" (pp. 212–28), Lynda S. Boren, comparing Atwood to American women writers such as Willa Cather, assumes that "Atwood's geography is the female body, which serves as a symbolic battleground for possession." The female body is analogous to region, i.e., Canada. Boren, however, is not sure whether Atwood or any other future Canadian woman writer will always be able to combine regionalism with feminism. Christine Strobel, dealing with Atwood's poetry in "'It's time to like men again': ueber Margaret Atwood (pp. 229–43), sees Atwood as a chronicler of patterns of behavior and structures but not as a caller for action. All in all, *Women's Studies and Literature* is a highly successful attempt under feminist perspectives to reinterpret American woman writers from two centuries.

Problems of canon and classic American literature are thoroughly discussed in two contributions to Hans-Joachim Simm, ed., *Literarische Klassik* (Frankfurt: Suhrkamp). Hans-Joachim Lang's "Kanonbildung in der Neuen Welt. Das Beispiel Vereinigte Staaten von Amerika" (pp. 69–87) succinctly searches for a classical national tradition, from John William De Forest, J. G. Holland, Van Wyck Brooks, Ezra Pound, T. S. Eliot, and F. O. Matthiessen to Robert E. Spiller's *Literary History of the United States* and Emory Elliot's *Columbia Literary History of the United States.* Although Lang is favorable to Poe, Hawthorne, Melville, Emerson, Thoreau, Whitman, and Twain, he diagnoses the problem of a literary canon in America as always being tied up with cultural, political, and future-oriented forces. Olaf Hansen in "Amerikanische Klassik" (pp. 299–323) understands the concept of the classic in American cultural history as a theoretical construct. Going back to Cotton Mather's *Magnalia Christi Americana* and drawing a fascinating comparison to Thomas Eakins's painting "The Gross Clinic," Hansen discovers a tendency in American culture to "transcend everyday life classisisticly." Hansen's conclusion is certainly surprising: there cannot be a classic tradition in America as long as the process of secularization has not ended.

c. Colonial Literature. A publication that has escaped my notice for far too long is David Eisermann's *Crèvecoeur oder Die Erfindung Amerikas. Ein literarischer Gründervater der Vereinigten Staaten* (Rheinbach-Merzbach: Clasen 1985). Written in German, it is truly a trinational book, with a summary in English and French. Though indebted to the achievements of Howard Crosby Rice (1933), Albert E. Stone (1962), and Thomas Philbrick (1970), it goes beyond these scholars in adding new perspectives. Eisermann shows clearly that Crèvecoeur who was widely read in Europe helped to rouse interest in the emergence of the United States. Yet why did the young French immigrant from Normandy, an officer in the French Canadian forces, who had taken part in the battle of Quebec in 1759, renounce his aristocratic origins? Eisermann holds that the carnage Crèvecoeur witnessed made him a pacifist and an unconditional believer in the equality of all men. This explains why he maintained his distance from both opposing factions in the War of Independence. Eisermann sees Crèvecoeur as a writer who created fictionalized accounts disguised as documentary prose and travel literature to catch the interest of his European readers. He idealized American society, built on the principles of equal opportunity and self-determination. In all his books, he praised American farmers, successful immigrants, and Nantucket whalers who wrested enormous profits from the sea, all of them prototypes of the self-made man, the citizen of a land of opportunity, who owed his status not to social rank but to industry. Eisermann discovers in the Nantucket chapters of *Letters from an American Farmer* the full definition of Crèvecoeur's concept of an ideal American society but also a disguised fantasy in the tradition of Thomas More's *Utopia* (1516). This optimistic trend, however, contrasts with those chapters that clearly illustrate Crèvecoeur's developing loss of confidence in the validity of such ideals. Yet although James Monroe refused to allow him to return to the United States, Crèvecoeur remained a faithful believer in the country's future greatness. Eisermann's meticulous account of Crèvecoeur's reception in Germany in the late 18th and early 19th centuries is an excellent illustration of how this writer helped to shape European public opinion of the promises of the new republic. Yet it is also interesting that most of Crèvecoeur's contemporary French and German critics were well aware of the fictional overtone in his works. Eisermann's excellent study ends with the German translation of a hitherto unpublished manuscript of Crèvecoeur's report of his years (1779–83) in New York. Eisermann's book should be noticed as soon as possible in the United States. Without its many astute observations, any scholarship on this binational writer will be incomplete.

Hans Galinsky, one of our few scholars frequently devoted to colonial literature, assesses a theme that has rarely been dealt with, namely, the relationship between printers/publishers and authors in early America. His essay "Amerikanische Drucker und Verleger als Autoren und Autorenfreunde im Neuengland des Kolonialbarock: Marmaduke Johnson und 'Philip Pain,' John Foster und Increase

Mather," *Einheit in der Vielfalt*, Owens's *Festschrift für Peter Lang* (Frankfurt: Lang), pp. 111–45, not only throws light on an important chapter of early American literary history but contains the convincing thesis that "Philip Pain," author of *Daily Meditations*, hailed by some critics as one of the earliest American poets (though of obscure origin) was none other than the self-made printer Marmaduke Johnson himself. In contrast to him, John Foster and Increase Mather, printer/publisher and author, were Harvard-trained men whose fruitful cooperation was the result of a close friendship.

d. **19th-Century Literature.** James Fenimore Cooper continues to hold German scholars under his spell. In her essay "Die Wildnis als historischer Ort und Heimat in *The Last of the Mohicans*" (*Archiv* 225:64–80), Maria Diedrich believes Cooper to be misinterpreted as an ethnochauvinistic writer who continued the Puritan view of a howling wilderness as well as the stereotyping of the Indians as either noble or ignoble savages. Cooper, she argues, created two different journeys into the wilderness in *The Last of the Mohicans*. For the white characters, even for Leather-Stocking himself, the wilderness becomes an unconquerable antagonist, slowly swallowing the ruins of Fort Henry. For the Indians, however, the journey through the wilderness helps them regain their identity and self-esteem. Even the renegade Magua, corrupted by contact with the whites, wins back much of his former status. That he turns into a destructive fiend is the fault of the whites who destroy the unity of Indian life. Ultimately, Diedrich concludes, Cooper did not create a confrontation between civilization and barbarism, but a coexistence of cultures. To him, the "errand into the wilderness" was not the legitimate conquest of an area without history and culture, but an invasion into and destruction of a territory that belonged to a living culture. Though Copper shared the belief in the necessity of Manifest Destiny, he was nevertheless a fierce critic of those who recommended the extermination of the Indians.

An important publication that I inspected only belatedly is Manfred Pütz's (with the assistance of J. K. Adams and J. Boeck) *Ralph Waldo Emerson: A Bibliography of Twentieth-Century Criticism* (Frankfurt: Lang, 1986). The bibliographical data cover the period from 1900 to 1985, with 2,941 titles. Reprints of essential publications before 1900 are also considered. Pütz's bibliography is undoubtedly a significant addition to Robert E. Burkholder and Joel Myerson's

Emerson: An Annotated Secondary Bibliography (1985), which ends four years earlier and does not contain publications produced in Europe.

Dietmar Schloss's " 'The Standard of One's Own Good-Humored Prosperity.' Henry James's Critique of American Innocence in *The American*" (*Archiv* 225:285–99) is, I think, a much-needed corrective to those critics who see Christopher Newman's story of a good-natured American businessman, cheated out of his marriage with a beautiful French aristocrat, as a work of a still pro-American author. Yet as Schloss intelligently demonstrates, the protagonist of *The American* is by no means a shining embodiment of America's virtues and none of its faults, though his European adversaries, the aristocratic Bellegardes, are products of a crime-ridden and murderous past. However, if James had wanted to make Newman the hero of a bildungsroman, he must have become aware that this character was ill-fitted for a process leading from innocence to experience and maturity. Newman's "ease" and "blankness"—two terms James frequently employed in describing this protagonist—made him not really open to experience, only complacent, and prevented him from probing too deeply into what he saw in Europe. Schloss holds that James introduced a minor character who serves as a critical foil to Newman. Babcock, the Puritan minister and travel companion, is not only the personification of a barren New England conscience but an American for whom Europe is a moral and intellectual challenge. This is something Newman in his ease and blank openness is unable to feel. Ultimately, *The American* is not so much a vindication of American innocence, but, as Schloss insists, a revelation of the "moral and epistemological shortcomings of American pragmatism."

***e.* 20th-Century Literature.** My overview will begin with some dissertations. Beate Engling's *Humoristische Elemente in den Kurzgeschichten und Romanen der Südstaatenschriftstellerin Eudora Welty* (Frankfurt: Lang), a solid, albeit pedestrian, study of Welty's humor, is heavily indebted to Walter Blair's *Native American Humor* and similar studies. Annegret Wemhöner's *"The Deeper Levels of Life and the Sense of Time and Place": John Cheevers Romanwerk zwischen Romance und Novel of Manners* (Amsterdam: Grüner) is one of the few longer studies on Cheever that have appeared in German scholarship. Wemhöner diagnoses a growing complexity in Cheever's novels resulting from employing both mythical and allegorical modes and, in addition, emblematic scenes, all of them part of Cheever's concept of romance. Small town life and middle-class society in *The Wapshot Chronicle*, still realistically presented, are turned into more universal human situations in later works. In his first three novels, however, the close affinity to the narrative constituents of the novel of manners as conceived by Howells, Wharton, and Sinclair Lewis is still obvious. It is only in *Falconer* and in *Oh What a Paradise It Seems* that the influence of the Hawthornian romance, the description of the "deeper levels of life," predominates.

Amerindian authors continue to attract German scholars, though much work is still in the stage of stocktaking and overviews. Frauke Zwillus's dissertation *"Today Talks in Yesterday's Voice": Zentrale Themen und ihre erzählerische Gestaltung im indianischen Roman der Gegenwart* (Frankfurt: Lang) is a case in point. Zwillus analyzes nine novels by Momaday, Welch, Roger Russell, Leslie Marmon Silko, Gerald Vizenor, Paula Gunn Allen, Louise Erdrich, and James Campbell Hale, besides minor classics like Momaday's and Silko's fairly recent novels that have not been discussed widely. Zwillus claims that the epistemological basis of Amerindian literature is rooted in the equality and interrelatedness of all organic matter as part of an "infinite and dynamic process of creation" and in an "Indian" concept of space and time. In all these novels contemporary America appears as a modern waste land in which man is alienated from nature, society, and the universe. Zwillus thinks that the female protagonists have a harder time than the males in finding identity, wholeness, and harmony in a life that has nothing to offer but violence, sexual discrimination, alcoholism, and disrupted families. In spite of all this misery, traditional ways of thinking—e.g., the belief in a mystical union of man and universe—survive. Whether the reservation becomes a kind of refuge in the face of the modern American waste land, as Zwillus also claims, is, however, highly debatable. But there is no doubt that her dissertation deserves praise, though from now on overviews like hers should be replaced by more detailed studies of individual authors or regional perspectives.

Restricted to black literature is Sabine Bröck's *Der entkolonisierte Körper. Die Protagonistin in der afroamerikanischen Erzähltradition der 30er bis 80er Jahre* (Frankfurt: Campus). Focusing on novels by Zora Neale Hurston, Ann Petry, Gwendolyn Brooks, Paule Marshall, Toni Morrison, and Alice Walker, Bröck uses literary, political, and social insights to demonstrate that the theme of the female black body is always the history of sexual violence against women. She sees in the emphasis on one's own body and one's sexual desire a liberation from patriarchal strategies of suppression. Erotic power and the conquest of mobility become touchstones beginning with dependence and ending in choice of place. But it remains for the protagonists of the seventies and eighties to appear as active subjects because of their emphasis on their own sexual desires.

A couple of substantial articles deserve mention. Monika Fludernik in "*Winesburg, Ohio*: The Apprenticeship of George Willard" (*Amst* 32:431–52) focuses on the central character of the novel, who in her opinion is the young aspiring artist, but at the same time one of the grotesques. His artistic development is shaped by his interactions with the other Winesburg characters, and the reader has to evaluate it against his knowledge of life in this small town. Anderson's disciple, Ernest Hemingway, will hardly ever lose his attraction for German scholars, as two articles amply prove. Susanne Opfermann in "A Laying of Ghosts: G. A. Custer and T. E. Lawrence in *For Whom the Bell Tolls*" (*Amst* 32:453–65) insists that Hemingway used Custer's last stand as a model for El Sordo's fight on the hilltop in order to demolish the Custer myth. In a similar vein, Hemingway battled the myth of Lawrence of Arabia. The Russian dynamiter Kashkin, Opfermann argues, is a malicious fictional portrait of Lawrence. That Hemingway, self-appointed military expert, criticized most military leaders, from Custer to Field Marshal Montgomery, goes without saying. It is equally true that he considered T. E. Lawrence, writer and man of action, as a rival. Yet I think it is also true that Custer and Lawrence simply provided him with two motifs, that of the last stand (reenacted in the El Sordo episode and in Jordan's heroic rearguard action), and that of the lone bridge-blower, personified negatively in Kashkin and positively in Jordan. Hemingway and the Spanish Civil War is also at the core of Hans-Peter Rodenberg's " 'The Moment of Truth'—Hemingway, Spain and the Civil War 1936–1939: A Study in the Psychoanalysis of Adventurism" in Bernd-Peter Lange, ed., *The Spanish Civil War in British and American Literature* (Braunschweig: Technische Universität), pp. 46–75. Rodenberg's psychoanalytical argument is that Hemingway's sexual identity was endangered by a dominating mother. His emphasis on masculinity and manly virtues were compensatory attempts to escape from this intolerable situation. The Spain of bullfights and, later on, the civil war, became a setting where he believed it possible to live out his psychic tensions by identification with an archaic Spain threatened by "mechanized doom" (fascism) and by a "cathartic nearness of death."

Two articles dealing with more recent American novels caught my attention. Heinz Tschachler's "James Dickey's *Deliverance* und George Batailles Metaphysik" (*ArAA* 12:123–45) interprets the protagonists' primitive regression in the light of Bataille's metaphysics of violence. Tschachler, however, comes to the conclusion that Dickey's intellectual and individualistic solution is closer to the triumph of rational consciousness over the Thoreauvian "animal in us" than to Bataille's irrationalism. Elisabeth Bronfen in "Between Nostalgia and Disenchantment: The Concept 'Home' in Jayne Anne Phillips' Novel *Machine Dreams*" (*ArAA* 13:17–28) takes on a literary trend that has made rural or small-town settings popular again. Bronfen singles out a novel about three generations of a lower middle-class family from West Virginia, which in her opinion expresses a yearning for a sense of belonging, a sense of home beyond the dream of machines, affluence, and national expansion. The sense of home does not necessarily mean the place where one was born; it rather denotes a sense of tradition, a sense of being rooted in a specific region, the feeling of sharing the same popular culture.

A major event in the scholarly landscape of 1988 was the long-announced publication of Gerhard Hoffmann's three-volume study of the contemporary American novel, *Der zeitgenössische amerikanische Roman* (München: Fink). It is a huge enterprise on which many German and foreign scholars cooperated. More than 1,100 pages, it is almost impossible to describe in my review-essay. Gerhard Hoffmann, Alfred Hornung, and Rüdiger Kunow join forces in an introductory essay entitled "'Modern,' 'Postmodern' und 'Contemporary': Zur Klassifizierung der amerikanischen Erzählliteratur des 20. Jahrhunderts" (pp. 7–43). This essay, a modernized and revised version of an article published more than a decade ago, tries to catch the various definitions of modernism, postmodernism, and contemporary as they have appeared in recent American criticism. Manfred Pütz follows suit with "Zum Fiktionsbegriff des amerikanischen Romans: Ein historisch-systematischer Überblick im Lichte von Autorenäußerungen" (pp. 81–107). Pütz deals with three problems: the theoretical debate of fiction as the constituting element of literature, the changing character of fiction through American literary history, and the programmatic statements of contemporary authors.

The largest part of volume 1 is taken by Gerhard Hoffmann's chapters on postmodernism (pp. 108–307). Hoffmann begins with the term "situationalism," which relates to the narrative structure of the contemporary novel as well as to its cultural matrix and its epistemological and ethical prerequisites. To him, "situationalism" is nothing less than the "epistémè" of postmodernism because the uncertainty and discontinuity of modern life can be traced back to the fact all epistemological, ethical, and organizational structures can cope only with "situations," i.e., segments of time, the social fabric, and value systems, without even trying to arrive at some totality of vision. The subject that in modernism was able to control or integrate the world around him is reduced to helplessness in a complex world in which the traditional categories space, time, figure, and event are replaced by attitudes, perspectives, concepts, and transformations, produced by the manipulation of fictional material. Fact and fiction become interchangeable in a world that does not seem to be realistic, but fantastic. So, with John Barth, fact becomes fantasy, and the story as a model of the world becomes a collage of situations dissociated from any "sequential continuum." Another of Hoffmann's special fields of interest is the satiric, the grotesque, and the absurd as major components of postmodern literature, which he pursues from Sinclair Lewis and Nathanael West to William Gass and Robert Coover. In contrast to Hoffmann's bulky chapters, Hartwig Isernhagen's contribution on "aesthetic negativity" in postmodern fiction (pp. 309–21), Heide Ziegler's on myth in the contemporary American novel (pp. 322–32), Malcolm Bradbury's on parody and authenticity in postmodernism (pp. 333–41), Rüdiger Kunow's on postmodern language experiments (pp. 342–63), Dietmar Claas's on playfulness in postmodern American literature (pp. 364–78) and André Le Vot's on the fiction of the sixties and seventies (pp. 379–91) sometimes seem curtailed, in spite of the valuable information they contain. Volume 1 ends with Jürgen Habermas's famous essay "Die Moderne—ein unvollendetes Projekt" (pp. 393–408).

Volume 2 combines chapters of social and literary history with studies of individual authors. Thus, Wolfgang Riedel deals with "affluence as crisis" between 1950 and 1980 (pp. 31–52), whereas Dieter Meindl takes on two main representatives of this period, Saul Bellow and Norman Mailer (pp. 53–101). Alfred Hornung singles out Bernard Malamud, Philip Roth, and John Hawkes as "writers between realism and anti-realism" (pp. 102–45). Peter Bruck takes care of documentary prose from Truman Capote's *In Cold Blood* (1966) to Tom Wolfe (pp. 146–64). Southerners Warren, McCullers, O'Connor, and Percy are dealt with as "Post-Renaissance writers" by Arthur Bartle (pp. 165–90). After two essays by Beate Neumeier on Mary McCarthy (pp. 191–213) and Gertrud Kalb on Joyce Carol Oates (pp. 214–33), the book ends with two overviews. Christopher Bigsby briefly sketches the black novel since 1945 (pp. 234–57); much more substantial is Gudrun Schindler's chapter on the contemporary Amerindian novel (pp. 258–345).

Volume 3 centers on postmodern writers. Richard Martin leads off with Walter Abish (pp. 7–21). Heide Ziegler discusses John Barth, "the ironic representative of postmodernism" (pp. 22–39), followed by Jochen Achilles on Donald Barthelme (pp. 40–59), whom he sees not only as stylistic innovator, composing his works from fragments and collages, but as a writer yearning for a better world. Marc Chénetier tackles Richard Brautigan's fiction and aesthetics (pp. 60–81), while Charles Russell assesses William Burroughs (pp. 82–93). Other writers discussed are Robert Coover by Heinz Ickstadt (pp. 94–114), Stanley Elkin by Kurt Dittmar (pp. 115–32), Raymond Federman and Ronald Sukenick by Alfred Hornung (pp. 133–56), William Gaddis by Johan Thielemans (pp. 157–74), and William H. Gass by Hartwig Isernhagen (pp. 175–90). Gisela Hoffmann turns to Joseph Heller (pp. 191–213), pointing out that only in *Catch-22* did he create a postmodern novel, whereas in his later works he resorted to more traditional modes of writing and tighter plot construction. Sepp Tiefenthaler's "Jerzy Kosinski" (pp. 214–30) and Horst Grabes's essay on Vladimir Nabokov (pp. 231–45) are condensed biographical studies. Heinz Ickstadt's and Klaus Poenecke's "Zum Romanwerk Thomas Pynchons" (pp. 246–76) is a revised version of earlier publications but by no means loses their qualities. The last four chapters are devoted to quite different writers. Richard Martin is the only scholar dealing with a black writer, namely, Ishmael Reed (pp. 277–91). Johan Thielemans writes on Gilbert Sorrentino (pp. 292–312), followed by Klaus P. Hansen on John Updike (pp. 313–33), and Peter Freese on Kurt Vonnegut (pp. 334–53). Two essays by Ihab Hassan on postmodernism conclude the book.

Many of the contributions are revised versions of studies published earlier in Germany or elsewhere. In this respect, the volumes of *Der zeitgenössische amerikanische Roman* provide the reader with a good survey of contemporary American literature and its criticism.

It is understandable that some of the essays collected are uneven. (Most contributors clearly focused on postmodern prose writers.) But the theoretical debate on what constitutes postmodernism is much too inflated and even sometimes repetitious. For readers interested in postmodern literature, *Der zeitgenössische amerikanische Roman* offers a wealth of information. Yet other aspects of the American contemporary novel and important writers are sadly neglected. To deal with black literature in only a 20-page survey and an essay on Ishmael Reed in an endeavor called "the contemporary American novel" leaves the reader a bit dissatisfied.

Universität Hamburg

iv. Italian Contributions

Massimo Bacigalupo

The number of Italian university chairs in American literature is at a standstill since 1987, while those of English literature have increased by 14, to be adjudged in 1990. If the situation does not change, which is likely, given the Italian university system (in which English is a main subject, American literature an optional one), fewer young academics will be concentrating on American studies if they are to hope for promotion. This may mean that only books inevitable to their authors will get written, which on the whole can have only baneful effects. However, I am happy to report that much work of merit appeared in 1988, including several significant books.

***a.* General Work, Theory, and Criticism.** Italo Calvino's *Lezioni americane* (Milan: Garzanti) is the original text of the Norton lectures published by Harvard as *Six Memos for the Next Millennium* (the essays being only five because the author did not live to finish them and deliver them in Cambridge in 1985). This is a most refreshing book on the qualities that make literature valuable, "Lightness" being the first of them. Calvino's comments on such diverse writers as Guido Cavalcanti and Emily Dickinson, Honoré de Balzac and Edgar Allan Poe, Giovanni Boccaccio and Henry James are rich with perceptions that bring us novel appreciation of their subjects. I admire the youthfulness and wisdom of the middle-aged novelist (b. 1923), who could still give so much and rely so little on cliché when preparing this testamentary account of what had been the business and, happily, the passion of his life: literature. He wrote that rare thing, a book which is equally rewarding for the jaded specialist and for the starry-eyed neophyte.

Marcello Pagnini's *Semiosi: teoria ed ermeneutica del testo letterario* (Bologna: Il Mulino) collects 15 essays by an elder master of Italian structuralism who also has not lost his capacity to make us *see*. Of the six theoretical essays only one, "La conoscenza del testo," is heretofore unpublished and offers a spirited critique of deconstructionism and its "pan-linguistic" weltanschauung. Pagnini reacts against the cynicism, the indifference, to meaning and value, which he detects in some deconstructionist criticism, and tells us bracingly that "there is still much to do to understand the ways in which men have lived and live, within the parameters of their culture. In our knowledge of the structures of Western culture we can draw near the 'truth,' with an approximation inevitable yet satisfactory, in relation to those parameters and to ours. This is why I believe in a hermeneutics that relates to the paradigms of history" (p. 97). And he quotes Umberto Eco's warning (1984) that in some cases post-structuralism "does not constitute an advance, but a return to the orgy of the ineffable." Pagnini's readings of chosen texts of Wallace Stevens ("Peter Quince"), Emily Dickinson ("I never told the buried gold"), Poe ("Usher"), and his more general observations on E. E. Cummings (see *ALS 1986*, p. 470) and Ezra Pound significantly contribute to our knowledge of these writers.

Guido Almansi and Claude Béguin include Ambrose Bierce, Elizabeth Bishop, Melville, Nabokov, Plath, Nathanael West, Whitman, and Wilder in their anthology of dreams, *Teatro del sonno* (Milan: Garzanti) and discuss their selections briefly in an ample introduction to the literary dream-world. Another thematic survey is my article, "Riscoprendo l'America" (*Columbus* 92 33 [December]:39–43), which sees Whitman, Dickinson, Kerouac, Nabokov, Pound, W. C. Williams, and Stevens as continuators of Columbus's voyages of discovery. As Dickinson put it (poem 555), "Trust in the Unexpected . . . 'Twas this—allured Columbus—/ When Genoa—withdrew / Before an Apparition / Baptized America."

Extracts of Stefano Rosso's doctoral thesis on post-structuralist criticism have appeared in *Quaderni di Lingue e Letterature* (Verona) 12 (1987):89–107 and in *Quaderni* (Bergamo) 4:105–24; the former article is a cogent discussion of Stanley Fish, the latter a clear and shrewd account of postmodernist tendencies, especially those of Ihab Hassan (whose conservative bias is noticed) and William V. Spanos. Luciana Pirè writes sympathetically and lucidly of "Un transito nel moderno: l'esempio di Susan Sontag" in *Contesti* 1 (Bari: Adriatica): 179–97.

b. Colonial Literature. In *L'idea dell'America nella cultura inglese (1500–1625). Vol. II: letteratura e teatro del '500* (Bari: Adriatica), Franca Rossi continues her survey of early English responses to America. Having treated historians and diarists in volume 1 (*ALS 1986*, p. 463), she turns to 16th-century writers (Thomas More, John Rastell, Philip Sidney, Edmund Spenser, Christopher Marlowe, and the University Wits). Her work will be useful for students of the roots of colonial literature. Marilla Battilana takes a further step in her enthusiastic booklet *The Colonial Roots of American Fiction: Notes Toward a New Theory* (Florence: Olschki). Her work on colonial diaries has suggested to her that the fiction of Bellow, Burroughs, Hemingway, James, Kerouac, Updike, Vonnegut, Nathanael West, and many more (there are 300 names in the index to her 90-page book) directly descends not from the European novel but from those early documents; she points to similarities of style, situation, and, yes, landscape. I think the main interest of her book is in its suggesting, though somewhat overemphatically, a new way of reading old texts, both colonial and modern, and in its sympathetic account of such forgotten treasures as Gouverneur Morris's *Diary of the French Revolution* (published 1939). But her treatment of diaries as if they were novels is surely questionable. For example: "The two great themes of [Morris's] book, love and politics, are already beautifully intertwining. Which will continue down to the very end of the diary. Perfectly in keeping with the concept of 'open form' we are now so familiar with, it is no *end* at all, but a sudden interruption. . . . Besides creating a true woman's fascinating character, G. Morris admirably struck the note of 'the American in Europe' (namely in Paris!). He gave birth, quite unaware, to the *international theme*" (pp. 56, 58). Perhaps Battilana's pamphlet should have been called not *Notes Toward a New Theory* but "A Reader's Journal," for she has caught the style of her beloved diarists.

I may mention here Rosella Mamoli Zorzi's useful collection of documents, *Gli Shakers: una comunità utopica americana* (Venice:

Fondazione Querini Stampalia, 1987), an attractive volume to accompany an exhibition of photographs, containing head notes by the editor and by Francesca Bisutti, Daniela Ciani, Alide Cagidemetrio (on Hawthorne's and Melville's negative responses to Shakerism), Silvana Cattaneo (on Howells), and Sergio Perosa (on Henry James), and an essay on Shaker music by Giovanni Morelli.

***c.* 19th Century.** In "'Plus Ultra': John the Baptist in Irving's *The Alhambra*," *LAmer* 27 (1985, but published 1988):15–36, Cristina Giorcelli writes generally about Irving's Spanish collection, focuses on "The Legend of the Enchanted Soldier," and takes off on an extraordinary excursus on the arcane implications of the figure of John the Baptist (the story is set on St. John's Eve). Perhaps in another essay she will pursue her researches into Ezra Pound's Canto 35 ("When the stars fall from the olive . . . Toward St John's eve"). An edition of Irving's book appeared, incidentally, early in 1989: *I racconti dell'Alhambra*, ed. R. M. Zorzi, trans. Biba Czerska (Pordenone: Studio Tesi), and was widely reviewed (for example, by Irene Bignardi, *Repubblica*, February 22, 1989). Francesco Marroni translated and wrote the narratological introduction to a story from *Bracebridge Hall, Dolph Heiliger* (Chieti: Marino Solfanelli).

Poe is given a somewhat free-wheeling postmodern treatment by Leo Marchetti in his *Edgar Allan Poe: la scrittura eterogenea* (Ravenna: Longo), which touches knowledgeably on recent critical debates. So does Roberto Cagliero in "La questione dell'origine in Gordon Pym" (*Quaderni di Lingue e Letterature* [Verona] 13:29–47), covering interpretations of Poe's novel and its relation to "Eureka." As things get more and more involved, there seems little chance for critics to admit that *Pym* is first and foremost a wonderful fairy tale for adults (and for children, by the way).

Interpretation would appear to be more controllable with Melville's "Benito Cereno" and *Billy Budd*, given the historical settings and issues, besides the metaphysical (or "metaquizzical"—Byron's word) ones. In the introduction (pp. 7–47) to my new edition of the two tales and of "Daniel Orme," published as *Gente di mare* (Milan: Mondadori), I provide sequential readings of the texts and concentrate on the criticism of romanticism (Goethe and, possibly, Wordsworth) in "Cereno" and on the growth of *Billy Budd* (this is the second Italian edition that follows, in the main, the Hayford-Sealts text), taking issue rather for than against Vere as a projection of authorial consciousness, and for the narrator, whom I do not see as an ironic persona. Melville had come around quite a bit by 1890 in his view of the Somers affair as aired in *White-Jacket*, though chapter 67 of that novel, for example, is very useful to an understanding of Billy's killing of Claggart. This paperback edition also includes critical excerpts, ranging from D. H. Lawrence and Gabriele Baldini to Hans-Joachim Lang (not Lange, p. 53) and John Updike (pp. 48–58), a bibliography, and, in the notes to "Cereno," details of Melville's changes of Amasa Delano's narrative. Unfortunately, there are more than 30 typographical mistakes (on p. 76 the oakum-pickers are said to be six, instead of four). Incidentally, in the introduction to "Cereno" I use a relevant Emerson quotation, borrowed from Edward H. Rosenberry's *Melville* (1979): "Let us honestly state the facts. Our America has a bad name for superficialness. Great men, great nations, have not been boasters and buffoons, but perceivers of the terror of life, and have manned themselves to face it." When I wrote Rosenberry asking for the source of the quotation, he answered that, as his notes implied, he in turn had borrowed it from Richard Hofstadter's *Anti-Intellectualism in American Life* (1964) and had written Hofstadter about it, but the latter had died before divulging the source. And there the matter rests. A review, by Alberto Lehmann, discussing rather carefully this edition of Melville in relation to previous ones appeared in *Cultura & Innovazione*, March 1989, pp. 127–32. Ahab's mysterious scar is the subject of Annalisa Goldoni's cogent "Cicatrici eccellenti: Odisseo e Ahab," pp. 151–67, in her collection of pieces by various hands, *Frammenti di corpi immaginati* (Rome: Carucci). Enrico P. Capodaglio takes a look at Ishmael's philosophy in "Un platonista sul Pequod: Nota su *Moby-Dick* e il *Fedone*," *Strumenti Critici* 58:439–52.

A new paperback selection of *Leaves of Grass* appeared under the capable editorship of Biancamaria Tedeschini Lalli: *Foglie d'erba*, trans. Ariodante Marianni (Milan: Rizzoli). Novelist Giorgio Manganelli wrote the witty and sympathetic preface (on Whitman as Hopkins's "scoundrel"), while Tedeschini Lalli in her introduction (pp. 11–25) concentrates on Whitman's language, and in the endnotes (pp. 483–503) gives a capsule interpretation of single poems. I'm only sorry that the opportunity has not been taken to use the 1855 text for the poems of the first edition rather than the 1892 text, already available here in the Mondadori paperback edition. A somewhat censorious but well-documented account of the good gray poet's politics is offered by Bruno Cartosio in "Whitman e le masse" (*Contesti* 1:61–8); he finds that F. O. Matthiessen's starry-eyed view of Whitman as a socialist throws more light on Matthiessen's will to believe than on Whitman.

Politics are also a central concern of Ludovico Isoldo in *L'immaginario sociale di W. D. Howells* (Naples: Istituto Universitario Orientale), which has chapters on *Silas Lapham*, *The Minister's Charge*, the Haymarket riots, *Annie Kilburn*, and *A Hazard of New Fortunes*, and in fact offers detailed readings of these works. The politics of literary appreciation are the subject of Donatella Izzo's careful study of the Italian reception of Henry James, *Quel mostro bizzarro: Henry James nella cultura italiana, 1887–1987* (Rome: Bulzoni). Part one chronicles the "absence" of James around the turn of the century, especially in the work of Gabriele D'Annunzio, though Izzo thinks that a case can be made for James's influence on Matilde Serao and, more positively, Italo Svevo. Svevo's younger friend Eugenio Montale mentions James in a 1928 review, and this is the beginning of a new phase of influence and study (*Daisy Miller e altri racconti*, the first Italian translation of James, appeared in 1930). However, by the 1930s the perceptive regard of such belletrist critics as Emilio Cecchi and Mario Praz was counteracted by the diffidence of engagé writers like Elio Vittorini, and this realist climate persisted into the 1950s. The first book in Italian on James, by Paolo Milano, was published in 1948 and is passionate but ambivalent; according to Izzo, Agostino Lombardo's 1956 edition of *Le prefazioni* was the turning point, after which James became safe for democracy. Part three is largely concerned with scholarly work, of which there is no lack; but there is an interesting section on James's influence on novelists Giorgio Bassani, Mario Soldati, and Giuseppe Tomasi di Lampedusa. Izzo's final exhibit (p. 157) is a January 23, 1986, politcal editorial (by Enzo Forcella) from the front page of *La Repubblica*, where James is brought in without excuse as a master of understatement. So an acquaintance with "that queer monster, the artist" (as James called himself in writing to Henry Adams) is now taken for granted among general readers. It is only to be regretted that Donatella Izzo's study, crammed as it is with names and bibliographic information, should lack an index. Speaking of Jamesian prefaces, Sergio Perosa has reprinted his translation of *La fonte sacra* (Turin: Einaudi) with a revised introduction; Agostino Lombardo has written an introduction to another reprint, *Le bostoniane*, trans. Marcella

Bonsanti (Milan: Rizzoli); and Luisa Villa has translated the late *Tre saggi su Balzac* (Genoa: Il Melangolo) and provided some introductory notes.

***d.* 20th-Century Prose.** Romano Giachetti, a well-known literary journalist, author, and translator, draws a composite portrait of the American writer in *Lo scrittore americano* (Milan: Garzanti, 1987), one of the best original surveys of 20th-century American writing that I have read. Giachetti uses a cameo technique, offering portraits, mostly accompanied by interviews, of 15 writers in the book's three sections: (1) Engagement (Farrell, Kerouac, Henry Miller, Ferlinghetti, Faulkner, Dos Passos, James Jones); (2) Chimera (Malamud, Styron, Vonnegut, Gaddis, Barth); (3) Essence (Carver, Leavitt, McInerney). There are also three connecting chapters on the writer as hero, as creator, and as stylist. These critical portraits are lively in their juxtaposing the writers' comments and milieu (for example, Farrell as an old man in his seedy New York apartment, Barth in his camper, Malamud talking at home while family and friends watch baseball on TV), with critical observations on their work. Giachetti has an enquiring and perceptive mind, and his conversations, craftily edited to be sure, are much better than the usual sparring of such occasions; he seems to be able to draw out the central concerns of his subjects, and at the same time to pursue his own critical thought, which is subtle and unpredictable. It is a revelation to find Malamud saying that his two great models are ("Ready for surprises?") Hemingway and Chaplin, and admit later that Henry Roth may have had an even vaster importance to him. Giachetti's last section is also very useful for what it tells us, critically, about the present: Carver's isolated stance, David Leavitt and his freshmen minimalist acolytes, Jay McInerney and the prevalance of media culture. Giachetti also offers perceptive comments on writers who do not have a chapter to themselves, such as John Hawkes. With its bandying of names and titles, his book may give a headache to any but the staunchest reader of the multifarious productions of the American writer, but he has done a good job of bringing together so much material and so many significant insights in 268 pages. We would be even more indebted to Giachetti if he rewrote his book in English, thus making his findings generally available.

A detailed portrait of one writer is *Album Hemingway* (Milan: Mondadori), a handsome and compact collection of 261 photographs, some little known, of Hemingway and his world, assembled by Eileen Romano, who wrote the scrupulous captions (in a picture of some library shelves at the Finca Vigìa, however, she erroneously identifies [pp. xiii, 206] the multivolume *Photographic History of the Civil War* [1911] as relating to the *Spanish* Civil War). The photographs are accompanied by an extended "biographic essay" by Masolino d'Amico, written with knowledgeableness and grace—under pressure, surely, d'Amico being among the most productive reviewer-critic-translators in the country. There is also a select bibliography, including Italian translations. The first of these, *Un addio alle armi*, appeared in 1945, when the Fascist ban on Hemingway was lifted. The writer Mario Rigoni Stern (b. 1921) remembers purchasing it for 500 lire, then a big sum, for the soldiers' library that he ran after returning from interment in Germany, then giving it to his father (who commented: "It's too true, but shameful"), then to other former soldiers and resistance fighters, students, and housewives. "For many evenings, as it snowed on our poverty, we talked of wars and defeats, of Hemingway, and set *Farewell to Arms* against the memoirs by generals, against the books on the Great War (of which our library had many) that spoke of great undertakings in rhymed couplets."

These telling reminiscences are included (pp. 1–16) in *Hemingway e Venezia*, ed. Sergio Perosa (Florence: Olschki), which gathers the proceedings of a 1986 conference at the Fondazione Giorgio Cini, Venice. According to Agostino Lombardo (pp. 7–16), despite the myth, Hemingway qua writer is relatively unknown in Italy, at least insofar as he has received less scholarly attention than others. Only one brief introduction to Hemingway is in fact available, by Giovanni Cecchin (1975), an indefatigable biographer and hunter of Hemingway arcana who provides new information in his article (pp. 57–71), starting from the two 1919 drafts (at the Kennedy Library, Cambridge), "The Passing of Pickles McCarthy" and "The Mercenaries." The latter makes fun of Fulco Russo, famous airplane pilot, because his aunt Rita had favored Agnes von Kurowsky's engagement to the Neapolitan aristocrat Domenico Caracciolo, and this had brought about Agnes' break with young Ernest. Cecchin also has turned up the story of Hemingway's relation to the Bellìa family of Turin: the father Pier Vincenzo is apparently the original of Count Greffi of *A Farewell to Arms*; the daughters Elda, Dionisia, and Bianca (to whom unflattering allusion is made in "The Mercenaries") were variously in love with the young American, and one (hush-hush!)

may even have borne him a son. The other essays collected in *Hemingway e Venezia* are less titillating (Cecchin notes in all seriousness that in the Milan hospital Agnes "preferred to do night-duty," p. 64), if less disconcerting. There are theoretical perspectives by William Boelhower (on "Hemingway's Cartographic Modernism," pp. 79–99), Sonja Bašić (on "Hemingway's Modernism: Troping and Narrating," pp. 111–18), Barbara Lanati (on the Paris experience), and Sergio Perosa (on the critics as sharks), more personal impressions by Fernanda Pivano and Gianfranco Ivancich, discussions of women characters (by Marilla Battilana), of Hemingway and Dorothy Parker (by Francesca Bisutti), and of the posthumous fiction, by Roger Asselineau and me. According to Asselineau, the received wisdom is wrong: "the late fiction of Hemingway . . . is at least equal and even in some respects superior to the fiction he wrote in the inter-war years" (p. 190). In sum, an uneven but surely stimulating volume.

Rosella Mamoli Zorzi, who contributed an article on Hemingway's "The Good Lion" and "The Faithful Bull" to the Venice conference, capably discusses Gertrude Stein's tale, *The World Is Round* in *Ritratto dell'artista come donna*, ed. Lilla Maria Crisafulli Jones, and Vita Fortunati (Urbino: QuattroVenti). Another unusual novel is the subject of Stefano Bronzini's "Viaggio nella memoria: note su *The Enormous Room* di E. E. Cummings" (*Contesti* 1:141–65), which is full of admiration for Mr. lowercase's flights of sentiment. Mario Maffi wrote the afterword to Tom Kromer, *Vagabondi nella notte* (Genoa: Costa & Nolan), a translation of *Waiting for Nothing* (1935); Roberto Cagliero the afterword to Jerome Charyn, *Metropolis*, and Thomas Pynchon, *Un lento apprendistato* (i.e., *Slow Learner*), both published by Edizioni e/o of Rome.

e. 20th-Century Poetry. *Robert Frost: Conoscenza della notte e altre poesie* (Milan: Mondadori), is a revised and enlarged edition of Giovanni Giudici's 1965 selection of 66 Frost poems (70 in this edition, which also includes a translation of "The Figure a Poem Makes"). I helped Giudici, one of Italy's better-known poets, in the revision and added an introduction (pp. 5–34) that sees Frost as a man of Falstaffian quips and quiddities and places him in a modernist context. The book got a thoughtful review, "La voce e il ridere di Eva," by Francesco Rognoni (*L'Indice* 9:29). A sensitive account of "Stopping by Woods" is provided by Gordon Poole in *Il Verri* nos. 3–4(1987):165–76.

Another volume that I edited is Wallace Stevens, *L'angelo necessario*, trans. Gino Scatasta (Milan: Coliseum). For this I wrote an introductory discussion of Stevens's poetics (pp. 3–31) and a documentary account (pp. 32–62), largely based on the *Letters* and on Peter Brazeau's research, of how the *Necessary Angel* essays came about and were read, received, and reviewed. I wanted to give the Italian reader a portrait of Stevens the man and poet, with his endearing (and occasionally forbidding) oddity, and his essential decency. ("The simplest personification of the angel of reality would be the good man," I quote him as saying on p. 32. He adds: "But I suppose that the good man would make a very uninteresting picture".) The volume also includes a capsule biography (pp. 63–69), a bibliography, and a few footnotes to Stevens's essays. This is the fourth Stevens book to appear in Italy. The first, *Mattino domenicale e altre poesie* (1954), ed. Renato Poggioli, which was also the first Stevens book published in a language other than English, and contained illuminating excerpts (in English) from Stevens's letters to the brilliant editor and translator, has been reprinted (Turin: Einaudi) with a new afterword by Guido Carboni. Poggioli's introduction and notes are still fresh and rich in suggestions despite the passage of 35 years, and in fact Stevens was very pleased with the volume. He died the year after, on August 2, 1955. My article, "Wallace Stevens trent'anni dopo" (*Verri* 8[1987]:21–34), is an homage to the poet on the thirtieth anniversary of his death and is written in the form of a dialogue between this scholar and a young woman, occurring on a sailboat on August 2, 1985, the point being that the seemingly forbidding poet that Heideggerians have claimed for their own is also one who "can please/A young girl in the indolence of her youth" (in Yeats's phrase) and is more accessible than his reputation would suggest. The young woman in the article, Vincentine, does not particularly care for poetry but reads selected passages from *The Palm at the End of the Mind*, making comments that show how she can interpret them in terms of her life, while the scholar watches in amazement and makes occasional digressions on the state of Stevens studies. Finally, a gust of wind separates a page from the book, and Vincentine dives to retrieve it, returning with the page in her mouth. On such a date this can only be a sign ("What syllable are you seeking,/Vocalissimus?"), and a happy destiny for a poet 30 years after God has made up his mind about him (as Stevens once joked in a letter). Well, I don't want to give the story away, but the article is in fact a recording of an actual, "real," sail after lunch, believe it or not, with a girl who may not have been called Vincentine but made some of the very comments I recorded. Does this prove that Stevens will become more popular than he is, and that the withering away of scholarly explication is in sight? Perhaps.

Stevens is usually claimed as an heir to romanticism, Pound less so, though he wrote from a "spontaneous overflow of powerful feelings" if ever anyone did, especially in *The Pisan Cantos*. In another article, " 'Lay in the soft grass': Wordsworth e Pound," in *Modernità dei Romantici*, ed. Lilla Maria Crisafulli Jones and others (Naples: Liguori):101–19, I investigate the connections between modernist and romantic poetics and see Pound and Wordsworth as comparable innovators, both as poets and as critics, and even find an analogy in their relation to a younger city-dwelling and neurotic poet-critic-philosopher, i.e., Eliot and Coleridge, respectively. Both Pound and Wordsworth wrote long autobiographical poems about paradise regained and were deeply affected by natural supernaturalism and the spirit of place, preferring rural settings. Incidentally, both had an illegitimate daughter for whom they cared deeply, as shown in "It Is a Beateous Evening" and in Canto 93, among others. So it is high time that Pound should be admitted to the post-romantic pantheon, and Wordsworth acknowledged as a premodernist innovator. Pound called him "that bleating sheep" but seems to have been reading him aloud to Yeats at Stone Cottage around 1914, picking up much in the process. (By the way, my article identifies and discusses the quotation from Wordsworth's "Plea for the Historian" in Pound's "Three Cantos I.") A better-documented but equally quizzing Poundian contact is glanced at in my "Pound/Joyce: Style, Politics, and Language" (*Joyce Studies in Italy* 2:161–70). Pound fans will be interested in G. Singh's memoir in the form of poems, *The Circle and Other Poems: Olga and Pound* (Udine: Campanotto), a series of compositions, imitative of Eugenio Montalé's *Xenia* (to his deceased wife), about Pound's lifelong companion, with good photographs by Elio Montanari. Pound himself dabbled in photography: four fine pictures he took of a young and quiet H.D. are reproduced in a neat little volume, *H.D.*, ed. Mary de Rachewiltz (Milan: Scheiwiller, 1986), which also includes in facsimile some notes Pound scribbled upon H.D.'s death (1961): "translate this for Vanni or some current obit of H.D. or I will if my signature is of use. set dead pyre flaming. . . ." "H.D.'s *Trilogy*, or the Secret Language of Change" is the subject of an article by Marina

Camboni (*LAmer* 27[1985]:87–106), which touches upon Christian, numerological, and alchemical symbolism. Raffaella Baccolini sees "*Hermetic Definition* di H(ilda) D(oolittle)" (*Ritratto dell'artista come donna*, pp. 19–42) as a kind of *Künstlerroman* in which "by an act of revision, the woman artist can finally free herself from the anxiety of comparisons with male predecessors and texts." At any rate, Baccolini is not anxious about the influence of Harold Bloom. Her discussion contains useful information and a sort of synopsis but seems to confuse, as criticism of H.D. often does, the theme (real or alleged) with the poem, which is quoted as if it were self-explanatory, straightforward, and of course morally uplifting. I hope that *Hermetic Definition* is better than that.

In the year of his centenary T. S. Eliot was the subject of careful scrutiny by Dario Calimani in *T. S. Eliot: lo spazio retorico* (Rome: Carucci), a structuralist reading the greater part of which is devoted to "Prufrock," but which also has a long chapter on *The Waste Land* (pp. 169–228). Calimani writes clearly and convincingly, will occasionally overinterpret a given passage (as when he points out that "Alfred" means "good counsellor," which Prufrock surely isn't—hence Irony!), but is usually helpful and thorough (without pedantry) in comparing previous readings. So this will be a usable book on Eliot the poet. Stefano Maria Casella's " 'Welding a poetic theft': da *Pericles* di Shakespeare a 'Marina' di T. S. Eliot a 'Marina' di Mario Luzi" (*Lingua e Letteratura* 11:6–40) seeks to compare Eliot's haunting poem with Mario Luzi's 1949 seascape, which Poe would have called a plagiarism ("Che acque affaticate contro la fioca riva,/ che flutti grigi contro i pali . . . Che sparse piagge navighi, che luci"), but is better understood as an imitation and transposition into another poetic language and context. Casella's research is praiseworthy, but the result is dense to the point of being unreadable, and his footnotes run away with him: he has cited *every*thing.

Roberto Birindelli manages well enough in "Il 'livido geroglifico': rileggendo una poesia di Hart Crane" (*Il confronto letterario* 9:141–55) to "reread" "At Melville's Tomb" and ask some pertinent methodological questions about trusting the tale or the teller, and Paolo Dilonardo offers some notes on *The Bridge* in "L'Arpa e il Telaio" (*Contesti* 1:83–139). Robert Lowell's "Water" is explicated convincingly with the help of biographical information by Maria Anita Stefanelli in "Analisi contestuale-dinamica di una lirica di R. Lowell," in *Analisi del testo letterario*, ed. Tatiana Slama-Cazacu (Rome:

Bulzoni):152–74). Gabriella Morisco adds a sketch of Elizabeth Bishop ("La memoria come itinerario," pp. 149–75) to the miscellaneous *Ritratto dell'artista come donna*, taking us back in the end from the waiting room of Bishop's poem of that title to "The Scream" of Lowell's *For the Union Dead*. In " 'The Stomach of Indifference': i *Journals* di Sylvia Plath," *LAmer* 29–31 (1985–86, but published 1989):115–30, Biancamaria Pisapia provides much light on Plath's journals (with sidelights from Maurice Blanchot, Elias Canetti, and others), and finds them finally to be a disappointing "pastiche, an erratic and disorderly miscellany, a deposit of different genres and writings . . . a literary space of passivity" (p. 128). "The Disappearance of the Self" of which Plath suffered is the titular theme of John Paul Russo's able survey of "Some Theories of Autobiography in the United States, 1964–1987" (pp. 5–42), which opens the same issue of *LAmer*, entirely devoted to what has been called the autobiographic pact.

f. **Ethnic Literature.** Gaetano Prampolini's edition of N. Scott Momaday, *Il viaggio a Rainy Mountain* (Milan: La Salamandra), is a substantial contribution to Native American studies in general, not only in Italy. His lucid and penetrating afterword ("Molti viaggi in uno," pp. 111–56) is one of the most sensitive discussions of Momaday's prose-poem novel and its structure, besides being an excellent introduction to the writer's background (there is also an ample bibliography). Prampolini stresses in particular Momaday's care for the oral tradition and for "the nature of language and the relation between language and human experience" (p. 141) and quotes Momaday's dicta, "We are what we imagine ourselves to be," "Man has no perfection of being but in language" (I am retranslating from the Italian, p. 142), and his definition of an Indian as "an idea that a certain man has of himself." Momaday's attitude toward nature, as evinced for instance in *Rainy Mountain*'s final section (24), is seen as confirmation of the book's universal qualities. A lesser work, James Welch's *La morte di Jim Loney*, was brought out by the same publisher, with an afterword, largely historical (on the Blackfeet tribes), by Cinzia Biagiotti (pp. 193–224).

Prampolini reminds us of Momaday's paradoxical association with Yvor Winters: a systematic account of the relation between the Native American and the modernist tradition is offered by Fedora Giordano in *Etnopoetica: le avanguardie americane e la tradizione orale indiana* (Rome: Bulzoni). Chapter 1 reviews anthropological research on Indian poetry (from Alix Fletcher to Franz Boas and Ruth Underhill); chapter 2 treats Indian-inspired work that appeared in the early *Poetry* and the writings of Frank Gordon, Lew Sarett, and others; chapter 3 discusses the "artist colonies" of Santa Fe and Taos, D. H. Lawrence's Indians, Jaime de Angulo, and Mary Austin; the final chapter attempts to define Ethnopoetics as a tendency related to Open Poetry and other modernistic modes. This appears to be a provisional survey that leaves us curious about a subject that escapes precise focusing.

Momaday's definition of an Indian as a state of mind is reminiscent of Malamud's definition of a Jew (by way of Morris Bober in *The Assistant*): "My father used to say to be a Jew all you need is a good heart"—which in turn may be compared with Stevens's identification (above) of the angel of reality with the good man. Guido Fink and Gabriella Morisco, editors of *Il recupero del testo: aspetti della letteratura ebraico-americana* (Bologna: CLUEB), suggest (with Harold Bloom) that "text-centerdness" may be germane to the Jewish tradition, and this is more or less the leitmotiv of the 15 mostly illuminating essays that they have collected (originally a series of talks given in 1986 at the University of Bologna). In his article Fink looks at the Jewish question through the writings of Henry James and Mark Twain; the other contributions are devoted to Jewish writers. Giordano De Biasio talks about the structure of Henry Roth's *Call It Sleep* as evident in its prologue (where he finds proof that David is not the son of his legal father Albert); Gabriella Morisco constructs an extended parallel between *The Assistant* and *Crime and Punishment*; other essays are devoted to Abraham Cahan (Marina Orsini), Saul Bellow's *The Victim* (Alessandra Calanchi), Joanne Greenberg (Liana Borghi), Karl Shapiro and other poets, including M. L. Rosenthal (M. L. Rosenthal), the Objectivists and Philip Levine (my essay), Allen Ginsberg (W. S. Di Piero), Stanley Elkin (Franco Minganti), Woody Allen and the Marx Brothers (Franco La Polla), and S. J. Perelman (Guido Almansi). A wide spectrum, as one can see. The book closes with an amusing and telling story (in English), collected by Mario Materassi: "Rabbi Kosseff's Answer," about the young man who wants to become a Jewish-American writer and brings the Rabbi his manuscript only to be told again and again that something is missing. The reader may look up what it is in this meaty and attractive book of 336 pages. By the way, a conversational introduction to Saul Bellow, given by Rolando Anzilotti in 1977, is included in the collection *Narratori contemporanei d'Europa e d'America*, published in Pisa under the auspices of the Comune.

It is only fitting that I should close with an Italo-American writer, John Fante (1909–83), who was represented in Elio Vittorini's 1942 anthology, *Americana*, but only recently has had a comeback both in the United States (*Dreams of Bunker Hill* and *The Road to Los Angeles*, both published by Black Sparrow) and in Italy, where Mondadori brought out *Sogni di Bunker Hill* with a preface by Pier Vittorio Tondelli, and Leonardo published (in 1989) *La strada di Los Angeles*. The latter, according to Claudio Gorlier's review ("John Fante, l'ora della rivincita," *La Stampa*, June 24, 1989), "has no development or plot but is a series of everyday sequences in which the hero Bandini seeks to establish for himself, both painfully and joyfully, an intentionally impoverished language. . . . It is a montage of everyday materials and of escapes into fantasy, as in the furious and horrible scene in which young Bandini destroys a mass of crustaceans to express his will to power, his resentment, by way of a hallucinatory transfiguration of himself and of his victims, which become a massed and hostile humanity. A superb piece of writing."

Fante's Bandini must imagine his lost identity, like Momaday's Native American or Malamud's Italo-Jewish Frank Alpine. Mark Twain, as Guido Fink reminds us, had already taken (in *Concerning the Jews*, 1898) a comparably generous view of cross-cultural patterns: "I am quite sure that (bar one) I have no race prejudices, and *I think* I have no color prejudice nor caste prejudice nor creed prejudice. Indeed, I know it. I can stand any society. All that I care to know is that a man is a human being—that is enough for me; he can't be any worse."

Università di Genova

v. Japanese Contributions

Hiroko Sato

It seems that recent tensions between the United States and Japan, either political or economic, have favorably affected Japanese interest in things American. Since the craze for Hemingway and Faulkner after World War II, Japanese interest in the contemporary American novel has never been stronger. Translations of works by writers of so-called minimalism, Raymond Carver, Ann Beattie, Jayne Anne Phillips, Tama Janowitz, Jay McInerney, Bobbie Ann Mason, and others, have been published and avidly read. Their influence on younger Japanese writers has been openly acknowledged. This tendency is reflected in the academic world, as will be noted. However, 1988 has something more to show. The papers read by Japanese scholars at various Emily Dickinson conferences in 1986 were compiled in one volume, and Eugene O'Neill's centennial was celebrated in the November issue of *EigoS*.

The articles examined here will be restricted to our major periodicals, *EigoS*, *SALit*, *SELit*, and *American Review*. Unless otherwise indicated, all books mentioned were published in Tokyo.

Japanese scholars' interest in American literature is biased in favor of 20th-century writers. However, some stimulating and suggestive books and articles were published on writers of "classic" American literature.

Before chronologically examining individual authors, however, I would like to refer to two books of great importance that came out in 1988. One is Shunsuke Kamei's *Waga Koten Amerika Bungaku* [*My Studies in Classic American Literature*] (Nanundo), the other Koji Oi's *Kinmekijidai Saiho* [*The Gilded Age Revisited*] (Kaibun-sha). Both Kamei and Oi have definite ideas about the study of foreign literature. Kamei studies such Puritan poets as Anne Bradstreet and Edward Taylor, then moves on through Benjamin Franklin, Cooper, Poe, Thoreau, Melville, Frederic Goddard Tuckerman, and Whitman to Mark Twain. He also pays homage to D. H. Lawrence, whose works acted as a catalyst in forming his book. Kamei's analysis is acute: Benjamin Franklin's complexity as an 18th-century intellectual and the important role played by country gentlemen in Cooper's novels are, for example, convincingly stated. The chapter on Tuckerman is the first article written in Japan on this reclusive poet. However, the book's most charming point is Kamei's almost fanatical belief in the subjectivity of literary studies, as shown in his title and by his affinity for Lawrence. Kamei believes that the concepts of "foreign" and "classic" contend with those of "domestic" and "contemporary" and that through this contention comes the energy to destroy the "objective" academic study that has deprived literature of life.

Oi's method is more sociological, strongly influenced by David Noble. Using the historian George Bancroft as a mirror to reflect individual writers' reaction toward the Gilded Age, he examines such novels as Henry Ward Beecher's *Norwood* and J. W. De Forest's *Miss Ravenel's Conversion from Secession to Loyalty.* He divides literary works into two groups, for or against Brancroftian optimism. The concept of children as "innocent saviors" appearing in Horatio Alger's novels, some of Twain's (*Tom Sawyer*), and books of children's literature by Burnett and others is contrasted with the idea of "a helpless child of nature" like Huck Finn. Oi regards the latter as a warning against the abounding optimism in that age and points out the ironical situation in which historians like Bancroft continued to entertain optimistic dreams for the American future, while writers like De Forest, Henry Adams, and Twain regarded the reality of America with pessimistic eyes. Oi says that this situation continues to the present when such writers as Saul Bellow penetrate to the core of the American myth, while some historians speak vaguely, afraid to face the passage of time and social changes. Oi also has written an article that supplements his book "The 'White City' and the American Writer" (*EigoS* 132:62–64). Here Oi thinks it significant that the Columbian Exposition in Chicago and Frederick Jackson Turner's declaration of the exhaustion of the American frontier came in the same year. Discussing W. D. Howells's *Letters of an Altrurian Traveller* and F. H. Burnett's *Two Little Pilgrims' Progress*, Oi proves how the "White City" provided Howells with another kind of American dream in the form of a technological utopia, while Burnett was given a kind of "secret garden."

***a.* Colonial Literature.** Few Japanese scholars have shown interest in the literature of colonial times, perhaps because of the difficulty of getting access to source materials. An exception is Naoki Onishi's "*Of Plymouth Plantation*: The Function of Typology" (*American Review* 22:113–30). First, Onishi points out that Bradford's use of biblical typology is infrequent and limited; he then compares Bradford's use of typology to that of John Winthrop and Edward Johnson. Bradford uses typology not to glorify or justify the Massachusetts Bay Colony, as did the "self-righteous" Winthrop and the "self-justifying" Johnson. Bradford was well aware of the natural disasters and criminal cases that afflicted the settlement, even in the early stage of colonization, but he never interpreted these happenings in terms of providential influence. Onishi contends that this shows Bradford "is open and honest to the dispensation of Providence."

b. **19th-Century Fiction.** Though few in number, the articles on 19th-century writers are interesting. Ryoichi Okada deals with paternity in Cooper's novels in "*Leather-Stocking Tales* and Paternity" (*EigoS* 134:495–97). Okada thinks that Natty's failure to be fathered or to be a father himself, and the lack of blood bondage in general, are expressions of Cooper's fear for the future of America as a country. In "The Hidden Intention of *The Blithedale Romance*" (*EigoS* 134:470–74), Junji Kunishige thinks the novel offers nothing new but is a kind of compilation of what Hawthorne had been doing technically and thematically in previous works; Hawthorne's intention in writing the novel is to perform a ritual of ablution to open up a new artistic sphere, while Coverdale's renunciation of the idea of being a poet is interpreted as a kind of substitute death for the novelist. Whether Hawthorne achieved rebirth through this ritual or not is uncertain, for after *Blithedale* he completed only *The Marble Faun*, which was written under the strong influence of his European experiences. The complex interaction of ambiguities, both biographical and fictional, in and around Melville's *Pierre*—Allan Melville's by-blows, the identity of Ann Allen, Isabel's identity, and Pierre's relationship with Isabel—is observed in Ginsaku Sugiura's "Biography and Text—Melville's *Pierre* Revisited" (*EigoS* 134:393–95). Yoshiko Tomishima's "Maisie through the Looking Glass—Henry James' Mastership" (*EigoS* 134:270–74) is an ambitious attempt to analyze the novel in its historical context. Taking a suggestion from William Veeder's book on James, Tomishima tries to see *What Maisie Knew* from new points of view—forms of popular literature, the topicality of the theme, and children's literature. Through this analysis, James's "mastership" in individuating the forms of popular literature becomes apparent. Tomishima, however, evades a definite conclusion by saying that whether James is a master or not depends on the question of literary canon. Reiko Maekawa's "James Studies Reconsidered—Van Wyck Brooks and F. O. Matthiessen" (*American Review* 22:131–51) is a study not of the novelist, but of two intellectual critics who believed "aesthetic criticism cannot be separated from social and cultural criticism." Maekawa tries to portray the hopes and frustrations toward the American cultural situation felt by the critics through an analysis of their attitudes toward James's Americanness.

What they felt and expressed about the novelist could be considered as typifying the intellectual agony of their time.

Two articles on the literature of the fin de siècle should be mentioned. One is Nobunao Matsuyama's "Henry Adam's Fin de Siècle—Toward the Science of History" (*American Review* 22:1–13), the other Taro Shimada's "The Aesthetics of Fin de Siècle—The Case of Stephen Crane" (*The Emergence of Modern America*, ed. Nagayo Homma, Tokyo University Press, pp. 27–43). In his article Matsuyama explains the significance of the fin de siècle in the life of Henry Adams, who tried to establish a scientific theory of history in the early 20th century. The most crucial year in Adams's life, according to Matsuyama, was 1893, in which three influential events—the panic, the Chicago Exposition, and his acceptance of his brother Brooks's theory of historical law—took place. These experiences prepared Adams to accept the 20th century. Shimada attaches three name tags to Stephen Crane as a writer of the fin de siècle—"naturalism," "impressionism," and "determinism"—and he places the greatest importance on Crane's impressionistic style. Using *The Red Badge of Courage* as a text, Shimada compares Crane's style with De Forest's *Miss Ravenel's Conversion*, Bierce's "Chickamauga," and Hemingway's *A Farewell to Arms*; he finds most of Crane's sentences simple and extremely short. This style, almost devoid of conjunctions of causal relationship such as "because" and "so . . . that," is clear evidence that Crane shares the conception of the limitedness of human perception with other writers of the fin de siècle.

c. 19th-Century Poetry. Two quite different books came out in 1988. Shigenobu Sadoya's *Poe no Meikai Genso* [*Poe's Fantasy of Hades*] (Kokusho-kankokai) is an exposition of Sadoya's unique aesthetics through a study of Poe's poetry. As such, it is too personal to be accepted universally. Sadoya says, "We seek an eternal spiritual bondage with the dead, not a temporal grief." Through an analysis of "The Raven," Sadoya asserts that Poe's poetry gives the illusion of combining the unseeable relationship between life and death with the love of life. *After a Hundred Years: Essays on Emily Dickinson* (Kyoto, Appollon-sha), ed. Emily Dickinson Society of Japan, is very different from Sadoya's book; it is solid, scholarly, and objective. Most of the 17 essays were originally presented at the International Emily Dickinson Centennial Conference at the University of Massachusetts in 1986. The book is divided into three parts: articles on recent trends in Dickinson studies; the relationship between Dickinson and Japanese and Oriental philosophy; and comparative studies of Dickinson. Tsuyoshi Omoto's "Emily Dickinson in Japan," which is an appendix to the book, supplies an extensive survey of the history of Japanese acceptance of Dickinson's poetry. Among the eight essays that make up the first part, Takao Furukawa's "Emily Dickinson's 'Finite Infinity' as a Double Vision" is worth special mention. Furukawa says that the idea of "finite infinity" is Dickinson's "final goal" as a poet and explains the idea of the double vision, using the conception of "circumference," one a vision around self/soul and the other a vision within self/soul. In Toshikazu Niikura's "Dickinson's Poetics: 'Disseminating Their Circumference,' " Niikura characterizes Dickinson as "the first poet to dive into the wreck of modern consciousness in the States." Far from being a confessional poet, she is the most accurate, detached observer of mental disintegration of her time. She is not an "autobiographical" poet, and "in her poems, the signifiers stand for the signifieds, which are also words," Nikura explains. Two studies of fascicles are included in this part: Tamaaki Yamakawa's "Emily Dickinson's Mystic Well—an Aspect of Fascicle 14" and Yoko Shimazaki's " 'Dare you see a Soul at the White Heat?'—a Study of Emily Dickinson's Inner World." Yamakawa notices that fascicle 14 begins with a dream and ends with anguish and thinks that "here is sure to be found Emily Dickinson's own world." Shimazaki sees that Dickinson's concept of the soul changed in the course of her life. By reading her poems following the fascicles as well as chronologically, Shimazaki concludes that "at one time her approach to the soul was almost psychological rather than moral or spiritual," but toward the end of her life it became highly spiritual. The book's second part includes such articles as Katsuhiko Inada's "Emily Dickinson and Japanese Sensibility," which deals with the Japanese way of accepting the poet, and Michiko Iwata's "Something from Nothing in Emily Dickinson's Poetry." Comparing her idea of "nothing" with the idea of "nada" in Oriental philosophy, Iwata points out the complex significance of "nothing" to Dickinson. Mary C. Miller pays attention to the fact that Dickinson's hometown, Amherst, had strong cultural ties with Japan in her time. In "Emily Dickinson's Oriental Heresies," Miller points out the similarities between Dickinson's concept of "enclosure" and the Japanese idea of "withdrawal." Miller also notices some similarities both in Dickinson and Japanese arts and literature in the use of intuition. However, Miller's conclusion that "Emily Dickinson's art and Japanese art have much in common" sounds a bit too facile. Masako Takeda tells of the difficulty she has faced translating Dickinson's poems into Japanese. Illustrating the problem by juxtaposing the Japanese translation with the original of "That I did always love" (p. 549), Takeda shows how Dickinson's poems resist translation. The third part of the book, which contains four comparative studies of Dickinson's poetry, is the most interesting. In " 'O, rare for Emily'—Dickinson and *Antony and Cleopatra,*" Keiko Beppu proves, through an examination of the text, Dickinson's letters, and other personal papers, that Shakespeare's Roman tragedy served as a catalyst to crystallize Dickinson's concept of love—a "love which is inextricably associated with death and immortality." Sachiko Yoshida's "Revolt Against the Absolute: Two Massachusetts Bay Colony Women Poets" compares Dickinson's poems with those of Anne Bradstreet; she defines the two poets' concept of immortality. As a whole, *After a Hundred Years* is a solid scholarly work, worthy of the centennial celebration.

d. **20th-Century Fiction.** The interest in southern writers is strong this year—three books and eight articles. However, several pioneering studies also have been done on other writers. In his article "Japanese Seen by Frank Norris" (*EigoS* 134:428–29), Kenji Inoue indicates the importance of historical context in the study of literature. He points out that, although Norris as an Anglo-Saxonist entertained a strong prejudice against nonwhite peoples, he treated the Japanese favorably in his novels. Inoue seeks the reason for this exception in a historical event—the Japanese victory over China in the Sino-Japanese War—and suspects that this victory might have corresponded with the idea that the superior race should govern the inferior, an idea that Norris shared with a majority of American whites of the time. Tadatoshi Saito's *Sinclair Lewis Joron—Ronko to Tekisuto Kenkyu* [*An Introduction to Sinclair Lewis—Studies and Textual Analysis*] (Ohshi-sha) is the first book on the novelist by a single writer. (A collection of critical essays was published in 1968.) Saito includes several critical essays dealing with the question of the "small town" in Lewis's novels, the influence of time, the process of the composition of *Main Street,* and Lewis's attitude toward racial questions. A charming essay on Saito's own visit to Sauk Centre is included. Although the topics may seem scattered, this part serves as an informative introduction to Lewis's world. The book's second half consists of textual studies. Saito traces the process of the composition of *Dodsworth* by comparing the finished novel with various manuscripts. Daiwa Izu's *Fitzgerald no Chohen-shosetsu* [*Fitzgerald's Novels*] (Ohshi-sha) justifies the biographical approach to Fitzgerald's longer fiction. Izu concludes that the novelist grasps the social condition around him intuitively and sensitively and then fictionalizes and historicizes what he perceives. Nobuaki Namiki's article "Thomas Sutpen and Jay Gatsby—Men Haunted by Dreams" (*EigoS* 134:128–32) examines the relationship between *The Great Gatsby* and "The Diamond as Big as the Ritz" and *Absalom, Absalom!* Namiki explains that Thomas Sutpen, Bradock Washington, and Jay Gatsby all possess "American innocence"; they choose to live fictional lives after their traumatic encounters with the rich, and so they never grow up spiritually. Although Namiki's point has some interest, it is regretable that he lacks the historical and social perspective to give it a deeper significance.

Book-length critical studies of Faulkner, Thomas Wolfe, Flannery O'Connor, and Eudora Welty were published in 1988. Katsuji Niki's *Faulkner no "Seikimatsu" to "Girisha no Tsubo"* [*Faulkner and the Literature of the Fin de Siècle and "Ode on a Grecian Urn"*] (Bunkashobo Hakubun-sha) first deals with the influences on Faulkner given by such fin-de-siècle poets, painters, and critics as Mallarmé, Swinburne, Housman, D. G. Rossetti, Pater, Beardsley, and Wilde. Niki observes the evidence of their influence in Faulkner's conception of time in his novels. The second part, "Keats and Faulkner," examines the influence of Keats's poems, especially "Ode on a Grecian Urn," on Faulkner's work from *The Marble Faun* to *The Mansion*. Keats's influence is quite obvious, but however much Faulkner was infatuated, there were essential differences between them. Niki's book seems to miss that point when he tries, for example, to explain Miss Emily Grierson's weird act as that of a transcendental, immortal love; Faulkner's grotesqueness can never be explained in this way. However, to see Faulkner through the literary personages of the fin de siècle may well open up a new aspect of Faulkner studies. In "Faun, Puppet and Pierrot; Some Basic Imagery in Faulkner" (*SALit* 25:51–66), Takako Tanaka asserts that Faulkner uses such common literary images as faun and puppet—"two images indicating man's battle against time"—to establish his own artistic vision. Rosa Coldfield is given a respectable place in Nobuaki Namiki's "Miss Rosa Coldfield in *Absalom, Absalom!*" (*SALit* 25:67–82). Namiki defines the role of

Miss Rosa as giving "one of the true aspects of [Sutpen] as he is absorbed in realizing his design."

Hiroshi Tsunemoto's *Aru Shosetsuka no Monogatari–Thomas Wolfe Hito to Sakuhin* [*A Novelist's Story: Thomas Wolfe–Man and Work*], published 50 years after the novelist's death, is the first on Wolfe to appear in Japan. The book supplies extensive information on Wolfe, with an analytical explanation of his work and an introduction to the status of Wolfe studies in the States. To supplement his book, Tsunemoto wrote an article on Wolfe in *EigoS*, "Thomas Wolfe: The End of the Kicking Season" (*EigoS* 134:439–41). Here, he surveys outstanding critical books on Wolfe by David Donald, Leslie Field, and John Idol; he concludes that the "kicking season" of Wolfe studies has come to an end. Hajime Noguchi's *Flannery O'Connor no Sekai* [*The World of Flannery O'Connor*] (Bunka-shobo Hakubunsha) is a handy introduction to the novels and stories. Noguchi's intention is to prove that O'Connor's starting point as a writer was not her experiences in her native town of Milledgeville, Georgia, but her experiences at the University of Iowa. Though a bit unconvincing on this point, Noguchi provides a thorough exposition of the background and contents of O'Connor's fiction. Ichiro Inoue's "'Parker's Back' and F. O'Connor's Artistic Problems" (*SELit* 65:33–45) deals with the question of "conversion" in O'Connor's stories. Conversion is too personal, supernatural, and mysterious an experience to be expressed in words, Inoue thinks, and this story is O'Connor's attempt to perform an almost impossible task. He concludes that O'Connor succeeded by dramatizing the spiritual changes in a visible form–in this case, a tattoo. Naoko F. Thornton's *Eudora Welty no Sekai* [*The World of Eudora Welty*] (Kobian-shobo) is a well-organized and persuasive book, which provides a biography and expositions of individual works. What gives unity is Thornton's view of Welty's work as in the stream of biblical, Greek, and Roman mythology, the archetypes of Western civilization. Thornton concludes, "Welty sees in the lives of the obscure people in her work something heroic and supreme, similar to that seen in the lives of the mythological heroes." What lies at the bottom of Walker Percy's novels is clearly shown by a comparison with a Faulkner novel in Ikuko Fujihira's "Beyond Quentin Compson's Ghost–A New Cosmos for Walker Percy's Novels" (*SALit* 25:83–102). Although born with the same kind of social background, Percy's Will Barrett in *The Last Gentleman* differs distinctly from Quentin Compson in that he tries to separate himself from haunted memories of the past. Fujihira points out that, in this way, Will is able to discover "a new cosmos of light, hope and the future."

Only one article on black literature was published. Hiromi Furukawa's "The Agony and Glory of James Baldwin" (*EigoS* 134:65–66) is a tribute to the versatile novelist who died in December 1987. Furukawa traces Baldwin's agony as an artist who could not ignore the social iniquities around him. Nabokov has never been a popular writer in Japan, but he is critically attractive as an experimenter. Michiko Maruyama uses reader-response theory in "Narrative Strategy and Its Failure in a Dramatized Confession—On the Former Section of Nabokov's *Lolita*" (*SALit* 25:119–35). Iwao Iwamoto's *Gendai Amerika Sakka no Sekai* [*The World of the Contemporary American Writers*] (Liber Press) is a collection of essays Iwamoto has been writing over the past 15 years on Malamud, Updike, John Barth, Mailer, Bellow, John Gardner, Kesey, Roth, Castaneda, and Brautigan. At the end come two dialogues Iwamoto had with Ihab Hassan and Tony Tanner, two noted scholars of American literature, one from an Egyptian and the other from a British cultural background. Iwamoto also writes a tribute on the death of Raymond Carver ("Raymond Carver's Novels—Immortality in Dailiness" [*EigoS* 134:492–94]); Iwamoto explains that the charm of the fiction lies in the fact that Carver, in spite of his knowledge that human existence is almost "unbearably light," saw immortal value in the dailiness of ordinary people. The literature of minimalism is a fad in Japan. In the January issue of *EigoS* there was a feature on it that consisted of a round-table talk by Iwao Iwamoto, Masao Shimura, and Konomi Ara, and four critical essays (*EigoS* 133:470–90). The talk gives a precise, skillful definition of minimalism, its social background, and its representative writers. Yoshiaki Koshikawa sums up the characteristics of Carver's art in "Raymond Carver and the Aesthetics of Short Stories." "Precise language" and a technical strictness like that of an artisan, as well as the elimination of dramatic effect and the adaptation of nonprivileged narration, produce the charm of Carver's stories, he says. Tobias Wolfe and Frederick Barthelme are discussed in Kenji Kobayashi's "Minimalists of the Vietnam Generation," while Ann Beattie's *Love Always* is regarded as a novel that suggests the future transformation of minimalism in Takaki Hiraishi's "The Poetics of Bubbles." Yoshiaki Sato's "Minimalism and Postmodern Spirit" sums up the situation: "good writers begin to produce enjoyable works, and a certain, though not large, number of constant readers are reading them; nothing more exciting and fabulous can be found in the world of literature."

e. **20th-Century Poetry.** Compared to 19th-century poetry, the 20th-century critical product was sparse this year. In *Robert Frost Ronko—The Figure a Poem Makes* [*A Study of Robert Frost*] (Kokubun-sha), Toshio Komamura defines Frost as an idyllic poet. Referring to about 140 poems, and comparing them with works of Chinese, Japanese, and European poets, writers, and philosophers, Komamura traces the development of an Arcadian philosophy. Junnosuke Sawasaki's "A Master and His Disciple—Pound and Eliot" (*EigoS* 134:383–85) observes Pound's influence on Eliot and how it affected Eliot's work. Sawasaki says that the publication of *The Waste Land* marked the liberation of Eliot from his master's influence. Eliot's later development is considered in Keiko Saeki's "From Poetry to Drama—T. S. Eliot in the Early Thirties" (*SALit* 25:33–49). Saeki contends that Eliot felt his capacities as a poet were exhausted in the early 1930s, but the favorable response to *Murder in the Cathedral* allowed him to pass through this crisis. His success gave him confidence in his ability to expand his activities as poet, dramatist, and critic. Wallace Stevens's resistance against the romantic, lyrical reading of his poems is observed in Tetsuo Koga's "Transcendence or Decreation—Some Notes on 'Abstraction' in Wallace Stevens Later Poetry" (*SALit* 25:17–31). Koga explains that Stevens's poems exist in "the marginal area where imagination and facts do not function reciprocally."

f. **20th-Century Drama.** The centennial of Eugene O'Neill's birth was celebrated by a feature in the November issue of *EigoS* (134:409–21). Mamoru Uchino in "O'Neill's Melodramatism" discusses how in the 1920s, when O'Neill was a popular Broadway playwright, he tried to satisfy the intellectual curiosity of his audience by the use of Greek tragedies; through analysis of *Desire Under the Elms*, Uchino shows how, under the surface of "high art," O'Neill uses melodramatic devices to please the taste of the bourgeois audience. In "*Hughie* as a Performance Text," Kazuo Ichinose sees an anticipation of modern absurd drama. Ichinose draws his conclusion from the play's unusual stage directions, which include interior monologues and psychological descriptions. Koji Ishizuka's "The Absence of the Author in an Autobiographical Play—*Long Day's Journey into Night* Reconsidered" takes up the problem of points of view. Ishizuka thinks that by discarding his own "ego" and adopting multiple viewpoints, O'Neill was able to liberate the play from the playwright's dominance. Consequently, he was able to make it highly realistic. A literary lineage of fauns in American literature beginning with Hawthorne and continuing through Melville, Whitman, O'Neill, and Faulkner is observed in Shuji Muto's "O'Neill and Faun." The last article in this feature is Toshiko Kusuhara's "The History of the Acceptance of O'Neill's Plays in Japan," in which the history of translations and productions is traced. *SALit* also carries an article on O'Neill, Akira Ito's "Literary Study and Biographical Information—The Case of Eugene O'Neill" (*SALit* 25:1–16). Ito observes how O'Neill's Irish heritage, the New England milieu, and his family experiences influenced his plays. Ito concludes that biographical information not only gives a richer, more intelligent understanding of literary works, but also helps reveal the creator's inner symbolic world.

g. Critical Theories. Although great attention has been paid to recent critical theories (feminist, deconstructionist, New Historicist), surprisingly few articles under such influences were published in 1988. This reflects the dilemma facing many Japanese scholars: they are interested, yet distressed by the variety and speed of change in the fashion of critical theories. Tadanori Iwase's "On Eliot's Criticism of James" (*EigoS* 134:386–88) deals with the question of how Henry James was regarded by Pound and Eliot. Both Eliot and James chose England as their home, and in their literary critical theory they have much in common—their emphasis on "observation" and sense of history. Iwase thinks these qualities sprang from their New England cultural heritage. Eiichiro Ohtsu defines modernism as a reaction against naturalism in "Modernism and Naturalism" (*EigoS* 134:402–04). Yoko Imaizumi's "Harold Bloom and Feminist Criticism" (*EigoS* 134:281–83) is the only article on contemporary criticism. Though Bloom is often regarded as a patriarchal critic who eliminates women completely and adopts a misogynistic attitude, Imaizumi points out an interesting similarity between Bloom's strategy in resisting bourgeois deconstructionists and that adopted by feminist critics in their attack on patriarchal criticism. Through this analysis, Imaizumi's article becomes a concise survey of feminist criticism.

Japanese scholarly interest in American literature was as avid as ever in 1988, and two interesting works that are currently being serialized in *EigoS* were to be completed sometime in 1989. One is Masao Shimura's "American Literature and Mysticism"; the other is Shunsuke Kamei's "The Lineage of the American Hero." Shimura's article began to appear in the June issue; Charles Brockden Brown, Jonathan Edwards, Hawthorne, and Thoreau have thus far been discussed. Kamei's series started in November; so far it has given a general survey of the history of hero worship in America and the conception of the "American Adam" in the wilderness. These two studies will receive full treatment in next year's report.

Tokyo Woman's Christian University

vi. Scandinavian Contributions

Jan Nordby Gretlund, Elisabeth Herion-Sarafidis, Hans Skei

The Scandinavian work in American literature during 1988 was mostly of a traditional nature. As usual, T. S. Eliot among American poets received the lion's share of attention, but Afro-American poetry was also introduced and considered. There is in Scandinavia an increased emphasis on seeing literature from a feminist point of view, this year in essays by men. The poet H.D. was singled out (together with Willa Cather) as a female modernist and subjected to a myth-oriented feminist critical approach, Djuna Barnes was praised for her imagist poetics, and the fate of "the American Girl" in male and female novels was brought to our attention. The preoccupation with a usable and viable past in American literature spawned essays on Henry James and Carlos Fuentes, Nathaniel Hawthorne and his Salem, John Dos Passos and the Russian novelist Andrei Bely. But Ernest Hemingway is still the most discussed American novelist in Scandinavia, in 1988 for his attitude to the father figure and male sexuality, his stance during the Spanish Civil War, and the codes of courage and will to survive. William Faulkner was considered for his use of humor, and Wright Morris for his creation of the photo-novel. There was some work on the reception of American literature in Scandinavia, and solid work on Scandinavian immigrant literature.

Jørgen Dines Johansen has written a long and ambitious essay on "T. S. Eliot's lyrik og litteratursyn" *Krystalgitteret: Den lyriske genres funktion* [The Crystal Lattice: the Function of Lyrical Poetry] (Odense) pp. 295–344. It is provocative in the tradition of Eliot himself. Johansen considers several of his essays and most of his poetry not only to point out what he finds worth celebrating, but primarily to tell us what should be rejected. It is an uneven effort, as the essay is both a very basic explanation of some of Eliot's ideas and a sophisticated and erudite attack on Eliot for the ways in which he used poetry. The essay opens and ends with a strong rejection of Eliot's conservative ideology: "How unpleasant to meet Mr. Eliot!" This is a well-documented attack that unfortunately deteriorates into self-revealing generalizing comments on "the narrowminded complacency of the Anglo-Saxon higher middle class." Johansen dwells on Eliot's definitions of poetry, the poet and language, the "dated" values and norms implied in the essays, the opposition between feeling/image vs. emotion/situation, the concept of the objective correlative, the idea of a dissociation of sensibility, and Eliot's thoughts on the individual poem and poetic tradition. In short, the essay attempts to cover Eliot's thinking on the creation, the form, the reading, the use, and the purpose of poetry.

The section on meditative verse is by far the best. Johansen admires the accepted classics of the Eliot canon. The Prufrock poem is analyzed in detail once again, and *The Waste Land* is read with the usual point of departure in the Grail story. The latter poem is called "heavy modernism" and "problematic," as the implied traditions are no longer felt as obligating and vital forces and because the poem is so hermetic that its ability to communicate can be called in doubt. Johansen singles out some passages for praise, e.g., the first part of "A Game of Chess." But he considers *Four Quartets* the crowning achievement of Eliot's meditative verse for its perfect and mature control, the universality of the theme, and the choice of the grand form that permits the rich modulation of theme. Considerable space is devoted to a convincing and useful reading of the poem, and the analysis is capped by a successful attempt to schematize the major themes and structure. Johansen accords *The Hollow Men* and *Ash-Wednesday* a mere mention, presumably for reasons of space; yet at the end he finds it worthwhile to repeat his attack on Eliot for conservatism and dogmatic Anglo-Catholicism. He finally considers Eliot's thinking unacceptable, which does not prevent him from appreciating the "inestimable" poetry that in its tension records the existential struggle and anxiety behind the thinking.

In his "The Setting of 'The Lovesong of J. Alfred Prufrock,'" *A Literary Miscellany Presented to Eric Jacobsen,* (P.D.E. Copenhagen, 16:304–14), Henrik Rosenmeier argues that Boston provides the poem with both framework and narrative coherence. Rosenmeier sees Prufrock as a true Bostonian "with respect to language, habit of thought and preoccupations." He compares Eliot's poem to Henry James's "Crapy Cornelia" and *The Bostonians*, describes the physical as well as psychological charts of Boston and Cambridge in both writers, and concludes that if the novel is "a brilliant social satire" on Boston and its high-mindedness, "Eliot's poem is at least in part a dirge on the same theme." Rosenmeier finally points out that what happens to Western Christianity and culture in *The Waste Land* is modeled on the vision of Boston's decay.

Olav Angell's *Masker og rytmer* [Masks and Rhythms] (Solum 1987) is a collection of translated Afro-American poetry from 1960 to 1985. The collection includes poems by Imamu A. Baraka, Alice Walker, James Baldwin, Sonia Sanchez, Etheridge Knight, Nikki Giovanni, Ishmael Reed, Langston Hughes, and many others. In "Black Is Beautiful," a preface by Olav Angell, who has translated much American literature from after 1960, a historical outline is offered of black American writing from the beginning, and Angell presents some of the most important black writers. In his conclusion he asserts that Afro-American poetry is structured in accordance with the "beat" of modern jazz. John Coltrane's music and the traditional blues are seen as closely associated with modern black American poetry.

Wishing to throw light on "the basic preconditions for female modernist art," Mark Troy juxtaposes Willa Cather and H.D. in "Secret Name: The Creative Realm of the Female Modernist" (*MSpr* 3:202–10). In their search for a muse to "embody the force or desire enabling—or driving—them to create," these two modernist writers have, Troy argues, enlisted the aid of ancient Egyptian lore, especially the goddess Isis. As female artists, their struggle was to redefine themselves, first as women and then as artists, to break loose from confining "patriarchal evaluations," and to fight the male version of "HER." A myth-oriented feminist approach such as Troy's might prove illuminating when applied to the work of the consciously experimental modernist poet H.D., but the success of the approach is more questionable in the case of the more conventional novelist Willa Cather, who only rarely made use of Egyptian mythology. The work of another original female writer, Djuna Barnes's *Nightwood* (1936), is the subject of Leif Dahlberg's perceptive "Nattens anatomi" [Anatomy of the Night] (*Tidskrift för litteraturvetenskap* 1:44–62). Seeking "the intention" of *Nightwood* (available in Swedish translation since 1954), Dahlberg focuses first on temporal relations, finding outer "objective" time to be of secondary importance to the characters' inner time, and then on what he sees as the imagist poetics of the novel. He concludes that the purpose of the novel, which is subtitled "anatomy of night," is to reveal the true nature of the night, it is "an exegesis of the anatomy of the night."

In his brief essay about "The American Girl from Howells to Chopin" (*ArAA* 13, ii:183–92), Per Seyersted traces the creation and further development of what has become known as "the American Girl" from William Dean Howells's *A Chance Acquaintance* (1873) to Kate Chopin's *The Awakening* (1899) and Chopin's even more outspoken story "The Storm." Seyersted shows the influence of European realism on American literature from 1870 to 1900, and he follows the fragile and rather limited literary creation "the American Girl" in books by Howells, James, Garland, Boyesen, Crane, and Dreiser. The development of a female character with a will of her own, who may even consider having a career instead of being married or trying to combine the two, is very limited in writings by men. Seyersted shows that it is much more noticeable in the writings of female authors of the same period, but only in works by Charlotte Perkins Gilman and Kate Chopin were the portraits of girls and women convincing and radically new. Seyersted argues that it was not until after World War II that the American Girl "was allowed to reach again and surpass that level of self-expression which was pioneered by [Mary Wilkins] Freeman, Gilman, and above all Chopin."

Helle Porsdam's "The Search for Identity—An Analysis of Henry James' 'The Aspern Papers' and Carlos Fuentes' *Aura*" (*AmerSS* 20: 27–39) takes its point of departure in Van Wyck Brooks's influential essay "On Creating a Usable Past" (1918). Brooks's essay deals with the topic that Porsdam wants to consider: "the need for the New World writer to create for himself a usable past upon which an American—whether North or Latin American—identity can be built." In the plot of *Aura* (1962) she recognizes the basic components of "The Aspern Papers" (1887). Porsdam argues convincingly that in spite of certain obvious differences, an essential issue for both James and Fuentes is that "the past can be creatively [re]constructed." This year also bears witness to the long-standing Swedish interest in Nathaniel Hawthorne. In "Hawthorne i häxornas och sjöfararnas Salem" [Hawthorne in the Salem of Witches and Seafarers] (*Horisont* 1:40–57), Jöran Mjöberg offers a reading of *The House of the Seven Gables*, a novel "obsessed by secrets." Salem's economic and social background of the time are emphasized.

Carl Pedersen's "Unreal Cities East and West: Bely's *Petersburg* and Dos Passos's *Manhattan Transfer*" (*AmerSS* 20:51–68) is a comparison of the image of Petersburg and New York. It argues that the images reflect in intensified form the situation of Russian and American culture during a period of profound crisis. Pedersen sees the two novels as attempts "to embrace and comprehend the kaleidoscopic nature of modern urbanism while recoiling from its implications." Bely and Dos Passos are supposed to have seen the unreality of their cities as a result of "a cognitive lapse in which beliefs no longer conform to the visual environment"; continuity snapped, and man was left without a meaningful past and without cultural reference points. The resulting anxiety is expressed in the two novels "in apocalyptic terms."

Harly Sonne and Christian Grambye use Hemingway's "Indian Camp" as the object for their analysis in "3-D: Fortælling og forløb," *Det fortaltes forløb*, ed. S. B. Jensen et al. (Basilisk) 8–39. After a survey of recent attempts at developing the Greimas and Rastier model, the authors demonstrate that traditional models of analysis and psychology-oriented additions tend to limit the crisis of a narrative to a point in the model with no consideration of its duration and possible internal structure. To overcome this problem, the authors suggest a triple rotation within the model. Nick Adams is the object who is transported in the suggested gender-oriented psychological model. The father's failure as a figure of authority is seen as the central fact of the story, as it leads to a focus on masculinity. The father fails to explain Uncle George's role in the tragic events. The authors claim that Uncle George is the father of the new-born baby and that this is the reason for the Indian husband's suicide. But Dr. Adams does not explain male sexuality to Nick; sexual urge is denied, and its role remains unintegrated. Nick is not initiated into an order, the argument continues; facts of life and death are withheld from him and he is locked in his position as a child without a chance to mature and accept his sex. As proof, the authors suggest a connection between the interchapter that precedes "Indian Camp" in the collection

("Everybody was drunk." etc.), in which Nick is still immature, has not come to terms with his masculinity, and still does not accept the presence of death. The use of the model helps the reader focus on the structure and duration of the crisis, but it fails to bring up anything new. Uncle George's probable role in the story was already described in Scandinavia in June 1975 by Erik Arne Hansen, *Meddelelser fra Gymnasieskolernes Engelsklærerforening* (Gyldendal), pp. 1–21.

Erik Arne Hansen's "Ernest Hemingway's the Fall of Troy in Spain" (*The Dolphin*, Aarhus, 16:54–87) confirms the continued Scandinavian interest in this writer's changing political awareness during the 1930s. Hansen offers an impressive reading of *For Whom the Bell Tolls*. In a well-argued assay that continues the discussion in Bent Haugaard Jeppesen's *Hemingway i hamskifte* (*ALS 1987*, pp. 492–93), Hansen argues that the novel can be profitably seen as "a complex, symbolic gesture" in which Hemingway tried to integrate "his artistic, personal, and political concerns at the time." According to this essay, Hemingway was always "a Middle American Republican" or "an apolitical Republic." Hansen traces the development of Hemingway's political thought before 1936 and concludes that Hemingway's alignment with the Left in Spain was caused also by marital and artistic problems. The essay evaluates the American mood during the Spanish Civil War, a summary of Hemingway's reasons for going to Spain (his problems with friends in the bullfighting world who were *for* Franco), and a reading of *The Fifth Column* as "a propaganda piece" that is primarily interesting for the possible biographical references. Hansen attempts to relate some of the fictional characters to historical figures of the war.

The analysis of *For Whom the Bell Tolls* is based on the idea that Hemingway had no desire to assign guilt to any individual officers for the miscarried Segovia offensive of May 1937: "the betrayal that pervades the novel as theme is ubiquitous and general in nature." Hansen considers Hemingway's handling of place, time, and perspective and concludes that it is "both journalism and fiction," both a personal reconstruction and "impersonal art above time." Robert Jordan's "ephebic education" through the various code characters is considered. Jordan is seen "as a political innocent abroad," for in spite of the novel's ideology, he is not a thinker; he is a bridge blower and he is ready for martyrdom. According to Hansen, there is more Freud than Marx in Jordan's make-up. The strength of this essay is its wealth of biographical, historical, and political information. Hansen demonstrates that with this novel the personal was becoming political for Hemingway, and he shows that the transmutation of the personal into art remains too sectional, the intellectual message too muted, and "the hymn to love, trust and brotherhood" too unconvincing to be fully successful. Hansen is probably right in seeing the novel as Hemingway's means toward a clarification of his stance in 1939–40, but if Hemingway was seeking the meaning of his experience of the war and his doomed idealism with the aid of his art, it is unfair (and this is the essay's weakness) to evaluate his novel primarily in terms of biography, political history, and ideology; for "there are no real people in this volume," as Hemingway warned in the colophon of *In Our Time.*

Daniel Anderson's "Om livsdyrkan och Nada hos Ernest Hemingway" [On the Worship of Life and Nada in Ernest Hemingway] (*Horisont* 6:45–57) is partly an attempt to illuminate the correspondence between the style Hemingway chiseled out for himself and the fictional world he created, and partly an exploration of the way in which the various protagonists handle the struggle for survival and their efforts to find some means to anchor their existence. Anderson points to the systematic portrayal of man as a creature of action whose full potential goes unrealized until he is forced into demonstrating his courage and his unique will to survive.

Hans Skei's essay "The Humor of William Faulkner" (*AmerSS* 20:83–89) sets out to prove that humor is an important aspect of Faulkner's writings. To perceive in Faulkner's long career a development from pessimism to optimism, from despair to acceptance, is seen as a career fallacy, since the comic is present in Faulkner's work from the beginning. Quoting from the Al Jackson letters (*The Hamlet* and *The Reivers*), Skei argues that the comic has varied central functions in Faulkner's work. It is often of the hyperbolic kind, but one may distinguish between the comic effects in stories by oral storytellers and the use of humor to achieve comic relief. Speculating, finally, on why he used comic effects so pervasively, Skei suggests that Faulkner may have used humor "to soften the impact of harsh criticism, to abate the agony of being alive and being a writer."

David E. Nye writes about the gray area between fiction and photography in his "'Negative Capability' in Wright Morris' *The Home Place*" (*W&I* 3, i:163–69). After a short introduction to the genre of the photo-novel, Nye considers *The Home Place* (1948) for its "self-consciously Jamesian" exploitation of point of view. The novel, which recounts a day in and around a farm, demonstrates Morris's "intimate knowledge of farm life." Although the novel has 90 photographs and only 88 pages of text Nye does not consider it a documentary novel; instead, it is "a series of discreet visions." As the photos are unnamed and unframed, they are not illustrations and do not have a stable relation to the text: "text and image offer the reader/ viewer the chance to infer the reality of *The Home Place* by triangulation." That the photo-novel will lose its subject with the passage of time and therefore become a story that cannot be continued in spite of the hyperrealism of the photos, Nye sees as a confirmation of the inadequacy of realism, "even when photography supplements language."

Jan Nordby Gretlund's "The American Within: Danes and American Literature" [Copenhagen: U.S. Information Service, 1989] is about the American literary canon from a Danish perspective. After introductory remarks on Danish-American relations since 1865, Gretlund considers the various forces that decide whether an American book is published in a Danish translation: publishers, translators, reviewers, book clubs, public libraries, academic critics. The essay enumerates the larger groupings of the canon in Denmark: the classics (Poe and Twain), the modern classics (Eliot, Hemingway, Fitzgerald), the southerners (Faulkner, O'Connor, Percy), the bestsellers (Updike, Oates, Le Guin, Vonnegut), the Jewish school (Bellow, Heller, Roth) the Beat writers (Ginsberg, Snyder, Burroughs), and the black writers (Walker, Morrison, Naylor). The essay concludes that despite constant efforts to market new writers, the canon in Denmark is surprisingly stable. "There is an obvious canon of the most widely read and studied, the best-received and the best-selling American writers, which clearly reflects the Danish sense of what American literature is."

The Norwegian emigrant experience in the United States has been the subject of numerous works of fiction, and it has also become a central concern for Scandinavian historians and literary scholars within the fields of American and Scandinavian studies. Ingeborg R. Kongslien *Draumen om fridom og jord* [The Dream of Freedom and Soil] (*Edda* 4:291–315 and Norske Samlaget, 1989). Kongslien's books deal with the emigrant novel, but she includes a consideration of O. E. Rölvaag, whose position in Norwegian-American literature is so obvious that although he is not the major figure in the study, the problematic nature of his position in the book's structure threatens to dwarf Kongslien's major concerns. From the point of view of American literary scholarship, only the chapters on Rölvaag are important.

In "Scandinavian-American Literature: The Last Phase" (*Cross-Cultural Studies: American, Canadian and European Literatures: 1945–1985* (Ljubjana) 371–78), Dorothy Burton Skårdal states that Scandinavian-American literature in their own languages completed most of its development before World War II, and that it peaked around the turn of the century. But Skårdal brings to light two overlooked Scandinavian-American writers who have published books of literary quality in their native languages: a collection of poetry by the Swedish-born Arthur Landfors, *Träd* [Trees] (1962), and a novel by the Danish-born Enok Mortensen titled *Den lange plovfure* [The Long Furrow] (1984). Skårdal gives biographical information, quotes extensively in translation from Landfors's poetry, and discusses the theme and structure of Mortensen's novel. The two books interpret the immigrant experience in different ways: Landfors emphasizes loss, whereas Mortensen's experience as a minister in strong Danish-American communities can be seen in his novel of alienation and faith. Skårdal comments that more than 40 years after he wrote it, Mortensen rewrote his novel and published it in Danish in Copenhagen. Skårdal also argues that "historians are justified in using such poems [by Landfors] as source material even though much, perhaps most, of their beauty is lost in the process." Even if literature is hardly a question of source material or beauty (either/or), this essay provides a good introduction to the last phase of Scandinavian-American literature.

Odense, Uppsala, Oslo Universities

vii. Spanish Contributions

José Antonio Gurpegui

In this initial Spanish contribution to *American Literary Scholarship* it seems appropriate to briefly review the study of North American literature in Spain.

The first course in North American literature was offered in 1965 at the University of Zaragoza. Thirteen years earlier Francisco Yndurain published *España en la obra de Hemingway* (Zaragoza: Publicaciones de la Facultad de Filosofía y Letras, 1952), a pamphlet of historical significance and indicative of the criticism that was to follow as Hemingway, the presence of Spain in the works of American authors, and the relationship between these and my compatriots, have been a constant presence in the Spanish critical approach to American literature.

Cándido Pérez Gállego and Javier Coy were among the first Spanish scholars to initiate studies of American literature. In 1966 Pérez Gállego published *El héroe solitario en la novela norteamericana,* (Madrid: Prensa, Española, 1966), the first serious study—and still of interest—of authors such as Melville, Hawthorne, Thoreau, Anderson, Faulkner, Hemingway, and Bellow.

In 1967 Javier Coy and Juan José Coy published *Teatro norteamericano actual: Miller, Inge, Albee* (Madrid: Prensa Española, 1967). More critical works appeared in the following years: Leopoldo Mateo, *Stephen Crane en el marco naturalista* (Madrid: Complutense, 1975); María Lozano, *El tema del regreso en la literatura norteamericana* (Zaragoza: Departamento de Inglés, 1977); Susana Onega, *Análisis estructural, método narrativo y sentido de* The Sound and the Fury *by William Faulkner* (Zaragoza: Libros Pórtico, 1979); Catalina Montes, *La visión de España en la obra de John Dos Passos* (Salamanca: Almar, 1980); Enrique García, *John Barth: el artifício de la técnica narrativa* (Salamanca: Almar, 1982); Bernd Dietz, *Tres calas en la novela norteamericana del siglo XX* (Madrid: Origines, 1985); José María Bardavio, *Fantasias uterinas en la literatura norteamericana* (Zaragoza: Libros Pórtico, 1987); and my own *Pequeña comunidad en la novela norteamericana* (Madrid: Complutense, 1987). An outcome of this activity was a growing interest in American authors among university students and general readers. At present, the writings of the most siginficant American authors have been translated into Spanish, as well as books by younger, lesser-known writers; however, very few critical works can be found in Spanish translation, a situation that has made histories of American literature indispensable. *Literatura norteamericana actual* de Cándido Pérez Gállego, Félix Martín, and Leopoldo Mateo (Madrid: Cátedra, 1986) is cited most often. This year the prolific Cándido Pérez Gállego published *Historia de la literatura norteamericana* (Madrid: Taurus), a historical survey that investigates the interrelation between different authors.

Parallel with the growth in interest and critical publications, mainly through university presses, more and more symposiums and conferences have taken place. This trend is reflected at the annual AEDEAN conference (Asociación Española de estudios anglo–norteamericanos). There is at present no American studies association, but steps to establish such an association are taking place; in previous years the University of Salamanca, where there is a Walt Whitman Institute, and the University of Valencia have organized conferences in American studies. In 1987 the University of Alcalá de Henares, in collaboration with the U.S. embassy, established CENUAH (Centro de Estudios Norteamericanos de la Universidad de Alcalá de Henares), the first center of American studies in Spain.

a. **Fiction.** In his comprehensive introduction to *Relatos* by Edgar Allan Poe (Madrid: Cátedra, 9–119), Félix Martín presents one of the year's most interesting studies, replacing Ramón Gómez de la Serna's obsolete *Edgar Allan Poe: El genio de América* (Buenos Aires: Losada, 1953). Félix Martín does not assess the artistic merits of Poe's work but limits himself to analyze various critical approaches, from Baudelaire to Shoshana Felman, including T. S. Eliot, Harold Bloom, and others. Felman's theories are essential to understanding Martín's perception of Poe. Martín proposes a new reading in which he goes beyond the merely aesthetic to give the contemporary reader a series of critical clues, the most important being the approach to Poe's persona through his use of language; the alphabetic characters can be understood as a decipherable system of hieroglyphs. Examining *The Narrative of Arthur Gordon Pym*, the theory reveals its essentially Viconian structure. Félix Martín argues that "a narrative trajectory as this one will not detain us in a concrete and fixed historical moment as the beginning and the end of the narrative merge. The return, then, to the original written enigmas, has as objective to situate the reader in an indeterminate historic, linguistic, and philosophical region in an original condition in which man's destiny and that of the universe merge."

Poe is also studied by Mónica Papazu in "Man, A Thought of God: An Essay on Poe's Tales" (*Atlantis* 10, i–ii:107–20), an essay that probes into the question of human identity. Papazu perceives language to be fundamental to the study of this identity, a dilemma that can be understood by confronting man with God or with his equals. She demonstrates how Poe's work comes close to the philosophy of Spinoza in which a pantheistic identification between God and the world exists; according to Papazu, spirit and matter become one in Poe's work. Abelardo Castillo published "Hesse, Poe, Lorca" (*CHA* 459:79–86). The title suggests a comparative study; however, Poe in this case is "the other Poe," that is, Charlie Chaplin. Castillo argues that Poe and Chaplin resembled each other physically and suggests that Chaplin was the dialectical resurrection of Poe.

Henry James is one of the best-known American authors in Spain. In 1975 Cándido Pérez Gállego devoted the most important chapter of his book-length study, *Circuitos narrativos* (Zaragoza: Departamento de Inglés, 1975), to examining internal structures in James's works; Javier Coy analyzes the critical approaches to James in "Henry James, su teoria del arte y el 'arte' de sus críticos." (*Atlantis* 5, i:65–83). This year also saw "Tensión entre 'presente' y 'pasado' en la obra de Henry James"; using (*Actas del X Congreso*, pp. 189–98), taking *The Wings of the Dove* as the focus of her study, María Antonia Alvarez explores James's concept of identifying Europe with the past and the United States with the present; and Sergio Perosa's "Henry James' 'The Aspern Papers': An Essay in Interpretation," pp. 81–90 in Enrique García Diez, ed., *American Studies in Spain* (Valencia: Servicio de Publicaciones Universitat de Valencia), analyzes the role of the narrator/protagonist, both as polarizing agent of the plot and as creator of the fusion between the gothic and the grotesque.

During the years of transition between dictatorship and the present democracy, *Junkie: Confessions of an Unredeemed Drug Addict* by William Burroughs was one of the most popular books among hopeful Spanish youth. Yet, as early as 1963, Javier Coy published "Sentido y alcance de la Beat Generation" (*Filologia Moderna* 4:21–23), a general but innovative essay at the time. More substantial is Bernard Dietz's "*The Naked Lunch*: o una distopía para la redencíon" (*Calle Mayor* 1 [1985]:53–70).

In "*The Naked Lunch*: la acogida de la critica y el proceso de Boston" (*Atlantis* 10, i–ii:79–92), Daniel Pastor meticulously surveys the difficulties this novel met with after publication. Pastor is also the author of *El individualismo anárquico y radical de William S. Burroughs* (Salamanca: Servicio de Publicaciones de la Universidad de Salamanca), which reviews Burroughs's artistic production and demonstrates how he adapted his work and his persona to American historical developments. Pastor analyzes this development from the individualism, and at times narcissism, of *Junkie* to the innovative experimentations of *Queer*. The chapter "Metodología de la rebelion" (pp. 115–35) reveals how the aesthetic and ideological development is not accidental or sporadic but reflects the author's concept of his role as a social critic.

Walker Percy has been generally neglected by Spanish critics. Julia Lavid amended this omission with *Lenguaje y conciencia en la obra de Walker Percy* (Madrid: Editorial de la Universidad Complutense). In "La teoría semiótica" (pp. 14–261) Lavid analyzes different theories of language: "El fundamento semiotico del yo: la relacion lenguaje-conciencia" (pp. 88–154) and "Hacia una teoría del lenguaje como fenomeno" (pp. 195–221). In subsequent chapters *The Moviegoer*, *The Last Gentleman*, *Love in the Ruins*, *Lancelot*, and *The Second Coming* are discussed. Lavid argues that to Percy language is the vehicle for achieving union between science and philosophy and the only medium through which man is able to know himself and the reality of his existence.

Edith Wharton has found her way into the criticism this year in a study by Bárbara Ozieblo, "Why a Woman Should Keep Her Feet Firmly on the Ground: Thoughts on Edith Wharton's *The House of Mirth*" (*Actas del X Congreso*, pp. 415–21), one of the more serious studies despite its ironic title. The undoing of Lily, and by extension of other heroines in Wharton's work, is, according to this critic, a consequence of her lack of pragmatism and her fanciful mentality. The conclusions Bárbara Ozieblo arrives at are interesting, but disturbing, particularly for those, myself included, who see the destruction of heroines and heroes alike as a result of the pressure that social rules and regulations exert on the individual. The feminine question is also subject for analysis in "Women in American Studies" (pp. 111–16) by Manuel Villar in Enrique García Diez ed. *American Studies in Spain* (Valencia: Servicio de Publicaciones Universitat de Valencia). The title could be misleading, as the essay actually examines the role that heroines play in North American narrative, whether the author be a woman or a man. Without analyzing the causes, exposing only the situations, Villar arrives at the same conclusions as Bárbara Ozieblo.

American Studies in Spain includes two further essays of interest to scholars of American literature. Javier Coy's "The Use of History in the Contemporary American Novel" (pp. 51–62) demonstrates how most American authors in their romances turn to the past, more or less removed from the present. His treatment of the historic novel and the war novel is particularly interesting. In "The 'Mediterranean' Character in American Literature" (pp. 139–48) Juan José Coy argues that the inclusion of the Mediterranean character and mentality in many works by American writers functions as an antidote to the barbarity of the "official Calvinism" in the United States. Emilio Serrano in "Walden como teoría literaria" (*Turia* 10:35–42) establishes a clear parallelism between Emerson and Thoreau and concludes that Thoreau goes beyond his master in the significance of his natural symbolism. John Hazlett's "Self Myths and the Autobiography of Renunciation in the 20th-century North America" (*Actas del X Congreso*, pp. 335–61), in which he opposes postmodern theories on the function of language. According to Hazlett, there exists a tradition of an autobiography of renunciation in American literature, its main characteristics being that it "bears no good news."

***b.* Drama.** North American drama is often represented on Spanish stages, yet criticism is not abundant. Only a few books and articles appeared in 1988, but one could say that the quality makes up for quantity. Ascención Gómez García *Mito y realidad en la obra dramática de Tennessee Williams* (Salamanca: Ediciones Universidad de Salamanca) examines the affinity between Greek myths and the characters in Williams's work. Part I, "Mitos antiquos en la obra de un dramaturgo contemporáneo" (pp. 17–75), and particularly its second chapter, "Heroes mitológicos-'freaks' Williamsiniano" (pp. 23–25), is, despite its brevity, incisive and original. Part II, "Mito y realidad, pasado y presente del sur de los Estados Unidos en la obra de un dramaturgo sureño" (pp. 83–122) abandons the shaky grounds of Part I and turns to the theater of Williams and the history of the South that still torments the modern characters of his work. Of particular interest are Goméz's observations on the staging of Williams's plays, analyzing the successes and failures alike, and the reason for these; listed in the appendix is detailed information—on the successful staging of his work.

Clifford Odets, practically unknown in Spain, is the subject of Miguel Angel Fernandez Soler's *Imagen de la sociedad em Clifford Odets* (Madrid: Editorial de la Universidad Complutense de Madrid). Each chapter in the book treats a single work by the author. Soler's conclusion is that Odets's artistic production was not influenced by his affiliation with the Communist Party. His idealism and social commitment lead him to the belief that man can improve the world through collective action, but he makes clear his repugnance toward writing according to the dictates of politically committed functionaries, an attitude that sets him apart from some other proletarian writers.

The centennial for Eugene O'Neill's birth occasioned a number of conferences and seminars, including general reviews in the Spanish media. However, only one article of interest appeared in the critical journals: Manuel Górriz's "Eugene O'Neill, o el conflicto fatal" (*Turia* 10:23–33). Górriz explores O'Neill's difficult personality and argues that the noted writer created his own narrative tradition that has been the cornerstone of an authentic North American theater. Górriz is also the author of "The Contrast, o la primera comedia norteamericana" (*Actas del X Congreso*, pp. 339–46), where he expands upon *The Columbian Muse of Comedy* (So. Ill. Univ. Press, 1974), a comparative study by Daniel F. Havens that draws parallels between Sheridan's *The School for Scandal* and Royall Tyler's *The Contrast*. Górriz examines the parallel development of the characters in these two comedies, lending only minimal attention to plot and content.

c. **Poetry.** North American poetry is unquestionably slighted by Spanish critics. Walt Whitman, Emily Dickinson, and Ezra Pound generally attract the most attention. Many critics engage in comparative studies of American poets and García Lorca, and this year was no exception. Only one book-length study and one article merit attention, both of them focusing on works by minority writers.

d. **Minorities.** The study of minority literature is a recent phenomenon in Spain, yet despite the newness of this field it has met with growing interest among Spanish scholars. The study of Afro-American literature and Chicano literature (the latter being officially encouraged prior to the celebrations of the Fifth Centennial of the Discovery) seem to have monopolized critical attention; however, initial conferences on Asian-American and Native American literature have taken place.

Joanne Neff Van Aertselaer examines the poetry of Paul Laurence Dunbar, James Weldon Johnson, Sterling Allen Brown, and Langston Hughes in *Estudio estilístico de la poesía negra norteamericana* (Madrid: Servicio de publicaciones de la universidad Complutense).

Van Aertselaer analyzes not only the purely textual character of the works under consideration, but also their relation to the history and cultural practices of Afro-Americans, placing special emphasis on oral traditions. Based on the grammatical norms of the Afro-American tradition, she demonstrates how the poetry has developed within that tradition: "the literary representation of Afro-American life through vernacular language carries certain implications which cannot be expressed in standard English," and it therefore continues to be the language of Afro-American poetry. Van Aertselaer continues her line of argumentation in "Repetition as a Feature of Afro-American Discourse" (*Actas del X Congreso*, pp. 407–14), in which she analyzes the objectives of repetition, such as to intensify dramatization or to set off a new event in the narrative.

Angels Carabí develops an excellent sociological study of the work of Toni Morrison in *Toni Morrison: Búsqueda de una identidad afroamericana* (Barcelona: Promociones y Publicaciones Universitarias). Carabí argues that Morrison through fictitious characters succeeds in rendering the true values of Afro-Americans. These values are not portrayed in comparison with those of the white population, but are presented as an integral part of a self-sustained cultural pattern. Included is an interview with the author.

The film *The Color Purple* turned the Spanish translation of the novel into a bestseller and its author, Alice Walker, into one of the most read American writers. In "Alice Walker's '1955': An Attack on the False Values of Our Times" (*Actas del X Congreso*, pp. 461–66), Justine Tally demonstrates sociologically how man's fixation on superfluous necessities is the reason for his disgrace.

Douglas E. La Prada develops a comparative study between Hughes and Lorca in "Langston Hughes and Federico García Lorca (*Actas del X Congreso*, pp. 371–75), focusing on the Gypsi Ballads. The difference between these two writers is evident, Hughes being more impressionistic and Lorca more realistic, but it becomes clear through La Prada's analysis that Hughes's accomplishment in translating Lorca into English influenced his own poetic voice.

Angels Carabí in "Developing a Sense of Place: Sandra Cisneros in *The House on Mango Street*" (*Anuari d'Anglés* [Barcelona] 10: 111–17) explores the cultural conditioning of an adolescent Chicana. Carabí concludes that the Chicana is doubly repressed, both by Anglo culture and male-dominated Chicano culture. In my own article, "La literatura chicana: una ilustre desconocida" (*Leer* 10: 111–14), I examine the development of Chicano writers, including those who write in Spanish, within the body of North American literature; the essay demonstrates regional differences among Chicano writers.

Universidad de Alcalá de Henares, Madrid

22. General Reference Works

James Woodress

Twenty general reference works came to my attention this year, making 1988 a rather average year for books of this sort. They range, as usual, from biographical compilations, to handbooks, to bibliographies, to dictionaries, to collections of criticism. There is in addition an index and a chronological outline of American literature. Reference works of a specialized nature are covered in the separate chapters of *ALS 1988*.

As every reference librarian has come to expect, Gale weighs in annually with a shelfful of tomes from its ongoing *Dictionary of Literary Biography* series. Two more volumes (*DLB* 64 and 71) in the series *American Literary Critics and Scholars* appeared in 1988 covering the years 1850–80 and 1880–1900, ed. John W. Rathbun and Monica M Grecu. The latter begins with Thomas Bailey Aldrich and ends with George E. Woodberry, including along the way Henry James, Bierce, Garland, and Norris among well-known authors and Basil Gildersleeve, the leading classical scholar of the 19th century, Bliss Perry, Barrett Wendell, Brander Matthews, and Fred Lewis Pattee, among the purely scholars. The former volume begins with James Burnell Angell, ends with Whitman, and gives coverage to Twain, Bret Harte, Paul Hamilton Hayne, Thomas Wentworth Higginson, Howells, Lowell, and Moses Coit Tyler. A third volume (*DLB* 67) covered *Modern American Critics since 1955*, ed. Gregory S. Jay, and includes 27 critics, all but Paul de Man alive in 1988. Leslie Fiedler, Northrop Frye, Irving Howe, Alfred Kazin, and Elaine Showalter are among those who made the volume.

From another series (*DLB* 73) comes *American Magazine Journalists, 1741–1850*, ed. Sam G. Riley, a work that begins with Park Benjamin and concludes with Frances Wright. Charles Brockden Brown, Paine, Franklin, and Poe get into the book, of course, along with Emerson as editor of the *Dial* briefly and Irving by virtue of his youthful lucubrations. Also included are N. P. Willis and Noah Webster.

Other Gale contributions this year are the *DLB Yearbook 1987*, ed. J. M. Brook; *DLB Documentary Series* (vol. 5): *American Transcendentalists*, ed. Joel Myerson; *Contemporary Authors Autobiographical Series*, Vols. 6, ed. Adele Sarkissian, and 7, ed. Mark Zadrozny. Brook's volume follows the previous format for yearbooks: essays of contemporary interest, updated entries (Hemingway, Welty, et al.), obituaries (James Baldwin, Richard Ellmann, Frederick A. Pottle). Myerson's volume focuses on the years immediately after the publication of Emerson's *Nature*, and among the writers whose work is included are Orestes A. Brownson, James Freeman Clarke, Margaret Fuller, Thoreau, and Hawthorne. There also are sections on Brook Farm and Fruitlands. The autobiographical volumes contain pieces by Kazin, W. P. Kinsella, Dan Wakefield, Walter Allen, René Wellek, Clarence Major, Ann Petry, Karl Shapiro, and two dozen lesser folk.

Four handbooks of various sorts appeared in 1988. M. Thomas Inge, a long-time contributor to *ALS*, has edited a *Handbook of American Popular Literature* (Greenwood). This useful volume contains 15 essays by various hands on a wide variety of topics: best-sellers, children's literature, comic books, detective and mystery novels, Gothic novels, historical fiction, westerns, to name some of the chapters. Each essay surveys the historic development of the genre, includes a guide to reference works and research collections, and ends with a bibliography.

Themes and Motifs in Western Literature by Horst S. and Ingrid Daemmrich (Francke) ranges widely in its coverage from classical Greek to contemporary American. About 150 of the themes that have most interested Western writers receive treatment: aggression, brother conflict, death, fear, friendship, incest, love, moon, night, *picaro*, and utopia are some of the subjects. The article on adultery ranges from Homer to Updike.

A very different sort of work is the third edition of the *MLA Handbook for Writers of Research Papers*, ed. Joseph Gibaldi and Walter S. Achtert. This is an update of a reference work too well known to need further description. *The Handbook of American-Jewish Literature: An Analytical Guide to Topics, Themes, and Sources*, ed. Lewis Fried, Gene Brown, and Louis Harap (Greenwood), contains chapters by various hands, each including a discursive essay followed by bibliography. There are three chapters on American-Jewish fiction; others include drama, poetry, "Yiddish Dreams in America," "American Yiddish Literary Criticism." The volume ends with a guide to European bibliography and selected reference materials and resources. There is a good index so that one can look up, say, Henry Roth or Budd Schulberg.

Another Greenwood publication is organized much like the previously described volume, but it calls itself *Humor in America: A Research Guide to Genres and Topics*, ed. Lawrence E. Mintz. There are chapters on literary humor, the comics, humor in periodicals, film comedy, broadcast humor, standup comedy, women's humor, racial and ethnic humor, and political humor. The coverage of literary humor from Franklin to Woody Allen in 21 pages is so sketchy as to be not very useful. There are bibliographies of secondary sources after each chapter.

Another resource guide is *Film and the Arts in Symbiosis: A Resource Guide*, ed. Gary R. Edgerton (Greenwood). The book consists of 11 chapters on film and some other art, but "Film and Literature" will interest *ALS* readers the most. There are, for example, brief discussions of Eric Von Stroheim's *Greed* and John Ford's *The Grapes of Wrath.*

Two general bibliographies were issued this year: *Asian American Literature: An Annotated Bibliography*, compiled by King-Kok Cheung and Stan Yogi (MLA), and *Comedy: An Annotated Bibliography of Theory and Criticism*, ed. James E. Evans (Scarecrow). The former covers Chinese-, Japanese-, Filipino-, Korean-, South Asian-, and Vietnamese-American literature and contains bibliographies of primary and secondary materials. The latter sweeps American literature into its larger concerns, devoting items 1658 to 1814 to American entries. One of the general sections of this work treats "Comic Theory after 1900" and includes work by Bergson, Ionesco, Sartre, and Thurber.

Two dictionaries worth calling to the attention of readers of *ALS* are *Loanwords Dictionary*, ed. Frank R. Abate and Laurence Urdang (Gale), and *Similes Dictionary*, ed. Elyse Sommer and Mike Sommer (Gale). The compilation of loanwords is a lexicon of 16,000 terms that are not fully assimilated into English. The editors have included many words I never would have suspected were loanwords such as the French *abricot* for apricot or the Spanish *chuleta* for chop or cutlet, though *ab ovo*, *adagio*, and *fait accompli* one certainly encounters often enough in the work of English writers. The similes dictionary also collects more than 16,000 items ranging from ancient to contemporary and is organized into categories such as patriotism, thrift, work, drinking, etc. The book is fun to browse through and discover that "tight as a tick" is attributed to Tallulah Bankhead and "as certain as that night succeeds the day" to George Washington. "As quiet as a mouse" was first uttered by someone who prefers to remain anonymous.

Gale's inexhaustible output of reference works also produced two collections of criticism in 1988: *Short Story Criticism: Excerpts from Criticism of the Works of Short Fiction Writers*, ed. Laurie Lanzen Harris and Sheila Fitzgerald, and vol. 50 of the series *Contemporary Literary Criticism*. The former is the first volume of a new series and includes 14 writers, mostly American and mostly important figures: Sherwood Anderson, Faulkner, Hemingway, Melville, Poe, and Welty, to mention some. More than 150 other writers will be covered in projected volumes. The contemporary criticism volume is the yearbook for 1987 and covers fiction, poetry, drama, the year's new authors, prizewinners, obituaries, and works of literary biography. In the last category Hemingway, Pound, and Plath made it, but not Willa Cather.

The final works to be reviewed are an *Index to Poetry by Black American Women*, compiled by Dorothy Hilton Chapman (Greenwood), and *A Chronological Outline of American Literature* by Samuel Rogal (Greenwood, 1987). The *Index* lists over 4,000 poems by over 400 poets, the most frequently represented being Maya Angelou, Gwendolyn Brooks, Lucille Clifton, Nikki Giovanni, Georgia Johnson, and Audre Lord. This is the first of two projected volumes. The chronology is a handy work organizing year-by-year births and deaths of literary figures, major literary events and activities, authors and titles of fiction, poetry, drama, and essays.

University of California, Davis

Author Index

Subject Index